The Black Urban Condition

THE BLACK URBAN CONDITION

A DOCUMENTARY
HISTORY, 1866-1971

BY

Hollis R. Lynch

Thomas Y. Crowell Company

NEW YORK   ESTABLISHED 1834

Designed by Vincent Torre

Manufactured in the United States of America

ISBN 0-690-14639-6

1 2 3 4 5 6 7 8 9 10

Library of Congress Cataloging in Publication Data

Lynch, Hollis Ralph, comp.
 The black urban condition.

 Bibliography
 1. Negroes—History—Addresses, essays, lectures.
 2. Urbanization—United States—Addresses, essays,
 lectures.   I. Title
 E185.L96   301.45'19'6073   72-13822
 ISBN 0-690-14639-6

ACKNOWLEDGMENTS

Grateful acknowledgment is made to the following copyright holders for permission to reprint selections in this book:

American Council for Nationalities Service for "I, Too, Sing America" by Jo Sinclair from *Common Ground,* copyright 1942 by Common Council for American Unity.

The American Sociological Association for "Profiles: Baltimore" and "Profiles: Detroit" by Dr. Edward S. Lewis from *Journal of Educational Sociology,* 1944, and "Profiles: Los Angeles" by Dr. Charles Bratt, from *Journal of Educational Sociology,* 1945.

Acknowledgments

Black World for "Americas's 10 Worst Cities for Negroes" by Ollie Stewart from *Negro Digest*, copyright © March 1948 by *Negro Digest*, "America's 10 Best Cities for Negroes" by Susan Cayton Woodson, copyright © October 1947, by *Negro Digest*, and "Black Metropolis" by St. Clair Drake and Horace Cayton copyright © 1945 by *Negro Digest*.

James Brown Associates, Inc., for "Image and Unlikeness in Harlem" by Albert Murray from *The Urban Review* (June 1967), copyright © 1967 by Albert Murray, reprinted by permission of the author and his agents, James Brown Associates, Inc.

Crisis Publishing Co., Inc., for "National League on Urban Conditions Among Negroes" (Sept. 1914), "Chicago and its Eight Reasons" (Oct. 1919) and "The Success of Negro Migration" (Jan. 1920) by Walter H. White, "The Growth of Colored Miami" (March 1942) by C. S. Thompson, "Chicago Schools Include Negro History" (Feb. 1943), "The Gestapo in Detroit" (Aug. 1943) by Thurgood Marshall, "St. Louis: Is It the Toughest Town for Baseball Players?" (Oct. 1950) by J. H. Hicks, and "Racial Trends in Seattle" (June-July 1958) by L. G. Watts, reprinted from *The Crisis* with the permission of the Crisis Publishing Company, Inc.

Ebony Magazine for "Baltimore: New Negro Vote Capital" by Simeon Booker (December 1969) and "Black Take Over of U.S. Cities" by Alex Poinsett (November 1970), copyright 1959 and 1970 by Johnson Publishing Company, Inc.

Earl G. Graves Publishing Co., Inc., and *Black Enterprise* magazine for "Birmingham" (Sept. 1971), "Memphis" (May 1971), "Houston" (Oct. 1970), "Baltimore" (Nov. 1971), "Philadelphia" (July 1971), "San Francisco" (June 1971), "Los Angeles" (Nov. 1970), copyright 1970 and 1971 by Earl G. Graves Publishing Co., Inc.

The International City Management Association for "Black Police in the Cities of the South" by Charles S. Johnson from *Public Management* (March 1944) and "City Takes Steps to Improve Interracial Relations" by Wilson W. Wyatt from *Public Management* (April 1945), copyright © 1944 and 1945 by the International City Management Association.

Mrs. James Weldon Johnson for "Harlem Renaissance" by James Weldon Johnson from *Black Manhattan*, copyright renewed 1958 by Mrs. James Weldon Johnson.

Alfred A. Knopf, Inc., for excerpt from *South of Freedom* by Carl T. Rowan, copyright 1952 by Carl T. Rowan.

David McKay Company, Inc., for excerpt from *The Long Shadow of Little Rock* by Daisy Bates, copyright © 1962 by Daisy Bates.

The Nation for "There Goes God!" (February 6, 1935) and "Harlem Runs Wild" (April 3, 1935) by Claude McKay, copyright © 1935 by The Nation.

National Planning Association for "Negro Employment in the Birmingham Area," Case Study No. 3, from *Selected Studies of Negro Employment in the South,* copyright © 1955 by National Planning Association.

National Urban League, Inc., for "Negro Employment in St. Louis War Production" by R. R. Jefferson from *Opportunity Magazine* (Summer 1944), copyright © 1944 by National Urban League, Inc., and "A Review of the Economic and Cultural Problems of Negroes in New Orleans" (unpublished manuscript), copyright © 1973 by National Urban League, Inc.

The New York Times for "Montgomery Bus Boycott" (Dec. 6, 1955), "Atlanta Negroes to Vote" (Sept. 7, 1949), "Negro Groups Boycott Mardi Gras" (March 1, 1957), "Cities Limit Negro Police Use" (July 27, 1959), "Greensboro Store Boycott" (Feb. 3, 1960), "Power in Harlem . . ." (Dec. 6, 1970) by Thomas A. Johnson, "Black Police Recruiting Fails" (Jan. 25, 1971) by Paul Delany, "Inner City Decay" (July 19, 1971) by J. M. Flint, and "Jackson Forms New Chicago Group" (Dec. 19, 1971) by Thomas A. Johnson, © 1943, 1949, 1955, 1957, 1959, 1960 by The New York Times Company, reprinted by permission.

Science & Society, Inc. for "Some Effects of the Depression on the Negro in Northern Cities" by E. Franklin Frazier from *Science & Society* (Fall 1938), copyright © 1938 by Science & Society, Inc.

Time magazine for "The St. Louis Economic Blues" by William S. Rukeyser from *The Negro And The City,* copyright © 1968 by Time, Inc., and "Business in Bronzeville," reprinted by permission from *Time,* the Weekly Newsmagazine, copyright © Time, Inc.

Transaction, Inc., for "The Making of the Negro Mayors 1967" by J. Hadden, L. Masotti, and V. Thiessen, from *transaction,* Vol. 5 (January/February 1968), copyright © 1968 by Transaction, Inc.

The Washington Post for "Richmond Quietly Leads Way in Race Relations" by Robert E. Baker (July 29, 1962), copyright © 1962 by The Washington Post.

To my daughters,
Shola, age three,
and Nnenna, age one,
and to all urban children:
may the inner cities
yet be restored for their
safe but exciting uses.

INTRODUCTION

Over the years innumerable projects have been proposed, plans made, and ideas brought to fulfillment in the cities of America. But one sober fact remains: the cities of the 1970's are little better places to live than the cities of the 1870's for those living in the rotting inner neighborhoods. Hunger, disease, unemployment, and prejudice still form the impregnable walls for thousands trapped in the urban condition. Housing, health, transportation, and other necessities are inadequate and deteriorating faster now than ever before.

The city has had contradictory effects on the minorities struggling to exist within its system—dehumanizing and demoralizing them even while sparking the creative energies needed to survive the expanded technology and population. The urban atmosphere pervades the spirit of its dwellers, breeding restlessness and cynicism at the follies of insufficient planning and poor direction.

But minorities have also had a profound effect on the cities, molding their growth, necessitating restructuring of institutions and frameworks, and providing the dynamic forces to spur economic, social, and political revolutions. Black Amercans have played an integral part in this process of urbanization in America. For over a century the redistribution of Black population from rural areas to the cities has paralleled the change in direction of the country as a whole. Through the period of great industrial expansion, the First and Second World Wars, the Depression and all the great movements on this continent, patterns of racial discrimination and economic development have fostered large concentrations of Blacks in the hearts of major cities, pressuring them into the segregated existence of the poor and the unemployed city residents.

From the poverty and despair a new power has become evident—a power born of the violence of institutions which serve only to perpetuate their own existence; a power bred of the frustrations of dealing with political, social, and economic pressures and hatreds; a power which has become clear as Blacks and others flex their muscles to fight for their humanity; a power which may prove to hold the key for survival for the cities themselves.

A full understanding of the implications of the Black contribution to our urban history has not been readily available, due in part to the scarcity of research into the background of the Black movements of the past. Today, however, that contribution is being explored more fully.

Introduction

Professor Hollis Lynch has made a noteworthy compilation of and commentary on historical documents relating to economic, social, political, and cultural aspects of Blacks in the American urban environment in all parts of the country. Compiling excerpts from contemporary accounts, some dating back over a hundred years, Professor Lynch has focused the light of awareness on the struggles of the past, adding new insights and new dimensions to the present and future efforts. The establishment of labor unions, sit-ins, marches and streetcar boycotts of the late 1860's, just like protests of 1920 or 1970, had as their end the freedom of all peoples from the bondage of poverty and prejudice. Civil rights crusades in this country did not begin with the present generation, but were brought with the generation that got off the slave ships. This book presents a splendid collection of accounts chronicling incidents and situations over a century of those crusades in America.

Cities today remain perplexing puzzles whose solution is essential to the future of this country. Answers must be found to the decay and the wasting of humanity that have taken root in the cities. The future of these areas demands a reshaping of our priorities and an end to the prejudices that lie behind them. For an urban community must, in the end, learn to live at peace with itself. Those who inhabit the homes, sidewalks, schools, stores, and parks of a city must believe that that urban area and environment are responsive to their needs. Public services—education, health care, housing, transportation, environmental protection, and crime control—must be reshaped and replanned to provide protection for all urban residents. Urban laboratories and experiments must be proposed and funded to find cures for the blight of the urban core.

This year more than 80 percent of Black Americans live within the boundaries of our urban areas. And the figures continue to increase. As the urban crisis grows in intensity, it is Blacks who suffer the consequences of inadequate planning and funding. And it is Blacks who must assert the power gained through generations of effort to reverse the tide and make America's cities livable once again.

Charles C. Diggs, Jr.
U.S. House of Representatives

PREFACE

Black migration and urbanization is a major but relatively neglected theme in American history. This volume is the first to try to present a well-rounded documentary history of blacks in American cities since their emancipation. As servants and slaves, blacks participated in the process of urbanization in America from its inception. But when slavery finally ended in 1865, over 90% of the blacks in the United States were rural, and they were overwhelmingly (95%) concentrated in the South. Since then, worsening farm conditions and an unprecedented rate of industrialization, intensified by the demands of two World Wars, have led to a massive urbanization and redistribution of the black population. Today, more than 80% of the blacks in America are urbanized, and almost half of them live outside the South. They have concentrated in relatively few areas, one third of the entire black population being located in fifteen major U.S. cities; and in more than a dozen of these, blacks comprise 40% or more of the total population.

Urbanization brought major opportunities as well as serious problems. The city provided blacks with greater economic, social, and cultural opportunities; it facilitated the rise of a significant middle class; it helped in the liberation of the black psyche, so long stifled by slavery and rural oppression; it proved a powerful stimulant to black creativity in music, dance, art, and literature; and for a long time it has been almost the sole base of black political power. But, historically, in the cities and elsewhere, blacks have faced pervasive discrimination and intense competition from the generally more numerous, better organized and favored whites, foreign born as well as native. In light of these persistent obstacles, and of the recent declining economic role of the city (with the correspondingly increasing economic role of the largely white suburbs), for the masses of urban blacks city life has also meant inferior employment, and, very often, underemployment or unemployment; substandard housing; inadequate health facilities; inferior education; and the problems of drugs, crime, and insecurity. For too many black people city life has been a continuous deadly ghetto trap, rather than the avenue to individual and group fulfillment and mobility that it was for European immigrants. It was the sorry plight of inner-city blacks, set against their rising expectations, that led to the devastating insurrections of the middle and late sixties. There is now wide agreement that the ravaged and decaying inner city is the major domestic problem facing the United States.

In this volume I intend to show the impact of cities on blacks historically, through the eyes of contemporary witnesses. I have taken special care to document all aspects of black life—social, cultural, economic, and political—as well as to achieve a regional balance. The materials are divided into six convenient time periods and into five geographic regions of the United States: the South; the Border States; the Northeast; the North Central; and the West (this last category being used from World War II only). Selections are arranged thematically and for the most part chronologically within each region. For each subsection, I have provided a short introductory analysis of the documents, indicating the trends they illustrate. I have also added some explanatory footnotes, which are numbered. Footnotes that were part of the original material appear with asterisks.

The materials in this book form a rich and fresh source on an important aspect of American history. The vast majority of them, to my knowledge, have not been reprinted before. Some are statistical, but most are descriptive and readable; some tell of frustration and despair; others, of hope and achievement; and still others, whimsically, of human foibles. The documents are drawn from about sixty different sources, black and white, although the former are more significant. The single most important source has been *Opportunity* (1923–41), the journal of the National Urban League; other black sources include the *Southern Workman, Crisis, Negro Digest,* the *Pittsburgh Courier,* and *Black Enterprise.* From the time of emancipation on, black leaders were aware of the process of urbanization; as a result, they themselves have made the greatest contributions toward documenting it. The list of writers represented in this volume includes some of the ablest black intellectual and political figures —more than forty—among them W. E. B. Du Bois, Booker T. Washington, Claude McKay, Walter White, Langston Hughes, Ralph Bunche, E. Franklin Frazier, Thurgood Marshall, St. Clair Drake, and Daisy Bates. Whenever I could, at the beginning of selections I have provided biographical information on the contributors.

For the reader's assistance and convenience I have included five appendices listing important and not readily available statistics of practical and political significance on black urban demography, literacy, and on

Preface

representation in municipal councils and police forces; I am grateful to the mayors' offices and police departments for supplying me with up-to-date information. It is my hope that this volume will appeal not only to scholars and students, but to professionals and laymen concerned with the plight of the city, and that, in addition, it will stimulate further major research on urban blacks.

Funds from the Program of Black and Urban Studies of Columbia University facilitated my research for this book, as did the encouragement of my colleagues in PROBUS, among them, Luther P. Jackson, who is himself doing a study of black towns. Stalwart research help came at various stages from four students and friends: Karla Spurlock, George and Grace Obiozor, and Pearl Robinson, and typing help from Mses. Doris Miller, Jeanne Goodman, Yvette Wilson, and Ruth Cooper. Editorial work was ably done by Ms. Penny Post. I here record my grateful thanks to all the above as also to several New York City librarians and most especially Ms. L. Lucille Chappelle of the National Urban League.

Hollis R. Lynch

Professor of History and
Director of the Institute
of African Studies
Columbia University

CONTENTS

PART ONE

THE NINETEENTH CENTURY:
RECONSTRUCTION AND AFTER

PART TWO

THE TWENTIETH CENTURY:
PRE-WORLD WAR I

Contents

BORDER CITIES
Political and Social Aspects

NORTHEASTERN CITIES
Social and Economic Aspects

NORTH CENTRAL CITIES
Political and Social Aspects

PART THREE

WORLD WAR I TO THE DEPRESSION

Contents

PART FOUR

THE DEPRESSION AND THE NEW DEAL

CITIES

General Aspects

SOUTHERN CITIES

Economic and Cultural Aspects

BORDER CITIES

Economic and Cultural Aspects

NORTHEASTERN CITIES

Social Aspects

Economic Aspects

PART FIVE

WORLD WAR II TO 1959

CITIES
General Aspects

SOUTHERN CITIES
Political and Social Aspects

TWO ALL-BLACK SOUTHERN TOWNS

Contents

PART SIX
THE SIXTIES AND AFTER

Contents

PART ONE

THE NINETEENTH CENTURY: RECONSTRUCTION AND AFTER

INTRODUCTION

Among the earliest problems the newly urbanized blacks in the post-Reconstruction South faced were their scant economic resources and limited bargaining power. They attempted solutions through cooperative economic ventures, unions, and fraternal and benevolent associations. Examples of these in the selections below are the Charleston Freedmen's Land and Home Society (Document 1); the Charleston Longshoremen's Protective Union Association (Document 4), an organization that was duplicated in all the major port cities on the Gulf and Atlantic coasts; and building and loan associations (Document 6). Out of the cooperative economic ventures of benevolent and fraternal associations were to come, toward the end of the century, the first major black economic institutions—banks and insurance companies. By 1900 there were four black banks: the Savings Bank of the Grand Fountain United Order of True Reformers in Richmond and the Capital Savings Bank in Washington, D.C., both founded in 1888; the Mutual Trust Company, organized in Chattanooga in 1889; and the Alabama Penny Savings and Loan Company, started in Birmingham in 1890. Two early examples of insurance companies were the Mutual Benefit Association of Baltimore, organized in 1885, and the North Carolina Mutual Life Company, which was organized in Durham in 1898 and was to develop into one of the largest black American businesses.

Document 6, which is the most comprehensive statement in this subsection, describes the substantial role black artisans played in southern cities despite increasingly active discrimination and prejudice; this was in contrast to the North, where the much more numerous European immigrants eliminated black competition as skilled workers in the post–Civil War period. The document also points out the growth of a new, and as yet small, college-trained professional middle class; the appearance of newly successful entrepreneurs and inventors; and the significant

3

increase in black newspapers. If Document 6 looks on the brighter side, Document 5 reminds us that most blacks in Charlotte, N.C., were "as poor as Job's turkey" and lived in ramshackle cabins in crowded, increasingly segregated parts of the city. And what was true of Charlotte held for the urban South generally.

SOUTHERN CITIES

Economic Aspects

Charleston, S.C. (1869)

1]   The Freedmen's Land and Home
                      Society *

. . . The question of permitting colored people to own land is of the greatest importance. In most places no obstacle appears if they have money . . . but as they have no money . . . the permission is of little importance.

Last year some 200 freedmen of Charleston formed a society for getting land and homes of their own. At a sale they bought a plantation of 600 acres on Remley's Point, opposite the city, for which they agreed to pay $6,000 or $10 an acre, which seems to me remarkably cheap. A part has been paid for and they have now 18 months to pay the remainder. Last year they planted 150 acres in cotton, but they got only one bale, because the cotton boll destroyed a part, and another part was stolen even after it was picked. This year they have put 30 acres in Sea Island cotton and about the same in corn. . . . They are doing their own work and are determined to watch the crop night and day until it is saved. The 30 acres of cotton of the Sea Island variety was cleared of timber during the Winter, and being too poor to buy a team, they dug up all this new ground with their hoes and planted it, and when I arrived I found 20 or more men and women busy in hoeing it. . . .

2]   *Georgia and South Carolina (1870)* †

Amongst the better class of emancipated slaves in the South, I found . . . provident habits rapidly forming. Savings' banks, friendly societies, and building as-

* SOURCE: *New York Tribune*, June 30, 1869.
† SOURCE: David Macrae, *The Americans at Home*, Vol. II, pp. 55–57. Edinburgh: Edmonston and Douglas, 1870.

sociations were springing up amongst them, and many were purchasing houses and land. In the single town of Macon, Georgia, they had purchased 200 buildings. In Savannah, during the month I was there, they laid past in the savings' bank $5,679, being $2,300 in advance of the previous year, notwithstanding the bad season. In their savings' banks throughout the South, they had deposited $1,500,000 since their emancipation three years before.

More recently the progress has been still more rapid. During this past year, 180 negroes have bought places around Augusta; 220 have built houses in Atlanta; at Columbia, where one black mechanic has already amassed a fortune of $50,000, forty heads of families have purchased city property for homes, at from $500 to $1,200 each, within six months; and on the islands near Charleston 2,000 freedmen's families have located themselves, built their houses and cabins, and paid for their little farms. I heard complaints from many colored men, who had saved some money and wanted to buy land, that landowners would not sell to negroes. But this evil is being remedied. The South Carolina Legislature, last year, appropriated $200,000 for the purchase of large estates, cut them up into farms, and offered them for sale to the freedmen and the poor of all colors. Forty thousand acres of this land have already been sold; and the Legislature has accordingly resolved on an appropriation this year of $400,000 more. . . . The freedmen's deposits in their savings banks have rolled up now to an aggregate of $12,000,000; and the cashiers who keep a note of the purpose for which sums are withdrawn report that in a large proportion of cases it is for the purchase of lands and houses. The deposited savings of the past year exceeded those of the year before to the extent of $558,000. And yet we are told the negroes are incurably thriftless.

3]   *Augusta, Ga. (1872)*

. . . Augusta contains about 15,000 inhabitants, one half of whom are colored, and of the remainder a large portion are of foreign origin, and many of them Germans. . . .

There are several banks in Augusta, one of which is the Freedman's Savings Bank; which is well patronized by the colored people. . . . These banks have been the means of great good to the colored people; having induced them to practise economy, and save their earnings to such a degree, that under their influence, great numbers of the freedmen have become the owners of houses and small farms. This bank occupies a large and handsome building in a prominent position on Broad street, which building was formerly owned by a Southern bank. . . .

The colored people in Augusta own four or five churches, principally of the Baptist order; and on Sundays these churches are well-filled with intelligent and well-dressed hearers. One of these churches was brilliantly lighted with

Source: Charles Stearns, *The Black Man of the South and the Rebels,* New York: American News Company, 1872, p. 128.

Charlotte, N.C.

gas, has a nice pulpit, with handsome cushions and a gallery on three sides; and will hold seven or eight hundred persons. Several of these churches were used for schools, and are hung around with maps, large mottoes, and supplied with other school appurtenances.

I am well acquainted with the pastors of two of these churches, the "Springfield" and "Central"; and am glad to be able to bear witness to the truly Christian character and eminently apostolic zeal of both of them. . . .

For several years there were eight or ten schools for the freedmen in Augusta, under the direction of the Am. Missionary Association. . . . So great was the desire for instruction on the part of the blacks, that these teachers were often compelled to resume their task in the evening, after the labors of the day were over. . . .

The intelligence of the blacks in Augusta is so far beyond that of the plantation blacks, that one would hardly suppose that they belonged to the same race of beings. . . .

Charleston, S.C. (1875)

4]   The Longshoremen's Protective
                Union Association *

The annual parade of the Longshoremen's Protective Union Association took place yesterday morning. The union met at Liberty Hall, Morris Street, at eight o'clock A.M., and formed the line. On the right were President Green and other officers, and Mitchell's Band of twelve musicians. Five or six hundred of the members were in the ranks. The line of march was through Morris, King, and Broad Streets to East Bay, thence to Market Street, and along Meeting, Calhoun and King Streets to the South Carolina Institute building at the Race Course. The parade was exceedingly creditable, the members being well dressed and a goodlooking body of men. Banners were displayed, and silver and gold badges were worn by the Longshoremen. The turnout was composed almost entirely of colored men. . . .

The Longshoremen's Protective Union Association has over eight hundred members and upwards of two thousand dollars in the treasury, besides some fifteen hundred dollars in the Freedman's Bank. They claim that they are conservators, rather than disturbers of the public peace, and have only associated themselves together for mutual benefit and protection.

5]   *Charlotte, N.C. (1889)* †

Charlotte, the third city in size in the State of North Carolina, has a population of about 13,000, of whom a fraction more than one-half are negroes. . . .

* Source: *Charleston News and Courier,* January 26, 1875.
† Source: *New York Tribune,* March 24, 1889.

Few of the negroes in and around Charlotte are prospering. There are about a dozen families of them thereabouts who have fine properties, but the land is too dear within a radius of five miles of the city for them to acquire much of it. In the town itself and in the suburbs, hundreds of them own their own homes—a lot or two and a cheap frame house. But the majority are as poor as Job's turkey, and have no prospects of rising from the depths of their penury. Many of them live in ramshackle cabins, of one or two rooms and in these squalid dwellings often a dozen persons crowd. . . .

In the town they follow the rudest vocations—laborers on the railroads, drivers of drays, stonebreakers on the roads, porters in stores, toilers at the cotton gins, etc. Whatever demands hard work and gives little compensation is theirs to do, although some of them are wheelwrights, carpenters, blacksmiths or shoemakers, and make out fairly well. One of them here is a physician. He is a graduate of Shaw University, at Raleigh, and appears to be building up a paying practice.

Labor is cheap in Charlotte, that is, negro labor. The men get from $20 to $25 a month; the women who live out as domestics get from $6 to $8 a month and dinner, and have to go home at night for supper and bed and return in the morning after getting their own breakfasts. Strapping big girls, from sixteen to thirty years, will give their services as children's nurses for two or three dollars a month and found. So keen is the competition for laundry work, that the negroes will offer to do the washing of an average family for seventy-five cents a week. . . .

The negroes have an excellent graded school in Charlotte, and in the Western suburbs Biddle University dominates the city, giving instructions to more than one hundred and fifty picked young colored men, who are nearly all aspiring to be teachers and preachers for their race. On Saturday afternoons, the colored people in the city and from the surrounding country take possession of the sidewalks of Charlotte. They assemble to do their "trading" and to hobnob with their acquaintances. Few whites go shopping on the day, consequently the town looks then as if it were inhabited almost exclusively by colored people.

6] Economic Progress of Blacks
in the South (1891)

. . . In the vicinity of Birmingham, farms are owned ranging from fifty to two hundred acres.

The home-buying that is going on in the agricultural districts is going on also in the cities. In Montgomery, street after street is owned by colored people. In Chattanooga, one third of the colored people own their homes. Suburban lots range in cost from $350 to $400. A cottage costs in the neighborhood

SOURCE: Samuel J. Barrow, "What the Southern Negro Is Doing for Himself," *Atlantic Monthly*, June 1891, pp. 807–14.

8

of $600 to $650. In Birmingham, colored people pay $10 or $12 a month rent. A number of householders have gardens with two or three acres of land. Some were fortunate enough to purchase land before the prices went up, and have profited by the rise.

The Negro is also venturing as a tradesman. In all the large cities, and even in the smaller towns, in the South, he is hanging out his sign. Two young men have engaged in the grocery business at Tuskegee, Alabama. Their credit is good at the bank. . . . The colored grocers in Birmingham are sharing the prosperity of this thriving city. . . . At Tuscaloosa, the livery stable man who drove me owns several horses and carriages, and is doing well. Thus, in whatever direction one goes, he can find Negroes who are rising by force of education and character. The influence of such schools as Hampton, Atlanta, and Tuskegee is felt all through the South in the stimulus given to industrial occupations. Tuskegee has turned out a number of printers, who have made themselves independent, and get patronage from both white and colored customers. One has a printing office in Montgomery. . . . In all the mechanical trades, colored men are finding places as blacksmiths, wheelwrights, masons, bricklayers, carpenters, tinsmiths, harnessmakers, shoemakers, and machinists. In Washington, colored brickmakers are earning from four to five dollars a day. Hod-carriers receive $1.50. . . . With industrial education and diversified mechanical pursuits, the Negro brain is becoming adaptive and creative. . . . A colored assistant examiner in the Patent Office department has . . . placed at my service a list of some fifty patents taken out by colored people, which show the scope of their inventive genius. In the list of things represented are an improved gridiron, a locomotive smokestack, a cornstalk harvester, a shield for infantry and artillery, a fire extinguisher, a dough kneader, a cotton cultivator, life-preserving apparatus, a furniture caster, a biscuit cutter, a rotary engine, a printing press, a file holder, a window ventilator for railroad cars, an automatic switch for railroads, and a telephone transmitter. The electric inventions are said to have a good deal of merit, and have been assigned to a prominent company. In Birmingham, a colored inventor is making money out of his patent.

With the purchase of homes and the accumulation of property, the colored people are gradually changing their condition of living. It is seen at its worst in the miserable one-room cabins of the country districts, and in the alley population of such cities as Washington and Baltimore. . . . Bad as the one-room cabin is, it is not so bad as the tenement house in the slums of the great cities. . . .

MONTGOMERY AND WASHINGTON

. . . The social progress of the Negro is well illustrated by two historic cities—the federal capital at Washington and the former capital of the Confederacy at Montgomery. The casual traveler, who sees the alley districts and the settlements around the railroads, forms no better idea of the social development of the Negro than he does of Northern whites, if he confines his inspection to similar localities. In Montgomery, under the guidance of Dr. Dorsette, a colored physician and a respected citizen, I had an opportunity to see the homes of the colored people at their best. In some of the streets, the whites occupy one side, and the blacks the other. Occasionally the colors alternate, like the squares on a checkerboard. It is not easy externally to tell one from the other. The interiors of these homes, especially of the younger and more progressive people, are comfortably and tastefully furnished. The rooms are as high as those of their white neighbors, well carpeted and papered, while the piano or the cabinet organ suggests loftier musical tastes than that of the plantation banjo. While in most respects the movement or development of the white and colored races runs on parallel lines, in music they seem to be going in opposite directions. Though I traveled all through the South, in urban, suburban, and agricultural districts, from Baltimore to New Orleans, the only banjo I heard was played in Atlanta by a white man. . . . In New Orleans, I was astounded at the strange phenomenon of a colored handorgan grinder. . . . It is estimated that there are from 250 to 300 pianos and cabinet organs in the homes of colored people in Montgomery. . . .

Immediately after the war I lived at the national capital. Thousands of destitute blacks from Virginia and further south had settled in the barracks around the city. They owned little more than the clothes on their backs, and most of these had been given to them. The change in these districts is remarkable. Large numbers of people live in their own homes. There is not much squalor outside of the alley population. Even the poorest houses have some comforts and show some endeavor to improve. A similar story may be told of Baltimore.

. . . There are no Negro millionaires that I know of; but there is growing up a class of men with fortunes ranging from $15,000 to $100,000. This accumulation has been going on in recent years with increasing rapidity. . . .

. . . Thus, in Montgomery, Alabama, a colored barber, originally a slave, has accumulated property amounting to $75,000 or $100,000. . . . In Baltimore, there are several colored men worth $15,000 each, three or four worth from $40,000 to $60,000, and the estate of a Negro recently deceased was appraised at $100,000. In Washington, also, colored men have profited by the rise of real estate, and a few are possessed of ample fortunes. These instances might be greatly multiplied from my notes.

RISE OF A PROFESSIONAL CLASS

The result of higher education is seen in the rise of a professional class. I remember the time when a colored doctor was a curiosity even in Washington; but colored physicians, lawyers, journalists, college professors, dentists, educated clergymen, and teachers are now to be found in all the large cities of the South. In Montgomery, Dr. Dorsette has built up a thriving practice. He has erected a three-story brick building, on the lower floor of which are two stores, one of them a large and well-equipped drug store. A hall above is used for the accommodation of colored societies. In Birmingham, there are two practicing physicians, one dentist, and one lawyer. At Selma, the practicing physician is a graduate of the university. There is also a pharmacist, owning his drug store, who studied at Howard University. There are six colored lawyers and seven colored physicians in Baltimore. The professional men command the confidence and support of their own people.

10

Economic Progress of Blacks in the South (1891)

Journalism is growing slowly. There are now about fifty-five well-established Negro newspapers and journals. Thirty-seven are in the Southern States; seven are monthlies and two are semi-monthlies. The aggregate weekly circulation of all is about 850,000 copies. There are other ephemeral journals, not included in this list. The largest circulation, 15,000, is claimed for the *Indianapolis Freeman*.

The colored people are determined to have their churches, and they subscribe, in proportion to their means, large sums to sustain them. . . . In the comparatively new city of Birmingham, there are seven comfortable colored churches, ranging in cost from $2000 to $15,000. In Washington, two churches cost nearly $30,000 each, and the money has been raised almost exclusively by the colored people. In Baltimore, there are forty-four colored churches, holding a large amount of property. . . . The colored people are also ambitious to pay their preachers as much as the whites pay theirs. In Montgomery, one colored preacher has a salary of $1200 a year with a parsonage. In another city in Alabama, $1800 is paid.

BENEVOLENT AND FRATERNAL SOCIETIES

. . . The colored people have developed a laudable disposition to take care of their own poor. In addition to the Odd Fellows, Masons, and Knights of Pythias, benevolent and fraternal organizations are multiplying. The city churches are feeling a new impulse to such work. Brotherhoods, Good Samaritan societies, and mutual benefit organizations are established. Members of these organizations are allowed a regular stipend when sick. In New Orleans, the colored people have started a widows' home, and have collected enough money to buy a piece of ground and to put up a respectable building. In Montgomery, I visited the Hale Infirmary, founded by the late Joseph Hale and his wife, leading colored citizens. It is a large two-story building, especially designed by the son-in-law of the founder for hospital purposes. . . .

BUSINESS ASSOCIATIONS

. . . Small stock companies for various purposes exist in a number of cities. A little has been done in the way of building associations. There is one at Atlanta, with branches and local boards elsewhere; others at Tuskegee, Montgomery, Selma, Baltimore, and Washington. In Baltimore there are three or four such associations, but the German organizations, managed by white people, have had much more of their patronage. A daily paper of Charlotte, North Carolina, in speaking of the loan associations there, said that the colored shareholders were outstripping the white. It was noticeable that they paid more promptly. A penny savings bank, chartered under state law, was organized at Chattanooga about ten months ago. It has already one thousand depositors, the amounts ranging from two cents to one thousand dollars. The white as well as the colored children are being educated to save by this bank. In Birmingham, a similar institution was opened last October, and has about three thousand depositors. . . .

Social and Political Aspects

During Radical Reconstruction blacks were able to wield a fairly substantial measure of power in the southern states for several reasons: they were completely franchised; they formed more than one third of the population of the eleven southern states and had a clear majority in South Carolina and Mississippi; they were in alliance with the largely northern Republican party. But even before the end of Reconstruction the violent determination of the white South combined with the fragility of the blacks' affiliation with the Republicans to remove blacks as an effective political force in the South. However, in the meantime blacks had held almost the whole range of local and state offices. Document 8 gives a vivid and fair-minded account by a visiting Northerner of black political performances in the legislatures of two state capitals—Jackson, Miss., and Columbia, S.C.—and in the municipal councils of Natchez, Miss., and Petersburg, Va. The report makes clear that among black leaders were some very able and well-educated men.

The selections also illustrate aspects of the social and cultural life of blacks. Document 7, on voodoo in New Orleans, attests to the continuing influence in southern city life of African customs. Document 8 points to the love of pomp and ceremony and the general social proclivities of urban blacks of Virginia who participated regularly in "excursions," "fetes," "reunions," and "revivals." Document 9 provides an interesting contemporary account of the origins and early history of Fisk, one of the best and most influential of the fourteen black institutions of higher learning that were established in the South within three years of emancipation.

New Orleans, La. (1872)

7]   Voodoo: An Eyewitness Account

On Monday morning (St. John's Day) I went to the French Market for the express purpose of finding out from an old negress, who sells in the market and whom I have known for years to be well posted—"she is one of them"—the exact spot where the Voudou Festival would be held this year. Knowing that I had attended many of them before, she told me immediately. She made me faithfully promise that I would tell no one.

Thus posted, I took the 8 o'clock train on the Pontchartrain Railroad. Arriving at the lake I fooled around a little; saw great crowds—all looking for the

SOURCE: *New Orleans Times*, June 28, 1872.

12

place, but very few, if any, knowing where it would be. I made up my mind not to walk or ride to the scene, so I hired a skiff and pulled to the mouth of Bayou St. John—the best way of getting there from the lake end—the festival took place near Bayou Tchoupitoulas. Upon arriving at the shanty I found congregated about two hundred persons of mixed colors—white, black, and mulattoes. I knew the larger portion of them, and was received with pleasure. The ceremonies had not begun. A few moments after my arrival a large crowd arrived in a lugger, say about one hundred more, making a total of three hundred. Soon there arrived a skiff containing ten persons, among which was the Voudou Queen, Marie Lavaux. She was hailed with hurrahs.

The people were about equally divided male and female—a few more females. The larger portion of the crowd Negroes and quadroons, but about one hundred whites, say thirty or forty men, the remainder women.

Upon the arrival of Marie Lavaux, she made a few remarks in Gumbo French, and ended them by singing, "*Saiya ma coupê ça,*" to which all hands joined in the chorus of "*Mamzelle Marie chauffez ça.*"

It was then about eleven o'clock. The song ended, orders were given by the queen to build a fire as near the edge of the lake as possible, which was "did," every one being compelled to furnish a piece of wood for the fire, making a wish as they threw it on. Then a large caldron was put on the fire; it was filled with water brought in a beer barrel; then salt was put in by an old man, who jabbered something in Creole; then black pepper was put in by a young quadroon girl; she sang while putting in the pepper; then a box was brought up to the fire, from which was taken a black snake; he was cut in three pieces (the Trinity), one piece was put in by Marie Lavaux, one piece by the old man who put in the salt, and one piece by the young girl who put in the pepper; then all joined in chorus of the same song: "*Mamzelle Marie chauffez ça*"; then the queen called for a "cat" [sic], it was brought, she cut its throat, and put it into the kettle.

Another repetition of the same chorus, then a black rooster was brought to the queen. She tied its feet and head together and put it in the pot alive. Repetition of the chorus. Then came an order from the queen for every one to undress, which all did, amid songs and yells. The queen then took from her pocket a shot bag full of white and colored powders. She gave orders for everyone to join hands and circle around the pot. Then she poured the powders into the pot, sang a verse of some oracle song, to which all joined in a chorus while dancing around the pot, "*C'est l'amour, oui Maman c'est l'amour,* etc."

She then looked at her watch, and shouted *Li minuit tous moune à l'eau*—it is 12 o'clock all hands in the water—and everybody went into the lake, remained in the bath about half an hour. Upon coming out they began singing and dancing for another hour, when all were halted to listen to a speech by the queen. She preached her sermon, ending with, "I give you all half an hour recreation." Then the crowd scattered promiscuously. In half an hour the horn was blown (a sea shell), and all hands hurried back to the queen, and set up another chorus to a verse she sang to the same tune as the first one.

After the song she said "You can now eat," [and] those who brought victuals, such as gumbo, jambalaya, etc., all began eating and drinking until the horn was again blown, when all hurried to the pot, the fire was put out from under it, water thrown on and around it by four nude black women, with white handkerchiefs on their heads. During this time the chorus was kept up of *"Mamzelle Marie chauffez . . ."* Then the whole contents of the pot was poured back into the same barrel the water was taken from, the queen saying, as this was done, *pour l'année prochaine* (for the next year).

The queen then said: "You must all dress up again," which was "did." The bugle was again sounded, all hands joined around the queen. She preached another sermon, at the close of which all knelt down to pray and receive her benediction. Another chorus of *C'est l'amour, oui Maman c'est l'amour*, during which day began to break. Then the queen said: "Here is day, we must welcome it with song, and all go home." I took my skiff, left them there, pulled to Pontchartrain Railroad, and came back into the city.

Natchez and Jackson, Miss., Columbia, S.C., and Petersburg, Va. (1873)

8]   Political Representation

NATCHEZ, MISS.

The negroes came into power in Natchez in 1867. The present sheriff, the County Treasurer and Assessor, and the majority of magistrates, and all the officers managing county affairs, except one, are negroes. The Board of Aldermen has three negroes on it. There is the usual complaint among conservatives that money has been dishonestly and foolishly expended; but the government of the city seemed, on the whole, very satisfactory.

JACKSON, MISS.

. . . [In Jackson, the state capital] . . . negroes lounge everywhere, and there are large numbers of smartly dressed mulattoes, or sometimes full blacks, who flit here and there with that conscious air which distinguishes the freedman. I wish here to avow, however, that those of the negroes in office, with whom I came in contact in Mississippi, impressed me much more powerfully as worthy, intelligent, and likely to progress, than many whom I saw elsewhere in the South. There are some who are exceedingly capable, and none of those immediately attached to the Government at Jackson are incapable. . . .

A visit to the Capitol showed me that the negroes, who form considerably more than half the population of Mississippi, had certainly secured a fair share of the offices. Colored men act as officials or assistants in the offices of the Auditor, the Secretary of State, the Public Library, the Commissioner of Emigration, and the Superintendent of Public Instruction. The Secretary of State,

SOURCE: Edward King, *The Great South*, Hartford, Conn.: American Publishing Co., 1873, pp. 293, 314–15, 460–61, 580–81, 583–84.

who has some negro blood in his veins, is the natural son of a well-known Mississipian of the old regime, formerly engaged in the politics of his State; and the Speaker of the House of Representatives at the last session was a black man. The blacks who went and came from the Governor's office seemed very intelligent, and some of them entered into general conversation in an interesting manner.

COLUMBIA, S.C.

But it is at the State-House in Columbia that one arrives at the truth. . . . In the poorly constructed and badly lighted corridors below are the offices of the State Government—that of the Governor, the Treasurer, the Secretary of State, and the Superintendent of State Schools—each and all of them usually filled with colored people, discussing the issues of the hour. The Secretary of State is a mulatto, who has entered the law school at the University, and carries on his double duties very creditably.

In the House and Senate the negro element stands out conspicuous[ly]. . . .

The House, when I visited it, was composed of eighty-three colored members, all of whom were Republicans, and forty-one whites; the Senate consisted of fifteen colored men, ten white Republicans, and eight white Democrats. The President of the Senate and the Speaker of the House, both colored, were elegant and accomplished men, highly educated, who would have creditably presided over any commonwealth's legislative assembly. In the House the negroes were of a much lower grade, and more obviously ignorant, than in the Senate. . . .

The negro does not allow himself to be abashed by hostile criticism. When he gets a sentence tangled, or cannot follow the thread of his own thought in words, he will gravely open a book—the statutes, or some other ponderous volume lying before him—and, after seeming to consult it for some minutes, will resume. He has been gaining time for a new start.

There are men of real force and eloquence among the negroes chosen to the House, but they are the exception. In the Senate I noticed decorum and ability among the members. Several of the colored Senators spoke exceedingly well, and with great ease and grace of manner; others were awkward and coarse. . . . The black pages fan to and fro, carrying letters and documents to the honorable Senators; and a fine-looking quadroon, or possibly octoroon woman, and the ebony gentleman escorting her, were admitted to the floor of the Senate, and sat for some time listening to the debates.

To the careless observer it seems encouraging to see the negroes, so lately freed from a semi-barbaric condition, doing so well, because their conduct is really better than one would suppose them capable of, after having seen the constituency from which they were elevated. . . .

PETERSBURG, VA.

The negroes were slightly in the majority in Petersburg at the time of my visit. As at Lynchburg, the Northerner is at first amazed by the mass of black and yellow faces. The hackmen who shriek in your ear as you arrive at the depot, the brakeman on the train, the waiter in the hotel, all are African. In the tobacco factories hundreds of dusky forms are toiling, and an equal number are slouching in the sunshine. On the day of my visit a colored Masonic excursion had arrived from Richmond, and the streets were filled with stout negro men, decently clothed, and their wives and sweethearts, attired in even louder colors than those affected by Northern servant girls. Each was talking vociferously; officials, in flaunting regalia and sweating at every pore, rushed to and fro; bands thundered and urchins screamed. The Virginia negro has almost the French passion for fete-days; he is continually planning some excursion or "reunion," and will readily consent to live in a cellar and submit to poor fare for the sake of saving money to expend in frolic.

At Petersburg the negroes are from time to time largely represented in the Common Council, and sometimes have a controlling voice in municipal affairs. The white citizens have readily adapted themselves to the circumstances, and the session of the Council which I attended was as orderly and, in the main, as well conducted as that of any Eastern city. There was, it is true, an informality in the speech of some of the colored members . . . but it was evident that all were acting intelligently, and had come to some appreciation of their responsibilities. Most of the colored members were full types of the African. . . . The Commissioner of Streets and the Engineer of the Board of Waterworks were both negroes. The mayoralty and the other city offices remained, at the epoch of my visit, in the hands of white Radicals, and the Negroes had made no special struggle to secure them, although they are to the whites in the city as eleven to nine. . . .

Revival Meeting

During our stay in this section a "revival meeting" was announced by the colored brethren of the surrounding country, to be held at a little station halfway between Richmond and Petersburg, and we determined to be present. On a beautiful Sunday morning we drove out through the fields, in which, the oak timber having been cut away, a rank growth of pine had sprung up; and stopping a massive coal black man, dressed in white duck, with a flaming red necktie at his throat, w· · .quired "the way."

"Ef yo' want to go to Zion's Hill, dat yer's de way; but ef yo' want to go whar de good preachin' is, dis yer road 'll take yo' to it."

Presently we arrived at a large frame building, much like a country schoolhouse, save that it was neither ceiled nor plastered, and therein the revivalists were gathered. A powerful spiritual wave had swept over the colored population, and dozens of carts, loaded with dusky searchers for truth, came rolling along the rough roads, and stopped before the primitive door. Entering, we found represented every shade of color, from the coal black full-blood to the elegantly dressed and well-mannered octoroon. The congregation was not large. Owing to the excitement which had prevailed for several previous Sabbaths, many had retired, worn out, from the spiritual feast. The women sat on the left side, the men on the right of a broad aisle, running to a plain wooden pulpit, in which were three moon-faced negroes, two of them preachers, and the third a State Senator.

In front of the pulpit, behind a little table, stood an olive-colored elderly man, neatly dressed, and with a wildness in his eyes, and an intensity written upon his lips. . . . The audience was breathless with attention as the preacher, a strolling missionary, supported by Quakers in Louisiana, took up the great Bible, and, poising it on his lean, nervous hand, poured forth such an impassioned appeal that I fairly trembled. I was not prepared for such vehemence. Never, in the history of New England revivalism, was there such a scene. The preacher stood with many of his hearers well around him; one of the deacons and exhorters, a black giant in spectacles, was his point d'appui, and to him he appealed from time to time, shaking him roughly by the shoulder, and hissing his words in his ear with fiery vehemence. The proposition with which he started was somewhat incomprehensible to us, viz.: "Christ is the creating power of God"; but the proposition was of no consequence, because every few moments he would burst into paroxysms of exhortation, before which the emotional audience rocked and trembled like reeds in a wind. He had a peculiar way of addressing himself suddenly and in a startling manner to some individual in the congregation, dancing, and pounding the table furiously with both hands, in the agony of his exhortation to that person.

From time to time he would draw in his breath with great force, as if repressing a sob, and, when speaking of love and salvation, he inevitably fell into a chant, or monotone, which was very effective. Under the hurricanes of his appeal, the fury of his shouting, the magnetic influence of his song, one of the old deacons went into a spasm of religious fervor, and now and then yelled vociferously. A milder brother ventured to remonstrate, whereupon the Quaker preacher turned upon him, saying loudly: "Let dat brudder shout, an' tend to dine own business!"

Then he began preaching against hypocrisy. He seemed especially to chide the women for becoming converted with too great ease. . . .

Nashville, Tenn. (1874)

9]   Fisk University:
                The Early Years, 1865–74

Fisk University is but one of a cordon of educational strongholds, reaching from the Ohio to the Gulf, and from the Atlantic ocean to the remotest borders of Texas, intended to break the supremacy of ignorance in the South, which have been established by the American Missionary Association of New York, during the last ten years, and are in various degrees of advancement, in build-

SOURCE: G. W. Hubbard (ed.), *A History of Colored Schools of Nashville, Tennessee*, Nashville, Tenn.: Wheeler, Marshall and Bruce, 1874, pp. 21–24.

ings and studies, according to the time they have existed and the labor bestowed upon them.

. . . . .

In October, 1865, Rev. E. P. Smith, who had just been appointed District Secretary at Cincinnati, and Rev. E. M. Cravath, came to Nashville for the purpose of opening a school in this city according to the general plan of the Association. After searching several days their attention was directed to the railroad hospital, west of the Chattanooga Depot, which was about to be given up by the Government. General Fisk was at that time Commissioner of the Freedmen's Bureau, and it was largely due to his interest and labor that the buildings were turned over to the Association for educational purposes. As a recognition of his services in behalf of the colored people of Tennessee, the name of Fisk School was given to the infant enterprise.

While the building belonged to the Government, the land belonged to Mr. Hines, and must be purchased before the school could be opened. Here was a great dilemma. The secretaries had been instructed not to invest in real estate, and here $16,000 must be paid, in order to secure a location for the school. After long and profound deliberation, the location of the deliberations being a convenient board pile, Rev. E. M. Cravath, Rev. E. P. Smith, and Prof. John Ogden purchased the land on their own responsibility, and gave their individual notes for the payment of the amount. It was some months before the Association assumed the notes. The buildings were at that time full of hospital stores; the dead house stood on the spot where the ladies' dormitory now stands; the officers were closing up their accounts preparatory to finishing their work. Under these circumstances, the opening exercises of the school took place amid such a blast of trumpets as indicated that the new work was to begin with a vigorous life.

The following persons were present, and delivered addresses:

Gov. W. G. Brownlow, General C. B. Fisk, Prof. John Ogden, Senator Wm. Bosson, Dr. J. B. Lindsley, Rev. R. H. Allen, Nelson Walker, Esq., and Mr. Richard Harris.

The school went forward under the efficient charge of Prof. John Ogden, with an attendance of about a thousand pupils during that year, and was recognized as a power in the city. At the close of the term of the next year, in the summer of 1867, a concert was given in Masonic Hall under the leadership of George L. White, now conducting the Jubilee Singers. This concert was a brilliant success, the building being crowded, and the audience most enthusiastic. Many of the best citizens of Nashville were present, and expressed themselves highly pleased with the quality of the music and the accuracy of its rendering. A few weeks afterward the City Council opened the city schools to the colored children, a result to the attainment of which it is believed the concert contributed not a little.

In August, 1871, the school took a step forward, and was chartered as a University, with a Board of nine Trustees, and the Academic and Normal Departments were opened soon after. This step was made possible by the fact that the city schools were opened for the colored people.

About this time General O. O. Howard, of the Freedmen's Bureau, donated

$7,000 to the school, thus rendering it advisable to incorporate it, and provide it with a Board of Trustees. At that time provision was made for a boarding department in connection with the school, into which students should be received, that they might be under good home influences. . . .

Fisk University since its beginning has made the preparation of teachers for the public schools of the State and the South a very prominent part of its work. From the first, an increasing number of its students have taught each year, and have uniformly done excellent work. From all sources have come most hearty endorsements of those who have received their training at this institution. These endorsements embrace not only the qualifications for governing schools, for imparting instruction, but also the moral character of the student teachers.

. . . . .

As the question of an adequate supply of competent teachers of the public schools will be for years to come an imperative one for the educators to answer, Fisk University proposes to address itself to this especial work in the future. It presents what has already been done as an earnest of its intentions for the future.

. . . . .

Its progress has been necessarily slow. Yet there are in actual operation College, Theological and Normal Classes. In the College Course, three classes, Freshmen, Sophomore and Senior are organized, and the students in them are studying the branches usually pursued. During the year just drawing to a close sixty-four students have studied Latin, and more than thirty Greek. In Latin, the Exercises, Caesar, Livy, Cicero and Horace have been studied. In Greek, the beginning books, *Anabasis* and *Iliad*. In Mathematics, Algebra, Geometry, Trigonometry; and in Science, Botany, Physiology and Chemistry; Vocal and Instrumental Music and French have also been taught. While it is not the policy of the University to urge all, or even the large part, of its pupils through the College Course, yet it is its aim to furnish the highest training to such young men and women as are by natural gifts and the force of circumstance justifiable in pursuing a College Course.

With the facilities for carrying on its extensive work, Fisk University is as yet imperfectly supplied. It has a library of one thousand volumes, to which important additions will soon be made. It has a cabinet of several hundred geological and mineralogical specimens; it has a small laboratory in which the classes become acquainted with practical chemistry, under the direction of a skilled manipulator. The students also conduct a vigorous literary society, for their improvement in the arts of writing and speaking, and in parliamentary usage.

The plans of the University will soon be enlarged, with the enlargement of its appliances for carrying on its work. The means for increasing its facilities have been secured by the Jubilee Singers, whose remarkable career has hitherto had no parallel in the history of institutions of learning.

In 1871, George L. White, Treasurer of the University, took a company of pupils in the school on a singing tour to the North, for the purpose of raising funds to purchase lands and erect buildings for the University. He spent two winters in the East, and gave concerts to over-crowded houses, with a net result of $40,000.

During the past year the company has been in Great Britain. Their concerts have met with the same enthusiastic receptions everywhere. £10,000 or $50,-000 were the net proceeds of the European tour. With these $90,000 twenty-five acres of most beautifully located land have been purchased, and on the site of old Fort Gillem, where the cannon of war once bristled, Jubilee Hall begins to tower upward. This hall is 128 feet south front, and 145 feet east front. It will consist of six stories from cellar to roof, and will accommodate one hundred and seventy pupils with rooms, and three hundred and twenty-five with table sittings.

Atlanta, Ga. (1894)

10]   After the Civil War

In 1867, by order of General Pope, the Constitutional Convention met in the city of Atlanta for the purpose of revising the Constitution of the State of Georgia, and reconstructing the political affairs concerning the government generally. And be it said to the honor of the Black Side, that the majority who composed that Convention were some of the noblest and most patriotic of the sons of Ham. This meeting brought about fiery, bitter speeches from both sides, which made this period almost as dangerous as any preceding it. . . .

It was, however, the year of jubilee for the Black Side. Nearly all public affairs were under their control or that of the party to which they belonged. . . .

All over the State, as well as at Atlanta, began the organization of leagues, which were for the purpose of inspiring and encouraging the Republican party in this State.

This league trumpet could have been heard from the mountains to the seaboard. The reinforcement of their energies and power was the backbone and the life-giving power of the Republican party. In Atlanta could be seen the sable sons of Ham, who a few days previous, handled a plow, saw, shovel or pick, crowding into the Legislature and Senate Hall, for the purpose of making laws for the government of their former owners. In nearly every seat in the old capitol hall were seated the ebony-faced men, once slaves, now free men and statesmen. There sat H. M. Turner, now D.D., LL.D., U. L. Houston, Madison Davis, Romulus Moore, Alfred Richardson, the martyr of the Republican party, James Simm, Jacob Fuller, Campbell and Bradley, and a number of others. . . .

. . . While the brothers in black were rejoicing in their sleeves over their

SOURCE: E. R. Carter, *The Black Side. A Partial History of the Business, Religious and Educational Side of the Negro in Atlanta, Ga.,* Atlanta: E. R. Carter, 1894, pp. 17–25. [E. R. Carter was a nineteenth-century Atlanta author.—Ed.]

freedom, they were at the same time trembling in their boots, from fear of losing their life, so great was the hostility between the two races. . . .

. . . . .

The many hardships and privations which he had so long . . . borne, energized him to strive to make a brighter future for himself and children; accordingly, James Tate, who is now one of the most successful wholesale and retail merchants of the Black Side . . . in the year 1866 commenced a grocery business on Walton street, near the First Baptist Church (white). His total stock at that time amounted to $6.00 (six dollars). He now carries a stock of more than $6,000 (six thousand dollars), in a neat, two-story brick building on Decatur street, where he has resided since 1867. This man was the first to open and teach a school in this city. He might rightly be called the father of the beginning of business and enterprise, as well as of the intellectual source. The first of the Black Side of this now thriving city to open a store, the first to open a school, the first to teach a school! From him no doubt came the inspiration for the many who have come after him. Business houses among the Black Side are now established all over this wonderful vestibule of the South; businesses of every class and kind, from the junk to the dry-goods store.

. . . . .

In the year 1868, under the leadership of Rev. Frank Quarles, the First Colored Baptist Church was organized. This body consisted of about twenty-five members, among whom were John Carter, Levi Allen, Jake Whittaker, James Tate, Orange Davis, Betsy Rucker, Mary Whitehead and others. They first held religious services in a car-box, in the northeastern part of the city, on Walton street. Here they worshipped for a considerable time. The next place of worship was somewhere on Luckie street, where they also held meetings quite a while. Finally a lot on the corner of Haynes and Markham streets was purchased, and a small wooden building was put up. The membership had by this time increased considerably, and wishing a still more desirable site, the present lot on corner of Mitchell and Haynes streets was, through the recommendation of John Carter, purchased, and upon this a more commodious structure of brick erected. . . .

. . . . .

On some of the most beautiful avenues and streets of this basin city are grand structures erected as altars to Jehovah, from which minarets, domes and steeples lift their heads to the azure sky. Along these same streets are many structures of brick, where various kinds of businesses are carried on.

Some of these structures are: Odd Fellows Hall, pointing upward four stories in height, on Piedmont avenue; Good Samaritan building, ascending four stories, on Ivy street; the Schell Opera House and Hall, of three stories in height, on West Mitchell street. On Marietta street, the erections of Rivers, McHenry and McKinley stand with neat brick fronts. The storehouses of Tate and Murphy occupy conspicuous places on Decatur street, while on West Mitchell street, near their beautiful residences, are to be seen the two-story structures of N. Holmes and W. H. Landrum, used as storehouses; and, in proximity to the same, on West Hunter street, is the handsome storehouse, with residence above, of M. V. James. The neat storehouse and dwelling of P.

Escridge, on Wheat street, deserves special mention, for the owner and proprietor is a man of acute business talent. Going in another direction, we arrive at the storehouse and dwelling of I. P. Moyer, on Peters street. Here he carries on a flourishing business. Also on same street are the storehouses and dwellings of King and R. N. Davis. Such are some of the brick buildings owned by the Black Side of Atlanta.

Returning to Wheat street, we come to the large fancy grocery of F. H. Crumbly, where he does business on an extensive scale. Above this place of business are his handsomely arranged apartments. On the same street are the business houses of Pace, and C. C. Cater; the storehouse and residence of Hagler & Co. Next in line is the pharmacy of Drs. Slater, Butler & Co. Then, on Fraser and Martin streets are the storehouses, near which are the dwellings also, of Watts, Graham, Emery, and Epps & Jones. . . .

Briefly we mention some other enterprises carried on by the Black Side of our business-like city of Atlanta. Among the most prominent is that of J. McKinley, which consists in rock-quarrying and dealing in sand and brick. In this enterprise he employs at times more than one hundred and fifty laborers, white and colored. Another, the Cooperative South View Cemetery Co. The Georgia Real Estate Loan and Trust Co., of which the Hon. H. A. Rucker is President. Atlanta Loan and Trust Co., of which W. C. Redding is President.

These enterprises show the marked ability of the Black Side in controlling and managing the most intricate forms of business, and is a firm denial of the assertion that the negro is non-progressive. It also demonstrates to the world what the negro will do if given a chance and let alone.

Just here may also be mentioned the professional pursuits. As lawyers we have the erudite Robert Davis and the cunning, shrewd M. E. Loftin. In dentistry the famous pedestrian, Robert Badger, and the sons of the late, much lamented Roderick Badger. . . .

. . . . .

. . . There is the firm of Drs. Asbury, Taylor & Co., known as the Friendship Drug-store. Then, that of Drs. Strong & Lockhart. All of these are skillful physicians and have an extensive practice among our people.

Those in the educational line, who are capable of filling chairs of languages and sciences at the colleges of to-day are: the scholarly, linguistic Professor Wm. E. Holmes, of the A.B.S.; Professor Wm. H. Crogman, who is considered, by all whose pleasure it has been to meet him, as a deep thinker, an able instructor and eloquent speaker; Professor St. George Richardson, the learned Principal of the Morris Brown College.

In the public schools we have as principals: the refined, cultured, gentlemanly instructor W. B. Matthews, of the Houston street school; the business-like and oratorical E. L. Chew, of the Gray street school; the eloquent "Boy royal of the times," F. Grant Snelson, of the Mitchell street school; and the witty, deep-thinking, progressive, self-made Carl Walter Hill, of the Martin street school. As lady principal, there is the inestimable Christian worker, well-informed Mrs. Allie D. Carey, of the Roach street school; and of her it is truly said that nowhere is there a more intelligent, better read or better informed person in all the languages than she.

After the Civil War

Having spoken of those who work with the mind, we now mention those whose lot it is to deal with the body. Our successful tailors are: the polite, artistic G. M. Howell; the venerable Wm. Finch; the successful Rufus Cooper; A. W. Finch, who does a flourishing business; and B. B. Brightwell, the steady. These are scarcely more than half of our successful tailors; but this number serves to show what the negro is doing in this line. We also have several artistic and fashionable dressmakers in our midst, and the gentle, obliging Mrs. Pennemone as milliner and hatter. Verily, the sons and daughters of Ham are applying themselves to the useful arts and professions of life.

Political and Racial Conflicts

Because urban riots in the South were partly political in origin, they were not exclusively racial, although the traditional hostility between whites and blacks was always a factor. The riots stemmed from the attempts of whites to nullify blacks as a political force, to diminish or eliminate them as competition for jobs, and to subordinate them socially. An additional aggravating factor— which also applied later to the twentieth-century urban industrial North—was the abnormally large jump in the black population of southern cities. As a result of the dislocation caused by the Civil War and emancipation, in the decade 1860–70 the black population in fourteen main southern cities increased by 90.7%, compared with a 16.7% white increase. In the New Orleans riot of 1866 (Document 12) although blacks were the main object of the fury of the white mob, it directed part of its anger and some of its bullets at the white Republican allies of blacks as well. And in the case of the Hamburg riot (Document 16), a black municipal judge headed a white state militia against a black and aggressive militia company that had apparently harassed two whites and defied the authority of the judge. The partly political motivation for the riots can also be illustrated by the fact that in three of the cases documented below—Vicksburg (1874), Hamburg (1876), and Wilmington (1898)—the riots led directly to a change from Republican municipal governments in which blacks were represented to all-white conservative Democratic governments.

The economic and social competition that helped cause these riots is best illustrated by the Memphis riot of 1866 (Document 11)—a bloody and destructive clash between blacks and the Irish.

In all of these riots blacks got much the worst of it; the police and militia either left blacks to the mercy of the furious white mobs or, sometimes, joined them in murdering and brutalizing blacks. Thus in the Memphis riots the Irish policemen and firemen were responsible along with the mob for the final black toll: 46 killed; five women raped; 91 homes, four churches, and twelve schoolhouses burned down. The Wilmington riot (Document 17), in which eleven blacks were killed, had such a traumatic impact on the town's black community that well over a thousand emigrated shortly thereafter.

23

Memphis, Tenn. (1866)

11]   Irish-Black Clash

From Headquarters Department of Tennessee,
Memphis, May 12, 1866.

Lt. Gen. U. S. Grant, U.S.A:

Your telegram of this date received.

The 3d colored artillery has been stationed here since its organization, and consequently was not under the best of discipline; large numbers of the men had what they call families living in South Memphis, contiguous to the fort in which the soldiers were stationed. These soldiers had been used as the instruments to execute the orders of government agents, such as provost marshal's bureau agents, &c, and consequently had been more or less brought directly into contact with the law-breaking portion of the community and the police, which is not far from being composed principally of Irishmen, who consider the negro as his competitor and natural enemy. Many negro soldiers have, from time to time, been arrested by the police, and many whites, including some of the police, have been arrested by the negro soldiers, and in both cases those arrested have not unfrequently been treated with a harshness altogether unnecessary. These remarks and hints will lead you to reflections which will explain and indicate to you the state of feeling which existed between the negro soldiers and their sympathizers and the lower class of whites and their sympathizers, in which last are included agitators, demagogues, and office-seekers. The testimony before the commission which I have assembled to investigate the circumstances connected with the riot shows, that about 4 o'clock Monday afternoon, April 30, four (4) policemen were walking down Cousey street and met three or four negroes; they jostled each other on the side-walk; an altercation occurred; one of the policemen struck a negro with a pistol, and was in return struck by another negro with a cane. There was no further trouble though a good deal of excitement among the negroes during that night. Incident on this encounter, about 4 o'clock p.m., Tuesday, May 1, a crowd of from fifty to seventy-five negroes, mostly discharged soldiers, were congregated together near the corner of Main and South streets; the greater portion of these negroes were intoxicated. Six policemen approached the crowd and arrested two of the most boisterous of the negroes; the policemen proceeded to conduct these two negroes towards the station-house, being followed by the crowd of negroes, which increased as proceeded, and who used very insulting and threatening language, and accompanied their threats by firing pistols into the air; the police turned and fired upon the negroes, wounding one; one of the negro prisoners escaped, and the other was released by the police. The ne-

SOURCE: "Riot at Memphis," 39th Congress, 1st Session, House of Representatives, Ex. Doc No. 122, Washington, D.C., 1866.

groes returned the fire, wounding one of the police. The police force of the city, together with a large crowd of citizens, congregated together in the vicinity of South street, and being very much infuriated, proceeded to shoot, beat, and threaten every negro met with in that portion of the city. This was continued until about midnight on Tuesday night, when it was quelled by the interference of a small detachment of United States troops. Wednesday morning arrived, and found large crowds of people collected together in South Memphis, most of whom were armed; they remained there until about 1 o'clock p.m., when they were dispersed by a detachment of United States soldiers which had been employed during the day in keeping the discharged negro soldiers in and the white people out of the fort. During the day several negro shanties were burned down. About 10 o'clock Wednesday night a party of mounted men began to set fire to the negro school-houses, churches and dwelling-houses. It is hoped that the investigation now being had will result in identifying the parties engaged. During Tuesday and Wednesday several inoffensive negroes were killed, and many maltreated and beaten in different parts of the city. The number killed and wounded in the riot, so far as can be ascertained by the commission, were one white man killed, shot by white man behind him; one white man wounded, shot by negroes. The number of negroes shot and beaten to death has not yet been ascertained. . . . Frequent applications were made for arms and for permission to organize a militia force, all of which were refused, and Thursday I issued an order prohibiting any persons, under whatever pretext, from assembling anywhere armed or unarmed. Great fears were entertained that other buildings, such as the Freedmen's Bureau buildings of the Memphis post, would be burned down, but if any such intentions were had, the disposition made of the small force at my disposal prevented the realization. An attempt was made by some parties to gain possession of the muskets which a few days before had been turned in by the 3d colored artillery. Every officer and man here was on duty day and night during the riot. On the 4th they were relieved by a detachment I had ordered over from Nashville.

As before stated, the rioters were composed of the police, firemen, and the rabble and negro-haters in general, with a sprinkling of Yankee-haters, all led on and encouraged by demagogues and office hunters, and most of them under the influence of whiskey. It appears in evidence before the commission that John Creighton, recorder of the city, made a speech to the rioters, in which he said: "We are not prepared, but let us prepare to clean every negro son-of-a-bitch out of town." Very few paroled confederates were mixed up with the rioters on Tuesday and Wednesday, the large portion being registered voters. Who composed the incendiaries on Wednesday night remains to be developed.

GEORGE STONEMAN,
Major General Commanding
Headquarters Army United States

12]   *New Orleans, La. (1866)*

I have already forwarded a number of disconnected despatches relative to today's fearful carnage, and now propose to give you a more connected account.
I only write what I can substantiate on the best authority. The Convention
met at 11 o'clock, twenty-six members being present, Judge R. K. Howell,
since missing, in the chair. King Butler, also missing, moved an adjournment of
an hour, during which time the Sergeant-at-Arms was directed to compel the
attendance of absentees. The Hall was densely packed with freedmen and
whites, the former having armed themselves extensively since their Friday's
demonstrations. Just after the adjournment a procession containing about a
hundred freedmen, carrying a United States Flag, and marching the streets
with martial music, arrived at the Institute, having had a slight disturbance on
Canal-street. At this juncture the merchants all over the city, fearing the coming riot, closed their stores. When the procession entered the building, a squad
of police followed and attempted to make arrests. A scene of the wildest confusion followed; pistols were fired, clubs and canes were used, and brickbats flew
in every direction. The policemen claim that they were merely attempting to
arrest the Canal-street rioters, above mentioned, but certain it is that they
mounted the platform, where a small body of the members yet remained, and
one of them presented a pistol upon their using offensive language. The policemen were finally driven out of the building, leaving inside Gov. Hahn, Judge
Howell, Mr. De Costie and other gentlemen, with Clark, attached to the State
Government, beside about fifty freedmen. Fortunately, Gov. Wells had just left
the building for the purpose of consulting with Gen. Baird about calling out
troops, Gen. Sheridan being out of town.

The Institute used now as the State Capitol is located in Dryades-street, between Canal and Common, and when the policemen were driven out they
were met by a large body of freedmen, who caused them to fall back to Canal-street. Hiring a furniture cart, I used it as an observatory on Canal-street.
The policemen rallied and drove the freedmen and their friends back to Common, and in turn were driven back to Canal-street, leaving Dryades-street perfectly clear of any vestige of humanity except the bodies of three dead freedmen. Up to this time one police officer had been mortally wounded, one
severely, others were slightly hurt with clubs and pistol shots. Police reinforce-
ments soon appeared in Canal-street, and the crowd of rioters accompanying
the police approached the Institute and commenced throwing stones through
the windows and firing pistols at any one they could see inside the building.
At the same time a detachment of police attacked the crowd of freedmen on
Common-street, and after sharp firing and wounding several blacks, they drove
them away. This gave the police and the mob which accompanied them, full
control of Dryades-street.

A fire-engine was brought out and placed in front of the Institute, for what

Source: *The New York Times*, August 1, 1866.

New Orleans, La.

purpose I do not know. Several attempts were made by the police to enter the building, but they were repulsed. The ammunition of the men in the Institute seemed to give out about this time, as they did not fire any more. They attempted to escape through the rear of the Institute into Baronne-street, but were met and either arrested or shot down. They also tried to escape through an alley which runs from Dryades to Baronne, on the Canal-street side. I do not know that any freedmen succeeded in getting away from the building alive, although I saw several at a distance from it being marched to Police Headquarters. I think that every one who tried to escape from it was killed, and I saw several brought in the alley above-mentioned,·and after they fell I saw crowds of ruffians beating them as they were dying.

The policemen, whatever their orders were, behaved well toward the white prisoners, comparatively speaking. A. M. Fish was the first member of the Convention captured, and I am happy to say that although the police could not prevent the crowd from abusing him badly, they did keep him from being lynched. A man mounted a lamp-post on Canal-street as Fish was being carried by under guard and got a rope ready to hang him, but the guard drove the crowd away with their pistols. The next member arrested was Capt. Haynes, a Texas scout for our army during the war. The crowd had been taught a lesson and did not interfere with him, although they grumbled deeply as he passed through, calling them rebels, traitors and other pet names.

Gov. Hahn succeeded in getting into the hands of the police unhurt, from out of the building where he had been, not as a member, but as one of the most prominent equal rights men in the State. While he was under guard, however, some coward shot him through the back of the head, inflicting a dangerous wound, and he was also stabbed. He was then placed in a hack and carried to Police Headquarters where I saw him sent into confinement. He was very pale and the blood trickled down his face from a wound which seemed to have reached his left temple.

Mr. Dostie, who had the reputation of being the most violent negro suffrage in the South, and who certainly was the most violent speaker on Friday last, was killed while attempting to get away. I am told that a policeman shot him in the back, and that after he fell a crowd jumped on him and cut him horribly with knives.

John Henderson and other members of the Convention were also captured, and were wounded—by stray shots, the local papers say, but more likely by cowardly rioters—while on their way to the stationhouse.

The riot commenced at 12:15 and ended at 3:30 o'clock. At 2:45 o'clock the military, under Gen. Baird, appeared on Canal-street and finally took possession of the whole city. Before night the riot was confined to Dryades, Baronne, Common, Carondelet and Canal streets, and the buildings and yards all around the Institute. I saw freedmen shot dead on all of the above streets except Canal, who could have been arrested uninjured. How many men have been killed, wounded, or even arrested, it is impossible to say, but my estimate is one hundred freedmen and twenty-five whites killed and wounded and one hundred altogether arrested.

The substantial men of the city deplore the occurrence, but all are very violent in their expressions, some glorying in the murder of Dostie and others in the murder of the freedmen.

Charleston, S.C. (1867)

13] Streetcar Revolt *

On Tuesday afternoon, March 7, after the adjournment of the Freedmen's mass meeting in Charleston, S.C., an attempt was made by some of them to test their right to ride in the street car, which is denied them by the rules of the Company. One of them entered a car, and declined to leave it when requested to do so by the conductor, who at the same time informed him of the Company's rules. The conductor, however, insisted that he should at least leave the inside of the car, and finally his friends, who found he was liable to be forcibly ejected if the resistance were offered, persuaded him to yield. On its return trip the car was filled at the same place by a crowd of negroes, who rushed into it, to the great discomfort of the white passengers, and although remonstrated with and appealed to by the conductor, declined to go out. The driver then attempted, by direction of the conductor, to throw his car from the track; and failing in this, unhitched his horses and left the car. The negroes attempted to push the car forward, and threatened personal violence to the conductor, but the arrival of the police and detachment of soldiers caused the negroes to disperse. Other cars were in the meantime entered in the same way, and the negroes, finding the conductors would not permit them to ride, endeavored to interrupt the travel of the cars by placing stones on the tracks. . . .

Memphis, Tenn. (1874)

14] Clash among Firemen †

Some weeks since Mayor Logue appointed negroes to take charge of a base carriage in Chelsea, which action was bitterly opposed by the firemen, and was annulled by the general council. Since then the feeling has been growing worse and last Sunday, in a dispute about the Civil Rights bill, a white man was dangerously cut by a negro with a razor. Some of the white man's friends, among them a number of firemen, seized and doubtless would have lynched the negro, but for an alarm of fire. The riotous proceedings on Decoration Day, and the arrest of Thomas Swan, President of the Pall-bearers and a leading colored politician, has embittered the negroes. Vague rumors of riots and

* Source: *The New York Times*, March 13, 1867.
† Source: *The New York Times*, June 6, 1874.

Vicksburg, Miss.

attacks by the blacks in revenge have been current for a day or two, which has been caused by the bravado of a few negroes to that effect. Most of the members of the Pall-bearers' Association served in the Union Army, and by some means they have secured Springfield rifles. The *Ledger* asserts positively that last night 150 of them were drilling beyond Chelsea from 11 till 3 o'clock, and had pickets thrown out, who halted several persons, and prevented any one approaching. . . .

15]   *Vicksburg, Miss. (1874)*

There has been for some time trouble brewing between the Tax-payers Association and citizens and the county officials. The sheriff was acting without a legal bond and the Board of Supervisors refused to order a new one, although the time for paying the taxes had arrived. Two or three officials were under indictment for forgery and embezzlements, and the citizens, despairing of any relief from the partisan courts, held a meeting last Wednesday, and in a body proceeded to the courthouse to demand the resignation of the Sheriff, Chancery Clerk, Treasurer, and Coroner. All fled except Sheriff Crosby, a negro, and he signed his resignation on Saturday. A card appeared upon the street signed Crosby and calling upon all citizens of Warren County, Republicans, white and black, to come to his aid and support him in his position. Crosby publicly and through the newspapers denied authorship of the card, yet this afternoon armed bodies of negroes appeared advancing on the city from six different roads. The alarm was sounded about 5 o'clock and the citizens gathered en masse, armed, and immediately advanced to meet the negroes on Baldwin Ferry road. The negroes were met just outside the city, on Grove Street, about 200 strong. The commanders of the citizens warned the Negroes to disperse, but they refused and immediately commenced firing on both sides. The negroes retreated about a mile and again made a stand in the old breastworks and a house, but were routed. The loss in this engagement was one citizen, Oliver Brown, killed, and about twelve or fifteen negroes killed, several wounded, and about twenty prisoners. On the Hills Ferry Road about 250 negroes were met and routed, after a short engagement, with several killed and wounded.

Andrew Owens, the negro who commanded the negroes on Baldwin's Ferry Road, was captured and committed to jail. In an interview with a Vicksburg *Herald* reporter, Owens said he was ordered by Sheriff Crosby to come to the city today with all the armed men he could get together.

Alexander Stockhouse, from Newton, one of the captured negroes, says the order for all the negroes to come to Vicksburg this morning was read in church on Sunday.

Crosby, who is under guard at the Court-house, denies that he gave such orders.

Source: *The New York Times,* December 8, 1874.

It is reported this evening that the negroes are committing depredation in the country.

The intense excitement which prevailed this morning has subsided to a great degree yet many citizens are under arms, and all the roads are picketed. . . .

16] *Hamburg, S.C. (1876)*

AUGUSTA, JULY 8.   There has been serious trouble in Hamburg. On the 4th Robert Butler and another citizen of Edgefield County, while driving to the town of Hamburg were interrupted by a colored Militia company, who blocked up the public highway and prevented them from proceeding on their way home. Complaint was made by Butler to Prince Rivers, colored, a trial Justice, who summoned witnesses to investigate the matter. "Doc" Adams, Captain of the company, was the first witness examined. Adams became so insolent Justice Rivers arrested him for contempt and continued the case until this afternoon. When the trial was resumed the company proceeded to the courthouse and rescued the prisoner Adams. Rivers, who in addition to being a trial Justice, commands the State Militia, ordered the company to disarm, and on [its] refusing to comply with his orders, he called upon the citizens for aid to enforce his orders. The citizens responded, and the Militia company took possession of a brick building and refused to surrender. Fire was opened by both sides, which continued for several hours with but little effect. One white man, Mackey Merriwether, was shot in the head and killed. His body was brought to Augusta. Another white man was reported wounded. One of the negroes is reported killed and nine taken prisoners. A small piece of artillery was taken from Augusta to Hamburg but after firing a few rounds the ammunition gave out. The citizens of Edgefield are aided by citizens of Augusta and a regular siege has been laid to the buildings in which the negro militia are entrenched. Prince Rivers is in command of the citizens. . . . There are about one hundred men in the building armed with rifles. There are hundreds of people on the bridge between Augusta and Hamburg witnessing the operations. . . .

AUGUSTA, JULY 9.   The riot at Hamburg has terminated disastrously. This morning between 2 and 3 o'clock, six negroes were killed and three wounded; one white man was killed and another wounded. After the whites fired four rounds from a piece of artillery, the negroes retreated from the brick building they held into the cellars and outhouses of adjoining buildings. Fifteen were captured and the others, including Captain Adams, escaped into the country. It is reported that some of the prisoners were shot after being captured. . . .

SOURCE: *The New York Times,* July 9 and 10, 1876.

.Wilmington, N.C. (1898)

After a day of bloodshed and turbulence Wilmington has subsided tonight into comparative peacefulness. Nine negroes were killed and three white men were wounded during the day, one of them, William Mayo, seriously.

Tonight the city is in the hands of a new municipal government and law and order are being established. This afternoon the members of the Board of Aldermen resigned one by one. As each Alderman retired the remainder elected a successor named by the Citizen's Committee until the entire Board was changed legally. The new Board is composed of conservative Democratic citizens. The Mayor and Chief of Police then resigned, and the new Board elected their successors according to law. Ex-Representative Waddell was chosen Mayor, and L. G. Parmelee, Chief of Police. The first act of the new government was to swear in 250 special policemen, chosen from the ranks of reputable white citizens. They are vested with all the authority of the law, and will take charge of the city. The citizens will remain on guard, however, throughout the town to prevent possible attempts at incendiarism. The new government will devote its attention to restraining recklessness among the white men, as well as keeping down lawlessness among the negroes. . . .

The trouble began at 8:30 o'clock this morning, when an armed body of citizens, numbering about four hundred and led by ex-Representative Waddell, chairman of the Committee of Twenty-five appointed for the purpose, proceeded to the publishing house of a negro newspaper, "The Record," to wreck it. The editor of this newspaper had published an article defamatory to white women, and a mass-meeting of citizens yesterday ordered his expulsion from the city within twenty-four hours and the removal of his press. Fifteen leading negroes were called in by the Committee of Twenty-five last night and directed to inform the chairman by 7:30 o'clock this morning whether or not they would agree to the removal of the press. They were informed that if no answers were returned the press would be demolished.

No answer was received by the chairman this morning, and after waiting an hour the citizens proceeded in a body and demolished the fixtures of the printing office. The building was also burned. . . .

The burning of the printing office created a great commotion among the negroes of the town. The rumor spread that whites were going to burn and murder in the negro quarter. This rumor reached the negro employes of a cotton compress, numbering three or four hundred, who quit work and hung about the streets in manifest terror. Other parties congregated in the negro section, and it was in one of these that the first tragedy was enacted. The men were standing on a corner and were ordered to disperse. They declined, . . .

A [fusillade] was immediately opened on them by the whites, and three negroes were killed. Two white men were wounded slightly. One negro ran

SOURCE: *New York Tribune,* November 11, 1898.

down the street, and while passing a house, fired a rifle at William Mayo, white, who was standing on the veranda, shooting him through the left lung. The negro was recognized, pursued and captured while hiding under a bed. It is said that he confessed to the shooting. He was riddled with shots by his captors and killed.

In the meantime the town was in a state of great excitement. The whites rushed to the scene from every direction, the local military company was ordered out and a battalion of United States Naval Reserves proceeded to the scene of the trouble with a rapid-fire gun.

About 1 o'clock some negroes in a house fired on a party of white men. The house was surrounded, and four negroes were captured and taken to jail. One negro broke away and ran, but he was shot down and killed before he had gone half a block.

In the afternoon there were other affairs of this kind, and eight negroes were killed in the disturbed sections. Their names are unknown.

As the news of the riot spread through the neighboring cities of the State, they offered to send help, but all the offers were declined except in the case of Fayetteville, from which about one hundred and fifty men came. As night fell the town was completely patrolled and guarded, a few negroes were on the streets, and they were not allowed to congregate anywhere. . . .

It was learned later in the day that the negro committee summoned last night had agreed to endeavor to have the press removed, although the editor had disappeared and they had no authority on the premises. Their letter, instead of being delivered to the chairman of the Committee of Twenty-five in person, was put in the mail, and did not reach him until three hours after the time which had been fixed for the reception of an answer had expired.

A crowd was formed tonight to take from the jail and lynch two negroes, Thomas Miller and Ira Byrant, who were arrested today charged with making threats and were regarded as dangerous cases. The Mayor, Colonel Waddell, promptly prohibited the assembling of the crowd at the jail and he himself headed a guard of twenty-five men with Winchesters to protect the prisoners.

Another negro was killed tonight at Tenth and Mulberry Streets. He was hailed, but refused to halt, and was shot by the guard.

BORDER CITIES

Economic and Social Aspects

After the Civil War, the numerical and percentage increases of the black population in the cities of the border states were among the highest in the nation. This urban population—unlike that of southern cities, which came primarily from within the state—was drawn from adjacent southern states and was early evidence of the general northward drift of the black urban population. By 1890 the three cities represented in the selections below—Washington, D.C., Baltimore, Md., and Kansas City, Mo.—ranked first, second, and seventeenth respectively in the nation in terms of the size of their black population.

It is not surprising, then, that the first major successful black cooperative business was established in Baltimore, which had had the largest preemancipation free black population (Document 20). Organized in 1866, Chesapeake Marine Railway and Dry Dock Company prospered until 1877, then declined, and finally collapsed in 1883. Documents 19 and 22 give the impression that job opportunities existed for skilled black tradesmen in the border cities during the 1870's, but this state of affairs did not long outlast Reconstruction; the situation in Baltimore in the 1890's, where blacks were "shut out of all the trades" (Document 23), makes this clear. Greater industrialization and a much larger percentage of foreign-born whites, who meant keener competition for blacks than they had in the South, were part of the reason.

Early in this period black workers saw the need to organize but were not permitted to do so on a basis of equality with whites. The first major attempt of blacks to organize nationally took place in Washington, D.C., in December 1869, resulting in the Colored National Labor Union (Document 18); but that came to a premature end in 1872. For the rest of the century and beyond, the vast majority of black urban workers either were not unionized or were mostly in segregated unions.

As the nation's capital, and hence the seat of power, patronage, and jobs in the federal bureaucracy, Washington, D.C., during this period was a mecca for blacks of all classes. Indeed, it was then regarded as the foremost political, social, and cultural center of all black America. However, as Document 21 indicates, the "colored aristocracy" suffered from pretensions and insecurity in the

33

face of increasing white hostility and the leveling impact of an influx of unlettered southern black peasants.

Document 23 indicates some of the general characteristics of black city life in the border states. The marginality of Baltimore is reflected in its social and political practices: unlike the North, its schools were officially segregated, but black and white schools here were more nearly equal in terms of both proportional representation and facilities than in the South; and, unlike the South, libraries, parks, and other public facilities were generally open to blacks and whites alike. Unlike most major southern cities, in Baltimore blacks had an elected representative on the municipal council. Yet Baltimore also reflected developments in black urban life that were to become a common pattern: the expansion and concentration of the black ghetto, the development of slums, and movement and mobility in the ghetto itself, with resulting marked social stratification.

Washington, D.C. (1869)

18]   National Labor Convention *

The Convention of colored men at Washington last week was in some respects the most remarkable one we ever attended. We had always had full faith in the capacity of the negro for self-improvement, but were not prepared to see, fresh from slavery, a body of two hundred men, so thoroughly conversant with public affairs, so independent in spirit, and so anxious apparently to improve their social condition, as the men who represented the South, in that convention. . . . The convention was called to order by Mr. Myers, of Baltimore, and Geo. T. Downing, of Rhode Island, was chosen temporary chairman. . . .

. . . rare tact [was] shown by their permanent president, the Hon. John B. Harris of North Carolina. . . .

. . . they formed a National Labor Union . . . and may be said to be fairly in the field as an organized body of laborers.

Isaac Myers, a member of the present Labor Union, was chosen their permanent President for the ensuing year, with a good list of other officers. . . .

Washington, D.C. (1869)

19]   Workmen in Navy Yard †

. . . Colored men have . . . been employed in the bricklayers' and joiners' gangs of the Navy Department here, and today [June 10] a colored man from

* Source: "The National Colored Labor Convention, 1869," *American Workman,* Boston, December 25, 1869, p. 2.
† Source: *New York Tribune,* June 11, 1869.

Business Cooperative

Baltimore was employed in the yard as a machinist, the first of his race to be employed in work of that character. The workmen in some branches at the Navy Yard are still on half-time, the work not justifying their full employment. The United States steamer Neipsic, now on duty in the Gulf Squadron, has been ordered to the yard for repairs. The excitement consequent upon the appointment of the colored bricklayers has subsided. . . .

Baltimore, Md. (1870)

20]   Business Cooperative

. . . Baltimore contains a larger proportion of skilled colored labor than any portion of the country, New Orleans not excepted. . . . One of the best evidences of thrift and enterprise I have noticed . . . are the building and other self-help associations which exist here. The first-named societies were inspired by the successful economy and activity of the Germans. There are at least 25 colored societies in the city. There are several known as "The National Relief Association No. 1," etc. The admission fee is $2.50 and ten cents a week is required thereafter. . . .

Among the noteworthy efforts is an operative brickyard, owned in five-dollar shares, and run by the share-holders themselves. It is doing very well. . . .

. . . The most interesting movement I have found is that known as the Chesapeake Marine Railway and Dry Dock Company, which, as it illustrates the tyranny of caste and the manner by which it can be defeated, when even energy, industry, skill, and determination [are] combined, deserves some extended notice. The company, or rather its leading corporators, have already attained more than a local fame, from the fact that from among them came the movement which resulted in the recognition last year at the Philadelphia Labor Congress of colored labor delegates, and subsequently of the organization at Washington, in December following, of the National Colored Labor union. Now for the origin of this enterprise. Baltimore had always been famous as a ship-building and repairing entrepot. In slave times a large portion of the ship caulkers especially were colored men, as were also many ship-carpenters. In all other trade connected with this interest, a considerable share of the skilled, and nearly all of the unskilled labor, was colored. As a rule they were and are excellent mechanics. Frederick Douglass once worked in the very yard now owned by colored men. When last in Baltimore, he visited the yard, and took the caulker's tool in hand once again. The slave power was strong enough to protect these colored mechanics, many of them being slaves. When the war terminated, however, the bitter hostility, hitherto suppressed, against colored labor, manifested itself in violent combinations. As Mr. Gaines, the present manager of the company, informed me, extermination of colored mechanics was openly declared to be the aim of their white rivals. The combination was

SOURCE: *New York Tribune*, September 1, 1870.

against all labor, but manifested mostly in the shipbuilding trades. The white mechanics all struck, even refusing to work, where colored cartmen and stevedores were employed. There was no antagonism or complaint on account of wages, as the colored men were as strenuous as the whites in demanding full pay. The Trades Unions, to which, of course, colored men were not admitted, organized the movement. In the yards on one side of the Patapaco River the colored caulkers were driven off in 1865. In 1866 the general strike was organized. The bosses did not sympathize with the white mechanics, and to the credit of many . . . they stood out as long as possible. Very soon the strike threatened to become general against all colored labor, mechanical or otherwise; the violence threatened to be extended even to hotel waiters of the proscribed race. This atrocious movement was industriously fomented by the active men in Andrew Jackson's reaction.

At last the leading colored caulkers, carpenters, and mechanics, seeing what the crusade meant, determined on a vigorous protective effort. Their conclusion was reached in the organization of the Maryland Mutual Joint Stock Railway Company, whose capital was to consist of 10,000 shares at $50. About 2000 shares were taken within a few days, and $10,000 subscribed, 100 shares being the largest amount taken by any one person. Most of the shares were taken in ones, twos, and threes, by mechanics, caulkers, laborers, even the barbers and washerwomen being represented. The shipyard and marine railway they now own belonged to Jas. L. Mullen and Son, earnest Union men and warm defenders of equal rights to their workmen. They offered to sell and asked no more than the place was worth—$40,000.[1] The bargain was closed; another honorable gentleman, Capt. Sipplegarth, ship-owner, builder and navigator, came forward and loaned them the remaining $30,000, on six years' time, at moderate interest, with the privilege of paying at any time within the six years, taking a mortage on the property itself.

. . . The Company was organized and got to work by Feb. 2, 1866, employing at first 62 hands, nearly all skilled men, and some of them white. Business was depressed, the outrageous strike having driven it away from the port, and the work did not average for some months more than four days per week, at the average wages of $3 per day. At the present time the Company are able to employ, fulltime, 75 hands. From Feb. 2, 1866, to Jan. 1, 1867, its business amounted to about $60,000, on which the profits were nearly or quite 25 percent or $15,000. The next year was better for them, though business was generally very dull. In carrying on their work and paying their men, they had to resort to borrowing as a rule. They never had a note protested. Within four years from organization they completed the payment for their yard and railway, lifting the mortgage in June last. In 1868 they were incorporated by the title I have given, having done business previously under the firm name of John H. Smith and Co. Most of their trade is with Eastern ship-owners and

[1] Blacks were actually duped: "They supposed they were buying the property in fee, [but] a cleverly inserted clause specified that it was being leased for 20 years. At the end of 20 years, most of which time was required to pay for it, the shipyard was taken away." See Charles S. Johnson, "Negroes at Work in Baltimore, Md.," *Opportunity*, June 1923, p. 16.

masters. At the present time they do, and have done for three years past, more repairing than any other company on the Patapaco River. This success has not been achieved without serious trouble. Intimidation has been practiced on their patrons. In two instances, where profitable jobs were pending they have been driven off by white mobs; in one case a white man who took charge of their working force was shot dead. What added point to the act was the fact that he was ordinarily one of their bitterest antagonists. On another occasion, having hired the Canton Marine Railway to take up a large ship which they were caulking and repairing, the whites threatened to strike, and so the Railway Company refused to allow its use. Still they have persevered, and today are masters of the situation. They have had some good contracts, in one case repairing Government dredges and tugs.

The managers think the feeling against them decidedly subsiding. They accredited this fact mainly to their ability to employ labor and pay for it promptly. They think that men have been forced to a sense of shame by finding no resentments cherished on the part of the corporators of the Chesapeake Company. To some extent, more recently, they believe that the dread of Chinese labor induces the ultra-trades unionists to desire their (the colored mechanics') favor. It is worth noting that they are not, and never have been, members of the trades unions. Their business rules, as stated to me by the manager, are simple. Asking why they did more ship repair work than other firms or companies possessing equal facilities, the reply was: 1st, because our labor is of the best; the men we employ are thoroughly skilled, and 2nd, we seek to retain custom as well as make money. We have never lost a patron except by outside intimidation. We try to accommodate, work hard and overtime to finish jobs, and always use the best materials. These are good rules, and this is a good record. . . .

Washington, D.C. (1877)

21]   The "Colored Aristocracy"

The . . . "fust families" with all the habits and customs of the "day before yesterday" hanging to them and about them as tenaciously and persistently as the barnacles on sea shells . . . live in old-fashioned homes way uptown, downtown and across town. They dress in the same style that their illustrious predecessors did half a century ago. It was from this class that the mother of George Washington procured nurses for her distinguished and immortal son—now called the "Father of his country." All the leading white washers, coachmen, *valets* and servants in *ordinaire* were furnished the "fust families" of the white race from this class, half a century ago. Those of them now living in Washing-

SOURCE: John E. Bruce, "Washington's Colored Society," 1877, pp. 12–17. (Thirty-page typescript in Schomburg Collection, New York Public Library.) [John E. Bruce, 1856–1924, was a leading black journalist and columnist.—Ed.]

ton wouldn't be caught dead with an ordinary Negro, if they could avoid such a dire calamity. The most of their company consists of antiquated old white people, many. of whom are so near death's door that they can hear the creaking of the hinges. The "fust families" of Washington Colored Society—keep a servant, two dogs, a tom cat and a rifle that saw service in 1776. They are pensioners provided they or their ancestors lived with the "bloods" of their day and generation. If they do not keep a servant—they are not pensioners. There is more family pride to the square inch in the hide of the "fust families" than there are fleas on a dog's back. To marry their children out of the circle in which they have been accustomed to mingle is decidedly out of the question and contrary to both their religious and social views. It has been said, whether truthfully or falsely I know not, that the species of misguided humanity with whose characteristics I am dealing, secretly hope to become absorbed by the white or Caucasian race—or as the distinguished editor of a prominent Negro Journal would say "swallowed up by the Anglo-Saxon race." I will here pause to remark that the Anglo-Saxon race do not manifest any perceptible desire to swallow the Negro "up or down" except by ways which are dark and tricks which are not always vain. In this connection, the reader will allow me an expression more significant perhaps than prudent—but nevertheless significant. It is the language of another,

> I could a tale unfold
> —only this and much more—

But I forbear as I have no desire to be personal or to enter into a discussion of the unholy alliances which were and are characteristic of Anglo-Saxon civilization and its peculiar code of moral *ethics*, my only object in thus referring to this matter is to show in a faint manner the peculiar relations which existed between the master class and their property and also to show that the evil is carried on to an alarming extent even at this advanced stage of our civilization and (as many of us believe) progress. The "fust families," some of them, are decidedly aristocratic in their notions—and may perhaps be a hundred years or so in advance of the "common herd" socially. Yet there are few marriages heard of between white men and black women, where the parties concerned were accepted with *open arms* into white society. This to my way of thinking is a "mighty" poor way of solving the social problem which has so long vexed the swelled heads of the colored races. There is another thing which I could never satisfactorily get through my cranium, and that is, that no white man or woman of any considerable importance on this side of the Atlantic at least has united his or her self by honorable marriage to a colored man or woman. The colored "big guns" show a greater anxiety in this direction than their Anglo-Saxon sisters and brothers. The "fust families" not infrequently (when they have the "coupons" which is a great inducement—to some white man of low degree) marry off a daughter—to one of this class of Negro lovers and make themselves believe that the white race is absorbing the black race and that very, very soon we shall have to petition our Heavenly Father to create a few more genuine Negroes. Such marriages in my humble judgment ostracize the woman if she be of Negro extraction, and isolate the man if he is honest and

Baltimore, Md.

means to be true to his troth. The "fust families" do not believe these homely observations. I care nothing for their opinions, I have simply stated mine. . . .

22]   *Kansas City, Mo.* (1879) *

In Kansas City . . . the negroes are more numerous than I have yet seen.[1] On the Kansas side they form quite a large proportion of the population. They are certainly subject to no indignity or ill-usage. They ride quite freely in the trains and railways alongside of the whites, as I myself experienced, and there seems to be no prejudice whatever against personal contact with them. I did not hear them at all abused or slanged. Coming along in the train-car a cart was found standing on the line, and detained us some time. When the owner at last appeared, he was a black man. A white waggoner in London would certainly have been most unmercifully slanged by a bus driver, and would have deserved it, but our driver said nothing that I could hear. He may have moved his lips or said something low, *but it was the negro* I heard defiantly call out "What do you say?" . . . The blacks are civil and attentive as waiters in the hotel and railway cars, but sometimes ill-mannered. . . .

Here the negroes seem to have quite taken to work at trades; I saw them doing building work, both alone and assisting white men, and also painting and other tradesman's work. On the Kansas side I found a negro blacksmith, with an establishment of his own; he was an old man, and very "negro," and I could extract a very little from him. He grumbled just like a white man—he made a living; did pretty well: "But things are dear." "But then you are expected to work cheaper." He came from Tennessee, after emancipation; had not been back there, and did not want to go. Most of the schools here are separate and not mixed. "Perhaps that suits best. Some black boys go, and some don't."

23]   *Baltimore, Md.* (1898) †

. . . Both to Washington and to Baltimore there has been, since the war, a steady flow of colored people; to the capital above all, for Washington is their Mecca. To-day, both cities are willing to see that the negroes are numerous within their limits. An ostrich-like policy has been followed for years, but the omnipresent negro . . . confronts the wise-acres of the nation, and the off-spring of the Maryland line, at every turn.

. . . . .

* SOURCE: Sir George Campbell, *White and Black—The Outcome of a Visit to the United States,* New York: R. Worthington, 1879, pp. 225–26.
† SOURCE: Rev. John R. Slattery, "Colored People in Baltimore, Md.," *Catholic World,* January 1898, pp. 519–24.
[1] According to the U.S. census the black population in Kansas City, Mo. in 1880 was 8,143. [Ed.]

. . . Again, out of Baltimore pours a constant stream of negroes northward and westward. In our travels we have met Catholic negroes from Baltimore in Philadelphia, New York, Boston, Buffalo, Chicago, and other places. . . .

Now, the first result is expansion. The colored people are rapidly spreading over Baltimore. Wherever we turn we meet them dwelling on new streets. Especially is this the fact in the north-west section. Without much effort we might name fully thirty streets where their presence, save as servants, was unknown ten years ago. One ward, the Eleventh, called the Shoe-string ward because of the peculiar shape which the politicians gave it, has a majority of colored people, so that in the Baltimore City Council there is nearly always a colored member. For natural site, the north-west section is in every way desirable; hence it seems strange that it should be so largely taken hold of by colored people. Small blame to them, however, for moving out of the alleys in the heart of the town and getting good streets, pleasant to the eye, especially when the rent is about the same. Yet as fast as one set vacate the alleys, another, and usually a lower, drift into them. Under our eyes there is the strangeness of our colored citizens reaching outward into new places and at the same time holding on to their old haunts. Save where an occasional factory or large warehouse has intruded itself, the colored people occupy the same streets they lived in twenty years ago; nay, one might name fifty other streets into which this unobtrusive race has quietly pushed its way. We cannot remember that a single street, once in their possession, was ever abandoned by them.

Not so the whites. Whenever a negro moves into a street the whites flutter away. They simply vanish. As the blacks vacate no streets, the whites verge more and more toward the suburbs. The outcome is, that to-day Baltimore is a city of valuable suburbs and ever-cheapening city homes.

The way that property values have gone down in the heart of the city is beyond belief. As the white race fear the negroes, so do the Gentiles the Jew. . . .

Just as patent as the growth of the population are the increase and development of the schools. The public-school system for the negroes is a post-bellum institution. From 1829, when they were founded, till after the war, the Oblate Sisters of Providence, a community of colored women, taught the three "R's" to . . . most of their race, Catholic as well as Protestant enjoying that knowledge. At present the middle-aged people of the colored race in Baltimore owe whatever education they have to the religious women of their own race. There are exceptions, however, the chief being the private schools. Nowadays they have almost gone. But twenty years ago they were still many. Five or six to twenty-five or thirty pupils would fill the roster. Almost the last, as well as the best liked by the Negroes, was a school kept by three sisters named Berry, who dropped off one by one, the school still holding on, till the last, known to every one of her race as "Cousin Lizzie," died some years ago. She was a very holy soul, and for a generation had been prefect of the women's sodality of St. Francis Xavier's. For six years the writer was its director. On taking charge he found the Vespers and Compline of the Little Office were recited at the meetings; when, not without a little pride of voice and air, they would intone the antiphon "I am black but beautiful." . . .

The public schools, however, have ended the private. Great strides have been made with them, although as yet they are far too few to receive the colored children of school age. Their growth has been slow but steady. Among the first changes was the handing over of some white schools to the negroes. Old family residences on old-time fashionable streets were hired by the authorities and used for colored schools, often to the great relief of their distressed owners. A next step was the high school, spick and span new from cellar to attic, on East Saratoga Street, within a stone's-throw of the fashionable Charles Street. More new schools were put up for the colored children. Nor was this all. Colored teachers were then brought into the city schools as teachers. Finally a department was added to the manual training school for colored boys. At present for the black school population of Baltimore are the high school, manual training school, and upwards of twenty grammar and primary schools. To these must be added the Catholic schools, in which there are about a thousand children. The number of schools might be doubled and no fear of over-crowding remain; the supply is far too little for the demand.

While all this is very encouraging, there is, however, one very harmful growth: the number, ever increasing, of liquor-stores in the colored sections of the city. In 1894 the United States Department of Labor issued a bulletin on "The Slums of Baltimore, Chicago, New York and Philadelphia." It shows that there are more liquor-stores, pro rata, in the slums of Baltimore than in any one of the other cities. Baltimore has more, pro rata, than New York or Chicago. The poorer parts of Baltimore are where so many colored people live, hence they become a prey to the saloon. Especially is this true of the Eleventh ward, known as the Black ward. Turn where you will, the saloon is ever before you. On the principal streets, on the cross streets, in the first floor of residences where the trouble to turn the dwelling into a store is not taken. Now, these saloons in the Eleventh ward are supported by the negro. Furthermore, twenty years ago there was hardly a negro keeping a saloon; but nowadays they are in the business, rivalling the white dealers in ruining their own race.

From all, or nearly all, trades the colored man is shut out. No negro apprentice will be found at bricklaying, carpentry, painting, tinning, smithing, etc. On this head the position of the Knights of Labor and the Federation of Labor is simply unintelligible. If organized labor say but the word, colored youth will get trades. The boycott goes further—it extends to factories, save the places for canning fruits and vegetables. Further still, the boycott shuts out all colored youth of both sexes from shop and store employment, save to run errands. Let the offspring of the most undesirable race of Europe appear in the streets of Baltimore, they may work at their trades and have their children master them; but when it is a question of the colored man, "No Admittance" is written over every trade shop. In the history of this world the negro has proved a never-dying Nemesis. In Time's whirligig it may be his turn to write over these same shops "Ichabod"—their glory is gone.

Factories are now being thrown open to colored women in the South; e.g., at Charleston, S.C., and Augusta, Ga. The day cannot be far distant when they will enter the factories of Baltimore. . . . The fact that the professions are open to them helps but little. Professional people are the few. Clergymen, lawyers, doctors, teachers are always in small numbers when compared to the bulk. Their presence widens not the ways of employment for the masses of their race.

THE POST-
RECONSTRUCTION NORTH

The cities of the urban Northeast, and in particular Philadelphia, New York, and Boston, contained a substantial portion of the free black population in the antebellum period. Thus they were the main centers of black protest against slavery and discrimination, and of agitation for civil rights. This protest tradition was carried on in the postemancipation period and was best exemplified in the late nineteenth century by the New York newspaper that was successively called The New York Globe, Freeman, and Age, and was edited by T. Thomas Fortune. Fortune himself illustrates the northward drift of black professionals during this period. He was born in 1856 in Marianna, Florida, attended Howard University, Washington, D.C., and settled in New York from 1879 until his death in 1928.

Fortune was unquestionably the best and the most militant black journalist of the late nineteenth century.[1] His newspaper assumed the role of national defender of blacks, and it was easily the best-circulated black newspaper in the late nineteenth century. But it was not alone. Other influential black newspapers of the time were the Chicago Conservator, founded in 1878, the Washington Bee and the Cleveland Gazette, both founded in 1883, and the Richmond Planet and the Philadelphia Tribune, both founded in 1884.

New York, N.Y. (1915)

24] Black Journalism

In 1879 . . . I took hold of Rumor, together with George Parker and William Walter Sampson, it was a weekly illustrated newspaper on the order of Harper's Weekly. . . .

I did not care for the name, and other things associated with it, and soon changed the shape from the magazine to the newspaper, and the name from

SOURCE: T. Thomas Fortune, The New York Negro in Journalism, New York: New York State Commission National Negro Exposition, (sic) 1915.
[1] See Emma Lou Thornbrough, T. Thomas Fortune: Militant Journalist, Chicago: University of Chicago Press, 1972.

Rumor to The New York Globe. For some time Mr. Sampson and I set the type of the Globe at night, working on the Weekly Witness in the day to be sure of our living expenses and that the paper would come out on time. There was no time to write articles, so I used to set one "out of my head" and dictate one to Mr. Sampson at the same time. We used to work in this way from 7 till 12 o'clock at night.

But the Globe grew in favor, and took the leadership in most things affecting the race in New York and the nation, but the expenditures always trod upon the heels of the receipts. Mr. Parker, who was not active in the management, thought otherwise, and sold his interest to Dr. William B. Derrick. When his notes came due Dr. Derrick failed to meet them, and, during my absence Mr. Parker foreclosed and the sheriff sold at public auction the plant of the paper. I thought it best to start again alone and did so, changing the name from The Globe to The Freeman. It was known far and wide as The Freeman in 1887, when I gave over the publication to my brother, Emanuel, and Mr. Jerome B. Peterson, and changed the name to The New York Age. I went on the staff of the New York Evening Sun, where I soon after became assistant to Editor Amos J. Cummings. The Globe had been very independent in politics, and very severe in criticism and denunciation of Republican men and policies, and the falling off of the receipts made a change necessary. To eliminate myself from the paper at the time was the best and wisest thing to be done. After the Presidential election of that year, in which I supported Grover Cleveland as against Benjamin Harrison, and upon the death of my brother, who died in Florida, as the result of exposure in the great blizzard in New York, as Roscoe Conkling did, I returned to The Age, and remained with it until 1907, when I disposed of my interest to Mr. Fred R. Moore, the present owner, having suffered a complete nervous breakdown. In September, 1911, I returned to The Age as associate editor and did its editorial work until August, 1914.

The national reputation that The Age enjoyed up to the time that the control of it passed to Mr. Moore it has maintained, under his editorial direction, to the present. He is ably assisted in the literary department by Mr. Lester A. Walton, Mr. Lucien H. White and Hon. James W. Johnson, a brilliant poet and essayist, and in the business department by his accomplished daughter, Mrs. Ida May Dudley.

During the stormy career of The Age, under the joint management of Hon. Jerome B. Peterson and myself, . . . it led in the demand and secured the adoption of the abolition of separate schools, first under Governor Grover Cleveland, and, finally, under Governor Theodore Roosevelt, and the adoption of a civil rights bill, which, amended up to date, is by far the best that we have secured in any other State. The Age also led in the agitation for and organization of the National Afro-American Press Association, which had its first meeting at Washington, in 1884, of the National Afro-American League, at Chicago, in 1890, out of which most of our civic organizations have since grown, and of the National Negro Business League, at Boston, in 1900, Mr. James H. Lewis of Boston having suggested the plan to me, and which I passed on to Dr. Booker T. Washington as I had more organization work at the time than I could creditably handle.

PART TWO

THE TWENTIETH CENTURY: PRE-WORLD WAR I

INTRODUCTION

The following two documents together reflect the increasing awareness in the early twentieth century of the significant increase in numbers of blacks in cities, the serious problems they faced—poor, congested housing; menial, inadequate jobs; and social dislocation—and the need for systematic and coordinated help to facilitate their adjustment to urban life. These circumstances led to the formation in 1911 of the National League on Urban Conditions Among Negroes (later and better known as the National Urban League)—an expression, albeit inadequate, of American progressivism.

The first document views city life as having a corrupting and demoralizing influence on blacks, and deprecates the fast rate at which they were moving to the cities. This was a point of view widely shared by such black leaders of the time as Booker T. Washington and Paul Laurence Dunbar, then the leading black poet. In his novel *Sport of the Gods*, published in 1902, Dunbar describes the disintegration of a black southern family in the "fast life" of "the great alleys of New York." It was not until after World War I that black leaders saw urban life as irreversible and, in many ways, advantageous for blacks.

It is worthy of note that the article on the National Urban League appeared in *Crisis*, the journal published by the then four-year-old NAACP and edited by the Harvard-trained scholar and activist Dr. W. E. B. Du Bois, who had pioneered in the field of black urban history and sociology with *The Philadelphia Negro*, published in 1899.

CITIES

General Aspects

1]   Blacks in Cities (1902)

Of the many complex problems growing out of the presence and persistence of
the Negro element in the United States none seem to be more immediate and
pressing than the congestion in large cities. The general drift of the population
at large towards overcrowded centers is portentous of evil rather than good.
In case of the Negro, the evil is accentuated. Being shut out from the controlling influences of municipal activities, he is relegated to the lowest order of
service and can only pick up the industrial fragments that remain after the preferred class has monopolized the choice of vocations. The lack of industrial opportunity necessarily enforces unwholesome modes of living which in turn en-
tail physical and moral decay. The Negro has little developed aptitude for the
commercial and industrial requirements of city life. A rural people can remain
embalmed, as it were, in a state of nature almost indefinitely. But if transferred
to the city, they are forced into a life and death struggle with the powers of
destruction.

   Why then, it might be asked, do Negroes join in this mad rush to the cities
in face of the fate which almost certainly awaits them? Every effect must have
an adequate cause. The Negro is attracted (1) by the general glare and glitter
of city life, (2) he deserts the country because of poor compensation for agricultural industries and the dearth of rural social attractions, and (3) because of the
better police protection and school facilities to be found at the centers of population. It is characteristic of a thoughtless people to enter upon a course of
conduct because of its alluring enticements, without giving thought to its disadvantages and dangers, until they are forced upon them by sad and bitter experience.

   The urban Negro constitutes a larger per cent of the race than is generally
supposed. It is a prevalent belief that ninety per cent of the race live in direct
contact with the soil. The census office limits the definition of a city to places

SOURCE: Kelly Miller, "The City Negro," *Southern Workman*, April 1902, pp.
217–22. [Kelly Miller, 1863–1939, was a Howard University educator and prolific social critic—Ed.]

48

having more than 8,000 inhabitants. But in the South, places of much smaller population are fully entitled to that rank. The following table shows the number of Negroes living in places of more than 2,500 inhabitants.

Number of Negroes in places having more than 2,500 inhabitants: 1900

STATE	NUMBER OF PLACES	URBAN LABOR POPULATION	RURAL POPULATION	PER CENT IN CITIES
1 Alabama	27	96,154	827,307	12
2 Arkansas	15	36,971	366,856	10
3 Delaware	4	11,537	19,100	38
4 District of Columbia	1	87,702	87,702	100
5 Florida	12	49,136	181,594	21
6 Georgia	31	161,246	873,752	16
7 Kentucky	34	100,145	184,501	35
8 Louisiana	15	116,954	533,850	18
9 Maryland	14	93,849	141,215	40
10 Mississippi	22	55,125	905,930	6
11 Missouri	50	89,247	161,234	55
12 North Carolina	28	76,169	548,300	11
13 South Carolina	20	84,358	782,321	11
14 Tennessee	22	131,144	349,099	27
15 Texas	56	123,775	496,947	20
16 Virginia	27	124,800	535,922	19
17 West Virginia	16	8,711	34,788	20

The table shows that there are nearly 400 places in the South containing more than 2,500 inhabitants with a total Negro population of about one and a half million. In Alabama, South Carolina, North Carolina, Arkansas, and Mississippi, the urban Negro constitutes 12 per cent or less of the race residing in those states. The per cent ranges from 6 in Mississippi to 55 in Missouri. It is quite noticeable that in the border states the city population is much larger proportionally than in the far South. It may occasion some surprise to note that more than half of the Negro population of Missouri, two-fifths of that of Maryland, and more than a third of that of Kentucky are found in the cities. These are all rich and varied agricultural states where the Negro was planted by the institution of slavery. The sense of social loneliness where the Negroes are thinly scattered among the whites is perhaps the principal cause which drives them to seek more congenial companionship with their own kind and color in towns and cities. In the North and West a still larger portion of the race is found in the cities.

. . . . .

The predominance of the female element is perhaps the most striking phenomenon presented by the urban Negro population. The accompanying table shows the female excess in cities of more than 20,000 colored inhabitants.

By consulting it we see that the females are in the majority in all of the cities except Chicago. Washington and Baltimore head the list with 126 females

CITY	FEMALES	MALES	EXCESS OF FEMALES	NO FEMALES TO 100 MALES 1890
Washington	48,354	38,348	10,006	126
Baltimore	44,195	35,063	9,132	126
New Orleans	42,585	35,129	7,456	121
Philadelphia	33,673	29,940	3,733	113
New York	33,534	27,132	6,402	124
Memphis	24,551	25,359	808	103
Louisville	18,842	20,297	1,455	108
Atlanta	21,017	14,895	6,122	142
St. Louis	18,020	17,496	624	104
Richmond	17,878	14,354	3,524	123
Charleston	17,552	13,970	3,582	125
Nashville	16,776	13,296	3,480	125
Chicago	14,077	16,073	1,997	88
Savannah	15,354	12,764	2,580	120
Norfolk	10,738	9,492	1,246	113

to 100 males. In the Western cities the excess is not so glaring. In Atlanta we have the startling result of 142 females to 100 males. It is suggestive to note that in such long settled cities as New Orleans, Richmond, Charleston, and Savannah, the proportion is about five to four. No such disproportion prevails among the whites. . . .

2]   Origins of the National Urban League (1914)

. . . When, during the spring of 1910, Mrs. William H. Baldwin, Jr., called representatives of the many social-welfare organizations working among Negroes to a conference at her New York City home, to consider means of preventing duplication of effort and overlapping of work, of promoting cooperation among the agencies and of establishing new organizations to improve neglected conditions, a new era was reached in the handling of the city problem as it affected the Negroes.

From this meeting resulted the National League on Urban Conditions Among Negroes, whose work of uplift is now being felt in ten cities, viz.: New York, Philadelphia, Pa., Norfolk, Va., Richmond, Va., Nashville, Tenn., Louisville, Ky., St. Louis, Mo., Savannah, Ga., Augusta, Ga., and Atlanta, Ga.; whose budget has increased from $2,000 to $18,000 per year and whose staff of paid employees has increased from one full-time and three part-time employees to sixteen salaried persons in New York City, three in Nashville and two in Norfolk. . . .

. . . . . .

SOURCE: "National League on Urban Conditions Among Negroes," *Crisis*, September 1914, pp. 243–46.

Origins of the National Urban League

The problem of the city Negro is but the accentuated counterpart of the problem of all urban inhabitants. Segregation and the consequent congestion, the evils of bad housing conditions with their inevitable accompaniment of dangerous sanitation and loose morals, the lack of facilities for wholesome recreation and the ill-regulated picture shows and dance halls combine to make conditions which demand instant relief. Add to this a population constantly augmented by Negroes from small towns or rural districts of the South, and the problem of the league is before you.

The most important achievement in the effort to prevent duplication of work and to inspire workers with a co-operative spirit was the consolidation of the National League for the Protection of Colored Women, the Committee for Improving the Industrial Condition of Negroes in New York and the Committee on Urban Conditions Among Negroes (the committee formed at Mrs. Baldwin's meeting) into the incorporated National League on Urban Conditions Among Negroes. Since this consolidation there has been close co-operation with practically every agency in the city working for colored people in the handling of numerous cases of destitution, in securing employment for worthy applicants, in getting knowledge of the work of the organizations disseminated through the community, in conducting boys' and girls' clubs, in making investigations, in placing neglected children in homes and in the securing of competent social workers. . . .

. . . . . .

The league has sought to establish agencies for uplift where needed. If no committee could be found ready to take over and conduct the particular undertaking, the league has handled the movement through its local office staff.

The Sojourner Truth house committee . . . has undertaken the task of establishing a home for delinquent colored girls under 16 years of age, because of the failure of the State and private institutions to care adequately for these unfortunates. The league made an investigation of this need and formed a temporary committee from which developed the present organization.

The League also inaugurated the movement for the training of colored nursery maids. A committee . . . has worked out the details for courses of study in hospital training in care of infants, kindergarten training, child study and household arts.

During the summer of 1911 the league conducted, in Harlem, a playground for boys, for the purpose of demonstrating the need of recreational facilities for the children of Harlem. As a result of this movement, and a continuous agitation for more adequate play facilities, the city has practically committed itself to the operation of a model playground on any plot of ground in the Harlem district, the use of which is donated to the City Parks Department.

The travelers' aid work . . . has consisted principally in the meeting of the coastwise steamers bringing large numbers of women and girls from Southern ports to New York City, who are without acquaintance with methods of meeting the competition of city life, and who are frequently sent to New York to be exploited by unreliable employment agents or questionable men. The league supports two travelers' aid workers in Norfolk, Va., which is the gateway to the North for hundreds of women and girls from Virginia and the Carolinas.

The preventive or protective work of the league consists of the visiting in the homes of school children who have become incorrigibles or truants, for the purpose of removing the causes of these irregularities. . . .

Probation work with adults from the court of general sessions is done. . . . In connection with this work with delinquents the Big Brother and Big Sister movements are conducted. The league seeks to furnish to each boy or girl passing through the courts the helpful influence and guidance of a man or woman of high moral character.

The league conducts a housing bureau for the purpose of improving the moral and physical conditions among the tenement houses in Negro districts. It seeks principally to prevent the indiscriminate mixing of the good and bad by furnishing to the public a list of houses certified to be tenanted by respectable people. It also seeks to get prompt action of agents and owners or the city departments whenever there is need for correcting certain housing abuses. . . .

A monthly conference of workers with boys and girls has been organized. Through this conference several neighborhood clubs have been formed, among them the Utopia Neighborhood Club. . . .

. . . . . .

Industrial organizations are formed along occupational lines. Public porters, mechanics (including carpenters, painters, plasterers, paperhangers, etc.), elevator men and hallmen and chauffeurs have been organized.

A vocational exchange, designed to refer Negroes to opportunities for training along vocational lines, and to refer applications for help and for positions to reliable philanthropic and commercial employment agencies, has been established, with Mr. John D. Jones in charge.

. . . Social work among Negroes has suffered not so much from the lack of movements as from the lack of conscientious, enthusiastic trained workers. This fact was emphasized by Dr. George Edmund Haynes when, shortly following Mrs. Baldwin's meeting, he was employed as director of the organization. The result was the establishment of two annual fellowships at the New York School of Philanthropy and Columbia University, and scholarships at Fisk University, where Dr. Haynes holds the chair of social science, and from which he seeks to influence other Southern Negro colleges to standardize their courses in sociology and economics and to encourage promising students to take up social work as a profession . . . .

SOUTHERN CITIES

Political and Social Aspects

The white movement to completely subordinate the black man in the South climaxed in the early twentieth century with the adoption by five more states (three had already done so) of new constitutions designed to disfranchise blacks, with the passage of jim crow legislation by state and local governments, and with increasing segregation and discrimination within cities.

Predictably, these measures sustained or further heightened tensions, resulting in race riots like those of New Orleans (1900) and of Atlanta (1906) documented below. Both riots provide examples of frenzied and unrestrained white mob violence against blacks, abetted by the police themselves. Unnecessary harassment by white police led Robert Charles, a crack black gunman, to kill two white police officers: this in turn sparked off white mob violence against blacks. In an incredible drama lasting four days, fugitive Charles shot to death nine whites, including eight law enforcement officers, before he was literally "shot to pieces" before a howling mob of 20,000 in a New Orleans square. At least two blacks were killed, dozens brutally beaten up, and thirty black homes and a major black high school burned down. The Atlanta riot, spurred on by the white desire for black disfranchisement, resulted from a vicious smear campaign and organized violence against blacks. Ten blacks were killed and dozens indiscriminately beaten up; the South's best black journal, the militant Voice of the Negro, was forced to close, and its editor, J. Max Barber, fled to Chicago.

Legislation providing for jim crow streetcars led to black boycotting between 1898 and 1906 in Atlanta, Augusta, Austin, Columbia, Houston, Jacksonville, Mobile, and Savannah, in addition to New Orleans and Nashville as documented below; and in three of these cities—Austin, Houston, and Savannah—serious attempts were made to organize independent black transportation systems. But white fraudulence, intimidation, and noncooperation led to the failure of the black companies, and to enforced acceptance of jim crow arrangements.

In other selections below, Atlanta provides evidence of further ills and some advantages of urban life. Its fast rate of growth and the neglect of blacks by the municipal authorities resulted in terrible slums (Document 8); and yet its *six black institutions of higher learning (Document 7) made it the foremost center of higher learning for blacks in the nation.*

New Orleans, La. (1900)

3] Race Riot

JULY 25. An armed mob, several thousand strong, has paraded the streets of New Orleans since 8 o'clock. Scores of negroes have been beaten and maltreated. Hundreds of shots have been fired and a number of casualties have been reported.

The outrages being committed tonight are the result of the murder of two policemen early yesterday morning, and the subsequent failure of the officers . . . to capture the murderer.

The mob began forming at 7 o'clock at Lee Monument on St. Charles Avenue, the heart of the aristocratic residence portion of New Orleans. They had no leader, though several men made incendiary speeches. A few citizens vainly made efforts to restrain the mob. When the crowd had increased to 500 the march up St. Charles Avenue was commenced. Street cars were stopped and negro passengers taken off and mercilessly beaten. Women and children were terrified and urgent appeals were sent to the police, but they were slow in responding.

The Carrollton and New Orleans Street Car Company then sent out orders to put all negroes off the cars before they got near the mob.

The mob learned of this, and marched up the avenue toward the scene of yesterday's trouble. Dozens of negroes who escaped the clutches of the mob caught safety in residences along the avenue.

The path of the mob was marked by scores of attack[s], wild yells, and the firing of many shots. Several times small squads of police made feeble efforts to drive them back, but the opposition seemed only temporary.

At 10 o'clock the mob changed its course and began a march on the Parish Prison with the avowed intention of lynching the negro Pierce, who was with Charles on Monday night and shot officer Mora.

By this time Sheriff Klock had geared . . . several hundred armed deputies and was prepared to defend the jail. The police were still making efforts to disperse the crowd, but frequent shots fired in the direction of the blue coats kept them at a distance.

All the way to the jail the mob assaulted every negro it could find, and at 11 o'clock the hospital ambulances were hard pressed to take them away. Three ambulances filled with wounded men, mostly negroes, were reported at one place alone. At the jail demonstrations were made, but no well defined attack was made, the Sheriff's force being too strong.

The mob then moved downtown to the negro section, where one negro was shot and killed and a newsboy was fatally injured. . . .

SOURCE: *The New York Times*, July 26–28, 1900.

Race Riot

When the mob left the jail the police adopted different tactics and got behind it, and instead of opposing its movements kept it moving. In this way the main body soon split up into smaller bodies of several hundred each.

The mob broke open numbers of stores on Rampart Street and secured a number of guns and ammunition. Raids were attempted on several large stores on Canal Street, but the police protected the buildings. Gradually the several mobs grew smaller and smaller, and one which passed down Newspaper Row was composed of some 400 men and boys.

By midnight there were no negroes left on the streets and the mobs, having no materials to work on, gradually dispersed.

JULY 26. Disorderly scenes following the rioting of last night prevailed throughout the city today and resulted in the swearing in by the mayor of 500 special policemen and the ordering out of 1,500 of the State militia, Gov. Heard responding promptly to the appeal of Mayor Capdeville for assistance in suppressing the existing lawlessness and in preventing tonight a recurrence of the violence of last night. Col. Wood, who commanded the first Louisiana Regiment in the Spanish War, was placed in command of the special police.

Throughout the day attacks were made by irresponsible mobs of whites upon the blacks. Before nightfall the negroes had been effectually hosed from the streets. The effect of the disorders was to put a practical stop on business in the wholesale districts and in the levee front. As this meant a serious crippling of the trade of the port, the business element rallied in force, and hundreds of the most prominent men of the city responded to the appeal of the Mayor for assistance in preserving order.

A summary of the casualties growing out of the disturbances last night and today shows that one negro was beaten to death, six were so badly wounded that their lives are despaired of and about a score of people white and black, male and female, have been more or less seriously wounded. In order to prevent the miscellaneous distribution of arms, the Mayor this evening ordered the closing of gunshops likely to supply the baser elements, and early in the day, for the better preservation of the public peace, issued orders to the police to close up every section in the city!

The police have been practically helpless during the disturbance. The force consists of some 300 men, including clerks and telegraph operators, and this is manifestly inadequate to the preservation of the peace of 310,000 people. But aside from this, the fierce indignance among members of the department of the ruthless murders of Capt. Day and Patrolman Lamb by the negro Robert Charles, to some extent made the police sympathetic with the mobs in their . . . efforts to avenge the murders. Several instances are actually reported where the police actually encouraged the rioters in their work.

Not a single arrest was made by the police throughout the night; nor were any of the rioters taken into custody up to noon today. The fact that there has been a strong feeling on the part of the working people against steamship agents and contractors employing negro labor to the exclusion of whites on public works and on the levee fronts also contributed to the disinclination of the police to do their full duty.

The noticeable feature of the crowd tonight is that these men are as a rule laboring men, the hoodlum element having to some extent disappeared. The feelings against the negroes by the white laborers is very intense, and their activity is regarded as a very serious phase of the trouble.

July 27. After a desperate battle, lasting for several hours, in which he succeeded in killing Sergt. Gabriel Porteous, "Andy" van Kuren, keeper of the police jail, and Alfred J. Bloomfield, a young boy, fatally wounding Corp. John F. Lally, John Banville, ex-Policeman Frank H. Evans, A. S. Loclere, one of the leading confectioners of the city, and more or less seriously wounding several citizens, the negro desperado, Robert Charles, who killed Capt. Day and Patrolman Lamb and badly wounded officer Mora, was smoked out of his hiding in the heart of the residence section of the city today and literally shot to pieces.

The tragedy was one of the most remarkable in the history of the city, and 20,000 people—soldiers, policemen and citizens—were gathered around the square in which Charles was finally put to death. Tremendous excitement reigned in New Orleans as the battle went on between the police and the citizens and the negro with his Winchester.

July 28. Last night the race troubles here took a new turn, when mobs set fire to the Thomy Lafon School, the finest negro school edifice in the city.

Thirty residences in the vicinity of St. Dem's and Sixth Streets were also set on fire. At 12:30 this morning the fires are burning fiercely. . . .

Atlanta, Ga. (1906)

4] Mob Violence

(The following article is from an educated negro, a life-long resident of Georgia, in whom, were it safe to print his name, our readers would have every confidence.—Ed.)

Atlanta, Ga., has again demonstrated that it is not a civilized community. Last Saturday the Atlanta *News*, hard pressed for existence in competition with two other afternoon papers, felt called upon to print sensational charges of assault upon white women by negroes. Not one of these charges has yet been proved, but the mere report was enough to call together all the white "toughs" in the city as soon as they had drawn their week's wages, and to give them license to set upon innocent and unsuspecting blacks wherever found and butcher them upon the spot.

The cause of all this violence, by careful inquiry, I have traced to four sources—one remote and three immediate.

The remote cause is the contest between Hoke Smith and Clark Howell for

Source: "The Atlanta Massacre," *Independent*, October 4, 1906, pp. 799–800.

Mob Violence

Governor, in which both men openly declared that negroes have no rights save those granted thru sufferance by the white people. The three immediate causes are: 1. There was circulated by the Atlanta newspapers—*The News* and *The Georgian* especially—the report that five assaults had occurred in one week and an additional one on Saturday—*not one of which charges has been proved.* 2. There is a sharp struggle for existence among three evening papers, which feel called upon to use any measures whatsoever to attract readers among a population that can be best attracted by abuse of the negro. 3. There is an increasing number of educated and prosperous negroes, whose business and whose success are an eyesore to some of the whites, who can in no peaceable way prevent that progress, as the facts here will show.

The facts about the most aggravating case of assault I have found to be as follows: A negro whose purpose was unknown was seen in the yard of a white woman; she drove him away with abusive language without asking him about his mission; the negro again returned and the woman again began to call him vile names and to scream and to cry that the negro was attempting to assault her. A mob at once assembled, and before they had well got together, all of the evening papers—*The News* and *The Georgian* especially—were circulating "extras" under the glaring headlines, "Another Assault." Then separate and extra editions of *The News* appeared hourly until dark, saying, "Another Assault." It seemed only necessary for a white woman to see a negro meeting her in the same street or looking at her on her front porch to make her cry out, "Assault!"

That is the evidence that drove the editors mad and made them advocate the gathering of a mob to murder peaceable negroes. It is coming out little by little that the whole affair was planned. A negro lad, the driver of a laundry wagon, told me that his employer said to him Saturday morning, "Well, Sammie, we are going to kill all the niggers tonight." The most horrible exhibition of savagery was in the treatment of negro passengers on the street cars as often as they came into the public square—negro men, women and children were beaten unmercifully. Even the negro barbers were dragged out of their shops while they were shaving white men, beaten and their shops demolished. One of the finest shops in the whole country had the glass front smashed because the owner was colored. It is believed that this violence upon the barbers was done by white barbers who were members of the mob and who have been unable to cope successfully in Atlanta in competition with negro barbers. They used the mob as a cover to destroy their competitors.

A hardware store and a pawnshop were broken into by the mob, and all revolvers and ammunition taken, but none of the stores would sell weapons to negroes. A negro fled thru a fruit house kept by Greeks, and when the Greeks attempted to defend their store against the mob, it was straightway demolished and the fruit taken. A stable owner, with revolver in hand, defied the mob to break open his door to take his horses to chase negroes to the suburbs. This only shows what one policeman might have done.

Where were the policemen? That is what all negroes asked at first, but when the bluecoats began to halt them on back streets, arrest them upon State charges for carrying concealed weapons, it became plain that the policemen

57

were not interested in quelling the mob. When one was seen in a crowd he made no effort to use his club or his gun to rescue a prisoner. One of the newspapers confesses that on Peachtree street, in the heart of the city, where the mob gathered, "only one policeman could be seen, and, of course, he could do nothing with such a mob."

Where were the conservative, good white people? That is not a question any one will ask when he knows that *ten* of the leading white pulpits in Atlanta are vacant because the pastors of moral courage have either been driven away or will not come to stifle their conscience in such service. On Sunday morning only one pastor stood up *positively* for law and order, according to statements published in the Atlanta *Constitution,* and that one was a Catholic bishop. All the others said it was what you might expect. . . .

New Orleans, La. (1902)

5]   Jim Crow Streetcars

On November 3 [1902], the "Jim Crow," or separate street-car, law went into effect in New Orleans. This law was passed at the last session of the Louisiana Legislature. By its terms the street railway companies are compelled to use separate cars for the carrying of white and colored passengers, or to fit the cars with wire screens or wooden partitions. . . .

Another group of intelligent negroes, the class that take the leading part in the various non-religious organizations, openly opposed the bill, and took steps, after it was passed, to prevent the law affecting the negro population. An association of women attached to the Masonic Order proposed to run 'bus lines to accommodate negro passengers, and issued a call to the fifty or more negro organizations in New Orleans to send representatives to a meeting at which the question would be considered. Unfeasible as the scheme was, it nevertheless appealed strongly to the negroes, and at the meetings representatives from nearly all the organizations were present.

It was apparent from the discussions that the "ruling passion" back of it all was a sense of deep humiliation that negroes as a race should be considered unworthy to ride in conveyances with white people. The railway companies had announced their intention of putting wire screens in every car, and to have negroes occupy the rear seats. This idea of sitting behind screens, as if they were wild or obnoxious animals, was another fact contributing to their mortification. Many of them, it was said, took pride in keeping clean, in wearing good clothes, and in behaving well, as much because they could feel at ease in decent company as because it gave them other personal satisfaction. To exclude such negroes from compartments occupied by white people would, they said, be as unjust as it would be to force them to sit in compartments with unworthy representatives of their own race, whom they, as much as the

SOURCE: A. R. Holcombe, "The Separate Street-Car Law in New Orleans," *Outlook,* November 29, 1902, pp. 746–47.

white people, despised. It would be equally unjust to admit obnoxious white people to white compartments and exclude respectable negroes from enjoying the same privilege.

Probably the next most pronounced sentiment of the meetings was a demand for negroes to support one another in business enterprises. To the negroes, the strongest argument in favor of a 'bus line was the fact that it would be a negro enterprise supported by negro capital and conducted for the general benefit of the race in New Orleans. Out of this assertion grew many an urgent appeal for negroes to acquire property and contribute to the general welfare of other negroes by patronizing them in their businesses. This sentiment is growing stronger and stronger every day, and the results of it are more and more apparent. Negroes no longer wish to send their children to white teachers; negro patients demand the services of negro physicians; drugstores, saloons, grocery-stores, coal and wood shops—in fact, almost every retail business in the city—are conducted on a small scale by negroes, and patronized almost exclusively by members of that race.

Of course the plan to establish a 'bus line failed. Opposition to it grew as its impracticable features became known, and at the third or fourth meeting nothing more was heard of the idea. The prevailing statement then was that the meeting was for the purpose of devising means to better the negro's condition in New Orleans.

The most sensible suggestion came from a band of ten or twelve negroes, who met several times to oppose the 'bus line movement. This suggestion was that eligible negroes register and vote, and that ineligible ones become educated or acquire property in order to be able to exercise the franchise rights granted under the Constitution of Louisiana. . . .

Several prominent negroes have refused to be seen on a "Jim Crow" car. They prefer to walk. Others ride on the cars, but stand on the platforms rather than be forced to sit behind the screens. . . .

Nashville, Tenn. (1905)

6] Boycott of Jim Crow Streetcars

. . . The spark of manhood in the breasts of the masses of the colored people in Nashville has been fanned into a flame by the inauguration of the Jim Crow car law. Great mass meetings were held and the colored people declared that they would not tolerate such an insult. The leaders of the colored people recognized the fact that the people could not get over a city like Nashville without some means of transportation. A Union Transportation Company was formed that pledged the people that some means of transportation would be secured without patronizing the electric-cars. This company decided to use automobiles in the conveying of colored people from one point in the city to another. Enough money was soon raised and a man was sent to New York to buy

SOURCE: "Nashville Revolt Against Jim Crowism," *Voice of the Negro*, December 1905, pp. 828–30.

five automobiles. . . . The subscriptions to stocks ran up from $10,000 to $25,000 ($9,000 have already been raised). Not only did the preachers, teachers, shopkeepers and other professional men give money to the concern, but the company is heartily supported by the cooks, the hod-carriers, the men with the pick and shovel and the wash women. The company has . . . purchased . . . fourteen twenty-passenger electric autos . . . by an expert machinist. They will be put in commission on the 25th of November. The company will have six lines, averaging two and a half miles each. One line will run to Fisk University which is on the suburbs of the city; one will go directly west; another will go southwest; a fourth will go south to Walden University [later renamed Meharry Medical College]; the fifth and sixth lines will go northeast and northwest respectively. The lines have been so planned as to pass through all of the thick settlements, principal places of interest, public schools, colleges, universities and churches of the city. Thus it will accommodate all classes of travel. Nashville has a colored population of 40,000 and yet hardly ever is a Negro seen on the street cars. Only those ride who do not live within reasonable distance of the place to which they desire to go. It is a fact that the Nashville Street Car Company is losing money since the inauguration of the separate car law at the rate of $7,500 per month or $90,000 per year. . . .

Atlanta, Ga. (1904)

7]   Black Schools and Colleges

Last year 2,188 colored students attended the several institutions of higher learning in Atlanta. . . . They come from all parts of the United States, from South America and Africa. . . .

The oldest of the Atlanta schools is the Atlanta University, founded in 1867 through the efforts of that prince of men, that man of God, Rev. Asa Edmund Ware. It has sixty-five acres of land and five brick buildings. Its enrollment last year was 282. Both sexes receive instruction. For a number of years this university was directly controlled by the American Missionary Board, but it is now entirely free from this management and regards itself as non-sectarian. Still Congregational influence prevails and the pastors of the University Church have thus far been Congregational ministers.

Clark University is an institution for the education of both sexes. It has 400 acres of land just beyond the city limits, has three brick buildings and a number of frame cottages. Its enrollment last year was 603. This school is owned and operated by the Northern Methodists, through the Freedmen's Aid and Southern Educational Society.

The Atlanta Baptist College is owned and controlled by the American Bap-

SOURCE: John Hope, "Our Atlanta Schools," *Voice of the Negro*, January 1904, pp. 10–15. [John Hope, 1868–1936, was president of Morehouse College and later of Atlanta University.—Ed.]

tist Home Mission Society. It has thirteen acres of land, three brick buildings and is devoted to the education of men. Its enrollment last year was 175.

Gammon Theological Seminary is dedicated to the education of Christian ministers. It has two brick buildings and a number of frame cottages for teachers and students. It is the only school in Atlanta with an endowment sufficient to support the institution without further financial assistance. The enrollment last year was 48.

Spellman Seminary, for the education of women, has twenty acres of land and eight brick buildings. Its enrollment last year was 635. This school also is under the control of the American Baptist Home Mission Society.

Morris Brown College, for the education of men and women, is owned and managed by the African Methodist Episcopal Church. It has one brick building which is in effect three buildings. Its enrollment last year was 545.

This brief statement by no means gives an idea of these schools; for, after all, institutions of learning less than almost any other organizations lend themselves to classification according to extent of grounds and the size of the buildings. The European University, with its meagre facilities, often without any fixed abode, has survived dynasties and created and guided the thought of centuries. It is rather in this light that the Atlanta schools are to be considered. For what do they stand, what is their contribution to the thought and life of the age?

In one respect they are all alike, they endeavor to give broad learning and liberal culture. They are institutions of higher learning for Negro youth. From the very outset Atlanta University has stood on this platform, and the fact of a well appointed building for manual training has never bedimmed or confused that idea that the boys and girls entering that school are expected to take those studies that make for higher education. It has also stood for equal privileges; and though the school was founded to give educational advantages especially to colored people, still its character does not hinder the youth of any other race, and the University rejected a state appropriation rather than be a party to the violation of the expression of the founder. The feature of the school today is the work it is doing in Sociology. This work is throwing light on the conditions of colored people in this country and giving the University new value and prominence among educational institutions.

No school in the state has had such a gradual evolution as the Atlanta Baptist College. Beginning as an institution for teaching colored ministers rudimentary English with a view to their interpreting the English Bible, the Augusta Institute found laymen seeking admission. To these the door was opened. However, still keeping to the original purpose, the school was later located in Atlanta. But gradually the literary side was developed until the ministerial department became overshadowed. A new charter changed the name from Atlanta Baptist Seminary to Atlanta Baptist College [today Morehouse College], and for the first time the Bachelor's Degree was conferred upon graduates. Then the school rehabilitated the seminary work, so that now there are two distinct departments, the academic course, with the bachelor of art degree, and the theological course with the bachelor of divinity degree. The academic work lays special stress on English and the natural sciences, these subjects finding place in every one of the eight years of preparatory and collegiate work.

Morris Brown College is the only one of the schools mentioned that has a faculty composed entirely of colored people and is operated by a board of trustees of colored people. In fact, it is a creature of that spirit of self-help for which the African Methodist Church has stood. When it is considered that Morris Brown College was the last of the institutions to enter the field in Atlanta, and that already there were a flourishing Methodist University and Theological Seminary in this city, it is questionable whether it was the wise course to locate the school here, when at the time other parts of Georgia were entirely without higher institutions of learning. The State College was not then in Savannah, Central City College was not then in Macon, not to mention several secondary schools, for example, Haines and Walker Baptist Institute at Augusta; Americus Institute at Americus. Here were localities at that time in need. Indeed, when the risk of establishing the college at Atlanta is realized, all the greater credit is due to those who have made Morris Brown a success. Now if it had failed, would that have been a proof of Negroes' inability to run their own schools, since the location was unfavorable? I think not. But it has shown its right to survive by its growth. This school has the academic and theological courses, besides a course in law; and is endeavoring to make nurse-training a feature, while there has been much doubtfully helpful effort recently to add industrial courses.

One of the most unique seminaries in the South is Spellman Seminary. Begun twenty-two years ago in the basement of Friendship Baptist Church by Misses Sophia Packard and Harriet Giles, who felt that colored women were being neglected, this school has had a phenomenal growth in the number of students and scope of work. It takes girls from the kindergarten through the college course. The trades and domestic sciences are taught. It owns and operates one of the best equipped hospitals in the South. Here trained nursing is taught. It has a normal school where student teachers have an opportunity to practice in a school numbering hundreds of students; and a missionary training school, from which women have gone to do home and foreign missionary work. To say what is the feature of this seminary is difficult, yet if all had to be excluded but one, not even excepting the nurses' course, we should say that the distinctive feature of the Spellman Seminary is its teachers' professional course. Spellman has revolutionized teaching in the grades and among colored people, and even its missionary success not only at home, but on the Congo in Africa has been due largely to this spirit of the teacher.

Clark University was blessed in being taken from its Crawford quarters in the city of Atlanta out to that unexcelled woodland of four hundred acres. Around it a community of colored people has grown owning their own homes. Since 1870 children have gone from the kindergarten through that University without having to leave the grounds for school advantages. If solid culture, sound scholarship and good morals ought to be found anywhere, surely South Atlanta must feel its duty in this particular. One of the attractions of this school is the model home for girls. In years past industrial training was a feature, and some of the most skilful Negro mechanics today are men who learned their trade at Clark University. Lately, however, this department has not been urged to its former limits, but it is still a part of the curriculum. Biology has within recent years held a strong place, and the impetus given this department may have much to do with shaping the future of Clark University.

While Gammon Theological Seminary has a fine record, both in its teaching and the life of the men who have gone out from it, yet the feeling is that it has not begun to reach the limit of its possibilities. Richly endowed, with an ideal situation, devoted to one work, and that work requiring only a minimum annual outlay for equipment, what may not be expected? If allowed its rightful growth, it will be a centre for research and investigation where men, regardless of race or denomination, will come to study with a view to increasing the world's store of learning. The Stewart Missionary Foundation to a man combining the student and missionary spirit gives one of the finest fields open to a man to-day, an opportunity to know Africa and to bring the United States and Africa in touch with each other. No more magnificent offer can be made to learning and consecration.

Here has been given the idea of the scope of six schools in Atlanta with an annual attendance of more than two thousand, with real estate, a conservative estimate of whose value is more than one million dollars. These are monuments to the insight and generosity of three great religious denominations. . . .

The total enrollment of the five colleges last year was 2,140. Of this number only 126 were in the college department, while 1,337 were in the grades. 557 were in the academic or normal course, and 26 were in the teachers' professional department. Atlanta University has the largest per cent of college students in proportion to its entire enrollment. The Atlanta Baptist College stood second, then Clark University, Morris Brown College and Spellman Seminary.

Here are five colleges with only 5.8 per cent of their entire enrollment in the college department, while 62 per cent. has not passed out of the grades. Almost any teacher in these schools would deprecate the fact that these higher institutions are compelled to do the work that cities and counties refuse to do for their school population. A glance at the catalogues will show that Atlanta, a most prosperous city, is very remiss. Not only does no Georgia town give Negroes a high school, but even in cities like Atlanta and Augusta the lowest grades are over-crowded.

Atlanta, Ga. (1908)

8]   Slums

Atlanta is a typical post-bellum city. . . . This growing city is built on the foot of the Alleghenies, a series of great round-topped mounds, which presents

SOURCE: W. E. B. Du Bois (ed.), *The Negro American Family,* Atlanta: Atlanta University Press, 1908, pp. 58–60. [W. E. B. Du Bois, 1868–1963, was an eminent scholar and civil rights leader.—Ed.]

many difficulties in drainage and grading. The city is circular in form and over half of the Negro population is crowded into two wards, one on the east and the other on the west side of the city.

The nucleus of Negro population in Southern cities is the alley. It is seen at its worst in slums of Charleston, Savannah, Washington and such cities. It represents essentially a crowding—a congestion of population—an attempt to utilize for dwellings spaces inadequate and unsuited to the purpose, and forms the most crushing indictment of the modern landlord system. Attention has lately been directed to the tenement-house abominations, but little has been said of the equally pestilential and dangerous alley. The typical alley is a development of the back-yard space of two decent houses. In the back-yard spaces have been crowded little two-room dwellings, cheaply constructed, badly lighted and ventilated, and with inadequate sanitary arrangements. In Atlanta the badly drained and dark hollows of the city are threaded with these alleys, usually unpaved and muddy, and furnishing inviting nests for questionable characters. The worst type of these homes is the one-room cabin with sidings of unfinished boards running up and down; no ceiling or plastering, no windows, no paint, an open fireplace, and the whole of this cheerless box set directly on the ground, without cellar or foundation. Next to these come two-room houses, built in the same way, but with one or two windows and still without porch, blinds, or fence. Such cabins are so crowded together that they nearly touch each other, and the sun must get high before it can be seen from these alleys. Sometimes such rooms are papered inside by the inmates. They are 14 or 15 feet square and 8 or 10 feet high. The furniture is scarce—a bed or two, a few chairs, a table, a stove or fireplace, a trunk or chest. The floor is bare, and there are no pictures. Sometimes six or eight persons live in two such rooms and pay $1.50 a month or more for rent; sometimes as much as $4.00. These houses have water outside in a well or street hydrant; the outhouses are used in common by several tenants. Probably twenty per cent of Negro homes in Atlanta fall into this class.

The surroundings of these homes are as bad as the homes. In the third ward most of the streets are in very bad condition, the longest of them having paved sidewalks only about half their length, while the shorter ones are not paved at all. The streets are of soft red clay, without gravel or cobble stones.

In the first ward, out of 25 typical homes,

> 4 had no water on the premises,
> 12 had wells (which are dangerous in Atlanta
>   and apt to be infected by sewage),
> 9 used hydrants in the yards or on the streets.

Only four had direct sewer connections. Conditions as to light and air vary, but in general there is less to complain of here, save that the careless construction of the houses makes the sudden changes of temperature in the winter peculiarly trying. This lack of protection in winter is made worse by the conditions of the foundations. Most of the houses are perched on wooden or brick pillars, allowing unchecked circulation of air beneath—a boon in summer, a danger in winter. The poor drainage of many of the hollows between the hills

Slums

where these alleys lie gives rise to much stagnant water, pools and the like, and the unfinished sewer system often leaves masses of filthy sediment near these homes.

In the fifth ward, one of the poorer sections, an Atlanta University senior made the following estimates:

30 per cent of the families live in 1 room
40   ″   ″   ″   ″   ″ 2 rooms
15   ″   ″   ″   ″   ″ 3 rooms

Of the houses,

60 per cent were plastered inside.
50 per cent were painted outside.

About half the population dwelt in districts which may be designated as "slums," although many of these were respectable people. Only 35 per cent of the homes looked clean and neat. There were five persons to every two rooms in the district, and three persons to every two beds. Sixty per cent of the homes had practically no yards, and 95 per cent of the homes were rented.

In the whole city of Atlanta the Negroes lived as follows in 1900:

In 1 room. . . . . . . 622 families.
In 2 rooms. . . . . .1654 families.
In 3 rooms. . . . . .1357 families.
In 4 rooms. . . . . .1039 families.
In 5 or more rooms. . .1902 families.

The great majority of the one and two-room homes and some of the others are thoroughly bad as places of shelter. In other words, a third of the black population is poorly housed and, as stated before, a fifth very poorly.

The result of all this crowding is bad health, poor family life, and crime. The actual physical crowding is often great, as for example:

42 families of 6, in one room.
15 families of 7, in 1 room.
12 families of 8 or more, in one room.
21 families of 10 or more, in 2 rooms.
6 families of 12 or more, in 3 rooms.

This crowding, however, is not nearly so bad or so dangerous as the close contact of the good, bad and indifferent in the slum districts. Vice and crime spread with amazing rapidity in this way, and its spread is facilitated by the prevalent vice of Southern police systems, which make little distinction of guilt or desert among the young and old, the criminal and the careless, the confirmed rascal and the first offender, so long as they are all black. The most pitiable thing of all is the breaking up of family life, even when the mothers and fathers strive hard to protect the home. The high death-rate of the Negro is directly traceable to these slum districts. In the country the Negro death-rate is probably low. In the healthy wards of Northern cities the Negro death-rate is

low; but in the alleys of Charleston, which are probably the vilest human hab-
itations in a civilized land, the wretched inmates die in droves, while the
country complacently calculates, on that abnormal basis, the probable extinc-
tion of black folk in America.

Economic Aspects

*As urban blacks encountered increasing disenfranchisement and jim crow prac-
tices, they sought to compensate by building up economic institutions and enterprises. Symptomatic of this spirit, and fostering it, was the National Negro
Business League, founded in 1900 by Booker T. Washington, the fervent and
influential advocate of black economic nationalism. Black banks and insurance
companies mushroomed in the first decade and a half of the twentieth century.
The four banks established by 1900 had increased to 31 by 1906, when the
National Negro Bankers Association was formed (Document 12) in Atlanta at
the meeting of the 1,200-delegate National Negro Business League. Document
11 describes the founding in 1904 and early optimistic phase of one of the institutions, the One Cent Savings Bank of Nashville. By 1911 there were "more
than fifty black banks" (Document 14). But the majority of these were to collapse within a decade because of mismanagement stemming from inexperience.*

*The bustling business attitude in the black urban communities during this
period is best exemplified in the selections below on Richmond (Document 9)
and Durham (Document 14). In 1904, Richmond's black population of about
40,000 boasted four banks, several insurance companies, and well-to-do individual proprietors who took pride in still being able to retain substantial
white patronage. By 1911 black Durham, with a large insurance company and
bank, a textile mill, an iron works company, and a brickyard company, among
other major businesses, was already gaining the reputation, later universally accorded it, of being the capital of black American business. This
would seem surprising in view of Durham's small population—in 1910, 6,869
blacks out of a total population of 18,241—but it was this smallness of proportion that permitted the paternalistic and wealthy whites to supply the blacks
of Durham with the normally elusive credit, expertise, and patronage.*

*Documents 9, 13, and 14 support the view that black artisans in the urban
South, although gradually losing ground, continued to play an important role
in the early twentieth century, while Document 10 lends weight to the thesis
that in the urban South segregated black unions were permitted by whites in
order to control black labor more easily.*

Richmond, Va. (1904)

9]   Black Business

The history of the business of Richmond extends far back beyond the war between the states. In the days of slavery there were "free men" and men who
"hired their time," who were engaged in various kinds of mercantile pursuits
on their own account, such as blacksmiths, barbers, carpenters, and tradesmen.
There are on record even cases of men who were in a small way Negro trad-
ers.

With the advent of freedom, men who had spent their lives in the tobacco
business formed companies for the manufacture of tobacco and as far back as
1868, James B. Burrell organized and operated the Virginia Loan and Trust
Company which for more than ten years did a creditable building and loan
business. To this latter company more than two hundred colored families are
indebted for their start toward the acquirement of real estate. Numberless mercantile firms were organized and operated for a time but, on account of ignorance of the rules of business, they all with one accord went to the wall. Notwithstanding these early failures, after persistent effort and knowledge born of
experience, there are now probably more Negroes doing business in Richmond
on their own account than in any other city of similar size.

Some of the concerns are of national importance and have played no small
part in the development of the business idea of the Negroes of the country.

ORGANIZATIONS AND INVESTMENTS

The most prominent organization in Richmond is the Grand Fountain of the
United Order of True Reformers founded by William W. Browne in 1881.
This organization, starting with a capital of $150.00 and one hundred mem-
bers for the purpose of caring for the sick and burying the dead, today numbers more than seventy-five thousand members and has affiliated with it under
separate charters, several business concerns. The oldest of these is the Savings
Bank of the Grand Fountain of the United Order of True Reformers with a
paid up capital stock of $100,000.00 and deposits of more than $300,000.00.
There are more than 10,000 depositors, all of whom are Negroes. This bank
opened in 1889 with deposits of $1,200. At that time the confidence of the Ne-
groes in banking institutions was at a low ebb and it was a long time before
this confidence was restored.

The Reformers' Mercantile and Industrial Association with its five stores in
Richmond, Manchester, Roanoke, Portsmouth, Va., and Washington, D.C., is
another flourishing branch of the True Reformers. The business of these stores
is conducted on a cash basis and amounts to over $100,000 a year. The com-
bined property of all the departments of the True Reformers is over $400,000

SOURCE: W. P. Burrell, "History of the Business of Colored Richmond," *Voice of the
Negro*, August 1904, pp. 317–22.

in value. Rev. W. L. Taylor, D.D., is the president of the system; R. T. Hill, cashier, and W. P. Burrell, secretary.

The next organization in importance to the True Reformers is the Knights of Pythias of which Mr. John Mitchell, Jr., is the head. This organization was started some years ago by Mr. Mitchell, and today spreads over every part of the state. There has been organized under his direction the second largest Negro bank in Virginia, known as the Mechanics Savings Bank. This bank commenced business in 1902 with a capital stock of $25,000 and $4,000 in deposits. The assets are now over $50,000. Mr. John Mitchell, Jr., is the president, Mr. Thos. Wyatt is the cashier, while Mr. Thomas Crump is the secretary. This bank, under Mr. Mitchell's direction, is coming rapidly to the front as a strong and reliable financial institution.

The Independent Order of St. Lukes is another organization with headquarters at Richmond, which is not only doing a Benevolent Society Business, but has connected with it a bank of growing importance known as the St. Lukes Penny Savings Bank.

The second oldest Negro bank in Richmond is the Nickel Savings Bank. Dr. R. F. Tancil is the president; Mr. E. A. Washington is cashier. Dr. Tancil is a hustling business man who enjoys a large medical practice and yet finds time to run a large brick yard and manage large real estate holdings of his own. Whole blocks of houses are owned by him and there is no more popular man in Richmond than he. He is the president of the Richmond Hospital Association of which I will tell you something later.

From the report of the Auditor of Public Accounts of the state of Virginia published in 1901 it appears that the whites of Richmond held property to the value of $40,044,000, while the Negroes held property valued at $924,000. In 1865 the property held in the name of Negroes did not exceed $20,000 in value.

The Richmond Negroes are engaged in many varied kinds of business other than banking, but time and space will not permit us to deal with them separately. We will give a list of the kinds of business and will then speak briefly of the most prominent men engaged.

The following is the list:

BUSINESS	NO.	CAPITAL INVESTED
Attorneys	10	5,000
Blacksmiths	19	4,500
Barbers	65	24,800
Boarding Houses	1	2,800
Broom Manufacturers	3	800
Butchers	4	2,500
Bakers	1	500
Chiropodists	8	500
Banks	4	125,000
Cabinet Makers	1	125
Caterers	3	500
Cigar Factories	2	750

Black Business

BUSINESS	NO.	CAPITAL INVESTED
Carpenters and Contractors	14	12,000
Coal and Wood Dealers	16	2,000
Confectioners	29	2,500
Druggists	4	8,000
Coopers	3	200
Dairies	2	1,250
Dressmakers	29	3,500
Dying and Cleaning	7	750
Eating Houses	53	2,000
Fish Dealers	18	3,600
Florists	2	2,500
Funeral Directors	11	26,000
Groceries	223	27,000
Insurance Companies	16	40,000
Ice Dealers	4	2,500
Junk Dealers	1	200
Horse Shoers	5	1,125
Harness Makers	1	50
Hay Dealers	1	500
Public Halls	19	121,500
Hotels	1	15,000
Hucksters	29	17,050
Liverymen	5	20,000
Music Teachers	8	1,500
News Dealers	5	150
Notaries	8	
Newspaper Routes	2	500
Trained Nurses	24	
Physicians	11	5,100
Poultry Dealers	3	500
Photographers	2	3,000
Paper Hangers	2	750
Plastering	7	1,925
House Painters	2	500
Sign Painters	3	
Artificial Makers [sic]	1	2,500
Teamsters	76	51,850
Tailors	2	4,500
Laundries (Steam)	2	22,000
Hospitals	2	21,000
Shoe Dealers	1	3,500
Real Estate Agents	1	4,500
Ice Cream Manufacturers	8	3,100
Business Colleges	1	5,000

From the foregoing list of individual business enterprises conducted by Negroes, it can be seen that they have a creditable showing.

MAJOR BUSINESS AND OWNERS

The space allotted to this article will not allow me to give very much of the history of what might well be termed "The Captains of Industry." In the undertaking and livery business, Mr. A. D. Price easily leads with a large, well stocked ware-room where can be found everything in the undertaking line. The stock is said to be worth over ten thousand dollars. He owns three up-to-date funeral cars, eighteen rubber tired carriages, twelve single and double rigs for pleasure and business, and forty-two horses. Mr. Price started twenty years ago with nothing but his trade as a blacksmith; he is now rated at more than $40,000. He is a hustler but very modest as to his own large business. He is a large property holder. His place of business covers a space thirty by one hundred and eighty feet and is three stories high.

Eighteen years ago Mr. S. J. Gilpin was a prominent shoemaker with a good custom. He decided to open a shoe store and today conducts one of the nicest stores in Richmond, which is patronized by both white and colored persons. Mr. Gilpin is a prominent Odd Fellow and a director in several important business enterprises.

Mr. R. T. Hill, the cashier of the Reformer's Bank, is one of the pioneer business men of the city, having conducted many years ago the first Negro book store in Virginia. Mr. Hill is a thorough business man and is the president of the colored Y.M.C.A., as well as the head of numerous other benevolent and religious bodies. He is a notary public and one of the directors and owners of the colored settlement known as Jonesboro.

Mr. Hill is a large property holder and lives in one of the finest residences owned by any Negro in this country.

One of the most striking examples of what a man may accomplish by pluck and push can be found in the person of Mr. Delware Bowles, who owns the largest furniture and piano moving outfit in the city. Ten years ago he was a day-laborer working for one dollar a day. He now owns ten double teams worth, in all, $5,000; has a good bank account and is kept busy at all times with his twenty assistants. He has no education but is respected by all as a man of sterling business qualities.

In the insurance business, Rev. W. F. Graham, the president and founder of the American Beneficial Insurance Co., stands almost without a peer. In two years he has built a company of more than forty thousand members and introduced many new features into the business. He is a director of the Mechanic's Savings Bank, and one of the leaders of the National Baptist Convention.

In the laundry business of Richmond, there is no more prosperous concern that the Richmond Laundry, conducted by Messrs. Geo. W. Bragg and Dorsey Bragg. A few years ago they started business in Farmville with a few tubs and flat irons. Their plant now employs more than thirty persons, three delivery wagons, and is valued at $20,000. Their patrons are mostly white and their work stands as the best in town.

There are only two colored dentists in Richmond and they have all the work they can do. Dr. D. A. Ferguson is a young man from Kentucky who graduated from Howard and opened an office here. His business is so large that he has often to go to his office at six in the morning and work until nine at night. There is no class of work with which he is not familiar.

The Richmond Hospital Association, of which Dr. R. F. Tancil is the president, owns and conducts one of the finest hospitals for colored people in the country. Located on East Baker street, it is prepared to care for all kinds of diseases. It is patronized by the best people and has charity beds, supported by charitable bands of ladies for the poor. Dr. M. B. Jones, the surgeon in chief, is a hustling business man and finds time from his large and growing practice to give much time to church work.

Mr. George Thompson and Mr. John M. Benson have been for many years associated in the drug business and have built up a large trade. They have many proprietary medicines of their own. Their prescription business is enormous. Mr. Benson now has associated with him his wife, Mrs. Nellie Benson, who is a registered pharmacist. These are the forerunners in the drug business.

Mr. John H. Braxton, the young real estate agent of Richmond, is pushing to the front. Entering on a new line of business for Negroes less than five years ago, he now stands among the leaders in his line.

For years the ice business in Richmond has been practically in the hands of white people and not until recently did any colored man dare to enter very largely into competition with them. It now requires a large double team to make his daily deliveries, and from selling a few hundred pounds a day he has built up a trade requiring several tons. Mr. E. E. Giles is a young man but of a type very plentiful in Richmond; with much push.

Until Mr. I. J. Miller came to Richmond ten months ago and on one of the most prominent streets next door to a large banking establishment opened a clothing store with a stock worth $20,000, Richmond had never had a colored clothier. Mr. Miller has built up a large business and now runs a branch store with a $15,000 stock in Newport News, Va.

The finest dressmaker in Richmond, regardless of color, is Mrs. Fannie Criss Payne. Her list of patrons is made up of the best white families in Richmond. So great is their confidence in her ability and taste that many leave to her the selection of their entire outfits. In the last six months she has made the trousseaus for the most popular brides.

She buys her patterns from New York where she goes twice a year to make selections. She employs eight girls regularly and her business amounts to more than $8,000 a year. She has recently fitted up a new home with every home-comfort and convenience for her business at a cost of $6,000 cash. A few years ago Mrs. Payne was a day cooker, earning one dollar fifty cents a day. Her dresses may now be seen at the most prominent watering places of the country and give the same satisfaction as many that are imported at a great cost.

Dr. R. E. Jones, the founder of the Woman's League Hospital and Training School, is also the founder of Jonesboro, a colored settlement of several hundred acres a few miles below Richmond. Dr. Jones is a good business man and is interested in all things that are for the interest of the race. In his daily visitations he uses a fine automobile.

Probably the oldest photographer in Richmond is a colored man, Mr. J. C. Farley. For years he worked in the Davis gallery where the best people of the town sat for his pictures. About ten years ago he went into business for himself and opened the Jefferson art gallery. The excellence of his work is recognized by everybody and his large list of customers is mainly white. His pictures have taken prizes at all the principal expositions. Mr. Farley is a director of the Mechanic's Bank.

Numbers of men and women in Richmond are working like beavers to hold their own in the great rush of business activity, and time will not permit us to name the many who are deserving of special mention, but the foregoing are fair samples of the mass of over one thousand.

Nashville, Tenn. (1904)

10]   Economic Conditions

. . . 1. The first test related to the wage-earning employment of the negro. The information supplied by the city directory, indicating the distribution among certain general lines of employment, was supplemented by personal inquiries to ascertain the wages earned and the steadiness of employment. The following table sets forth the results:

Black Males with Jobs in Nashville °

KIND OF LABOR	NO.	WAGES	REGULARITY OF EMPLOYMENT
UNSKILLED LABOR.			
Laborers: Working on streets, ditching, etc.	3,970	One to two dollars per day.	Intermittent, hired by the job.
Porters, house boys, waiters, bootblacks, etc.	2,450	$7 to $7.50 per week without board, or $15 per month and board.	Steady employment.
Expressmen, hackmen, drivers, and coachmen.	1,090	Drivers and Coachmen same pay as porters. Expressmen and hack drivers estimated as having the same net income.	Steady employment. Intermittent, by the job.
Stationary firemen.	100	$2 per day.	Steady employment.

SOURCE: Richard Davis Smart, "The Economic Condition of Negroes in Nashville, Tenn.," *Vanderbilt University Quarterly*, April 1904, pp. 108–13.
° According to the 1900 U.S. census, Nashville had a black population of 30,044. This table is based on information in the Nashville City Directory, 1902/3.

Economic Conditions

KIND OF LABOR	NO.	WAGES	REGULARITY OF EMPLOYMENT
SKILLED LABOR.			
Carpenters.	186	$2.50 to $3.50 per day.	
Stone masons.	135	$2.50 to $3.50 per day.	
Mechanics (mostly black-smiths).	116	$2.50 to $3.50 per day.	
Bricklayers.	81	$3.15, $3.60, $4.50 per day, according to ability.	
Plasterers.	61	$2.50 per day.	
Painters.	82	$3.50 per day.	
Barbers.	212	Receive a percentage of their earnings—difficult to estimate.	
Merchants (including hucksters and shopkeepers in about equal numbers).	230	Incomes varying with individual merit.	
PROFESSIONS.			
Ministers.	88	$455 per annum . . .	
Teachers.	(19)†40	$300 to $540 for teachers, $700 to $1,200 for hall teachers and principals in the city schools.	
Doctors.	26		
Lawyers.	18		
Students (adult).	422	Some employed as house boys, etc.	
All other occupations (clerks, printers, etc.)	525		
No occupation.	91		
Total in Directory.	9,923		
Total twenty years and over (census of 1900).‡	7,818		
Number fifteen to nineteen years.	1,435		

Females

Laundresses.	2,595	Average, $10 to $12 per month; maximum, $15.	The greater freedom from restraints enjoyed by the

Females (Continued)

KIND OF LABOR	NO.	WAGES	REGULARITY OF EMPLOYMENT
Cooks.	2,150	$10 to $15 per month and board.	laundresses will proba-bly count as offsetting
House girls and nurses.	850	$8 to $12 per month and board.	the smaller wages.
Seamstresses.	230		
Teachers.	(48)†80	$300 to $340 for teach-ers, and $700 to $1,200 for hall teach-ers and principals.	
Students.	250		
All other occupations (store-keepers, boarding house keepers, etc.).	95		
No occupation (over one-half being widows).	960		Presumably supported by their chil-dren.
Total.	7,210		
Total twenty years and over (census of 1900).‡	10,666		
Number fifteen to nineteen years.	1,913		

† In the city schools.
‡ The Directory includes a larger area than the census, which is limited to the bounds of the corporation. Census figures added by the editor.

2. The relation of the negroes to organized labor. The unions affiliated with the American Federation of Labor are prevented by constitutional provision from barring the negro on account of race. In reality, however, negroes are frequently excluded by the "black ball."

The labor leaders of the city are in favor of organizing the negroes to control the formidable array of "scab" labor which this race might furnish in a strike and also to keep wages up, for the negro, being able to live so much more cheaply than the whites, could easily underbid the latter under free competition in the labor market.

It is generally considered preferable to have the negroes organized in separate unions, and to maintain the very necessary relation with them by allowing them representation in the city Trades and Labor Council. There are six unions composed exclusively of negroes—barbers, stone masons, carpenters, colored laborers, hod carriers, and stationary firemen. In the bricklayers' and plasterers' unions both races are found.

74

Economic Conditions

The barbers' union has thirty-three members, with three delegates in the Trades and Labor Council. The barbers of this union cater to white trade exclusively, leaving the negro trade to the non-union shops. Their minimum wage is sixty per cent of their earnings. They provide a sick benefit of five dollars per week for not more than sixteen weeks, and in case of death a sixty-dollar burial benefit. The same general provisions exist in all of the unions. Thus the stone masons' union does not provide a burial benefit, but gives a sick benefit of two dollars per week for an unlimited time; and the bricklayers' union has no sick benefit, but provides a one-hundred-dollar burial benefit. None of them omit altogether to make provision for mutual help in time of need.

3. Closely allied with this feature of the labor unions, and holding an important place in the life of the negro, are the benevolent organizations. There are a dozen or more of these which, beneath the surface of parade and show, have some features of real worth. The organization of the "Immaculates," which will serve as a good example of them all, has dues of fifty cents per month, with extra assessments amounting to two or three dollars more during the year. The sick benefit varies from one dollar and fifty cents to seven dollars and fifty cents, according to the degree taken in the lodge. In case of death there is a fifty-dollar endowment, and funeral expenses are paid. Furthermore, these advantages are not limited to the men alone, for quite a number of the organizations have "branches" for women and for children. The women's branch is called the "Court" and the children's branch the "Juveniles," or the "Gem." . . . Relying chiefly upon the personal knowledge of the tax assessor, about 11.3 per cent of the total value of taxable property was gone over and it was found that about $2\frac{1}{2}$ per cent of it belonged to negroes. At the same rate the negroes would own $742,068 [1] in a total assessment of $29,682,740. The $83,950 actually ascertained to be the property of negroes was distributed according to size among one hundred and forty-two owners as follows:

Under $200	28 items; estimated for whole city	248 items
$200 to $399	49 items; estimated for whole city	221 items
$400 to $599	25 items; estimated for whole city	433 items
$600 to $999	23 items; estimated for whole city	203 items
$1,000 and upward	17 items; estimated for whole city	150 items
TOTAL	142 items; estimated for whole city	1,255 items

Most of the items are seen to be small, and none exceeded $10,000.

It is an interesting fact that most of the property in the vicinity of Fisk University is owned by negroes. When we reflect that the property-owning negroes form the better class, we see in the circumstance mentioned a very strong indication, if not a proof, that the more enlightened negroes appreciate the institution, and are giving it their moral support.

It is also to be noticed that the property owned by the negroes is not usually of the poorest grade. The negroes who live in the meanest parts of the city are not able and have not the thrift to own their homes, but rent from

[1] The estimated total, $742,068, would represent about 1,255 owners.

some white owner. The negro who has succeeded well enough to own his home is not generally content to live in the lower quarters of the city, but moves to a better neighborhood.

4. Industrial education. In the higher institutions of learning for negroes in the city some instruction in manual training and the trades is given: in carpentering, printing, bookeeping, and other similar trades for the men; and in dressmaking, plain sewing, housekeeping, etc., for the women. But the number of students in these institutions is not large, and most of them come from without the city and return thence. Manual training has not been introduced into the city free schools for blacks, indeed only tentatively into the free schools for whites. Altogether the facts show that a large percentage of the negro artisans in the city have learned their trades by practical experience in them. . . .

Nashville, Tenn. (1909)

11] The One Cent Savings Bank

Among the cities of the "New South" that are enjoying the distinction of having banking institutions doing a thriving business is Nashville, Tennessee. The name of the concern is the One Cent Savings Bank. It was organized and chartered under the laws of the State of Tennessee and opened its doors for business on January 16, 1904. The first day's deposits convinced the promoters that there was confidence already awakened in the race which guaranteed success. It took some time, however, to get the people of this city to see the advantage of such an enterprise, because of the disastrous failure of the Freedman's Bank in Washington, some years ago. The Negroes of Nashville grew into a state of lethargy towards organizing and supporting a bank of their own but the demand for such an institution continued to grow until it became apparent long before an institution was organized that the day had dawned when a bank owned by Negroes must sooner or later be put into operation in Nashville. Finally the citizens awoke one morning to find that a number of them had gathered and were discussing the advisability of organization. This proved to be the first distinctively Negro banking concern, operated under the laws of Tennessee in its capital city. It took several months to complete the plans of the organization, because the issue at stake seemed to be, first, success; second, the stability of the same; third, to put it upon a financial basis backed up by successful men whose business genius had guided safely their individual efforts. An organization was perfected and the significant name, the One Cent Savings Bank, was given and a charter secured. The failure of the institution was predicted time and again, but the personnel of the officers, together with the Board of Directors, have worked hard to see to it that this prediction would not come true.

SOURCE: Henry Allen Boyd, "The One Cent Savings Bank of Nashville, Tennessee—Its Organization and Progress," *Alexander's Magazine*, March–April 1909, pp. 252–53.

The One Cent Savings Bank

The capital stock of the bank was placed at $25,000. This was divided into five thousand shares, to be sold at $5.00 per share. The wisdom of making the capital stock this amount and of putting the shares of stock within reach of the common people proved a success, as admitted by the promoters; hence, as a result, the most humble citizens in the city of Nashville, working at meager salaries, were permitted to become stockholders in what is known as the financial back-bone of the Negro population of this growing city. No effort has been made by the wealthy Negroes to buy up the unsubscribed stock in order that those of smaller circumstances would be left out; to the contrary, liberal inducements have been held out to the masses to buy stock and become directly interested in the growth and the management of the institution.

No bank operated exclusively by members of the race can claim the distinction of having among its stockholders and officers such an array of local, state, national and international characters. Beginning with the president and going down the entire list of officers and directors, it will be seen that the hands and the brains lent to guide this concern have been instrumental in helping to shape the destiny of a people not only along business and educational lines, but in the religious world as well. Frequent changes of officers is avoided, from the beginning the same officers, elected five years ago when the bank was organized, were re-elected last January when the institution held its fifth annual meeting. It might be interesting to the readers to know the names of the men who have been entrusted with the management. The names of the Board of Directors elected at the last stockholders' meeting with the position or profession followed by each, which is evidence of itself that it is to be the greatest of any in the South, are as follows:

Directors: Mr. Lewis Winter, who has been in the poultry business in Nashville for more than a quarter of a century, worth more than $50,000, and today the largest poultry dealer in the city; J. W. Grant, attorney-at-law and a property owner rated at $50,000, prominent secretary and secret Order promoter; T. G. Ewing, Sr., attorney-at-law, one of the pioneer Negro attorneys of Tennessee, interests in almost every enterprise started in this city, stockholder in several large manufacturing concerns; C. A. Cullum, a modest, yet enterprising citizen of Tennessee rated at several thousand dollars; J. B. Bosley, who quite a number of years ago was reputed to be worth more than $150,-000; R. F. Boyd, M.D., who built the magnificent three-story building on Cedar street, known as the Boyd Building, proprietor of the Mercy Hospital, a large real estate owner, worth $100,000; C. N. Langston, grandson of the late ex-Congressman John Mercer Langston, who has served as teller; C. S. Randalls, a pioneer and one of Nashville's contractors, worth more than $20,000; Preston Taylor, proprietor of Greenwood Cemetery, the Taylor Undertaking Company, Greenwood Park and pastor of the Lea Avenue Christian Church, reputed to be worth $200,000; R. H. Boyd, D.D.. LL.D., founder and secretary of the National Baptist Publishing Board, an institution of international reputation, valued at $300,000; J. West Bostic, proprietor and large stockholder in the Economical Steam Laundry, proprietor of the Old Reliable Buffet, rated at $50,000; J. P. Crawford, M.D., Grand Chancellor of Knights of Pythias of Tennessee and principal of the Knowles School, estimated at

$20,000; E. B. Jefferson, D.D.S., long ago given up to be one of the leading dentists of the city, worth $20,000; G. W. McKissack, brick contractor, whose estate is valued at $25,000; J. C. Napier, attorney-at-law, owner of building in which bank is located and of several large business buildings, worth fully $200,000; William Beckham, D.D., Field Secretary of the National Baptist Convention, who is said to be worth in Texas holdings and in other states $50,000; Henry A. Boyd, Assistant Secretary of the National Baptist Publishing Board, manager and treasurer of the Globe Publishing Company; Rev. William Haynes, president of the Tennessee Baptist State Convention, pastor of one of the largest churches in Nashville, worth fully $20,000.

Officers: R. H. Boyd, President; J. West Bostic, Vice President; J. C. Napier, Cashier; C. N. Langston, Teller.

The bank has been able to keep such a reputation and standing with every financial institution in the city that it is looked upon as one of the best managed concerns in Nashville. . . . The fifth annual report is interesting. It shows that, notwithstanding the recent panic, the business had increased above that of the previous year. It showed a clearance of $663,948.25 and a clearance in five years of more than two million and a half dollars. The bank has been by careful management not only able to lay up a surplus and undivided profit equal to its paid up capital, but has declared an annual dividend of 6 per cent. The stock has had constant and regular sale upon the market, and while discretion has been exercised to see that it was placed strictly in the homes of people, no limitation has been placed or put upon the amount to be purchased by an individual.

Atlanta, Ga. (1906)

12]   First National Black Bankers' Meeting

. . . the National Negro Bankers' Association . . . held its first meeting in Atlanta a few days ago, in connection with the annual meeting of the National Negro Business League. . . . At the meeting . . . there were present fourteen bank officials, most of them being either the cashiers or the presidents of negro banks.

The growth of the negro in commercial and business directions is indicated by the growth of banks under the control of negroes. . . . fifteen years ago there were only two banks in America under the control of negroes—one in Richmond, Va., and one in Birmingham, Ala. At the present time there are thirty-one banks operated by negroes, and others are being organized each year.

There have been very few failures of negro banks; in fact, I only know of the failure of one.

SOURCE: Booker T. Washington, "A Most Encouraging Convention," *Independent*, September 20, 1906, pp. 684–86. [Booker T. Washington, 1856–1915, Tuskegee educator, was the most powerful black man in American history.—Ed.]

Skilled Labor

Up until our last meeting, the bankers had been meeting in connection with the regular session of the National Negro Business League. . . .

Of the thirty-one banks, fourteen were represented at the Atlanta meeting. It may sound strange, but nevertheless it is true, that eleven of these banks are in the State of Mississippi. . . .

Memphis, Tenn. (*1908*)

13]   Skilled Labor

For several months it was the privilege of the author to visit factories and plants of every character and note with his own eyes just what the opportunities of the colored people really are along the line of employment; and the results of his observations were as astonishing as they were gratifying. His investigations were particularly directed along the line of skilled labor. . . . He visited the candy factories and found some of their most efficient and reliable workmen colored men. In one of the factories the foreman is a colored man of intelligence and culture, Mr. Charles Taylor, and practically the whole working force are colored men. Very much the same may be said of the other candy factories in Memphis. Mr. James Wooten, Donald Hayden, Chas. Taylor and many others have been creditably identified for years with the candy making business and enjoy the confidence of their employers. Possibly the oldest candy maker in Memphis and the pioneer in that business is Mr. Charles Morton, who has made candy for nearly 45 years.

The author visited the broom factories and found some of their most expert operatives to be colored men. He found similar conditions in the mattress factories. It is hardly probable that two more efficient mattress makers than Maurice Larry and Garnett Hopkins can be found in the whole country; and there are others quite as skillful in the same line of work. The author visited several blacksmith and horse-shoeing shops and found no one white except the proprietor. In the great lumber yards he found many colored men holding the most responsible positions and that not a foot of lumber is carried out of these yards without their inspection. He visited the slaughter houses and found the veteran butchers to be colored. At one of the largest slaughter houses he found a colored man the foreman, Mr. Fred Smith, a very kind and courteous gentleman. He found that many of the engineers running the various plants are colored men of experience and ability. In many of the best white tailoring establishments may be found first-class colored tailors doing everything that is to be done in that business. Without further elaboration it may be repeated that the results of the author's observations were as astonishing as they were gratifying.

It is quite probable that no part of the great northern section of this country gives to the colored man such great opportunities along the lines of skilled labor. It is a common occurrence for colored contractors to erect buildings for white people, notwithstanding fierce competition from white contractors of

SOURCE: G. P. Hamilton, *The Bright Side of Memphis,* Memphis: G. P. Hamilton, 1908, pp. 11–17.

ability who feel that racial considerations alone entitle them to the work. In the laying of brick and the erection of buildings in general skilled workmen of both races work side by side and no serious objection is made. . . .

     . . . . .

In many respects the city of Memphis has a distinct advantage over most of the other cities of the South, but in few other respects is the advantage for colored people more pronounced than in business opportunities. Having the largest colored population in the far South,[1] it is very natural that the business outlook for energetic, capable and shrewd business men should be of the most favorable character. . . .

In the past few years the colored people have awakened to the fact that it is commendable in them to patronize the business enterprises of their own people and there is at present a general inclination to do so. . . .

In the city of Memphis no serious effort has ever been made by the colored people to go into the dry goods business on a scale that would enable them to compete with the big concerns that are already in the field. It has always been a question of doubt whether the colored man would be able to compete successfully with the Hebrews who seem to have an instinctive knowledge and mastery of the dry goods business. . . .

The colored people are well represented in the grocery business and have many examples of mercantile success. There are attractive drug stores, photograph studios, tailor shops, feed stores, restaurants, barber shops, blacksmith shops, undertaking establishments, jewelry stores, dental parlors, coal and wood yards, laundries, shoe shops, shoe stores, ice cream manufactories, shoe shining parlors, news paper plants, printing offices, silk and lace cleaning establishments, harness making stores and many other kinds of business establishments in Memphis.

The greatest and most successful competitor that the colored business man must meet is the Italian. We are not able to account for the Italian's complete mastery of the patronage of the colored people; but he holds it nevertheless as if in the hollow of his hands. The Italian lunch houses and grocery stores will be packed to suffocation with colored patrons while colored establishments of a similar character would be practically empty. . . . The general explanation . . . is that the Italian is much craftier as a business man. He is a good mixer with colored people and a great jollier. . . .

Durham, N.C. *(1911)*

14]   Black Business

. . . Now, Durham is one of the large cities of North Carolina, and knowing from my early experiences something of the superficial and hand-to-mouth liv-

SOURCE: Booker T. Washington, "Durham, North Carolina, a City of Negro Enterprises," *Independent,* March 30, 1911, pp. 642–50.
[1] It was actually the second largest; New Orleans' black population was in fact significantly larger.

ing of the average city Negro, I became more and more curious to see what Durham had in store for me.

Arriving there about four o'clock on a bright afternoon in October, I found every preparation that was necessary to sweep me from my feet with the conviction that sure enough this was the city of cities to look for prosperity of the Negroes and the greatest amount of friendly feeling between the two races of the South. . . . Well, and not foolishly, dressed colored people, colored people representing all manner of business, from the small store to the thriving, thorogoing business enterprise, colored people seated in one and two horse carriages with rubber tires, stood eager to welcome me. . . .

In addition to many prosperous doctors, lawyers, preachers and men of other professions, I found some of the most flourishing drugstores, grocery and dry goods stores I had ever seen anywhere among Negroes. I found here the largest Negro insurance company in the world, with assets amounting to $100,000, owning its building, a large three-story structure, and being operated with nothing but Negro clerks and agents. Here is located the Durham Textile and the Whitted Wood Working Company, manufacturers of doors, window frames, mantels and all kinds of building materials. Here, too, is the Union Iron Works Company, a Negro company which manufactures general foundry products, turning out plows, plow castings, laundry heaters, grates and castings for domestic purposes, and it was refreshing to learn that in this enterprise as in others that I shall mention there was no evidence of the color line drawn on the part of the purchaser. Each groceryman, each textile manufacturer, each tailor, in fact, all the Negro tradesmen and business men numbered many white customers among their most substantial purchasers.

I began by this time to believe that Durham was a city of Negro enterprises, and quite convinced now, I was ready to go home, but they wanted to show me one more successful Negro plant. This was the plant known as the Durham Textile Mill, the only hosiery mill in the world entirely owned and operated by Negroes. Regularly incorporated, they operate eighteen knitting machines of the latest pattern, working regularly twelve women and two men and turning out seventy-five dozen pairs of hose each day. The goods so far are standing the test in the market, being equal in every way to other hose of the same price. They are sold mainly by white salesmen, who travel mostly in North Carolina, New York, Indiana, Georgia, South Carolina and Alabama, ...

Aside from these flourishing enterprises Durham had many individuals, such as tradesmen and contractors, who were shining examples of what a colored man may become when he is proficient and industrious. I found that Payton Smith, a general contractor, had put up some of the largest buildings in the city, that P. W. Dawkins, Jr., who had learned the carpenter's trade at Hampton, and Norman C. Dadd were not only never out of work, but kept jobs always waiting for them.

It was exceedingly interesting, too, to find here two individuals owning and operating brickyards. . . . With a business amounting to $16,000 per year, R. E. Clegg, manufacturer of all kinds of bricks, turns out per season in brick two million brick. But the pioneer in brick making in Durham is R. B. Fitzgerald.

Beginning thirty years ago, Mr. Fitzgerald has supplied the material for many of the largest brick structures in the city. . . . Fitzgerald . . . not only turns out 30,000 bricks a day from his $17,000 plant, but owns besides 100 acres of land within the city limits and has $50,000 worth of real estate.

A Negro bank is no longer a novelty, there being more than fifty in America at the present time, but the one at Durham, in addition to carrying resources of $400,000 and deposits of $20,000, is an instance of what the white Southerner often does to help Negroes. When this bank was opened, the cashier and teller of the leading white bank came over and, without charge, helped the colored bankers open and close their books.

With all this prosperity, with flourishing insurance companies, a bank, brick-masons and men in the professions, it was not remarkable that this class of persons should own beautiful homes. . . .

I must here call especial attention to Mr. John Merrick, recognized as the leading Negro of Durham. Mr. Merrick began as a poor man, borrowing money from General Julian S. Carr, a leading white man, to begin his first business. During all the years he has lived in Durham, he has continually expended time and money to promote the interests of colored people, aiding them in securing homes and in establishing organizations of protection. In 1883 he founded the Royal Knights of King David and in 1898 he founded the North Carolina Mutual and Provident Association. He aided in establishing a hospital here for Negroes, is a trustee of the bank, a steward in the St. Joseph A. M. E. Church and president of the Christian Endeavor League. In addition to this he is the largest Negro owner of residence property in the city, collecting per month rents amounting to $550. . . .

But what of the poor man, the unlettered man, . . . ?

. . . I drove through their section of the city, observing closely their homes inside and out, their yards, their fences, their window curtains, their furniture, and I own that in many cases I almost doubted my eyes. The one-time hovel and the shack with rags sticking in the windows and fences rotting away, with little gulleys washed in the yards and half-clad children standing in front of the door, were all gone. I saw no dead dogs or cats or dead fowl in the streets as I sometimes see in our larger Southern cities and I sniffed no feverish odors from dens and dives. Neat cottages stood where in many cities still stands the tubercular shack, and well cared for children in clean yards, many of which were adorned with flower beds, everywhere greeted me. . . .

. . . Of all the Southern cities I had visited, I found here the sanest attitude of the white people toward the black. Disabused long ago of the "social equality" bugbear, the white people, and the best ones too, never feared to go among the Negroes at their gatherings and never feared to aid them in securing an education or any kind of improvement. I have already stated that the wealthiest and best thought of Negro in Durham began his business career upon a loan of money from General Julian S. Carr. Perhaps a still stronger instance is that of the Duke family, the famous tobacco manufacturers. The members of this family have always given generously to support the colored schools and churches of the town. . . .

. . . I never saw in a city of this size so many prosperous carpenters, brick masons, blacksmiths, wheelwrights, cotton mill operators and tobacco factory workers among Negroes.

In the larger white mills and the like the Negroes in several instances are the only ones employed. The hook and ladder company of the fire department is manned entirely by black men. . . . I have referred to the hosiery mill owned and operated solely by Negroes; there is one here also owned by a white man, but operated exclusively by colored men. The proprietor is Gen. Julian S. Carr. . . .

But the company that has done most for the Negro, both in employment and in general help, is the W. Duke Sons & Company, branch of the American Tobacco Company. This company employs more colored laborers than any other firm in the city, keeping steadily at work 1,548 negro men and women, at an average of 93 cents per day, or paying out $1,400 per day or $440,000 a year to colored people. And it is highly to the credit of the colored people that thru all the changes in the system and in the introduction of new and complex machinery they have been able to hold their positions and give increasing satisfaction to their employers.

. . . The Lincoln Hospital here, a place for the sick colored people and for the training of colored nurses, received its grounds and building, valued all told at $75,000, from Mr. Washington Duke, the founder of the Duke Tobacco Company. . . .

. . . That so large a proportion own their homes, that the most of those renting rented from Negro landlords, that the southern part of Durham has been inhabited almost entirely by colored people, and that Negro possessions in the city amounted to one million dollars, was the key that unlocked for me much of the mystery of prosperity and good feeling between the two races. . . .

BORDER CITIES

Political and Social Aspects

From 1900 to 1915 the border cities became increasingly segregated, due both to social custom and to legislative attempts to enforce residential segregation. Before St. Louis's historic use of the referendum in 1916 to vote for residential segregation (Document 21), the municipal councils of Baltimore and Louisville had passed similar legislation in 1910 and 1912 respectively. Although in 1917 the Supreme Court declared housing segregation ordinances unconstitutional, residential segregation was maintained through race-restrictive covenants in the border states and in fact nationally for decades to come.

Rigid social and institutional segregation in Cincinnati—northern in location, but southern in orientation—was both painful and inconvenient to the small black middle class of a city with a proportionately very small black population (Document 18). In Washington, D.C., where "there are more colored people who are well educated and well-to-do than in any city in the world" (Document 16), blacks could more easily fall back on their resources but this did not make less humiliating to them the segregation of the races that took place in several departments of the federal government under President Woodrow Wilson (Document 20).

Some black leaders viewed all-black communities as one way of avoiding white prejudice and of providing better opportunities for the talents and abilities of blacks. Boley, Okla., is typical of the attempts to establish such all-black communities. It was the most famous of some 25 all-black towns founded in Oklahoma between 1891 and 1910 as part of a plan to make the state all black. But the counterambitions of whites were to lead to the disfranchisement of blacks in 1910—four years after statehood was achieved.

Growing segregation and magnified social problems led urban blacks to establish more social, cultural, and religious institutions (Documents 15 and 19), but these were inadequate to meet rising needs.

St. Louis, Mo. (1903)

15]   Social and Cultural Institutions

The Negro is learning organization; the most obvious evidence of this fact exists, I suppose, in the churches. The colored people of St. Louis have between thirty and thirty-five churches of their own and they rarely intrude into any others. Of this number one is Catholic, one Episcopalian, two Presbyterian, and the rest Methodist and Baptist. . . .

In point of education and social standing of members the Episcopalian church undoubtedly heads the list, and the others follow in the order given. St. Paul's and the Central Baptist church have the finest buildings. There is a third building that should be classed with these, that of the Metropolitan A. M. E. Zion church, but I have not succeeded in getting any statistics about it. The $1700 received by the pastor of St. Paul's is the largest salary paid, and it is safe to assume that the Central Baptist is the only colored church in the city that is entirely free from debt.

The primary function of the church—the satisfaction of spiritual demands and the development of the spiritual life—is fulfilled perhaps as well as in Negro churches anywhere. Several of the clergymen, as has been said before, are men of high ideals and noble character; one in particular, who has been working here quietly and faithfully for twenty years, has done much to raise the standard of morality, not only in his own congregation, but also in the community at large; and there are several others who deserve to be classed with him. But, as a rule, the spiritual leaders are little above the level of their flocks. Immorality is countenanced, and questionable amusements are allowed, and the emotionalism which is apt to pass with the Negro for religion is encouraged by the character of the instruction given, all for the sake of making the church "popular" and raising enough money to pay expenses. The importance of the Negro church as a social center has often been noticed. Far more than is the case in white churches, the members of any congregation are in the same social "set" and most of their amusements are connected with the church.

Even more important than the churches in regard to the number affected are the secret and benevolent societies; it is estimated that there are over a hundred and fifty of them in the city and many Negroes belong to seven or eight. They are attracted by the mystery and the processions and titles and regalia of the secret organizations, and by the expectation of getting a substantial return, in the way of burial or sick benefits, for a very small outlay. . . .

There are many social clubs among both men and women. The Forum Club deserves mention; it had a membership in 1901 of 186, including most of the professional and prominent business men, and it owns a good club building; its

Source: Lillian Brandt, "The Negroes of St. Louis," *Journal of the American Statistical Association*, March 1903, pp. 256–64.

object is the study of race problems; lynchings are investigated by agents, and reports on many points of interest are made at the monthly meetings.

During the summer of 1901 a Negro Business League was formed, with the object of improving the "commercial interests of the Negro business men of the city"; the membership at the beginning was 36.

The Afro-American Young Men's Christian Home Association is a creditable organization that has been in existence six years. There were 105 members in 1901; their building is a three-story ten-room brick house which they were buying for $3300; they had paid $800 on it in the last two years. Their income amounted for the year to something over $1000, derived entirely from membership dues and entertainments. The members gather for a devotional meeting on Sunday afternoons, and for a literary and social evening once a week, and the building serves as a clubhouse. There is a "Young Ladies' Auxiliary" society [also]. . . .

There are also among the Negroes several organizations looking towards social improvement. The Provident Hospital and Training School for Nurses is the most considerable of these; it was organized and incorporated in 1894 and has been very successful; the management is in the hands of a board of directors composed of eighteen colored men who are prominent in various ways; the staff includes most of the colored physicians of the city, a head nurse, and a lecturer on domestic science; there is a consulting staff of fourteen prominent white physicians and surgeons. The hospital is pleasantly situated in a three-story brick building, apparently well kept and in good repair; there is equipment for twelve patients, which comes far short of meeting the demands; there is no endowment and the association owns no property. The hospital building is rented. On the other hand, there is no debt; the current expenses, amounting to about $260 per month, are met by the pay from the patients and by money raised by the board of directors and the Ladies' Auxiliary. The patients pay from $5.00 to $7.00 per week if they are able; if they are not able they pay as much as they can, sometimes nothing. The cost per week per patient in 1901 was $7.14 and the receipts were only $3.60 per week from each patient. The deficit is made up by the directors and by the efforts of the Ladies' Auxiliary; this society undertakes to provide for the salary of the head nurse and all the hospital linen; it has sixty members, and raises the money by "entertainments." A few contributions have been received from outside, but no general canvas of the white philanthropists of the city has ever been made; the largest single contribution ever received was $100. There are generally five nurses in training; three were graduated in June, 1901.

The Colored Orphans' Home was founded by the colored W.C.T.U. immediately after its organization in 1889. At present the Home is located in three dilapidated old buildings, comprising fifteen rooms, in a very poor part of the city. A project is on foot for buying a desirable piece of property in the western part of the town, but no immediate realization of it seems probable. The mortality among the babies under present conditions is frightful, though, of course, the provision made is better than nothing. Abandoned colored children are boarded here by the city at the rate of $12 per month, and "half-orphans" are sometimes paid for. The only other sources of income are voluntary contributions, annual boat excursions, and occasional "concerts"; no trustworthy financial report could be obtained. The children attend the public school regularly while at the Home, and are under the care of a matron who seems to be wise and kind, and who does as much for them as any one could with the equipment she has. Homes are found in the country districts of Missouri when possible, and the matron keeps track of the children as long as she can after they leave. In August, 1901, there were 33 inmates; of these 14 were girls, and 19 boys; two of the 33 were under one year of age.

The colored W.C.T.U. numbers fifteen active members, and carries on work along several lines; a sewing school, with incidental temperance features, was conducted on Saturday afternoons last winter in a Negro quarter; certain members visit the jail, the work-house, the poor-house, jnd the hospitals, where they give "spiritual talks" and distribute creature comforts, in the way of flowers, food, and literature; one member gives temperance talks at the colored Sunday-schools. The finances of the Union are inconsiderable, but it seems to be an active body and to accomplish a certain amount of good.

The Old Saints' Home has been maintained for seven years by the Central Baptist church, and in that time has cared for about twenty old persons, presumably "saints." A seven-room house is rented for the purpose, but more room is needed and a fund for building has been started. The running expenses are between $700 and $800 per year. In the summer of 1901 there were seven inmates, including a man and his wife who had been married eighty-one years. Nominally any needy old Negro is received, but practically the limited equipment restricts the beneficiaries to members of the Central church. An applicant sent there recently by the Provident Association was refused.

The Nazareth Home is an interesting institution. It was started five years ago by a young colored girl who has since died, and is run by Negroes, though several white women are interested in it and have a general supervision. It is a non-sectarian home for old women and girls who come to the city to find work. The building occupied has eleven rooms, a good laundry, and a large yard. In July, 1901, there were 9 residents, 5 old women and 4 girls. The "staff" consists of a matron and a laundry superintendent. The aim of the promoters is to make the institution self-supporting, and to that end a laundry is carried on. The girls pay $1.25 per week and work a day and a half in the laundry. The old women do what they can. I was told that the income from the laundry and the fees from the girls amount to enough to cover all current expenses except the rent of the building. The principle is good, certainly, and the attempt bids fair to be successful.

A Penny Savings Bank has been carried on for four years by the pastor of one of the churches. . . . An employment bureau is conducted in connection with the bank, primarily for members of the church. No fees are asked, but help is given as far as possible.

A day nursery has recently been established; it is due to the colored kindergartners of the city, who secured furnishings for the house and the contribution of a year's rent from a white philanthropist. They expect to have three attendants, and to have accommodations for from thirty to fifty children. A charge of five cents a day will be made.

A Rescue Home for Colored Girls was in existence for six months two or three years ago; it was established through the efforts of a poor, ignorant, colored woman who believes that she has a definite "call" to do that sort of work. During the six months she received and cared for fourteen girls and six babies. She says that the most encouraging feature of the work was the gratitude and humility of the girls, one of whom "was actually converted and baptized in the Mississippi river." The work lapsed through lack of funds but its divinely "called" promoter has not lost her enthusiasm and she is working now to get enough money to start again.

. . . . . .

The recreations and amusements vary in the four classes of society. For the lowest classes there are only the saloons, gambling-dens, houses of ill-fame, low dance-halls, and the streets. The upper class has its social and literary clubs, church entertainments, and pleasant homes. For the mass of the people there are steamboat excursions, barbecues, cake-walks, picnics, balls, and church "sociables," all of them ranging from respectable, well-conducted functions down to orgies of vice and sensuality. I think that it is only in the very lowest sort of amusements that there is any contact with the whites. A Negro is rarely seen at a theatre, or even at any of the summer gardens, which are resorts unrivalled in popularity among all classes of white society.

Washington, D.C. (1904)

16]   "Colored Society"

. . . In Washington there are more colored people who are well educated and well-to-do than in any other city in the world. . . . Like other human beings all colored people who are of equal culture, intelligence and affluence do not care to mingle with one another socially. . . .

The old citizens think they are elect, the chosen, and dare anybody to dispute it. They believe that longevity coupled with culture and affluence should count for more than any other combination. . . .

Then there are the new comers who laugh in their sleeve at the old citizens. "Verily we are the social salt of this Capital earth," they say "while the old settlers are wrapped in the drapery of their scorn and contempt for us, we are up and doing things." "If you ask who are the Sunday-school superintendents," says an interloper, "or if you inquire who is the president of almost any literary society, or who originates, executes to perfection, and mans anything creditable to the colored people of the District, you will discover that the individual who does all these things is a new comer.". . . In spite of this rivalry between the old citizens and the new comers, they occasionally exchange social courtesies with one another, tho' the line of demarcation is never wholly eradicated.

SOURCE: Mary Church Terrell, "Society Among the Colored People of Washington," *Voice of the Negro,* April 1904, pp. 150–56. [Mary Church Terrell, 1863–1954, was a learned leading advocate of women's and black rights.—Ed.]

"Colored Society"

Besides these two grand divisions of old citizens and new comers there are subdivisions ad infinitum. If all colored people look alike to some folks, they all do not look alike to one another, when it comes to drawing the social line. However many social wheels within a wheel there may be among the colored people at Washington, there is one general rule of admission into all, to which there has never been an exception, so far as I know. It would be as difficult for a bore or a moral leper to obtain social recognition among the educated, refined colored people at Washington, as it would be for a camel with a hump to pass literally through a cambric needle's eye.

Tho' it is impossible to tell which social circle stands at the head, there is one that comes more prominently before the public than the others, because it fathers and mothers most of the big social functions given on special occasions and contributes much to the pleasures of those within the charmed circle throughout the season.

In this set oil and water mix, for it is a combination of old citizens and new comers. The club which stands sponsor for this circle gives a grand ball during inauguration week, during a D. A. R. encampment or any such notable occasion. Attendance at any of these parties would be an eyeopener to one whose education concerning the society of colored people had been neglected. Here he would see women as tastefully arrayed, as refined, as correct in their use of the English language, and as graceful in carriage as ever rivaled Terpsichore in the mazy dance.

To one unaccustomed to such a gathering, the variety of types might appear odd at first, but soon this very feature of the affair would please him most of all. Is not variety the spice of life? At any dance given by the club to which reference has been made one might rub elbows with a doctor, whose practice is lucrative and large, who owns a beautiful home tastefully furnished, and who together with his wife, a member of the school board, has been whisked to the ball in his own automobile.

It is impossible to circulate very freely at such a function without meeting graduates who hold diplomas from Harvard, Cornell, Oberlin and other renowned institutions of learning.

It would be hard to find a bevy of a dozen young women among whom there was not one or more who had graduated from college or from the normal or high school. Of this number might be one distinguished in appearance and prepossessing in manner, who married a short while ago and has gone to Philadelphia to live. Both by ancestry and by marriage this young woman is connected with two as remarkable men as the race has produced. Twenty-five years ago her own grandfather kept the finest and most exclusive hotel in the Nation's Capital.[1] A list of the titled diplomats and distinguished statesmen who stopped there, together with the important conferences held under its roof, would furnish an excellent history of the times. The grandfather of the young woman's husband amassed a great fortune in Philadelphia and was worth a million and a half dollars when he died a few years ago. In going the rounds a visitor might be introduced to a distinguished looking gentleman with a

[1] Wormley House, owned by James T. Wormley.

magnificent physique, whose name was perfectly familiar to him, but whom personally he had never met before.

While cudgeling his brain to fix the status of this man, if the stranger should thrust his hand inadvertently into his pocket and pull out a $10.00 bill, the mystery would be solved, for upon that very bill, perhaps, the name of the man in question would be written, and the stranger would know that he had just been presented to a high official in the Treasury Department—the Register of the Treasury. A bald-headed judge, who for the nonce had thrown off his judicial dignity, might be seen tripping the light fantastic as gracefully as a man no longer so young that he would tear under the wing could be expected to dance. That genial gentleman with the contagious laugh is the man whose signature is necessary to all documents conveying real estate and all instruments establishing corporations in the District of Columbia. His official title is Recorder of Deeds. The daughter of a man who has a congressman and Minister to Hayti and who is the wife of one of the best lawyers in the State of Tennessee might be in the gay throng. A handsome man who was once lieutenant governor of Louisiana [P.S.B. Pinchback], and who was really elected to the U.S. Senate, tho' he was not seated, is rarely absent from such an affair. The son or the grandson of one of the greatest orators this country has ever produced [Frederick Douglass] would probably be present. That young man with a fine intellectual face and an unassuming manner is the son of a former United States Senator [B. K. Bruce] from Mississippi. Altho' he is but a few years beyond his majority he is a graduate of Harvard University and is Principal of the Academic Department of Tuskegee. The man with the bright piercing eyes and the enthusiastic manner is a prosperous real estate dealer, who numbers among his clients and friends men holding some of the highest positions in the gift of the nation. Among the teachers present there might be a principal of a building, a supervisor or so, and other school officials, both on the trustee board and off. A clerical looking gentleman with dignity, benignity and intelligence written on his brow, would probably rivet a stranger's gaze. This rector received his education in Oxford, England, and numbers among the communicants of his church some of the best families in Washington.

It would not do to fail to mention the literary lights which some times shine at a representative social function. No one enjoys dancing more than a certain literary celebrity, whose short stories have appeared in the Atlantic Monthly and whose novels are widely read. And the latter have been commended not only by the "Dean of American Letters," but by other distinguished writers as well. Tho' this author [2] lives in Cleveland, Ohio, he is a frequent visitor in Washington, particularly when the city is celebrating some event of national importance, like an inauguration, say. Those young women sitting at a table near the window are daughters of a prosperous business man in Baltimore. The lady who has just risen and who looks as tho' she might be a beauty from Madrid has an interesting history. Some years ago a teacher's examination was held in the State of North Carolina. A large number of white teachers took the examination but she was the only one who had African blood in her veins.

[2] Charles W. Chesnutt, 1858–1932.

"Colored Society"

When the papers were marked she stood first—far ahead of all the white teachers. Since that time colored teachers have not been allowed to take the examination with their white brothers and sisters. It was deemed unwise by the powers that be, no doubt, to permit the Negro to show his intellectual superiority over the whites. The tall young man conversing with her is a prosperous druggist and is the son of a man who was once Secretary of State of South Carolina. That fine young fellow with the shoulder straps was a lieutenant in the Spanish American war and is now practicing law in Pittsburgh. He is also a graduate of Harvard University. The older man to whom he is talking was awarded a medal by the Congress of the United States for distinguished bravery during the civil war.

"I have heard and read of the 'poetry of motion,'" said an Englishman of title who had attended an assembly, "but I have never seen it till to-night." This burst of enthusiasm, so unusual from an Englishman, was poured forth, after our British friend had seen the fanciers danced by some young people whose feet, like the old flag, "never touched the ground!" Each and every member of the club which gives these assemblies makes it a matter of conscience and religion that every woman, old or young, married or single, gets her share of the dances, if she wants it. There is the usual belle, perhaps, who receives more attention than the rest of her sisters and there is the beau ideal, with whom most of the women like to dance. The club which gives the assemblies to which reference has been made is by no means the only one worthy of mention. There are others which contribute similarly to the pleasure of their friends, even tho' they do not entertain so frequently. In addition to the functions given by the various clubs, there are card parties, luncheons, dinners, and receptions, given by individuals on a large scale, or small scale, as the case may be. If a matron or a maid from a sister city visits Washington, her hostess will probably give a reception in her honor, so that the stranger may meet her Washington friends. Then there will be a succession of luncheons, dinners, card and theatre parties and small dances given for the stranger by the friends of her hostess. She will certainly enjoy one or more drives and the chances are that she will be taken in a conveyance owned by the friend who invites her.

Some of those seen at the leading social functions during the winter spend a portion of the summer at the sea shore, in the mountains or at some quiet country resort. There is a charming spot in the Chesapeake Bay, which has been converted into a summer resort by one of the most progressive and useful colored men in Washington. Here some of the flower of the social flock of Washington and neighboring cities take their summer outing in pretty little cottages which they themselves own. Boating, fishing and crabbing are the order of the day, together with an occasional dance, to which a few of the sweltering friends of Washington are invited. At Cape May, or Atlantic City or Newport or Saratoga, some of the social contingent are sure to while away a portion of the summer.

Among the colored clubs formed by the colored men of the city, there is none more interesting than the Pen and Pencil Club, which is composed of some of the cleverest and most intellectual men of the race. As its name indicates, the members are men who wield the pencil and push the pen for the various magazines and newspapers published by the race. This club usually celebrates the birthday of Frederick Douglass by giving a banquet, at which speeches laudatory of the services of this Moses of his people are delivered. At the expense of the invited guests quips, jokes and witticisms are indulged in, which are worthy of the efforts of leaders in this line. There is a club composed entirely of women, who call themselves the Brownies. The social functions of this club are always noted for the originality of their conception and the cleverness with which the conceits are executed.

While the colored people of Washington believe that all work and no play makes Jill as well as Jack very stupid and dull, they have a serious side which presents itself in many ways. There are many literary clubs, composed of people who like to study and read the best literature. One of these has held together for nearly ten years. There are musical organizations, the purpose of which is to both cultivate a taste for good music and to learn to sing it as well. Generally speaking the representative colored people of Washington take a deep interest in all the great questions of the day. The race problem is constantly discussed, of course, wherever two or three are gathered together. Whenever an interesting subject is to be presented at the Bethel Literary, which by the way, is the oldest literary society established by the colored people of this country, or at any similar organization, there is sure to be a goodly number of the leading lights in Washington society.

Boley, Okla. (1908)

17]   An All-Black Town

Boley, Indian Territory, is the youngest, the most enterprising, and in many ways the most interesting of the negro towns in the United States. A rude, bustling, Western town, it is a characteristic product of the negro immigration from the South and Middle West into the new lands of what is now the State of Oklahoma.

. . . . .

In 1905, when I visited Indian Territory, Boley was little more than a name. It was started in 1903. At the present time it is a thriving town of two thousand five hundred inhabitants, with two banks, two cotton-gins, a newspaper, a hotel, and a "college," the Creek-Seminole College and Agricultural Institute.

. . . . .

. . . It was, it is said, to put the capability of the negro for self-government to the test that in August, 1903, seventy-two miles east of Guthrie, the site of the new negro town was established. It was called Boley, after the man who built that section of the railway. A negro town-site agent, T. M. Haynes, who

SOURCE: Booker T. Washington, "Boley, A Negro Town in the West," *Outlook*. January 4, 1908, pp. 28–31.

is at present connected with the Farmers' and Merchants' Bank, was made Town-site Agent, and the purpose to establish a town which should be exclusively controlled by negroes was widely advertised all over the Southwest.

Boley, although built on the railway, is still on the edge of civilization. You can still hear on summer nights, I am told, the wild notes of the Indian dancers among the hills beyond the settlement. The outlaws that formerly infested the country have not wholly disappeared. Dick Shafer, the first Town Marshal of Boley, was killed in a duel with a horse thief, whom he in turn shot and killed, after falling, mortally wounded, from his horse. The horse thief was a white man.

There is no liquor sold in Boley, or any part of the Territory, but the "natives" go down to Prague, across the Oklahoma border, ten miles away, and then come back and occasionally "shoot up" the town. That was a favorite pastime, a few years ago, among the "natives" around Boley. The first case that came up before the Mayor for trial was that of a young "native" charged with "shooting up" a meeting in a church. But, on the whole, order in the community has been maintained. It is said that during the past two years not a single arrest has been made among the citizens. The reason is that the majority of these negro settlers have come there with the definite intention of getting a home and building up a community where they can, as they say, be "free." What this expression means is pretty well shown by the case of C. W. Perry, who came from Marshall, Texas. Perry had learned the trade of a machinist and had worked in the railway machine shops until the white machinists struck and made it so uncomfortable that the negro machinists went out. Then he went on the railway as a brakeman, where he worked for fifteen years. He owned his own home and was well respected, so much so that when it became known that he intended to leave, several of the County Commissioners called on him. "Why are you going away?" they asked; "you have your home here among us. We know you and you know us. We are behind you and will protect you."

"Well," he replied. "I have always had an ambition to do something for myself. I don't want always to be led. I want to do a little leading."

Other immigrants, like Mr. T. R. Ringe, the Mayor, who was born a slave in Kentucky, and Mr. E. L. Lugrande, one of the principal stockholders in the new bank, came out in the new country, like so many of the white settlers, merely to get land. Mr. Lugrande came from Denton County, Texas, where he had 418 acres of land. He had purchased this land some years ago for four and five dollars the acre. He sold it for fifty dollars an acre, and, coming to Boley, he purchased a tract of land just outside the town and began selling town lots. Now a large part of his acreage is in the center of the town.

Mr. D. J. Turner, who owns a drugstore and has an interest in the Farmers' and Merchants' Bank, came to Indian Territory as a boy, and has grown up among the Indians, to whom he is in a certain way related, since his brother married an Indian girl and in that way got a section of land. Mr. Turner remembers the days when every one in this section of the Territory lived a half-savage life; cultivating a little corn, and killing a wild hog or a beef when they wanted meat. And he has seen the rapid change, not only in the country, but in the people, since the tide of immigration turned this way. The negro immigration from the South, he says, has been a particularly helpful influence upon the "native" negroes, who are beginning now to cultivate their lands in a way which they never thought of doing a few years ago.

A large proportion of the settlers of Boley are farmers from Texas, Arkansas, and Mississippi. But the desire for Western lands has drawn into the community not only farmers, but doctors, lawyers, and craftsmen of all kinds. The fame of the town has also brought, no doubt, a certain proportion of the drifting population. But behind all other attractions of the new colony is the belief that here negroes would find greater opportunities and more freedom of action than they have been able to find in the older communities North and South.

Boley, like the other negro towns that have sprung up in other parts of the country, represents a dawning race consciousness, a wholesome desire to do something to make the race respected; something which shall demonstrate the right of the negro, not merely as an individual, but as a race, to have a worthy and permanent place in the civilization that the American people are creating.

In short, Boley is another chapter in the long struggle of the negro for moral, industrial, and political freedom.

Cincinnati, Ohio (1910)

18] Rigid Segregation

. . . the following facts about the situation in Cincinnati are, in a broad way, typical of all the cities of Ohio, the nearest to an exception probably being Cleveland.

In the first place, no colored man is allowed to enroll in the Ohio Medical College, which is a branch of the University of Cincinnati, a public institution, nor can he enter the Eclectic Medical School. In fact, there is no school in the city where he is privileged to equip himself for the medical profession. If he leaves the city and secures his training elsewhere and then comes back again, he finds the door of opportunity closed. The colored doctor, no matter what his training has been or what his ability and standing may be, is not allowed to operate in the large City Hospital, a public institution maintained by taxation to which colored people contribute their share. He is debarred from the Seton Hospital, on West Sixth Street, and, in fact, from all hospitals save two small charity concerns. Colored people, received with reluctance into separate wards in the City Hospital, are refused the privilege of having a physician of their own race attend them.

. . . . .

There is not a Negro to be found in the city fire department, which employs hundreds of men, all, of course, paid out of public taxation. The reason given for their absence is that white firemen will not work with them, as they would

SOURCE: Frank U. Quillin, "Cincinnati's Colored Citizens," *Independent*, February 24, 1910, pp. 399–403. [Frank U. Quillin was a turn-of-the-century Ohio historian and sociologist.—Ed.]

be compelled to eat and sleep alongside of them under the present manner of conducting the department.

The officers controlling the Municipal Bath House now forbid all colored people to bathe there. The privilege was granted for a short time recently under Democratic administration, but the house became practically a colored institution so quickly that the reform party had to withdraw the privilege.

All the popular parks, such as Chester, the Lagoon and Coney Island, exclude the Negroes. Some of them have one "nigger day" each year, when the colored people are allowed to pass the sacred portals which are forbidden them the rest of the year. Some Negroes are employed as waiters and porters at Coney Island, a leading park, six miles up the Ohio river. These are compelled to ride on the deck of the steamboat, going and coming.

Hotels, restaurants, eating and drinking places, almost universally are closed to all people in whom the least tincture of colored blood can be detected. . . .

At the Sinton Hotel, where Mr. Taft made his campaign headquarters, the colored man is not welcome even to standing room in the lobby. No matter how prominent he is, if he desires to see a white man on one of the upper floors he must take the freight elevator, or the lower compartment of the elevator, the "Jim Crow" compartment, we may call it.

The Pullman Car Company refuses to sell berths to colored people going South. Under stress, they will offer to put them in the drawing room, which costs more than they can afford to pay, and which if occupied would segregate them from the whites. Trains pulling out of Cincinnati for the South have their "Jim Crow" coaches, into which the colored people are asked to go. . . .

The Y.M.C.A. refuses them either active or associate membership. Recently some young colored men established a Y.M.C.A. on Walnut Hills, a prominent suburb of the city. The white Y.M.C.A. rose in holy wrath at this defilement of their name, and caused the colored organization to change its name to the Y. B(oys) C. A.

The Ohio Mechanics' Institute, probably the largest school of its kind in Ohio, has recently decided to deny them admission.

In the Children's Home, on Ninth Street, another large public institution, colored children are permitted to stay but twenty-four hours, after which they are sent to the Colored Orphans' Asylum. . . .

Theaters universally exclude the Negro, or at the best give him a gallery seat, and that possibly at an advanced price. The large city workhouse, reformatories, city and county prisons, and hospitals, separate white and black as much as they possibly can.

The Negro can neither rent nor buy a house in a decent section of the city without paying an exorbitant price. If he does succeed in buying a desirable piece of property, his white neighbors will endeavor by all possible means to get him out of it. Sometimes they even threaten his life, but more often they buy him out, generally paying him considerably more than the property cost him. . . .

. . . . . .

But all of these prejudices, galling as they might be and would be to any white man, are small ones in comparison to one other. . . . The colored man in earning his living is hampered on every side by race prejudice. The labor unions as a whole do not want him and will not have him, and their members will not work by the side of him. The result of this is that he is practically debarred from all mechanical pursuits requiring skill. He can join the hod carriers' union only, and this is due to the fact that not enough white men can be found to do the work. The bricklayers' union, the painters', the carpenters', the lathers', the plumbers', the barbers', the bartenders', the printers' unions, and many others deny him admission. The white man can not employ them in any skilled work if he has so large a job that he has to employ white men along with them. The white men will not work with them, there are not enough colored people prepared to do the work to do it alone, and the result is that no matter how much the white employer himself is free from prejudice, his hands are tied, he must of necessity, generally speaking, refuse to employ the colored man in any skilled capacity. Many colored men who had come from the South told the writer that there was no such condition as this existing in the South; that if a colored man became capable of laying brick or doing carpenter work or any other skilled work, he was as freely employed in it by the whites as the white laborers themselves were.

Besides their being debarred from skilled labor, they are not employed as stenographers, bookkeepers or office men in any capacity except that of janitor. Not one is employed as teacher in the public schools, none are employed as clerks in stores or factories.

The post office work is open to them because of its being under civil service rules, and we find them generally measuring up to the possibilities in this line. In the Cincinnati post office there are twelve employed as clerks and twenty-eight as carriers, making a total of forty out of a grand total of seven hundred employees, or about 5 per cent, which is the per cent of colored people in the city to the total population. In the police department there are twelve colored patrolmen out of a total of six hundred and ten, which is one-half their quota according to population. They get these places as policemen solely as a price for the colored vote.

The learned professions—the law, the ministry and medicine—are open to them, but the few who are brave enough to attempt these find that they can hardly make an honest living. The white people, of course, will not employ them, and, strange to say, their colored brothers are almost as much against them, but for different reasons, one of which is jealousy . . . , and the other is lack of confidence. . . .

What are the causes of this strong prejudice in the City of Cincinnati? In general they are the same as are found in other cities of the state. The one big cause is that—"well, just because."

The other causes are:

(1) There is a large number of ignorant colored people coming in from the South, seeking the land of the free, where they can have "their rights," many of whom mistake liberty for license.

(2) When a Negro commits a crime the newspapers always emphasize his race connection by such headlines as "A Big Black Burly Brute of a Negro" does such and such, and the whole race gets a share of the blame; while if a crime is committed by a white man, race is not mentioned, and the individual gets the blame.

Religious Life

(3) The mixing of the lower classes of the two races causes jealousy and ill feeling in these very classes, and much revulsion of feeling and fear in the higher classes.

(4) Cincinnati has always catered to the Southern trade and still does; therefore she adopts much of the South's attitude toward the Negroes.

(5) An unusually large number of Cincinnati's population very probably has been in the South for a time and then returned to the North. It is almost the universal observation that such people, after their return, forever despise the Negro.

(6) The white people constantly complain of not being able to depend upon the Negro; they say he is shiftless, careless, and too prone to appropriate little things belonging to other people.

(7) The Negro more and more is entering politics as a Negro, and demanding rewards for the Negroes, in the way of positions and public offices. Naturally they are meeting with strong opposition and much secret resentment.

(8) The fact that so many Negroes appear in the police court and prisons certainly hurts their cause greatly. . . .

Kansas City, Mo. (1913)

19]   Religious Life

. . . The following table reveals the numerical and financial strength and the benevolent activities of the Negro churches of Kansas City, Missouri. It will be seen that the Roman Catholic Church has not made . . . progress among Negroes . . . . Only a small number are members of the Episcopalian and the Christian Churches, while the majority belong to the Baptist Church. The rest are divided among the four branches of the Methodist Church, the African Methodists being decidedly the strongest:

Black Churches of Kansas City

DENOM-INATIONS	NUMBER OF CHURCHES	NUMBER OF MISSIONS	TOTAL MEM-BERSHIP	VALUE OF PROPERTY	TOTAL DEBT	BENEV-OLENCES	INCI-DENTAL EXPENSES	PAID TO MINISTERS
Baptist	9	8	3,900	$190,300	$15,300	$1,250	$ 6,050	$ 5,045
A.M.E.°	4	3	1,958	163,010	35,665	858	7,864	4,109
M.E.	1	1	750	25,000	2,600	350	600	1,405
C.M.E.	1	0	125	5,000	1,600	100	150	700
A.M.E.Z.	1	2	93	2,000	1,900	125	225	850
Christian	2	0	180	12,000	8,400	60	275	100
Episcopal	1	1	150	12,000	—	205	2,000	620
Catholic	0	1	—	—	—	—	—	—
TOTAL	19	16	7,156	$409,310	$65,465	$2,948	$17,164	$12,829

A.M.E.—African Methodist Episcopal.
M.E.—Methodist Episcopal.
C.M.E.—Colored Methodist Episcopal.
A.M.E.Z.—African Methodist Episcopal Zion.

SOURCE: Asa E. Martin, *Our Negro Population* (1913), New York: Negro Universities Press reprint, 1969, pp. 179–84.

The table above shows that there are in Kansas City 19 Negro churches and 16 missions, with a total membership of 7,156. These 7,156 Negro church-members own church property valued at $409,310, or $57.19 for each individual member. These figures are indeed gratifying, since the per capita wealth of the Kansas City Negro is only $80.61.

The total church indebtedness is only $65,465, which, it seems to me, is rather remarkable. The Second Baptist Church, located on the southwest corner of Tenth and Charlotte Streets, of which Samuel Bacote has been pastor for nearly thirty years, has a church plant valued at about $100,000, which is entirely free from debt. The Vine Street and the Pleasant Green Baptist churches, valued at $27,000 and $17,000, respectively, are also free from debt. . . .

. . . . .

Only 10 of the 19 Negro preachers of the city devote their entire time to the church work, while the remaining 9 follow various lines of work, contributing to the Church as much time and ability as they have at their disposal. A majority of the regular ministers are college men, possessing a marked degree of ability, of whom Wm. H. Peck, of Allen Chapel African Methodist, Samuel W. Bacote, of the Second Baptist, and Rev. E. S. Willett, of the First Episcopal Church, are the most prominent. These men, together with several others, are doing a work that would be creditable to any church, regardless of race or color.

Washington, D.C. (1914)

20] Federal Segregation

Delegates representing the National Independent Equal Rights League, an organization of negro citizens, called at the White House last week to protest against segregation orders, which separate the negro employees from their white associates in two or three executive departments at Washington. Their spokesman was William Monroe Trotter, of Boston, the editor of a newspaper [the *Boston Guardian*] devoted to the interests of his race. His attitude and remarks were so offensive that he was sharply rebuked by the President, who told the delegates that if he should ever consent to see them again they must have another spokesman. Before the interview came to a disagreeable termination, Mr. Wilson said he had made inquiry about the segregation orders and was convinced that their sole purpose was to prevent race friction and promote the comfort of all. He admired the progress made by the colored people and he desired to aid them.

Mr. Trotter said they were not asking for aid or charity, but for justice and equal rights. He asserted that the segregation movement in the Treasury Department and Post Office Department, where whites and negroes had worked

SOURCE: "Race Segregation at Washington," *Independent,* November 23, 1914, p. 275.

Segregation by Election

side by side without any separation for fifty years, had been due to the race antipathies of Secretary McAdoo, Postmaster-General Burleson, and Comptroller Williams, Southern men. He virtually predicted the opposition of all negroes at the polls to the Democratic party. This kind of argument, as well as his manner, his questions, and the cross-examination to which he sought to subject the President was emphatically disapproved by Mr. Wilson, who said that never before, since he entered the White House, had he been addressed in this way.

St. Louis, Mo. (1916)

21]   Segregation by Election

The first popular vote by use of the initiative under the new St. Louis city charter, and the first popular vote in the United States on negro segregation, resulted in adopting the segregation ordinance by a three-to-one vote on February 29. Seventy thousand voters, one-half of the total registered, cast their ballots. Of the eighteen thousand votes cast against segregation, about nine thousand were those of negroes. The only white wards which voted against it were two in the downtown district inhabited by citizens of foreign birth.

The election marked the end of a six-year fight led by small property owners and real estate dealers, to secure the segregation of the races. Every attempt to get the city's legislative body to pass such an ordinance has failed. The advocates of segregation were among the foremost supporters of the initiative and referendum amendment to the old charter and the direct-legislation features of the new. It has been the consensus of opinion all along that negro segregation would be one of the first propositions submitted under direct legislation.

The ordinances were not vigorously opposed because it was apparent from the start that it would be almost impossible to make much headway against almost universal race prejudice and the interests of small property owners. However, a strong citizens' committee of one hundred was formed, composed of leading white men who believed segregation a violation of American principles. The *Post-Dispatch* was vigorous in its opposition, but the other daily papers either let the subject as much alone as they could or were inclined to favor it in their news columns. The leading Republican organ made no editorial mention of the issue at all, and the local Republican party failed to oppose it actively. The Socialist party and the entire foreign press were unanimously against the ordinance. Although the churches were appealed to, very few ministers took any stand.

Much prejudice against the negro had doubtless been aroused by the long run of the "Birth of a Nation," [1] which was shown only a few months ago.

SOURCE: Roger N. Baldwin, "Negro Segregation by Initiative Election in St. Louis," *American City*, April 1916, p. 356.
[1] The film was based on *The Clansman*, by the virulently antiblack novelist Thomas Dixon.

NORTHEASTERN CITIES

Social and Economic Aspects

New York, Philadelphia, and Boston were the cities in the Northeast in which blacks had the longest and most active history. By 1910, they ranked second, fifth, and thirty-first respectively in the nation in terms of black population. However, blacks averaged only 3% of the population of the three cities, compared to an average of 34% formed by foreign-born whites. The competition from European immigrants resulted in blacks losing the virtual monopoly they had possessed of such semiskilled jobs as barbers, waiters, etc., and in the debarring of skilled black artisans from joining unions. Thus in New York in 1905, although a comparatively high 5% of black males were in unions (Document 25), very few of these were in skilled trades; overwhelmingly, they were in menial jobs. Politically, blacks carried little or no weight—although, as Du Bois shows in the case of Philadelphia (Document 22), the corrupt political machines were open to them and brought participants modest patronage.

Of special interest in this subsection is the selection "Early Harlem," which provides a unique example of the capture of the essentially upper-class white neighborhood by blacks. Second only to Birmingham, New York had the largest increase of any American city in its black population between 1900 and 1910. This produced terrible congestion in mid-Manhattan between 20th and 64th streets on the West Side, where most black New Yorkers were concentrated in substantial pockets, the best known of which were the Tenderloin and San Juan Hill. Genteel Harlem was to provide the answer to black overcrowding in mid-Manhattan. Construction of new subway routes to Harlem in the late 1890's had led to an incredible wave of speculation in land and property in Harlem, and it became glutted with luxury homes and apartments that could not find white renters or buyers. Impending ruin for white speculators, plus the initiative of black realtor Philip A. Payton and his Afro-American Realty Company, led to the introduction of the first new group of blacks (black servants had had scattered homes there before) in 1904–5, which was followed by white panic selling and flight. By 1914, there were 50,000 blacks in Harlem, and it had been transformed into the most glamorous, elegant, cultured, and creative black metropolis.

100

Philadelphia, Pa. (1905)

22]   The Black Vote

The typical Philadelphia colored man is a young immigrant from the South, from twenty to forty years of age, who has come to the city to better his fortune. . . .

. . . . . .

About 5,500 Negroes were eligible to vote in Philadelphia in 1870. In 1900 there were 20,000 Negro voters and in 1905 there are perhaps 25,000 voters.

Nothing in the Negro immigrant's earning of a living is apt to direct his attention to government unless, of course, he is employed by the city. He is usually employed as servant or laborer by private parties and sees little more of government than when he was in the South. When, after work, and on Sundays and holidays, he starts out for recreation he is apt in the denser parts of the city to run upon two and only two rival claimants for his interest: the church and the club. . . .

As he saunters up Lombard street, then, of evenings, he may drop into the church if it is Sunday, and other days he stands lonesomely about, gaping and longing for a fellow soul. But he finds soon that at one place he is welcome and that is at the club. He may be introduced to the club accidentally or by design, through the medium of the saloon or corner pool-room, or by chance companions. At any rate he finds here and there throughout the city ten or fifteen little groups of good fellow—gay young blades, roystering tellers of doubtful tales, well-dressed connoisseurs of the town's mysteries, and they welcome the newcomer cordially and make him feel at home. No where in Philadelphia is there such a welcome for the friendless, homeless black boy, no where is so much consideration shown for his feelings, his wants, his desire for pleasure. He easily joins therefore the crowd of loafers and idlers and laborers who circle and congregate about these clubs.

What is a "club"? He finds that it is a suite of rooms more or less elaborately furnished where a crowd of men can always be found smoking and talking and drinking. Usually, too, they play cards for small stakes and sometimes gamble with various devices for sums mounting up to $25 or more. Here one may make all kinds of acquaintances from honest laborers to drunken debauchees—and the clubs grade from semi-criminal haunts to respectable well-furnished quarters. Nearly all of them, however, and particularly the lower grades, are above all "political," and they give our young immigrant his first introduction into "politics." He comes to know gradually that these pleasant quarters where his friends meet and enjoy themselves are furnished through "politics"; that if it were not for "politics" they could not have beer to

SOURCE: W. E. B. Du Bois, "The Black Vote of Philadelphia," *The Negro in the Cities of the North*, New York: Charities Publication Committee, 1905, pp. 31–34.

drink or play cards in peace. Moreover, there is poor John So and So arrested last week—he'll get clear by "politics." Is the new Philadelphian willing to help along the folks who are doing these kindnesses to him and his? Why, certainly. And when election day comes he receives a bit of printed paper with unknown names and deposits it in a place indicated.

It may be now that he becomes one of the constituent members of the club, being invited by the president. This president selects his own membership of tried and true men warranted to do as he says: he keeps his hold over them by furnishing them amusement if they are honest laborers, or by giving them money if they are poor laborers out of a job, or loafers, or by protecting them if they fall afoul of the police. The newcomer soon sees that he is in a network of intrigue, influence and bribery. The policeman on his beat, the magistrate, the criminal, the prostitute, the business man, all fit in their little circle in the great "machine," and this is "politics";—of certain questions as to the ownership of gas works, the payment for franchises, the reform of the civil service— of these things he has never heard; he is submerged in a sea of mud and slime called politics which the great and good and wise city of Philadelphia has prepared for him; he has never seen its shores or surface, and of its clearer, sweeter waters he has never heard.

Of the 25,000 Negro voters in Philadelphia from one-half to two-thirds fall into the class I have described. There are, of course, other Negro voters in the city—or rather men eligible to vote. There is, first, the native Philadelphian of Negro descent—member of an educated and well-to-do group of people. There are the better class of immigrants from the country districts of the state, Maryland, and Virginia. These men come into politics from a different angle. A large number of them, especially of the better class of immigrants, neglect to vote—the campaign of contempt for civic duties and civic privileges has been preached to them assiduously. They have seen those of their number who preached political suicide for the Negro vociferously applauded and they have come to think it a virtue to neglect the exercise of the right of suffrage. Thus the result of the foolish campaign against the Negro in politics has been simply to drive out of political life the very class of Negroes needed most, and to deliver political life and activity into the hands of the political clubs and their ignorant or debased followers.

Then, too, the Negro voter even of the better class feels no civic pride. Philadelphia is not his city; it grants him nothing in particular save what he struggles for in sweat. It shows him no kindness unless he be a criminal or pauper, and under the political organization preceding the recent upheaval, it did not need his vote or seek it. The Negro feels in Philadelphia and in America few promptings of patriotism, and he looks upon all local questions from the standpoint of his social and individual interests. His greatest hardship is difficulty of employment; his characteristic, poverty. This is due to present and past conditions, i.e., prejudice and lack of skill and application. Both these handicaps can be overcome, but it takes hard work. To such a class the direct or indirect bribery of money is a tremendous temptation. Direct distribution of money to Negro voters at the polls is therefore considerable, but this does not touch the upper half or third of the voting population. This part is influenced by the indirect methods of bribery. There are in the employ of the city to-day, approximately:

1 member of the common council
3 clerks in the city service
10 or more messengers
65 policemen
30 school teachers

These persons on the whole represent the better class of Negroes and with a few exceptions have given first-class service; but so far as the office-holders themselves are concerned these are the best jobs they could get; probably in no other way could these people get employment that would give them half their present incomes. Their jobs are "in politics," and their holders must and do support the "machine." Moreover, such civic pride as the Negro has is naturally expended on these representatives of his race in public life and they support the party that puts these men in office. Thus office holding is both a direct and indirect bribe to the Negroes and to the better class of them.

It happens, however, that the political hold of the "machine" in Philadelphia has been so great and far-reaching, their majorities so overwhelming, and the white citizens so supine in their bondage, that the "machine" cares little for the 25,000 Negro votes and has cut down their patronage lately in some respects; Negroes used to have three counsellors: now they have one, and Boss Durham before his fall said that this "would be the last one." "There are some Negroes in my division," said a ward politician, "and they've been coming to me and telling me what they want, but I tell 'em to go to hell. We don't need their votes." If on finding their support not sought or needed, perhaps the better class do not vote. This makes little difference, for the ward bosses having the registration lists vote the names of all who do not appear at the polls. A colored man, headwaiter at a large hotel, went down to the polls; pretty soon he came back. "Did you vote?" he was asked. "No," he said, "I find that I had already voted—I'd like to know which way!"

Suppose now one of the better class of Negroes should determine to go into politics with a view to better conditions. . . . Men of Negro blood like Henry L. Philips, one of the most public-spirited of Philadelphia's citizens, white or black, and Walter P. Hall, a member of the present reform Committee of Seventy, have continually and repeatedly sided with reform movements. And others have, too. . . . [But] the Negroes have always been suspicious that the reform movements tended not to their betterment but to their elimination from political life and consequently from the best chance of earning a living. And the attitude of some of the reformers and their contempt for Negroes has not improved this race opinion.

It might be asked—Could not the better element of Negroes outvote the worse element and support an independent movement? This has been tried and the machine beat it. A few years ago a clean young colored lawyer, Harry W. Bass, revolted against the machine and ran for the legislature. He made a good run in the seventh ward, receiving a large vote but not a majority. A little later he ran again and the machine was alarmed. Immediately they nominated another Negro of fairly respectable character on another independent ticket and finally nominated a white candidate on the regular ticket. The result of this three-cornered fight was that Bass received but 400 votes, the white machine candidate was elected, and the other "independent" candidate was given a political job at Harrisburg.

In the present latest upheaval the Negroes are represented on the Committee of Seventy by a business man, Walter P. Hall. In a few of the wards they have organized under the new city party of reform. In the great Negro ward, the seventh, there is one Negro member of the ward committee. While it is uncertain how far the Negro will support reform at present, yet it is certain that an influential part of the better class will cooperate and that there is a great opportunity to give 70,000 Negroes the best chance of education in politics that they have ever had. . . .

New York, N.Y. (1905)

23] The Black Family

The great majority of the Negroes of New York live in poverty. Sixty-two per cent of the men, according to the last census, are in domestic and personal services, and in large stores and factories they do the work of porter or general utility man, not the better paid tasks. Only a few practice a trade. The women have not been able in any numbers to gain entrance to the factory or the shop. The result is a group of people receiving a low wage, and the character of their homes must be largely determined by their economic position.

Like all the New York poor the Negro lives in a tenement. The lower East Side, famed for its overcrowding, does not know him. His quarters are West, but there he finds conditions that are often quite as bad as those among the Italians or the Jews. In the most thickly segregated Negro section, that between West Fifty-ninth and West Sixty-fourth streets and Tenth and West End avenues, the tenements are of the old double-decker and dumbbell types, with no through ventilation and with twenty and twenty-two familes to a house. The air-shafts in these tenements are so small as to be only "culture tubes" except on the top story, where the rooms gain something of air and light. In the lower part of town, about the thirties, we still find a number of rear tenements occupied by the colored race. The sunlight enters these houses, but they are very old, impossible to keep clean, and dangerous because of their distance from the open street. Again still further south, about Cornelia street, the race lives in dilapidated former dwelling-houses. These West Side districts have little of the picturesqueness of the lower East Side, and have been more or less neglected by those interested in the moral and civil welfare of the community.

Rents are high for everyone in New York, but the Negroes pay more and get less for their money than any other tenants. Every week in the warm weather hundreds of them come from the South. They must find shelter, and

Source: Mary W. Ovington, "The Negro Family in New York," *Charities*, October 7, 1905, pp. 132–34.

the places that they may rent are few and those not tenements of the better sort. The many attractive and healthful houses that have been built since the creation of the Tenement House Department are not open to them. They are confined to certain localities, and usually to only a few houses in each block. Forced to crowd into small and uncomfortable rooms, their opportunities for making a home are much restricted.

Like the dweller on the East Side, the Negro knows enough to get out of his house and into the fresh air when he can. In the summer the streets, while not so filled with people as in the neighborhood about Rivington and Delancey streets, are well crowded. The roofs, too, offer breathing-places. Day as well as night many men and women are to be seen about, especially in the vicinity of the Sixties. The presence of men in the daytime gives an appearance of idleness among the population that is not as great as it seems, as about fifty per cent of the colored men of this city are engaged at jobs tha give them leisure when other people are at their tasks.

Study closely the tenants in any of these streets and you will find every grade of social life. Their difficulty in procuring a place to live compels the colored people to dwell good and bad together. . . .

It is impossible to give an idea of the home of the Negro in New York without touching upon his relations with the rest of the city's population. . . . He has to meet the Irish, the German, the Hebrew, the Italian, the Slav. These maintain varying attitudes of animosity and friendliness. The Irish is the most boisterously aggressive, though when once the Irishman really knows the Negro he can be a very good comrade. New York seems to demand that all the laborers who come to her must endure a period of abuse and ridicule; there must be street fights and biting nicknames and the refusal to work with the detested race. All this the Negro must endure, as other races have endured before him, but his case is an exaggerated one. There those who wish to deny him opportunity because they believe in his inherent and eternal inferiority. . . .

While the Negro is an able and respected member in some of the labor unions, and while his children occasionally have playmates among the boys and girls of other races in the schools, he does not usually see the white workingman at his best. Too often white and colored meet only in the saloon of a low type or in the rough jostle of the street. . . .

The contact that the colored people have with the monied people of the white race is varied. In the domestic service Negro men and women often have the opportunity to live in good and honorable homes, but it is not always so; and from people whom they are taught to regard as belonging to the upper class they learn low standards of married life. Those who are not in domestic service see from their tenement streets much that is base in the dominant race. There must be a world of irony in the heart of the seeing Negro who reads in the papers the lurid descriptions of his own crime, while he lives in the Tenderloin district and looks out upon its life. He sees the daily danger attending the attractive women of his own and other races. . . .

Yet, despite these handicaps, there is much of good and honorable living in the homes of the race. Choosing at random fifty families living in the most demoralizing neighborhood of New York, I found that seventy per cent of the mothers are known to be moral by those charitable workers who for many years had been in close touch with them. These people live a life apart from the roughness about them, but close to their church and their children. . . .

There is in New York, in proportion to the population, a fairly large class of professional colored men and women; and also a class of business men of some means. The homes of these do not differ essentially from the homes of all good Americans in the city. There is nothing by which to especially characterize them. Their hospitality is very pleasant and their family life is very harmonious and sweet. The young women are, perhaps, brought up in more sheltered fashion than those of the white race. Very much emphasis is laid upon education, both for the boy and for the girl. The music-loving character of the race is shown in these homes, as indeed it is in all colored households; but here we have much ability, for there are among the race in New York musicians of no mean gifts. . . .

Boston, Mass. (1905)

24]   Black Occupations

In 1900 there were in the city of Boston 11,500 Negroes. At present. . . . there are probably about 15,000. In the metropolitan district, including Cambridge with its 8,000 there are perhaps 26,000.

. . . there are in the entire metropolitan district in the neighborhood of 9,750, and in the city of Boston . . . about 5,625 Negro men who can be and may be at work.

. . . in 1900, according to the census, no less than seventy-six per cent of the Negro males in Boston were in gainful occupations. . . .

. . . in the following discussion, the writer will attempt a rough presentation of the Negro's occupations according to grade, using . . . the census findings as a base. The presentation will comprise four groups: the first, certain inferior occupations in which most of the Negroes are found; the second, waged, salaried, or commissioned occupations of higher grade; the third, business proprietorships, and the fourth, the professions.

The first of these industrial groups comprehended, in 1900, the following occupations and number of individuals [table on page 107]:

. . . . . .

Well, in this group were comprised in 1900 no less than seventy-three per cent—3,288 out of 4,510—of the Negro males at work in Boston. . . .

Of the bootblacks, hostlers, messenger boys, railway laborers and porters, there is nothing to be said that the reader will not understand for himself. These occupations command, of course, only the wages of rough, unskilled work. Of the "laborers" and the "servants" a goodly proportion are what have already been referred to as "men-of-any-work"—floorscrubbers, window-

SOURCE: John Daniels, "Industrial Conditions Among Negro Men in Boston," *The Negro in the Cities of the North*, New York: Charities Publication Committee, 1905, pp. 35–39.

Black Occupations

Bootblacks	36
Janitors	319
Laborers	665
Servants and waiters	1,676
Stewards	29
Hostlers	61
Messenger, errand and office boys	64
Porters (in stores)	404
Steam R.R. laborers	34
TOTAL	3,288

cleaners, garden-trimmers, barbers' boys and what not—scratchers here and there for a living. As before mentioned, these Negro men-of-any-work constitute a large class in the city. Many of them are by training skilled artisans, but having come here to this Northern city they are forced to take what they can get. This is the class of industrial scavengers. The waiters and stewards are classes of skilled laborers—much more skilled than the uninformed would imagine—and their income, chiefly from tips, is such—in the case of waiters most fortunately situated as much as $115 per month—as to constitute them the aristocracy of wealth in this particular industrial group. A number of the wealthiest Negroes in Boston are waiters. It is true, also, that many of the leading Negroes of the country have risen from the ranks of waiters. The janitors, however, are the aristocracy of respectability. The responsibility placed upon them calls out their best . . . traits, their often resulting long tenure of position gives them a good place in the esteem of their employers, and altogether they are a steady, dependable class who are helping their race by the force of example.

There are these differences between the occupations in this group. But on all these occupations alike there is, in greater or less degree, this brand of inferiority. . . .

The . . . waged, salaried or commissioned occupations of a higher grade . . . was in 1900 constituted as follows:

Barbers and hair-dressers	106
Miscellaneous "domestic and personal service"	65
Clerks, salesmen, agents, stenographers, etc.	152
Teamsters	167
Miscellaneous "trade and transportation"	48
Engineers and firemen (not locomotive)	53
Carpenters and joiners	37
Painters	25
Masons	30
Other building trades	43
Metal working trades	38
Printers	19
Tailors	26
Miscellaneous "manufacturing and mechanical pursuits"	66
TOTAL	875

. . . diversity is one of the striking features of the Negro's industrial situation here, showing as it does that at present there is no distinct relegation of the Negro to merely a few pursuits of this class.

There is the Negro barber, who once had such a grip in the North, but who now, in Boston as elsewhere, is being excluded by the wide-spreading anti-Negro feeling, and the apparent economic incapacity of the Negro to set up as pretentious an establishment as his competitors of other races. There are no first-class Negro barber shops in Boston now. Many of the Negro shops, however, get a good deal of white patronage. Then there is the clerk class among the Negroes. There are many Negroes who by personal qualities, education and ability, are fitted for such positions as clerks, salesmen, and the like; but the difficulty usually is that the white employes raise objections to working with Negroes, and so the employer is not entirely a free agent. None of the department stores, for instance, ever employ Negro salesmen or saleswomen, for this reason. The teamsters, who are now a large and well-paid group, originally came into their position as strike-breakers. A few being called in some years ago to fill the places of strikers, they formed an opening for others of their race, who got into the unions and prospered. So far as the writer has observed they are on an equality with the whites in the teamsters' unions; a number of the officers of these unions are Negroes. The Negro carpenters, masons, painters, and the like, are mostly immigrants from the South, having the skilled trade, but being unable to get better than intermittent occupation here in the North, largely because white artisans dislike to work with them.

. . . In 1900 there were in this group 875 of the 4,510, or about twenty per cent of the working Negro men. . . . figures seem to show that in the entire state of Massachusetts the number of Negroes in this group is increasing, both absolutely and as a percentage of the total Negro male population. The writer . . . must say that all he has ascertained thus far indicates that the unions are treating the Negroes fairly and helpfully.

Now we come to the group of commercial and industrial proprietorships. So far as the census represents the facts, this group was in 1900 thus composed:

Agricultural proprietors	3
Boarding and lodging-house, hotel, restaurant and saloon keepers	47
Hucksters	7
Livery stable keepers	3
Merchants (retail)	50
Merchants (wholesale)	3
Undertakers	1
Boot and shoemakers	20
TOTAL	134

Observation leads us to the belief that one cannot, however, get from the census an adequate representation of this group. . . . Doubtless 200 Negro men, or two and one-half per cent of the total, were in 1900 independent proprietors.

Black Occupations

This is the most picturesque of the industrial groups. All over the city, chiefly in districts where Negroes live, of course, but also in the other districts, these Negro business establishments are found. A few are of such proportions as to stand out above the rest. For instance, one of the leading tailors in the city is a Negro who got his start by being especially clever in the making of the "bell" trousers in vogue a dozen years ago, and who became so prosperous as to be able to move into fashionable quarters. Again, the largest wig manufactory in Massachusetts is operated by a Boston Negro, and a very reputable undertaker of the city is a Negro.

Most of the Negro business establishments, however, are of unpretentious and humble proportions. . . .

Of Negro establishments . . . there are a number of barber shops, poolrooms, restaurants, newstands, tailor shops, a men's furnishings store, printing shops, and lodging houses. . . .

Finally, we arrive at the professional group, the make-up of which was in 1900 as follows:

Actors and showmen	29
Artists and art teachers	3
Dentists	10
Engineers and surveyors	2
Lawyers	12
Musicians and teachers of music	31
Teachers	4
Architects and designers	3
Clergymen	13
Electricians	4
Journalists	5
Literary men	2
Officials (government)	1
Physicians and surgeons	12
TOTAL	131

Naturally, most of the prominent Negroes in the city are found in the professions. Boston has two Negro journalists of national name, a young poet of great promise, and several other Negroes of literary distinction. Among the dentists, physicians and surgeons are some most of whose practice is among the whites, and two, at least, who have attained high distinction in their professions. In the ranks of the lawyers are a number of not only prominent Negroes but prominent citizens. The number of Negroes in the professions is increasing from year to year.

These Negroes of the professions are admirably fitted, by education and present position, to be leaders of their race and interpreters standing between the ranks of the Negroes and the white. But it seems to be true that many of the Negro professional men, and likewise of the Negroes who through other occupations have risen to positions above their fellows, prefer to use their position to get as far away as possible from their race, and as near as possible to the whites. . . .

New York, N.Y. (1906)

25] Blacks in Trades Unions *

The following is a list of Negro union men in New York City. With the exception of some of the building trades, only organizations affiliated with the American Federation of Labor are counted:

Asphalt workers, 320; teamsters, 300; rockdrillers and toolsharpeners, 250; cigar makers, 121; bricklayers, 90; waiters, 90; carpenters, 60; plasterers, 45; double drum hoisters, 30; safety and portable engineers, 26; eccentric firemen, 15; letter carriers, 10; pressmen, 10; printers, 6; butchers, 3; lathers, 3; painters, 3; coopers, 2; sheet metal workers, 1; rockmen, 1. This makes a total of 1,386 men. . . . We . . . have today a working male population of 27,039 Negroes; 1,386 of these, a little over 5 per cent, being union. . . .

· · · · ·

. . . One union owes its large membership and its strong organization to a colored man. The asphalt workers have for their agent, or walking delegate, Mr. James L. Wallace, a Negro from Virginia, who helped to organize his union and has worked for it with much ability. Mr. Wallace has increased the membership from 250 in 1903, when he assumed control of it, to 850 in 1906. The colored men of this union constitute a little over a third of the members, the other workers being chiefly Italians. . . .

· · · · ·

But while we find the proportion of union Negroes in strong organizations gratifying, we also see that there are numerous omissions, and that colored men are in few skilled trades. There are no machinists, no structural iron workers, no plumbers, no garment makers. I find 102 different trades, or divisions of trades, on the list of the Central Federated Union which, as far as I have been able to ascertain, have no Negroes in their membership. . . .

New York, N.Y. (1914)

26] Early Harlem †

In one district in New York City a Negro population equal in numbers to the inhabitants of Dallas, Texas, or Springfield, Massachusetts, lives, works, and pursues its ideals almost as a separate entity from the great surrounding metropolis. Here Negro merchants ply their trade; Negro professional men follow

* SOURCE: Mary W. Ovington, "The Negro in the Trades Unions in New York," *Annals of the American Academy of Political Science*, May 1906, pp. 89–91.
† SOURCE: E. F. Dyckoff, "A Negro City in New York," *Outlook*, December 23, 1914, pp. 949–54.

their various vocations; their children are educated; the poor, sick, and orphaned of the race are cared for; churches, newspapers, and banks flourish heedless of those, outside this Negro community, who resent its presence in a white city. The progress which the Negroes have made in their own district is indeed little understood by those who, fearing the encroachment of a Negro slum, have done their best to thwart the growth and the progress of New York Negroes in obtaining better housing and living conditions and opportunities for racial advancement for the responsible colored people of New York City. That this prejudice manifested by their white neighbors is largely unwarranted both on moral and economic grounds, may be seen from a rehearsal of the facts.

If one stands at the corner of One Hundred and Thirty-fifth Street and Fifth Avenue, in four directions can be seen rows of apartments or flat houses all inhabited by Negroes. This is virtually the center of the community. The houses are in good repair; windows, entrances, halls, sidewalks, and streets are clean, and the houses comfortable and respectable inside to a degree not often found in a workingman's locality. The ground floor of the buildings in every case is occupied by a store or business office. Here and there one sees the name of some nationally known firm whose agent, always a Negro, has opened a branch business among the people of his own race. From the juncture of One Hundred and Thirty-fifth Street and Fifth Avenue can be seen the business signs of Negroes and Negro firms whose holdings and interests reach an aggregate of four million dollars.

Philip A. Payton, a Negro and a wealthy real estate operator, may be rightly termed the father of this Negro community, since it was he who, despite violent opposition, first installed his people in tenement property in this section ten or twelve years ago. It was Payton's theory that living conditions equal to those available for the white man were what the Negro needed to give him the realization of white progress and white standards.

Payton first bought three tenements. At that time a wealthy syndicate of whites owned a near-by tract, known as Olympic Field, where athletic meets had been held for several years. The syndicate intended cutting the tract into building lots, and, thinking to improve their selling chances, bought the tenements controlled by Payton and evicted the Negroes. But Payton and another Negro, J. C. Thomas, thereupon bought three other tenements on the same block and evicted the whites. The result of this skirmish was merely an exchange of tenants. After a series of shrewd business dealings in which the syndicate was worsted, the Negroes were left in possession of the nucleus of their future community, and Payton's dream of progress among his people had begun to be realized. The Negro section proper now extends for ten blocks between Seventh and Park Avenues, with a generous fringe of colored tenants reaching out in all directions from the community center—evidence of quiet growth and expansion. In this community of tenements and apartments are about fifteen hundred private houses of very good grade. One prominent member of the settlement recently paid fifty thousand dollars for one of these. The most prosperous of the Negroes, however, do not all live in private houses, by any means, since the apartment-houses, as in similar white districts in New York City, offer equal advantages for good living.

Examples of Negroes who have attained success in this community may be found in Mr. George W. Harris, a Negro who worked his way through Harvard University and two years in the Harvard Law School. Mr. Harris is editor of "The News," a paper whose entire staff of twelve men are all colored. Among these twelve men are Fenton Johnson, a writer of verse and a recent graduate of the University of Chicago; the sporting editor, Leslie Pollard, who as a Dartmouth student was rated as a member of that somewhat nebulous organization the All-American Football Team: a clever cartoonist, E. C. Shefton; and a Washington correspondent in the person of Ralph W. Taylor, an auditor in the navy under both President Roosevelt and President Taft. The clerks, stenographers, and advertising solicitors of "The News" are also all Negroes.

In the professions this Negro community has some twenty physicians who received their medical training at various universities and colleges. Harvard, the University of Pennsylvania, Dartmouth, Howard, the College of Physicians and Surgeons, Long Island Medical College, and the Flower Hospital School are all represented. One West Indian who is resident in the community was a student at Oxford.

In the legal fraternity there are fifteen lawyers from Harvard, Yale, Syracuse, Columbia, the New York Law School, and Northwestern University. One of these men is a deputy Assistant District Attorney for New York County, and one is Assistant Corporation Counsel for the city of New York.

There are eight dentists from Howard and New York Dental Colleges, two architects from Cornell University, four registered pharmacists from Columbia and the New York College of Pharmacy who conduct large drug stores in the districts, and twenty-five registered trained nurses.

In the business world the community possesses Negro real estate firms which enjoy the confidence of some of the largest and most conservative financial institutions in the city. One of these, Nail & Parker, may be taken as an interesting example. This firm has full charge of the property holding of St. Philip's Church, which is valued at well over a million dollars. In addition to this they manage for individual owners some seventy-five to eighty separate parcels of real estate, and collect over thirty-five thousand dollars a month in rent. St. Philip's Church, built, by the way, from the plans of a Negro architect, was erected a few years ago at a cost in land and building of $255,000. It carries a mortgage now of only twenty-nine thousand dollars. In addition to this the church owns a block of ten apartment-houses valued at $620,000. These carried a mortgage of $393,000 in April, 1911, when they were acquired by the church; this has since been reduced to $311,000. From this and other property owned by the church is derived a yearly income of over $25,-000. A study of the history of St. Philip's from its founding and establishment in Sullivan Street one hundred years ago, and its steady growth, reveals a system of business management of which any religious community might well be proud. In this Negro district there are eight other churches, some wealthy, all in good circumstances, and all with interesting histories of growth and administration.

Such success is not obtained without economy and well-directed saving. Indeed, as may be supposed from such a record as is shown by this brief account of St. Philip's Church, thrift is encouraged and practiced by the more substantial element of the community to a very great degree. In many instances all members of a family are engaged in some definite form of work. One family representative of this class may be instanced. The father is a chef in the Pullman service, a son is a "red-cap" in the Grand Central terminal, a daughter has charge of a theatrical dressing-room, the mother makes appointments for hair-dressing among well-to-do people in white localities and acts as treasurer for the family. A younger daughter looks after the home. Each member of the family deposits his or her entire earnings with the treasurer, and when in need of clothing or moderate spending money draws on the treasurer, who issues the money and keeps strict account of all expenditures. This family has accumulated a savings account of over $46,000 and is buying property on Long Island.

The thoroughgoing business attitude of a majority of the community is witnessed in the small percentage of saloons. The city of New York numbers its saloons at the ratio of one to every thousand of population, and in poorer class neighborhoods a much higher average obtains. The Negro community has less than one to every two thousand of population, and only five of these are owned or conducted by Negroes.

There are no very definite data on which to base the per capita wealth of the community. Some statistics published three or four years ago gave as the savings bank deposit of all Negroes in New York City the sum of fifteen million. Since three-fourths of the Negro population of New York City and practically all of their prominent men now live in this uptown community, it would seem reasonable to estimate their savings deposits at least as high as ten million. Business men of the section, however, insist that this is too low by at least fifty per cent, and point out that the Union Dime Savings Bank carries alone one and a half per cent of Negro savings.

Of public institutions run for and by Negroes the community possesses an old folks' home, a day nursery, a home for graduate nurses, a house for boys which is the headquarters for sixty Boy Scouts and their major, a union rescue home for girls, and a music school settlement. Of these, perhaps the music school settlement deserves most special attention. It occupies a fine double brown-stone house, and is under the management of Mr. J. Rosamond Johnson, a Negro and member of the New England Conservatory.

Of clubs and organizations; for social purposes and civic betterment the Negro community has also its full share. The list of these includes such familiar sounding titles as the Business Men's League, the Civic League, the United Democracy, the Republican Club, and colored branches of the Boys' Camp and Big Brother movements. There is a musical club called the Tempo, of which James Riese Europe, a composer of modern dance music, is president. There is a theatrical club known as the Frogs, of which no less a person than Bert Williams, late of Williams and Walker, and now known as one of the most popular of Broadway comedians, is the head.

Among the opportunities available for the young Negroes of the district,

113

Public School 89 plays a most important role. There are some two thousand pupils in this school, and eighty per cent are Negroes. Like white cities of equal size, this Negro settlement has its slums, in which the vicious element prevails; but the citizens, through the medium of their civic organizations and groups of workers, try hard to cope with that element.

NORTH CENTRAL CITIES

Political and Social Aspects

The striking feature of black urban life in the documents below is the relatively advantageous position blacks occupied in Chicago and Cleveland, although they formed a very small percentage of the population.

Before World War I and after, blacks wielded more political power in proportion to their number in Chicago than in any other city in the United States. This was due to the following combination of factors: concentration of blacks in a few wards; the high ratio of young, unmarried men; the large foreign-born population disadvantaged by temporary lack of franchise, illiteracy, and language barriers; the potential of the black vote to swing elections; and aggressive black leadership. All this resulted in blacks gaining "a large number of minor political positions and some offices [state and municipal] that carry with them honor as well as emolument" (Document 28).

In pre-World War I Cleveland, as Document 30 shows, there existed exceptional opportunities for the small black population (in 1910, 8,448 formed 1.3% of whole): "almost complete economic equality with the white man," including admission to unions and skilled jobs; unsegregated public institutions, including schools; and reasonably good political and professional preferment. A literate black population, a strong city economy, and a native white population then largely derived from relatively unprejudiced New England at least partially accounted for this.

If Cleveland was the nearest thing to paradise for urban blacks in the pre-World War I years, Springfield, Ill., during the riot of August 13–29, 1908, and for months after, was a nightmare and a vivid reminder that vicious white victimization of blacks was not confined to the South. The riot, caused by the standard factors of intense black/white competition for jobs, housing, etc., and precipitated by the attempted lynching of a black man, outraged the sensibilities of some northern liberals and radicals and led to the founding of the interracial NAACP in 1910.

Chicago, Ill. (1905)

27]   Social Bonds in the "Black Belt"

The last federal census showed the Negro population of Chicago to be about
35,000. The present population is estimated to be over 50,000,[1] an increase of
about forty per cent in five years. The colored people who are thus crowding
into Chicago come mostly from the states of Kentucky, Tennessee, Alabama,
Mississippi, Louisiana, Arkansas and Missouri.

The underlying causes are easily traceable and are mainly as follows:

1. Primarily to escape laws of race discrimination that have steadily increased during the last few years.

2. To obtain better school privileges.

3. On account of the good news circulated by the hundreds of young colored
men and women who have been educated in the Chicago and Northwestern
Universities and the professional schools, that Chicago offers the largest liberty
to citizens of all colors and languages of all communities in the North.

4. Because of the many industrial strikes which in the last ten years have
brought thousands of colored people to Chicago, either for immediate work as
strike breakers, or with the prospect of employment through the opportunities
for both skilled and unskilled workers. Whatever the cause, the fact remains
that thousands of Negro men and women are now employed in the stockyards
and other large industrial plants, where ten years ago this would not have
been thought of.

This increase of Negro population has brought with it problems that directly
affect the social and economic life of the newcomers. Prevented from mingling
easily and generally with the rest of the city's population, according to their
needs and deservings, but with no preparation made for segregation, their life
in a great city has been irregular and shifting, with the result that they have
been subject to more social ills than any other nationality amongst us. Notwithstanding the disadvantages suggested, the colored people of Chicago have
shown in their efforts for self-help and self-advancement a determination that
is altogether creditable.[2]

. . . . . .

. . . The organizations created and maintained by them in Chicago are numerous and touch almost every phase of our social life.

SOURCE: Fannie Barrier Williams, "Social Bonds in the 'Black Belt' of Chicago," *The
Negro in the Cities of the North*, New York: Charities Publication Committee, 1905,
pp. 40–43. [Fannie Barrier Williams was a Chicago-based social critic and social
worker.—Ed.]

[1] The 1910 federal census put the black population at 44,103.

[2] The Negroes of Chicago support some twenty lawyers, as many physicians, about a
dozen dentists, about twenty school teachers in the public schools, and an ever-increasing number of them are carrying on successfully many small business enterprises that give employment to scores of educated young colored men and women.

116

Social Bonds in the "Black Belt"

First in importance is the Negro church. There are 25 regularly organized colored churches. This number includes 9 Methodist, 8 Baptist, 1 Catholic, 1 Episcopal, 1 Christian and 1 Presbyterian. In addition to these there are numerous missions in various parts of the "Black Belt." These churches are for the most part housed in large and modern stone and brick edifices that cost from $7,000 to $40,000 each, and have a seating capacity of from 300 to 2,000 people. Most of these churches are burdened with oppressive indebtedness, and because of this their usefulness as agents of moral uplift is seriously handicapped. For example, the members of one of the largest have raised and paid in over $60,000 during the last five years, but the church still carries an indebtedness of over $24,000.

Despite this serious handicap of a slowly diminishing debt, the colored church is the center of the social life and efforts of the people. What the church sanctions and supports is of the first importance and what it fails to support and sanction is more than apt to fail. The Negro church historically, as to numbers and reach of influence and dominion, is the strongest factor in the community life of the colored people. Aside from the ordinary functions of preaching, prayer, class meetings and Sunday-school, the church is regarded by the masses as a sort of tribune of all of their civic and social interests. Thousands of Negroes know and care for no other entertainment than that furnished by the church. Theatres, concert halls, and art galleries mean nothing. What they fail to learn of these things in the churches remains unlearned. Nearly every night the church building is open, either for worship, or for concerts, lectures, and entertainments of all kinds. Even political meetings, of the most partisan sort, are not barred. The party leaders find it to their advantage, if they want to secure a large audience of colored people, to hold their meetings in the colored church. In a purely social way, the church leads in setting standards of social conduct. Weddings and receptions of all kinds, except those including dancing, are held within its walls and in this respect the church has become progressively liberal. Among other nationalities, there are Young Men's Christian Associations, social clubs, gymnasiums, reading-rooms, university extension lecture courses, etc. The colored people, generally speaking, have none of these . . . except as they are supplied by this single institution.

Within the last six years, the colored churches of Chicago have begun to recognize the larger social needs of the people, and as much as their intense denominationalism will permit, they are endeavoring to enlarge their influence as a factor for betterment. One of the large churches has carried on such activities as a kindergarten, a day nursery, a boys' club and reading-room, a penny savings-bank, gymnasium, a kitchen garden, mothers' club and sewing school.

Nearly all of the large churches have literary clubs which have become attractive to hundreds of young colored men of intelligence. The effect has been a wider and more intelligent interest in things that concern the progressive life of the people.

In fine the colored churches must be reckoned with in every movement of a social character that aims to reach and influence life. . . .

Next to the Negro church in importance, as affecting the social life of the people, are the secret orders, embracing such organizations as the Masons,

Odd Fellows, Knights of Pythias, True Reformers, the United Brotherhood (a fraternal insurance association), the Ancient Order of Foresters, and the Elks. Nearly all of these secret orders have auxiliary associations composed of women. The Masons and Odd Fellows are strongest in point of number and influence. There are about fourteen lodges of Odd Fellows and about as many Masons. Their estimated membership is respectively 2,000 and 1,600.

The colored people believe in secret societies. I believe it is safe to say that fifty per cent of the better class of Negro men are enrolled in some secret order. These affect every phase of their social life and represent the best achievements of the race in the matter of organization. In no other way is the organized Negro so reliably responsive to the requirements of his social obligations. In no other form of organization do the terms brotherhood and mutual obligations mean so much.

Thousands of dollars are paid into the treasuries of these societies every month, and it is very rare that we hear of any charge of dishonest dealings in money matters. They take care of the sick and provide for the dead with a promptness, fidelity and abundance of sympathy that is not to be found in any other form of society amongst us. The lessons of right living, of charity and truthfulness are enforced in these societies more rigidly even than in the churches.

Most of the colored men belong to more than one secret order and many belong to as many as four or five at a time and live up to their obligations in all of them. In nothing does the colored man live such a strenuous life as he does as a lodge man. The lodge, more than any other merely social organization, is a permanent and ever-increasing force.

There are other social organizations among the colored people of Chicago that are indicative of a desire for progress and improvement. For example there is one organization that supports an institution known as the "Old Folks' Home," in which some twenty-five old colored men and women are comfortably cared for and saved from eking out their existence in the dreaded almshouse.

There is a Choral Study Club composed of about one hundred young men and women under competent leadership and devoted to the study of music. A business league, composed of colored business men and women, is a part of the National Business League of which Booker T. Washington is founder and president. A physicians' club has undertaken a campaign of education as to the cause of tuberculosis and methods of prevention, together with lessons on domestic sanitation and kindred subjects.

And there are, of course, numbers of purely pleasure clubs. Love of pleasure is in good part a hopeful characteristic of the Negro people. Painfully conscious as we all are of our present position, which tends to exclude us from things that are most prized in human relationships, there is an all-pervading light-heartedness which saves us from the pessimism that must inevitably banish from the soul all hope and joy. Young men's social clubs, young women's social clubs, fellowship clubs, whist clubs and social charity clubs fill nights and holidays with laughter, song and dance.

. . . In the matter of employment, the colored people of Chicago have lost in the last ten years nearly every occupation of which they once had almost a monopoly. There is now scarcely a Negro barber left in the business district. Nearly all the janitor work in the large buildings has been taken away from them by the Swedes. White men and women as waiters have supplanted colored men in nearly all the first-class hotels and restaurants. Practically all the shoe polishing is now done by Greeks. Negro coachmen and expressmen and teamsters are seldom seen in the business districts. It scarcely need be stated that colored young men and women are almost never employed as clerks and bookkeepers in business establishments. . . .

The increase of the Negro population in Chicago . . . has not tended to liberalize public sentiment; in fact hostile sentiment has been considerably intensified by the importation from time to time of colored men as strikebreakers. Then again a marked increase of crime among the Negro population has been noted in recent years. All these things have tended to put us in a bad light, resulting in an appreciable loss of friends and well-wishers. . . .

Chicago, Ill. (1907)

28]   Blacks in Politics

. . . Probably no class of citizens in Chicago exercise in larger degree their right to vote than Negroes.

Some Negroes here make politics an occupation and these are not the dreamers that long for perfect states; they, just as the whites, who "do politics," make no loud pretentions to a high sense of civic duty . . . they are in politics for offices; or, for what is better than offices, for the control and distribution thereof.

For a Negro to be a successful politician in the accepted sense of the word, it is necessary that he be in a community where there is a number of Negro votes. This may not always be so; there have been instances of colored men elected to office by almost wholly white constituencies; but the waxing prejudice has reduced those cases to the vanishing point and a Negro politician nowadays without a black constituency would be like a general without an army.

This constituency exists in a very substantial form in Chicago. For the past two decades, at least, Chicago has been a Mecca for Negroes fleeing from injustice and seeking the blessings of liberty that are supposed to abound here. The thirteen thousand Negroes in 1890 grew into thirty-one thousand by 1900. Seven years have passed since the last census and one may safely guess that at present there are above forty thousand Afro-Americans in Chicago. It is true that the colored population of Chicago does not measure its voters at the ratio of one to every four and a half or five persons, because of the large number of young and unmarried men that have come here seeking work and the

SOURCE: Edward E. Wilson, "The Chicago Negro in Politics," *The Voice*, March 1907, pp. 98–103. [Edward Wilson was a Chicago lawyer and author.—Ed.]

119

small number of children. Frequently in a house one finds several men lodgers who run on the railroad, as the phrase goes, while there may be but one woman and no children.

The Negroes of Chicago wield most political influence on the South Side in the first, second and third wards. Here are perhaps eight thousand voters in a very small compass known as the Black Belt. In this Black Belt are located all the large churches—and numberless little ones—most of the business enterprises and many of Chicago's most solid Negro citizens. So fast have the colored people flocked to Chicago that the Black Belt has long since overflowed and Negroes are scattered all over the South Side; many having invaded exclusive portions of the city much to the disgust of their aristocratic white fellow citizens.

Outside the Black Belt there are hundreds of Negro voters in Englewood and Hyde Park and on the North and West Sides. Taken all in all one may be conservative and say the Negro politician in the city of Chicago alone has some fifteen thousand votes to back up his demands. These, in a close campaign, could play havoc with either party could they be for their own interests swung solidly, or in a large measure so, one way or the other as occasion demanded. Most of them, however, have plighted their faith to the Republican party, though they appear to be wakening up to the fact that their affections are not wholly reciprocated. A few more such shocks as came from the cutting of Negro candidates in the last election and they will be led to an estrangement that may result in temporary if not permanent divorce.

The political freedom of Chicago has produced some notably good Negro political leaders. Of course their field is limited just as in other walks of life. Still by their aggressiveness they have secured much recognition and tolerance; the tangible result of which is a large number of minor political positions and some offices that carry with them honor as well as emolument. A proof of this is found in the fact that we have living in the City of Chicago seven colored men who have served from one to two terms in the legislature. The first member, J. W. E. Thomas, is dead. The seven living ex-members referred to are the Honorables E. H. Morris, John C. Buckner, James E. Bish, George Ecton, John G. Jones, W. L. Martin and Edward D. Green. The present member is Dr. Alexander Lane. All these are men of more than common ability and most of them reflected credit not only on their own people but on the community at large that had honored them. To Thomas, Morris and Buckner are due the Civil Rights Statutes that do so much to protect the Afro-Americans in Chicago. Mr. Green signalized his term in the legislature by securing the passage of a strong law against lynching.

In the Republican party a member of the legislature and a county commissioner are regularly accorded to Negroes in nominating conventions. Of course they have to run the gauntlet of a campaign which in these days of growing prejudice is not without its dangers. It was because of this fact that the biggest office yet tendered to Negroes slipped away from them, as many whites could not stomach addressing a Negro as "Your Honor." Growing feeling against Negroes in the Republican party (together with the importance of the office) left Barnett off the bench.

Blacks in Politics

Among the politicians who have been intelligently active in Chicago one might name Edward H. Wright, ex-County Commissioner and State central committeeman; Oscar DePriest, County Commissioner; Edward D. Green; Edward H. Morris; John C. Buckner; F. L. Barnett, Assistant State's Attorney; Louis B. Anderson, Assistant County Attorney; Theodore W. Jones, ex-County Commissioner; W. L. Martin; S. Laing Williams; B. F. Moseley; and A. H. Roberts. Robert T. Motts, the owner of *The Pekin Theater*, puts in his oar at times so as to cause him to be eagerly sought as a valuable ally. I ought not fail to mention D. R. Wilkins, Editor of *The Conservator;* S. B. Turner, Editor of the *Illinois Idea,* and Julius F. Taylor, Editor of *The Broad Ax.* Besides the above newspapers quite a number of others spring up here and there, called forth by the warmth of a campaign. Such papers, however, die in the chill of every day affairs.

I do not pretend to have mentioned all the Negroes influential in politics when I have given the above names, but only representative ones such as have, in one way or the other, done things in politics. Moreover I do not mention all those that think themselves great men in politics; their name is legion. Nor do I mention any representative of the myriads of hangers-on who talk loud, boast of their power and then wait for orders and vote as they are told.

Of this last class many amusing stories might be told. From campaign to campaign some loiter about county buildings, living heaven knows how. Others seem to hibernate like a bear. When a campaign comes on they are in their glory. They attend political meetings and shout "hear, hear"; they hold forth from corners with pot-eloquent fervor; they show mysterious letters from a senator or representative calling on them to come to his district and help him out. These gentlemen go about rather shabby, having refused, as they will tell you, a job paying a thousand dollars a year. A marked characteristic of this kind of statesman is that he is always armed with a number of newspapers—literally weighted down with them—and refers to them on every occasion to prove his prophetic vision and the infallibility of his stand on this or that question. It is gentry of this kind that have given the Negro a bad name in politics; for not a few of these, though burning with patriotism have a burning palm also, and are not seldom found refusing to vote without having been persuaded thereto by some other than patriotic influences.

One should not, however, jump to the conclusion—as is so often done where a small part of the Negroes is censurable—that any considerable portion of the colored electorate is corrupt. It is here, as elsewhere, that the few have been instrumental in fastening a stigma on the many and given an excuse to those who consult their prejudices before deciding any question to charge a whole race with obliquity. The corrupt colored vote in Chicago is exceedingly small, but thrusts itself forward so as to be greatly noticeable. Of one thing I am certain—corruption is by no means confined to Negroes; for among the whites whole wards are given over to bribery and every year in certain white wards hobos and nondescripts are regularly housed, fed and enrolled that they may participate in elections. Not long ago there was a furious contest in Chicago for control of the republican party. In a ward where lived almost exclusively the so-called better class of whites and but few Negroes, the leader of the win-

121

ning faction said he spent forty-two thousand dollars for his victory. I heard a white leader say once that if the amount of money necessary to carry primaries was any sign of the venality, then Negroes were, on the whole, the least purchasable among his constituents.

It has always appeared to me that the fact that so large a proportion of the Negroes—as elsewhere—have voted one way all the time is at least a point against any wider spread corruption among them.

While the great majority of Chicago Negroes are Republican there is a respectable and growing element that has allied itself with the Democratic party. There is but little difference—save in name—between a white Chicago Democrat and a white Chicago Republican. Because of tradition and of the support given it, the Republican party has granted the Negro most of his political recognition, but this party shows manifest restlessness at Negro demands. A Democrat of liberal leanings always commands some Negro votes in city elections and it is a good guess to say that henceforward there will be fewer Negroes of the unalterable Republican faith in local contests. . . .

So far as patronage and personal treatment are concerned, the old line Democrats of Chicago treat Negroes with commendable fairness. With the small per cent of the Negro vote that goes to the Democrats, they, controlling the city, have given Negroes some very good places. Mr. S. A. T. Watkins has such a place as assistant city attorney and Mr. W. H. Clark represents colored Democrats in the Corporation Counsel's office. Mr. Julius F. Taylor conducts a Democratic newspaper among the colored people and has the favor and confidence of his white Democratic allies.

The number of Negroes in Chicago, though giving a basis on which Negro politicians can work, has also had the effect of lessening the political esteem for Negroes even of the white Republican voter. This is according to the rule in America that prejudice increases as the number of Negroes grows in any community. Then the general increase of race feeling; the coming North of many Southern whites; the constant talk of the Negro's keeping out of politics and of the mistake of making him a voter; the effect of the floating, corrupt element, small as it is; the number of mountebanks that under our political system inevitably get to the front—these things have made the election of colored men more difficult than in days past. Perhaps greater reasons than any of the above are the easy victories of the Republicans everywhere. They have in some measure come to think that the colored vote is not so needful as it once was.

The Negro vote alone would of course effect but little. It must make combinations with the controlling forces in the parties. He who gets closest to the powers that be is for the time being the biggest leader. Negro political leaders like those among the whites rise and fall as their faction is up and down; and he that is so situated as to pass through a desert of official and political obscuration is in the long run the most successful politician. One must necessarily have the ability to bring in delegates to nominating conventions, or greatly influence bringing them in, in order to get any serious consideration from the big leaders or "bosses" as they are sometimes called. In this matter, social, intellectual or other admirable qualities count for nothing if you cannot "deliver

the goods." Hence very often men of very limited capacity and of none too savory reputations get to the front; a thing which is not only true among Negroes but even more so among the ruling classes.

One finds among Negroes a reformer here and there just as among the
whites, and these reformers are pretty much alike; they are for reform until
they can get into office or can climb on the band-wagon with the victorious
faction. Some of our most active white reformers have ceased to see evil in the
community the moment they were given a place at the official table.

It is not the intention of the writer to leave the impression that the Chicago
Negro is in politics merely for the offices. Practical politicians are such the
world over. The politicians among Negroes form but a small per cent of the
vast number of voters who interest themselves in politics because they are
property-owners and wish to have a say about who shall levy their taxes and
what their taxes shall be. Others try to vote for what they consider the best interests of the community and are found on the right side of most public questions. Moreover they realize that they gain consideration everywhere—even in
the courts—because they have a say in making public officials; that they gain
in a measure the respect of their fellow citizens; that their own self-respect is
sustained by being kept civilly and politically on a plane with all other Americans; and that by intermingling with other citizens they learn much of civic
duty and have the stimulating advantages that come from the interchange of
ideas.

Charges are often made that the Negro is not loyal to his own. During every
campaign there are endless rumors that knives are being prepared for the
Negro candidates. These rumors arise from a few disgruntled ones who would not
find satisfaction in heaven itself. When the colored candidates are men of fair re-
spectability, as they usually are, no race shows a finer loyalty to its own than the
Negroes of Chicago.

Springfield, Ill. (1908)

29]   Race Riot

. . . On August 13, Mrs. Hallam, the young wife of a street car conductor, alleged that she was attacked while in her home, in bed, dragged into the yard
and outraged.[1] She accused George Richardson, a Negro who had been working on a house near her home. The Negro was taken into custody by the sheriff about noon. At two o'clock he was identified by Mrs. Hallam. Before the
sheriff was satisfied with the identification he was compelled to take the Negro
to the jail because of threats of violence to his prisoner. The mob began to assemble about the jail, and at four o'clock the crowd numbered about three

SOURCE: "The So-called Race Riot at Springfield, By an Eye-Witness," *Charities and
Commons*, September 19, 1908, pp. 709–10.
[1] Two weeks later Mrs. Hallam said that her "attacker" was a white man whose
identity she refused to divulge.

thousand people. At five o'clock, after an alarm of fire was turned in, the two Negroes, James and Richardson, in view of part of the crowd, were placed in an automobile owned and driven by Mr. Loper who had frequently done automobile service for the sheriff or his deputies, and taken a few miles north of the city, where a train was flagged, and thence carried to Bloomington, sixty miles north. A large number of persons in the crowd, not believing the Negroes had been taken away, demanded to go through the jail. The sheriff permitted them to select a committee of three, though they wanted seven, who about seven o'clock went through the jail. The mob was still unsatisfied and a half hour later three others were allowed to make the search. Those outside were still not satisfied but the sheriff then told them emphatically that he would not permit any more foolishness and he began clearing the streets about the jail. The members of Company C. and Troop D, I. N. G., who had begun assembling at the jail about 6:30 P.M. assisted the sheriff in dispersing the mob, firing two volleys over the heads of the crowd. The officers and soldiers were stoned by the rioters. Some of the crowd, among them the woman, Mrs. Kate Howard, who was later arrested, indicted for murder for participating in the lynching of Scott Burton, and who committed suicide on the way to the jail,—started to cry, "To Loper's"—Loper's being the restaurant owned by the man who had taken the Negroes away in his automobile.

About 8 o'clock the mob reached Loper's restaurant. The obnoxious automobile was standing in front. The rioters demanded of Mr. Loper that he tell them where the Negroes were. This he refused to do, in spite of their threats. Then they broke in the front of the building with bricks and stones, upturned the automobile and set fire to it, and looted the place. The basement was used as a saloon, and they drank the liquors. I saw one group carrying off a tub of bottles of champagne; all were drinking from bottles. The money was stolen from the cash register, and even the silver and table linen were carried off, many of those arrested being found with the loot in their possession.

It took about three hours to wreck Loper's place. From there the now drunken mob went to East Washington Street, the "Levee," where it demolished and looted the Negro saloons and stores. One pawn shop was looted, on the pretext—purely fabricated,—that the owner had furnished fire arms to the Negroes, and here a number of revolvers were secured by the rioters who then went to the "bad lands" and began burning the houses of the Negroes. All the houses occupied by Negroes were burned from Ninth eastward to Twelfth street where Burton was hanged to a tree, after being shot, he having fired three shots at the mob from his door.

30]   Paradise for Blacks?

I have thought of heading this article, "The Negro's Paradise," owing to the fact it pictures a condition in such contrast to the situation in so many cities of Ohio. . . .

.   .   .   .   .

In the city of Cleveland, the largest city of Ohio, according to the census of 1900, the negro has almost complete economic equality with the white man. By this I mean that he is permitted to earn his bread by the sweat of his brow, working in that calling for which he is equipt and for which he has a liking, just the same as is permitted to the white man. In the other cities of the State the same privilege is not granted him so fully, for various reasons. Not the least of these reasons is that the white people cannot bring themselves to think that the negro can do anything else than carry their suitcase or serve them at table. To some of these people the following facts will be startling.

A colored man by the name of George D. Jones has recently invented a trolley-wheel that is said to be one of the best on the market. He has patented it, interested a few of his colored friends in it, and is now engaged in its manufacture on a considerable scale. Several white capitalists have tried to purchase an interest in the business and conduct it on a larger scale, but they have not been successful. He has faith in himself to carry on what he has so well begun.

A colored man is the manager of a large manufactory, employing about one hundred white men and one hundred black men. The Leonard Sofa Bed Company is a good-sized factory, owned exclusively by colored people and colored people only are employed by it.

The superintendent of construction of the immense Hippodrome Building, in which the National Educational Association held its meetings in 1908, was a colored man and of most unusual ability.

A colored citizen of Cleveland is the private secretary of the president of the Nickel Plate Railroad, and has filled the same position for three of the latter's predecessors.

Cleveland has honored several colored men with high political offices. A few years back she sent a colored man by the name of Green to the State Senate as her representative—something that has not been done elsewhere in the North, to my knowledge. Mr. Green now occupies a Government position in the postal service and is a lawyer by profession. Two other colored men have been sent as Cleveland's representatives in the lower house of the State Legislature, and these were sent at the same time. One negro has been a city justice of the peace for many years.

Source: Frank U. Ouillin. "The Negro in Cleveland, Ohio," *Independent*, March 7, 1912, pp. 518–20.

Besides those engaged in manufacturing pursuits and political work, we find many in the professions, and many of these doing well. There are several lawyers, one of whom is an author of considerable note [Charles W. Chesnutt] having written several novels and some more serious works. He has a large practice, and it is not confined by any means to his own race. He is honored and esteemed by many of the leading white men of the city.

There are some colored physicians. Their practice is confined almost exclusively to the colored population. There are also some dentists. There are several colored teachers, and these teach, not in colored schools, for there has not been a colored school in Cleveland since it was founded. (This statement can be made of no other city in Ohio.) These colored teachers are engaged in instructing white and colored children alike in the regular public schools. One colored girl, a graduate of Smith College, teaches Latin and algebra in the Central High School, and is very satisfactory in her work. Eleven other colored girls, graduates mostly of Western Reserve University, located in Cleveland, teach in the grades. The Superintendent of Schools and others informed me that their work is wholly satisfactory, and that there had been scarcely a complaint from a white parent against his child being taught by a colored person. The head librarian of Western Reserve University is a colored man. He has held the position fourteen years.

The colored men are admitted to trades unions on the same equality as the white men, receive the same wages and work on the same jobs with the white men without any friction.

As many white men and many colored men told the writer, the negro is given a clear field in which to work out his own welfare, and, if he "makes good," he is respected for it by the white people. The colored men feel that they are fairly treated and have no complaint to make. Feeling also that it is "up to them to make good," they are steadied in life and get down to business more than they otherwise would. To illustrate how this feeling permeates the average man of the race in this city of Cleveland, consider the following fact: The proprietor of the barber shop in the leading hotel, the Hollende, a colored man himself, and the leading colored henchman of the late Senator Marcus Hanna in the city of Cleveland, employs fifteen colored men in his shop, each one of whom owns his own home and besides has a comfortable bank account. . . .

. . . . .

The negroes live by themselves in Central avenue, Cedar avenue and Doan street. According to the census of 1900, there were 6,000 of them. The two races prefer to live by themselves in their home life. As the negro population increases and new land is needed to accommodate it, adjacent property is always ready for sale at a cheap price.

Men of the two races may meet as friends on the streets or in business, but it is never carried to the home life. . . .

Each race shows regard for the rights and desires of other, and the result is a most happy one for all concerned, and Cleveland stands out today in a class by itself so far as the cities of Ohio are concerned, and possibly there are few like it in this regard thruout the country.

Black Housing

The question now naturally comes up, Why is Cleveland's attitude toward the negro as it is? The following facts will help to answer this question: According to the census of 1900, her population of 381,768 was made up of 124,631 foreign-born people, 163,570 native whites of foreign parents. The last mentioned class was composed of those born of American parents, most of whom came from Connecticut and the New England States, where little prejudice was felt against the negro. The other two classes came from countries not so recently afflicted with the curse of African slavery and hence felt less antipathy toward its victims. The only other thing that I might mention is that this city has been unusually wise in solving a most distressful question and gives to the colored man full economic equality and lets social status rest upon natural law and ordinary good sense.

Chicago, Ill. (1913)

31]   Black Housing

. . . In a recent investigation of general housing conditions in Chicago, the problem of the Negro was found to be quite different from that of immigrants. With the Negro, the housing dilemma was found to be an acute problem not only among the poor, as in the case of the Polish, the Jewish, or the Italian immigrant, but also among the well-to-do. The man who is poor as well as black must face the special evil of dilapidated insanitary dwellings and the lodger evil in its worst form. But for every man who is black, whether rich or poor, there is also the problem of extortionate rents and of dangerous proximity to segregated vice. The Negro is not only compelled to live in a segregated black district, but this region of Negro homes is almost invariably the one in which vice is tolerated by the police. That is, the segregation of the Negro quarter is only a segregation from respectable white people. The disreputable white element is forced upon him. It is probably not too much to say that no colored family can long escape the presence of disreputable or disorderly neighbors. Respectable and well-to-do Negroes may by subterfuge succeed in buying property in a decent neighborhood, but they are sure to be followed soon by those disreputable elements which are allowed to exist outside the so-called "levee" district.

In no other part of Chicago, not even in the Ghetto, was there found a whole neighborhood so conspicuously dilapidated as the black belt on the South Side. No other group suffered so much from decaying buildings, leaking roofs, doors without hinges, broken windows, insanitary plumbing, rotting floors, and a general lack of repairs. In no neighborhood were landlords so obdurate, so unwilling to make necessary improvements or to cancel leases so that tenants might seek better accommodations elsewhere. Of course, to go

SOURCE: Sophonisba P. Breckinridge, "The Color Line in the Housing Problem," *The Survey*, February 1, 1913, p. 575.

elsewhere was often impossible because nowhere is the prospective colored tenant or neighbor welcome. In the South Side black belt 74 per cent of the buildings were in a state of disrepair; in a more fortunate neighborhood, partly colored, only 65 per cent of the buildings were out of repair, but one-third were absolutely dilapidated.

Not only does the Negro suffer from this extreme dilapidation, but he pays a heavy cost in the form of high rent. A careful house-to-house canvass showed that in the most run down colored neighborhoods in the city, the rent for an ordinary four-room apartment was much higher than in any other section of the city. In crowded immigrant neighborhoods in different parts of the city, the median rental for the prevailing four-room apartment was between $8 and $8.50; in South Chicago near the steel mills it was between $9 and $9.50; and in the Jewish quarter, between $10 and $10.50 was charged. But in the great black belt of the South Side the sum exacted was between $12 and $12.50. That is, while half of the people in the Bohemian, Polish, and Lithuanian districts were paying less than $8.50, for their four-room apartments; the steel-mill employes less than $9.50, and the Jews in the Ghetto less than $10.50, the Negro, in the midst of extreme dilapidation and crowded into the territory adjoining the segregated vice district, pays from $12 to $12.50. This is from $2 to $4 a month more than the immigrant is paying for an apartment of the same size in a better state of repair. . . .

PART THREE

WORLD WAR I
TO THE DEPRESSION

INTRODUCTION

The great demand of American industries for labor during World War I, the disaster to southern agriculture caused by flooding and the boll weevil, plus a sharp decline in European immigration, all provided new opportunities for blacks as industrial laborers in northern cities. Throughout the entire black South—from Florida to west Texas—the gospel of migration was spread by aggressive northern capitalist agents, crusading black northern newspapers, especially the *Chicago Defender*, cunning but cautious black scouts, and by letters of migrants. There was also a constant rumor that, at its best, the North was the "promised land" and, more soberly, was a place where blacks could get much better wages, a better education, more even-handed justice, could vote, and generally could be "a man." The result was that an unprecedented 500,000 blacks migrated to the North between 1910 and 1920, the vast majority coming after 1915. This migration firmly established the pattern of blacks settling in a relatively few northern cities. Thus in the three major industrial cities of the Midwest—Chicago, Detroit, and Cleveland—there was an average increase of 355.8% in the black population for the decade. It is interesting to note that, unlike the older black commentator Kelly Miller (Part Two, Doc. 1), the young NAACP official Walter White took a positive view of black migration and urbanization.

The growth of the black population in the cities led in the North, most notably in Chicago, to active black involvement in municipal politics. By 1928 blacks had been elected to municipal councils in three northern cities: Chicago, New York, and Cleveland (Document 2). Although blacks' political participation in a few cities in the South and border states was minimal, in some, like Memphis and St. Louis, their vote was strong enough to swing elections and to assure their access to minor elective and appointive offices.

CITIES

General Aspects

1]   Black Migration (1920)

Seldom has there been a more interesting change of attitude than that of the
South with regard to the migratory movement of Negroes during the past four
years. When the war caused an appreciable decrease in the number of European immigrants and created an industrial void, an economic opportunity in
northern industrial centers was offered to the southern colored man for the first
time. The departure of a small number of Negroes caused some southern newspapers to utter paeans of praise, whether sincere or not. They felt that the old
doctrine of settling race relations by deporting Negroes to Africa, long since
abandoned by sensible persons, might be of value still and that the journey
North was but one step towards ridding America of the "vicious, indolent, and
criminal blacks."

A second stage occurred when the employer of the South found that he was
unable to employ as many Negro laborers as formerly, and when his wife discovered, much to her horror, that she no longer could secure house servants
with the ease of former years. About this time southern papers began carrying
pitiful and heartrending tales of deluded southern Negroes starving and freez-
ing in the North and editorials appeared, gloatingly based on such stories, re-
peating the moth eaten story of the South being the Negro's best and only
friend.

When this propaganda failed to check the increasing exodus, southern employers became frantic and began a persecution of the few labor agents working in the South, who were "fooling our Negroes to their doom by urging
them to leave." Not realizing that the movement was a leaderless one and that
it was the natural result of the economic law of supply and demand, affecting
the labor world in the North, they failed utterly to appreciate that the eco-

Source: Walter F. White, "The Success of Negro Migration," Crisis, January 1920,
pp. 112–15. [Walter F. White, 1898–1955, was a prolific author and long-time secretary of the NAACP.—Ed.]

nomic pull from the North, added to the oppressive push from the South, was taking the Negro away.

A welcome aid to their theories, or lack of them, was the race riots of Washington, Chicago, and Omaha. Played up by the southern press, these riots were used to urge Negroes to return southward and to keep those who yet remained in the South. News articles appeared in profusion, headed: "NEGROES ANXIOUS TO RETURN SOUTH," "TO GIVE LOUISIANA BLACKS IN CHICAGO CHANCE TO RETURN," "CHICAGO NEGROES ASK HOMES IN SOUTH AGAIN," and a few with captions such as "CAROLINA WANTS BLACKS, LESS 'EQUALITY' DREAMS," "NEGRO LABOR WANTED," and "MAGNOLIA STATE INVITES WANDERING NEGROES HOME."

Commissions were sent from southern states—Mississippi, Louisiana, and others—to furnish railroad fare to those Negroes who had found northern opportunity an illusive mirage. To their surprise, they found that instead of wanting to return, Negroes were well content, earning good wages, comfortably housed in many cities, and saving money. When reminded of race riots in the North, their answer was similar to that of a Chicago colored man, who replied, "If I've got to be killed, I would rather be killed by my friends." The universality of this feeling is evidenced by an inquiry made by the Chicago Branch of the National League on Urban Conditions Among Negroes into the motives actuating all Negroes who left that city on railroads during the week of the riot in July and August. During that week 261 Negroes came to Chicago and 219 left. Of the latter number only 14 left the city on account of the riot and not one was going South, but to other points in the North. Eighty-three of the 219 were going South, but in every case they were either returning from summer vacations, visiting, or going on business.

So much has been said and with so little foundation in fact about the Negro migrant that an inquiry has been made by the National Association for the Advancement of Colored People into his progress in certain industrial centers of the North. These include Chicago, Pittsburgh, Detroit, Cleveland, the Atlantic Coast shipbuilding plants, the steel and manufacturing sections of Pennsylvania, Ohio, and adjoining states.

In Chicago 40,000 colored men and 12,000 women have been added to the industrial population since the migration began. According to T. Arnold Hill of the Chicago Urban League, the stockyards employ 8,000 of these; the Corn Products Refining Company has increased its force of colored employees in one year from 30 to 800; the International Harvester Company employs 500; and the Pullman Car Shops, 400. The Industrial Department of the Urban League places about 1,000 a month. Many of the industrial plants endeavor to maintain a ratio of one Negro to every three white workmen, although the population ratio in Chicago is one Negro to thirty whites. The outlook for retention of this labor is excellent, according to all reports, and no encouragement was given to southern labor agents in their efforts to induce Negroes to return. Negroes are rapidly adjusting themselves to the new industrial and social environment; they are saving money, which is evidenced by the large number of depositors in the banks located in the Second and Third Wards, where most of the colored population live; they are conducting an increasing number of business enterprises, and real estate dealers are reaping a rich harvest in selling homes to Negroes. In spite of the serious rioting of July and August, there is yet a marked influx into the city and jobs are secured with little difficulty for all who want to work. Employers who have had no experience before with Negro labor are, in the main, finding that the old belief about the inefficiency of Negro labor is a myth. The greatest proof of this is the eagerness with which colored applicants for jobs are received.

In Pittsburgh competent observers, who are in close touch with labor conditions, state that fully 12,000 Negroes have been placed during the past two and a half years. One large employer of labor states that Negro labor as a whole is far superior to any type of immigrant labor which he has used. Thrown into the rigorous industrial life, working in mills with roaring machinery overhead and all around him, the man who has been used only to the quiet life of the rural South finds it difficult at first to adjust himself to the new order of things. Yet the testimony is almost unanimous that after a period of adjustment, the vast majority soon shake off habits of tardiness, of indolence, of unreliability, and of carousing at night, and are rapidly absorbed into the industrial life. It is evident in Pittsburgh that prohibition has had a beneficial effect, for there is less disorder and savings bank deposits are growing larger. All signs indicate a bright outlook for the retention of those who have already come and many more who are planning to come North.

Five thousand migrants have been placed in Cleveland. Recently a questionnaire was sent to 150 industrial plants, asking for specific information on the question of the efficiency of migrant labor. Practically all of the questionnaires were answered and only a few expressed any dissatisfaction. In the main, the answers were highly laudatory, and due to rigid citizenship requirements which employers have adopted, the outlook is exceptionally good for the Negro in preference to the immigrant population upon which employers have been largely dependent in the past.

One Detroit automobile firm employs some 1,200 to 1,500 Negroes. Another similar plant employs over 1,100. In this latter plant a most interesting situation has taken place, which is a valuable commentary on the efficiency and adaptability of Negro labor. In one of the departments of this establishment prior to the introduction of Negro labor, 70 white men of various nationalities were producing an average of 18 chassis a day. The official records of this plant show that within six weeks after an all-Negro force was placed in this department, 50 men were turning out from 40 to 50 a day—a clear gain in efficiency of over 300 per cent. Another blow to the exponents of the doctrine of race inferiority!

According to Dr. George E. Haynes, of the Department of Labor, 24,647 Negroes were employed in shipbuilding on the Atlantic Coast during the war and 14,075 since the war ended. Of this number a large percentage was employed in those lines of employment classed as skilled labor, and this number is increasing as the Negro is given the opportunity to prove his worth.

2]   Blacks in Municipal Politics (1928)

. . . No group in the nation has paid a heavier toll to corrupt municipal politics than the black man. He has paid it not only in bad housing, inferior
schools, poor lighting, paving and sewage, but he has been used as a political
football on the gridiron of municipal politics. Largely on account of residential
segregation, however, the urban Negro is rapidly acquiring political wisdom,
and with wisdom comes power. In American local government, political power
depends to a large degree upon the domination of areas into which the political domain is divided. The alderman must hold sway over his ward, the state
legislator over his district, the Congressman over his congressional district.
Now, in all of the northern cities where the Negro resides in large numbers, he
constitutes the majority of the population in one or more wards, or "Black
belts," as they are popularly designated. In several instances he controls state
legislative districts, and in one or more cases he holds a majority in a congressional district. As a matter of fact, his position in many parts of the North is
such that it has evoked the following assertion from Professor Jerome Dowd of
the University of Oklahoma, in his interesting volume, *The Negro in America:*

> At present [1926] the Negro vote is large enough to hold the balance
> of power in Indiana, Rhode Island, Illinois, Pennsylvania and Delaware,
> and could turn the scale of the presidential vote in any of these states.

This potentially decisive vote has not failed to attract the favor of municipal
rings and bosses. Although 250,000 of any group is not many people in New
York City, this number of Negroes has political significance to Tammany because of the compactness of the group. The great preponderance of these people live in the small and crowded area known as Harlem. It is quite widely
recognized that were it not for a lack of cohesion, due largely to dissensions
between the American and West Indian or "foreign" Negroes,[1] this race would
hold a clear balance of power in three districts and dominate two others. Tammany has regularly made overtures to them, and New York Democratic leaders
as far back as Croker have proselyted among them. The "Wigwam" applies the
same methods to the Harlem voters as to the New York immigrant groups—
Irish, German, Jew and Italian; that is, patronage and favor are exchanged for
ballots. There have been two Negro Tammany aldermen, one member of the
municipal civil service commission, a fire lieutenant, 54 policemen, an assistant
district attorney, over 100 school teachers, and a host of minor appointments.
    Chicago affords another interesting illustration of the profitable exercise of
the franchise by Negro citizens. There the Thompson forces have consistently
courted the Negro vote, and it is largely through the enthusiastic response of

SOURCE: R. J. Bunche, "Negro Political Laboratories," *Opportunity*, December 1928,
pp. 370–73. [Ralph Bunche, 1904–71, Harvard educated UN official, won the Nobel
Peace Prize in 1950.—Ed.]
[1] In 1930 there were 91,677 foreign-born blacks—overwhelmingly from the Caribbean—
residing in U.S. urban areas and 65% of these lived in New York City.

135

the "south side" or Negro wards that the Thompson administration has remained so long in the ascendancy in Chicago politics. It is conceded that the Negro vote won the mayoralty for Thompson in 1927 in Chicago's most exciting campaign. "Big Bill" was victorious over the incumbent, Dever, by a plurality of 82,938 votes, of which 59,215 were rolled up in the Negro strongholds.

Because of its potency in municipal affairs, the Chicago Negro population enjoys a greater degree of political participation and representation than any Negro group in the nation. A Negro serves as member of the civil service commission of three—a cabinet office; another holds position as legal adviser to the city in matters pertaining to state legislation of vital interest to Chicago. Six of the best trained young lawyers of the group hold appointments as assistant corporation counsels. An assistant city attorney sits in the city attorney's office. In the office of the city prosecutor are five more as assistant city prosecutors. Two Negro representatives are also found as assistant attorneys for the board of local improvements; another, an appointee as member of the library board with no salary, having jurisdiction over approximately 3,000 employees. These men are all entrusted with responsible positions. Additional appointments in the many city departments as teachers, clerks, police, et cetera, total hundreds.

But, as in New York, all representation is not only by appointment. In the two strong Negro wards the majority group has elected two of its members aldermen. A municipal court judge, with a salary of $10,000, has been nominated and elected. The natural outcome of such local political activity has increased Negro influence in state affairs. Four Negroes have been elected to the lower house of the state legislature, and one to the state Senate. A Negro serves as the Governor's appointee on the powerful Illinois industrial board, and another as state commerce commissioner. Furthermore, it seems almost a certainty that Oscar De Priest, the Republican nominee to succeed the late Congressman Madden of the first congressional district of Illinois, who so long held his seat in the House by Negro votes, has been elected to the Seventy-first Congress.

The situation in New York and Chicago finds duplication in most other large municipalities of the East and Mid-west. So much so in fact, that a leading Negro has pointed out that with the 1930 enumeration and a probable reapportionment of congressional seats throughout the country, a plausible estimate indicates that 125,000 Negroes ought to command the political fortunes of a congressional district. Such being the case, New York, Philadelphia, Chicago, Baltimore, St. Louis, and possibly Detroit and Cleveland would meet this requirement.

Negroes of St. Louis have evidenced remarkable political progress in the past decade. In 1922 the first Negro justice of the peace was elected in the fourth district, defeating a white opponent by more than 25,000 votes. By the expiration of his first term, despite public predictions that his court would be boycotted out of existence, his cases had increased from 150 to 400 per month. He succeeded himself, and on both occasions he carried three Negro elective constables into office with him. From the third district a Negro was elected to the fifty-first, fifty-third and fifty-fourth General Assemblies as state representative, and in 1926 two Negro representatives were returned. Another has been appointed assistant circuit attorney. One more, a young attorney, was the Democratic nominee for representative from the twelfth congressional district, in opposition to the incumbent Republican candidate. The sixth ward alone boasts more than 300 Negroes employed by the city with salaries ranging from $110 to $250 a month.

Wyandotte County, Kansas, including Kansas City, employs 125 Negroes in the city departments, and one has been appointed assistant health director. In the governmental departments of Jackson County, Missouri, including Kansas City, 330 Negroes are employed.

Cleveland, Ohio, has three Negro members in the city council, has had a representative in the eighty-fourth, eighty-fifth, eighty-sixth and eighty-seventh General Assemblies, who was chairman of the committee on codes in the eighty-sixth and eighty-seventh assemblies, and who in 1928 was elected by the city council as a member of the Cleveland civil service commission for a six-year term. New Haven, Newport, New York, Wilmington, Annapolis, Chicago and Cleveland, have all recently had Negro members of their respective city councils. Pittsburgh has had an assistant city solicitor, Boston four Negro members on a city planning board. The following states have lately had Negro members of their state legislatures, all of whom were elected by city groups and gave capable service: New York, two; Ohio, one: Pennsylvania, two; New Jersey, two; Missouri, one; California, one; Illinois, Senate one, and House four.

It is also of interest to note in passing that there are 64 towns and 21 settlements in the United States populated and governed entirely or almost so by Negroes. These are not all located in the South, as might be expected. One of them, Robbins, Illinois, whose government is by Negroes from mayor to janitor, has just erected a new modern-equipped schoolhouse costing $65,000 and accommodating 800 students.

In the South the Negro has made far slower political progress, for the southern policy of disfranchisement has been a stern barrier. The Negro has become, however, eager to grasp every opportunity to vote, and in local elections, where issues are sharply drawn and the white vote is split, the Negro ballot is not infrequently the deciding factor. This was the case in an Atlanta bond election a few years ago, and the Negro colony received its first and only high school building as a reward for its winning support.

In Memphis, Tennessee, where the Negro votes freely, since Tennessee makes no serious effort to restrict the franchise, a recent mayoralty election witnessed the Negro vote turn from the incumbent candidate who had won to office through Negro support, but who had failed to keep pledges, and virtually elect his opponent, who won by a plurality of 15,000. There were approximately 20,000 Negroes registered in Memphis at the time, most of whom voted. Bob Church, Negro business man who controls the Negro vote, is probably the most bitterly assailed and vilified political leader in the country. Coincident with this newly exercised power, Negroes have appeared on the federal grand jury in Memphis for the first time in forty years; a court crier is a Negro, and it is anticipated that a Negro will very shortly be sent to the state legislature. In Mississippi, one of the most oppressive of the southern states in its attitude toward the black race, Negro voters have in rare instances held a balance of power in special school and bond elections, and early in 1926 a Vicksburg mayoralty contest was determined by Negro ballots.

To a large degree, however, the Negro in the South is disfranchised. In Birmingham, Alabama, with a Negro population now in excess of 100,000, there exists what amounts to an unwritten law that not more than 400 Negroes be registered for any single election. A Negro, no matter how prominent or how well qualified, must, in order to register, "fetch" a note of recommendation from some responsible white person! (or irresponsible, it matters little, since *all* white persons would be reputable where any Negro is concerned there). The wretched condition of the Birmingham Negro quarters pathetically but graphically relates the complete helplessness of the group—streets unpaved, without street signs, poor lighting, inadequate water and gas service, and indifferent police protection. And the Negro "citizen" is deprived of all effective means of voicing protest, although he must pay his taxes promptly and fulfill the other duties of citizenship.

SOUTHERN CITIES

Political and Social Aspects

The documents below highlight two aspects of southern urban life: a new, formal attempt at cooperation between black and white leaders to ease racial tension and conflicts; and the rural superstitions—the belief in black magic and in voodoo—of the majority of blacks living in southern cities (Documents 4 and 5).

The Atlanta Inter-racial Committee (Document 3) was one of a number of local and state committees that came into being following the lead of the Commission on Interracial Cooperation, a southern regional body, founded in 1919. The ultimate purpose of the committees was to protect the business interests of southern whites. The race riots and lynchings of which blacks had long been victims had increased during and after the war and had in part been responsible for the unprecedented increase since 1916 in the migration of blacks to the North. This movement thoroughly alarmed southern white business men who could ill afford to lose so cheap a labor supply. Out of these circumstances had come the interracial committees and minor concessions to placate blacks: for instance, in Atlanta, the first public park and high school for blacks (Document 3); and, in highly industrialized Birmingham, the largest black high school in the nation (Document 6).

Atlanta, Ga. (1920)

3]   Interracial Cooperation

In view of the unsettled racial condition of the country, white and Negro men of Atlanta came together recently and decided to form an inter-racial committee for mutual helpfulness. They agreed that Negro and white ministerial un-

Source: H. H. Proctor, D.D., "The Atlanta Plan of Inter-Racial Co-Operation," *Southern Workman*, January 1920, pp. 9–12. [H. H. Proctor was pastor of the First Congregational Church (Black) of Atlanta, Ga.—Ed.]

ions should appoint an equal number from their bodies to meet together for common counsel in the matter. These, in turn, named two committees of twenty-five each of ministers and laymen from both races to be the permanent body for action. The white and Negro committees meet separately each week and jointly each month. The committee of each race is a sort of clearing house for that race on these matters, but nothing is to be done until the joint committee decides. The general committee is subdivided into eight standing committees, made up in parallel numbers of each race. They are as follows: Racial Relationship, Civic Betterment, Law Enforcement, Education, Evangelism, Industrial Relations, Finance, and Resolutions. These sub-committees of the races work conjointly.

One of the first things done by the organization was to adopt a declaration of principles ["of Christian Democracy"] which was read for adoption in all the churches of both races in the city.

· · · · · ·

But the Alanta Plan has more to its credit than mere words. I give three instances. One is that it has secured for the Negroes of Atlanta their first park for recreation. Although there are two public parks in the city, Negroes have never been welcome in them and one of the first things this committee realized was the necessity of recreation facilities for this pent-up people. Another thing is that it has secured the first public high school for Negroes in Atlanta. Public education for blacks had not gone beyond the seventh grade there, the private institutions of the city being depended upon for the higher training of Negro youth. With the beginning of the New Year there is to be in this city the first public high school for Negro youth. This has come about through the agency of this committee. And there are many other reforms contemplated.

But I think the chief result of the work of this organization has been the spirit it has generated. Here in this chief city of the South where in 1906 the great Atlanta riot raged, there was much unrest a few months ago. This is the gateway between the sections, and many Negroes passed through here bound for the North. Through the assurance of this organization there is noticeable lessening of the tension. Negroes are venturing out into new lines of business, and an air of prosperity and contentment pervades the Negro section. Its reflex influence is felt through the whole community of a quarter of a million souls. It would be impossible, under present conditions, for an outbreak between the races to occur here. This is remarkable, being in the heart of the State that has so often led the Union in her red record of lawlessness.

New Orleans, La.

4]   Church of the Innocent Blood: A Cult

Mother Catherine Seals, the High Priestess of New Orleans Negro cults, was born in Huntsville, Kentucky, and came to New Orleans at the age of sixteen.

SOURCE: Federal Writers' Project, *New Orleans City Guide*, Cambridge, Mass.: Houghton Mifflin, 1938, pp. 199–202.

Church of the Innocent Blood: A Cult

In 1922, Catherine left the kitchen of a Mrs. Nettles to organize her "Church of the Innocent Blood," which was the forerunner of the many "spiritualist" churches among the Negroes in New Orleans.

Brother Isaiah, the white prophet who astounded New Orleans in 1921–22 by curing sick and lame persons with a magic touch and prayers on the levee of the Mississippi River, may be indirectly responsible for the Church of the Innocent Blood. It is said that because of her color he refused to cure Catherine of a paralytic stroke resulting from a fight with her third husband. This inspired her to pray more intensely for religion and better health. "De Lawd heahed me," she later contended. "He healed me; Ah heals all colors." A spirit told her that her prayers would be answered and suggested that she hold a religious meeting of sinners as soon as she became well. She cured by "layin' on ob hands and anointin' dere innards" with a full tumbler of warm castor oil, followed by a quarter of a lemon to kill the taste. "Ya gotta do as Ah says ef ya wants to be healed an' blessed," she told those who objected.

Without any money or followers, on a large lot beyond the Industrial Canal, Mother Catherine started her Manger and the Church of the Innocent Blood. Mother Catherine declared, "De Lawd tol' me to have a twelve boaded fence round ma Manger but de contractors give me only ten. Ah's been gypped." Each "boad" represented a nation. The extraordinary height of the church fence was intended to keep curious persons off the grounds. The Manger is sixty feet long, fifty feet wide, and can accommodate 300 people. It was started November 4, 1929, and completed January 4, 1930. It was planned in minute detail by Mother Catherine herself. She even made most of its statues, and painted the pictures that adorned its walls. The room was dominated by an altar as centerpiece, surrounded by the fourteen stations of the Cross and banners of the Sacred Heart, Jehovah (whom Mother Catherine called "Jehovia") and the Innocent Blood. Flanking this were several feast tables from which blessed lemonade in summer and blessed coffee in winter were served. Twenty feet from the altar a large choir balcony hung, containing a single piano and enough chairs to accommodate the Manger's numerous singers. Small clay figures of Mother Catherine were scattered about the Manger, and in the rear stood a five-foot statue of the priestess. To the congregation this statue represented a messenger of fear and fate, and they prayed to it for forgiveness.

The High Priestess slept in the Manger in an ornate brass bed, from which, late at night, she conversed with spirits. An array of weaponless bodyguards watched over Mother Catherine while she slept. At midnight, as in the blaze of day, persons came to her to be prayed over and blessed.

The Church of the Innocent Blood was approximately forty feet from the Manger. Flags of the Sacred Heart, Jehovah, and the Innocent Blood flew from atop the building. Rituals borrowed in part from the Roman Catholic Church were used, and the building was crowded with holy pictures, statues, and altars; five hundred oil lamps burned constantly. "Wish Lamps" were interspersed among them. The petitioner put water in the lamp instead of oil; if the water turned dark—as it usually did—the wish would come true. In the center of the church, a small manger, surrounded by miniature animals, hung seven feet from the floor.

Mother Catherine had no particular uniform. The Lord told her what to wear, and it was usually spectacular. One of her favorite costumes was a voluminous white dress and white cap. A large key dangled from a blue cord tied around her waist. The members were permitted to kneel at her feet and make wishes as they kissed this key. Mother Catherine did not wear any shoes on her grotesquely large feet during the church services; she reminded her people that "de Lawd went widout shoes."

Mother Catherine always entered the church through a hole in the roof of a side room, intimating that she was sent down from Heaven to preach the gospel. The men of the congregation helped her to the top of the church by means of a ladder, and she made a very solemn entrance; all remained quiet until she had blessed everyone. Then a rhythmic outburst of chanting voices and stamping feet began as she started preaching. The High Priestess stood in the center of the altar and raised her hand in blessing. "Chillen, Ah's come heah to do good, not evil." The response was unanimously favorable. Such statements as "She sho did"; "Look a heah, she done cured me"; and "Ah believes in ya, Mother," came from whites as well as blacks. Mother Catherine did not bother with the Bible: she could remember everything in it. "Ah's read de Bible all de time. Ah's gonna gib ya facts." She began her talks with a short history of the church. For every "Amen" from Mother Catherine came a chorus of, "Yas," and "Preach it." When the congregation started singing much improvising was done, chiefly by Mother Catherine and her co-workers, who were clad in long white robes and sat in the front pews.

When a brother or sister wanted to be healed, he was escorted to the altar by a co-worker. Mother Catherine surveyed the candidate closely and asked, "Has de Lawd got His rod [curse] on ya? Ah can't cure anyone what's got de rod on dem." The candidate first took his castor oil or black draught, then Mother Catherine prayed over him, making various motions and calling, "Heah me, Sperrits," while he stood silently before her. If he were not healed, someone would say, "Sumpins wrong wid him. Boy, clean yo soul 'fo de debbil gits ya too much." Paralytics were rubbed and prayed over with the assistance of unseen spirits; the lame were often whipped with a wet towel and told to run out of the church. The most spectacular cures were those of the blind. Easy cases were treated with blessed rainwater; in stubborn cases, Mother Catherine "called lightnin' right down from hebben" to clear the clouded visions of her patients. To the statue of Jehovah women prayed that their men would "do whut's right"; but the men told their troubles directly to Mother Catherine. The High Priestess did not charge a fee for her services or remedies but with a finger pointed towards the voluntary contribution box said, "Ah's gotta pay ma expenses an eat, ya know."

Mother Catherine often invited prominent people to dine at the Manger, saying that she liked to have "letter red" people around her. At dinner, she would sit at a table apart from the guests, remarking, "In de nex' worl' Ah will be high up in things, but in things of dis worl', Ah knows ma place."

Mother Catherine died in 1930 believing she would rise from the dead as did Jesus Christ. She contended, "Ah's gonna sleep awile, not die. De great Gawd Jehovia, he's callin' me to come an rest awile. But on de thud day Ah's comin' back; Ah's gonna rise agin. Ah's gonna continue ma good wuk." Thousands attended the funeral, at which many feeble and timorous guests fainted. The congregation of the Church of the Innocent Blood intended that the High Priestess should be buried in the middle of the Manger next to the statue of Jehovah, but the city health officials objected and Mother Catherine was buried in the St. Vincent de Paul Cemetery, vault number 144, 4th tier.

Many of the persons Mother Catherine cared for still inhabit three dilapidated houses on the grounds. Eliza Johnson, better known as Mother Rita, and actually the mother of fourteen children, is Mother Catherine's successor. Eliza came to New Orleans from Baton Rouge. She states that she suffered with lumbago prior to her visit here, but "Mother Catherine looked me in de face an de lumbago it disappeared." Mother Rita left a career as cook for a wealthy family to become the favorite co-worker of the High Priestess. She is past seventy and stands ready to bless or ban anyone who visits the old Manger and church, now called "the Church of the True Light." The old "mammy mother" says that Mother Catherine prays and sings with her every night but never talks about the church, for "Mother Catherine's wuk is done. She's restin'."

Birmingham, Ala. (1929)

5]   The Harlem of the South

While New York's Harlem wears the high silk hat of sophistication, Birmingham's sepia settlement—the Harlem of the South—flaunts the red bandanna of superstition with a silver luck-piece knotted in the corner. In this little city-within-a-city, booming voices often hoist a hymn on crowded corners. Shoppers empty their purses in exchange for magic black cat bones. All the women who are not swathed in rusty mourning swagger in firecracker-red dresses.

The stroller who plunges into the dusky crowds on Saturday afternoon is caught up in a carnival gaiety. Two blocks behind him he leaves Birmingham's somber streets where package-laden persons are hurrying with little preoccupied frowns between their eyes.

Within two blocks all dignity and diffidence vanish. Here crowds jostle riotously. Strangers banter with each other. Vermilion silks rustle. Shiftless feet shuffle to the tempo of a jazzed spiritual. Brilliant colors flash in the sunshine, in pink shirts and garish green ties, in purple turbans and red glass beads.

From skyscrapers to squatty red buildings, from nervously swift traffic to happy-go-lucky loitering, the stroller changes landscapes and civilizations in the distance between Twentieth Street and Eighteenth. This little Harlem, within sound of Birmingham's traffic roar, within sight of its skyscrapers, huddles within itself as separately as if a taboo line had been chalked around it.

While New York's Negroes quickly assume the veneer of urbanity, these Southern city-dwellers betray their nearness to the soil—in ribald laughter and

SOURCE: Lucia Giddens, "The Happy-Go-Lucky Harlem of the South," *Travel*, July 1929, pp. 40–41.

in careless hand-to-mouth existence. The city's promise of high wages in mines and mills and its lure of amusement have sucked these people from south Alabama's cotton fields. But they cannot in one generation shake off their country outlook, even under the city's goad of competition.

Birmingham's Eighteenth Street becomes merely a waystation between the South's "Black Belt" and large Northern cities. That dapper idler with pearl-colored gloves and jaunty cane wears a sneer of discontent which presages a railroad ticket North. But even his face forgets its wryness when the blare of a phonograph sets his cane and spatted feet tapping in unison.

All the naive joy and elemental tragedy in the history of these people is reflected in the crowds which drift on Saturday afternoon along the four square blocks of little Harlem.

A blind man squeezes out of a squeaky accordion, "Hallelujah, I shall see the Lawd face to face." "Nobody knows the trouble Ah've seen—" soars a husky voice, not from a decrepit hag but from a frolicsome flapper, whose greatest trouble at the moment is the smudging of a rough spot on her right cheek to balance the one on her left. White teeth and whites of eyes flash in burnished brown faces. The sharp smell of frying fish reeks with burning grease. Watermelon rinds, gnawed to the rim, clutter the curb.

Under a bedraggled awning a gaunt man pours a jumble of incantations into the ear of a gangling boy. The glazed staring eyes of the man, his constant twiddling of a little red flannel sack mark him as a voodoo doctor. Suddenly he loosens the sack and solemnly draws forth the potent talismans, one by one: a twist of horsehair, a blue bottle filled with graveyard dirt, a false tooth from the "seventh son of a seventh son." The wide-eyed boy parts with a packet of bills and hurries blithely away armed with luck. The voodoo doctor slips another red flannel bag out of the suitcase at his feet. And the game begins with the next passerby.

Musk rose perfume hangs in the air as thickly as a cloud. Rattletrap autos splutter above the hubbub of beggars' cries and tiny phonographs. The cloying whiff of aromatic hair-strengthening oils assails one at every breath. Cheap pearls out-glisten gold teeth. Coins jangle in the pockets of men who have asked for their wages in small silver. Against the windows of a beauty parlor is silhouetted an immobile ebony face, grotesque enough to be a gargoyle.

The crowd bubbles slowly—clotting around show-windows to match purses and price tags, around fireplugs to jeer and jostle. Conversations flutter like lazy pennants in the humid air.

"You kin git away the fastes', stay the longes' and bring back less 'n any pusson Ah evah saw!" Thus a woman of circus-tent proportions with a face like the ruddy harvest moon, rebukes the small slouching man who has just extricated his wizened body from the throng.

"Honey, I mus' go to the pawn shop and git me a dress to wear to meetin' tommorrer," drawls a slinky girl to the man hovering at her elbow.

A phonograph droning "Railroad Blues" is surrounded by a fringe of squirming backs. Hand-clapping and jigging spatter a stuttering answer to the plaintive tune.

The Harlem of the South

Another circle of idlers, almost overlapping that one, encompasses a man gesticulating with knotted hands and with flapping ministerial coat-tails. He is patting his hands with revivalistic fervor while a crippled woman in the crowd lifts her wail in testimony: "Oh, I done cleanified myself . . . tull now mah life is jes' like a clothesline. Everything is hangin' out plain, so you can see how spot-t-t-tless it is!"

In front of the Frolic Theater taut backs are pasted against gaudy posters proclaiming the "Hairbreadth Escape of Blond Bess." All the pent-up emotion of a drab dishwater week overflows in gaping faces and twitching hands.

Next door in a stuffy pawn shop, a leering caramel-colored woman haggles over the miserly appraisal of her dingy ostrich boa and battered suitcase. Around the dim walls perch the trophies of numberless crap games and flat purses. An Indian tomtom, bristling against the foot pedal of a bass drum, collides with a plaster plaque, "Crucifixion of Christ."

A tall bronze Negro stalks into the shop and out of his shoes.

"What'll you gimme?" he queries, peering down at his shining tan shoes.

"Two dollars," snaps the pawnbroker.

"Aw, boss, mek it three. I done los' that much in a crap game outside. Soon's I win it back, I'll come and claim 'em. See ef I don't!"

But their babble is lost in the clamor of two men arriving at the counter simultaneously.

"Gimme a deck of cyards. None o' them red-back uns. They're an unlucky hoodoo. It's the blue uns I wants."

"Put and take!" blurts out the other man, as he pays out one suit by pawning another. "I got six goin' and comin' in and out." He grins, displaying an amphitheater of gold teeth.

In the shadow of Booker T. Washington Library, the settlement's citadel of learning, a scrawny little white man has set up a booth of patent medicine. A glass of reddish liquid is being passed from hand to hand, while the creaking voice quavers: "For men, women and children! Whatever's the matter with you, this'll cure it. Just name your disease and this medicine'll go to work!"

The listeners savor the liquid slowly with faint smacks, as if they expect some instant magical transformation. Several amble away with bottles smugly bulging in their hip pockets.

Blocking the doorway of a second-hand shop, a photographer's tripod crouches before a scenic back-drop of Dutch windmills. The waiting line is preening its plumed hats and smearing rice powder, while a gawky girl poses with arms akimbo.

"Twing, twang" booms a plantation tune through the flopping door of a meat market. Inside, two jovial minstrels, sitting on meat blocks, are luring customers with a rollicking version of "Massa's in the Cold, Cold Ground." At the moment a shriveled little man is buying three porterhouse steaks with a condescending flip of his bankroll. But the next customer, a brawny man with baggy trousers and a pouchy umbrella, is meekly asking for ten cents' worth of white meat.

In the throng outside the door a legless beggar moans, revolves piteous eyes and extends a dented spittoon for coins. An incessant mumbling—an effectual ballyhoo—seesaws through the grizzled beard of an old man, roasting peanuts in a rusty oil heater on the sun-baked sidewalk.

If any snobbery lurks in the South's Harlem, it masquerades behind wide-lipped smiles of friendliness. A girl, rigged out like a bargain show-window, hobnobs without condescension with a sartorial scarecrow in overalls and flop hat. But he does boast the dazzling virtues of a polished cane, mammoth stud horseshoe set with brilliants and an artificial sunflower boutonniere. Nearby a man with resplendent white vest whispers fraternally with the driver of a tottering fruit wagon.

These folk can even lament "hard times" with laughter. Yet their noisiest hilarity over a whispered joke leaves their eyes dull and dreary. Always their faces are strangely incongruous—stolid, staring eyes overshadowing minstrel-show grins.

Returning to the grim aloofness of Twentieth Street, one remembers the South's Harlem as a country town where joy and sorrow openly play an endless game.

Birmingham, Ala. (1931)

6] The Largest Black High School
in the Nation

Down in Alabama, surrounded by cotton fields and smoke stacks, in the city of Birmingham, is located the largest regular four-year high school in the entire country for colored youth. Spreading over an entire city block, the Industrial High School serves a Negro population of 99,000 with an enrollment of nearly 3,000 pupils.

The whole State of Alabama reported to the Office of Education 5,260 Negro high-school pupils for the year 1927–1928. It is significant to note that more than 50 per cent of these pupils were enrolled in the Industrial High School of Birmingham, although the Negro population of the city constituted only about 9 per cent of the Negro population of the State.

The Industrial High School was one of the first public high schools for Negroes established in the South. It first offered secondary work in 1900, and by 1903 it was offering a full four-year program of high-school work, which was accredited by the State department of education in 1929.

The Industrial High School building is one story high. Broad inside courts provide for play space, insuring both protection and privacy.

Source: Ambrose Caliver, "The Largest Negro High School," *School Life*, December 1931, p. 73.

BORDER CITIES

Economic and Social Aspects

During World War I and the immediate postwar years, blacks gained a foothold in the industries of the border cities, as the following selections on St. Louis and Baltimore (Documents 7, 8, 9) indicate. But it was a slight foothold. Blacks had disproportionately high representation among industrial laborers with seasonal, dirty, or difficult jobs in brickyards, packinghouses, steel and ship-building plants. In spite of modest gains, they remained grossly underrepresented among semiskilled and skilled laborers, and not represented at all in many industries. For the first time black women entered industrial life, but minimally, at the lowest level as elevator operators and "stock girls." At the same time, increasing exclusive unionization of white workers caused blacks to lose ground in the building trades and as waiters and barbers.

Documents 10, 11, and 12 highlight aspects of the social life of the border cities. St. Louis continued to exhibit the mixed social traditions of border cities: schools were formally segregated, but black and white teachers received the same pay—an equalization that did not come until much later for most southern cities. In Washington, although well-to-do blacks could buy new houses, these were made of inferior materials and were priced exorbitantly. And "the wonderful [black] society" of the nation's capital continued to take itself seriously enough to draw barbed and satirical comments from a brilliant young black poet named Langston Hughes, who obviously thought that Harlemites were more mature and sophisticated.

St. Louis, Mo., and East St. Louis, Ill. (1920)

7]   Migration and Conflict

It will be both interesting and profitable to follow these migrants into their new homes in the North. Among the most interesting of these communities is

SOURCE: Emmett J. Scott, *Negro Migration During the War*, New York: Oxford University Press, 1920, pp. 95–101. [Emmett J. Scott was a college educator and high government official.—Ed.]

Border Cities: Economic and Social Aspects

the black colony in St. Louis. St. Louis is one of the first cities of the border States, a city first in the memory of the unsettled migrant when the North was mentioned. During a long period thousands had gone there, settled down for a while and moved on, largely to Illinois, a sort of promised land. Conservative estimates place the number of negro migrants who have remained there at 10,000. . . .

The composition of the city's population is significant. It has a large foreign element. Of the foreign population Germans predominate, probably because of the brewery industry of the American white population. The southern whites are of longest residence and dominate the sentiment. The large industrial growth of the town, however, has brought great numbers of northern whites. The result is a sort of mixture of traditions. The apparent results of this mixture may be observed in these inconsistencies; separate schools, but common transportation facilities; separate playgrounds, but common bath houses; separate theaters and restaurants with the color line drawn as strictly as in the South. There has been considerable migration of whites to this city from Kentucky, Tennessee, Alabama, and Mississippi.

. . . . . .

How St. Louis secured her migrants makes an interesting story. . . . Large industrial plants located in the satellite city of St. Louis sent men to Cairo, a junction point, to meet incoming trains and make offers. There developed a competition for men. They were first induced to accept jobs in smaller towns, but lack of recreational facilities and amusements and the monotony of life attracted them to the bright lights of St. Louis. The large alien population of this city at the beginning of the war made some employers anxious about the safety of their plants. The brick yards had been employing foreigners exclusively. When war began so many left that it was felt that their business was in danger. They advertised for 3,000 negroes, promising them $2.35 per day. The railroad construction companies sent out men to attract negroes to the city. They assert, however, that their agents solicited men only after they had started for the North.

The industries of St. Louis had much to do with the migration. In this city there are more than twenty breweries. None of these employ negroes. St. Louis also has a large shoe industry. In this line no negroes are employed. A short while ago a large steel plant employing foreigners in large numbers had a strike. The strike was settled but the management took precautions against its repetition. For each white person employed a negro was placed on a corresponding job. This parallel extended from unskilled work to the highest skilled pursuits. The assumption was that a strike, should it recur, could not cripple their industry entirely. About 80 per cent of the employes of the brick yards, 50 per cent of the employes of the packing houses, 50 per cent of the employes of the American Car and Foundry Company are negroes. The terra cotta works, electrical plants, united railways and a number of other foundries employ negroes in large numbers.

The range of wages for unskilled work is $2.25 to $3.35 per day, with an average of about $2.75. For some skilled work negroes receive from 35 cents to 50 cents an hour. Wages differ even between St. Louis and East St. Louis, because of a difference in the types of industries in the two cities. Domestic service has been literally drained, and wages here have been forced upwards to approximate in some measure the increase in other lines.

The housing facilities for negroes, though not the best, are superior to such accommodations in most southern cities. There are about six communities in which the negroes are in the majority. Houses here are as a rule old, having been occupied by whites before they were turned over to negroes. Before the migration to the city, property owners reported that they could not keep their houses rented half of the year. According to the statements of real estate men, entire blocks stood vacant, and many vacant houses, after windows had been broken and plumbing stolen, were wrecked to avoid paying taxes on them. Up to the period [of the riot] in East St. Louis (July 1–3, 1917), houses were easily available. The only congestion experienced at all followed the overnight increase of 7,000 negroes from East St. Louis, after the riot. Rents then jumped 25 per cent, but normal conditions soon prevailed. Sanitation is poor, but the women coming from the South, in the opinion of a reputable physician of the city, are good housewives. New blacks have been added to all of the negro residential blocks. In the tenement district there have been no changes. The select negro residential section is the abandoned residential district of the whites. Few new houses have been built. An increase of rent from $5 to $10 per month is usually the sequel of the turning over of a house to negroes.

Community interest in the situation was at first dormant but not entirely lacking. The migration was well under way before there was any organization to make an adjustment in this unusual situation. Interested individuals made sporadic efforts to bring pressure to bear here and there, but the situation was not really appreciated until the outbreak in East St. Louis. . . .

East St. Louis, another attractive center for the migrants, is unique among northern industrial cities. It is an industrial offshoot of St. Louis, which has outstripped its parent in expansion. . . .

. . . . .

Long before an influx was felt, it has been foreseen. . . . The East St. Louis plants had been going to Ellis Island for laborers. When this supply was checked, steps were taken to secure negroes. Agents were sent to Cairo to get men en route further North. One advertisement which appeared in a Texas paper promised negroes $3.05 a day and houses. It is estimated that as a result of this beckoning the increase in population due to the migration was 5,000. A number of other negro migrants, however, work in East St. Louis and live in St. Louis, Lovejoy and Brooklyn, a negro town. The school registration of the city showed that the largest numbers of these blacks came from Mississippi and west Tennessee. Despite the advertisement for men in Texas newspapers, few came to this city from that State.

The industries requiring the labor of these negroes were numerous. The packing plants of Swift, Armour, Nelson and Morris employ large numbers of negroes. In some of the unskilled departments fifty per cent of the employes are black. The Aluminum Ore Works employs about 600 blacks and 1,000 whites. This is the plant in which occurred the strike which in a measure precipitated the riot. The Missouri Malleable Iron Works makes it a policy to keep three classes of men at work and as nearly equal numerically as possible. The usual division is one-third foreign whites, one-third American whites and one-third blacks. The theory is that these three elements will not unite to strike. Negroes are also employed in the glass works, cotton presses and transfer yards. Their wages for unskilled work ranges from $2.75 to $3.75 generally for eight hours a day. Semiskilled work pays from 35 cents to 50 cents an hour.

The housing of the negro migrants was one of the most perplexing problems in East St. Louis. The type of houses available for negroes, before being burned during the riot, were small dilapidated cottages. The incoming population, consisting largely of lodgers, was a misfit in the small cottages designed for families, and they were generally neglected by the tenant and by the local authorities. The segregated vice district was located in the negro locality. The crowding which followed the influx forced some few negroes into the white localities. Against this invasion there was strong opposition which culminated in trouble.

The roots of the fateful horror that made East St. Louis notorious, however, are to be found largely in a no less notorious civic structure. Politics of a shady nature was the handmaiden of the local administration. The human fabric of the town was made up of sad types of rough, questionable characters, drawn to the town by its industries and the money that flowed from them. There was a large criminal element. These lived in a little corner of the town, where was located also the segregated vice district. Negroes were interested in politics. In fact, they were a considerable factor and succeeded in placing in office several black men of their choice.

Trouble started at the Aluminum Ore Works which employed a large number of whites and blacks. In February of 1917 the men struck while working on government contracts. Immediately, it is claimed, negroes were sought for in other States to take their places. An adjustment was made, but it lasted only a short while. Then followed a second strike at which the employers balked. In this they felt reasonably secure for negroes were then pouring into the city from the South during the spring exodus. There followed numerous evidences of brooding conflict such as insults on the street cars, comments and excitement over the daily arrival of large numbers from the South. On one day three hundred are said to have arrived. Standing on the streets, waiting for cars, lost in wandering about the streets searching for homes, the negroes presented a helpless group. The search for homes carried them into the most undesirable sections. Here the scraggy edges of society met. The traditional attitude of unionists toward negroes began to assert itself. Fear that such large numbers would weaken present and subsequent demands aroused considerable opposition to their presence. Meetings were held, exciting speeches were made and street fights became common. The *East St. Louis Journal* is said to have printed a series of articles under the caption, "Make East St. Louis a Lily White Town." It was a simple matter of touching off the smoldering tinder. In the riot that followed over a hundred negroes were killed. These for the most part lived away from the places of the most violent distrubances, and were returning home, unconscious of the fate that awaited them. The riot has recently

150

been subject to a congressional investigation, but few convictions resulted and those whites convicted escaped serious punishment.

Baltimore, Md. (1923)

8]   Black Employment

. . . The 1920 census reports 108,390 Negroes in a total of 733,826, or 14.8 per cent. The per cent. of the Negro population in Richmond, Virginia, is 31.5; in Birmingham, Alabama, 39.31; in Atlanta, 31.3, and in Memphis, 37.7. Of northern cities: in Chicago it is 4.1; in New York City, 2.7; in Pittsburgh, 6.4, and in Philadelphia, 7.4. The Baltimore Negro population, therefore, is just large enough to be a factor in the social structure of the city, but not quite large enough to constitute an independent support for the city's industrial structure as they do further south.

The struggle for existence in the Negro group registers first and most prominently in the number of Negroes at work. They represent the largest element of the population gainfully employed.

TYPE OF OCCUPATION	NO. MALE NEGROES ENGAGED	NO. FEMALE NEGROES ENGAGED	TOTAL
Professional Service:			
Actors and Showmen	31	—	31
Authors, Editors, etc.	6	—	6
Chemists, Assayers, Metallurgists	4	—	4
Civil Engineers & Surveyors	2	—	2
Clergymen	187	—	187
Dentists	24	—	24
Draftsmen	1	—	1
Electrical Engineers	1	—	1
Lawyers	27		27
Musicians and Teachers of Music	142	41	183
Photographers	13	—	13
Physicians and Surgeons	107	—	107
Religious, charity and welfare workers	—	21	21
Teachers	53	396	449
Trained nurses	—	41	41
All other occupations	62	44	106
TOTAL	660	543	1,203
Entrepreneurs:			
Builders and Building Contractors	34	—	34
Commercial Brokers and Commercial Men	3	—	3

SOURCE: Charles S. Johnson, "Negroes at Work in Baltimore, Md.," *Opportunity,* June 1923, pp. 13–19. [Charles S. Johnson (1893–1956) was a Chicago University–trained sociologist, urbanist, and college president.—Ed.]

Border Cities: Economic and Social Aspects

TYPE OF OCCUPATION	NO. MALE NEGROES ENGAGED	NO. FEMALE NEGROES ENGAGED	TOTAL
Jewelers, etc.	10	—	10
Manufacturers	8	—	8
Commercial Travelers	10	—	10
Milliners and Millinery dealers	—	9	9
Proprietors and Manager Transfer Companies	47	—	47
Real Estate Agents and Officials	18	—	18
Restaurant, Cafe and Lunchroom Keepers	91	90	181
Retail Dealers	519	78	597
Saloon Keepers	5	—	5
Wholesale Dealers	5	—	5
TOTAL	750	177	927
Managers and Foremen:			
Captains, Masters, etc.	28	—	28
Foremen and Overseers (Manufacturing)	74	—	74
Foremen and Overseers (Other Trans.)	30	—	30
Foremen and Overseers (Steam R.R.)	10	—	10
Forewomen and Overseers	—	14	14
Inspectors	2	—	2
Managers and Superintendents	1	—	1
Officials of Insurance Companies	4	—	4
Officials (Manufacturing)	1	—	1
Proprietors, Office Managers	7	—	7
United States Officials	5	—	5
TOTAL	162	14	176
Clerical Workers:			
Agents	3	—	3
Bookkeepers and Cashiers	16	39	55
Canvassers	12	—	12
Clerks (Except in Stores)	282	79	361
Clerks in Stores	76	26	102
Collectors	23	—	23
Messengers, bundle and office girls	—	16	16
Insurance Agents	41	—	41
Salesmen	81	—	81
Saleswomen	—	40	40
Stenographers and Typists	4	31	35
Telephone Operators	—	13	13
All other clerical operators	—	5	5
TOTAL	538	249	787
Skilled Workers:			
Bakers	39	—	39
Blacksmiths	37	—	37
Brakemen	10	—	10
Brick and Stone Masons	43	—	43

Black Employment

TYPE OF OCCUPATION	NO. MALE NEGROES ENGAGED	NO. FEMALE NEGROES ENGAGED	TOTAL
Boiler Makers	7	—	7
Cabinet Makers	10	—	10
Carpenters	191	—	191
Compositors, etc.	26	—	26
Conductors (Steam R.R.)	2	—	2
Coopers	16	—	16
Cranemen, Derrickmen, etc.	95	—	95
Dressmakers and Seamstresses	—	661	661
Electricians	15	—	15
Engineers (Stationary)	96	—	96
Firemen (except Locomotive and Fire Dept.)	545	—	545
Furnace Men, etc.	44	—	44
Guards	86	—	86
Iron Molders	120	—	120
Locomotive Engineers	2	—	2
Locomotive Firemen	31	—	31
Machinists	109	—	109
Mail Carriers	80	—	80
Mechanics	122	—	122
Painters, Glaziers, etc. (Bldg.)	84	—	84
Painters, Glaziers, etc. (Factory)	15	—	15
Paper Hangers	15	—	15
Plasterers, Cement, etc.	115	—	115
Plumbers, Gas and Steam Fitters	37	—	37
Policemen	3	—	3
Shoemakers and Cobblers	47	—	47
Structural Iron Workers	40	—	40
Switchmen and Flagmen	8	—	8
Tailors	130	—	130
Tailoresses	—	13	13
Telegraph Operators	2	—	2
Tinsmiths	7	—	7
Upholsterers	31	—	31
TOTAL	2,260	674	2,944
Apprentices	23	—	23
Extraction of Minerals	97	—	97
Semi-Skilled Workers: (Manufacturing Industries)			
Blast Furnaces, etc.	119	—	119
Broom and Brush Factories	60	—	60
Candy Factories	15	13	28
Car and Railroad Shops	24	—	24
Chemical and Allied Industries	78	6	84
Cigar and Tobacco	15	182	197
Furniture Factories	37	—	37
Glass Factories	45	—	45
Food Industries	—	33	33
Iron and Steel Industries	—	13	13
Ship and Boat Building	262	—	262

153

TYPE OF OCCUPATION	NO. MALE NEGROES ENGAGED	NO. FEMALE NEGROES ENGAGED	TOTAL
Other Food Industries	212	343	555
Other Clothing Industries	258	241	499
Other Metal Industries	19	—	19
Other Industries	287	315	602
Other Iron and Structural Industries	114	—	114
Printing, Publishing, etc.	20	8	28
Shoe Factories	11	—	11
Slaughter and Packing Houses	86	—	86
Shirt, Collar and Cuff	22	427	449
Straw Factories	—	18	18
Suit, Coat, etc.	119	244	363
Textile Industries:			
Cotton Mills	—	53	53
Other Textile Industries	—	44	44
Tinware, etc.	30	—	30
TOTAL	1,833	1,940	3,773
Domestic and Personal Service:			
Barbers, Hairdressers, Manicurists	291	224	515
Bartenders	54	—	54
Boarding and Lodging House Keepers	—	112	112
Chauffeurs	1,831	—	1,831
Charwomen and Cleaners	—	243	243
Elevator Tenders	178	—	178
Housekeepers and Stewardesses	212	—	212
Janitors and Sextons	884	198	1,082
Laundresses (Not in laundry)	—	7,716	7,716
Laundry Operatives	117	733	850
Messengers	336	—	336
Porters and Helpers in Stores	1,602	—	1,602
Porters (Except in Stores)	1,299	—	1,299
Servants	1,876	12,333	14,209
Nurses (Not trained)	—	150	150
Waiters	1,476	—	1,476
Waitresses	—	746	746
All other occupations	640	185	825
TOTAL	10,796	22,640	33,436
Unskilled Workers:			
Blast Furnaces and Steel Rolling Mills	1,024	—	1,024
Brick, Tile, Terra Cotta Factories	265	—	265
Building (General)	4,879	—	4,879
Car and Railroad Shops	55	—	55
Copper Factories	145	—	145
Fertilizer Factories	919	—	919
Gas Works	172	—	172
Glass Factories	167	—	167
Helpers in Bldg. and Hand Trades	459	—	459
Laborers	—	14	14

Black Employment

TYPE OF OCCUPATION	NO. MALE NEGROES ENGAGED	NO. FEMALE NEGROES ENGAGED	TOTAL
Lumber and Furniture Industries	144	—	144
Other Chemical and Allied Industries	510	—	510
Other Industries	1,089	—	1,089
Other Food Industries	302	—	302
Petroleum Refineries	81	—	81
Ship and Boat Builders	1,008	—	1,008
Slaughter and Packing Houses	216	—	216
Textile Industries	53	—	53
Tinware, etc. Factories	123	—	123
Other Iron and Steel Industries	483	—	483
All other occupations	—	314	314
TOTAL	12,094	328	12,422
Unskilled Laborers Transportation:			
Deliverymen	819	—	819
Laborers (Coal Yards)	341	—	341
Laborers (Elevators, etc.)	303	—	303
Laborers (Lumber Yards)	298	—	298
Newsboys	71	—	71
Other Transportation Industries	311	—	311
Road and Street Building, etc.	1,412	—	1,412
Sailors and Deck Hands	373	—	373
Steam Railroad	721	—	721
Stevedores	3,151	—	3,151
Teamsters and Draymen	1,712	—	1,712
TOTAL	9,512	—	9,512
Public Service:			
Laborers	491	—	491
Farm Laborers	114	—	114
TOTAL	605	—	605

In two principal lines of work it will be observed that Negroes are practically in control. These are (1) Domestic and Personal Service in which field they furnish 65.6 per cent. of the workers, and (2) Unskilled Labor, where in spite of their 14.8 per cent. in the total population they contribute 47. per cent. of all the unskilled laborers. This differentiation is still more clearly apparent in certain specific positions. Seventy per cent. of all the building and repair laborers; 64 per cent. of all the unskilled laborers in blast furnaces and steel rolling mills; 71.8 per cent. of all the porters in stores; and 92.5 per cent. of all other porters; 78 per cent. of the waiters; and 73 per cent. of the stevedores are Negroes.

. . . . .

Where certain industries, for any reason whatever, do not employ Negroes in their manufacturing processes almost invariably Negro porters and janitors are to be found. Employers with the most pronounced objections to Negro workers in plants employing whites because of the contact involved, do not object to these Negro porters, cleaners and janitors. It is an established custom that seems never to have been seriously questioned.

The situation is similar in domestic service in which field 33,436 Negroes out of a total of 50,446 are employed.

. . . . .

. . . The plants included in the Survey divided thus are as follows:

	NO.	WHITE		NEGRO		TOTAL
		Male	Female	Male	Female	
Plants Employing Negroes	113	21,217	2,539	5,809	716	30,281
Plants Not Employing Negroes	62	18,233	2,502			20,735
TOTAL	175	39,450	5,041	5,809	716	51,016

The establishments represent a wide diversity of product. . . . Each of the principal types of industries in which Negroes are employed therefore, is briefly and separately treated.

Of these industries the most important group is composed of those predominantly Negro. These include the fertilizer industry, which is the largest in the country, the docks, construction labor, tanning, and brick making.

The outstanding features of the fertilizer industry are as follows:

1. It is seasonal and thus must depend upon a large drifting labor supply.
2. It is disagreeable work because of its strong, offensive odors and dust.
3. Most of the manufacturing processes call for unskilled labor.

The preponderance of labor in all of the plants is Negro. Eight fertilizer plants and one chemical plant were visited. In the eight plants there were employed 367 whites and 1,108 Negroes. With few exceptions all the processes except that of supervision are done by Negroes. The work is easy to learn, but requires considerable physical strength. On these jobs they are preferred to white men.

. . . . .

The second group, the longshoremen, have a most interesting history in the city. Before the Civil War practically all the longshoremen were Negroes. . . . At present there are 4,290 men employed in the city as longshoremen and stevedores, of which number 3,151, or 73 per cent., are Negroes. Employers agree that, considered as a group, they are superior to any other class of workers available for the type of labor. They have the physical strength, agility and dexterity of the larger muscles necessary for the work, and familiarity with longshoremen work acquired over a long period of employment in this field.

Their ready adaptability and selection for this kind of work, however, suggests an outstanding feature of their general industrial status. Dock work is extremely irregular and uncertain. It demands a large body of casual labor and casual employment is for the ordinary worker demoralizing. . . .

. . . . .

Third in this group are the brick-yard laborers. The Census reports but 369 persons engaged in this work in 1920 of which number 265 were Negroes. The intensive survey located 450 brick-yard laborers, 75 per cent. of whom were Negroes.

Fourth in the list are construction laborers. This includes street paving, excavation, and general building contract work. Practically all of this work is unskilled. There are 2,204 such laborers in the city, of which number 1,412, or over 50 per cent. are Negroes.

The fifth is tanning. There is but one tannery in the city, but over 90 per cent. of its employes are Negroes.

Of the 5 types of industries these factors are common:

1. The work is seasonal and requires a large, mobile labor supply.

2. Over 90 per cent. of the processes are unskilled.

3. The basic wage paid for unskilled work is 25 cents per hour.

4. Opportunities for advancement are limited first by the predominantly unskilled character of the work, second by the racial division which, with but few exceptions, decrees that the skilled work and supervisory positions including that of foreman shall be performed by white workers.

5. The labor turnover is high.

6. The work generally demands a cheap class of labor and is not attractive to white laborers.

Of these plants all found Negro labor satisfactory for the work on which they were engaged, and in most instances preferred them to white laborers, since as between the two races the chances for good workers were greater among the Negroes whom they were able to employ.

The next group of industries are those employing Negroes on special processes. . . . In the metal industries Negroes have the highest percentage of semi-skilled workers, averaging about 10 per cent. of the semi-skilled workers. Most of these are at Sparrows Point. Included in the intensive study were 12 plants with a total of 16,416 workers of whom 3,194 or 20 per cent. were Negroes. Although there are both white and Negro skilled and semi-skilled workers in these plants, there is frequently a racial division of jobs. For example, in one of the shipbuilding plants it is understood that Negroes should do the ground riveting, while white workers did the riveting on the ship's hull.

Of the Negro workers employed in the metal trades, 2,715 are unskilled and 588 are skilled or semi-skilled. Fortunately for them, the opportunities provided in this work in Baltimore as well as other parts, particularly Newport News, Virginia, have made possible the acquirement of a considerable degree of skill and experience. It will be recalled that the world's record for speed and accuracy in riveting was won by Charles Knight, a Negro employed in a Baltimore plant. . . .

. . . . .

In the steel mills and shipbuilding plants where they are employed, their range of work is wider, perhaps, than in any other forms of employment in the city. Proportionately, there are more skilled Negroes employed than in any other line of work. Aside from furnishing from 15 to 20 per cent. of the general labor supply and approximately 40 per cent. of the unskilled labor, they are semi-skilled workers in fairly large numbers, riggers, crane operators, riveters, reamers and drillers. In one plant a Negro is foreman of the erectors, a highly responsible position. They also perform semi-skilled and skilled work connected with the coke and blast furnaces, coke ovens and open hearths.

In the principal food industries of the city there are employed 4,322 workers of whom 575 or about 13 per cent. are Negroes. Included in the more intensive inquiry were 18 establishments employing a total of 3,529, of whom 543 were Negroes. These establishments included bakeries, wholesale packing houses, canning, preserving, meat packing plants and candy manufacturers. The duties of the Negroes employed fall generally into three classes: (1) ordinary cleaners, (2) laborers, and (3) workers engaged on manufacturing processes. The distribution of these workers among these classes of work, however, discloses an interesting situation. Strictly speaking, though classed as workers in the food products industries, only a small proportion are actually doing work that could not as well be performed in any industry. The distribution is as follows:

Unskilled Labor	334
Semi-Skilled	130
Skilled	11
Porters, Cleaners and Scrub Women	78
TOTAL	543

. . . . .

In the clothing industry Negroes are used to manufacture cheap shirts and overalls, as pressers, stitchers and power machine operators. In the manufacture of suits, hats, shoes, and fine ladies' wear they are excluded entirely. There is a racial division of jobs with fixed wages, which, though operating without discrimination in actual wages paid for certain work, in effect yields a difference of from 2 to 4 dollars weekly more for white workers on piece work which Negroes are not permitted to do.

There are 13,792 persons engaged in this industry of which number 1,371 are Negroes and most of these Negroes women.

In the manufacture of glass 850 employes were listed, of whom 220 were Negroes. The employers have definite reasons for their use of Negroes and have found them suitable for the positions in which they are employed. In the two principal plants Negroes are used as mold shutters and carriers. The peculiar "adaptability" of Negroes for this type of the work was explained by the manager of one of the plants as follows: "We found that Negroes were best adapted to the work of carrying and mold shutting, because there is no incentive on the job, nothing to look forward to, and the white boys won't stay on it. The Negroes learn quickly and stay."

. . . . .

Black Employment

The history of the Negro laborer and the Trade Union Movement is but another aspect of his struggle for status in the industries of Baltimore. . . .

. . . . . .

The Baltimore Federation of Labor lists 114 locals in the city affiliated with the American Federation of Labor. This list divides itself into three parts: (a) those crafts in which Negroes are not employed; (b) those crafts in which Negroes are employed but are not admitted into the unions, and (c) those lines of work in which Negroes are employed and are permitted to organize separate locals.

Fifty-four unions fall into this first group. The second is made up largely of independent crafts unions—carpentry, brick masonry, plumbing and steam-fitting, painting and decorating, paper-hanging and mechanics—all of which exclude Negroes from membership.

In the third group are locals in which Negroes have membership but are organized without exception in separate locals. They are as follows:

UNIONS	MEMBERSHIP
The Longshoremen	800
International Hod Carriers and Common Laborers No. 644	250
Station Employes Association (Under the jurisdiction of the Brotherhood of Railway Clerks)	150
Musicians Association	60
Freight Handlers No. 17393	700
Federal Employes	20
TOTAL	1,980

These are affiliated with the American Federation of Labor.

There are other independent labor organizations as follows: the Consolidated Hod Carriers No. 1; the International Building Laborers Protective Association No. 3; the National Hod Carriers and Common Laborers No. 124; the Railway Men's Benevolent and Protective Association.

The independent labor organizations, although figures on membership were not available, have a combined membership estimated at 1,900. This totals about 3,880.

. . . . . .

Despite the comparatively low range of income, the Negro population pays relatively the highest rents of any group in the city. Over 100% more Negro women are forced to work away from home than native white of mixed parentage of foreign-born whites.

The experiences of employers of Negro labor indicate that in a majority of instances, satisfactory results have been obtained. There is, however, a disposition to avoid breaking with the tradition of using Negroes only for certain grades of work. The Negro population on the other hand, while chafing under these restrictions, is immersed in the community's policy of conservatism and their protests, weak and scattered, as a result, have little effect.

St. Louis, Mo. (1927)

9]   Economic Status

St. Louis enjoys a greater diversity of industries than any large city in the country. Not more than eight per cent of the total labor employed in the city will be found in any one industry, although this metropolitan city boasts of leading the world in a few industries. It is the largest fur market in the world. . . .

The shoe, brick, drug, lead, terra cotta, stove, lumber and steel manufacturies are among the chief industries of the city. The shoe industry, although it runs Boston a close second in production, is practically closed to Negroes because of union control. The brick industry absorbs several hundred Negro men, who work about the kiln and stacks and who haul brick. The lead and chemical industries, regarded dangerous to health, have their quota of Negro workers. The steel industry employs more Negroes than whites in proportion to population. The Negro proportion ranges from one-fourth to one-third in the steel mills and foundries. Negro men work at all the skilled trades except that of machinist. In some instances, they do work as machinists' helpers. At Scullins Steel Company, Negroes operate steam locomotives. This company also has Negroes as foremen, who actually act in that capacity.

The Pullman Company employs about 500 men in its shop. Ninety per cent of these men are doing highly skilled labor. The company is operated on a high plan of efficiency. Incidentally, it is the only company employing a large number of Negroes having a Negro welfare worker.

Since 1920, one hundred and ninety-six new industries have entered St. Louis demanding additional factory floor space of 14,000,000 square feet.

It can be truthfully said that Negroes are employed in all the industries in the St. Louis Industrial District. But when such statements are indulged in by over-zealous boosters of St. Louis as the forty-ninth State and the like, the mental behavior of the average Negro is likely to shift the scene of *Nigger Heaven* [1] from Harlem to Market Street.

Were it not for the geographical location of St. Louis, one might feel that the city had every right to be ashamed of its treatment of Negroes in the industries.

The steel, brick, tobacco, chemical and glass industries stand out as the chief employers of Negroes in large numbers. It is very true that Negroes are employed in practically every industry in St. Louis, but as porters, janitors, messenger boys and maids. The 269 passenger trains operating over 28 railroads into St. Louis, draw considerably upon Negro labor as train and sleeping car porters and dining car waiters. In the large department stores Negro girls

Source: William V. Kelly, "Where St. Louis Negroes Work," *Opportunity*, April, 1927, p. 116. In 1927, it was estimated that there were 95,000 blacks out of a total St. Louis population of 835,000.—Ed.]
[1] A popular novel of Harlem life by Carl Van Vechten, published in 1926.

are employed as elevator operators and stock girls. They can hope for nothing better though they stay for years. On the other hand, the clerks and sales-ladies in these stores present an apparent range in age from 16 to 17 years to 60 to 70 years. So well worked out is the general order of things in St. Louis that a girl with promise, but without financial backing to continue in school after finishing the high school, aspires, as a matter of course, to becoming an eleva-tor girl or a stock girl in a big down-town store where she can earn $9.00 to $12.00 per week and get a discount on her purchases, where she is employed and has her charge account.

Domestic and personal service is probably the backbone of the Negro's finan-cial existence in St. Louis. This statement is not made to give the impression that most Negroes do this type of work. The truth is, however, that the men generally doing porter's work are so underpaid that the woman in the family must find a job in order to supplement the income of the man. This, of course, gives rise to serious social problems within the family.

There is a greater outlet for working Negro women than there is for men. The fruit and nut industry is handled almost exclusively by Negro women. The rag and bag factories find Negro women very useful and employ them in large numbers. Steam laundries are quite satisfied with Negro labor.

In many hotels, where white waiters and bell boys are employed, the maids are colored. It is far easier for a woman to find employment than it is for a man.

Although St. Louis has in the past been regarded as an open shop town, it is rapidly becoming unionized and at the same time forcing Negroes out of the building trades. The Negro brick-layer, who has come to St. Louis with a card from some other city, becomes a member of the local Hod-Carrier's Union and is not permitted to lay brick.

The electrical and plumbing work must be done by registered electricians and plumbers before the city inspectors will look the work over. In 1926, there was not a registered Negro plumber in the State. With such a situation union strength is obvious.

There is a Waiters' Alliance, which claims some strength despite the fact Negro waiters have been replaced by whites in one of the large hotels and a few of the smaller ones.

It is very evident from the foregoing statement of facts that the union labor is threatening the Negro's already threadbare existence in this community. In or out of the union, they are placed at a decided disadvantage.

St. Louis, Mo. (1927)

10]   Cultural Institutions

. . . The 95,000 Negroes of St. Louis present problems not essentially different from those of any other group. The minority of this group is for the most part

Source: Gladys Carrion Gray, "A Social Worker Looks at St. Louis," *Opportunity*, April, 1927, pp. 112–13.

native born, and accustomed to the modes and manners of a complex urban life. The majority are migrants from the rural districts of the adjoining Southern States, Arkansas, Tennessee, Mississippi, Alabama, Kentucky. Clearly, both classes have problems in common, but the migrant has the added difficulty of transition from a simple rural life to an urban life, demanding much more in every line of activity.

The institutional activities of St. Louis are not unlike those of any other urban community, except that they have to keep in harmony with the problems of rapid industrial development such as St. Louis is experiencing. We have most institutions which the average American city provides—churches, schools, recreational facilities, agencies for the care of the sick and disabled, and agencies for social work. The churches meet the needs of every modern form of worship. The Blue Book, a church directory, published in 1926 by the Metropolitan Church Federation of St. Louis, lists Negro churches as follows: Adventist, 1; Baptist, 76; Catholic, 2; Christian, 2; Church of Christ, 5; Congregational, 1; Methodist, 25; Presbyterian, 2; Protestant Episcopal, 2.

The education system of St. Louis provides training for Negro youth from the Kindergarten through the high school; and a Teachers' College for a selected group of girls who wish to become teachers in the St. Louis Elementary Schools. The Sumner Teachers' College is located in the high school building. It is supervised by the principal of Sumner High School and has a faculty of four teachers. Both two and four year courses are offered. The enrollment for 1926–1927 is 135.

The Sumner High School, the only high school in the city for Negroes, is modern and well-equipped for the various courses of instruction of a recognized and accredited high school. Its faculty consists of a principal and fifty-six teachers. The enrollment in September, 1926, was 1,842.

The fourteen elementary schools are, for the most part, so located as to be easily accessible to every Negro school child. The enrollment at the opening of school in September, 1926, was 13,885, with a teaching staff of 335.

In addition to the educational facilities already mentioned, St. Louis provides eight special schools for children who are handicapped mentally and physically. Notable among these is the Turner Open Air School which was opened in 1925. This school provides instruction and care for children who are underweight and mal-nourished, and for tubercular contacts.

The salary schedule for colored and white teachers in St. Louis is the same, and ranks second in salaries paid throughout the country. The demand for increased school facilities for Negroes is being met, gradually. Two elementary schools were turned over to Negroes in 1926, and there is a million-dollar Junior High School under construction.

The health of Negro school children is supervised by a staff of two colored physicians and two nurses, who visit the schools daily.

There are three parochial schools, two conducted by the Catholic Church and the third by the Lutheran Church.

The city maintains two playgrounds for Negro children. During the past two summers, the Board of Education has added to this number of conducting playgrounds in school yards in some of the congested districts.

Cultural Institutions

The city parks, museums, and libraries do not differentiate between white and colored patrons. The St. Louis Symphony Orchestra gives free concerts for school children, and one is given for Negro children.

The social problems of our community are so numerous and the agencies handling them so many that it is impossible to mention all. An effort is made to give a brief sketch of the agencies dealing chiefly with the problems of Negro life, with the understanding that there are many other agencies in the city which are doing very effective work with Negroes.

The Pine Street Young Men's Christian Association and the Young Women's Christian Association are well established in St. Louis and carry out effective programs. The Pine Street Young Men's Christian Association conducts a social and educational program for men and boys. Its departments are: Religious work, physical work, and educational work. An average monthly attendance in the religious work department is 175 men, and 791 boys; in the physical work department, 853 men and 2,840 boys; in the educational work department, 647 men. The dormitory has a capacity for 173. There is a modern and well-equipped cafeteria in the building. Plans are already under way for the construction of another Young Men's Christian Association building for Negroes.

The Young Women's Christian Association was organized in St. Louis in 1912. It maintains employment, industrial, educational, and recreational departments. During 1926, the employment department placed 4,460 women in business and industry. The total enrollment was given as 145. The educational department has organized mothers' clubs, to foster the improvement of neighborhood conditions and give instruction in the care and training of children. The enrollment is 83. The club slogan is "better homes." There is also a well-organized cooking school. The Welfare Department of the Association co-operates with the Board of Religious Organizations and the Juvenile Court, in giving service to delinquent girls. Seventy-six girls were helped through this department last year. The recreational department conducts the gymnasium class, skating, tennis, swimming, volley ball, baseball, music and dramatics. In the Girl Reserves, there are 396 girls of 'teen age. The total number of contacts of service with persons, recorded last year, was 89,000. There are five secretaries and two clerical workers with the Association.

The St. Louis Colored Orphans' Home was organized in 1888. It now occupies one of the most modern and best equipped buildings of its kind in the country. It has a capacity of 100 and accepts orphans, half orphans, and neglected children up to the age of twelve years. It also takes children for temporary care.

The Colored Old Folks Home was incorporated in 1901. Its purpose is to care for dependent Negro men and women over the age of 50 years. Its capacity is 20. A nominal fee is charged at the time of admission.

The St. Louis Urban League conducts a Day Nursery and Dental Clinic. The Nursery charges ten cents a day for the care of children, and is meeting a long-felt need of working mothers. The Dental Clinic is located in one of the public schools and is in charge of a dentist who has one nurse as an assistant. This clinic is used exclusively by school children.

People's Hospital, the only private hospital in St. Louis for Negroes, was organized in 1918. It gives both medical and surgical care, but does not treat contagious or mental diseases. Its capacity is 50 beds.

St. Louis City Hospital No. 2 was organized in 1919, and is endorsed by the American College of Physicians and Surgeons. There are sixteen internes on the resident staff and there are eighteen Negro physicians on the Associate Visiting Staff. The Hospital maintains a social service department and nurses' training school. Its capacity is 275 beds.

The Visiting Nurses' Association of St. Louis employs fourteen Negro nurses, who give skilled nursing care to the sick in their homes.

The municipal Visiting Nurses employ four colored nurses, who work in health centers and give medical supervision in child welfare, pre-natal and tuberculosis cases. They give public health instructions in the homes, but provide for no bedside nursing.

The St. Louis Tuberculosis and Health Society employs one colored case worker. This Society is largely responsible for the success of the Turner Open Air School.

The Juvenile Court of St. Louis has two officers in the Probation Department. This court deals with delinquent and dependent children, and carefully studies the individual needs of children coming to their attention.

Another city institution, the Board of Children's Guardians, an agency which grants mothers' allowances to widows for the support of dependent children, has recently employed a colored case worker. St. Louis Provident Association, a family social work agency, numbers among its employes fourteen Negroes, eleven as professional case workers, and three as stenographers. The work of this organization is done through ten district offices, two of which are supervised by colored superintendents. Throughout the entire organization, during 1926, more than a thousand Negro families received the services of the organization, which included not only provision for material need of families, but also help with problems of health, education, domestic difficulties, housing and employment. St. Louis is, without doubt, destined to become one of the nation's greatest industrial and commercial centers, and the attending problems of human welfare must become more complex. The various community resources, which have handled these problems in the past, undoubtedly will respond to the increasing demands on them with more efficiency and understanding.

Washington, D.C. (1927)

11]   Black Society

As long as I have been colored I have heard of Washington society. Even as a little boy in Kansas vague ideas of the grandeur of Negro life in the capital

SOURCE: Langston Hughes, "Our Wonderful Society: Washington," *Opportunity*, August 1927, pp. 226–27. [Langston Hughes, 1902–65, was an internationally known poet.—Ed.]

found their way into my head. A grand-uncle, John M. Langston,[1] had lived there during and after the time of colored congressmen and of him I heard much from my grandmother. Later, when I went to Cleveland, some nice mulatto friends of ours spoke of the "wonderful society life" among Negroes in Washington. And some darker friends of ours hinted at "pink teas" and the color line that was drawn there. I wanted to see the town. "It must be rich and amusing and fine," I thought.

Four or five years passed. Then by way of Mexico and New York, Paris and Italy, through a season of teaching, a year at college, and a period of travel, I arrived at Washington. "Of course, you must meet the best people," were almost the first words I heard after greetings had been exchanged. "That is very important." And I was reminded of my noble family ties and connections. But a few days later I found myself a job in a laundry carrying bags of wet-wash. The dignity of one's family background doesn't keep a fellow who's penniless from getting hungry.

It was not long, however, before I found a better place in the office of a national Negro organization. There I opened up in the morning, did clerical work, took care of the furnace, and scrubbed floors. This was termed a "position," not a "job." And I began to meet some of the best people. The people themselves assured me that they were the best people,—and they seemed to know. Never before, anywhere, had I seen persons of influence,—men with some money, women with some beauty, teachers with some education,—quite so audibly sure of their own importance and their high places in the community. So many pompous gentlemen never before did I meet. Nor so many ladies with chests swelled like pouter-pigeons whose mouths uttered formal sentences in frightfully correct English. I admit I was awed by these best people.

Negro society in Washington, they assured me, was the finest in the country, the richest, the most cultured, the most worthy. In no other city were there so many splendid homes, so many cars, so many A.B. degrees, or so many persons with "family background." Descendants of distinguished Negroes were numerous, but there were also those who could do better and trace their ancestry right on back to George Washington and his colored concubines: "How lucky I am to have a congressman for grand-uncle," I thought in the presence of these well-ancestored people.

She is a graduate of this . . . or, he is a graduate of that . . . frequently followed introductions. So I met many men and women who had been to colleges,—and seemed not to have recovered from it. Almost all of them appeared to be deeply affected by education in one way or another, and they, too, had very grand manners. "Surely," I thought when I saw them, "I'll never be important unless I get a degree." So I began to spend ten cents for lunch instead of fifteen,—putting the other nickel away for college.

Then I met some of the younger colored people, sons and daughters of the pompous gentlemen and pouter-pigeon ladies, some of them students at North-

[1] John M. Langston, 1829–97, was an important educator and political figure. Between 1869 and 1875, he was Howard University's first Dean of Law and in 1890/91 was the first and still the only black man to represent Virginia in Congress.

ern colleges or at Howard. They were not unlike youth everywhere today,—
jazzy and loud. But, "They are the hope of the race," I was told. Yet I found
that their ideals seemed most Nordic and un-Negro and that they appeared to
be moving away from the masses of the race rather than holding an identity
with them. Speaking of a fraternity dance, one in a group of five college men
said proudly, "There was nothing but pinks there,—looked just like 'fay
women. Boy, you'd have thought it was an o'fay dance!" And several of the
light young ladies I knew were not above passing a dark classmate or acquaintance with only the coolest of nods, and sometimes not even that. "She's
a dark girl but nice," or similar apologies were made by the young men for the
less than coffee-and-cream ladies they happened to know. These best young
people had, too, it seemed, an excessive admiration for fur coats and automobiles. Boasts like this were often to be heard: "There were more fur coats in
our box at the Thanksgiving game than in anybody else's." Or concerning the
social standing of a young lady: "Her father owns two cars." Or of a sporty
new-comer in town: "He's got a raccoon coat just like a 'fay boy." Or as the
criterion of success: "He's one of our leading men. He has a Packard and a
chauffeur."

But cars or fur coats or fine houses were not more talked about, however,
than was culture. And the members of Washington society *were* cultured.
They themselves assured me frequently that they were. Some of those who
could pass for white even attended down-town theatres when "The Scandals"
or Earl Carrol's "Vanities" came to town. But when a concert series of Negro
artists including Abbie Mitchell and other excellent musicians, was put on at a
colored theatre, the audiences were very small and most of the members of
cultured society were absent.

I knew that Jean Toomer's home was in Washington and I had read his
book *Cane* [2] and talked about it with other readers in New York and Paris and
Venice. I wanted to talk about it in Washington, too, because I had found it
beautiful and real. But the cultured colored society of the capital, I mean
those persons who always insisted that they were cultured, seemed to know little about the book and cared less. And when the stories of Rudolph Fisher
(also a colored Washingtonian) appeared in *The Atlantic Monthly*, what I
heard most was, "Why didn't he write about nice people like us? Why didn't
he write about cultured folks?" I thought it amazing, too, that a young play-
wright of ability and three or four poets of promise were living in Washington
unknown to the best society. At least, I saw nothing being done to encourage
these young writers, for the leading women's clubs appeared to be founded
solely for the purpose of playing cards, and the cultured doctors and lawyers
and caterers and butlers and government messengers had little concern for
poets or playwrights. In supposedly intellectual gatherings I listened to conversations as arid as the sides of the Washington monument.

There appeared, also, to be the same love of scandal among the best folks as
among the lower classes. Sometimes I heard how such-and-such a pompous
gentleman had struck his wife or how this or that refined couple had indulged

[2] Published in 1923, *Cane*, a combination of prose and poetry, has been regarded as
one of the major literary productions of a black American.

Black Housing

in physical combat,—all of which was very amusing but hardly compatible with a society which boasted of its gentility. Such consciously nice people ought never to let down the bars, I thought, but they did.

. . . . .

Washington is one of the most beautiful cities in the world. For that I remember it with pleasure. Georgia Douglass Johnson [3] conversed with charm and poured tea on Saturday nights for young writers and artists and intellectuals. That, too, I remember with pleasure. Seventh Street was always teemingly alive with dark working people who hadn't yet acquired "culture" and the manners of stage ambassadors, and pinks and blacks and yellows were still friends without apologies. That street I remember with pleasure. And the few fine and outstanding men and women I met who had seemingly outgrown "society" as a boy outgrows his first long trousers,—those men and women I remember with pleasure. But Washington society itself,—perhaps I am prejudiced toward it. Perhaps I had heard too much about it before hand and was disappointed. Or perhaps I didn't really meet the best society after all. Maybe I met only the snobs, and the high-yellows, and the lovers of fur coats and automobiles and fraternity pins and A.B. degrees. Maybe I'm all wrong about everything. —Maybe those who said they were the best people had me fooled. —Perhaps they weren't the best people,—but they looked tremendously important. Or, perhaps they *were* the best people and it's my standard of values that's awry. . . . Well, be that as it may, I have seen Washington, of which city I had heard much, and I have looked at something called "society" of which I had heard much, too. Now I can live in Harlem where people are not quite so ostentatiously proud of themselves, and where one's family background is not of such great concern. Now I can live contentedly in Harlem.

Washington, D.C. (1929)

12]   Black Housing

In general, there are two types of houses in which Negro families in Washington live. First, those that are built originally for white people and have been taken over by colored renters or buyers. Second, houses built especially for Negro occupancy. The first type of house is in nearly every instance superior in quality to the latter, and is generally preferred by Negroes who desire durable homes. This preference, however, has resulted in the renting and selling of these homes by real estate companies at excessive prices.

Many of the large construction companies in the city—such as the Kite Realty Company, Cafritz Company, B. F. Saul Company, Wardman Company, and Grady & Company—have taken advantage of the tendency of the Negro

Source: William Henry Jones, *The Housing of Negroes in Washington*, Washington, D.C.: Howard University Press, 1929, pp. 91–95.
[3] Atlanta-born poet, 1886–1966.

167

population to concentrate in Northwest Washington, and are rapidly developing "business quarters" and new homes and communities for Negroes. Within a period of twelve years, the Kite Realty Company has built approximately four hundred houses and two or three apartments for colored people. The Wardman Company is now renting approximately five hundred houses to colored families. Feeling the lure of these new modern homes, Negroes are renting and purchasing them as fast as they are completed.

These new houses, when first erected, display a rather attractive appearance, because of their extreme modernity and their improvement in facilities over the old houses, equipped with oil lamps and built-in stoves, known as "latrobes." However, certain strong objections have been made to these new structures, and severe criticisms have been launched against the building programs. . . . The slightest comparison shows that these new houses, which are being so rapidly constructed for Negroes, are of material much inferior to those which can be purchased from white owners at similar prices. Most of them contain an inferior grade of brick, cheap fixtures and floorings, and ceilings and walls that crack within a few months after the houses are completed. It also seems to be a practice among construction companies to use very cheap labor. For these reasons, many of the loan companies—according to information given the writer—are hesitant about making loans to builders who erect homes for Negroes. . . .

In addition to the matter of cheap materials, there is the question of exploitation. In practically every instance, the new homes that are built for Negroes sell for prices that vary from one to two thousand dollars more than similar homes built for white people. A comparison of the purchase prices of similar types of houses purchased by Negroes and white people established the fact that there is a very noticeable difference in the costs of these homes along the lines of race. It also substantiated the charge of unnecessary exploitation of Negroes. The following table is a summary of a comparative study of the purchase prices of practically identical houses sold to Negroes and white people:

SIZE OF HOUSE	PRICE PAID BY NEGROES	PRICE PAID BY WHITES	NO. OF HOUSES COMPARED
Six Rooms	$7,250	$6,500	15
Six Rooms	8,250	7,500	12
Five Rooms	5,650	5,500	8
Eight Rooms	12,500	10,500	20
Seven Rooms	9,500	9,000	10
Six Rooms	7,500	7,000	15

Building programs for Negroes are becoming extremely popular, for the reason that they are profitable commercial enterprises. The real estate companies confess that they usually charge Negroes more for these homes than they do white people, not because they realize that Negroes are compelled to find new homes—on account of the housing shortage—but solely because the financial risks are much greater in the case of Negroes; in other words, because Negroes

168

are not as likely to be able to keep up their payments. The writer, however, subjected these theories to a critical investigation, and secured statements from experienced and impartial real estate dealers to the effect that the facts show that, above a certain cultural and economic level, the risks are not as great in the case of Negroes as they are in the case of white people. Below this average standard of culture, the risks were very great in the case of both races—but somewhat greater in the case of Negroes.

In view of the fact that these homes are built solely for responsible colored families, as alleged by the realty companies themselves, and indicated by the prevalent sign, "New Modern Homes for Progressive Colored Citizens"— families that are more prompt in meeting their financial obligations than white people of a similar cultural level—the theory of "greater risks" becomes untenable. . . . White retail grocers and shopkeepers state that the upper classes of Negroes are better buyers and much more responsible and reliable customers than are white people of similar economic and social status.

The houses which Negroes occupy in Washington vary in quality and structure from the well-appointed, almost palatial residence of twenty or more rooms, equipped with all the modern facilities—even to the extent of outside servant's quarter—to the one-room shack without flooring and plastering.

Nothing so clearly indicates the wide class stratification among Negroes, resulting from economic achievement, as these marked differences in the homes which they occupy. It is not unusual to encounter cases of Negro families which have purchased their homes on a cash basis of from $10,000 to $25,000, and repaired and furnished them at a cost of several thousand dollars. There are doubtless as many Negroes living in well-appointed homes, enjoying comfort, in Washington, as in any other urban center in the United States— Chicago and New York not excluded. There is, however, no strict cultural determination of the well-appointed home. It is not determined entirely by the economic and social status of the family, for it was found that frequently the best furnished homes were those of persons employed in domestic service— maids, porters, chauffeurs, or Pullman porters and dining car employees. The largeness or smallness of the family's income does not necessarily condition the nature of the appointments of the home. There are other factors besides that of economic status—cultural factors—that determine the type of the home. Brick masons were found to have larger family incomes than government workers, yet, in the majority of instances, their homes were found to be inferior in appointment to those of the latter group of wage earners.

Chauffeurs and house servants—though unable to boast of the kind of culture that is found in the schools—frequently enjoy more genuinely cultural contacts than persons of higher social status. Their contacts are with the atmosphere of cultured white homes, and they quickly imitate and assimilate the models and forms of life which they encounter.

NORTHEASTERN CITIES

Economic and Cultural Aspects

The documents that follow describe the way in which blacks edged into the industrial labor market of the Northeast (Document 13) as well as their vigorous political and cultural activities (Documents 14, 15). The various movements were partly precipitated by very large-scale black migration.

During World War I Pittsburgh, as the leading iron and steel center of the Northeast, attracted a large number of migrant blacks from the South Atlantic seaboard. Since few new houses were built to accommodate them, this influx led to one of the earliest instances of dramatic deterioration of urban housing due to overcrowding. The situation was hardly helped by the fact that in the decade 1920–30, as in 1910–20, the black population of Pittsburgh increased almost 50%.

During the decade 1910–1920 New York's black population surpassed that of Washington, D.C. as the largest in the country, and by 1930 it was greater by almost 100,000 than that of Chicago, its nearest rival. The size of its population, plus the fact that it was in one of the largest and most vital cities of the world, gave New York's black community unusual confidence and sophistication. Harlem, the glamorous New York City black metropolis, contained an unrivaled concentration of black talent whose achievements spread its fame virtually worldwide. Harlem was the headquarters of Marcus Garvey's United Negro Improvement Association, the first major urban black mass movement in the United States; it emphasized racial pride and self-sufficiency and had an impact throughout the black world. Simultaneously Harlem was the main venue of an unparalleled flowering of black American literary, artistic, and musical talent known as the Harlem Renaissance. Document 14 gives a sympathetic view of the Marcus Garvey movement by the best-known black freelance journalist of his time, while Document 15 gives an excellent synopsis of the literary expression of the Harlem Renaissance by one of its main participants.

170

Pittsburgh, Pa. (1918)

13]   The Black Migrant:
          Housing and Employment

The Negro population of the Pittsburgh districts in Allegheny County was 27,753 in the year 1900 and had increased to 34,217 by the year 1910, according to the latest United States Census figures available. The increase during this period was 23.3%. Assuming the continuation of this rate of increase, the total Negro population in 1915 would be about 38,000.

From a canvass of twenty typical industries in the Pittsburgh district, it was found that there were 2,550 Negroes employed in 1915, and 8,325 in 1917, an increase of 5,775 or 227%. . . . the number of Negroes now employed in the district may be placed at 14,000. This means that there are about 9,750 more Negroes working in the district today than there were in 1915, an addition due to the migration from the South.

A schedule study of over five hundred Negro migrants indicates that thirty percent of the new-comers have their families with them, and that the average family consists of three persons, excluding the father. Adding to the total number of new workers (9,750), the product obtained by multiplying thirty percent by three (average family), we find a probable total new Negro population of 18,550 in 1917.

This sudden and abnormal increase in the Negro population, within so short a time, of necessity involves a tremendous change, and creates a new situation, which merits the attention of the whole community. Before this great influx of Negroes from the South, the Negro population, which constituted only 3.4% of the total city population, lived in a half dozen sections of the city. Although not absolutely segregated, these districts were distinct.

Because of the high cost of materials and labor, incident to the war; because the taxation system still does not encourage improvements and because of investment attractions other than in realty, few houses have been built and practically no improvements have been made. This is most strikingly apparent in the poorer sections of the city. In the Negro sections, for instance, there have been almost no houses added and few vacated by whites within the last two years. The addition, therefore, of thousands of Negroes, just arrived from Southern states, meant not only the creation of new Negro quarters and the dispersion of Negroes throughout the city, but also the utmost utilization of every place in the Negro sections capable of being transformed into a habitation. Attics and cellars, store-rooms and basements, churches, sheds and warehouses had to be employed for the accommodation of these new-comers. Whenever a Negro had space which he could possibly spare, it was converted into a sleeping place; as many beds as possible were crowded into it, and the

SOURCE: Abraham Epstein, *The Negro Migrant in Pittsburgh*, Pittsburgh: University of Pittsburgh Press, 1918; New York: Arno Press, 1969, pp. 7–8, 30–32.

171

maximum number of men per bed were lodged. Either because their own rents were high, or because they were unable to withstand the temptation of the sudden, and, for all they knew, temporary harvest, or, perhaps because of the altruistic desire to assist their race fellows, a majority of the Negroes in Pittsburgh converted their homes into lodging houses.

Because rooms were hard to come by, the lodgers were not disposed to complain about the living conditions or the prices charged. They were only too glad to secure a place where they could share a half or at least a part of an unclaimed bed. It was no easy task to find room for a family, as most boarding houses would accept only single men, and refused to admit women and children. Many a man, who with his family occupied only one or two rooms, made place for a friend or former townsman and his family. In many instances this was done from unselfish motives and in a humane spirit.

. . . . . .

The great majority of the Negro migrants come North because of the better economic and social opportunities here. But even here they are not permitted

Industrial Concerns Studied in the Pittsburgh District
[during July and August, 1917]

NAME OF CONCERN	NO. OF NEGROES EMPLOYED AT PRESENT	NO. EMPLOYED PRIOR TO 1916	% DOING UNSKILLED LABOR	HOURLY WAGES OF UNSKILLED LABOR (CENTS)	NO. OF HOURS PER DAY
Carnegie Steel Co. (all plants)	4,000	1,500	95	30	8–12
Jones & Laughlin	1,500	400	100	30	10
Westinghouse Elec. & Mfg. Co.	900	25	90	28–30	10
Harbison & Walker	250	50	80	27½	10
National Tube Co. (all plants)	250	100	100	30	10
Pressed Steel Car Co.	25	25	50	23	11
Pgh. Forge & Iron	75	0	100	30	10
Moorhead Brothers	200	200	75	30	10
Am. Steel & Wire	25	25	100	28–30	10
Clinton Iron & Steel	25	25	75		
Oliver Iron & Steel	50	0	100	25–28	10
Carbon Steel Co.	200	50	75	30	10–12
Crucible Steel Co.	400	150	90	28–33	10
A. M. Byers Co.	200	0	60		10
Lockhart Steel Co.	160	0	95	27½	10
Mesta Machine Co.	50	0	100	30	10
Marshall Foundry Co.	15	0			
U. S. Glass Co.			No Negroes employed		
Thompson-Sterret Co.			No Negroes employed		
Spang-Chalfant Co.			No Negroes employed		
TOTAL	8,325	2,550			

to enter industry freely. They are kept in the ranks of unskilled labor and in the field of personal service. Until the present demand for unskilled labor arose, the Negroes in the North were for the most part servants. There were very few Negroes occupied otherwise than as porters, chauffeurs, janitors and the like. The Negro at present has entered the productive industries, but he is kept still on the lowest rung of the economic ladder.

From a study of colored employees in twenty of the largest industrial plants, in the Pittsburgh district, arbitrarily selected, we find that most of the concerns have employed colored labor only since May or June of 1916. Very few of the Pittsburgh industries have used colored labor in capacities other than as janitors and window cleaners. A few of the plants visited had not begun to employ colored people until the spring of 1917, while a few others had not yet come to employ Negroes, either because they believed the Negro workers to be inferior and inefficient, or because they feared that their white labor force would refuse to work with the blacks. The Superintendent of one big steel plant which has not employed colored labor during the past few years admitted that he faced a decided shortage of labor, and that he was in need of men; but he said he would employ Negroes only as a last resort, and that the situation was as yet not sufficiently acute to warrant their employment. In a big glass plant, the company attempted to use Negro labor last winter, but the white workers "ran them out" by swearing at them, calling them "Nigger" and making conditions so unpleasant for them that they were forced to quit. This company has therefore given up any further attempts at employing colored labor. . . .

About ninety-five percent of the colored workers in the steel mills visited in our survey were doing unskilled labor. In the bigger plants, where many hundreds of Negroes are employed, almost one hundred percent are doing common labor, while in the smaller plants, a few might be found doing labor which required some skill.

New York, N.Y. (1922)

14]   The Marcus Garvey Movement

I have been studying Marcus Garvey for the past four years, and I have studied some of his opponents for thirty or forty years, and find that my estimate of Marcus Garvey is much higher than it is of many of those whom I have personally known in all these years. To me, two of the tests of true leadership are the absence of the love of money and a desire to help the masses to get on and up. I haven't discovered such altruism in the ethics of many of these leaders whom Mr. Garvey is putting out of business by his straightforward methods and bull-dog tenacity.

When Mr. Garvey first came to this country from his island home in Jamaica, B.W.I., I was one among the first American Negroes on whom he

Source: John E. Bruce, "Marcus Garvey and the U.N.I.A," 1922. (Ms., B 5–14, Schomburg Collection, New York Public Library.)

called. I was then residing in Yonkers on the Hudson, New York. He was a little sawed-off and hammered-down Black Man, with *determination* written all over his face, and an engaging smile that caught you and compelled you to listen to his story. Like all other Negroes who feel deeply the injustices of the White Man, whether they are committed by individuals or by the State, he had a grievance, and I listened with interest to its recital, which is much too long to repeat here, but the substance of which was, that the Negroes in the West Indian Island, from which he came, were not receiving fair play at the hands of the Whites, either in the matter of education or in the industries, in that the school facilities were inadequate, and that the workers were underpaid, thus preventing them from doing for themselves what they would like to do to improve their educational and economic condition. All they needed was a fair opportunity and the Organization which he was then endeavoring to form, he believed would give them, in some slight measure, this opportunity, if the Negroes on this side of the World would lend a helping hand.

Mr. Garvey is a rapid-fire talker, and two reporters are necessary to keep up with him at his meetings here in Liberty Hall on Sunday Nights, when he speaks to audiences of 5000 or more; I was able to catch enough from his rapidly spoken story, however, to convince me that he had a real mission, and I promised him such aid in the furtherance of his plans as I could give him, morally and substantially. We parted the best of friends. I had given him a list of the names of our leading men in New York and other cities, who, I felt, would encourage and assist him. Some of them were Clergymen; some professional men; and some of them private citizens. He called on some of these, and among them, Prof. Du Bois, who did not think well of his plan, but he kept on.

The Jamaica Club of New York City hired St. Mark's Hall on 138th Street, near Lenox Avenue, for a public meeting and announced that Mr. Garvey would speak on his favorite subject. He spoke with so much vigor and earnestness that he stepped off the platform to the floor. The tickets were $5.00 and I gladly purchased one and went to hear him. Since I had seen him in Yonkers, he had been *seeing things* in and around New York, and his vision had become enlarged. His address in St. Mark's Hall indicated, from its tenor, that his plan for Racial uplift was not to be wholly confined to his Island Home. The problems which it embraced were universal, because the Negro in the United States of America was but little better off than the Negro in the West Indies. Later on, he *reasoned* that the Negroes throughout the World had as much to complain of as those of Jamaica, and to prove that he was right, he made a trip into our *Southern Shambles*, and mingled freely with the humble and lowly classes, "who, in the Halcyon days of politics, served as 'meal tickets,'" for the scalawags of the White Race, seeking office and power through their Black accomplices, in the dirty game of American politics, which has at last come to a period in that section of the Country, and left the Negro political leader on the outside looking in.

Among these leaders were many men calling themselves ambassadors of God, who made a good living out of the political game, by using their Congregations as weavers use a shuttle-cock, for their personal gain. Garvey saw all

174

the rottenness and deceptions of both White and Black leaders. He saw his Race being used as a plaything by these men, who had no other aim than to advance themselves politically at the expense of these Blacks, and then to pose as their Champions and defenders. Their hollow pretensions, their mock heroics, their false zeal and their rank hypocrisy set him to thinking, and after months of travel in the West Indies and the United States, where he used his eyes and kept his own counsel, he finally changed his plans, and began a vigorous soapbox campaign in Negro Harlem, out of which grew the Universal Negro Improvement Association, the original membership of which was thirteen (13), and which now numbers four millions in the United States, with 800 Divisions throughout the United States and the World which include Africa, the West Indies, and South and Central America. The Divisions which are established are growing by leaps and bounds in every part of the World where Negroes are to be found.

In the incipiency of this newer Movement of Garvey, the old leaders paused, and snorted; the preachers, who found their Congregations thinning out and slipping away from them, and the Professional leaders for Revenue only, discovering that majorities for the candidates who had paid them to get results in Negro districts were growing more and more uncertain, combined and united in a campaign of slander and abuse of the Garvey Movement, and threw all sorts of obstacles in the way, to prevent the accomplishment of his plans. But they continued to develop, despite these handicaps, and, like the proverbial steamroller of the G.O.P., they will all of them be flattened out, if they wait long enough.

Mr. Garvey is very busy now working out the larger details of his plan, jailing crooks who have robbed his Association, and finding and fitting men to take up the work of spreading the Gospel of the U.N.I.A., among those who sit in darkness.

I was among those who opposed him at the start and who wrote against him, and I tried my best to defeat his aims, which, I confess, I did not then thoroughly understand. They seemed to me wild, chimerical and impossible of accomplishment. I stood, one night, at a corner of Lenox Avenue and 135th Street, when Garvey, standing on an especially built platform—a step ladder— with which he could take liberties without falling, unfolded, in part, the plan of his Organization, which was to draw all Negroes throughout the World together, to make one big brotherhood of the Black Race for its common good, for mutual protection, for commercial and industrial development, and for the fostering of business enterprises. This sounded not only good to me, but practical. The things he proposed were easy of accomplishment under a leader as full of his subject as he, and, "Why not?" I said to myself, "let him try out his plan; since no one else has submitted a better one, why oppose him?" and from that cold night, in October, I ceased writing and talking against Garvey.

His street corner audiences were larger than those of the Socialist Orators on the other corners a few blocks away, and they stayed longer. The people hung upon his words, drank in his messages to them, and were as enthusiastic and earnest about this business as their doughty little Black Orator. To me, this connoted that Marcus Garvey was more than the average Street Corner

Orator and that his work and mission had more than an ordinary significance. The people to whom he spoke heard him gladly, pondered his words, and acted wisely by organizing what is today the most powerful Negro Organization in the World. There is absolutely no corner of the earth where there is a Black or Brown or Yellow face, where there is not a Branch of the U.N.I.A. There are branches in Germany, London, Wales, Scotland, and recently, I saw a letter from far off Peru, requesting the literature of the Organization. What does this mean? It means clearly, that Mr. Garvey has caught the vision, that the people of Color, throughout the World, believe in his leadership and want him to lead them. Nothing could be plainer.

The old leaders were not able or were too lazy or indifferent or both, to work out a plan for the redemption and regeneration of the Race, as attractive and practical from any angle in which it is viewed, as that of Marcus Garvey. It has progressed too far now for any of them singly or all of them combined to stop it, and it will be a hazardous undertaking for those who think they are powerful enough to do so. They have had their chance and failed, and the wisdom of prudence suggests that they let Garvey alone. Let him carry on the work to which he has put his hands and to which he, in the greatness and bigness of his heart, is inviting them now to put their hands, their brains, and their money to make the Big Negro World Brotherhood, the accomplished *fact* that he intends it to be, with or without the consent of any Negro leader or leaders who now think they are IT.

Garvey is neither a rum drinker, a user of tobacco in any form, a social bug, nor a grafter. He is scrupulously honest in the handling of the funds of the Organization, and exacts the strictest accounting of its funds from those holding subordinate positions in the Organization, and through whose hands its money passes. "His spear knows no brother." The man caught stealing the people's money is promptly cut off the payroll and headed for jail, if the offense is sufficient to justify such action. He is branded a thief in the "Negro World," and must change his name and complexion to do business elsewhere. Garvey is relentless with crooks and fakers, and he is the idol of the masses of the common people, of whom he is one.

New York, N.Y. (1930)

15]　　　　　Harlem Renaissance

The most outstanding phase of the development of the Negro in the United States during the past decade has been the recent literary and artistic emergence of the individual creative artist; and New York has been, almost exclusively, the place where that emergence has taken place. The thing that has

Source: James Weldon Johnson, *Black Manhattan*, New York: A. A. Knopf, 1930, pp. 260–80. James Weldon Johnson, 1871–1938, was an author, composer, and NAACP official.—Ed.]

happened has been so marked that it does not have the appearance of a development; it seems rather like a sudden awakening, like an instantaneous change. The story of it, as of almost every experience relating to the Negro in America, goes back a long way. . . .

　　　·　·　·　·　·　·

Towards the close of the World War there sprang up a group of eight or ten poets in various cities of the country who sang a newer song. The group discarded traditional dialect and the stereotyped material of Negro poetry. . . . What they did was to attempt to express what the masses of their race were then feeling and thinking and wanting to hear. They attempted to make those masses articulate. And so the distinguishing notes of their poetry were disillusionment, protest and challenge—and sometimes despair. And they created, each in accordance with his talent and power, authentic poetry. The poems of the Negro poets of the immediate post-war period were widely printed in Negro publications; they were committed to memory; they were recited at school exercises and public meetings and were discussed at private gatherings. These revolutionary poets made black America fully aware of them.

But there was among them a voice too powerful to be confined to the circle of race, a voice that carried further and made America in general aware; it was that of Claude McKay, of the Harlem group. Here was a true poet of great skill and wide range, who turned from creating the mood of poetic beauty in the absolute, as he had so fully done in such poems as "The Harlem Dancer" and "Flame Heart," for example, and began pouring out cynicism, bitterness, and invective. . . . Later his work appeared in other magazines, principally in the *Liberator*. He published *Harlem Shadows* in 1922. Claude McKay's poetry was one of the great forces in bringing about what is often called the "Negro literary renaissance."

In 1922 *The Book of American Negro Poetry*, edited by James Weldon Johnson, was published. This anthology contained an essay on "The Negro's Creative Genius" by the editor, and presented to the general reading public a representative collection of poetry by American Negroes from the earliest writers down to and including that written by Negro poets immediately following the World War. The book was effective in following up the work of making America at large aware.

Within five or six years after the close of the war there had sprung up a group of younger Negro poets. Like the immediate post-war group, they were scattered in different cities. Of these younger poets there were some fifteen writing verse of distinction; and four-fifths of that number belonged either to New York or Washington. Two of the poets belonging to the Harlem group rose above the level and gained, almost simultaneously, a recognition for themselves which carried the Negro literary movement far forward and succeeded greatly in focusing national attention upon it. These two poets were Countee Cullen, born in New York in 1903, and Langston Hughes, born in Joplin, Missouri, in 1902.

　　　·　·　·　·　·　·

Mr. Cullen is a true lyric poet. . . . The best of his poetry rises out of the idea of race and is permeated with it. But it is through his ability suddenly to deepen and heighten these very experiences that his race-conscious poetry becomes the thing of beauty, at times almost insufferable beauty, that it is; it is through this ability that he achieves some of his finest effects. . . .

Mr. Cullen published his first volume of poems, *Color,* in 1925, when he was twenty-two; the book placed him at once in the list of American poets. He has followed it with *The Ballad of the Brown Girl, Copper Sun,* and *Caroling Dusk,* an anthology of verse by Negro poets from Paul Laurence Dunbar down to and including the younger group, and *The Black Christ,* a long narrative poem.

Langston Hughes is a cosmopolite. Young as he is, he has been over most of the world, making his own way. Consciously he snaps his fingers at race, as he does at a great many other things. He belongs to the line of rebel poets. He is a rebel not only in the matter of poetic form, but also in the choice of poetic subjects, for, of subjects, he is as likely to take one from the gutter as from any other place. On this point he has met with the disapprobation and censure of some in his own race who feel that the subject-matter of his poems is not sufficiently elevating. Yet Mr. Hughes, too, falls under this idea of race, and most of his best work springs from it. It is by taking this idea and shooting it through with a cynicism and a sardonic humour peculiarly his own that he secures some of his finest effects. These effects are very unlike Mr. Cullen's but have a quality of equal finality.

Mr. Hughes writes a poem which has for its title and its subject "Brass Spittoons." Here, if ever there was one, is an "unpoetic" subject. But the poet takes it and tells of the black porter at his distasteful task of cleaning brass spittoons; tells of him in Detroit, Chicago, Atlantic City, Palm Beach; cleaning spittoons in Pullman cars, clubs, and hotel lobbies; picking up nickels, dimes—and a dollar, two dollars a day. . . .

No matter how Mr. Hughes handles this idea of "race," he is very seldom sentimental and never pathetic. But this is not due to any flinty quality in his poetry. In much of his work the throb and the tear lie close to the surface. As a conscious artist he has in a large measure adopted the philosophy of the folk-bards, makers of the blues. That philosophy consists in choosing to laugh to keep from crying. Mr. Hughes might even subscribe to the philosophy summed up in that line in one of the blues:

"Got de blues, an' too dam' mean to cry."

. . . . . .

Mr. Hughes has published two volumes of poems: *The Weary Blues* in 1926, and *Fine Clothes to the Jew* in 1927. In the latter year *God's Trombones—Seven Negro Sermons in Verse,* by James Weldon Johnson, was published.

Early in the decade a fresh start was made in fiction. There had been the stories of Paul Laurence Dunbar and Charles W. Chesnutt. And later *The Quest of the Silver Fleece,* a novel by W. E. Burghardt Du Bois, and *The Autobiography of an Ex-Coloured Man,* by James Weldon Johnson, appeared. In 1923 Jean Toomer published *Cane,* a string of stories of Negro life, interspersed with original lyrics. The book was in no degree a popular success, but it made a great impression on the critics. It is still often referred to as one of the finest pieces of modern American prose. The poems in the book stamp the author as a lyricist of the first order. Mr. Toomer was the prose pioneer in the work done in the past decade to make America in general aware of Negro artists and what they were doing; it is regrettable that he has written so little since.

In 1924 there appeared a novel that struck both the critics and the general public. It was the first piece of fiction written by an American Negro to accomplish this double feat with so large a degree of success. The book created a sensation and was the subject of heated controversy wherever it was discussed. It was *The Fire in the Flint* by Walter White. *The Fire in the Flint* was a realistic novel dealing in a fearless manner with the contemporary conditions surrounding Negro life in a small town in the South. Mr. White was well prepared to write such a book; he was born in Atlanta, Georgia, and educated at Atlanta University. In 1918 he came to New York to become assistant secretary for the National Association for the Advancement of Colored People. In that capacity he travelled through many parts of the South to make investigations of lynchings, race riots, and civil and social conditions among Negroes. Being a man who can be white or coloured as he may choose, he gathered a great deal of curious information. All of this experience he packed into this book and produced a story of extraordinary power. *The Fire in the Flint* was followed by *Flight*, a novel with "passing" as its theme. Last year Mr. White published *Rope and Faggot*, the most authoritative study of lynching yet made.

Just prior to *The Fire in the Flint* a novel by Jessie Fauset, *There Is Confusion*, made its appearance. Miss Fauset's book was a story of conditions surrounding contemporary Negro life in a Northern city. Her next novel was *Plum Bun*, a story with a similar theme. . . . Within the past ten years more fiction has been published by Negro writers than had been brought out by them in the preceding two hundred and fifty years. And every bit of this fiction—that is, every bit that has been published in a way calculated to reach the general public—has been written by writers of the Harlem group. Nella Larsen published two well-written novels: one, *Quicksand*, the story of a coloured girl, with the scene laid in the South, in New York and in Europe; and the other, *Passing*, a story of "passing." Eric Walrond published *Tropic Death*, a volume of colourful stories of West Indian and Panamanian life. Rudolph Fisher brought the first light, satirical touch in *The Walls of Jericho*. W. E. Burghardt Du Bois published *Dark Princess*, a novel that was fantasy and satire. Wallace Thurman published *The Blacker the Berry*. In 1927 *The Autobiography of an Ex-Coloured Man* was re-published in New York. In 1928, Claude McKay broke his silence with a book of prose, *Home to Harlem*, a novel of life in Negro New York. This book appeared on the list of best sellers and was one of the successes of the season. McKay followed with another successful novel, *Banjo*. In 1929 Taylor Gordon published *Born to Be*, a story of his life, but at the same time containing, probably, an element of fiction. William Pickens published *Bursting Bonds*, an autobiography, in 1923. Apart from fiction but closely related to the literary and artistic movement, were the *First and Second Books of American Negro Spirituals,* edited and arranged by James Weldon and J. Rosamond Johnson, and published respectively in 1925 and 1926.

There are writers in Harlem who do a regular newspaper stint and contribute to the magazines; among them is George S. Schuyler, a brilliant writer and a first-class journalist and publicist. J. A. Rogers is another excellent newspaper and magazine contributor. The Negro novel of the World War is still unwritten.

In making America aware of the Negro artist and his work an important part was played by the Harlem number (March 1925) of the *Survey Graphic.* This number of the *Survey* contained a hundred pages. There were twenty contributors, fifteen coloured and five white; twelve of the coloured contributors belonged to the Harlem group. Some of the articles were: "Enter the New Negro," "The Making of Harlem," "Black Workers and the City," "The Tropics in New York," "The Black Man Brings His Gifts," "Jazz at Home," "Negro Art and America," "The Negro Digs Up His Past," "The Rhythm of Harlem," "Color Lines," and "Ambushed in the City." There were also poems, drawings, and photographs. This issue of the *Survey* had the largest circulation of any in the history of the magazine up to that time; several editions had to be run off before the demand was satisfied. It was a revelation to New York and the country. Later the symposium, somewhat enlarged, was brought out as a book entitled *The New Negro,* under the editorship of Alain Locke. It remains one of the most important books on the Negro ever published.

Another decided impulse to the literary movement was furnished by the establishment in 1924 of cash prizes for original literary work. These prizes were offered through the two New York magazines, the *Crisis,* organ of the National Association for the Advancement of Colored People, under the editorship of Dr. Du Bois, and *Opportunity,* the organ of the Urban League, under the editorship of Charles S. Johnson. . . .

In the other arts some advance, though not quite so marked, has been made in the decade just passed. In music the Harlem group has been a strong factor in giving a fresh interpretation and a new vogue to the Spirituals. The Spirituals have been sung before audiences for a long time. It has been sixty years since they were first introduced by the Fisk Jubilee Singers. But a change has been wrought in the reaction they call forth. Fifty years ago white people who heard the Spirituals sung were touched and moved with sympathy for the "poor Negro." Today the reaction is less of pity for the Negro's condition and more of admiration for the creative genius of the race. This higher evaluation and truer appreciation of the Spirituals are due in a very direct way to the work done by the Harlem group. Paul Robeson and Lawrence Brown, and J. Rosamond Johnson and Taylor Gordon have sung programs made up exclusively of Spirituals before the finest concert audiences in New York and other principal cities of the country. The Hall Johnson Choir has sung with great orchestras at the Lewisohn Stadium and has appeared in connexion with theatrical productions and on the bills of the big moving-picture theatres. And all of these have broadcast Spirituals. In addition, soloists like Jules Bledsoe, Charlotte Murray, Minnie Brown, and Abbie Mitchell have included these songs in their concert programs. The efforts of these artists have had a far-reaching effect on this new and popular appreciation of the Spirituals. And behind and supplementing the efforts of these and all other artists who have taken the Spirituals to the public has been the work of Harry T. Burleigh and J. Rosamond Johnson in making large numbers of these songs musically available. Because of their work, between two and three hundred Spirituals are in a form that makes them interesting to musical people.

Some creditable work in painting is being done by younger artists, but neither in Harlem nor in the whole country has there been produced in this decade or any other, for that matter, a Negro painter who has achieved anything like the eminence of H. O. Tanner, for some time now dean of American painters in Paris. Aaron Douglas of the Harlem group has won recognition for his black and white drawings. His work has marked originality and has gained for him a place as an illustrator of books. Some creditable work has been done by several students in sculpture, but here, as in painting, the Negro must go back to a former generation for outstanding achievement. But the strangest and most surprising lack is that with all the great native musical endowment the race is conceded to possess, the Negro in New York has not in this most propitious time produced an outstanding composer. The American Negro composers of prominence belong, too, to a former generation.

NORTH CENTRAL CITIES

Social and Economic Aspects

In the period between World War I and the Depression the black population of the major industrial cities of the north central region—Detroit, Chicago, and Cleveland—grew at a faster rate than that of major cities in any other region of the United States. Between 1910 and 1920, the average increase of the black population in these cities was 355.8%, most of it occurring during and after the war; in the period 1920–30, the average growth was 138.9%.

The phenomenal increase in the black population of these cities reflected the fact that they offered blacks comparatively greater economic opportunities and greater advancement in industry than did other cities. These three were the centers of rapid expansion in the steel, automobile, oil, chemical, and food industries, resulting in a relative shortage of labor. Managements encouraged black/white labor competition, but at the same time exercised relatively less discrimination in hiring policy. Also, the Urban League performed an excellent job not only of placing migrants in jobs but in general of facilitating their social adjustment to big city living (Document 17).

Although blacks in Detroit, Chicago, and Cleveland as in other cities were used mainly in unskilled positions, a relatively higher per cent of them were to be found in semiskilled and skilled positions. For instance in 1926, mainly due to the liberal policy of the automobile industry, some 35% of the black laboring force was to be found in semiskilled and skilled positions, perhaps then the highest per cent of any city in the nation.

In these cities, too, black women were used to a much greater extent than elsewhere as industrial workers. They were to be found in the needle trades and in the garment, packing, and foundry industries, but they were generally nonunion and underpaid. Both black men and women were comparatively well represented in public services, the former primarily as clerks, postal carriers, and accountants, the latter as clerks, typists, and telephone operators.

Chicago blacks for reasons already indicated (Part Two, Document 28) continued to enjoy "comparatively excellent political representation" throughout this period. But heightened racial consciousness and pride, stimulated by the industrial opportunities opened up during World War I, combined with racial prejudice, police unfairness, and inequality of opportunity in housing, to pro-

duce the dastardly Chicago riot of 1919 (Document 16), which resulted in 38 dead (23 blacks and 15 whites) and some 537 injured. The Chicago race riot was one of at least 26 urban explosions in 1919—all stemming from the same basic causes.

Chicago, Ill. (1919)

16]   Race Riot

Many causes have been assigned for the three days of race rioting, from July 27 to 30 (1919) in Chicago, each touching some particular phases of the general outbreak. Labor union officials attribute it to the action of the packers, while the packers are equally sure that the unions themselves are directly responsible. The city administration feels that the riots were brought on to discredit the Thompson[1] forces, while leaders of the anti-Thompson forces, prominent among them being State's Attorney Maclay Hoyne, are sure that the administration is directly responsible. In this manner charges and counter-charges are made, but, as is usually the case, the Negro is made to bear the brunt of it all—to be "the scapegoat." A background of strained race relations brought to a head more rapidly through political corruption, economic competition and clashes due to the overflow of the greatly increased colored population into sections outside of the so-called "Black Belt," embracing the Second and Third Wards, all of these contributed, aided by magnifying of Negro crime by newspapers, to the formation of a situation where only a spark was needed to ignite the flames of racial antagonism. That spark was contributed by a white youth when he knocked a colored lad off a raft at the 29th Street bathing beach and the colored boy was drowned.

Four weeks spent in studying the situation in Chicago, immediately following the outbreaks, seem to show at least eight general causes for the riots, and the same conditions, to a greater or less degree, can be found in almost every large city with an appreciable Negro population. These causes, taken after a careful study in order of their prominence, are:

1. Race Prejudice.
2. Economic Competition.
3. Political Corruption and Exploitation of Negro Voters.
4. Police Inefficiency.
5. Newspaper Lies about Negro Crime.
6. Unpunished Crimes Against Negroes.
7. Housing.
8. Reaction of Whites and Negroes from [sic] War.

Some of these can be grouped under the same headings, but due to the prominence of each they are listed as separate causes.

Source: Walter White, "Chicago and Its Eight Reasons," *Crisis*, October 1919, pp. 293–97.
[1] William Hale Thompson was mayor of Chicago 1915–23 and 1927–31.

Prior to 1915, Chicago had been famous for its remarkably fair attitude toward colored citizens. Since that time, when the migratory movement from the South assumed large proportions, the situation has steadily grown more and more tense. This was due in part to the introduction of many Negroes who were unfamiliar with city ways and could not, naturally, adapt themselves immediately to their new environment. Outside of a few sporadic attempts, little was done to teach them the rudimentary principles of sanitation, of conduct, or of their new status as citizens under a system different from that in the South. During their period of absorption into the new life, their care-free, at times irresponsible and sometimes even boisterous, conduct caused complications difficult to adjust. But equally important, though seldom considered, is the fact that many Southern whites have also come into the North, many of them to Chicago, drawn by the same economic advantages that attracted the colored workman. The exact figure is unknown, but it is estimated by men who should know that fully 20,000 of them are in Chicago. These have spread the virus of race hatred and evidences of it can be seen in Chicago on every hand. This same cause underlies each of the other seven causes.

With regard to economic competition, the age-long dispute between capital and labor enters. Large numbers of Negroes were brought from the South by the packers and there is little doubt that this was done in part so that the Negro might be used as a club over the heads of the unions. John Fitzpatrick and Ed Nockels, president and secretary, respectively, of the Chicago Federation of Labor, and William Buck, editor of the *New Majority*, a labor organ, openly charge that the packers subsidized colored ministers, politicians and Y.M.C.A. secretaries to prevent the colored workmen at the stockyards from entering the unions. On the other hand, the Negro workman is not at all sure as to the sincerity of the unions themselves. The Negro in Chicago yet remembers the waiters' strike some years ago, when colored union workers walked out at the command of the unions and when the strike was settled, the unions did not insist that Negro waiters be given their jobs back along with whites, and as a result, colored men have never been able to get back into some of the hotels even to the present day. The Negro is between "the devil and the deep blue sea." He feels that if he goes into the unions, he will lose the friendship of the employers. He knows that if he does not, he is going to be met with the bitter antagonism of the unions. With the exception of statements made by organizers, who cannot be held to accountability because of their minor official connection, no statements have been made by the local union leaders, outside of high sounding, but meaningless, protestations of friendship for the Negro worker. He feels that he has been given promises too long already. In fact, he is "fed up" on them. What he wants are binding statements and guarantees that cannot be broken at will.

With the possible exception of Philadelphia, there is probably no city in America with more of political trickery, chicanery and exploitation than Chicago. Against the united and bitter opposition of every daily newspaper in Chicago, William Hale Thompson was elected again as mayor, due as was claimed, to the Negro and German vote. While it is not possible to state that the anti-Thompson element deliberately brought on the riots, yet it is safe to say that they were not averse to its coming. The possibility of such a clash was seen many months before it actually occurred, yet no steps were taken to prevent it. The purpose of this was to secure a two-fold result. First, it would alienate the Negro set from Thompson through a belief that was expected to grow among the colored vote when it was seen that the police force under the direction of the mayor was unable or unwilling to protect the colored people from assault by mobs. Secondly, it would discourage the Negroes from registering and voting and thus eliminate the powerful Negro vote in Chicago. Whether or not this results remains to be seen. In talking with a prominent colored citizen of Chicago, asking why the Negroes supported Thompson so unitedly, his very significant reply was:

"The Negro in Chicago, as in every other part of America, is fighting for the fundamental rights of citizenship. If a candidate for office is wrong on every other public question except this, the Negroes are going to vote for that man, for that is their only way of securing the things they want and that are denied them."

The value of the Negro vote to Thompson can be seen in a glance at the recent election figures. His plurality was 28,000 votes. In the second ward it was 14,000 and in the third, 10,000. The second and third wards constitute most of what is known as the "Black Belt."

The fourth contributing cause was the woeful inefficiency and criminal negligence of the police authorities of Chicago, both prior to and during the riots. Prostitution, gambling and the illicit sale of whisky flourish openly and apparently without any fear whatever of police interference. In a most dangerous statement, State's Attorney Maclay Hoyne, on August 25, declared that the riots were due solely to vice in the second ward. He seemed either to forget or to ignore the flagrant disregard of law and order and even of the common principles of decency in city management existing in many other sections of the city.

All of this tended to contribute to open disregard for law and almost contempt for it. Due either to political "pull" or to reciprocal arrangements, many notorious dives [are] run and policemen are afraid to arrest the proprietors.

During the riots the conduct of the police force as a whole was equally open to criticism. State's Attorney Hoyne openly charged the police with arresting colored rioters and with an unwillingness to arrest white rioters. Those who were arrested were at once released. In one case a colored man who was fair enough to appear to be white was arrested for carrying concealed weapons, together with five white men and a number of colored men. All were taken to a police station; the light colored man and the five whites being put into one cell and the other colored men in another. In a few minutes the light colored man and the five whites were released and their ammunition given back to them with the remark, "You'll probably need this before the night is over."

Fifth on the list is the effect of newspaper publicity concerning Negro crime. With the exception of the *Daily News*, all of the papers of Chicago have played up in prominent style with glaring, prejudice-breeding headlines every crime or suspected crime committed by Negroes. Headlines such as

"Negro Brutally Murders Prominent Citizen," "Negro Robs House" and the like have appeared with alarming frequency and the news articles beneath such headlines have been of the same sort. During the rioting such headlines as "Negro Bandits Terrorize Town," "Rioters Burn 100 Homes—Negroes Suspected of Having Plotted Blaze" appeared.

In the latter case a story was told of witnesses seeing Negroes in automobiles applying torches and fleeing. This was the story given to the press by Fire Attorney John R. McCabe after a casual and hasty survey. Later the office of State Fire Marshal Gamber proved conclusively that the fires were not caused by Negroes, but by whites. As can easily be seen, such newspaper accounts did not tend to lessen the bitterness of feeling between the conflicting groups. Further, many wild and unfounded rumors were published in the press—incendiary and inflammatory to the highest degree. . . .

For a long period prior to the riots, organized gangs of white hoodlums had been perpetrating crimes against Negroes for which no arrests had been made. These gangs in many instances masqueraded under the name of "Athletic and Social Clubs" and later direct connection was shown between them and incendiary fires started during the riots. Colored men, women, and children had been beaten in the parks, most of them in Jackson and Lincoln Parks. In one case a young colored girl was beaten and thrown into a lagoon. In other cases Negroes were beaten so severely that they had to be taken to hospitals. All of these cases had caused many colored people to wonder if they could expect any protection whatever from the authorities. Particularly vicious in their attacks was an organization known locally as "Regan's Colts."

Much has been written and said concerning the housing situation in Chicago and its effect on the racial situation. The problem is a simple one. Since 1915 the colored population of Chicago has more than doubled, increasing in four years from a little over 50,000 to what is now estimated to be between 125,000 and 150,000. Most of them lived in the area bounded by the railroad on the west, 30th Street on the north, 40th Street on the south and Ellis Avenue on the east. Already overcrowded, this so-called "Black Belt" could not possibly hold the doubled colored population. One cannot put ten gallons of water in a five-gallon pail. Although many Negroes had been living in "white" neighborhoods, the increased exodus from the old areas created an hysterical group of persons who formed "Property Owners' Associations" for the purpose of keeping intact white neighborhoods. Prominent among these was the Kenwood-Hyde Park Property Owners' Improvement Association, as well as the Park Manor Improvement Association. Early in June the writer,[2] while in Chicago, attended a private meeting of the first named at the Kenwood Club House, at Lake Park Avenue and 47th Street. Various plans were discussed for keeping the Negroes in "their part of the town," such as securing the discharge of colored persons from positions they held when they attempted to move into "white" neighborhoods, purchasing mortgages of Negroes buying homes and

[2] Walter White, secretary of the NAACP (1933–1955), although admitting to part African ancestry, was blond, blue-eyed, and indistinguishable from white.

ejecting them when mortgages fell due and were unpaid, and many more of the same calibre. The language of many speakers was vicious and strongly prejudicial and had the distinct effect of creating race bitterness.

In a number of cases during the period from January, 1918, to August, 1919, there were bombings of colored homes and houses occupied by Negroes outside of the "Black Belt." During this period no less than twenty bombings took place, yet only two persons have been arrested and neither of the two has been convicted, both cases being continued.

Finally, the new spirit aroused in Negroes by their war experiences enters into the problem. From Local Board No. 4, embracing the neighborhood in the vicinity of State and 35th Streets, containing over 20,000 inhabitants of which fully ninety per cent are colored, over 9,000 men registered and 1,850 went to camp. These men, with their new outlook on life, injected the same spirit of independence into their companions, a thing that is true of many other sections of America. One of the greatest surprises to many of those who came down to "clean out the niggers" is that these same "niggers" fought back. Colored men saw their own kind being killed, heard of many more and believed that their lives and liberty were at stake. In such a spirit most of the fighting was done.

Detroit, Mich. (1917)

17]   Adjustment Problems of Newcomers

During the past twelve months the colored population of Detroit has increased by about 100 per cent through migration. The experience of this city in the absorption of this large new population of Negro citizens and the program of work for its assimilation springing, as it did, from actual experience rather than speculation may be of use to other communities which face a similar problem. The subject may, perhaps, best be considered under the separate headings of employment, housing, recreation, crime prevention, cooperation and aids to efficiency.

The first prerequisite in the task of organizing a local community is the establishment of a vocational bureau. In the past, when labor agencies brought the majority of Negroes who came north, the problem of employment was simple. They were assured of jobs before they arrived. But now the majority of immigrants come without such inducement. They come in larger numbers and at all times of the year, when the demand for labor is strong and when it is slack. Moreover, the majority come knowing nothing of the city which is to be their home and unacquainted with any of its citizens. Impossible as it may seem, it is not uncommon for factories in one part of the city to be crying for labor while many of these strange Negroes wander about other parts of

SOURCE: Forrester B. Washington, "The Detroit Newcomer's Greeting," *The Survey*, July 14, 1917, pp. 333–5. [Forrester B. Washington was director of the Detroit Urban League.—Ed.]

the city to find employment. This situation is fraught with danger because in a few days idling about the city in search of a job the immigrant may come into contact with conditions and people whose influence is demoralizing and may destroy his chance of ever becoming a useful citizen. The immigrant needs more bolstering up in the first week than at any future time. Until he gets his first pay at the end of two weeks, he finds it difficult to get anybody to trust him. He is apt to become a charity seeker and a dependent.

Moreover, in a rapidly growing industrial center like Detroit, where the demand for houses is greater than the supply, few landlords will rent a house or room to a prospective tenant who has no job. The vocational bureau should strive to make itself acquainted with every possible industrial opening for Negroes in the city and, on the other hand, make its presence widely known so that the immigrant Negro will be directed to it immediately on arrival. The Detroit League on Urban Conditions among Negroes, therefore, has not been content merely with locating vacant jobs but has approached manufacturers of all kinds through distribution of literature and personal visits and has been successful during the last twelve months in placing 1,000 Negroes in employment other than unskilled labor. It has made itself known to immigrants by cards of direction placed in the hands of Negro employes about railway stations and intends, as soon as its funds permit, to station a capable, level-headed representative at each of the railway stations of Detroit to direct Negro immigrants to the league's office or to other responsible individuals and societies who will look after their welfare. It has persuaded the proprietor of a local moving picture theater, which is a great gathering place for colored newcomers, to run lantern slides nightly announcing that employment and other services can be secured free at the office of the league.

In order to care for the women and girls who are beginning to appear in appreciable numbers, five cigar manufacturers in the city were induced to experiment in employing only colored help. To solve the difficult problem of the first week's board, the league has arranged with certain factories a system of checks issued to guarantee payment for bills incurred at restaurants and boarding houses. Some direct arrangements previously made between certain factories and boarding-house keepers resulted in exploitation of the immigrant by the latter.

The establishment of a bureau of investigation and information regarding housing comes next in importance. The character of the houses into which Negro immigrants go has a direct effect on their health, their morals and their efficiency. The rents charged determine whether the higher wages received in the North are real or only apparent, whether the change in environment has been beneficial or detrimental. The tendency is to exploit the Negro immigrant in this particular. Rents charged him in Detroit have risen by from 50 to 200 per cent in one year. He is forced into a district inhabited by colored people where housing accommodation is inadequate for those already there. The proximity of the colored district in most northern cities to the center is responsible for the imposition of the vice district upon the Negro. This bureau should, therefore, scour the city for every available house, tenement or room inside or outside the recognized Negro district. It should make also a thorough investigation of comparative rents charged Negroes and white and give the findings the fullest publicity. The bureau should constantly remind employers of Negro labor that it is to their advantage to see that the Negro is well housed and that, if nobody else will build, it is good business for them to do so.

The Detroit Urban League has induced one of the largest foundries to build low-priced homes for its colored employes near the plant. It also has somewhat relieved the housing problem by the purchase of leases from the proprietresses of a number of disorderly houses which were closed by the police. In each case the league persuaded some manufacturer to take over the lease, and in this way a large number of colored families were accommodated. It also keeps a list of empty houses and has been surprised to find how many of them are not listed by commercial real estate agents. It uses the daily and Negro press in appeals for more notifications. A list of furnished rooms also is kept and immigrants are kept away from those connected with disorderly houses. Lists of these rooms are furnished to factories.

With the shorter working hours, recreation is more important for the Negro in the North than in the South. On the other hand, he is beset by many vicious attractions entirely new to him, and there is not the restraining influence of his family, friends and those that know him. I am sorry to say, but it is true, he does not receive a warm welcome from the great majority of colored citizens of the better class in the city to which he migrates. While they try to decide whether his coming is a benefit or an injury to them, he gets a royal welcome from another element of the Negro community—the saloon keeper, the pool-room proprietor, the owner of gambling club and disorderly house.

The only way to counteract these vicious influences is to provide the immigrant Negro with wholesome recreation that will satisfy his natural instinct for active amusement and society of his own kind. This is no simple affair and can be met by existing institutions in only a few cities. The hard-working laborer recently from a rural section of Alabama cannot be attracted away from saloon or pool-room with art lectures or literary forums or even the facilities of the average Y.M.C.A. The first demand he makes of recreation is that it be active and practical, to a certain extent primitive. If he does not get it under wholesome conditions, he will seek it under evil ones.

The Detroit league some time ago inaugurated a ten-cent newcomers' community dance, held every Tuesday in a public school in the heart of the Negro district. A Young Negroes' Progressive Association has helped in promoting this dance as well as in all other plans for adjusting the newcomers to the city. A committee of the association handed printed cards about the street where most of the immigrants collect and placed them in the hands of newcomers, inviting them to the community dance, where another committee welcomes them—the rougher the type, the heartier the welcome. This committee also introduces the newcomer to the more desirable people present who have been longer in Detroit. Certain dances are introduced which are calculated to lead to better acquaintance. The school auditorium has already been outgrown, and the use of the gymnasium of a neighboring high school has been promised for these dances.

The league also develops athletic features for the immigrants, especially bas-

189

ket-ball. The first colored basket-ball team, not a member of which was a native of Detroit, last winter played against strong white teams and lost only one game. It has played against colored teams as far away as Pittsburgh. Teams have been created in the various industrial plants of the ctiy, and the recreation commissioner was so pleased with the progress made that he offered to persuade certain business men to donate a silver cup for the team which wins the supremacy of the league.

Camp-fire girls, mostly the children of newcomers, also have been organized. There are only twenty-one regular members—the regulations do not permit a larger number in one camp. All the expenses for these girls, such as rent, refreshments, etc., are paid by the Young Negroes' Progressive Association from the proceeds of the community dance. It is very encouraging to find these young men take upon themselves the responsibility of providing decent recreation for young girls of their own age.

A department for the suppression of crime is necessary in a program for the assimilation of the Negro immigrant. The increased crime among Negroes has had two bad results: it has made both white and native colored citizens believe that the southern Negro is more criminal by nature than his northern brother; and it has created a general distrust against all Negroes. The assistance of the local police should be solicited from the outset. It should be impressed upon them that they must not, as they are prone to do, let matters go from bad to worse in a colored community until conditions are so acute that drastic and unusual measures are necessary. The appointment of colored detectives should be urged to filter from the community as soon as possible the inevitable floaters, crooks, bums and adventurers who are parts of every hegira.

The league has persuaded the police commissioners to appoint a special officer, selected by the league, to work entirely with the newcomers. It is his duty to mingle with crowds on the streets where the newcomers congregate and urge them not to make a nuisance of themselves by blockading sidewalks, boisterous behavior and the like. He is also provided with cards directing newcomers to the office of the league when in need of employment. The league itself keeps a close watch on the Negro underworld of Detroit and immediately apprises the police when dives are developed especially to prey on the immigrant.

Much strength can be added to the program and much energy saved by enlisting the aid of every possible organization in the city whose functions can in any way be construed as touching on Negro migration. The urban league found the Board of Commerce exceedingly willing to cooperate in a movement for the investigation and improvement of working conditions of Negro employes in the various manufaturing plants in the city. The Board of Health gave considerable assistance in obtaining better and more sanitary housing conditions. The aid of several mothers' clubs among the colored women was enlisted to instruct immigrant mothers in the proper diet and clothing for children in a northern climate. From the outset, the aim was not only to put each immigrant in a decent home but also to connect him with some church. Many times the churches have reciprocated with considerable material as well as spiritual assistance.

190

Adjustment Problems of Newcomers

But the greatest cooperation received has been that of the Young Negroes' Progressive Association to which reference has already been made. This is a body of thirty-four young colored men, most of them attending the various schools and colleges about Detroit. They have been the finest possible agent in the development of all the different activities.

In the adjustment of the Negro, a definite place must be given to the development of industrial efficiency. This is perhaps the most important feature in the program; the welfare of the Negro in his new environment depends upon the opinion that the community has of him. If the community can be convinced that the Negro is and always will be a business asset, we need not worry much about his housing, employment and recreation. But the Negro has got to convince the captains of industry. This he can only do by developing to a maximum his industrial efficiency. The more trades and occupations Negroes become familiar with, the more efficient they will be as a race, and the greater an asset to the community. Therefore the league has endeavored to get them into as many different kinds of employment as possible. It also uses every opportunity to develop individual efficiency by calling the attention of Negro employes to the fact that they must be punctual, zealous and ambitious in their work: These points are always emphasized when a Negro is sent to a job.

In pursuance of this object the league, with the assistance of the progressive association, is carrying on a movement which, I think, is unique. Representatives of the two organizations visit the various factories where large numbers of Negroes are employed and talk to them during the noon hour on the necessity of creating the best possible impression at the present time so that they may be certain of retaining their jobs in the future. At the same time, the speakers circulate these cards:

WHY HE FAILED

He watched the clock.
He was always behindhand.
He asked too many questions.
His stock excuse was "I forgot."
He wasn't ready for the next step.
He did not put his heart in his work.
He learned nothing from his blunders.
He was contented to be a second-rater.
He didn't learn that the best part of his salary
    was not in his pay envelope—SUCCESS.

Note: By not paying strict attention to the above
    details you may not be able to keep your
    job after the war is ended and foreign
    labor is again available.

Detroit, Mich. (1926)

18] Black Employment After World War I

In 1920 Detroit had a population of 993,678 of whom 40,838 or about 4% were Negroes. Of these 18,472 were males over 21 years of age and 12,107 were females over 21 years of age. On the basis of a previous study (made in 1919 by F. B. Washington) it is a conservative estimate that there were 16,-000 Negroes in the industries of Detroit. They were engaged in 36 skilled occupations, 79 semi-skilled occupations and 66 unskilled occupations. About 50% of the skilled jobs were in the automobile factories.

Since 1920 the Negro population of Detroit has more than doubled. The 1925 census showed there were 81,831 Negroes in the city; 30,948 adult males, 26,009 adult females. The results of the present survey give the basis for an estimate that there are between 25,000 and 30,000 Negroes employed by Detroit establishments today.

Questionnaires were sent to most of the Detroit business establishments. With one exception exact figures were given as to the number of Negroes employed, one large manufacturing firm giving only an approximation.

Returns from Employer's Questionnaires

Total questionnaires sent to Detroit firms	276
Total replies received	151
Total firms employing Negroes (out of 151)	120
Total number of Negroes employed	
(one approximation)	21,571
Males	21,004
Females	498
Sex not given	69

Processes Employing Negroes

Manufacturing and Foundry (one firm gave an approximation)	16,549
Public Service	2,745
Personal Service	893
Building Trades	675
Department Stores, etc.	295
Miscellaneous	414
TOTAL	21,571

SOURCE: Mayor's Inter-racial Committee, *The Negro in Detroit*, Vol. 1, Detroit: The Detroit Bureau of Governmental Research, Inc., 1926, pp. 2–11.

Black Employment After World War I

Firms Employing Negroes

NAME OF COMPANY	NUMBERS OF NEGROES EMPLOYED MALES	FEMALES	PERCENT OF TOTAL FORCE
Ford Motor Co. (Approx) (Fordson)	6,000		10
Ford Highland Park	4,000		10
Dept. of Public Works	2,200		40
Dodge Brothers	850		3.5
Studebaker Corporation	530		10
Packard Motor Co.	500		—
U.S. Post Office	454	31	16.4
Detroit & Clev. Nav. Co.	438		39
Morgan & Wright	393		12
Cadillac Motor Car Co.	300		5
Mich. Copper & Brass Co.	275		30
U.S. Aluminum Co.	230		65
Murray Body Co.	215		4
Midland Steel Products Co.	200		35
Hudson Motor Car Co.	200		1.2
Detroit Steel Products Co.	180		25
Detroit Steel Casting Co.	179		54
H. G. Christian Co.	179		27.8
Whitehead & Kales Co.	175		20
Parker-Webb Co.	172		36
Chevrolet Motor Co.	159		3.5
Buhl Malleable Co.	140		36
(Name withheld)	140		14
McCord Radiator Mfg. Co.	125		10
Detroit Seamless Steel Tube	125		33.5
Everett-Winters Co.	121		58.7
Albert A. Albrect Co.	120		15
American Radiator Co. of Mich.	118		20
W. E. Wood	118		27.9
Tryant-Detwiler	111		43.7
Riley Stokes Corp.	105		32
Hupp Motor Car Co.	100		12
U.S. Radiator Corp.	100		33.3
Hotel Tuller	90	70	35
Detroit Athletic Club	80	20	70
Chrysler Corp.	75		1.5
Bohn Aluminum & Brass Corp.	75		14.3
Detroit Lubricator Co.	75		6
Federal Mogul Corp.	75		100
Hammond-Standish Co.	70		16
Mich. Smelting & Refining Co.	70		15
Webster Hall	67	8	40
Timken Detroit Axle	65		2.5
Chicago Pneumatic Tool Co.	57	6	1.5
Detroit Stove Works	55		5.5
Detroit Forging Co.	50		25
Burroughs Adding Machine	46		1
Lincoln Motor Co.	40		1
Bowen Products Co.	40		—

NAME OF COMPANY	NUMBERS OF NEGROES EMPLOYED MALES	FEMALES	PERCENT OF TOTAL FORCE
Crowley-Milner Co.	40	35	5
Fisher Body Corp.	38	2	1
Hotel Palmetto °	35		33.3
Peoples Outfitting Co.	34	9	8.7
Capital Brass Works	30		8
Atlas Foundry Co.	28		8
Union Belt Co.	26		12
Detroit Edison Co.	25		.3
Michigan Valve & Foundry	25		10
County Offices	24	4	0
D. J. Healey Shops °	20		2
Evening News Assn.	18	2	70
A. W. Kutsche & Co.	18		35.3
Peninsular Stove Co.	17		3
Long Mfg. Co.	16		3
Pemberthy Injector Co.	16		5
Gemmer Mfg. Co.	14		2
J. L. Hudson Co.	13	92	2.9
Ternstedt Mfg. Co.	12		.3
Standard Peninsula Brawler	11		10
Newcomb-Endicott	11	22	2.5
Custodian Service	11	15	44.8
Eureka Vacuum Cleaner Co.	10		1
Corrick Brothers	10		78
Michigan Bell Telephone Co. °	10		.007
Madison-Lenox	10	65	90
Detroit Range Boiler & Steel	8		10
Ireland & Mathews Mfg. Co.	8		2.5
S. S. Kresge Co. (Store 1)	7	10	5
Paige Detroit Motor Car Co.	6		.5–1
Diamond Power Spec. Corp.	6		.5
Great Lakes Eng. Wks.	6		1
Schneider Brothers	6		15
Himelhocks Bros. & Co.	6	6	4
Times Publishing Co.	6		—
Forest Cleaners & Dyers	6	35	40
Rickenbacker Motor Co.	5		—
Weller Laundry Co.	5	60	80
Cable Draper Baking Co.	5		1
Hotel Lincoln	4	22	45
Hotel Brookins °	4		66.6
American Brass & Iron Co.	4		10
Demby Motor Truck Corp.	3		25
Richmond-Backus Co.	3	1	2
U.S. Customs	3		22
Parke, Davis & Co.	2		.01
Banner Laundry Co.	2		—
White Eagle Laundry	2		6
Gregory, Mayor & Thom	2		—

° Sex not given.

Black Employment After World War I

NAME OF COMPANY	NUMBERS OF NEGROES EMPLOYED MALES	FEMALES	PERCENT OF TOTAL FORCE
American Lady Corset Co.	2		—
Detroit Graphite Co.	2		—
Bureau of Immigration	2	1	—
Russell Wheel & Foundry Co.	1		—
Terns Coal & Lumber Co.	1		—
Geo. G. Martin	1		33.3
Cross Laundry Co.	1	2	3
TOTAL	21,004	498	Sex uncertain 69

There were some alleged cases of firms discontinuing the use of colored labor. Most of these proved on investigation to be myths, or if true were attributable to the normal reduction in working force, or to the reinstatement of returned soldiers.

. . . The majority of Negroes are found in the processes involving unskilled manual labor. Many employers felt that all the Negro could do was manual labor, and many gave him no opportunity to get into any other kind of a job. Suffice to say, the Negro is not only a good manual laborer, but he has proven his ability to do more skilled jobs.

Although the great bulk of Negroes employed in Detroit are still used in unskilled positions, there are many in skilled positions in industry.

In three large automobile plants employing a total of about 11,000 Negroes, the Negro workman was found in practically every department. He is given an opportunity to make progress if he studies and shows himself capable. In these plants some colored men have supervisory jobs, although as yet the number of colored supervisors is not proportionate to the number of colored men hired.

There are many skilled Negroes in the various trade groups such as carpenters, bricklayers, masons, plasterers, stationary engineers, structural iron workers, molders, auto mechanics, machinists, etc. Then there are the larger classes of skilled or semi-skilled such as clerks, barbers, motormen, chauffeurs, waiters, chefs, and so on. Add to this the large force of skilled and semi-skilled employed on skilled jobs in the automobile industry and receiving a fairly high wage, and Detroit's quota of Negro workers who are distinctly above the level of manual labor is considerable. A study of the returns on the questionnaires sent out indicates that about 35% of the Negro employees would come under the class of skilled or semi-skilled workmen. . . .

In the Public Service in and around Detroit there were 2,745 Negroes employed with a salary range of from $12,000 (paid to at least one Negro head of a department), down to $1200 per year. There are 486 Negroes employed in the Post Office, of whom 31 are women; 28 in the County offices of whom 4 are women. The work in these departments is that of accountant, clerks, carriers, etc. and the unskilled work of janitress, window washers, etc.

In the Department of Public Works there are some 2200 Negroes employed at an average wage of $26.40 per week, with the exception of garbage truck drivers and collectors who receive $6.50 per day (members of Garbage Handlers Union). Most of the work in this department is unskilled labor such as street cleaning, repairing, etc.

In the Bureau of Immigration there are two Negro border patrolmen who receive $1800 per year and one or two charwomen at 45¢ per hour.

In the Customs Service there are two Negroes employed as clerks at $2000 a year, and one janitor at $480.

In the United States Treasury Department (custodial service) of Detroit there are 16 Negroes employed, of whom five are women, mostly in the unskilled positions.

The Public Service seems to be a place where the Negro is entrenched and making progress. This is due no doubt to the fact that these positions are based on Civil Service Examinations and naturally he cannot very well be discriminated against. . . .

Chicago, Ill. (1923)

19]   Blacks in Industries

. . . The problem of the colored worker in Chicago is a complex one. His industrial background would hardly permit automatic adjustment to a situation so new and so different from anything in his previous experience. His adjustment to plant and shop, then, was attended with difficulty requiring patience and intelligence. He had the barrier of race prejudice to overcome which sometimes resulted in his undoing. Wartime production gave him a place—did he keep it? In most instances yes, there can be no doubt that he lost positions of skill in one place only to gain them in others. For instance, skilled positions were lost to colored men in the steel mills in the period of depression following the armistice, but were recovered during the steel strike of a year later. In the Stock Yards colored men also lost positions of skill only to recover them during the strike of 1920–1921 and gain others they never had. The great strike of 1919 and 1920 headed by John Kilkuski was lost by Polish workers, but resulted in promotions from unskilled to skilled positions in the plants of the International Harvester Company, Corn Products & Refining Company, and many other industries which are still held by colored men.

Today the grey iron industry, insofar as molding is concerned, is practically all in the hands of colored men. Foundry after foundry has introduced the colored molder and when the white molder objects and leaves, the colored man gets control and keeps it. Colored foremen over men of their own race are not uncommon.

The strike of the Stock Yards Union offered a chance for occupational advancement to colored men which was accepted. Carpenters, electricians, and steam fitters positions were given colored men, but were soon lost, in most in-

SOURCE: William L. Evans, "The Negro in Chicago Industries," *Opportunity*, February 1923, pp. 15–16. [William L. Evans was industrial secretary of the Chicago Urban League in the 1920's.—Ed.]

stances, to returning strikers. Employers gave reason for this as lack of experience on the part of the colored men. A few, however, have held on so that the result is not a complete loss to the colored worker. The Landis Award Committee sought him wherever he could be found. Bricklayers, carpenters, hoisting engineers, cement workers, and other tradesmen were placed with the committee. Colored tradesmen may now be seen working side by side with whites in all sections of Chicago—in some cases as union workers, in others, on the open-shop plan, while previously he worked only as a member of the Building Laborers and Hod Carriers Union.

The recent strike of the railroad shop employees has, like all the others, brought advantages to colored workmen. Skilled positions formerly closed to him are now his. While no figures are available, it is known that many are working as boiler-makers, steam-fitters, carpenters and painters in shops in Chicago.

Similar advantages to the colored workman may be shown from every industrial dispute where colored persons are not members of the striking unions. There is no reason to conclude that the Negro is by choice a strikebreaker any more than other men, but the fact is that in most instances where he has risen above the ranks of common laborer, the strike has furnished the medium thru which his advancement is accomplished. To our notion, the policy of white unionists is more to blame than all else. White unionists must sooner or later realize that their own security consists in the acceptance on equal terms of the colored workman. When he is a member of the union, the colored man is as loyal as any other, but like others he must be shown that his best interest is in the union rather than out.

. . . . .

Employers did not take the recent depression period as an opportunity to drive the colored men out of industry. When it became necessary to reduce working forces, colored men suffered only a proportionate "lay-off." A few instances were recorded on the other hand which showed an increase of colored employees. Early in 1922 officials of the stock yards reported from 25 to 30 per cent increase in colored employes, while recent reports show this proportion remaining about the same.

In September, a conference was held in the office of one of the large steel plants on the subject of increasing its colored working force. Here the increase was from less than 100 in 1914 to 800 in 1922. There are several others which will register similar increases. On the other hand, we know of not a single instance in which an industry has been lost to colored workers, with the exception of Sears Roebuck and Company and Montgomery Ward & Company where 2,000 colored girls were employed as clerks, typists and operators. These two firms have not recovered from the depression period. One promises to reemploy its colored force if business justifies the re-opening of its branch office. As neither company has re-opened its branch office, it cannot be said that these companies have been lost. At least, the colored workers have not been replaced, which leaves the decision to some future day.

Colored women have gained even more than the men. They have not only held all gains they made during the past four years in industry, but have successfully invaded and held new territory. Today they are a real factor in the needle trades and must be counted by the thousand. Though segregated, they are working in every branch of the trade from overalls to costly silk gowns. They have proven competent in the arts of beading and embroidering. They are decorators of parchment shades. Three hundred and fifty may be found in a single plant, while many plants have more than a hundred in skilled occupations. They are both union and non-union. Hundreds of others are in the packing industry on skilled and unskilled jobs. One large foundry employs 50 as core makers where they work without friction with twice as many white women.

The garment workers unions accept colored women without discrimination and have even made feeble attempts to unionize them. Most of the interracial shops are union. Colored women are generally non-union. They have not, as yet, learned the value of collective bargaining and are generally underpaid. Often their apprentice weekly wage is $7.00 to $9.00, at which they are unfairly held for unreasonable periods by unscrupulous employers. There is not much doubt that colored women, in most cases, represent "cheap" labor. Whenever they are well-paid, they are cheerful and dependable, when working for less than a living wage, they are restless and unreliable. In a certain factory in which the management had declared their colored girls unreliable, it was found that if a girl ever reached the earning power of $15.00 per week, she usually became a satisfactory worker. Fifteen dollars a week is the minimum upon which a woman living in Chicago may be self-supporting. Thus their unreliability is easily explained. Those falling below fifteen dollars produce a high and expensive turn-over. The dependability then of colored girl workers depends, at least in some measure, on her chance to earn a living wage. Is this not true of all workers regardless of sex or race?

Many employers are beginning to see that industrial efficiency is not confined to the white race. Proof of this is shown in the thousands of colored workers and the demand for more which cannot be met. Even while writing this article there comes a call for 75 young colored women to work as merchandise inspectors in one of Chicago's largest department stores. Another company manufacturing spring cushions has increased its colored women employees from 25 to 350 in four years and has recently engaged a well-trained colored woman as welfare secretary with supervisory power over all its colored workers and announces its intention of increasing its present force from 350 to 600 in the near future. These instances serve to demonstrate the colored woman's possibilities in industry. . . .

Finally we would say that Negroes have taken advantage of their opportunities in industry at least in Chicago. They have retained successfully most of the gains made during war times, steadily advancing from unskilled to skilled positions in spite of handicaps which are not known to white workers. . . .

Cleveland, Ohio (1924)

20]   Migrants in Industry

The *New York Economic World* reprints in its issue of May 3, 1924, an article published by the Union Trust Company of Cleveland, Ohio,[1] giving the experience of manufacturing concerns of that city with the southern migrants. The article, written by John B. Abell, is based on an inquiry carried on among industrial employers of the Greater Cleveland district.

Migration from the South has been constantly increasing, "until in 1923 there were more than 43,000 Southern negroes who settled in Cleveland alone, as against 2,000 for the year 1880." To a large extent the negroes are now coming from the southern cities, not from the agricultural regions. They are a mixed group, including the good and the bad, the industrious and the lazy, the capable and the inefficient, much as any other cross section of the population would show. "However, they check up well with the average for other races who come as immigrants to help make up the great American industrial life." From the employer's point of view they have one great advantage over the foreign immigrants in that they understand the language and the basic ideals of the country.

The survey on which the article is based covered 75 of the larger employers of the district, and the findings of this inquiry were checked up by an investigation of conditions in 20 large factories of the city. The author dwells particularly on the questions of the steadiness of the negro as a worker and his fitness for skilled work.

As to steadiness, the first and most persistent complaint against the colored worker is that he is unreliable and shiftless, prone to be absent on slight occasion, and fond of changing from one employer to another. Investigation, however, fails to show that this charge is generally true.

To be sure, there has been a large turnover in some of the plants where these colored men have been employed. In some instances firms report that where 25 per cent of their workers are negroes, the turnover among them has sometimes been as high as 75 per cent of the turnover for the entire plant. On the other hand, an equal number of firms state that the turnover has never, even at the start, been greater than for other racial groups.

It is suggested that where the turnover is large there are several reasons, quite apart from the character of the colored workers, to account for it. The newcomer has often been obliged to take the first job he could get, and naturally, if this does not suit him, he leaves it as soon as he can get something

Source: "The Southern Negro in Cleveland Industries," *Monthly Labor Review*, Vol. XIX, No. 1, July 1924, pp. 41–44.
[1] It has not been possible to locate the original article.

better. Also the employers, it is said, have in general taken little pains to try to fit the colored migrant into the place for which he is qualified. They have taken on negroes when they were hard pressed for help and put them at "what might be termed turnover work—work not fitted to the man's training, and upon which there would be a constant change of employees under any circumstances."

As an incidental proof of the tendency of the negro worker to hold on to his job, the results are cited of an inquiry made by a local manufacturer who employed both races.

Picking 200 colored and a like number of white workers at random, he found that 150 of the negroes had savings accounts, while only 35 of the other employees had such reserve resources. This condition, he asserts, shows that the colored man must have been fairly regular at work in order to lay aside weekly earnings.

In another plant, employing 445 colored people out of a total of a little more than 1,000 it was found that 140 colored men were putting money in shop savings accounts. Many of them reported that they were doing this in order to purchase homes here in the North—or in other words, that they might establish themselves permanently as a part of the community.

The actual situation as to turnover for 15 plants was found to be as follows:

Per cent of Employees who are Colored and per cent of Total Turnover due to Colored Workers in 15 Cleveland Plants

NATURE OF PLANT	PER CENT OF TOTAL EMPLOYEES WHO ARE COLORED	PER CENT OF TOTAL TURNOVER DUE TO COLORED WORKERS	NATURE OF PLANT	PER CENT OF TOTAL EMPLOYEES WHO ARE COLORED	PER CENT OF TOTAL TURNOVER DUE TO COLORED WORKERS
Metal working	50	35	Paints	15	20
Chemical	15	15	Castings	25	30
Railroad labor	40	80	Foundry	25	15
Foundry	50	20	"	30	20
Chemical	25	35	Machinery,		
Steel mill	10	60	castings	35	10
Machinery	10	75	Foundry	50	20
Foundry	35	55	"	55	60

The experience of these 15 firms is typical of those included in the survey of the 75 plants.

Accepting these plants as typical of general conditions in Greater Cleveland, we find the average factory employment among them for the negroes is $32\frac{1}{3}$ per cent of the total, while the average per cent of turnover among them is $36\frac{2}{3}$ per cent. Thus, in spite of the fact that the negro in industry is a comparatively new factor in this territory, he is but slightly more responsible for the shifting of jobs than is the native of the district or the foreign born, who on the whole has had a longer time to adapt himself to local conditions.

Turning to the question of the future possibilities of negro labor, the author states that it is almost impossible to find any authoritative answer. Some employers consider that the negro's capacity is strictly limited and that he can not make good on skilled work; others prefer him to members of any other race. In considering the opportunities and the negro's ability to take advantage of them, it must be remembered that in general, on arriving in the North, he has had to start at the very bottom of the industrial ladder, and that any progress he may make is due both to his own ability and to the willingness of his employer to recognize that ability.

So far, the railroads have offered very little opportunity for negroes, except as track workers, in which capacity they are said to prove highly satisfactory. A few have worked into skilled and semiskilled jobs in roundhouses. "The number here will increase as rapidly as race prejudice can be overcome, for the colored men are making good."

In hotels, restaurants, and the like, opportunities are very limited, and few of the southern negroes have gone into this work.

The greatest number of the southern negroes have gone into foundry mills and machine-working plants. A number of them were taken on as war emergency help, and many of these were dismissed at the close of the special need, though in some plants the foreign workers were dismissed and the negroes retained, as being more desirable.

Twelve foundries or plants primarily engaged in foundry work report that from 10 to 60 per cent of their plant employees are colored. The average for these plants is 33 per cent negro workers. An equal number of important machinery factories report but a slightly smaller average of all employees as being colored migrants.

In all but one of the foundries it was found that the negroes have advanced from labor to semiskilled work, and finally to skilled positions. . . . One such plant reports that there is no opportunity for the negro beyond semiskilled work. This is not due so much to his inability to qualify, but rather to a distaste of other workers to working alongside of him.

Practically all of the machine-working plants stated that the negro is finding his place in nearly all factory jobs, from common labor up through foremanships and mechanical maintenance work. They say that while some of the migrants have not made good on certain skilled work, that it is not due to racial traits but rather to lack of fitness of the particular individual.

The suggestion is advanced that the one place in production work to which the negro does not seem to be so well fitted as the white is the semiskilled or routine machine work. In Cleveland, at least, the newcomers "have landed in large numbers and for longer times on either straight labor work or the highly skilled trades." Several examples are given of the ability which negroes have displayed on skilled work, and in what might be called professional lines, such as industrial chemistry, for instance. On the whole, the conclusion is reached that the negro is likely to be a permanent and an important factor in the industries of Cleveland.

While it would be pure guess to state now what positions may or may not be efficiently handled in the future by the Southern negro, experience thus far has established the fact that they have not as a race failed in any class of work upon which they were given a fair trial. Although during the last five years their range of opportunity has been greatly widened, their field is still limited because of lack of understanding by both employer and employee, and in some instances because of the colored prejudice.

It is almost unanimously agreed that during the time they have been used to any great extent in northern industry, the negroes have made as rapid progress to better jobs as have immigrants who came in on the same footing. It is generally acknowledged the negro is no longer an emergency factor in industrial employment, but that he is here to stay, with the probability that his numbers will increase as years go by.

PART FOUR

THE DEPRESSION
AND THE NEW DEAL

INTRODUCTION

The economic boom of the 1920's had produced among blacks of the urban industrial North, especially for the middle class, their highest standard of living. But the Depression hit the North more quickly and with greater intensity than the less industrialized South and, added to continuing discrimination, it had a shattering effect on northern blacks. Black unemployment in cities ran two to three times as high as that of whites, and those blacks who did get jobs were paid an average of 30% less than whites. The black professional, proprietary, and managerial groups, economically dependent on their own people, also suffered a catastrophic financial decline. Some lost their property; others sought to hold on to it by taking in roomers, which resulted in a rapid deterioration of middle-class housing. Other consequences were a modification in the structure of the black family, with an increasing number of women as heads of families, and a new political militance, expressed partly through boycotts of white businesses to end employment discrimination against blacks and generate new jobs. The contemporary findings of E. Franklin Frazier (Document 1) have generally been confirmed by subsequent research.

CITIES

General Aspects

1] Northern City Blacks and the Depression (1938)

. . . concerning the effects of the depression on [black] newcomers to modern industrial society very little systematic information is available. In this paper, an attempt will be made to bring together and interpret the available information which we have been able to secure from various sources.

. . . In fourteen of the sixteen northern and western cities included in the unemployment census of 1931, the percentage of Negroes unemployed was higher than that of either native or foreign-born whites. This was true for women as well as men. For example, in Chicago, 40.3 per cent of the employable Negro men and 55.4 of the women were reported unemployed, whereas only 24.6 per cent of the foreign-born white men and 12.0 per cent of the foreign-born white women; and 23.4 per cent of the native white men and 16.9 per cent of native white women were reported unemployed. Klein, in his recent survey of Pittsburgh, reported that in February 1934, "48 per cent of the employable Negroes were entirely without employment . . . while only 31.1 per cent of the potential white workers were unemployed." . . . this situation was [also] generally true in regard to Negro women. . . .

Although there is a rather general but uncritical acceptance of the belief that the "Negro is the last to be hired and the first to be fired," it is difficult to make any generalization concerning practices during the depression in northern cities. In a paper read before the Conference on the Economic Status of the Negro held in Washington, D.C., in May 1933, it was reported that in the meat packing industry, "Reductions in the working force due to the depression have in general left these Negro workers in relatively larger proportions than other workers." On the other hand, Dr. Joseph H. Willits of the University of Pennsylvania, in a study of unemployment among several groups in Philadel-

Source: E. Franklin Frazier, "Some Effects of the Depression on the Negro in Northern Cities," *Science and Society*, Fall 1938, pp. 489–99.]E. Franklin Frazier, 1894–1962, was a prolific and controversial Howard-based sociologist and historian. —Ed.]

Northern City Blacks and the Depression

phia, found the following situation during the years 1929 to 1933. "In 1929 when 9.0 per cent of all white employables were unemployed, 15.7 per cent of the Negroes were unemployed. In 1930 it was 13.8 per cent for whites and 19.4 per cent for Negroes; in 1931 it was 24.1 per cent for whites and 35.0 per cent for Negroes; and in 1932 it was 39.7 per cent for whites and 56.0 per cent for Negroes." It is likely that these figures are typical of northern cities since the vast majority of Negro workers are employed on jobs which are generally susceptible to fluctuations in industry.

We are on much surer ground when we consider the incidence of relief. When the unemployment relief census was taken in 1933, there was in New York, Chicago, Philadelphia, and Detroit, a total of 78,027 Negro families on relief or 32.5 per cent of the Negro families in these four cities. Measured in terms of population, New York with 23.9 per cent and Detroit with 27.6 per cent had smaller percentages of Negroes on relief than Chicago and Philadelphia in each of which cities 34 per cent of the Negro population was on relief. The situation was even worse in Pittsburgh and Cleveland each with 43 per cent and Akron, Ohio, with 67 per cent of the Negro population on relief. After the census of 1933 was taken, the situation in these cities undoubtedly became worse. For example, by February 1935, "practically three out of every five Negroes in Allegheny County," where Pittsburgh is located, were on the relief rolls. A study of the situation in the Harlem area of New York City in 1935 revealed that 24,293 or 43.2 per cent of 56,157 Negro families were receiving relief. In addition to these relief families, 7,560 unattached Negro men had registered with the Emergency Relief Bureau over a period of four years.

. . . as the depression lifted momentarily, Negroes were not reabsorbed into industry to the same extent as white workers. . . .

Negro workers who have not lost their jobs have suffered a reduction in earning power. In Kiser's study of 2,061 Negro households in a section of Harlem in New York City, it was found that the median income of skilled workers had declined from $1,955 in 1929 to $1,003 in 1932 or 48.7 per cent. The decline in the incomes of semi-skilled and unskilled workers was slightly less or 43 per cent. This study also gave information on the effect of the depression on the earning power of the Negro middle class which had rapidly emerged in response to the varied demands of large Negro communities in northern cities. It was found that among the white collar workers, who comprised 16 per cent of the households studied, "the income decreases were 35 per cent in the professional class, 44 per cent in the proprietary class and 37 per cent among clerical and kindred workers." First hand observations and reports of college students indicate that this was representative of the Negro middle class throughout the North. Their savings and incomes, and investments from business, which gave this class a favored position in the Negro community, were largely wiped out and even Negro doctors were forced to seek relief.

Concerning the effects of the depression upon the Negro family in the northern city, . . . it appears that "well organized families met the depression with less catastrophic consequences than families that were already disorganized." That this was true of upper-class Negro families was revealed in the documents furnished by college students who come from the more stabilized elements in the Negro population. Although, in many cases, savings were lost or consumed, homes were mortgaged or lost, and the children had to delay their college education for one to three years, these families maintained their solidarity and by pooling their resources were able to achieve some of their major family objectives. But since family disorganization among the masses has been one of the main problems resulting from the migration of the Negro to the northern city, it is not unreasonable to assume that family disorganization increased as a result of the depression. First among the consequences of reduction or loss of income was the seeking of cheaper living quarters or the crowding of families and relatives in a single household. We have a record of a case of mass housing in Chicago, where 67 families were permitted to move into an old apartment building that had been partially destroyed by fire and was without heat and light. For heat, they used coal stoves such as are used in the rural districts, and for light, they burned kerosene lamps. The owners of the building operated the house through a committee of Negroes and collected rents from those families who were able to pay. In some cases, the men in the families made payments in terms of various services. Although thousands of Negro families in northern cities, who had constantly lived close to the margin of existence, had been crowded into slum areas, the depression made their condition worse and reduced thousands of others to their level. . . . Although even under normal conditions from 10 to 30 per cent of Negro families in northern cities have women heads, it is probable that the number increased during the depression. Among the relief families in Chicago, Detroit, New York, and Philadelphia, we find that only from 29 per cent (in Chicago) to 50 per cent (in New York City), were normal family groups; i.e., man, wife, and children. Among the relief families in these same cities, a fifth to a fourth of the families had a woman head. . . .

The next question to which an answer has been sought is: What effect has the depression had on the health and survival of the Negro in the northern city? . . .

In this connection, we can cite the results of a statistical study . . . of Harlem, which deals with the relation between dependency and birth and death rates. . . . [The] explanation of the tendency of the infant mortality to decrease as the dependency rate mounted was as follows:

The Home Relief Bureau made available medical services to the recipients of relief which they had been unable to afford previously out of their own earnings; the fact that a trained investigator visited the home periodically, was able to advise and instruct the families in the proper care of their children, refer them to the community pre and post natal clinics, arrange for their hospitalization, and distribute and explain literature on the proper care of mother and infant before and after birth proved to be a very helpful factor in overcoming some of the above mentioned things which contributed to the very high rate of infant mortality. There is also the factor that the mother, if employed prior to the family's going on relief, worked several months during pregnancy and returned to work within a minimum time after the birth of the child whereas the mother on relief remains at home and is thus able to take greater precautions in regard to her own health during pregnancy, and devote more care to her child after its birth. . . . It is much easier to get an expectant mother to visit the clinics regularly and exercise the proper precautions to insure the good health of her offspring, but the problem becomes more difficult when persuading an adult to exercise proper care about his own health, visit clinics regularly, take preventive measures, and seek medical attention and advice.

If the author's explanation of these correlations may be taken as valid, and if the situation in Harlem is typical of other northern cities, then it appears that the Negro child has been afforded a better chance of survival because of relief measures than if he had been born into a family existing upon the sub-standards of living of the great body of Negro workers who make their own livelihood.

We turn, finally, to those changes in the Negro's philosophy and outlook on life which may reasonably be attributed to the depression. First, among the changes, one might mention the disillusionment of the Negro middle class. Probably no section of the middle class in America had such high hopes as the Negro middle class during the years of prosperity. Their dream of reaping the rewards of individual thrift and foresight which had had only a partial fulfillment in the South seemed to have come true in the northern city. The Negro professional and business man had prospered upon the earnings of the black masses in northern cities. Moreover, the political power of the Negro had opened the way to political patronage and the civil service held out a substantial living for many educated Negroes. Then, suddenly, the purchasing power and savings of the masses began to melt. Doctors' and lawyers' fees dwindled and finally ceased, and the hothouse growth of Negro business behind the walls of segregation shrivelled and died, often swallowing up the savings of the black masses. Fine homes and cars and other forms of conspicuous consumption were given up. In their disilluisonment, some of the very professional men in New York who had laughed at the small group of radical intellectuals now formed a class to study Marx. But disillusionment did not breed radicalism among a very large group. It appears that more often, they turned to racial chauvinism as a way of realizing their dreams. In Chicago, those of the middle class who had laughed at Garvey's grandiose ideas of a back to Africa movement began to talk of a Forty-ninth State which according to their specifications would be a Black Utopia where the black middle class could exploit the black workers without white competition. In New York City, small Negro business men pointed to the Jewish merchant as the cause of their failures and began to demand that Harlem be reserved as their field of exploitation.

Closely associated with the chauvinistic aims of many members of the middle class have been the efforts of Negroes in a number of northern cities to organize cooperatives as a solution of the Negro's economic problems. However, little or no success has attended these efforts which tended in some instances to nurture if not encourage racial chauvinism. Another movement of greater significance so far as it reflects the growth of militancy directed toward immediate economic ends, has been the picketing and boycotting of stores in order to enforce the employment of Negro workers, usually as clerks. In Columbus, Ohio, the Housewives League assumed the leadership in this movement. Although in some cities white storekeepers have made concessions to the demands of the Negroes, they secured relief for a time through court injunctions. But the recent ruling of the United States Supreme Court on a case in the District of Columbia has removed legal barriers against this type of picketing. Inasmuch as the demands for employment in stores where Negroes were the chief customers involved the employment of Negroes as clerks and salesmen, it implied a demand for status, which redounded also to the economic advantage of the middle class.

. . . . .

In summing up the effects of the depression on the Negro in northern cities, one can say, first, that the depression has laid bare the general economic insecurity of the Negro masses. It has tended to destroy the high hopes that were kindled during the War period when it appeared that the Negro, though at the bottom of the industrial ladder, had secured a firm foothold in the industries of the North. From a position of increased earning power, unequalled during his career in America, the Negro has become the ward of the community with from a third to a half of his numbers dependent upon relief. His family life, which had been shattered by the impact of the modern metropolis upon his simple folk life, had scarcely had time to recover and reorganize itself before the shock of the depression shattered it once again. The struggle for survival, always precarious and in doubt, became even more uncertain, though relief has probably enabled children to survive who otherwise would have died. . . .

SOUTHERN CITIES

Economic and Cultural Aspects

One of the most significant developments for black urban workers was the concerted new drive to unionize them. The new spurt of union activities had been facilitated by New Deal legislation—the Wagner Act (1935) and the Wages and Hours Act (1938), which was intended to protect labor laid low by the Depression as well as to restore the nation's purchasing power. The initiative for unionizing black urban workers came from the Congress of Industrial Organizations, which was founded in 1935 as the result of a breakaway from the American Federation of Labor. Initially imbued with idealism, the CIO organized industries rather than crafts and genuinely sought to discountenance racial discrimination. Its primary targets were the steel, auto, mining, packinghouse, rubber, and other mass-production industries in which blacks were represented in large numbers. The CIO drive forced the AFL to adopt more liberal policies and to enter the competition to organize black workers. Although the drive was met by suspicion from some black workers and opposition from the conservative middle class and from company unions, it did succeed in unionizing tens of thousands of black workers. The CIO goal of fully integrating the black workers ran counter to social practices of the South and so could not succeed there; but unionization did lead to much greater cooperation than hitherto between black and white workers. The early efforts of the CIO to organize black workers in three major southern cities is well captured by Document 3 below.

With regard to southern black business, Durham maintained its reputation as the "Capital of the Black Middle Class" (Document 4), while Richmond's early twentieth-century promise as a black business center was not sustained. Richmond blacks had reacted to discrimination and jim crow arrangements by heading north, with the result that it was the only major southern city to lose black population in the decade 1920–30. Those who were left, hard hit by the Depression, followed the lead of blacks in Gary, Ind. (Document 17), and formed a cooperative store to combat high prices (Document 5).

There is a main street in every black metropolis, and one of the most celebrated is Beale Street. Memphis had a large and relatively prosperous black population, which still retained a good deal of its African cultural heritage,

211

and a strategic location on the Mississippi, the commercial and cultural route that led from New Orleans on to St. Louis and Chicago. So it was natural that Memphis—and "gay and raucous" Beale Street in particular—should play a vital role in the creation of two major Afro-American musical forms—the blues and jazz.

Memphis, Tenn. (1934)

2]   Beale Street and the Blues

Beale Street is where the blues began. Rising out of the Mississippi River, it runs for one mile straight through the busy heart of Memphis and loses itself in the muddy bottoms of East Street. The echoes of its fantastic music have been heard around the globe, for this colorful little thoroughfare is known the world over; its fame has penetrated into every nook and cranny where sound carries the echoes of the English voice. It has been talked about, written about, sung about so much that sightseers from every quarter are lured there in search of adventure or to gaze upon the scenes and surroundings that represent its vanished glory.

Beale Street, owned largely by Jews, policed by the whites, and enjoyed by the Negroes, is the Main Street of Negro America. There are many other streets upon which the Negro lives and moves, but only one Beale Street. As a breeding place of smoking, red-hot syncopation, compared to it, Harlem, State Street, and all the rest of the streets and communities of Negro America famed in story and song are but playthings.

. . . . . .

That part of Beale Street which is generally considered as "underworld" is a short block from Hernando to Fourth Street. Here a gay and raucous night life that includes gambling, streetwalking, and every kind of vice known to the demimonde flourishes, though outwardly it looks innocent enough: a noisy and congested block in which guitar players stroll up and down filling the night with music, in which blind men sing on the street corners, and preachers bark in Handy's Park. Throughout the day this underworld block on Beale Street sleeps peacefully, but when the sun sinks beyond the river and the stars come out it sings, laughs, drinks and dances until early morning. On Thursday nights the block belongs to the white people. They come in evening dress in high-powered cars, in overalls and Fords, to see the scantily clad brown beauties dancing across the stage in the midnight show at the Palace.

All day long every Saturday Beale Street is thronged by country people from Arkansas, North Mississippi and West Tennessee who arrive in the early morning in their wagons, their Fords, or on horseback. They bargain with the Jews for clothing, buy groceries at the Pigglywiggly and fish and pork chops of

Source: George W. Lee, *Beale Street*, New York: Robert O. Ballou, 1934, pp. 13–14, 24–25, 26, 27–28, 62–66, 119–20.

the Greek, and sometimes moonshine in the "blind pigs." They leave at sun-down to cross the Arkansas bridge or journey down the Hernando Road to their homes sleeping along the banks of the muddy Mississippi.

Saturday night belongs to the cooks, maids, houseboys and factory hands. For on this big night of the week, when large cars roll up and down the ave-nue and long parallel lines of them are parked against the curb, the color and tempo of the street reaches its highest point. The sidewalks then are crowded with carefree humans enjoying the magic of the night, and great throngs move leisurely down the street to pack the Daisy Theater and enjoy a thrilling West-erner. Some of them leave the crowd to dodge in and out of alleys, where syn-thetic gin and corn liquor flow freely, or stop to witness a fight, fascinated by a glimpse of gun or knife. The more adventurous ones find their way to crap games where they stake their week's wages against galloping dice.

On this night Elmer Atkinson's stag poolroom is crowded with loud-talking throngs. Golden browns, high yellows and fast blacks, some gorgeously dressed and others poorly clad, move together down the old thoroughfare. The work-ing folks are on parade; going nowhere in particular, just strolling, just glad of a chance to dress up and expose themselves on the avenue after working hard all the week. In the course of their rambling they will meet old friends; more than that, there is also a good chance of picking up a new "sweetie" down at the New Orleans or at Sim's Beer Garden. This makes the Saturday night stroll on Beale Street a thrilling adventure which the cooks in the kitchens and the men at the big plants on the Wolf River looked forward to all the week.

It must have been one of these Saturday night scenes that inspired W. C. Handy to write his "Beale Street Blues":

> The Seven Wonders of the World I have seen
> And many are the places I have been;
> Take my advice, folks, and see Beale Street first.
> You see pretty browns dressed in beautiful gowns,
> You will see tailor-mades and hand-me-downs;
> You will meet honest men and pick-pockets skilled,
> You will find that business never closes until
> Somebody gets killed.
> You will see hog-nosed restaurants and chitterling
> Cafes and jugs that tell of by-gone days.
> You will see golden balls enough to pave the new
> Jerusalem.
> I would rather be there than any place I know.
> It is going to take a sergeant just for to make me go—
> I am going down to the river maybe by and by,
> 'Cause the river is wet and Beale's done gone dry.

Beale Street is many years from Africa. . . . Yet in some quarters the habits and customs of jungle life still linger.

On East Beale, wrinkled old witch doctors and medicine men sit before boil-ing pots mixing strange concoctions which, they assert, will cure any disease of the flesh and drive away the evil spirits. Hanging on the walls of their dingy

213

huts are red "luck bags" to be worn around the neck. It is claimed that these bags will protect their wearer against the malicious designs of his enemy and bring good luck. Because of the many superstitions of the people these dealers in the occult do a flourishing business.

If a black cat runs across their path, if they are struck with a broom, if some one brings peanuts into the house and drops the hulls on the floor, if by mistake a third person lights his cigarette with a match from which two others already have lighted theirs, or if a policy player is desirous of a lucky number, they all seek the advice of these "voo-doo" doctors and medicine men.

. . . . .

The musical heritage of the southern Negro has been preserved largely through the activities of a group of band and orchestra leaders on Beale Street. . . .[1]

Beale Street . . . is where the blues began, the birthplace of America's most popular music. Up from the docks of the Mississippi River, up from the saloons, the bawdy houses on Beale, up from the honkytonks of the sawmill towns, up from the white cotton fields of Dixie, accompanied by banjo strumming and hand-clapping, rose the sorrow songs of the Negro toiler. Beale Street band masters emphasized the native and nationalistic elements of these songs and sent their echoes floating around the world. Handy set them to music and the jazz age was at last a reality.

Memphis, Tenn., Atlanta, Ga., and Birmingham, Ala. (1937)

3]   Black Unions

The almost hysterical vehemence with which the Southern press denounces the "Communistic" CIO, is a barometer of the rising fear of labor unionism and its more enlightened attitude toward union labor in Memphis, Birmingham and Atlanta. The Southern employers who have waxed sleek and fat off the proceeds of quasi-slave labor and lured numerous sweat shops from Northern industrial centers with the bait of colonial wage standards, grew jittery as both AF of L and CIO invite the Negro to march with them toward industrial democracy. They know only too well that levelling up the wages of black and white workers, long fooled into fighting each other, marks the beginning of the end of the halcyon days of industrial feudalism. . . . Already the Negroes, they see, are restive.

SOURCE: George S. Schuyler, "Industrial South Shaky as Unions Woo Labor," *Pittsburgh Courier*, September 13, 1937. [George S. Schuyler was a leading journalist and author.—Ed.]
[1] Among the most prominent of these band leaders between the Civil War and the first World War were Sam Thomas, James L. Harris, Mat Reynolds, Robert Baker, John R. Love, West Dukes, Jim Turner, and W. C. Handy, the best known to posterity.

Black Unions

THE MEMPHIS AF OF L

It is obvious that the Memphis AF of L has seen the "Mene, Mene, Tekel Upharsin" of the new labor deal on the industrial wall, and is heeding the handwriting. With the town serving as a "refuge" for CIO organizers working to emancipate the work slaves in Mississippi and with a CIO office scheduled to open this month with Attorney Robert Tillman of Mississippi in charge, the AF of L hears the hounding of competition baying on the heath and is tossing the burden of Negrophobia aboard.

When Frank Hargrave, International Longshoremen's Association organizer, from St. Louis, visited the town about six years ago [and] organized a strike of low-paid Negro stevedores who defied efforts of the bosses to prevent picketing, the AF of L Memphis Trades and Labor Council came to the men's assistance and aided them in negotiations with the employers.

The men, who won their rights to organize, went back to work, their Local No. 27 became affiliated with the Council and they now meet regularly in the Labor Temple where all the city's organized workers meet.

Negotiations are now going on with reference to wages and hours. Being young to the labor movement, most of the men are lacking in labor education and are said not to be paying dues or attending meetings as they should, but labor officials are optimistic about the future of this union.

Up historic Beale Avenue, immortalized in the affable George W. Lee's "Beale Street: Where the Blues Began," I strolled early one morning to the imposing, castle-like Labor Temple on the corner of Lauderdale. There I interviewed President Levi G. Loring of the Memphis Trades and Labor Council who was most courteous and obliging.

Mr. Edw. Smith, a veteran Negro laborite, is president and business agent of Local 52, International Hod Carriers and Building Laborers Union, which has a membership of 200. This union now has a minimum wage of 63½¢ an hour for an 8-hour day. A year ago the minimum scale was 50¢ an hour.

Back in 1934, the whites did not pay much attention to this union. "They are much more cordial now than ever before," declared Mr. Smith. "Race relations have unquestionably improved in the labor movement here." At one time, not far back, it was common to use the epithet "nigger" in union meetings. Mr. Smith and others protested against the practice and it has ended. This labor leader feels that "history is being made" in Memphis.

There are two locals of the longshoremen with a total membership of 300. All officers from president down are Negroes.

Local No. 427 of the International Ladies Garment Workers Union is composed of some 20-odd colored girls who are pressers in a clothing factory.

There has as yet been no organization drive among building service employees or laundry workers. Local 521 of the cement finishers has 25 Negroes in a total of 60 members. There are about 25 Negroes in the 150 members of the bricklayers' union, while 12 of the 50 organized plasterers are colored. There are two locals of carpenters, one is colored with about 30 members and the other white with about 400.

The Coopers Union has 175 Negroes out of a total of 250 while the Firemen and Oilers group is entirely Negro with a Negro president.

The bricklayers meet separately according to "race."

While a few Negro steamfitters have been taken into the union, it is charged that Negro painters have been given the runaround.

The Switchmen's Union is mixed but Negroes predominate. Among the structural iron workers, there are a few Negroes as helpers, so-called. Efforts are being made to organize the iron works where some Negroes are employed.

Last year a federal labor union was established at the American Finishing Co., with 500 members, of whom 200 are colored.

Concerning the painters, I learned that efforts were being made to organize a separate Negro local. Some Negroes want it but some do not. The whites are similarly divided.

Of the 16,000-odd organized workers in Memphis, more than 3,000 are Negroes.

Indicative of the attitude which labor must overcome in Memphis is the story told me about Firestone's tire plant where both white and colored are employed. The company opened schools for members of both groups to prepare them for upper bracket jobs, according to the story. When this news came to the attention of the Chamber of Commerce, a committee was delegated to take up the question with the company and voice the strenuous objection to Negroes being prepared for or assigned to upper bracket jobs.

At McCollum and Robinson Mop Factory, the white workers refused to work in the same department with Negroes. When the whites went on strike, the Negroes stayed on, joined the company union and refused to have anything to do with the labor union.

Such incidents reveal the distance that has yet to be traveled in Memphis. But there is no doubt that such attitudes are not so general as before and do not today represent the viewpoint of organized labor in the city. Quite likely they will almost disappear when the CIO begins to supply the competition which elsewhere has been like a breath of fresh air to the labor movement. Meantime, Negro workers are slowly awakening.

ATLANTA UNIONS

There is, of course, little of the *new* labor drive in Memphis as yet. Conditions in Atlanta are almost identical, so much so that it is scarcely necessary to dwell at length on them. There, as in Memphis, Negroes dominate the building labor and are in a mixed plasterers union. Painters, bricklayers and carpenters, however, are in separate unions. Recently Frank R. Crosswaith, brilliant general organizer of the International Ladies Garment Workers Union, organized Local No. 207 in Atlanta which has 300 girls in it. Aside from this, the labor picture in Atlanta varies little from that in Memphis. But CIO organizers are now at work in the city and ere long it is probable a great deal will be heard from the capital of Georgia.

BIRMINGHAM UNION PARTICIPATION

In contrast to Memphis and Atlanta, there has been much new union activity in Birmingham, the Pittsburgh of the South. Not only have Negro workers

216

joined the unions in great numbers but they have met with bosses' representatives to negotiate contracts.

At the headquarters of the Steel Workers Organizing Committee in the Steiner Building, I interviewed Thomas Pate, the field director, whom I found quite cordial and cooperative. Of the 32 steel lodges in the district, all except one have Negro members. In many of the lodges Negroes predominated, and several have Negro officers, among them a number of vice-presidents. In a number of lodges, I learn that Negroes could have all of the offices from president down, but seemed to prefer to elect white men to the leading office. Among the Negro organizers employed by the SWOC in the Birmingham district are Ed. Cox, A. G. Johnston, Rev. Alonzo Walker and James J. Israel. Mr. Pate told me the Negroes on the whole had responded as good [sic] as whites and sometimes better.

The SWOC has signed contracts with the Tennessee Coal and Iron Company, a subsidiary of the U.S. Steel, of which 10,000 workers (55 per cent) are Negroes. Approximately 40 per cent of the Negroes are in the union. It has also signed contracts with the Woodward Iron Co., and the Continental Co., Virginia Bridge Co., and various scrap iron firms.

At the Continental Company the 340 Negroes are almost all union men. After a five-week strike they won raises of 11 cents an hour.

The Ensley SWOC Lodge, of which a Negro minister, the Rev. W. M. Hall, is vice-president, has a total membership of 1,800 of whom half are Negroes. Union activities have boosted the wages from $2.68 a day to $3.60 a day.

The McWain Pipe Shop, with 400 workers, mostly Negroes, organized a lodge even before the SWOC came. Efforts to force them into the AF of L failed. Jesse Gill, a core worker of eight years' experience, said there were 275 Negroes and 100 whites in the McWain plant. The lodge has a colored vice-president and secretary. Mr. Gill told me the treatment of the men had vastly improved and the wages are much better as a result of the union. They used to work from dawn to dusk and were constantly cussed out by the foremen. That has been ended. Common labor which formerly received 30 cents an hour is now getting 40 cents.

There are 450 employees at the plant of the Birmingham Stove and Range Company. Most of them are Negroes and all but two are in the union. Last winter they staged a five-week strike. Other lodges in the district sent food and money to help out, but singularly enough no white striker was given anything. It was explained that the whites had been getting better wages than the Negroes and consequently were in less need than their colored fellow workers. That seems to be a new high in solidarity.

Mr. Pate showed me some of the pay envelopes the men had received prior to the strike: 50 hours $7.94; 60 hours, $8.86; 30 hours, $4.55; 27 hours, $3.02; 54 hours, $6.98. Other weekly salaries were: $10.93, $11.51, and $11.76 for a six-day, 54-hour week.

The strike won the men a general 20 per cent increase.

Mr. Pate deplored the fact that there were Negro moulders in the city getting $25 a week who should be getting the union scale of $8 a day, but who refused to join the union.

At the Virginia Bridge Company, with 349 workers, of whom only a seventh are members of the union, the few Negroes have been slow to join as, it would seem, have the whites.

There are two scrap iron yards in Birmingham and environs employing a total of some 400 men, mostly Negroes. Before the union came along they were getting $1.50 for a ten-hour day. Now they are getting $2 for an eight-hour day. In addition to winning recognition of their union, they have won seniority rights. Most significant of all, their contracts call for no cussing out of Negroes by their bosses. That alone would seem to be worth the union fee and dues.

At two of the plants where extensive "welfare" is furnished the workers, the SWOC has made no headway. The plants are the Stockham Pipe and Fittings Company, which hires 1,300 men, mostly Negroes, who get half of what white men get elsewhere, and the American Cast Iron Pipe Company of whose 1,000 workers 650 are Negroes.

Several Negro workers said the Negro welfare worker at the Stockham Plant is more reactionary than his brother, Congressman Mitchell [1] of Illinois, which is certainly a grave charge. He has long been a bitter opponent of unions.

The ACIPCO is one of the country's outstanding examples of "employee ownership," with welfare features difficult to find elsewhere. While all the facilities are strictly segregated, they appeared to be identical and adequate. A $100,000 dispensary has recently been completed with a staff of the finest physicians and dentists (white, of course) obtainable in the city. Free hospitalization is given not only to employees, but to their families. There are three colored nurses, each supplied with a personal Ford touring car.

There is a well-stocked company store allegedly "co-operative" where the best quality goods are said to be sold to workers at the lowest cost. All the clerks are white, I noticed.

There are 53 company-owned houses renting from $9 to $15 monthly, and the company has a real estate agent to arrange home buying on terms for the workers.

One is justified in dwelling somewhat at length on this company because it is unique. The plant was left by its founder to the workers in it, and every worker is a stockholder, and an equal one under the so-called Eagan plan. Almost all are industrial veterans, a large number having been working there for fifteen or twenty years. New men are on probation for six months until found "desirable" to receive benefits. Each man is insured for $500.

There is an apparently democratic arrangement, something new in American industry, until you examine it carefully. There are, as I have said, 650 Negroes out of 1,000 employees, yet the Negro workers, even though employed there for 25 years, have no say whatever in the administration of the business built by their brain and brawn.

There are three boards in the company. Two are white: the Board of Management, which is the highest, and the Board of Operatives; and one, the Colored Auxiliary. The Board of Operatives cooperates with the Board of Manage-

[1] Arthur W. Mitchell, black Chicago-based Illinois congressman, 1935–43.

ment in administering affairs, but the colored board is only advisory, and the colored officers would not seem to possess any real power.

Thus, 350 whites with the higher-paid jobs run the plant, while 650 Negroes have no voice whatever. Which probably isn't strange in Alabama.

With a minimum pay of 42 cents and a maximum of 58 cents an hour, it cannot be said that the Negro workers are growing rich under the Eagan plan, but they seem satisfied and have spurned all overtures of the SWOC organizers. The majority of the supervisory jobs are held by white men. Negroes are not employed in the moulding and machine shops, but are everywhere else except, of course, in the administrative offices. The mimeographing office, however, is run by Negroes.

At the CIO office on the seventh floor of the National Bank Building (reached via jim-crow elevator) N. B. Swick, field representative, boasted that the Alabama CIO leads the U.S. in activities. He told of the four-week strike of 87 Negro workers at the Grayson Lumber Company, and the manner in which they picketed the plant. He said, "They stacked up 100 per cent." It was the same, he reported, in the American Bakeries strike.

In nine out of ten cases, he said, a Negro is the vice-president of the union, and there are always several Negro officers. The CIO seems determined, according to its officials, to eliminate every possible trace of color discrimination. This is admittedly difficult when the vicious Alabama laws do not permit mixed racial meetings.

American Bakeries workers are 60 per cent Negro, Martin Biscuit, 85 per cent; Grayson Lumber, 98 per cent, and Nehl Bottling, 65 per cent. These figures indicate the importance of Negro labor in Birmingham.

There are a number of saw mill and timber workers in and around the city and 75 per cent of them are Negroes. These men have responded 100 per cent to the union call and several Negroes are serving as officers of the union. The workers were formerly getting 14, 15 and 16 cents an hour, but a minimum base pay of 38 cents an hour has been established, regardless of color or race.

The United Agri. and Cannery workers recently held a convention at Johnstown, Alabama. About 35 of the 50 delegates from 16 locals were Negroes.

United Soft Drink and Bottling Workers' Local No. 220 has a majority of Negro workers. The vice-president and most of the committeemen are Negroes.

A CIO official said: "These local unions here are really functioning."

There are some Negroes in the unionized skilled crafts, but not very many. Here as elsewhere, the old spirit of race reactionism is said to dominate the thinking of craft union officials. No particular advances have been made in that direction. The United Mine Workers, with its large Negro membership, Negro officers and organizers, is flourishing.

According to young James J. Israel, who has been doing organizing work for the SWOC among Negroes for 9½ months, "The majority of the Negroes really want the CIO."

H. D. Coke, managing editor of the *Birmingham World* who has done much to enlighten Negro workers, thinks "the CIO drive is teaching the Negroes in industry the value and necessity of cooperation and mass action. Its weakness here lies in the lack of trained organizers. I believe they shipped A. Q. Johnson away from here to Chattanooga recently, mainly because he insisted upon the same wage scale for whites and Negroes."

In this connection Mr. Coke cited the strike at the H. W. Smith foundry, which was finally settled after 45 days. The Negroes got a 5-cent increase while the whites got a 15-cent increase on hourly pay. Organizer Johnson, a Negro, protested against this and was promptly transferred.

Mr. Coke feels that the CIO has been lax in organization and has failed to touch many plants as yet. It needs a little zip and life, he asserted.

. . . . .

Marvelous progress has been made in this new labor drive. Much greater progress can be made if the two major labor groups will not take the Negro for granted and will not forget that the 1937 Negro is no fool.

Durham, N.C. (1937)

4]   Black Business

Durham is known as a center of business activity. Tobacco products have earned universal recognition for the city. The North Carolina Mutual Life Insurance Company has also given it more than local significance.

. . . the North Carolina Mutual Life Insurance Company, which today operates thirty-two districts in the States of North Carolina, South Carolina, Alabama, Georgia, Tennessee, Virginia, Maryland, and the District of Columbia . . . has $42,000,000 worth of life insurance in force, as of June 30; and total assets of $4,837,107. It employs 1,153 people as follows: 460 agents, 115 managers, cashiers, clerks and assistants, 93 persons in its home office, and 485 medical examiners. It owns without encumbrance a six-story pressed brick and limestone office building in downtown Durham.

The allied business interests of the North Carolina Mutual Life Insurance Company combine nearly another $2,500,000 in assets. The Mechanics and Farmers Bank was begun in 1908 with a paid-in capital of $10,000, which has been increased to $214,000. It occupies the first floor of the Mutual Building in Durham and its own building in Raleigh. The deposits as of June 30 amounted to $1,224,991; its resources were $1,529,702. Included among the depositors of the bank are the City and County of Durham, and the State of North Carolina; also a large number of white citizens.

There are now two real estate corporations in Durham. One is doing approximately $130,000 worth of business a year, and the other $100,000 worth. The Bankers Fire Insurance Company (1920) started with $100,000 paid-in capital, which has increased to $200,000. The Mutual Building and Loan As-

SOURCE: C. C. Spaulding, "Business in Negro Durham," *Southern Workman*, December 1937, pp. 364–68. [C. C. Spaulding, 1874–1952, was a leading Durham, N.C., businessman.—Ed.]

A Black Cooperative

sociation has a capital of $224,000. The latter has won its way with the public on account of its service in helping to secure homes for people who have meagre incomes. The Southern Fidelity Mutual Insurance Company is a bonding company with assets of $69,000. It bonds the agents of the Negro companies and writes several kinds of casualty insurance. All of these business enterprises and others such as barber shops, tailoring establishments, shoe shops, grocery stores, and filling stations, hinge around and can in some way attribute their successes to the major institution, the North Carolina Mutual Life Insurance Company. Scarcely has a professional man come to Durham who has not secured his start from our business institutions.

These businesses have brought forth most unusual acclaim, and Durham has been called the "Capital of the Black Middle Class." Various reasons for the business success of Negroes in Durham have been assigned. Some tell of the racial good will and understanding that exist between all groups of business and professional people in Durham. They begin with John Merrick whose barber shop catered to the leading white families of the town, including the Dukes, and the Watts, and the Carrs. These were his friends, and they, with a widening circle of liberal white people, have taken pride in us. Our supporting consitituency is interracial. Others say that our Durham institutions were simply a part of the national era of big business. In this connection they name our white contemporaries, the leaders of American finance, of steel, of railroads, of oil, of meat packing, of farm machinery, of tobacco and cotton, and of labor. Another explanation is that our business groups owe much to the Negro churches. While each of these explanations contains much of truth, the ability of Negroes in Durham to coöperate in business enterprises must not be ignored. Leaders like W. G. Pearson of fraternalism and public school education, and James E. Shepard of the North Carolina College for Negroes have coöperated with us.

Richmond, Va. (1940)

5]   A Black Cooperative

Jackson Ward is one of the most densely populated parts of Richmond, Virginia. Here Negroes live under almost all known economic handicaps, of which a lack of Negro business is the most noticeable. On every other corner, and sometimes in the middle of the block, is a business establishment conducted by members of some other race at the expense of the Negro.

For years attempts have been made to place some of this business in the hands of colored persons, but with little success. As early as 1927 one civic-minded citizen, Mr. E. R. Storrs, presented a limited cooperative plan to the people of Richmond. But he found it impossible to arouse enough enthusiasm among the citizens to launch such a movement. The idea remained dormant in

SOURCE: Samuel A. Rosenberg, "Richmond's New Negro Cooperative," *Opportunity*, April 1940, p. 118.

his mind, however, and when in the spring of 1937 he heard the Executive Secretary of the Richmond Urban League speak during Bigger and Better Negro Business Week on the cooperative movement, and particularly the success of the cooperative store operated by Negroes in Gary, Indiana, it occurred to him that such an enterprise might be the answer to the need he saw in Richmond.

On June 17, 1937, thirty-five men met in response to a call he had issued to one hundred persons. Data on the cooperative movement and the history of the Gary system had been secured, and was outlined in detail. The enthusiasm of the group was such that the Red Circle Cooperative Association, Inc., was born, with all present joining and paying a membership fee of $1.00.

A campaign was launched immediately for additional members and stock subscriptions. An educational drive was started and continued throughout the year. At the end of the period one hundred and twenty-five members had been secured and $1,200 collected. The president of the association, its secretary, and one other member spent a day each in Washington, D.C., Baltimore, and Greenbelt, Maryland, inspecting cooperative stores and getting ideas and plans of organization and operation. They reported their findings to the board of directors, and the decision was made to open the proposed store. Furniture and fixtures were bought on credit, and the cash was used for stock. The store opened on October 11, 1938, doing $380 worth of business the first day.

The store is located in the heart of Jackson Ward, across the street from a unit of the largest grocery chain in the United States. This chain had for years positively refused to employ Negro clerks in Richmond. After the Red Circle Store had been in operation three months, however, a Negro clerk was employed by the chain. When this did not cut into the cooperative's business, the chain store started a cut-price war. Wholesalers came to the assistance of the Red Circle Cooperative and sold goods to it at cost in order to meet this competition. In a short time the chain management notified the owner of the building which its store occupied that it was sacrificing its yearly lease and would take only a two month's lease. The manager was discharged and a new one employed, who now operates the store alone except on Saturdays, when an additional clerk comes in.

Today the Red Circle Cooperative has 400 members, and the store is doing a weekly business of $700. A manager, two clerks, and a delivery boy are employed. During 1939, 100,000 customers were served and a 1 per cent dividend was paid on purchases. A committee is now working on the advisability of organizing a credit union, a service station, and a second store.

BORDER CITIES

Economic and Cultural Aspects

Blacks in the border cities—major industrial centers—were also hit hard and early by the depression. In Cincinnati in 1931, blacks formed 11% of the population and made up 45% of the relief rolls (Document 6). And in Baltimore in 1934, 40% of the black population was on relief compared with 13% of the white population. Here, as in other border cities, the Depression brought a collapse in the large number of marginal black businesses. But the new CIO drive in the "notoriously non-union" border cities began making modest gains. Whereas in 1935 blacks were found for the most part only in the unions of jobs in which they had substantial representation, e.g. as longshoremen and postal workers, by 1937 the CIO had begun to organize the steel and other mass industries in which blacks had less substantial representation (Document 10).

Social progress of blacks in the border cities was uneven. Although Baltimore possessed "one of the most representative [black] middle-class communities" in the United States and had added substantially to its number of black social workers, it was still without black policemen, firemen, and librarians. In Louisville, on the other hand, through the influence of its interracial committee, blacks were more generally represented in public service, including the police and fire forces.

The Depression had witnessed a deterioration in the housing of blacks that reflected the disastrous economic decline as well as the shortage of housing. There were, however, community efforts among some members of the middle class to prevent the decay of their neighborhood, and Document 7 well illustrates one such successful effort.

Washington, D.C., remained an important educational and cultural center, but its continued boast of "cultural supremacy" lacked conviction or foundation (Document 9). Although itself disfranchised, it assumed new political significance in the 1930's when a black congressman from Illinois—Republican Oscar de Priest, 1929–34—arrived; he was later replaced by Democrat Arthur Mitchell, 1935–43. Washington also secured significantly greater and more influential black administrative appointments in Roosevelt's New Deal government.

*Richmond, Va., Louisville, Ky.,
and Cincinnati, Ohio (1931)*

6] Black-White Coexistence and Conflict

Richmond is the only Southern city reported to have lost in Negro population during the decade 1920–1930.[1] While the white population increased 10 per cent, the Negro population declined 2 per cent, giving the city an aggregate of 52,988 Negroes who represent 29 per cent of the total population, whereas in 1920 the ratio was 31.5 per cent. Richmond is exceptional also, in that its city government is the most backward in employment opportunities for Negroes. There are no principals of schools, even where there are colored teachers. There are no clerks in city offices. There are no Negro policemen, although many Southern cities find this an advantage. Janitors of public buildings, street sweepers, and garbage collectors are white.

Static in race relations, Richmond permits of no infiltration of new ideas on Negro-white problems. It is inhabited by a dominant group of "die-hards" who are constantly discriminating against Negroes in politics, housing, and industry. They lose in court, but this deters them temporarily, for they bob up again with a new clause or an altered phrase which forces Negroes again to resort to the courts for justice. The few whites who want conditions improved are up against an impregnable wall of indifference and the "well enough" spirit—and so the Richmond of today is the Richmond of twenty-five years ago.

While Richmond was losing, Louisville was gaining. Contrast Louisville with Richmond and though there may be practices to be complained of in it, there is at least a moving spirit that is not recognized in Richmond. The schools are manned by a colored personnel. There are now in Louisville a normal school and a city college. There are Negro policemen, detectives, and firemen. There is an active interracial group that has overcome barriers. Louisville is not stagnant. The city authorities are by no means as listless and recalcitrant as are those of Richmond, and there are liberal and unafraid people in the white group who do not have their light under a bushel.

The Negro population of Cincinnati is now 47,816, an increase of 59 per cent in ten years. Here conscious effort is being made to raise the status of Negroes as workers and as citizens. Recently the Mayor said: "Being Mayor one acquires a sense of the high honor that has been conferred on him and one likewise acquires a sense of responsibility—a sense of responsibility to all the citizens of a great city without regard to creed or race."

While Cincinnati has had an abnormally large number of unemployed Negroes amounting to approximately 45 per cent of the total unemployed, the city authorities and private agencies have measured up to their responsibilities.

Source: T. Arnold Hill, "Richmond–Louisville–Cincinnati," *Opportunity*, July 1931, p. 218.
[1] Savannah, Ga., also suffered a slight loss of black population. See Appendix I.

Urban Renewal

The vocational forces of the city schools are working with sympathetic heart and intelligent technique to improve the occupational status of the potential man and woman in the Negro group. The Department of Public Welfare is especially interested in the placement problems of this group. Relief agencies are rehabilitating as well as giving food and funds, and the whole system of welfare is coordinated—recognized as an obligation and not as an expedient, regardless of race or religion.

If Richmond wishes to hold its Negro population it might send a commission to Louisville and Cincinnati—all three cities are removed from extreme Southern or Northern atmosphere—to observe the working out of practices and policies which inspire young Negroes and make them delight to live in the city of their birth; or, it might contrast its treatment of Negroes with the injunction of its own *News Leader*, which admonishes the city fathers in this fashion:

No mystery surrounds the departure of the Negroes. No municipal magic will keep them here. Three things the Negro asks. One is as good a house as his money will procure, with no discrimination in streets, city service or rents. The second is justice in the courts of law, with no presumption against him because of his color. And the third is a standard of wages based on the value of his labor, and not on the theory that a Negro can contrive to live on nothing. Give the Negro these three things and he will stay in the South. Deny him these things, and the alert, ambitious Negro will certainly go where he can get them.

St. Louis, Mo. (1934)

7]   Urban Renewal

The highly segregated areas of Negro residents in St. Louis present about the same picture to be found in any of our larger cities to which thousands of Negroes migrated after the war. Deterioration in old houses occupied by Negroes in "interstitial" areas was hastened by the congestion which followed. This pressure for more housing space naturally brought into the situation economic competition for neighboring areas of houses occupied by whites. Spearheads of invasion made the greatest headway in two directions; first, in areas where with Negro tenants, the net rent income was possibly greater than that paid by whites and second, in better areas where more solid white residents with "peculiar notions" about Negro neighbors rapidly gave ground when one or more perfectly respectable Negro families bought property in their midst. One class of real estate dealers played an important part in helping Negroes invade new areas and another class helped set up Improvement Associations of white property owners to check the spread. Gradually these enlarged areas have become

SOURCE: John T. Clark, "When the Negro Resident Organizes," *Opportunity*, June 1934, pp. 168–71.

sharply defined "black belts" with a somewhat awakened group consciousness on the Negro's part. Within these well defined limits the ambitious Negroes invested their savings, bought their homes and helped create their social environment.

Especially during the depression the usual elements of neighborhood disintegration began to appear—residence zoning laws were completely forgotten, properties owned by white absentee landlords were subject to every kind of remodeling for any use whatever, so that they might yield their maximum earning power. Vacant lots built up with barracks-like flats contrary to the laws for such areas—city streets and alleys cleaned less regularly, garbage collections miserable. Then in addition "Hawkers" and door-bell pushing salesmen infested the areas, disregarded fences, lawns and flowers in a feverish determination to oversell each household as the real estate dealers too frequently had oversold each house. Such forces without the control of the group were augmented in this slow neighborhood deterioration by the influx of many Negro families likewise ambitious but unaccustomed to certain standards of living, or whose uncertain incomes made congestion and carelessness a natural result. Of course complaints were numerous but always whispered and behind drawn curtains. But soon the disgust of property owners in one block on Enright Avenue reached a ferment and the St. Louis Urban League was asked to do something about these complaints.

During May 1932 eleven residents in that block met and formed Block Unit No. 1. Invitations to membership were extended to every resident in the block. Committees were formed and they vigorously set out to correct nuisances which had been imposed upon them by outsiders and thoughtless residents in their own block. They waited upon department stores, theatres and merchants whose advertising pamphlets and bills daily littered lawns and streets. They challenged and checked postmen, ice men and salesmen who were crossing lawns and ruining fences and flower beds and then they joined in an effort to improve their lawns. All signs on houses in that block that were not in keeping with certain artistic standards were condemned and their removal requested. Within two months Block Units 2, 3, 4, and 5 were organized. One block in particular kept behind the superintendent of streets during the whole summer and saw to it that avenues in that area were cleaned and flushed daily. Another developed especially a neighborly care of every case of illness in their block and the whole block's sympathy in each case of death. It was immediately obvious that the kind of cooperation necessary to obtain results depended upon a real neighborly acquaintance and understanding. There was no block unit formed, however, in which every person who attended the first meeting did not have to be introduced to several persons of their group.

Mrs. Patty Cox Hall, assistant neighborhood secretary, in charge of Household Demonstrations with the St. Louis Urban League, was placed in charge of this phase of neighborhood service. Under her enthusiastic direction the block unit idea became an instant success. The constitution worked out by these first units, assisted by the Urban League, states that the general purposes of a block unit organization are: to improve the general aspect and cleanliness of lawns, streets and alleys; to obtain group action in checking the development of unwholesome influences in a block and to give support or to arouse opposition to proposed city ordinances or other statutes which would affect the residential values of their neighborhoods.

The simplicity of its organization might be shown by the following: membership is extended to every resident in the block, including lodgers, if they are sufficiently interested in helping to carry out these purposes. There are no initiation fees for joining, no dues or assessments, except when unanimously agreed upon at a regular or special meeting. Partisan politics, religious sectarianism are considered matters over which neighbors can legitimately differ and hence such discussions are not tolerated in any part of a block unit program.

Several blocks were organized during the fall, winter and spring of 1932 and 1933. In April 1933 twelve units had been organized. A federation of units was effected at this time, to coordinate block unit action on neighborhood projects. There were two definite projects launched last spring—cooperative buying of coal and a "front and rear lawn beautiful" contest. The Urban League initiated an open contract with a mine operator that saved an average of $2.00 per ton to every resident of blocks organized up until December 1, 1933. Nearly one thousand tons of coal were purchased by unit members through this channel.

The "front and rear lawn beautiful" contest was conducted in each block through the months of May, June and July. At the end of July, each unit selected two of its front lawns and two of its rear lawns, to enter into competition with lawns similarly chosen by other block units. The Missouri Horticulture Society volunteered to supply the judges. The results were most satisfying even though most of these residents were passing through the worst period of the depression. Prizes were presented at a lawn party and consisted of a handsome loving cup donated by Mayor Bernard Dieckman for the first prize and an assortment of useful tools donated by landscape gardners and commercial houses as the other awards. Refreshments for the lawn party were provided by an assessment of one penny levied against each family residing in the 16 blocks organized at that time. Three hundred and sixty-five people attended the lawn party. At this lawn party the Federation of Block Units presented to the City Administration the following recommendations for improvements which it felt ought to be granted to Negro citizens as their share in St. Louis' New Deal:

1. That this administration abrogate all remaining discriminations against Negroes using all facilities for recreation provided in our public parks.

2. That the city replace all trees destroyed by the tornado on the residential streets in this area and that trees be planted also on the important streets in the Elleardsville district, especially in the neighborhood of the new City Hospital.

3. To have corrected all violations of the zoning law committed in this area since 1930 against which the residents have protested. This includes the present use made of the old Deaconess Hospital for congregate housing.

4. That Tandy Park be made a playground for adults only, by remodeling the shelter house into a bath house and making a large open air swimming pool out of the present wading pool.

5. That a separate children's playground be acquired by the city within this vicinity and upon a portion of the grounds a sufficient number of additional tennis courts and a community center should be provided.

6. That wider opportunities for employment of Negroes are most imperative to retain self respect and maintain standards of decency and citizenship.

Committees from the different units were appointed to follow through each of these requests. The following are outstanding results already achieved: The Administration had an investigation made of specific complaints, especially of recreation facilities in the parks and ordered them corrected. Two Community Houses exclusively for Negroes to cost $500,000 were included in a City Bond Issue. This was recently voted upon favorably. An ordinance was introduced and passed to replant trees in the tornado area. Seventeen thousand trees were planted on residential streets throughout the city but the first trees were planted in the Negro areas which sponsored this ordinance.

Block units continued to be added until there are now twenty-seven, each with its own organization looking after the particular problems presented in its own block. There are a variety of activities within the blocks. Two blocks took the initiative in clearing up vacant lots as playgrounds for their children. Another held a cut flower show of flowers grown in the block. Several units held Open House receptions on New Year's Day for all residents in their respective blocks. Others gave children's block parties at various times throughout the year.

The potential economic strength of such an organization of consumers is obvious, but little or no effort as yet has been encouraged to use this power until the basic principles of the federation are well grounded. The cooperative buying of coal was tried out on a voluntary use of an open contract. Two units threatened and successfully used the boycott on unsanitary markets in each of their respective blocks. Others sought relief from "odorous" butcher shops by calling sanitary officers. Four units joined in a ten day boycott against a chain grocery store which had replaced its only regular Negro clerk with a white clerk who had been employed at another one of its stores until it closed. Two other units joined in a boycott against a market because it constructed an extension past the building line for a curb market. After a few months the market was bankrupt and the extension removed.

A most interesting example of the power of such an organization was shown when assessments were levied averaging up to eighteen dollars a front foot by the City for widening a boulevard fully one-quarter of a mile away at the nearest point from some of these organized blocks. Two hundred and twenty-three Negro property owners on Enright Avenue who were assessed for being in the "benefit zone" signed a petition denying any benefits from the widening, and so forcibly argued their points, that all assessments in "benefit zones" were abrogated. The Board of Aldermen promptly cancelled seven other street widening projects and stated "That no further street widening would be made until more modern and fair methods were developed to pay for widenings."

The usual personal differences, neighborhood feelings and individual prejudices arose very frequently to halt the development of various block units. In one instance the officials of one block, eager to improve the appearance of their garages and rear lawns which faced a car line, were determined to have each old garage rebuilt and all of them painted. Six new garages were built in that block but not until some feelings were aroused and the peace of the block organization threatened. Members in some blocks objected to and stopped efforts being made to have their avenues resurfaced with Public Works Administration funds for fear the cost would ultimately be assessed against each property owner. Numerous differences of opinions have arisen over block programs, etc., but none has permanently checked a gradual development of each block unit organized.

During the two years existence of these block units, their members, through committees, have learned for what purposes different city departments are created and how to use them. They impressed city officials with the fact that there are so many intelligent and determined Negro citizens whose requests must not be so easily ignored. The police department especially has been compelled to close up lottery headquarters, hooch joints, and other suspicious places located within these resident areas. The City Legal Department, Sanitary and Streets Department, Zoning Commission, Health Department, Forestry Department, etc., all have been intelligently approached by committees from time to time with most gratifying results.

This experiment in community organization by blocks has in the two years of its existence served in many civic welfare projects—during Health Education campaigns, in spreading knowledge of the purposes and plans of the NRA and its various agencies, in giving nonpartisan information to members about political issues and methods in cooperation in order to make their neighborhoods more attractive. Mr. Harold Bartholemew, St. Louis' City Planning Commissioner, stated that "efforts made by residents themselves to check general neighborhood deterioration are extremely important to the cultural development of any city and frequently offset expensive paternalistic plans to supply with local or federal funds, model housing which is so widely discussed now."

It might prove interesting to know that the total valuation of this residence property occupied by Negroes in these twenty-seven blocks is well over six million dollars—that Negroes own or control slightly more than five million dollars of this amount. So far there has been little or no political representation obtained through group action. There are no Negro members of the Board of Aldermen, Board of Education, Welfare Commissions, commercial or trade bodies. Perhaps an awareness of the power of group understanding and action in matters so close to one's living is necessary first for that power to be extended and used in a larger civic way. This is the hope of the St. Louis Urban League as a possible reward for the small part we have had in initiating this movement.

Baltimore, Md. (1935)

8]   Blacks at Work

. . . The job, to the mass of Baltimore Negroes, means only three types of work: common labor, personal service, and domestic service. The only jobs on which Negroes have a monopoly are in the fertilizer and chemical plants, on streets, roads and railroads as laborers, as porters in stores, in coal yards, lumber yards and as servants, janitors and waiters. Female workers are essentially laundresses, servants and waitresses. In normal times 676 of 1,000 Negroes are workers. In the total population, only 543 out of every 1,000 persons are workers. . . .

In the employment of Negroes in the mechanical and manufacturing industries, Baltimore increased from 4.2 per cent. of the total in 1900 to 17.8 per cent. in 1930. They were for the first time performing a proportion of the industrial work that was equal to their incidence in the population. Of course, they did not have the higher type jobs, but at least there was representation. And then came the depression.

. . . . .

In 1934, approximately 1,350 Negroes were employed in the field known as public service. While more than half of these were school teachers, it also included probation officers, health officers, nurses, dentists, clerks, stenographers and recreation workers. Others were employed as clerks, carriers, chauffeurs and laborers in the Post Office.

Negroes of Baltimore frequently complain that they do not have jobs in the municipal government in proportion to their incidence in the population. Baltimore, the largest city in the South Atlantic states, employs no Negroes as policemen or firemen. In fact, in no department of the city government does the number of Negro workers approach the 17.7 per cent. which is the city's proportion of Negroes. If we exclude the number of Negro teachers, which is required by law in separate schools, the remaining workers represent 1.7 per cent. of the total.

Approximately 3,000 Negroes are engaged in some phase of professional employment in Baltimore. For some years this group has been one of the most representative middle-class communities in the country. Its journalists, clergy men, lawyers, educators and diplomats have attained national recognition. But two features of this occupational distribution are particularly noticeable: (1) it includes no librarians, and (2) within the past three years there has been an enormous increase in the number of Negro social workers.

Negroes' wages invariably tend to be lower than the wages of white workers. . . .

. . . . .

SOURCE: Ira De A. Reid, *The Negro Community of Baltimore*, Baltimore: The Baltimore Urban League, 1935, pp. 11–15, 39–40. [Ira De A. Reid is a Columbia-trained sociologist and former Urban League official.—Ed.]

Blacks at Work

LABOR UNIONS

Baltimore labor unions, in the main, have put forth no effort to secure Negro members. Where such efforts have been made, they have resulted from the fact that Negroes were engaged in the trade in sufficient numbers to severely threaten the power of the union in its jurisdiction. It is significant that in the unions composed of white and colored members, the Negro membership was relatively large. The strongest group of Negro workers is found in the Longshoremen's Union. Of the five International Longshoremen's Association locals in Baltimore, Negroes are prominent in four. The other union, composed of checkers and shipping clerks, bars not only Negroes but certain foreign-born workers as well. Other unions in which Negro workers are strong include the International Hod Carriers, Building and Common Laborers, the Marine Workers Industrial Union, the National Federation of Post Office Clerks and the National Association of Post Office Laborers.

Organized labor has had little success in its efforts to organize the steel industry in the Baltimore area. . . .

In periods of prolonged unemployment, it is especially true among Negroes that if there is any work at all everybody will work but father. The one bulwark of sub-minimum security is the domestic service employment of the female worker. The only basis for establishing the volume of unemployment is the size of the relief roll. Based upon the number of families receiving relief in 1934, 60,791 or approximately 40 per cent. of the Negro population was being cared for by the relief agencies. Among the white population, 87,118 or 13 per cent. of its population was affected. . . .

. . . . . .

BUSINESS

Baltimore, the fourth largest center of Negro population in the United States, ranked ninth in the number of retail stores under Negro proprietorship. It ranked third among these cities in the ratio of stores to the population, with 504; New York was highest with 838 and Washington was second with 541.

The report of value of sales for the year for 282 retail stores conducted by Negroes was smaller than in any other city having a population of 100,000 or more Negroes. Its 282 retail stores gave employment to 491 persons, including 283 proprietors and firm members not on the payroll. These firms paid out $123,198 in wages on part-time and full-time workers during the year.

The average annual sales per store was $3,769. Bakeries, bakery goods stores and caterers reported the highest average sales per store, $13,647. Filling stations, a relatively new business, had a net average of $2,465 during the year. Lunch rooms, the largest single business enterprise among Baltimore's colored population, had average sales of $2,836. Stores handling a combination of groceries and meats had the second highest average annual sales, $7,490. Drug stores with fountains had average annual sales of $7,295.

In 1931, the Urban League listed 698 colored business enterprises in Baltimore. These concerns were chiefly of the personal service variety or allied with foods. Barbers and hairdressers were the largest ones, numbering 142.

This study reported 6 concerns with annual gross incomes in excess of $100,000, and 2 concerns with incomes exceeding $150,000. The leading business concerns in Baltimore are given as the Afro-American Publishing Company, publisher of the weekly *Afro-American,* the American Bottling Company, the Druid Hill Laundry, the Dunbar Theatre Amusement Company, the Metropolitan Finance Corporation—a financial concern reporting in June, 1933, a net worth of $75,000,—and Harry O. Wilson, banker. The depression has adversely affected a large number of the marginal business enterprises among Negroes.

It is estimated that in normal times Negro workers in Baltimore earn $45,000,000 annually in salaries and wages. This amount is regarded as the nucleus upon which Negro business must build. Yet, the 1931 survey, previously mentioned, reported "less than ten companies in which more than six people have productive investments. The noticeable successes in business establishments here have been individually-controlled concerns which started with limited capital and grew over long periods of development."

Washington, D.C. (1937)

9] Education and Culture

Out of more than $11,000,000 appropriated in 1936 to the public schools of the District of Columbia, approximately one-third was devoted to the colored schools. Education for Negroes in the District has come a long way from the first school founded by illiterate ex-slaves to the teachers' college, 3 senior high schools, 2 vocational schools, 6 junior high schools, and 40 elementary schools, with 1,004 teachers and 35,739 students. These schools are under the direction of Garnet C. Wilkinson, First Assistant Superintendent, divisions 10 to 13. Two other Negroes serve as second assistant superintendents, there is a Negro examining board and there is proportional membership on the Board of Education. The teaching force is unusually well prepared and the salaries are on the same scale as the salaries of the white teachers. The fact of segregation, however, must still be reckoned with. The theory of equal, though separate, accommodations breaks down into the fact of unequal facilities and equipment. Negro high schools are badly overcrowded and too often, instead of new structures, school buildings abandoned by whites are used for Negroes.

Howard University, called by some the "capstone of Negro education," is for the first time headed by a Negro, Dr. Mordecai W. Johnson. Under President Eugene Clark, Miner Teachers College, in spite of its youth, has received high rank from accrediting agencies. Frelinghuysen University, with Mrs. Anna J. Cooper as president, gives college instruction to students who must attend night classes. Miss Nannie Burroughs is the founder of the National Training School for Women and Girls, the school of the three B's: the Bible, the Bath,

Source: Federal Writers' Project, *Washington: City and Capital,* Washington, D.C.: U.S. Government Printing Press, 1937.

and the Broom, called the "nickel and dime school" because it depended for support almost wholly on contributions from Negroes who could not afford to give more.

Because of these universities there are many Negroes of ability in the humanities, and the social and natural sciences. Frequently their influence is greater than academic. At Howard University the *Journal of Negro Education* is ably edited. Carter G. Woodson edits the pioneering *Journal of Negro History* and directs the Association for the Study of Negro Life and History in this city. The weekly *Afro-American,* with a Washington edition, and the semi-weekly *Washington Tribune* are the city's Negro newspapers, both tending to develop race consciousness.

These give some point to the boast of Washington's "cultural supremacy" among Negroes, but the boast is not too well founded. There is little literature even attempting to do justice to the facts of Negro life in Washington. There have been literary circles with a few poets, dramatists, and writers of fiction. The Little Theatre movement, initiated among Negroes by Alain Locke, editor of the *New Negro,* and Montgomery Gregory at Howard University, has only partially succeeded.

. . . Of national popularity is the Howard University Glee Club under the direction of Roy W. Tibbs and Todd Duncan. The latter carried the role of "Porgy" in Gershwin's *Porgy and Bess.* Among jazz composers and orchestra leaders there are many Washingtonians; chief among these are Claude Hopkins and Duke Ellington, who has as one of his "hot" numbers, *The Washington Wabble.*

Although politically voluble, Negroes in Washington are still politically ineffectual. The hey-day of important political figures has passed. Oscar De Priest, Republican Congressman from Illinois, was followed by Arthur Mitchell, Democratic Congressman from the same State. There are still staunch Republicans and a Young Republican Club, and some of the old school have espoused the Liberty League; but there are many Democrats as well. The number of Negro appointees to administrative posts in the New Deal, while by no means adequate, is greater than in previous administrations. Many of these appointees are Washingtonians. Although political disquisitions may still stir the somnolence of barber shops, or break up friendships quadrennially, and although job-seekers abound, disfranchisement makes most of the Negroes politically apathetic. There is likewise a civic apathy. Civic organizations bringing grievances are often treated with scant courtesy by municipal authorities; without the vote they have little redress. There is a growing liberalism among Negroes who understand their plight, but the urging of such groups as the National Negro Congress and the N.A.A.C.P. too often meets with inertia and confusion. Segregation in Washington seems an accepted fact. Public buildings and public conveyances are not segregated, although on every southbound train Negro passengers are "jim-crowed." Negroes are not served in restaurants, saloons, hotels, movie-houses, and theaters, except those definitely set aside for them. Some stores will not accept their trade. Some governmental departments have separate accommodations, and some discriminate in the type of work offered to Negroes.

One boast, perhaps better founded than those of culture or civic status, is that Washington Negroes have a good time. Dances range in full plenty from the "house shouts" to the "bals masques" of Washington's mythical Negro "400." Social scribes flatteringly speak of Negro "Mayfair" with no sense of incongruity. Social clubs are legion; the What-Good-Are-We Club (composed of ex-Howard students) is widely known for intensive hilarity. Though college sororities and fraternities seem to be awakening to social realities, their lavish "formals" are still the most important events on their schedules. Washington Negroes are great "joiners"; the largest orders are the Elks, Odd Fellows, Knights of Pythias, and the Masons, but some with an ancient history like "Love and Charity" linger on. The Musolit Club and the Capital City Pleasure Club have large memberships.

The movie-houses attract great crowds of Negroes. Of the chain theaters owned by the Lichtmans, three are located on U Street, the thoroughfare of Negro businesses and pleasure-seekers. The Howard Theater, something of a theatrical institution, affording both movies and fast-stepping, high-hearted shows, attracts an audience of both races. Poolrooms, short-lived cabarets, beer gardens, and eating places, from fried-fish "joints," barbecue, and hamburger stands to better-class restaurants, do an apparently thriving business. And yet, when the outsider stands upon U Street in the early hours of the evening and watches the crowds go by, togged out in finery, with jests upon their lips—this one rushing to the poolroom, this one seeking escape with Hoot Gibson, another to lose herself in Hollywood glamour, another in one of the many dance halls—he is likely to be unaware, as these people momentarily are, of aspects of life in Washington of graver import to the darker one-fourth. This vivacity, this gayety, may mask for a while, but the more drastic realities are omnipresent. Around the corner there may be a squalid slum with people jobless and desperate; the alert youngster, capable and well trained, may find on the morrow all employment is economically proscribed, and segregated nearly as rigidly as in the southern cities he condemns. He may blind himself with pleasure seeking, with a specious self-sufficiency, he may point with pride to the record of achievement over grave odds. But just as the past was not without its honor, so the present is not without its bitterness.

Louisville, Ky., St. Louis, Mo., and Indianapolis, Ind. (1937)

10] Slow Unionization

The current unionization drive has so far touched Indianapolis, Louisville and St. Louis only lightly. The Steel Workers Organizing Committee has been active for many months in Indianapolis and St. Louis, but CIO offices have only

SOURCE: George S. Schuyler, "Union Drive Slows in Border Cities," *Pittsburgh Courier*, September 11, 1937.

recently been established in those cities and Louisville and the general drive is only in its initial stages.

This is due in part to the CIO strategy of concentrating major organizational efforts in the great industrial centers, in part to the fact that these border cities are notoriously non-union communities where low wages and long hours are the rule, and in part to the Southern tradition of segregation and discrimination which hangs heavily in the atmosphere of all of them and has been so instrumental in perpetuating industrial peonage.

Thus the labor conditions in these border cities reflect the instability, insecurity and uncertainty of this social and economic No-Man's Land.

The newspapers are mostly opposed to the new union drive and busily working the Communist scare against the CIO. The Negro professional class, with a few notable exceptions, reflects the views of the editorial writers of the daily press. The Negro workers are, in the main, scary and hesitant. Nevertheless, from the point of view of the laborites, the gloomy picture is illuminated by a few bright spots that give some promise of better things to come. Here and there Negro labor is displaying a new spirit, a new solidarity, a new pioneering enterprise that strengthens the view that the working masses are beginning to think fundamentally about the basic problems of food, clothing and shelter.

THE CIO IN INDIANAPOLIS

At the CIO headquarters in Indianapolis, Joseph D. Persily, the regional director, told me something of their progress in the two months the office had been open.

The Wadley Poultry Company, with 200 workers, of whom 35 per cent are Negroes, is completely organized, the local being affiliated with the United Cannery and Agricultural Workers of America. One of the five members of the negotiation committee which arranged the contract with the company is a colored woman. Mr. Persily, a young white man with the new labor viewpoint, assured me that "our policy is to bring out Negro leadership wherever possible."

Negroes constitute 25 per cent of the 200 workers in the Piel Bros. Starch Company, which is 100 per cent organized. There, it is said, a number of Negroes have blossomed out as leaders. The plant is at present completely closed down. Two of the seven members of the union's negotiating committee are Negroes.

One of the guiding spirits in the organization of the United Municipal Employees is Mr. Robert Obelton, a Negro. There are 200 Negroes out of 1,100 members. Colored members are said to be very active and two of them are on the union's negotiation committee.[1] The Negroes played a prominent part in a recent demonstration against the decision of the city to cut wages.

At the plant of the Century Biscuit Company, where 10 per cent of the employees are colored, the most important and influential member of the union next to the president is a Negro named Shirley, who is on the negotiation com-

[1] Hod Carriers and Building Laborers Local 86 had all Negro.

235

mittee. She is a former coal miner. The union, now on strike, is the United Bakery Workers No. 86.

Half of the members of the United Ice and Fuel Workers Union No. 87 are Negroes and some are serving as officers.

This is also true of United Grain Workers No. 88, which covers the different plants in the city.

The local of the Hod Carriers and Building Laborers has a two to one Negro membership and practically all of the officers from the president down are colored.

Of the total of 4,000 workers employed in the meat packing plants of the Kingan, Armours, Swift and smaller companies about 35 per cent are colored. The main plant is Kingan, where the AF of L union has obtained a contract, but the CIO union is contesting it before the National Labor Relations Board. It is, or should be, of interest to Negro workers to know that as a result of Negro workers having shunned the union, over 40 per cent of the 800 men recently laid off in the industry were Negroes.

At the Indianapolis Glove Company, which employs 300 colored women, the leading spirit for unionization is a Miss Louisa Dawson, who has been responsible for the little bit of success obtained in organization there. Although these 300 Negro girls are getting much less than 800 whites in the company's other plant, they are refusing to join the union and are positively hostile to all efforts to improve their working status.

Harry G. James of Huntington, W. Va. and Local 6006, District 11, United Mine Workers of America, is an experienced labor unionist, a worthy representative of that fine type of honest, upstanding Negro workman supplying so much of the new militant leadership among the masses. I had a long talk with him in the fine offices of the Steel Workers Organizing Committee in the Amalgamated Clothing Workers building on West Ninth Street. He is at present Field Representative of the SWOC, trying to organize the Negro workers in the various steel fabricating plants in Indianapolis.

It has been a hard fight to organize these Negroes. At the plant of the National Malleable & Steel Company, 50 per cent of the 866 workers are colored and only about 125 have joined the SWOC drive. The plant has a company-fostered union, which is using the usual pressure on the workers to keep them out of the legitimate union. Most of the Negroes are as frightened as rabbits, although it is said they are favorably inclined. No contract has as yet been secured.

At the foundry of the Link Belt Company, 400 of the 900 workers are colored. They have almost all remained in the company-fostered union. At the Dodge plant of this same company, where Negroes are 85 per cent of the 800 workers, the majority of the whites have joined the new steel union, but only 40 Negro workers have done so. A contract is now being negotiated between the union and the company.

At the Switzer-Cummings Company, where there are only 23 colored out of a total of 800 workers, only 4 Negroes have joined the overwhelming majority in the union.

It is illuminating that while segregation is not the law of Indiana, the colored workers at National Malleable are segregated in the washrooms as if they were in Mississippi. Most of the Negroes are reported to be in debt to the company, which uses the old loan shark method of keeping the workers enslaved and thus docile. Many of them are so deep in debt that they draw practically nothing for their killing labor. The colored women workers are terrorized by the white woman who hires them and she threatens to fire anyone who joins a union. Colored women get 40 cents an hour in this plant, while white women get 48 cents an hour. Men get 50 to 65 cents.

Henry Ford, whom certain Negro leaders in Detroit think is in love with Negroes, has one of his assembly plants in Indianapolis. Not a single Negro is employed there.

"All we have met from the Negro preachers," said a union official, "is discouragement. They don't seem to care anything about the low wages and bad working conditions their people suffer, nor the feudal conditions existing in the plants here. We have been assisted by Dr. Cable, the Negro city councilman, and Secretary F. E. DeFrants of the Y.M.C.A., but by no one else." The attitude of the rest of the leading Negroes allegedly runs from indifference to hostility. They quote the local N.A.A.C.P. head as saying, "I have come to the conclusion Negroes had better stay out of the union."

Nevertheless, the union organizers are optimistic. "I believe we'll be successful in getting the Negro here lined up," Mr. James stated. He pointed out that since last Labor Day the CIO had signed up 12,000 members in Indianapolis and environs and that there was evidence of a definite change taking place in the attitude of the Negro workers.

LOUISVILLE REMAINS DORMANT

Most of the Negroes in Louisville are employed in the tobacco industry, in domestic service, building construction for the various railroads and miscellaneous pursuits. It is a typical border anti-CIO town, where union labor has never had much of a foothold.

There is one colored AF of L tobacco local of which a Negro, William Brown, is president. Some idea of labor conditions in the tobacco industry may be gleaned from the fact that stemmers range from $7 to $10 a week with the first figure the most prevalent. But this is better than the $5-a-week average paid for domestic service.

I went to the CIO office in the Starks Building at Fourth and Walnut, where I talked with Peter Campbell, a former AF of L official who is now the regional director of CIO.

The office has just recently opened and he had little to tell me. Moreover, he was the first big CIO official I've met who seemed to be completely steeped in the traditions of the old South so far as Negroes are concerned.

Hod Carriers and Building Laborers Local No. 86 has all Negro officers and George Dougherty is president. There are 200 members and in recent months it has grown 100 per cent. It has managed to boost wages from 75 cents to 87½ cents an hour, according to Mr. Dougherty.

Building and Construction Laborers No. 576 is a mixed union with 2,300 members, of whom better than 50 per cent are colored. The secretary is

Border Cities: Economic and Cultural Aspects

Charles J. Newton, a Negro. These workers, allegedly less skilled than the hod-carriers, are now getting 50 cents an hour. They were getting 35 cents and 40 cents before unionization.

Both these locals belong to the AF of L. There are three Negroes on the Louisville District Council. There are about a half dozen Negro carpenters belonging to the local union.

The only work of the CIO so far has been the organization of a local of the Iron, Steel and Tin Workers' Union. There are said to be 100 Negro members of this school.

STIRRINGS IN ST. LOUIS

Labor is marching forward on many fronts in St. Louis. But owing to the Southern traditions that hang like a miasmic pall over the metropolis that sprawls from the Mississippi to the Missouri river, and to the previous dominance of reactionary AF of L officials, labor is not marching forward very fast. Nevertheless, all things considered, much progress is being made in organizing steel, furniture, electrical manufacturing and automobiles. Of the 900,000 population of the city, Urban League officials estimate that there are 110,000 Negroes, 40 per cent of whom are from Mississippi and Arkansas. Just like the whites, they have brought the Dixie mores along with them. They are slow to heed the appeals of labor organizers, having obtained what they consider a favorable position in steel plants by scabbing years ago. Then, too, they have noted the manner in which the AF of L building trades in the past have driven the ablest Negro mechanics out of the city or out of their trades. As one intelligent Negro said: "It is a crime the way the building trades choke off the Negro artisans."

Just two Negro preachers out of the hundreds in the city have taken any favorable interest whatever in the strengthening of Negro labor through unionization. The Negro educated (?) class as a whole is lying low, indifferent or outspokenly anti-union. By comparison, the Urban League is radical in its labor interests and activities. One reason advanced for the indifference or hostility of most of the Negro preachers to organized labor is that they are constantly begging small sums (or large ones if they can get them) from various business concerns and so feel indebted to them.

There are 25,000 steel workers in and around St. Louis and the SWOC started in August, 1936, to organize them. There are a large number of Negroes in the industry and realizing this, the SWOC early sent George Edmonds, a veteran Negro organizer, into St. Louis. He considers the area very complex and difficult and different from any other place in the country. The Negro workers, he holds, play a most important industrial part.

There are 26 locals of the SWOC, and Negroes are active members in all of them. All have Negroes as officers when they can get them, but many Negro members, it is asserted, are too timorous to serve in positions of responsibility and reluctant even to attend meetings.

The largest lodge is that at the American Car Foundry, where Negroes are 50 per cent of the 1,700 workers. At the Scullins Steel Company, 60 per cent of the 1,400 workers are colored, and great difficulty has been experienced in

238

organizing them because of the diversity of work offered them and the fear of unions instilled by the company's propagandists.

There are 2,000 Negroes at the Granite City Casting Company, where a total of 3,800 workers are employed. The SWOC is now struggling to become sole bargaining agent. There has been no great rush of Negroes to join the union.

At the Missouri Rolling Mill, Negroes constitute half of the 600 workers. The plant is 85 per cent organized and a colored man is vice-president of the union.

The Sheffield Steel Company recently signed a contract with the union. Five hundred of its 700 workers are Negroes, and there are a number of colored members serving as union officials. They are on all committees.

Most of the other steel plants are small fabricating concerns which do not employ many Negroes.

About 400 of the 4,000 auto workers in the city are colored. At the time of the strikes no effort was made to organize them and only 15 Negroes joined. Negroes were openly used as scabs during the strikes. The union, it is said, has now changed its policy.

The situation in the laundry industry also reveals how the Southern white attitude works to the detriment of labor in this border city. The AF of L is directing the current drive to organize the 100 laundries in the city. Negroes constitute the majority of the workers, and yet there is not a single Negro organizer or official in the union. Moreover, the laundry drivers in the Truck Drivers' Union will not support the inside laundry workers. As a result, only 12 laundries have been organized and the bulk of Negro laundry workers are not joining the union. Of course, some of this is due to sheer inertia more than anything else—inertia and fear.

The Hotel and Restaurant Employees' Association has 3,000 members, of whom well over 600 are colored. It is an AF of L outfit. While there are some Negroes on committees, there are no officials or organizers. The Negro maids, who have a virtual monopoly in the city's hotels, were wise enough to get through a clause safeguarding their position.

Of the 500 Negroes in the Local No. 603 Teamsters' Union, most of them are moving van men. There are, however, 20 Negro milk-wagon drivers traveling routes for big dairy companies. There are no Negro organizers or officials in the union. One intelligent Negro member said, "Just dumb Irish Catholics run the outfit."

The Amalgamated Association of Street and Electric Railway Employees has about 50 Negro members, all car cleaners. It is said that Negroes are being gradually squeezed out of this work.

There are reported to be many Negroes in the AF of L Cleaners' and Dyers' Union.

The Textile Workers' Organizing Committee has been very active in St. Louis, but there are few Negroes in the industry. In one plant, the Burkhardt Manufacturing Company, they are credited by observers with having done a "phenomenal thing." This company manufactures auto seat covers and employs 300 workers, half of them Negroes. The T.W.O.C. organized the plant, the officials of the local are equally divided between the races, and race relations have improved greatly. When the company recently fired a Negro checker, the whole working force, white and black, pulled a 90-minute strike of protest, which led to the man's reinstatement, it is said.

The workers in garages and auto agencies have been organized by the CIO and there are about 100 Negroes in the union. The AF of L has the repair shops.

The International Longshoremen's Association has two locals, No. 1400 in St. Louis, of which Frank Hargraves is president, and No. 1401 in East St. Louis, of which Jones is president. The membership of the two locals is entirely Negro and numbers around 250. Mr. Hargraves is special organizer for the ILA.

These workers were formerly getting 25 cents an hour and often had to borrow from the commissary, to say nothing of enduring "lay time." They pulled several successful strikes and today they are getting 50 cents an hour.

There are two rival unions of shoe workers, AF of L and CIO. One factory has about 100 colored workers, but Negroes in the industry are mostly janitors and laborers. Few are as yet in either union.

The AF of L Tobacco Workers' Union has about 50 per cent Negroes. There are a large number of Negro women in this industry but they are said to be indifferent to labor organization.

A drive is on to organize city and government employees in whose ranks there are many Negroes, including 500 employed by the Board of Education. But as elsewhere this type of Negro seems timorous and ultra-conservative as a result of his "education."

The Building Service Employees Union is headed by Mr. Messingale, a colored man. A drive is in progress to organize the many Negro elevator operators, porters and maids in department stores. A union official declared that "the Negro is becoming more labor conscious and tends to react favorably." This union, which is 50 per cent colored, is credited with having more contact with Negroes than any other in the city.

It is interesting to note that the Negro beauticians are trying to set up a separate (Jim Crow) union. It is equally significant that the strong local branch of the Brotherhood of Sleeping Car porters refused to pay an assessment to fight the CIO.

I met W. Sentner, national representative of the United Electrical and Radio Workers of America, a CIO affiliate, which covers the plants manufacturing electrical and radio equipment. He reported 6,600 workers in the industry in St. Louis and 5,600 are in the union. Of this number approximately 400 are Negroes. The current drive got well under way in March, 1937.

When the workers struck at the Emerson Electric Co. on March 8, the 46 Negroes in the plant went out 100 per cent with the other workers. They are all in the union. Very few Negroes are in production, being mostly porters. . . .

The Wagner Electric Co. has 3,110 employes, 10 per cent colored. A Negro member was recently elected to the executive committee of 17, and one is on the negotiating committee.

Slow Unionization

At the Century Electrical Co., a Negro, Lawrence Young, is one of the seven members of the union's negotiating committee, although only four of the 50 Negroes in the plant are members of the union. Young has spoken over the radio more times for the union than any other member.

Meat packing is an important industry in this city and while many workers are organized the CIO is preparing to launch a determined drive to get all of them.

The Hod Carriers and Building Laborers group is almost exclusively colored, but aside from that Negroes are virtually barred from the building trades. By some necromancy a Negro was recently permitted to join the plasterers' union and everybody viewed it as a nine-day wonder.

After a long struggle with the reactionary AF of L motion picture projectors union, during which time Negro projectors [projector operators] were getting $8 to $18 weekly, the 20 Negro operators were finally admitted to the union. They now earn from $32 to $55 a week.

Many of the more enlightened Negroes of St. Louis like Sidney Williams, Industrial Secretary of the Urban League, and Arnold Walker, also of the League, have realized the necessity of labor education and the significance of the current labor drive, and have sought through the St. Louis Negro Labor Committee to inform and guide the bewildered Negro workers. The committee has done excellent work in this direction. It is directed by a board of 15. The president is the well-known E. J. Bradley, the vice-president of the Brotherhood of Sleeping Car Porters.

At CIO headquarters in the Title & Guarantee Building, I talked with Bert Taventer, regional director, who claimed 40,000 CIO members in the St. Louis district. As to the Negro's reaction to the current labor drive, Mr. Taventer said, "We have found that they have been very reticent in coming out. We understand that that is because they have been bulldozed in the past. When we get them in the movement and they find that we don't discriminate because of race or creed, they become enthusiastic supporters of the union. They make it a religion."

Concerning the objection of some of the St. Louis white workers to associating with Negroes in the union halls, he said, "Race has undoubtedly interfered with the organized work here. But our position is that if Negroes are good enough to work in the industry, then they are good enough to meet with for the common good."

Mr. Taventer there reflected the spirit prevalent in all of the many CIO offices I have visited.

NORTHEASTERN CITIES

Social Aspects

Among the notable trends in black urban communities in the 1930's were the proliferation of religious cults and the use of coercive methods—the boycott, destruction and pillage of property—to end white discrimination against and exploitation of urban blacks. Both were responses to the difficult times created by the Depression. The cults were invariably led by charismatic and flamboyant figures, doctrinally and ritually unorthodox, and offered a religion at once more personal and truly communal than that offered by the regular church: a religion emotional yet morally austere, one that was supposed to guarantee good health and material well-being, and was politically and socially militant. No wonder the combination appealed to the urban masses living in material and psychological misery.

The Father Divine cult (Document 11) was certainly the most striking and successful of its time. It was led by George Baker, known to his followers as "Father Divine . . . the true and living God." It was uniquely interracial; untypically, it did not exact tithes, at least openly, from its members, and yet catered admirably to their material as well as their emotional needs; it showed a developed social as well as political consciousness. The cult itself continued to thrive well beyond the 1930's, and Father Divine himself assumed an unearthly form in 1965. Other major cults of the thirties and forties were Daddy Grace's United House of Prayer for All; Bishop Ida Robinson's Mt. Sinai Holy Church of America, Inc.; the Black Jews; and the Moorish Science Temple of America.

The Harlem riot of 1935 (Document 12) was directed at property, not people. Triggered by rumor, it was a spontaneous expression of frustration at being exploited by white businessmen. One of the main issues at stake was the hiring of black clerks in the predominantly Jewish-owned Harlem stores.

The third document below describes the southern and Caribbean origin of Harlem's cuisine and indicates how savory dishes were created out of unpromising materials.

242

New York, N.Y. (1935)

11]   Father Divine

The most African characteristic of Harlem, after the color of its people, is the multitude of amazing cults. Native African churches (so-called), groups of Ne-gro-Jews, and a host of straight Christian and revival sects pullulate in Harlem. To say that there is a cult to every block would be no exaggeration.

It is through religion, more than any other channel, that primitive African emotions find expression in our modern civilization. Indoors and along the pul-pit pavements of Harlem, black men and women, some singularly robed, ec-statically prance and reel and writhe with a fervor that is tolerated simply be-cause their exhibitions bear the label of religion. No Negro cabaret or Ne-gro theater could permit the display of such very African antics.

Returning to Harlem after three years spent in North Africa, I had a queer, topsy-turvy sensation when I mingled with folk who were so similar physically to those of North Africa (and from the same cause—miscegenation) but in spirit so different, though they have precisely the same strenuous preoccupa-tion with religion. My arrival in Harlem coincided with a big religious parade. The streets were massed with marching people, led by bands of music, shout-ing, singing, bearing banners proclaiming "Father Divine Is God," "God Al-mighty Is Father Divine." Automobiles loaded with enthusiastic disciples were bright with pennants praising Father Divine. Spectators jammed the pavements. Excited black and brown faces, framed in apartment windows, beamed down on the scene. Suddenly an airplane droned through the clouds, and looking up the people shouted: "God! God! There goes Father! Father Di-vine is God! The true and living God." Never had I seen such excitement in Harlem except in the days of Marcus Garvey's Back-to-Africa movement.

Father Divine is God! With that one phrase Father Divine stands out above all the other leaders and their cults. God, who was invisible to all before, is now personified in him. He has created "Kingdoms" of Heaven in Harlem and elsewhere. "He is sweet, so sweet," chant his "angel" followers, "God, so sweet, Father Divine." According to them Father Divine is the source of all things. He gives his "angels" work, health, food, happiness, prosperity—everything. Accepting nothing, he gives all, being God.

Father Divine was a name unknown to the large public a little more than two years ago. As the leader of a holy-rolling kind of black-and-white cult, he was known only in Sayville, Long Island. There Father Divine had acquired property, upon which he had built a house. The house was called a "king-dom." He had lived there for about ten years. Actually he was supposed

SOURCE: Claude McKay, "'There Goes God!' The Story of Father Divine and His Angels," *The Nation*, February 6, 1935, pp. 151–63. [Claude McKay, 1890–1948, was a poet and leading literary figure of the Harlem Renaissance.—Ed.]

243

to be in retirement after many years of preaching. But some of his faithful white and colored disciples, mainly from New York, continued to visit him, eating, sleeping, and worshiping in his house. As their numbers increased, their presence disturbed the respectable white residents, and Father Divine was prosecuted for maintaining a public nuisance. That colored and white persons of both sexes were united under a Negro leader seemed particularly to incense the presiding judge. In his preliminary examination of Father Divine he laid special emphasis upon that fact.

Meanwhile the case had attracted wide attention, especially among Negroes, because of its white-with-black feature. A clever Negro lawyer with some political influence offered his services free to Father Divine. In Harlem his followers organized large protest meetings. At one of these meetings, held at the Rush Memorial Baptist Church, a leading disciple exhorted the assembled congregation to hold together and be not dismayed, for their Father Divine would sentence the judge to death if the judge dared to sentence him to prison.

The court was unable to elicit anything about the antecedents of Father Divine, since he insisted that he had been divinely projected into existence and had no record of his life. Thereupon the judge committed him to jail, to obtain further information and to have his mental condition determined by a psychiatrist. When the case came up for final trial, the judge sentenced Father Divine to a year in prison and $500 fine. Curiously, three days after the sentence the judge died suddenly. He was very old and had been stricken by heart disease. To the Divine disciples the hand of their Father had struck the judge dead. They even reported that Father Divine had said that he regretted having to make an example of the judge. The news spread through the country.

Father Divine's attorney appealed the sentence. The verdict was reversed by the Brooklyn Supreme Court, which ruled that the presiding judge had injected prejudice into the minds of the jurors. Upon being released, Father Divine entered into his apotheosis. Overnight his following had developed into a vast army. The man who had retired to Sayville emerged as God. He came to New York again and thousands flocked to the Rockland Palace to hear him speak.

"Peace!" he cried to them; "Good health, good appetite, prosperity, and a heart full of merriness. I give you all and everything." And his people responded: "God! It is wonderful! I thank you, Father." Such is the essence of the Divine message and the response it calls forth. And so greatly grew that response that Father Divine alone could not handle it as he had done at Sayville. More and greater "kingdoms" had to be created. Father Divine declares, and his followers believe, that he is in all of them at the same time. "I am here and I am there and I am everywhere," he says. "I am like the radio voice. Dial in and you shall always find me."

Fifteen Divine kingdoms are maintained in New York City alone. In fine buildings all. The finest is the former bath premises in 126th Street, now known as the Faithful Mary Kingdom. Other kingdoms are in Jamaica, Brooklyn, and White Plains, in New Jersey and Connecticut. From Washington, D. C., to Seattle, Washington, centers have been established by Father Divine enthusiasts. Headquarters Kingdom, where Father Divine has office and residence, is in 115th Street. In whichever "kingdom" he eats, Father Divine himself serves his flock. The food goes through his hands before it is served. He pours and passes the coffee and cream in the grand style of a maître d'hotel. And he has more dignity and naturalness doing that than when he is haranguing an audience.

The kingdoms are sanitary and apparently well managed. They pay their way. The secret of their financing is Father Divine's. Rooms are rented to individuals at a dollar a week, but there is more than one person to a room. In the restaurants meals are served for ten and fifteen cents. The food is good and plentiful. A good piece of meat and two vegetables cost ten cents; a piece of cake or ice-cream, five cents; coffee or soft drink, three cents. There are separate kingdoms for men and women. For in the kingdoms sex is proscribed.

The decorative motif of all the kingdoms is the apotheosis of Divine. His enlarged photographs dominate the walls. Large posters with black and red lettering proclaim his virtues: "Father Divine is God." "Father Divine is the living Tree of Life, Father, Son, and Holy Ghost." "We all may take of the words of Father Divine, eat and drink and live forever." Other posters make a queer melange of social and religious statements. They reveal that Father Divine is aware of social problems and that he has a special approach to them. Framed newspaper clippings advertise Father Divine's letters to firms doing business with him, from which he solicits jobs for his people. Also displayed are letters to the mayor referring to Father Divine's secret service, which is investigating racial and color discrimination and segregation in New York City institutions. One poster reads:

> We the Inter-racial, International, Inter-denominational and Inter-religious Coworkers . . . as being called Father Divine's Peace Mission Workers . . . do demand the release through commutation of the life sentence of the Scottsboro boys, and other means of releasing the nine boys. And also we demand freedom, and extermination of the mistreatment of the Jews in Germany and all other countries, and we demand the equal rights and religious liberty according to our Constitution.
>
> I thank you, Father.

Enthusiastic masses of colored people, with a sprinkling of whites, West Indians, and Latin Americans, make up the kingdoms. Women predominate, forming about three quarters of the whole number. It is largely a middle-aged crowd. No prayers are said at the meetings. Praise has taken the place of prayer in Father Divine's religion. He often quotes: "Prayer is the heart's sincere desire, unuttered or unexpressed." And instead of praying, his people testify, praising and thanking him. Of music and singing and dancing there is no end—a riotous, prancing, antic performance that "it is wonderful" indeed to see and to feel. Loosely the women fling themselves about, with a verve and freedom that would startle a cabaret. They toss up their skirts and contort their limbs, dancing and singing to Father Divine:

> I don't know why, I don't know why,
> I don't know why you love me so . . .
> You put your arms around me and you took me in. . . .

With nervous, petulant gestures they turn from the men, the forbidden, and dance extravagantly with one another, colored with colored and colored with white. After they are exhausted from singing and dancing in chorus, they give individual testimony—amazing testimony, whether openly given in the kingdoms or privately related.

At Headquarters Kingdom I saw a little, wiry black man cleave through the jam to reach and kneel a moment against the back of Father Divine's chair. Standing up again with uplifted hand he cried: "Peace—O Father, thank you, Father, for what you have done for me. Father, I used to think I was smart. But I was all wrong and bad. I used to take the Jew man's furniture and then change my address and sell it. But Father, you showed me where I was wicked and I don't do that no more. And I mean to pay back all what I stole. And Father, I used to make the women pay. I was a mean feller, Father. Until I find one woman what was different and wouldn't pay off. And I wanted her, Father. And wanted her that bad I couldn't help falling for her. But I had to take it the way she wanted to give. And she made me go housekeeping together like an honest couple and I changed my ways and worked like a man. Then we both heard about you, Father. And we came to you. And you stopped us from living in sin, thank you, Father it is wonderful. Peace. And you put me in one kingdom, Father, and put her in another. And you did right, for Father Divine is always right. But oh, Father, she been coming to my room every night in my dreams. It was powerful awful, Father, and I was afraid and asked you to guide me. I concentrated on your spirit, Father, and last night when I was dreaming she come again and all at once you just descended into the room like a lightning bolt between us. Oh, thank you, Father. It was wonderful."

"It is wonderful!" everybody echoes and joined in singing: "All hail the power of Father's name, let angels prostrate fall."

From a mulatto young woman standing behind Father Divine's chair escaped a frightening yell. "Father, you did call me," she cried, "call me all the way from Seattle, Father, let me confess the truth that I had sinful thoughts about you, sinful, deceitful woman as I am. I imagined that you were just another colored minister. I said, Father can't be so different, he is just another one. For I have lived my life, Father, as a sample and example of a free woman among men and counted my victims. All the long way from Seattle I came, Father, thinking evil. And when I entered your presence and tried to fix you, you fixed me instead. You saw straight through me, Father, the lust that was in me, and you drove it out of me into the Gadarene swine. And, oh, Father, you were God in the place of the man I was looking for. You put your spirit in me and made me pure, one of your 'angels,' Father. I thank you, Father. It is truly wonderful."

California and other points west have supplied most of the white followers. An old man in his sixties said that he had left California doubting that Father Divine could be more than a prophet, because there is a passage from the Bible which says that no man can look upon God and live. But as soon as he saw Father Divine he was convinced that he was in the presence of God. And he immediately experienced a transformation from a mortal to an angel. He lives now in one of the kingdoms.

246

Father Divine

The skeptic part of Harlem's population, whatever its opinion of Father Divine, is excited over his success and the financing of it. Unlike other evangelists Father Divine never collects any money at his meetings; he delights in making a mystery about the source of the funds he uses to run his Divine Trust of large, well-appointed kingdoms, cheap restaurants (where hundreds of hungry out-of-work persons are fed free daily), and the splendid buses and automobiles which convey his disciples from kingdom to kingdom. He waxes sharply waggish when inquiries are made. He told a group of white parsons, professors, and students that he got his money from the Treasury in Washington, just like other people. At his meetings he jokes with his followers about "people who want to know where I get my money." "They want to know how I get my money. But you all know I take absolutely nothing." "Right, Father! Yes, Father!" the people cry. "I give everything, because I am omnipotent. I give you plenty of good food, clothes, shelter, work. And you are fat and merry." "Yes, Father! Thank you, Father!" the people shout. "It is wonderful!"

Graciously granted an interview, I could not ask Father Divine how he got his money. His white secretary had explicitly stated to me beforehand: "Father Divine does not accept money from his followers. Rich people interested in his work have offered large sums of money which Father Divine has refused, because he does not want to be limited in the conception of his work." The secretary also intimated that inquiries about the source of his income were annoying to Father Divine. I said that primarily my interest was in Father Divine's work.

In his sumptuous living quarters, African in the gay conglomeration of colors, Father Divine in a large easychair appeared like a slumping puppet abandoned after a marionette show. He seemed shrunk even smaller than his five feet four, which is not unimpressive when he is acting. He pointed to a seat near him, and said he thought he had said enough at his meetings to give me an idea of his work and mission. I told him that I was interested mainly in his ideas about social problems and interracial relations and would like a special pronouncement from him as a Negro leader and pacifist. Father Divine replied: "I have no color conception of myself. If I were representing race or creed or color or nation, I would be limited in my conception of the universal. I would not be as I am, omnipotent."

I said that I accepted his saying that he was above race and color, but because he happened to have been born brown and was classified in the colored group, the world was more interested in him as a Negro. And I asked him what was his plan for the realization of peace and understanding between the masses and the classes. Father Divine said: "I am representative of the universal through the cooperation of mind and spirit in which is reality. I cannot deviate from that fundamental. The masses and the classes must transcend the average law and accept me. And governments in time will come to recognize my law."

I drew his attention to an editorial in the *Daily Worker* referring to the demonstration against war and fascism, in which the Communists had paraded in company with Father Divine at the head of thousands of his people carrying banners bearing Divine slogans. The editorial was an explanation to critical readers of the necessity of cooperating with Father Divine and his followers, "carrying such strange and foolish placards." Father Divine said that he was always willing to cooperate in his own way with the Communists or any group that was fighting for international peace and emancipation of people throughout the world and against any form of segregation and racial discrimination. But what the Communists were trying to do he was actually doing, by bringing people of different races and nations to live together and work in peace under his will. He had come to free every nation, every language, every tongue, and every people. He did not need the Communists or any other organization, but they needed him. For he had all wisdom and understanding and health and wealth. And he alone could give emancipation and liberty, for he was the victory. I thanked Father Divine for the interview, and he dismissed me with the gift of a pamphlet.

The followers of Father Divine are always ready to testify to his divinity, the glory of the kingdoms, the sweetness of the fellowship, and the wonders of his works. But ask a pertinent question about the Divine finance and immediately they clamp their lips. That is something as taboo with them as it is with Father Divine.

Some cabalistic thing, such as exists in a secret society, may be at the bottom of this. The Divine disciples are called "angels." And Father Divine has said, "Denial of money is Angelship degree." Even those who have ceased to be followers will not discuss it. There is a story of a Negro petty shopkeeper who disappeared taking $1,500 of his own money. Investigating, his wife discovered him in one of the kingdoms, but without the money. Finally he was persuaded to return home. But neither he nor his wife will discuss the incident or what has become of the money.

Perhaps a clue to the Divine method of finance may be found in Faithful Mary. She was the first disciple of Father Divine. At all his big meetings she sits at his right. In striking contrast to him, her brown-moon face shines with a disarming otherworldliness. She is middle-aged, a fine-fleshed, compact, and balanced motherly woman. She testifies that she had been insane from drink for ten years, had been discharged from hospitals as incurable. She was living soddenly in the gutters of Broome Street in Newark, eating out of garbage cans, when she heard about Father Divine. She concentrated upon him, believing that he was God. He lifted her up and cured her. And now she belongs to God. Faithful Mary's sincerity strikes you; her story is convincing.

Father Divine's little white secretary, who unlike Father Divine does talk about the material side of the Peace Mission, had this to say of Faithful Mary: "She is blessed with the love of the people and they give her great gifts. They have given her houses to be converted into kingdoms, clothes, and automobiles. The largest kingdom in 126th Street was given to her." If Father Divine as God takes absolutely nothing, his first disciple, Faithful Mary, is not like him. And she declares that she belongs to God.

"It is truly wonderful," even as the "angels" of Harlem sing-song, this frantic, prancing expression of black emotionalism in the heart of the great white city.

248

New York, N.Y. (1935)

12]   Harlem Riot

Docile Harlem went on a rampage last week, smashing stores and looting them
and piling up destruction of thousands of dollars worth of goods. But the mass
riot in Harlem was not a race riot. A few whites were jostled by colored people in the melee, but there was no manifest hostility between colored and
white as such. All night until dawn on the Tuesday of the outbreak white persons, singly and in groups, walked the streets of Harlem without being mo-
lested. The action of the police was commendable in the highest degree. The
looting was brazen and daring, but the police were restrained. In extreme
cases, when they fired, it was into the air. Their restraint saved Harlem from
becoming a shambles.

The outbreak was spontaneous. It was directed against the stores exclusively. One-Hundred-andTwenty-fifth Street is Harlem's main street and the
theatrical and shopping center of the colored thousands. Anything that starts
there will flash through Harlem as quick as lightning. The alleged beating of a
kid caught stealing a trifle in one of the stores merely served to explode the
smoldering discontent of the colored people against the Harlem merchants.

It would be too sweeping to assert that radicals incited the Harlem mass riot
and pillage. The Young Liberators seized an opportune moment, but the explosion on Tuesday was not the result of Communist propaganda. There were,
indeed, months of propaganda in it. But the propagandists are eager to disso-
ciate themselves from Communists. Proudly they declare that they have agi-
tated only in the American constitutional way for fair play for colored Harlem.

Colored people all over the world are notoriously the most exploitable material, and colored Harlem is no exception. The population is gullible to an
extreme. And apparently the people are exploited so flagrantly because they
invite and take it. It is their gullibility that gives to Harlem so much of its
charm, its air of insouciance and gaiety. But the facade of the Harlem masses'
happy-go-lucky and hand-to-mouth existence has been badly broken by the depression. A considerable part of the population can no longer cling even to the
hand-to-mouth margin.

Wherever an ethnologically related group of people is exploited by others,
the exploiters often operate on the principle of granting certain concessions as
sops. In Harlem the exploiting group is overwhelmingly white. And it gives no
sops. And so for the past two years colored agitators have exhorted the colored
consumers to organize and demand of the white merchants a new deal: that
they should employ Negroes as clerks in the colored community. These agitators are crude men, theoretically. They have little understanding of and little
interest in the American labor movement, even from the most conservative

SOURCE: Claude McKay, "Harlem Runs Wild," *The Nation*, April 3, 1935, pp.
382–83.

trade-union angle. They address their audience mainly on the streets. Their following is not so big as that of the cultists and occultists. But it is far larger than that of the Communists.

One of the agitators is outstanding and picturesque. He dresses in turban and gorgeous robe. He has a bigger following than his rivals. He calls himself Sufi Abdul Hamid. His organization is the Negro Industrial and Clerical Alliance. It was the first to start picketing the stores of Harlem demanding clerical employment for colored persons. Sufi Hamid achieved a little success. A few of the smaller Harlem stores engaged colored clerks. But on 125th Street the merchants steadfastly refused to employ colored clerical help. The time came when the Negro Industrial and Clerical Alliance felt strong enough to picket the big stores on 125th Street. At first the movement got scant sympathy from influential Negroes and the Harlem intelligentsia as a whole. Physically and mentally, Sufi Hamid is a different type. He does not belong. And moreover he used to excoriate the colored newspapers, pointing out that they would not support his demands on the bigger Harlem stores because they were carrying the stores' little ads.

Harlem was excited by the continued picketing and the resultant "incidents." Sufi Hamid won his first big support last spring when one of the most popular young men in Harlem, the Reverend Adam Clayton Powell, Jr., assistant pastor of the Abyssinian Church—the largest in Harlem—went on the picket line on 125th Street. This gesture set all Harlem talking and thinking and made the headlines of the local newspapers. It prompted the formation of a Citizens' League for Fair Play. The league was endorsed and supported by sixty-two organizations, among which were eighteen of the leading churches in Harlem. And at last the local press conceded some support.

One of the big stores capitulated and took on a number of colored clerks. The picketing of other stores was continued. And soon business was not so good as it used to be on 125th Street.

In the midst of the campaign Sufi Hamid was arrested. Sometime before his arrest a committee of Jewish Minute Men had visited the Mayor and complained about the anti-Semitic movement among the colored people and the activities of a black Hitler in Harlem. The *Day* and the *Bulletin,* Jewish newspapers, devoted columns to the Harlem Hitler and anti-Semitism among Negroes. The articles were translated and printed in the Harlem newspapers under big headlines denouncing the black Hitler and his work.

On October 13 of last year Sufi Hamid was brought before the courts charged with disorderly conduct and using invective against the Jews. The witnesses against him were the Chairman of the Minute Men and other persons more or less connected with the merchants. After hearing the evidence and the defense, the judge decided that the evidence was biased and discharged Sufi Hamid. Meanwhile Sufi Hamid had withdrawn from the Citizens' League for Fair Play. He had to move from his headquarters and his immediate following was greatly diminished. An all-white Harlem Merchants' Association came into existence. Dissension divided the Citizens' League; the prominent members denounced Sufi Hamid and his organization.

In an interview last October Sufi Hamid told me that he had never styled

Harlem Soul Food

himself the black Hitler. He said that once when he visited a store to ask for
the employment of colored clerks, the proprietor remarked, "We are fighting
Hitler in Germany." Sufi said that he replied, "There is no Hitler in Harlem."
He went on to say that although he was a Moslem he had never entertained
any prejudices against Jews as Jews. He was an Egyptian and in Egypt the relations between Moslem and Jew were happier than in any country. He was
opposed to Hitlerism, for he had read Hitler's book, *Mein Kampf* and knew
Hitler's attitude and ideas about all colored peoples. Sufi Hamid said that the
merchants of Harlem spread the rumor of anti-Semitism among the colored
people because they did not want to face the issue of giving them a square
deal.

The Citizens' League continued picketing, and some stores capitulated. But
the Leaguers began quarreling among themselves as to whether the clerks employed should be light-skinned or dark-skinned. Meanwhile the united white
Harlem Merchants' Association was fighting back. In November the picketing
committee was enjoined from picketing by Supreme Court Justice Samuel Ro-
senman. The Court ruled that the Citizens' League was not a labor organization. It was the first time that such a case had come before the courts of New
York. The chairman of the picketing committee remarked that "the decision
would make trouble in Harlem."

One by one the colored clerks who had been employed in 125th Street
stores lost their places. When inquiries were made as to the cause, the managements gave the excuse of slack business. The clerks had no organization behind them. Of the grapevine intrigue and treachery that contributed to the debacle of the movement, who can give the facts? They are as obscure and
inscrutable as the composite mind of the Negro race itself. So the masses of
Harlem remain disunited and helpless, while their would-be leaders wrangle
and scheme and denounce one another to the whites. Each one is ambitious to
wear the mantle of Marcus Garvey.

On Tuesday the crowds went crazy like the remnants of a defeated, abandoned, and hungry army. Their rioting was the gesture of despair, of a bewildered, baffled, and disillusioned people.

New York, N.Y. (1935)

13]   Harlem Soul Food

The song writers, the story writers, even the columnists have glorified Harlem
as a place that is redolent with the aroma of fried chicken (Southern style of
course), and golden-brown crispy waffles. But that is the restaurant olfactory
teaser. Drop a smell-detective (blind-folded, please) into the middle of a residential block about dinner time. Ask him where he is, and why he thinks so.
He will tell you Harlem because he smells pork-and-greens cooking. Pork-and-

SOURCE: Viola Glenn, "The Eating Habits of Harlem," *Opportunity*, March 1935, pp.
82–85.

251

greens is as characteristic of the Negro race as sauerkraut of the Germans or fish pudding of the Finns.

The culinary history of the Negro race in America is a tale of an heroic struggle of a food loving people against the grimmest of economic conditions. Ruthlessly tossed into a strange, new land; hard worked, and poorly fed, then freed to enjoy pinching poverty, they have nevertheless survived, and out of their survival has grown a cookery as distinctive as that of any nation.

In pioneer days hogs were raised with practically no effort or expenditure; they roamed the woods for food or were fed on swill. Thus pork, fresh, salted and smoked, was the ideal meat to feed Negroes. They grew to love its sweet fatness. But good cuts of meat were meagerly doled out: so, with the ingenuity of the truly hungry, Negro women evolved tasty dishes out of the parts that were considered waste. Under skilled hands chitterlings, hog's maw, tails, heads, ears, spareribs, backbones and feet were made into palatable, filling meals.

Cornmeal was cheap, so they used plenty of that too, and busied themselves finding new ways and means of including it in the menu.

Greens grew wild or thrived luxuriantly with little cultivation; they too became everyday food.

Most of the cabins in the South had only one pot and a tiny fire with no oven. The cooking of the greens and the pork together was necessary. In the absence of an oven pones and potatoes were buried in the ashes to bake or roast.

When the Negro had become fairly well adjusted to the life in the new land there came "The Wah." After it ended, amid the groans of the hungry and a cloud of general misery, the Negro need call no man master. But he was left with only the Lord and his own resourcefulness to provide his daily corn pone. He soon learned.

If he helped around at "hawg killin'" he could take home the "innerds," and the tails and other such no-'count parts. Sometimes he was given a whole head or a slab of fat belly meat as a reward. If he had a few pennies pork was the cheapest meat that he could buy. And he learned the art of raising a hog or two himself.

Greens could still be picked in the fields or along the roadsides. With very little cultivation they grew in almost any soil, with very few crop failures. Sweet potatoes were easy to grow too.

Cornmeal was filling and still cheap—many pennies cheaper than white flour.

Even to-day you will find chitterlings, maws, tails, heads, ears, spareribs, backbones and feet in great quantities in the butcher shops of Harlem. Indeed a nationally known packing house is putting chitterlings on the market in tin pails. Many slaughter houses make a specialty of selling these various parts to butchers who sell to the Negro trade. Plenty of tripe, liver, kidney and some lung are sold as well. Salt pork is a big seller. It is boiled with the greens or is freshened, sliced, fried and served with cream gravy. A small piece may be used just to flavor the greens, or a sufficient quantity to make the meat course of the meal. For the latter purpose it is served over the greens in thin slices, and enough "potlikker" to insure thorough dunking for the cornbread.

Regardless of a feverish pork market most of the above mentioned articles are still sound economic buys.

Bacon is also a good seller among Negroes. When in funds they buy ham, preferably the blackened looking, smoky smelling kind known to the trade as "Virginia Cured Style." This is fried or boiled with cabbage or collard greens —a green of the cabbage family that doesn't head up—and potatoes. Pork chops and fresh roast ham are in high favor. From the latter is usually obtained the cracklin' for the cracklin' bread.

Of course lamb and beef are used to some extent. Beef stews and beef steak are the two most popular dishes. At the street stands hamburgers and frankfurters vie with the oldtime favorite pork chop sandwiches. To-day rotisseries and barbecue places are the favorites.

During the season rabbits are much in demand for stew.

Chicken is a favorite food, but a chicken in the pot or on the frying pan means money in the family, and money is scarce.

Negroes rank second in fish eating among the three groups who consume the greatest quantity of fish in the city. The other two are Italians and Jews.

Negroes are especially fond of the smaller, sweet-tasting oily fishes. This preference too can be traced back to the years when streams were well stocked, and it was restful to sit quietly on a river bank after the day's work and wait for a fish to grab at the line: an easy way to provide today's supper or tomorrow's dinner. It was easy, too, to roll the cleaned fish in cornmeal and fry it a golden brown.

All sorts of fish that are oily are popular, especially if they are fried. Good sellers are spots, porgies, mackerel—the Spanish mackerel is well liked but is usually rather expensive—butterfish, weakfish and blues.

Southern Negroes are fond of catfish, but about the only cats that are marketed in New York are the bullheads, although a few sea-going cats are brought in by trawlers from Southern waters.

The Southern Negro also likes the pompano, which is rated cheap on this market when it sells at fifty cents the pound.

Smoked fish doesn't as a rule appeal to Negroes, nor does most of the salt fish. He has however a fondness for salt mackerel, and there is some sale for salt herring.

Shrimps are the most popular and best liked of the shellfish. Here too we must consider history. In the South shrimping was exclusively a Negro industry, and the little shellfish were plentiful and cheap.

Today a dime a pound is the average price of raw shrimp. The usual dish prepared with them is Shrimp à la Creole, which is a mixture of rice, shrimp, onion, peppers and tomatoes highly seasoned and cooked together.

Fried scallops are well liked.

Those who have been brought up near tide water like oysters; first fried, then in stew and lastly raw. Clams are not favored at all.

In the vegetable line, greens and yellow yams pile the stands. The best liked

253

greens are these: kale—the pale green summer variety in preference to the darker green winter kale; cabbage, collards, turnip and mustard greens. In fact all the greens are liked although the bitter ones such as dandelion and escarole are not rated as highly as the others. In some neighborhoods there is a good sale of spinach. But on the whole it has to be very cheap to be considered by the majority. This is undoubtedly due to the fact that spinach is one green that does not cook to the best advantage with meat. During the past two or three years both the early spring broccoli heads have advanced in popularity and are now a good selling item on the markets.

Broccoli is a delightful green cooked as Negroes cook it. They will tell you that the proper way to cook greens is to put on your meat, which is usually salt pork or bacon, with enough water to cover it. After it has cooked 30 or 45 minutes you add the greens and let the whole dish simmer until all is cooked. The mixture is served, as before mentioned, with the slices of pork over the top of the greens and plenty of "pot-likker." Sometimes cornmeal dumplings are cooked with this. If other meat is to be used then the greens are cooked with a generous spoonful of bacon fat or pork drippings added to flavor. Salt pork or jowl is usually served with turnip greens, and ham or spare ribs accompany cabbage or collards.

String beans and snap cow peas are both sure, fast sellers, Both should be cooked as are greens with a piece of meat or a spoonful of fat. Green peas, lima beans, tomatoes, okra and corn are good sellers. All the commoner vegetables such as carrots and turnips are also bought in good quantities. Of the potato family sweets and yams are the most used although there is a fair sale of whites. Many breads, pones, and at least two kinds of sweet potato pie—a mashed and a sliced—are their contribution to sweet potato cookery.

When it is necessary to skimp the diet the first item to suffer a cut is the fruit. Blackberries, peaches, apples, bananas, melons of all kinds, grapefruit and oranges are the best sellers. Again going back to history we know why blackberries and peaches are made into such lovely dishes, including the dumplings and the cobblers. The rest of the fruits are usually regarded as something to have in a dish around the house or buy on the street to help fill in between meals.

Of the legumes the black-eyed or cow pea which is really a bean is the heaviest seller. The pink bean is the next best seller followed by the white and the lima. The much-heard-of dish called Hopping John is created by combining salt pork or pig's head with black-eyed peas and rice.

Of the cereals, rice is easily in the lead, followed closely by cornmeal, then hominy grits and hominy.

Many hot breads are used, and loved, as are the highly seasoned spicy foods. Molasses, eggs and milk are used in fairly good quantities.

On the whole the diet of American Negroes is quite adequate to supply all the bodily needs as to calories, vitamins and minerals. It is true that they live on all the cheaper stuffs, but they are plentifully supplied with all the elements needed by the body for growth and maintenance.

A few years ago welfare workers told pitiful tales of undernourishments, rickets and other nutritive derangements found in Harlem. But in spite of the fact that we have a depression and Harlem is still suffering from some of these ills the condition probably is not a matter of diet primarily. It was, and is still, caused by housing conditions, inadequate financial earnings, and, in part, to uneducated mothers.

Negroes are becoming more cosmopolitan in eating. They are branching out and trying all sorts of new foods and new ways of preparing the old standbys. One of the dishes that they have wholeheartedly adopted into their dietary [habits] is the Italian dish of spaghetti.

But, dietetically speaking, Harlem is beginning to see the light. Today those who have money know better how to spend it. Daughters of the well-to-do are being educated at schools, and mothers are instructed at clinics or by the family doctor or the visiting nurse in the district. As a result bad food habits at least among the employed are changing into good ones. Balanced diets are served in many homes, even if they are the homes of the poor.

The West Indian Negro [1] coming up to "the States" has built up a beautiful dream: a dream of a job that will provide three good meals a day.

Once off the ship and into the town he begins to feel that the only difference between himself and his ancestors who came from Africa is that he had a much pleasanter boat ride.

Usually he speaks Spanish, although he may speak French, Dutch or English. He quickly gets into a neighborhood where his own language is spoken.

Even if the language barrier is pushed aside he is faced with a very hard problem: that of getting used to a complete change of diet. Some of the everyday foods that he has been used to are not available, or the price is beyond the limited family income. The price that the market man asks for a couple of rosy-cheeked Hayden mangoes, little fellows just the right size to snuggle comfortably in the hand, is the price of a basketful down home. So, until he gets used to the American ways, if he decides that he ever will, he sticks to the same old diet of rice and beans, with fried eggs and tomatoes when he has the eggs and the tomatoes.

The West Indians have been reared in the semi-tropics where a blazing sun and lack of refrigeration combine to discourage the use of left-overs. Frequently they throw away, regarding it as likely to be unfit for use next day, enough food to make an excellent second-day dinner for an American Negro.

They use a great deal of beef. This is due to the fact that oxen ran wild on the Islands as did the hogs in America. The term "buccaneer" which finally came to mean pirate originally referred to those who captured the "boucans" or wild bulls of Haiti and used them for food.

The West Indies are close to the great cattle raising countries of South America. These countries ship in beef that is frozen, sun-dried or corned.

Fresh beef is for stews, roasts and beefsteak; and what beefsteak! The slices are cut as thin as steak can be cut, then they are rubbed with just a little smashed garlic and left to soak all night in plenty of sour orange juice. Next

[1] According to the 1930 census, there were 54,754 foreign-born blacks in New York City (16.7% of the black population), of which the vast majority were from the Caribbean.

255

day, seasoned with salt and pepper, these steaks are fried in a frying pan, and boiled rice is put into the pan afterward to be mixed with the rich steak gravy. It is a dish for an epicure.

The dried beef is very hard with a smoky-yellow outer-surface, and inside it looks very black. It is used in stews by just cutting into pieces and stewing. But the usual way is to cut it into pieces then pound the pieces until they can be shredded and pulled apart. This is cooked with garlic, onions, sweet and hot peppers, and tomatoes. But in New York beef is dear, and dried beef if procurable at all is in the luxury class.

Although they use lard a great deal for frying, West Indians are not versed in the art of cooking the cheaper cuts of pork to advantage. However they love the taste of pork and use it when they cannot afford beef. But they usually want chops, ham or bacon; so little other pork is sold in West Indian neighborhoods.

Of course they are fond of chicken. Is not "arroz con pollo"—chicken with rice—one of the dishes that one might say are traditional?

A great many eggs are used if the prices are fairly low. They are fairly fond of cheese, and much more accustomed to oleomargarine than they are to butter. But the use of fresh milk is not common. They are used to the canned milk, which keeps will in the tropics.

They use more molasses, brown sugar and oil in their cooking than does the American Negro.

They are fond of fish. It is cheap in the Islands and they eat a great deal, both dried and salt fish especially if they come from the interior. Fish soups and stews are not only well made but well liked. Fish and rice with or without tomato sauce is a favorite dish, as is the dried codfish cooked in hot tomato sauce. Some of the Islands make fishcakes of salt fish and yellow cornmeal cooked together and seasoned with plenty of freshly ground black pepper. When this is cooked it is made into flat cakes and fried in lard. These are often sold at the roadside stands.

Now let us talk about the semi-tropical produce that can be bought in New York. The Department of Markets ought to do a great deal of talking along that line if the jumble of misinformation that the *New York Times* allowed to be printed in their Sunday Magazine on December 23, 1934, is any yard stick to measure the knowledge of John J. Public. But reporters who have tramped the markets know that the public are looking, asking intelligent questions, and buying semi-tropical produce.

Just at present the average price of this semi-tropical foodstuff is high, the supply is limited and often not first quality. However the supply is ever increasing, and the prices are being hammered down. Not only are the natives of semi-tropical countries demanding this sort of stuff but Northerners who have tried it are also asking for more.

Florida and Georgia are slowly waking up to the fact that they too can produce this type of produce. But it is high time for them to progress out of the experimental into the profitable shipping stage. If they would make efforts as fast as Nature could be induced to cooperate there should shortly be a fairly reasonably priced, dependable supply of first class stuffs on the Northern markets.

Employment in Industries

Until then the West Indian on a limited budget will try to exist on a diet not only of inadequate value but of very limited variety.

Economic Aspects

The selection below on Pittsburgh (Document 14) exemplifies the precarious economic position of blacks in the industrial North East. Document 16 points to the growth of black business cooperatives in Philadelphia—in the absences of access to white capital—to provide loans for home building, while Document 15 describes the relative success in the same city of the new CIO unionization drive.

Pittsburgh, Pa. (1935)

14]   Employment in Industries

Where the Negro Works: By Types of Firms:
(excluding, for the moment, firms
not employing any Negroes)

	TOTAL EMPLOYEES	NEGRO EMPLOYEES	PER CENT NEGRO IS OF TOTAL	PER CENT OF NEGROES IN EACH CLASS
Builders' supplies	645	75	11.62	.69
Building construction	459	67	11.59	.61
Domestic (hotels, etc.)	4,248	1,235	29.07	11.42
Education (janitors, not teachers)	1,216	74	6.08	.69
Manufacturing	81,642	6,055	7.41	55.96
Mining	10,712	1,149	18.19	18.01
Printing, Publishing	2,397	24	1.00	.22
Professional (hospitals, etc.)	929	130	13.99	1.21
Trade	17,445	806	4.62	7.44
Transportation	11,237	406	3.61	3.75
TOTALS	130,930	10,821	8.25	100.00

SOURCE: R. Maurice Moss, "The Negro in Pittsburgh's Industries," *Opportunity*, February 1935, pp. 40–42, 59.

What the Negro Worker Does:

	MALE	FEMALE	TOTAL
Supervisory work	11	0	11
Professional and clerical	7	1	8
°Skilled work	77	0	77
Semi-skilled	737	90	827
Common labor	9,443	455	9,898
TOTALS	10,275	546	10,821

° In counting workers as "skilled," "semi-skilled," etc., the rate of pay (rather than the operation performed) was used as the basis for classification.

Practically all of the firms covered were operating under NRA codes. *Not a single instance of differential in pay* on the basis of race was reported. But the vast majority of the Negro workers, as may be seen by the above table, found themselves in the types of work, or on those processes, which pay the minimum under the codes. The highest paid Negro employee reported upon received $236.00 per month; the next highest received $180.00. The bus companies hire Negroes as porters on tips only. They reported an average income of but $5.00 to $6.00 per week.

The total weekly pay-roll for these 10,821 Negroes would not exceed $200,000, even if each and every one of them worked full time at the "rate of pay" shown by the pay rolls. Actually at least one-quarter of them were working only "part-time" so that the total weekly income of the group was thereby considerably reduced. We believe that the figure of $170,000 is a generous estimate of the actual earnings of this group of ten thousand workers each week.

The survey showed that comparatively few Negro women are employed by Allegheny County's larger industrial or commercial firms. Of the 731 firms studied, 679 employ women in some capacity. But only 52 of these same 679 concerns that had women employees had any Negro women on their pay rolls. Their Negro female employees totaled only 546 and only one of these was reported to be an office-employee. It apparently "just does not occur to the employees that Negroes can do office work."

The largest employers of Negro women were the department stores (104), the hotels (102), the hospitals (97), the clothing trades (86), and the laundries (72). Practically all of those employed in the clothing trades worked in one plant.

The major classification for these 546 Negro women workers were maids (100), needle workers (86), laundresses (93), tobacco strippers (18), elevator operators (15), janitresses (5), and checkroom attendants (5). The others were scattered as cleaners and dyers, cooks, dishwashers, matrons, wrappers, pressers and scrubwomen. There was one office-clerk, one saleslady, and one seamstress.

Of the 731 firms studied, 282 (38.1 per cent) employed no Negroes whatever. They covered the entire field of business activity in the County and

Blacks in Unions

frequently were found to be located very near to competing firms which do hire Negroes. Of the 282 firms which do not employ Negroes in any capacity 86 come under the heading: "Firms employing fifty or more persons," with an aggregate employed force of 18,289. The ten largest of these firms alone have 10,044 employees on their payrolls, ranging from 4,600 to 400.

The reasons given for not employing Negroes varied, and were frequently ridiculous in the extreme. One firm reported that it could not hire Negroes because "the nature of our work makes it necessary for our employees to go into the intimate recesses of homes." Thousands of the same homes are occupied by Negro families while Negro servants certainly go into "the intimate recesses" of thousands of the white homes of the city. Another said: "The mill next door hires Negroes; therefore, we shouldn't."

The replies from the 86 largest firms (not employing Negroes) showed: No special reason (40); Negroes never applied (11); Specialized work at which no Negroes are skilled (9); Unions supply help and no Negro members of the particular union (5); racial prejudice (21). "No work that can be segregated," "white help better," "in white locality," were some of the other answers to this question of why the pay rolls are lily-white.

Philadelphia, Pa. (1937)

15]   Blacks in Unions

Negro workers of this city are living up to the tradition of intelligent militancy established over a century ago when the first conferences of free Negroes were held. This may be "Sleep Town" in common parlance but the activities of Negro workers belie this nickname.

Accompanied by Donald W. Wyatt, industrial secretary of the Armstrong Association, I visited the CIO headquarters on North Broad street to find out just what part Negro labor is playing in the drive now on to organize the workers of this metropolis.

An old 4-story building with stone facade and ornate entrance, the place is a beehive of activity with clerks busy and telephone bells jangling. One gets the impression of money, skill and brains in this important nerve center of the CIO. The young white men who are directing things are not the type commonly associated with labor unions. Here is none of the indifference toward Negro investigation commonly experienced in the past. Everyone is courteous, helpful and understanding.

From a young white man, George Steele, organizer of the Credit Salesmen and Outside Collectors Local of the United Retail Employees Union, a CIO affiliate, who is also a member of the organizing staff and educational committee of the local CIO, I learned something of the manifold activities going on in the busy headquarters.

Source: George S. Schuyler, "Philadelphia Negro Workers Are Rallying to 'New Deal' Call of Unions," *Pittsburgh Courier*, August 14, 1937.

He gave me a sidelight on the militant attitude of Philadelphia Negroes. When a strike was recently declared on an installment house whose patrons were largely Negroes, the striking collectors asked them not to pay their installments until the company had signed with the unions. "The colored people gave us 100 per cent cooperation," Mr. Steele declared.

The contagion of the union drive in this city has so spread that even the boy bootblacks have formed a union, demanding a 10-cent shine. A large number of Negro bootblacks have joined and a colored boy is president. While it is more like a club than a union, it is an indication of the attitude prevailing in the city.

The Association of Educational and Recreational Workers' Local No. 474 of the American Federation of Teachers has as president, Mr. Charles Hunt, a colored man.

The station cleaners, chiefly Negro, has as organizer a colored man, Townsend Johnson.

From Frank Hellman, president of Local No. 344 of the United Auto Workers, I learned that a big membership drive had been in progress for three months. There are a large number of Negro workers in the industry employed in the various agencies as washers, laborers and dealers. Negro workers, I learned, were easily organized. Some Negroes are on the executive committee of the union, which is Local No. 258. The United Bedding and Glider Workers Union has organized some 20 firms in the present drive, and its membership includes a considerable number of Negro workers. According to a woman official, no difficulty has been experienced in getting Negroes into the union.

From George Nott, president and organizer of the local union of the United Mine Workers which is organizing the Philadelphia Gas Works, I learned that a considerable number of Negroes are employed in the gas works. While Negroes were at first reluctant to be organized, little difficulty is now being experienced in doing so. One Negro is trustee of a station and another is trustee at large. Both serve on the executive committee of the union. Approximately 500 Negroes are employed in this industry in gas and coke plants.

"The Negroes," said Mr. Nott, "are very faithful and militant union members. They make good organizers and prove their sincerity."

The CIO lost the election in the Philadelphia Gas Works and this is attributed to the fact that the company used anti-Negro propaganda, telling the white workers that it was the union policy to put Negro workers over white workers.

In the office of the United Food Workers' Independent Union Local No. 107, David Biltman, one of the business agents, told me of the result of the nine-week drive in the industry. He declared that of the 1,300 organized in the union, 65 per cent are working under the closed shop, and 35 per cent of these members are Negroes. This union covers all the handling of food except in bakeries.

"We have experienced no difficulty at all in organizing the Negroes in the industry," he declared. "They are as fine a bunch of fellows as imaginable. They have given us 100 per cent cooperation."

Of the 14 members on the executive board of the union, seven are colored workers. Two Negroes are shop chairmen and one is slated to become a paid organizer.

"We are proud of our Negro members," declared Biltman. "They are the first to join as soon as we start organizing a store. They have a fine spirit. They are most interested to know what it is all about."

This union has succeeded in reducing working hours . . . and whereas wages ranged from $6.00 to $15.00 a week, the minimum is now said to be $22.

Mr. Daniel Elkins, young president of the Cleaning and Dyeing Workers Industrial Union, a CIO affiliate, was even more enthusiastic about the result of the drive among Negro workers in the industry.

Of the 2,500 workers in the trade, he declared that from 70 to 80 per cent are colored. Of the 600 members of the union 500 are Negroes. An organizing drive has now been in progress for two months. The two largest shops and three of the smaller ones of the total of 29 have signed contracts with the union.

Mr. Elkins was very frank about the problems of the union as they pertain to colored workers. "We must prove to our people in the trade," he said, "that we are sincere and above board. Of our executive board of fifteen, 10 are colored workers. The vice-president is a Negro and so is the chairman in the largest shop, the United Tailors Association. So also is the shop committee of five in this plant.

"We are putting four full time organizers in the field," said Mr. Elkins, "and two of them are colored men. This is the third union to enter the field in this city in the past five years. The two previous unions were affiliated with the AF of L. The organization was killed by the mistakes of the leadership which was weak and undemocratic. As a result we are hampered by a perfectly justifiable watching and waiting policy on the part of the workers. We are not collecting dues or initiation fees from anyone until we get a closed shop. Our union is run democratically. Every position is an elected position and we tolerate no discrimination against Negro workers.

"James Shorter (Negro), shop chairman in the North Cleaning Plant and chairman of our organizing committee," said Elkins, "actually made negotiations for affiliation with the CIO. He organized his own shop of 90 people in three weeks time. Indeed, Negroes initiated this whole organization. Mr. Shorter, who is also a musician, is a member of Local No. 274, American Federation of Musicians, of which he is the business agent. When he had difficulties with the white union he fought for a separate charter. Joseph H. McCoomer (Negro), our vice-president, kept together the remnants of the former AF of L union and used it as a nucleus of our present organization.

"We have brought hours down," he continued, "from 55 to 75 hours a week to 44 hours a week. When the industry is organized, we will boost the wages. We are calling for a sharing of work and a living wage. The union scale will represent an increase of from 15 to 25 per cent."

The Amalgamated Meat Cutters and Butcher Workmen of North America, Local No. 195, AF of L has been conducting an organization drive for over two months. Because of past discrimination against colored workers, organizers report a certain reticence of Negro workers in joining but claim that it is being overcome.

Of the 2,300 workers in the local industry, comprising 10 different nationalities, about 30 per cent are Negroes. A colored man, Dewey Bucannon, is vice-president. William Banks is shop steward at Duffy Bros. and Emmanuel Wyatt at Cross Bros. and Samuel Elliott at the Consolidated Dressed Beef Company. All are trustees of the union. The Negroes in the industry are both laborers and craftsmen.

George Rooney, organizer of the Transport Workers Union, a CIO affiliate, declared that "it is taking a considerable effort to persuade Negro workers to go along with us. The response has been slow. However, we have succeeded to a certain extent in breaking down the terrific fear of the union. There is a very definite need of a union. While our principal effort is organizing the Philadelphia Rapid Transit, we are taking in all transportation. The cab drivers are being organized by the AF of L."

This union has just started its drive and no local has as yet been set up. So far as Negroes are concerned, they are mostly porters in the subway system and laborers.

Of the 3,500 hod carriers and building laborers in Philadelphia in Local No. 332 of the International Hod Carriers and Building Laborers Union, approximately 75% are colored. The union has four business agents of whom two are Negroes. One of these Negro business agents is Harry Murray, said to be a former AF of L organizer.

Half of the members of the chemical workers union are Negroes.

Of the 200 members of the Building Service Employees International Union, Local No. 125 AF of L, 100 are Negroes. This includes the president, vice-president, treasurer and recording secretary.

In the International Brotherhood of Teamsters, Chauffeurs, Stablemen and Helpers of America, Local 107, the Negro membership has risen from 50 in 1933 to over 500 at present. Negroes are trustees and members of the executive board of the union.

Of the 600 members of Pennsylvania State Employes Association, Local No. 6, 70 are Negroes. The union is affiliated with the CIO.

Almost 80 per cent of the members of the laundry workers union are colored.

Drives are in progress among the tobacco workers, the woodworkers and the hotel and restaurant workers, all of these groups having a large Negro representation. Indeed, aside from the CIO activities, of the 50 AF of L unions organized since the NRA, half of them have Negro membership.

All in all it is evident that Negroes are responding as well to the union drive as the white workers. This is the more remarkable since widespread discrimination against them in the past has engendered a feeling of skepticism about labor organization. They have been tricked in the past and accordingly are wary.

This is said to be especially true in the building trades where in the past there has been marked discrimination against Negro craftsmen. Often Negro artisans have been sent to the worst jobs and then only after white artisans had been placed. Difficulty has been experienced by Negro craftsmen in getting jobs on PWA projects. Many Negro plasterers failed for this reason to pay their dues and were dropped from the union.

At the same time there has been until recently the usual feeling on the part of white workers that Negroes could not be trusted and would desert in the first struggle.

But there is general agreement that the coming of the CIO has made a difference. It has made the AF of L outfits wake up and do the organizing work that should have been done long ago.

Competition, it seems, is not only the life of trade but also the life of the labor movement.

Among the strongest and oldest unions in Philadelphia are those of the coastwise and deepwater longshoremen. They have always been among the most militant in the United States, and a large proportion of them are Negroes, with Negro officers and business agents.

If any proof were needed of the essential oneness of humanity and the equality of black and white, it is demonstrated by the manner in which the black workers of Philadelphia have organized in unions to improve their standard of living and increase their economic power.

Philadelphia, Pa. (1937)

16]   Black Business Associations

At the present time there are twenty-three building and loan associations in Philadelphia operated by Negroes and their total resources at the end of 1935 were more than $2,000,000. . . .

The major part of the associations' funds is invested in mortgage loans on homes which are being purchased by their members. More than $1,200,000 has been placed in such loans. The borrowing members who used these funds to acquire homes are repaying their mortgages in monthly installments. Stock loans, representing advances made to members on the security of their own savings in the associations, amount to $59,000. Real estate, consisting of properties taken over through foreclosure in cases where the former owners could not keep up their monthly payments, is carried at a valuation of $293,000. This property will be disposed of by the associations as the real estate market revives sufficiently to enable them to get a fair price for it. Delinquent payments to be collected from members amount to $143,000. The cash holdings of the associations amount to $59,000. The balance of the resources includes United States Bonds, judgment notes, taxes advanced for stockholders and miscellaneous items.

Members or stockholders of the association have paid in the sum of $900,-

Source: I. Maximilian Martin, "Philadelphia's Building and Loan Associations," *Crisis*, June 1937, pp. 173–74.

000 and in addition have been apportioned earnings amounting to $131,000. . . . Members who have given notice of their intention to withdraw from the associations are due $212,000. The amount of borrowed money owed by the associations is very small, amounting to only $33,000.

In order to safeguard their members against any losses to be suffered in the future on mortgage loans which turn out to be bad or real estate which declines in value, the building and loan associations have set aside special reserves amounting to $489,000.

The associations vary in size from several associations with assets of approximately $27,000 up to one association with assets of over $600,000. Seven associations have assets of from $25,000 to $50,000; eight, assets of from $50,000 to $100,000; three, assets of from $100,000 to $150,000, and one association has assets of over $150,000.

The earnings of the associations were divided among their members at rates ranging from about 1½% to 7%. The typical rate, however, was 3%. This rate is much lower than that earned in former years by these associations because of present economic conditions. It compares favorably, however, with the present rate of interest allowed by Philadelphia banks on savings accounts.

Philadelphia's Negro-managed building and loan associations have rendered a valuable service to the community by encouraging thrift and helping people to own their own homes. By and large these associations have been managed as efficiently as those operated by any other group in the city. In fact, it seems that these associations have fared better than many others because their loans were principally confined to residential properties occupied by their owners, whereas other groups have loaned on commercial and speculative properties and suffered losses on them.

Unfortunately, a condition has grown up in Philadelphia whereby many of the major lending agencies have adopted a policy of refusing to consider mortgage loans on properties owned by colored people or else offering to lend only a ridiculously small amount, regardless of the value of the property or the character and financial responsibility of the prospective borrower. This will throw an even greater responsibility on the Negro-managed association.

NORTH CENTRAL CITIES

Economic Aspects

Economic distress among blacks in Gary led to the successful formation of the Consumers' Trading Company, a cooperative effort to provide cheaper food. This kind of effort was widespread among blacks in border and northern cities.

Property in northern ghettoes was mostly owned by whites who also got the bulk of black business patronage. Document 18 describes the efforts of some black businessmen in Chicago—the city which then had the greatest black purchasing power—to gain a greater share of the black market.

Gary, Ind. (1935)

17]   A Consumers' Cooperative

. . . In January of 1932 a group of Negroes of Gary, Indiana, representing some twenty families, met at the Roosevelt High School of that city and decided to make a study of some of . . . [its economic] problems. The principal of the school and several of the teachers attended the first meeting. At that time not only were the Negroes at the bottom of the economic ladder but the town itself was practically dead. With a total population of 100,000, some 21,000 were being fed by relief agencies. About one-half of the total Negro population of 20,000 were on relief. Gary is a one-industry town and at the beginning of 1932 the steel mills were all but closed. Only one of the city's thirteen banking institutions remained open at that time. The whole situation looked very hopeless. At the first meeting of this Negro group someone suggested that a newspaper should be started in order to better inform the people of their economic situation, but after meeting weekly for some time they decided that the only hope of the group was to organize themselves as consumers. . . . About twenty-four dollars had been collected from donations at the first few meetings. This money was used to do some publicity work and to

Source: J. L. Reddix, "Consumers' Cooperation in Gary," *Opportunity*, October 1935, pp. 301–3.

start a cooperative buying club. The depression was at its worst by this time and people were not easily persuaded to put their few remaining dollars into a "new fangled" scheme. Capital was collected very slowly. The buying club activities were kept alive by having one of the members, Mr. H. T. Smith, who later became the first manager, visit each family weekly and collect orders. Arrangements were made with one of the local Negro grocerymen to fill and deliver these orders. Needless to say that practically no savings were made by this method of operation. About three months later the group was fortunate enough to rent a closed store with fixtures where a more auspicious capitalist venture had failed sometime before. It was the plan of the club at that time to use the store only as a clearing point for collecting and filling orders. But due to the fact that wholesalers would not sell to the group unless they had a bona fide store, the buying club was opened as a full-fledged grocery store on December 15, 1932. The store had a clerk and a manager. Arrangements were made with a member who had an ancient Ford truck to make deliveries. No one of the sales force had any previous grocery store experience. Needless to say that with the antiquated fixtures of this store and with little or no stock the organization was laughed at by all the merchants of the neighborhood. These were trying times for this young cooperative. Many members did not have faith in the future of the organization. But due to the spirit of Christmas and because a large number of persons came to the store with the expressed purpose of having a good laugh, the Christmas week's sales totaled $275. The organization was chartered as the Negro Cooperative Stores Association December 17, 1932. The store struggled along through the spring and summer of 1933 with a turnover of about $200 per week. A few of the members were loyal and other loyal members were added slowly. However, some of the members would act as if to say: "How can a dingy little grocery store help a race group to solve its problems when it cannot help itself?" On August 7, 1933, Mr. Leslie Joseph, who had acted as secretary up to this time, was elected the manager. But due to the lack of capital the turnover of the store did not increase to any extent.

In the fall of 1933 the Educational Committee made arrangements with the director of Adult Education of the Gary schools to start a class in Cooperative Economics as a regular course in the evening school curriculum. This class was instructed by the author, who is one of the regular teachers in the Roosevelt High School. The creation of this class proved to be a tremendous stimulus to the success of the organization. Some of the most loyal officers and members of the organization were converted to Cooperation after having studied its history and philosophy. The women members of the class organized a very active guild. The class was continued during the winter of 1934–35. It had the largest attendance of any academic class of the evening schools.

With the added interest of the Women's Guild, 1934 saw a much increased interest in the affairs of the organization. In the spring of that year the Educational Committee published a pamphlet entitled: "A Five Year Plan of Cooperative Action for Lifting the Economic Status of the Negro in Gary." The first item on the program was the opening of a large modern grocery store and meat market. This has already been done. The first store, which was not much more than a buying club, was closed and the new store was opened on August 17, 1934. At this time, the name of the organization was changed to the Consumers Cooperative Trading Company. The five year plan calls for the organization of a second store and a Credit Union in 1935. The development is ahead of the schedule in that the Credit Union was organized in November, 1934. . . .

. . . . .

The Consumers Cooperative Trading Company has now reached the stage of rapid and healthy growth. Persons who a few months ago were skeptical are now becoming loyal supporters. The organization has over 400 members. The turnover for the first year will be more than $35,000.

As stated previously, the Consumers Cooperative Credit Union was organized in November of 1934. Although it is less than one year old, yet it has more than one hundred members and has on deposit several hundred dollars. The Credit Union has been a valuable supplement to the store. Since the store is operated on a strictly cash basis, all credit accounts are handled through the credit union.

The social side of the movement is not being neglected. The organization has a Women's Guild of about thirty members and a Men's Council, both of which meet weekly in their own club rooms. The Youth League is one of the most active in the Central States territory. The Youth League members are getting practical cooperative education by operating their own ice cream parlor and candy shop. This business is a miniature consumers cooperative with youths holding offices. This experiment is proving invaluable in training young people for future leadership in the cooperative movement.

Chicago, Ill. (1938)

18]   Business in Bronzeville

Although Chicago has 100,000 fewer Negroes than New York, it is the centre of U.S. Negro business; last census figures showed Chicago's Negro establishments had annual net sales of $4,826,897, New York's were only $3,322,274. Chicago's Negroes all hail from the South, work generally as laborers in packing plants and steel mills, have a community feeling; New York's are less homogeneous, work mostly in hotels and apartments. Great majority of Chicago Negroes live in a south side section known as Bronzeville. Here the principal shopping districts are on 43rd, 47th, 51st and 57th streets. Virtually all of this property belongs to whites, most of them Jews, and they make it tough for Negroes to go into business in these prize areas. Leases generally have clauses forbidding Negro tenants; and if a Negro manages to wangle a lease anyway, he is apt to find his rent tripled when the lease comes for renewal.

When the Jones Brothers started the world's only Negro-owned department

Source: "Business in Bronzeville," *Time*, April 18, 1938, pp. 70, 72.

store they had to buy the property to get onto 47th Street. When dapper little Frank Howell Jr. started Mae's Dress Shoppe, he was forced to pay six-and-a-half months' rent in advance. This smouldered in Negro Howell's breast and continued to as he prospered. After Marva Trotter, fiancée of Prizefighter Joe Louis, bought her trousseau from Frank Howell, four other Mae's Dress Shoppes were started by rivals eager to cash in on the publicity; but Frank Howell's Original Mae's Dress Shoppe is today the biggest and most fashionable in Bronzeville.

Now something of a tycoon, Frank Howell decided to organize other Bronzeville bigwigs, hold a two-day Exposition of Negro Business for the double purpose of spurring Negro business and arranging a program to fight "fleecing" by whites. So last week to the shabby 8th Regiment Armoury trooped no less than 110,000 Negroes to watch fashion shows, finger fancy caskets, see demonstrations of pressing the kink out of Negro hair, listen to church choirs and hot bands, munch free handouts or purchase raffle tickets from the 75 booths. No Negro gathering is complete without Joe Louis and he was on hand opening day to cut a ribbon across the door. As usual he was surrounded with admiring pickaninnies who well know his bodyguard's penchant of giving dollar bills to moppets so they will leave Joe alone.

PART FIVE

WORLD WAR II TO 1959

INTRODUCTION

The following documents present selections by two well-traveled black writers of the ten best and the ten worst cities for blacks in 1947–48. As they themselves concede, there is some arbitrariness about their choice. Not surprisingly, the best cities for blacks in terms of educational, cultural, and economic opportunities as well as personal freedom were the major ones in the North and West. But even in these, the writer points out, the black traveler or resident was not always free from slights, insults, and discrimination in public life.

It was equally predictable that all the worst cities for blacks would be found in the South. What is striking is that the nation's capital and two cities that today would be regarded as among the most liberal in the South, Atlanta and Houston, were then listed, apparently with good reasons, among the worst cities for blacks.

One obvious reason why southern cities were distasteful to blacks was the fact that the police were almost exclusively white and highly prejudiced. In 1944 most cities had no black police, and those that did employed them on highly discriminatory terms and for limited purposes within the black community (Documents 3 and 4). Across the nation in 1959, blacks were still grossly underrepresented on urban police forces; Birmingham was still without a single black policeman. And various forms of discrimination continued to be practiced against those on the forces.

CITIES

General Aspects

1]   The Ten Best Cities for Blacks (1947)

Anyone who travels much in the United States soon begins to realize that
there are good and bad cities for Negroes. Curiously, the traveler with few
connections and friends learns this much faster.

My experience is a case in point. As I was reared in the isolation of the Pacific Northwest, I had few friends in the East and Middle West and, hence,
was not a part of the intricate and involved system of reciprocal entertaining
through which Negroes soften the impact of prejudice on the Negro traveler.

This system of entertaining visitors, and expecting to be entertained when a
visitor, is of course not only a social ritual but a method of avoiding insults in
restaurants, refusals in hotels, and discrimination in places of public entertainment. Not having such connections, I soon learned to size up a city with a
quick look-see and a few questions directed toward persons who had specialized knowledge of the area.

Here's the way I found myself operating. Just before we pulled into a city
which was new to me, I would ask the porter rather casually, "Is this a good
town?" He would generally answer "yes" or "no" and then drop his voice a little to give me a few pertinent facts on what I should or should not expect; i.e.,
as a Negro. This information I quickly added to the general background of
facts which I had gathered from friends before taking the trip. With this much
knowledge I could then make such decisions as whether to try a downtown
white hotel or retreat immediately to the local Black Ghetto.

My next source of information was the Red Cap. With him I was much
more specific. I would get his judgment as to what downtown hotel to try, the
name of a small, clean Negro hotel to use if refused, and, finally, the name and
address of the local Baptist preacher so that I could throw myself on his mercy
if nothing else worked out.

SOURCE: Horace R. Cayton, "America's 10 Best Cities for Negroes," *Negro Digest*,
October 1947, pp. 4–10. [Horace R. Cayton, recently deceased sociologist and social
critic, was coauthor of the classic *Black Metropolis*.—Ed.]

272

The Ten Best Cities for Blacks

From then on I was on my own. If the decision had been to stay downtown, my behavior had to have a certain amount of bravado which might pass for self-assurance, but at the same time I had to be alert to every cue which would help orient me to the etiquette of race relations which prevailed in that city. The attitude of the taxi driver when I got into the cab—his reaction, or lack of reaction, when I asked to be driven to a first class hotel, the behavior of the hotel clerk in assigning my room, and, finally, the service I was accorded in the dining room, all told me much about the temper of race relations in that locality.

Having obtained some notion of the extent to which Negroes enjoyed civil liberties and acceptance to public places, my next step as a social investigator was to inspect the Negro community. There I would interview its leaders and observe its physical appearance in an effort to test the more basic and important reasons why this was or was not a good town for Negroes.

. . . I can state in general that the cities I consider best for Negroes are those in which the majority of Negroes have an opportunity to live a fairly well-rounded life which approximates that of the ordinary American citizen.

Certainly the first question any person would ask is: What are the chances for making a living? What about chances for obtaining a job, establishing a professional practice or opening a business? There is a "job ceiling," a level in industry and governmental service above which Negroes will not be hired, in every city. Here are a few hints on how to check this ceiling. What is the highest rank Negro policemen hold? Are Negroes in the fire department, [and] if so, are they segregated into one fire company? Are Negroes hired in large numbers in the basic industries of the city or are they concentrated in the service industries? Do Negro professional men have offices in downtown buildings and do they have white clients? What percentage of the businesses in the community are owned or operated by Negroes?

Living conditions constitute the second important criterion. All cities have some residential segregation but it is important to note its rigidity and method of enforcement. The answers to these questions will give you a quick fill-in on this picture. Is the Negro community overcrowded? Are restrictive covenants, simple agreements between realtors, or the threat of violence responsible for locking the black population in a ghetto? Where, in relation to the topography of the city, is the Negro community located—behind the railroad tracks, near swampy and low ground, away from the lake or river front? What is the physical appearance of the community, the homes, stores, streets, and alleys?

Next to be taken into consideration in one's judgment of cities are the educational and cultural advantages which they offer, and the extent to which, and the conditions under which, Negroes may use them. Of prime importance, of course, would be an adequate, unsegregated public school system, and a university, preferably a good state or privately endowed institution with low tuition. Almost as important to many would be the presence of art galleries, libraries, theaters, and music halls. Ten years ago one was surprised to see a Negro at a symphony concert (unless Marian Anderson was a soloist), but now it is surprising not to see numbers of darker citizens. If these necessities of cultural living are denied the Negro, it certainly is not a good city for me.

Freedom of speech, press, and assembly, religious freedom, the right to security against unreasonable search and seizure, against double jeopardy and excessive bail, against self-incrimination, the right to trial by jury before an impartial judge are things which many Negroes migrated from the South to obtain. They are basic necessities for a life without fear and with respect and dignity. But my conception of civil liberties also includes civil rights: the right of persons to accommodations in hotels, restaurants, common carriers, other places of public accommodation and resorts, the right to employment, especially buttressed by a local or state Fair Employment Practices Act. If a city affords these rights and privileges to its Negro citizens, even with the disadvantage of color they can live a dignified, cultured, and well-rounded life.

These are the standards by which to choose the ten best cities for Negro citizens. Given the criteria, for obvious reasons I am ruling out all Southern and border towns. I have tried to pick cities which would have the same relative attraction to Negroes of all economic classes. A small town might be good for the old settlers who have been there for years, but not for the migrant Negro from the South; a wealthy suburb might not object to a well-known Negro artist living there in semi-seclusion, but would object violently to anyone else; a wealthy community might welcome polite, discreet Negro servants, but would be very antagonistic to a Negro doctor. All of these I have ruled out as they are good towns only for a special group or segment of Negroes.

Place a pencil on a map of the United States and, starting with Boston and New York on the East Coast, draw a line west through Chicago, northwest to Seattle, and due south to Los Angeles. All of the cities of my choice would fall along this imperfect triangle. Of the ten cities, four are located in the East, three in the Middle West, and three on the Pacific Coast. Every large city on the Pacific Coast is included except Portland, Oregon (which is still suffering from a hangover caused by an early influx of pro-slavery settlers), and San Diego, California (which suffers from being too close to Texas). Only two states, New York and California, have two cities of my choice.

Here, reading East to West, is the list:

BOSTON

On a scale running from Bad to Excellent, I would place Boston at the top of the list for its educational and cultural advantages and civil liberties. There are remnants of the old Abolitionist zeal for obtaining full rights for Negroes which has made this so. The city deserves only a rating of Good for job opportunities and chances for economic advancement. There are, however, as in most eastern cities, unusual cases where individuals have been able to pierce the job ceiling and obtain positions of great responsibility and prestige. Like most eastern and older cities, it has horrible slums although there is not the strict segregation of the Negro middle and upper classes.

NEW YORK

In the first place, as the song from *On the Town* states, "It's a hell of a town." Both here and in the song, this is intended to be a compliment. In educational and cultural advantages, it rates an Excellent, in spite of some rather

274

low standards in some of the elementary public schools in Harlem. Although there are frequent infringements of civil liberties (one of the most ironic being the arresting of light-skinned Negroes, who were thought to be white, for being up in Harlem late at night), a Negro not only has civil liberties, but a great degree of civil rights. The economic situation is just Good, except for the chosen few, and living conditions are from Bad to Fair, again except for the chosen few.

PHILADELPHIA

In this town if you have the money, you can hear a lot of good concerts, and it shouldn't be too hard to get a fairly decent job. In spite of the near riot about putting Negroes on the street cars as platform men a few years ago, Philadelphia rates a Good as far as civil liberties are concerned. But don't think that just because they have the Liberty Bell there you can go into every restaurant—it's tightening up a bit lately. Living conditions, except for the Black Bourgeois, are pretty sordid.

BUFFALO

The last World War brought a great influx of Negroes into Buffalo to work in the steel mills. This migration has continued, but even with the constantly growing population, Buffalo still is a good town. A job is not too hard to get and the Negro community is gradually being taken more and more into the social and political structure of the city. The civil liberties of Negroes are fairly well respected, and certainly anyone who wants an education can get excellent training. Housing and living conditions are spotty. There are some nice neighborhoods and many perfectly awful ones. If you are interested in classical music, however, I would suggest that you live in Rochester.

CLEVELAND

As one leaves the East Coast, living conditions become markedly better. Cleveland has some slums but they can't compare with those of New York and Philadelphia. Besides, within the past few years, Negroes have acquired homes in a section of the city which has beautiful parks and boulevards. Perhaps some of the finest Negro homes in the country are located there. With its varied industries, there is plenty of work, and a liberal labor movement and political party have seen that the Negro has gotten ahead. You can't go to a symphony concert every night, but there is good music, a smattering of plays in the winter time, and an excellent educational system.

DETROIT

Detroit is a wonderful town for automobiles. Negroes can buy them—wages aren't bad and even Negroes can make them. Neither management nor the liberal CIO United Automobile Workers would attempt to put Negro workers out of that city's basic industries. Negro neighborhoods vary from slums (not as bad as the East, however) to racially mixed middle class residential areas. Detroit has a history of violence from the Sweet case over Negro housing to the more recent race riot. It's still dynamite, but, paradoxically, also a good town for Negroes.

CHICAGO

Chicago had a race riot in 1919 and everyone expects it to have another one. However, Chicago, like England, somehow just muddles through. Living conditions for ninety per cent of the population are bad but the other ten per cent have rather fabulous private dwellings and apartments. It's a good town for work or for business. Civil liberties are fair (not as good as Boston or New York) and the Negro voter throws his weight around a bit. Next to New York and perhaps Boston, it has the best educational and cultural advantages in spite of its double and sometimes triple shift elementary schools in the Black Belt.

SEATTLE

Up until now Seattle has been a city without slums. Further, the sharp residential segregation which characterizes most eastern and middle western cities is not present, although there is a movement in that direction. But if the Pacific Coast cities have, on the whole, better living conditions, there are fewer job opportunities or chances for economic advancement (i.e., except for Los Angeles which follows no set rule). The educational system from grammar school through the university is topflight, but if you like music—boogie or otherwise—you had better take along some phonograph records.

SAN FRANCISCO

You may have to look around a while for a job in keeping with your training, but if you find one, you can find a house outside of "Little Tokyo," which the Negroes took over from the Japanese during the war. You will find San Francisco (never Frisco) a wonderful, quaint, European-like town. Most people prefer Los Angeles but that just shows their bad taste. The University of California is just across the Bay and the police will not bother you if you happen to walk down the street with a very light complexioned colored girl.

LOS ANGELES

Los Angeles is overcrowded, tense, and tawdry. Everyone from the shipyard workers to the doctors made lots of money during the war. There is a bad slum section in its "Little Tokyo," but most of the middle class and upper class Negroes, as well as a good number of just common folk, have purchased attractive private dwellings in nice, quiet neighborhoods. There are good public schools (the public schools of the Pacific Coast are the best in the country) and plenty of universities and colleges. Civil liberties are good, i.e., by American standards, although a Negro is not always sure of securing his civil rights (Los Angeles is vying with Chicago in the matter of writing and enforcing restrictive covenants—they even use them against American Indians out there).

But in spite of all this the people up and down Central Avenue seem very happy and boost just as hard for their city, and feel just as superior toward the East, as do the white Los Angelenos. So it, too, I must conclude, is a good town for Negroes.

2]   The Ten Worst Cities for Blacks (1948)

I had been off the boat less than ten days, and it was my first assignment in
America after more than three years abroad. My boss called me in and said:
"Get down to Columbia, Tennessee, as soon as you can. There's a trial
going on. Thurgood Marshall is handling it. You'll probably find him in Nashville. I understand he—er—doesn't stay in Columbia overnight."

I got down to Nashville and found Marshall in a huddle with Z. Alexander
Looby,[1] who was also on the case. With them was Maurice Weaver, a white
lawyer from Chattanooga, and another young attorney named Reed. As we left
the office, Looby's secretary said dolefully: "From the moment that car leaves
the parking lot for Columbia, until it comes back, I'm going to have a funny
feeling inside. Every time the phone rings, I'll probably be too nervous to answer."

I fell in step beside Marshall. "Look, chum," I said. "Is this trip really necessary?" He didn't even bother to answer me.

We covered the forty-odd miles from Nashville in almost complete silence.
Then, on the outskirts of Columbia, as we crossed the bridge over Duck River,
somebody with a misplaced sense of humor remarked: "And here, gentlemen,
is the muddy water in which our bodies are supposed to float!"

That was my introduction to one city in America, which for sheer brutality,
prejudice and downright savagery in its treatment of Negroes would be hard
to beat. Blood, mud and wholesale destruction in Europe hadn't made me
shudder the way Columbia did. Tobacco-eating characters with necks that
were dirt-creased and dirt red, stood around and spat almost in unison as we
rolled up to the courthouse. Their eyes were hard and openly hostile. They
threatened even while they slouched, having already sent word that they
would "get" the so-and-so lawyers before the trial was over.

We got out and marched inside in a tight little group. At lunch time, we
marched out in an even tighter little group—food having been prepared in the
home of one of the men being tried. And when court adjourned for the day,
we dived into the car and raced pell-mell back to Nashville.

What about the trial?

Well, it seems that a veteran and a member of his family had words with a
clerk in a store. The words led to something else—and the clerk came out
loser. So, that night, a delegation went to Mink Slide to call on the veteran. It
turned out, though, that the veteran had friends who had a few German Lug-
ers and an assortment of GI Equalizers, and knew how to use them. The delegation left Mink Slide in a hurry.

Later, a bigger delegation, led by the local law (&) [sic], returned to take
care of the veteran. But in their eagerness (and viciousness) they took care of

SOURCE: Ollie Stewart, "America's 10 Worst Cities for Negroes," Negro Digest,
March 1948, pp. 44–49. [Ollie Stewart was a staff reporter of the Baltimore
Afro-American.—Ed.]
[1] Black Nashville lawyer and later (1951–71) councilman.

everybody and everything in Mink Slide. Stores, homes and a funeral parlor were wrecked with axes. Whole families were routed from bed and men, women and children scattered into the night. But it wasn't all one-sided. Mink Slide fought the wrecking crew, and when it was all over, two men were dead and a deputy wounded.

Quickly, near thirty Mink Sliders were rounded up and lodged in jail. Twenty-one were swiftly charged with attempted murder. Local authorities were all set to rush through a conviction and hang them all, when the NAACP moved in and saved their lives in a long and bitter trial—but only after the trial had been moved to a different place.

Columbia, then, becomes the first on my list of the ten worst cities in America for Negroes. It cannot be omitted because it has proved to the world that there is no personal safety for Negroes in Columbia. The very men sworn to uphold the law have shown themselves willing to head a mob and take the lead in wielding axes and crow bars on the property of Columbia citizens. And in addition, this Tennessee city must be included because its ghetto, Mink Slide, means that it has second class citizens who are restricted and tolerated only so long as they "stay in their place."

It goes without saying that a list of this kind must be a personal thing. . . .

What makes a city bad—for Negroes?

Terror, for one thing!

Any city in which a lynching, near lynching, kidnapping or other act of terrorism by a mob occurs, or is likely to occur, is a bad city.

．　．　．　．　．

Does this city have libraries and schools and hospitals and parks to which Negroes have free access? Are there too many churches, and too few youth centers? What about juvenile delinquency? Is there a decent hotel? Are there colored policemen and firemen? Can one vote without intimidation? Or catch a bus or street car in front of the door, or a train, and take the first seat that's empty?

．　．　．　．　．

GREENVILLE, S.C.

"Everyone is entitled to life, liberty and equal protection under the law." Believing this, and remembering how twenty-six mobsters recently lynched a man here, confessed to it and were freed, Greenville gets a special place on my list.

ALEXANDRIA, LA.

Surrounded by red clay hills and piney woods, Alexandria was indelibly etched into my mind during two hectic visits to Camp Claiborne and Livingston, while the woods around were swarming with GIs. Bad before the war, Alexandria, the last time I saw it, only allowed colored people on a few of its streets. Soldiers were restricted to two streets—and on one occasion the whole city was off limits to them. Only a handful of Alexandria Negroes vote, the whites receive five or more times as much for education as the coloreds, the

The Ten Worst Cities for Blacks

hospital situation is nauseating—and in short, it has all the viciousness of a southern city, with none of the redeeming features.

ATLANTA, GA.

It's a shame about Atlanta. It's a shame that it has to be in Georgia—and a shame that it offers such fertile soil for the type of racial animosity this country can least afford to cultivate. Atlanta is beautiful, has a marvelous climate, several top-flight schools for Negroes and from what I hear on good authority, some honest-to-goodness colored millionaires. But it still does little more than cross its fingers in solving its acute housing shortage among Negroes. Negro policemen were just voted in in December, on shameful conditions. The Columbians still terrorize, though driven underground. Atlanta has long been the cradle of the Klan. Segregation insures second-class citizens, and votes are not used to gain for Negroes the recognition due them by virtue of their wealth and intellect.

JACKSON, MISS.

Like Kilroy, Bilbo [2] was here—and Rankin lives not too far away. But these two are only symbolic. When Bilbo ranted against Negroes during his Senate investigation trial, a packed courtroom in Jackson cheered his every vitriolic utterance. Here there is no personal safety, no equal justice under the law, in education, health or exercising of the ballot.

ANNAPOLIS, MD.

This capital city is a hostage to southern prejudice, and so long as the U.S. Naval Academy remains here, so long will it stay in hock to the boys from below the line. Shot through with prejudice itself, the Academy furnishes work to three-fourths of the working people here, and sets the pattern for the town. Colored sailors have no place to go for recreation, hospital maternity wards are closed to Negro mothers, and there is no comparison between the educational facilities of the two races.

BIRMINGHAM, ALA.

A lot of Negroes have made a lot of money in Birmingham, but a quarter of a million Negroes have still to make noteworthy progress politically. Professional Negroes, with nice homes and purring cars, are not bothered by little things like the lack of a decent hotel, over-crowded elementary and high schools, no representation in the city government, lack of colored policemen, a high rate of crime and a higher rate of juvenile delinquency. Birmingham has a great big beautiful park high on a hill in its midst. Some friends once drove me up to see the park, but we got no farther than the gate. "This park isn't for you people," the big policeman shouted at us.

[2] Theodore C. Bilbo, racist U.S. senator from Mississippi.

MIAMI, FLA.

"It's a crime," a man said near the airport here. "It's a crime that one of the finest parts of this country has to be messed up by prejudice." It is indeed a crime that a garden spot like Miami offers Negroes more terror than beauty. At night, a Negro must not be caught on most of the streets of Miami. No equality under the law, only menial jobs, inferior hospital and school facilities, and prejudice that warps both the hater and the hated.

HOUSTON, TEXAS

The new school now being built here,[3] which embraces the ideal of segregation, is a dodge, a deliberate subterfuge. It is a denial of constitutional rights. The spirit of Texas is crystallized here in this monument which can never be dedicated to anything but inequality. Houston remains politically impotent, economically insecure—with a great need for rescuing its youthful delinquents, curbing its adult law breakers and cleaning up its ghettos. Prodded by an aggressive newspaper editor, the people of Houston have only begun to use the ballot as an effective weapon.

WASHINGTON, D.C.

All the monuments, the thousands of Negroes in government jobs and the high salaries paid school teachers cannot wash away the stain. Even the cherry blossoms cannot erase the blot of discrimination. It is worse here because all the world can see it. Ask those who wanted to hear Marian Anderson or Hazel Scott in Constitution Hall. Ask those who cannot attend the National Theatre, or have picketed restaurants. Washington has Negro firemen and policemen— but restrictive covenants lie in wait for those who would exercise their constitutional right to buy and live where they please, or send Junior to the nearest school. The Jim Crow policy for the Army and Navy originates here, and so do the disgraceful filibusters that defeat an anti-lynch bill or a permanent FEPC. On these and many other counts, Washington has earned a high place among the nation's worst.

3]   Black Police in the South (1944)

While complete information is not available it is known that at least 18 southern cities of more than 20,000 population employ a total of 110 Negro policemen, ranging from one such officer in each of the cities of Raleigh and Winston-Salem, North Carolina, and Owensboro, Kentucky, to 24 in St. Louis, Missouri. In most instances Negro officers patrol only Negro sections and are limited to Negro arrests. Negro police form a small percentage of the total police force in the 18 cities except in Galveston, Texas, where there are 13 Negro policemen (10 uniformed and 3 plain clothes) who compose one-sixth of

SOURCE: Charles S. Johnson, "Negro Police in Southern Cities," *Public Management*, March 1944, pp. 79–80.
[3] Texas Southern University.

280

the force and in Daytona Beach, Forida, where four officers compose one-seventh of the total force. The work of the Negro policemen has proved generally satisfactory and recently there has been increased interest in several other southern cities with large Negro populations in employing several Negro officers.

Little Rock, Arkansas, put eight Negro policemen on the regular force after an unfortunate incident in which a Negro Army sergeant was shot to death by a city policeman who was subsequently exonerated. However, the Negro population was aroused and a number of Negro M.P.'s were assigned to patrol the Negro business district. At the request of the city government the Urban League of Little Rock submitted the names of 10 Negro men they recommended for the police force and after special training eight were appointed to the force without examination and at regular salary. Since their appointment crime has been greatly reduced in the Negro section, there have been no racial clashes, and public pride in policemen of its own has brought effective cooperation from the Negro community.

Charlotte, North Carolina, has four Negro police on the regular force; they operate only in Negro districts where their work has been very satisfactory in relieving the race tension. The Negro officers are paid $110 a month compared to $165 a month paid white officers but equalization of salaries has been promised. In addition, Charlotte employs two Negro policewomen to handle Negro juvenile cases.

High Point, North Carolina has two Negro policemen in the Negro section; the one Negro policeman in Winston-Salem works mainly with juveniles.

In Texas, Austin has three Negro patrolmen who are assigned to one-way radio police cars; Beaumont has two; Houston four; San Antonio seven, and Galveston 13.

Daytona Beach, Florida, has employed four Negro policemen for the past 10 years; they work in the Negro section and are not permitted to deal with any situation in which a white person is involved even though the offense occurs in the Negro section.

In Lexington, Kentucky, three Negro patrolmen operate as plainclothesmen in a police car in Negro districts. In addition the city has one Negro policewoman. Of the 18 Negro policemen in Louisville four are in plain clothes.

Other cities which have Negro policemen are Muskogee, Oklahoma, two in plain clothes; Tulsa, Oklahoma, eight, only one of whom is in plain clothes; and Knoxville, Tennessee, five. Negro police have been employed in Tulsa for more than 15 years and are selected through the civil service system.

In St. Louis, Missouri, Negro policemen have been employed for 42 years. There are 24 policemen, nine uniformed men who patrol beats, nine special officers, one sergeant, one lieutenant, two policewomen, and two prison guards.

Macon, Georgia, has no regular Negro police but has 70 Negro auxiliary police who work two nights a week under white officers and furnish their own equipment and uniforms. . . .

4]   Black Representation on City
                      Police Forces (1959)

Correspondents of *The New York Times* have made a spot check in several cities with large Negro populations to learn whether Negro districts have Negro
or white policemen.

The survey showed that Negro policemen were assigned to both white and
Negro sections in Washington, Chicago and Detroit. Chicago and Detroit,
however, use them mostly in Negro areas.

Detroit has recently integrated patrol cars in eight of its fifteen precincts,
sending out a mixed team of one white and one Negro policeman in each car.

In Memphis, Atlanta and New Orleans, Negro policemen serve in Negro
neighborhoods and white policemen in white neighborhoods. There are no
Negro policemen in Birmingham.

Most of the cities employing Negro policemen say the results have been
good. In some of the cities there seems to be a growing demand for further integration in police departments. This is especially so with respect to proposals
for the use of mixed pairs in police cars.

The survey was made as result of recent tensions reported in Harlem following a July 13 incident in which two white policemen were accidentally shot
while dispersing a crowd after they had arrested a woman.

Some Negro leaders later demanded the assignment of more Negro policemen to Harlem. Police Commissioner Stephen P. Kennedy rejected the demand. He said that his policy was to integrate the department and that he
would not make assignments on the basis of color or religion.

WASHINGTON, D.C.

It is not the policy of the Metropolitan Police Department of the District of
Columbia to use Negro policemen largely in Negro areas. Acting Chief George
R. Wallrodt says all policemen are assigned where the department believes
they will be most effective and that Negro policemen are assigned to both
white and Negro areas.

The authorized strength of the department is 2,508 men, of which 326, or
about 13 per cent, are Negroes. This percentage holds for both the uniformed
force and the detective force, Mr. Wallrodt said.

In recent years the Negro population has grown, so that now Negroes outnumber whites. This growth has been accompanied by a great expansion of
Negro residential areas. Now there are Negro areas of substantial size in all
but one of the city's fourteen police precincts.

CHICAGO

The Chicago Police Department does not have a policy of assigning Negro
policemen exclusively to Negro areas, but there is a heavy concentration of

SOURCE: *The New York Times*, July 27, 1959.

them in such districts, according to Tom Shannon, secretary to Police Commissioner Timothy J. O'Connor.

"Negro policemen in Chicago are assigned to all areas of the city," Mr. Shannon said. "They are assigned in the same manner that white policemen are. They work on traffic duty, including the post at the world's busiest corner (State and Madison Streets); they ride three-wheeled motorcycles and squad cars and cover beats."

There is no doubt that most of the Negro policemen work in the Negro belt, partly because they know their own people and command respect from them. It has sometimes appeared that Negro policemen are more severe with Negroes than are white policemen.

Negroes work out of the detective bureau. Many of these plainclothesmen are in the narcotics division. Two of the best pickpocket detectives in the city are a team of Negroes.

There is one Negro police captain, Kinzle Blueitt: he is in command of the Wabash Avenue station, the district most heavily populated by Negroes.

In recent years Negro policemen have been assigned in increasing numbers to districts populated by white residents. Most, however, are assigned to traffic duty and cruising on three-wheelers.

DETROIT

Negroes make up 3 per cent of the Detroit police force—133 of 4,365 policemen. Most are assigned to districts heavily populated by Negroes, none to all-white districts.

Thirty-nine Negroes work at headquarters. Ninety-four are assigned to fifteen precincts. Six white precincts have 1,000 white policemen and no Negroes. Three precincts where the population is 80 per cent Negro have sixty-three Negro policemen, 437 white policemen. Thirty-one Negro police and 965 white policemen are assigned to six precincts with a mixed population.

Integration within precincts was begun this year. Scout car crews previously consisted of two white policemen or two Negroes. On March 1, in one precinct only, crews were assigned regardless of race, a move that stirred resentment among white officers. For three days, policemen throughout the city ignored traffic violations and issued fewer than one-tenth the normal number of tickets. Pressure by the Mayor, the Police Commissioner and leaders of the Detroit Police Officers Association ended the slowdown. No incidents have been reported since, and seven more precincts were integrated smoothly on April 1.

Leaders of the Negro community have welcomed the move as a step toward reducing complaints of discourtesy, brutality and unlawful arrest.

Arthur L. Johnson, executive secretary of the Detroit chapter of the National Association for the Advancement of Colored People, said he was pleased by integration within the precincts but wanted Detroit to hire more Negro policemen and to assign them to all precincts.

MEMPHIS

Negro policemen have been employed for eleven years in Memphis, but Negro leaders are now demanding that more be hired. First hired after *The*

Commercial Appeal editorially suggested the idea and the late E. H. Crump endorsed the plan, Negro policemen began patrolling the beats in the vicinity of Beale Street Nov. 6, 1948.

There are now ten Negroes on the force, all serving in predominantly Negro districts. Negro applicants must meet the same general requirements for jobs as white policemen. They receive the same salary and are under Civil Service.

Russel B. Sugarmon, a Harvard-trained Negro lawyer, has called for more Negroes on the police force here. "Negroes give much more cooperation to policemen of their own race," he said.

Police Commissioner Claude A. Armour praised the work of the Negro policemen. "I feel they have done a very good job," he said. "Colored policemen have a place in our law enforcement."

BIRMINGHAM

Birmingham's City Commission has consistently rejected petitions by Negro groups and others to employ Negro policemen. The city has never employed a Negro in any police capacity.

The three-member commission generally goes along with the wishes of the commissioner in charge of a particular phase of governmental activity. In this case police jurisdiction is in the hands of the Public Safety Commissioner. The incumbent is Eugene Connor, an outspoken segregationist.

Negroes have undertaken legal efforts under the city's Civil Service Code to qualify for openings but have made no real headway. Arguments against the use of Negroes even in Negro areas are that other Southern cities have had little success with that effort.

ATLANTA

White policemen patrol white sections of Atlanta, and Negro policemen patrol Negro sections.

Mayor William B. Hartfield, whose position in such matters is more liberal than that of most Southern officials, said: "We have had a very good experience with our Negro policemen as a whole. Though lower-class Negroes despise them, better-class Negroes respect them."

This was considered a reference to reports that some Negroes think Negro policemen are harder on them than white policemen are.

Police Chief Herbert Jenkins said white and Negro policemen worked well together. "They are police officers first and put race and color second," he said.

Atlanta has thirty Negro policemen, of whom four are detectives and the rest patrolmen. The Negro patrolmen are used exclusively in Negro residential areas. In cases where both whites and Negroes are involved, they call in white policemen to help them. Negro policemen work under a white captain.

NEW ORLEANS

This city's small number of Negro policemen are assigned to areas heavily populated by their race and handle only crimes committed by Negroes.

Black Representation on City Police Forces

This system, in operation just over a year, has been "extremely effective," according to Provosty A. Dayries, Superintendent of Police.

New Orleans has thirty-seven Negro policemen on its 710-man "on-the-street" force, which is divided into three eight-hour watches.

Twenty of the Negro patrolmen are scattered through the six police districts, working either afoot or in radio cars in the Negro housing projects.

The remaining Negroes are assigned to the juvenile, detective and traffic bureaus.

Only Negro officers handle Negro juvenile cases, Negro detectives working only in Negro districts are responsible for solving a large number of Negro homicides, assaults and robberies.

SOUTHERN CITIES

Political and Social Aspects

The period following World War II saw a resurgence of black political activities in southern cities, as well as a vigorous new civil rights thrust. At the same time there was a series of important NAACP Supreme Court victories; the most important were those that outlawed the white Democratic primary, (Smith v. Allwright in 1944), and the segregation of schools (Brown v. Board of Education in 1954). In southern cities there was fairly vigorous black voter registration. New political organizations were formed to promote black interests; one of these was the Atlanta Negro Voters League, founded in 1949 (Document 7). The marked rise in the political consciousness of southern blacks is illustrated in another way by the fact that New Orleans blacks chose to give up their traditional and much-loved Mardi Gras (Document 8) in protest against continuing discrimination (Document 9).

Of course, the most far-reaching political event of this period was triggered off on December 1, 1955, when a tired Rosa Parks refused to give up her bus seat to a white man (Document 12). Montgomery blacks went on to demand the desegregation of buses, courteous treatment for black riders and black drivers for black routes. The city's resistance was finally overcome by the Supreme Court ruling of November 13, 1956 that segregation on buses was unconstitutional. The boycott brought national fame to the late Dr. Martin Luther King, Jr., an advocate of nonviolent direct action and one of the founders of the Southern Christian Leadership Conference.

However, other documents show how far southern urban blacks were from removing their disabilities. The attempt to implement the 1954 Supreme Court desegregation decision met with formidable southern white opposition, which gained national and international attention through the resistance in 1957 of "moderate" Little Rock. In Atlanta, the proportionately small number of black medical personnel had access only to segregated and inferior facilities (Document 6), and Birmingham still bore proudly its appellation of "capital of Jim Crowism" (Document 11).

Miami, Fla. (1942)

5]   The Black Community

Miami is a cosmopolitan city. Colored Miami is none the less so. Here are found peoples from South Africa, central and East Africa, India, South America, Central America, Canada, Bermuda and all the islands of the West Indies, composing a city of about 40,000 colored inhabitants. Being a tourist city colored Miami enjoys benefits coming from 1) America's leading Negro business and professional men and women whose vacation is regarded as incomplete without a stay in the "Magic City." 2) America's leading white men—statesmen, millionaires, educators, business men—most of whom bring their colored help whose intelligence has been keenly sharpened by contact with some of the highly cultured Americans. 3) They are inspired by contact with and help from America's leading sportsmen, society leaders, philanthropists et al who make it possible to see, hear and work with the best the world produces at first hand.

In religious and spiritual affairs colored Miami is a bumper. There are 70 churches as follows: A.M.E., 8; African Orthodox, 1; American Catholic, 1; Baptist, 30; Christian, 1; Church of Christ, 2; Church of God, 13; Episcopal, 3; Roman Catholic, 2; 7th Day Adventist, 1; Spiritualist, 2; miscellaneous, 6.

Miami has been very liberal in providing schools for its colored population. The only exception, which is as prevalent among the whites, is that the population increases faster than the authorities can produce school facilities. In the city are 2 senior high schools, 1 junior high, 2 primaries and 3 elementary. Both high schools are accredited and one of them boasts the finest high school building in Florida.

In business colored Miami is excellent. The city directory enumerates the following colored business. Barber shops, 18; beer and wine establishments, 27; bar rooms, 2; cleaners and pressers establishments, 26; beauty parlors, 38; confectionery and ice cream, 32; druggists, 3; fish dealers, 14; grocers, 48; garage, 4; gasoline stations, 5; hospitals, 2; hotels, 7; newspapers, 3; photographers, 3; restaurants, 31; real estate, 4; shoe repairers, 7; tailors, 7; funeral homes, 5. Colored Miami has also 3 Federal Housing Projects, a public library, a Social Welfare Department and a City Welfare Home. In social affairs local and federated women's clubs abound. There are Greek letter clubs, college clubs, men's social and business clubs, professional men and women's organizations, colored insurance agencies, secret societies, 2 lawyers, 10 physicians and surgeons, 4 pharmacists, 4 dentists and a host of teachers from the nation's best colleges.

Source: Charles S. Thompson, "The Growth of Colored Miami," *Crisis*, March 1942, p. 83.

Atlanta, Ga. (1947)

6] Black Doctors, Dentists, and Nurses

There are 37 Negro physicians in the City of Atlanta, or a ratio of approximately one physician to each 3,074 Negro persons. It is generally accepted that one physician cannot adequately serve more than 2,000 persons for medical care, and one physician for each 1,000 to 1,500 persons is considered a more desirable standard.

In addition to an extremely heavy case load, the Negro physician in Atlanta is seriously handicapped by three other factors:

1. The lack of facilities which may be necessary for diagnosis of patients requiring hospital care.
2. The lack of sufficient facilities for hospital treatment and care of private patients.
3. The lack of learning opportunities which staff membership in a good hospital affords its physicians to learn from each other and from other members of the profession with greater proficiency.

The Negro physician is denied an opportunity to obtain post-graduate training in any hospital in the city of Atlanta. The only exception to this practice may be the occasional inclusion of Negro physicians in a professional seminar. The Negro physician is barred from membership in the county and state medical societies, and is consequently barred from membership in the American Medical Association. The fact that Negroes do not share in the internships, residencies and fellowships of the municipal hospital, restricts seriously the growth of the medical profession in the city. No recruits to the Negro medical group are possible through local training.

The general professional calibre of Negro physicians in Atlanta is shown in the following analysis based upon data supplied by thirty-four of the thirty-seven Negro practitioners.

The majority of Atlanta's Negro physicians are graduates of Meharry Medical College. Twenty-five (67.5%) received medical training from that institution, six from Howard University, four from Leonard Medical School of Shaw University and one from the University of Chicago. A few more than half of these physicians reported having had internship training. Of the eighteen physicians with internship training, nine interned at Homer G. Phillips Hospital, St. Louis, Missouri; two at Freedman's Hospital, Washington, D.C.; two at Hubbard Hospital, Nashville, Tennessee; and one at each of the following—St. Agnes Hospital, Raleigh, N.C.; Cook County Hospital, Chicago, Illinois; Kansas City General Hospital, Kansas City, Mo.; Mercy Hospital, Nashville,

SOURCE: A Report on the Hospital Care of the Negro Population of Atlanta, Georgia, 1947, Atlanta: The Atlanta Urban League, 1947, pp. 39–41.

Black Doctors, Dentists, and Nurses

Tennessee; and, Kingston Public Hospital, Kingston, Jamaica. Of the sixteen physicians who interned, four did further advanced study, after they had practiced medicine for several years. Two studied at Harvard, one at Howard University and one at the Royal College of Physicians and Surgeons in Edinburgh. Twelve physicians are now practicing medicine in Atlanta without having had any internship training or study beyond the requirements for the M.D. degree. A total of seventeen physicians reported post graduate medical study (not including one year internship) in various fields of medicine. Several have taken advantage of clinical study at the University of Georgia, at John Andrews Hospital, Tuskegee, and at other places. In the main, this post-graduate study has not been intensive or specialized.

Thirty of Atlanta's Negro physicians received their premedical or college education in Southern colleges and twenty-three of them are graduates of Atlanta's colleges for Negroes. One physician received his premedical education outside of the United States.

The majority of the Negro physicians in Atlanta (26) are between forty and sixty-five years of age, while four are sixty years of age and over. Most of the time that these physicians have been practicing medicine has been spent in Atlanta. Of the twenty-seven physicians who have been practicing medicine ten years or more, twenty-three have done so in Atlanta. Three physicians who are under thirty years of age have been practicing in Atlanta one year or less. No one of the Negro physicians practicing in Atlanta has received any professional graduate or post-graduate training or experience in Atlanta's hospitals, clinics, or medical schools.

There are even fewer Negro dentists than physicians. There are nine dentists, or one for each 11,614 Negro persons. When this ratio is compared with the accepted standards of one dentist to every 2,000 persons, it is found that approximately forty-three additional dentists would be required to provide adequate dental care for the Negro propulation, assuming a strict pattern of racial services.

There are 111 Negro registered nurses in Atlanta. Forty-eight are employed in public health nursing, 22 in institutional services, 22 in private duty, and 6 in educational, office or industrial nursing. Thirteen of them are inactive.

The City of Atlanta employs 42 Negro nurses in its clinics and public health programs. Fulton County employs five, and DeKalb County employs one. Grady Hospital employs between fifteen and twenty graduate nurses for services in the "colored side" of the hospital. Seven of these fill semi-supervisory positions in the wards and clinics.

There are seventeen schools of nursing in Georgia which are approved by the Board of Examiners of Nurses for Georgia. Only three of the approved schools in the State accept Negro students, Grady Hospital, Lamar School, affiliated with Paine College, and City Hospital, Columbus, Georgia. None of these schools offer courses leading to the Bachelor's degree or offer advanced training for graduate registered nurses. Such advanced training opportunities are available for white nurses at Emory University, and the University of Georgia.

Grady Hospital School of Nursing has a Negro enrollment of approximately

200. Though it is possible to accept only forty-four students in each class, there were more than 300 applications for admission to the beginning class in the fall of 1947.

Sixty of the 111 registered nurses in Atlanta reported Grady Hospital as their school of nursing. The other fifty-one were from seventeen other schools, several of which no longer exist. . . .

It is evident that additional training facilities are needed within the State. In view of the complete absence of any opportunities for advanced study beyond the basic nursing course, it would seem advisable to consider ways in which advanced nursing education for Negro nurses may be offered at acceptable educational centers.

Atlanta, Ga. (1949)

7]   Black Voting *

Negroes will vote for the first time in a city primary tomorrow in which four candidates seek the Democratic nomination as mayor.

Weeks of campaigning built up tension that resulted in the Negro Voters' League closing its meetings to the four mayoralty candidates and the public.

About 22,400 Negroes are on the list of 94,744 persons eligible to ballot in the primary. Nomination is equivalent to election.

New Orleans, La. (1948)

8]   Mardi Gras King †

When Johnnie J. Smith was King Zulu in 1947 he ruled with a mighty hand. "Ain't having no foolishness, just having fun," he said. "Don't send me no champagne. I'm strictly a scotch and bourbon man." Even before Mardi Gras, Negro night clubs wanted Johnnie to appear on their premises, but he postponed that. "Maybe later," he said, "but I'm too busy now. We got dates in every funeral parlor in town and a lot of other high-class places. Can't mess with that cheap stuff. It's gotta be high-class or nothing."

Weeks before Mardi Gras, Johnnie accomplished what few white carnival kings have done. He practically made himself the king. His fellow members in the Zulu Social Aid and Pleasure Club began talking about who was to be king. "Who you think?" Johnnie asked. "I'm gonna be king."

It was only fair, Johnnie argued. The year before he had been the royal

* SOURCE: *The New York Times*, September 7, 1949.
† SOURCE: Robert Tallant, *Mardi Gras*, New York: Doubleday & Company, Inc., 1948, pp. 230–41.

290

Mardi Gras King

witch doctor, and a mule had eaten part of his grass skirt. "A man that goes through that ought to be the king," he said.

And so it came to pass that Johnnie was king

Days before Mardi Gras Johnnie rode around New Orleans in a glittering limousine driven by a chauffeur, distributing the autographed coconuts that are part of the bounty always bestowed upon favorite subjects by King Zulu. Coconuts were rather scarce that year, too.

"The way them people go for my coconuts," Johnnie said, "I'd have to buy out the French Market and a couple of other places to have enough to go around and the king's gotta have enough. People get jealous."

He bought out something, for few Zulus have been more generous. "A king's gotta advertise too," Johnnie said. "You ever meet a cheap king?"

Johnnie left his coconuts in bars, night clubs, barbershops, restaurants, funeral parlors, and private homes all over the colored sections of New Orleans. Many went to his white friends, too, who were just as eager to have them for souvenirs. One always goes to the mayor at the City Hall. "From the black mayor to the white mayor," is the way that coconut is usually inscribed. But of course not all were given away before Mardi Gras. Many were retained to be thrown from the Zulu floats during the parade. It's good luck to catch one of the Zulu's coconuts on Mardi Gras, and Johnnie wanted to spread good luck all over town.

"I'm gonna be the biggest king in Zulu history," Johnnie predicted as Mardi Gras approached. "I hear lots of people are coming from cities like Hollywood and New York to see me. They ain't gonna be disappointed. They gonna really see something."

The boastful manner of this King Zulu is part of the tradition of the ruler of Negro Mardi Gras, which has in its way just as much tradition as does the Mardi Gras of white New Orleans, and which deviates even less from its traditions year after year. Zulus will tell you that "There Never Was and Never Will Be a King Like Me!" is always their theme.

Many white Orleanians and visitors agree that there is no carnival king like Zulu, and the first thing many of them do early Mardi Gras morning is to go out to the New Basin Canal and South Caiborne Avenue to see King Zulu and his cohorts arrive on the royal barge.

In 1947 the Zulus boarded their barge, the Lawewyn, in the New Basin Canal at South Carrollton Avenue, some blocks from South Clairborne Avenue. King Johnnie Smith, who weighed more than two hundred pounds, was helped into a chair in the center of the barge, and his dukes, the royal witch doctor, and the Big Shot of Africa encircled him. All the Zulus wore the traditional costume of the krewe—long black underwear that covered them to wrists and ankles, grass skirts, and woolly wigs. Faces were blackened and eyes and mouths were circled with white. The royal witch doctor wore, in addition, a horned headdress and a golden ring in his nose, and carried a spiked mace. The Big Shot of Africa wore a high silk hat, a "diamond" stickpin with a stone as big as an egg blazing on the starched white dickey he wore over his black union suit, and another piece of glass of doorknob proportions on the little finger of one hand. He smoked a cigar a foot long. But the most magnificent of all, of course, was King Zulu. His Majesty wore a gold paper crown, dangling earrings, and strings of gleaming beads about his neck. His mantle was dark blue velvet trimmed in gold and edged with white rabbit fur. He carried a jeweled scepter, with which he now and then threatened the small page boy who kept pulling at his mantle. He also wore a leopard-skin vest.

As the barge moved slowly down the canal the royal prince—who always does this job—began to distribute coconuts among the crowds who lined the banks. The others held a conference with His Majesty. What about liquor? was the principal question.

"I know you all got some," said King Zulu, winging that scepter. "But I want you to hold it down, and not to be drinking too much. We got a long day ahead. There's been too much intoxication in the court and I decree it's gotta stop."

There were not too graceful movements of bulging grass skirts as attempts were made to further conceal the bottles hidden beneath them.

"All the gifts along the route come to my float," said King Zulu. "That's so I can watch what you all are doing." It is customary for saloons along the royal route to present the Zulus with bottles.

"That ain't never been done before," protested the Big Shot of Africa, who always feels he is pretty important.

"It's being done now," said King Zulu coolly. "I'm the king."

Colored girls and women along the shore began to yell greetings to His Majesty, and he waved his scepter genially, then directed the royal prince to give a special coconut to one young woman who was leaning so far over the water that she could nearly touch the barge. The royal prince obeyed, tossing it. King Zulu turned on him and berated him mildly. No coconuts were to be thrown this year, he ordered. They were to be handed. People had been hurt in other years, when Zulus had exuberantly heaved them into the crowds.

One of the dukes pulled out a bottle filled with colorless liquid and lifted it to his lips. King Zulu looked at him but said nothing. Another bottle appeared. "Okay," said His Majesty. "I told you all to hold it down. That's all I'm telling you." The bottles vanished beneath grass skirts, and no others appeared for a while. The crowd along the canal bank were in agreement that they had never seen the Zulus so sober in any year within the memory of anyone present.

The tug began to belch thick black smoke from its funnel, and the king brushed soot from his mantle. "Somebody shut that thing off," he commanded. "I'm gonna be ruined before we get started." The funnel obeyed him and stopped its annoying belching and coughing.

Someone remarked to His Majesty that during the coming year the New Basin Canal was to be filled in and that one of the oldest Zulu traditions would have to be discarded. The king snorted. "If they does that to us," he said, "they're gonna have to let us use the river, that's all. We'll just come floating down the lazy Mississippi."

When the barge docked at South Claiborne Avenue the crowd waiting on the shore, which is in the center of the most thickly populated Negro neighborhood in New Orleans, was so immense that the Zulus could scarcely see the end of it. Mostly Negro, there were, nevertheless, many white faces grinning up toward the royal entourage. About half of those who had come to view the arrival were in costume, the others in ordinary clothes. Right in front were a group of Baby Dolls, who are bands of Negresses who dress like dolls in short pleated skirts, silk bloomers, and little bonnets from which always dangle false curls of varying shades—sometimes golden blond.

The Baby Dolls shrieked at the Zulus.

"Hiyah, honey!"

"Come on, Daddy. Let's you and me go someplace!"

"Whatcha say, foots!"

"That king got it!"

Some of the dukes were impressed. "Look at them old gals," they remarked. "Man, what I couldn't do with that!"

"Shut up," said King Zulu. "Keep your mind on me!"

A Negro band, part of the parade to come, began playing, and one of the fattest of the Baby Dolls began doing a shake number. She accomplished what is called "going all the way down," lowering herself to the ground, shaking violently all the time, until she was stretched out on her back, resting upon her shoulders and feet, with her hips gyrating violently and her breasts quivering like jelly under the pink satin halter she wore above her brief skirt.

The parade began to form. One by one, the mule-drawn floats were lined up, four of them, each decorated with straw and palmetto. The band took its place in front, and then a number of Negroes dressed as policemen swung their clubs at the crowd and forced them back so that the regal maskers could board the floats. King Zulu, followed by the royal prince and the pages, climbed on the first float and sat himself carefully in the armchair in the center of the jungle that the float represented. When his mantle and crown had been arranged, someone handed him a Coca-Cola highball and he raised it high and toasted the crowd. The witch doctor and several other Zulus mounted the second float. Now the witch doctor waved his mace and warned all within hearing distance that he was present to guard the health of all. "I'll cure or kill anybody that gets sick along the route," he said with a fierce expression. "If I can't find the cure I'll use the royal mace."

"Listen to him!" shouted a Baby Doll.

"I mean you too, gal!" growled the witch doctor.

The Big Shot of Africa took over the third float for himself and no one else was allowed aboard, as is the custom. The Big Shot sat himself in the armchair beneath the palmetto canopy, crossed his legs, and assumed an expression of supreme hauteur, puffing at his huge cigar and flashing his gigantic glass jewelry with exaggerated gestures and affectations.

All the rest of the Zulus crowded aboard the fourth float, and at last the parade was under way. In front were some of the dukes on horseback, surrounded by the "policemen." Then came the Young Tuxedo Brass Band, now rendering a hot number. After the floats was the property wagon, loaded with old and worn trunks labeled "Fragile, Handle with Care." What is in these trunks has always been a Zulu secret and is not to be divulged.

Negro maskers streamed behind the parade. The Baby Dolls walked the way they call "raddy," which is a strutting, sexy gait that includes much shaking and rolling of the hips. Other women imitated them. Men, both masked and unmasked, left the crowds edging the banquette and joined the women, flinging careless arms about their waists. The Baby Dolls greeted them with cordial expressions like "Hello, ugly. How you doing?" and "Man, we're gonna get it today. And I mean we're gonna get it, Papa." In front of the king's float a sign proclaimed the subject of the parade as "Let the Good Times Roll," and the good times were rolling. One of the "policemen" demanded of everyone he passed, "Gimme a drink!" "Gimme a drink! If somebody don't gimme a drink, I'm gonna call the wagon and send you all to the precinct for loitering around here." It was obvious that one duke had already disobeyed the royal decree of His Majesty, for he could not sit erect upon his horse, but kept sliding forward and slumping over the horse's neck, his white-painted eyelids drooping. Some-one found a rope and the duke was carefully tied into his saddle to prevent an accident. But King Zulu was too busy to notice. He kept leaning down to shake hands with his subjects as the float rocked through the street, and the spectators crowded close to reach up and touch the royal palm.

"I'm the people's king," he explained. "We gotta law against being high-hat. That's one thing a Zulu can't be. I gotta be friendly[!"]

A Baby Doll wanted to be friendly with king, too, and she tried to climb aboard his float. "No women," said one of the "policemen," slapping her lightly on the posterior with his club. "King Zulu's too busy today."

New Orleans, La. (1957)

9]   Black Boycott of Mardi Gras

New Orleans Negroes have started a boycott of Mardi Gras festivities as a pro-test against segregation, it was disclosed today.

Negro leaders have asked that money that would have been spent on fun-making at the Mardi Gras be turned in to support legal fights for integration on buses and in public schools in Louisiana.

"We want to destroy the myth that we are satisfied," said Raymond B. Floyd, an instructor at Xavier University, a Negro school. "By denying our-selves we can dramatize our cause."

Mr. Floyd and Dr. Leonard Burns, leaders in the Negro United Clubs, Inc., a social and civic organization, said that the "Mardi Gras blackout" was cut-ting deeply into the sale of carnival ball luxury items.

They said that many long-established Negro pleasure clubs, including Bon Temps and Plantation Revelers, had canceled traditional balls and elaborate costuming.

Mr. Floyd said that an effective boycott on luxury items would show how important Negro buying power was in New Orleans, whose 650,000 popula-tion is one-third Negro.

SOURCE: *The New York Times*, March 1, 1957.

Improved Status of Blacks

New Orleans has been celebrating a pre-Mardi Gras period since last Sunday. The big day is next Tuesday.

Houston, Texas (1950)

10]   Improved Status of Blacks

Preliminary census reports place Houston's population at 600,000, of which 150,000 are Negroes. Half of this number came during the war to take the jobs created by war industries. Sheffield Steel, Howard Hughes' tool plant and his Grand Prize brewery employ large forces of Negroes. Others work in the southern Pacific Railroad yards, on the docks and in the many oil refineries on the outskirts of town. Hundreds are on the civil service payrolls of city, state and federal governments.

More than 2,500 Negro businesses are scattered throughout the city. Largest employer is Louis Dickerson, who has 254 persons on his payroll. He came to Houston in 1930 without a cent. Today, they refer to him as the "sepia Glenn McCarthy." He's now working on plans for a $100,000 supermarket.

Richest Negro businesses are the insurance firms, which include Watchtower, Universal, Lone Star, Golden State and Excelsior. They carry over $80 million insurance on at least 50 per cent of the Negro population.

Political awareness and a wide awake Negro Chamber of Commerce are responsible for many of the economic gains made by Negroes here. "You can't speak and be heard unless you have the power to vote," says Dickerson, who is a bigwig in Democratic affairs. Carter Wesley's militant *Informer* newspaper also is a big factor in fighting for Negro rights. Directed by hustling Roscoe Cavitt, executive secretary, the Negro Chamber of Commerce has an effective all-around program. It works closely with city officials in trying to solve the many problems of the Negro community it serves.

One of the city's worst slum areas is a section of dirty, smelly streets called Shrimp Alley. Here Negroes and Mexicans live side by side in tumbled down shacks that have outhouses in garbage-littered back yards. Many of the kids born here have never seen a bath tub. Over 50 per cent of the TB victims, disease, arrests and major crimes stem from this area, Mayor Oscar Holcomb recently told civic workers.

Although the Fifth Ward is the largest of the six in which Negroes live, most of the crimes are committed in the "Bloody Fourth." Since 30 Negro cops have been assigned to patrol the colored neighborhoods, the crime rate has been somewhat reduced. But there is still a tendency on the part of white police to beat up Negroes without reason, a situation which the NAACP is protesting vigorously.

In contrast to the squalor of the slums is the well-kept Upper Third Ward and Sugar Hill district. There are homes, some costing over $15,000, which

SOURCE: "Houston," *Our World*, October 1950, pp. 11–19.

are a source of pride to their owners. Most of them are members of the Professional group.

Although Negroes are one quarter of the population, they have the use of only two of the city's 62 parks, Finnegan and Emancipation. Other recreational outlets for them are movies, church socials and the usual beer parlors. The ritzy set does most of its entertaining at home. In the winter they attend formals at the El Dorado ballroom. On week-ends they trek to wealthy divorcee Mattye Hillard's country club. Several doctors . . . own private clinics, although city and state hospitals serve Negro patients. . . .

. . . . .

The city's 33 schools for Negroes employ more than 600 instructors. Salaries, which were equalized in 1942, range from $2400 to $4200. When the newly built Senior High School opens, Dr. J. E. Codwell will head it. He is the city's first Negro Ph.D.

Ten years ago the outlook for Negroes here wasn't bright. That Negro Houstonians today can vote or attend the white state university is a tribute to those who fought for these rights. From these battles they learned if they hope to get their share of democracy in Houston, it's everybody's fight.

Birmingham, Ala. (1952)

11] The Capital of Jim Crowism

Birmingham, Alabama, is the capital of Jim Crowism in America. Birmingham, industry's Pittsburgh of the South, is Jim Crow in birth, life, and death. It is, with apologies to Johannesburg and Capetown, South Africa, the world's most race-conscious city. Birmingham is a city of gross tensions, a city where the color line has been drawn in every conceivable place; Eugene "Bull" Connor, white-supremacist police commissioner, sees that no man, white or black, crosses the line.

I visited Birmingham because of its industry, its labor unions, and my knowledge of the racial friction that manifested itself at intervals in house bombings and police brutality. I wanted to see if Birmingham's industry meant the same thing to the Negro as did Alcoa's industry in Tennessee or if the labor movement in Birmingham meant to the Negro what some Americans predicted it would.

I arrived in Birmingham by Jim Crow train . . . on a Sunday afternoon. I spent a little more than two days in the city. During those hours I tried to find just one aspect of Birmingham life not dominated by a segregation decree. I failed. I found only countless examples of the inconsistency, the irony, the pathos, and accompanying evil that is segregation. Here is Birmingham as I met and lived it:

SOURCE: Carl T. Rowan, *South of Freedom*, New York: Alfred A. Knopf, 1952, pp. 158–67. [Carl T. Rowan, 1925–   , has been a journalist, author, diplomat, and U.S. cabinet member.—Ed.]

The Capital of Jim Crowism

For about half a block after leaving the train I walked toward the station among white passengers. Then it ended. We came to steps of which one set was for Negroes, one for whites. Any notion of ignoring the distinction faded quickly, for there was a policeman standing at the steel gate for whites, seeing to it that Negroes went through the other gate, which led into the Negro waiting-room. It was like a stockyard loading: once in the enclosure, the animals can go but to one place.

I had no idea where I would stay in Birmingham. I asked the woman at the Traveler's Aid desk (a Negro "branch" was set up in the Negro waiting-room) what hotel she recommended. She named the Rush. Then I called the parents of an Oberlin classmate to get their opinion as to whether it was a place infested with thieves, prostitutes, and bedbugs. They, too, said the Rush is as good as anything available to Negroes in Birmingham. I had doublechecked because I knew enough about Negro so-called hotels that are no more than "love pads," operating under the eye of the police so long as the proprietor deals out the customary "cut" and so long as no Negro takes a white woman in.

I found that I would have to ride a cab driven by a Negro. I looked out for one and saw a sign, WHITE CABS ONLY. Even a segregated parking-place is set aside for Negro cabs. I hailed a driver who took me to the Rush, where a huge, red-lettered sign hung over the sidewalk, leaving no doubt that the hotel was FOR COLORED. I got a clean room, although it was without bath or telephone. Despite the apparent cleanliness, I was cautious not to make the mistake that I made in Atlanta. There I left my toothbrush out of its plastic container, and when I returned to my room roaches and waterbugs were having a jolly time nibbling on the toothpaste-sweetened bristles.

I edged into the teeming streets of Birmingham's Negro business-section, and my immediate feeling was that I never had seen so many Negroes in my life. I had, of course, but not crowded into so small an area. The street scene made it evident that housing and other facilities are far inadequate for Birmingham's Negro population. The junkiest little sweets shop was crowded. All along the streets, dumpy little places, many of them operated by whites, were reaping a bonanza.

I ran into food trouble for the first time on my journey. Either Birmingham has no eating-places comparable to those for Negroes in Atlanta, Miami, and Washington, or I asked the wrong people for recommendations. The place labeled "tops" by three people had been closed by policemen, I found upon arrival. I went to a place described as second best. It was so small and crowded that it was almost impossible to walk between the tables. I was hungry, so I ordered fried chicken, an old Southern stand-by. To my woe, the chicken was tough, the rolls were baked hard and crumbly, and the sweet potatoes must have been three-day leftovers, the syrup having thickened and become white. In general, the food was lousy, I informed the proprietor, who sat behind the cash register.

She took my money with nonchalance and told me: "In Birmingham, particular people eats at home." When I stepped back on the street I knew what she meant. You could poison all the "particular" people in overcrowded Birmingham and she still would have enough customers to do a profitable business. I ate at a little ice-cream parlor until I left Birmingham.

I looked for Sunday-afternoon entertainment and ended up heading for a movie. I found three all-Negro (owned by whites) movies, two of which were showing third-run, third-rate features. . . . One white theater in Birmingham admits Negroes, but only to the balcony. I got a wry chuckle from the sign at the side door of this theater: "Balcony kept open continually for your convenience and entertainment."

I decided against the movies, and walked on down the streets, watching the many faces that mirrored joy and sadness, hope and resignation. For blocks I just looked and listened. At one corner I saw a policeman, one hand on his hip, the other on his gun holster, giving an aged Negro peanut-vender a tongue-lashing. A few Negroes leaned against the aged buildings and watched silently. Others paraded by as if nothing out of the ordinary was taking place.

I tired of walking and decided to ride a city bus downtown. I found that both races enter through the front door, as is customary in most cities of the South. I did not read fast enough, however, and had to be told by a gruff motorman that "Nigras step up on the left side, white people on the right side" of the steps. Sure enough, painted side-by-side on the single set of steps were the words COLORED and WHITE. There was only one money box; the fares were the same for both races.

I sat behind a wooden bar near the rear of the bus. The bar is the official "segregator," and a sign on it warned both whites and Negroes not to move it. Although it was not the case on my bus, I saw others on which Negroes stood packed in behind the segregator although there were many empty seats in front of the bar. This can work the other way, of course, but drivers usually see that the bar is where no whites will be inconvenienced.

Instead of riding downtown, I got off at the street where my hotel was. Again I erred by starting out the front door—down the colored side of the steps. The motorman closed the door in my face and ordered me to go to the back door. Only whites could exit at the front. I followed his instructions, and then went to my room.

Monday was a busier day, but it was the same Birmingham. And I was the same Negro, fenced in by law and custom, confused by paradox, left aghast by obvious fear in the eyes of innocent people. All this at one time. I stopped to take a picture of a uniquely Jim Crowed restaurant called George's. This place, in the Negro section but run by a white man whom I assumed to be Greek, lived up to the letter of the law by having whites eat on one side of a horseshoelike counter and Negroes on the other, but in full view and chatting range of each other. The same Negro waitresses served them all. I noticed that a white and a Negro man were conferring across the few feet of space that performed the imaginary segregation. They said that although they worked side by side in Fairfield, a Birmingham suburb and steel-mill center, they could not eat together. I wanted to take their picture but found the room too small to get the shot I wanted, so I stepped outside, planning to take my picture through the window. As I adjusted my camera an old Negro woman caught my arm. "Don't let 'em see you, don't let 'em see you," she cautioned.

"Don't let whom see what?" I demanded hastily.

She nodded her head toward town, where I saw two policemen approaching. I mustered up a "policemen-be-damned" look and snapped the picture. The policemen looked at the camera but said nothing. Later I found that the trembling old woman's fear and excitement had affected me. I had forgotten to take the cover off my lens.

I called a taxi to take me to a few places I wanted to see. I carried a bundle of shirts along in hopes of finding a one-day laundry. The first laundry to catch my eye was the Imperial. A sign painted high on the building proclaimed proudly: WE WASH FOR WHITE PEOPLE ONLY.

"Nothing working in there but colored, neither," said my taxi driver, Samuel Clemens, who knew by my exclamation that I had seen the laundry sign.

"I'd sure like a word with one of the workers," I said. Clemens said he knew a girl in there and would take me in the back way. "I'm Army bound, what the hell have I got to lose?" he philosophized.

Clemens parked and we walked into the laundry. "Why do you work in a joint like this?" I said boldly, trying to catch a worker off guard. The perspiring washerwoman was not surprised, however. She knew to what I referred and acted as if she had been criticized before. "Shucks, the joke's on the owner," she countered. "They do wash some Negroes' clothing here, 'cause mine's in one of them tubs there."

Clemens and I returned to the taxi and he drove me to Birmingham's monument to bigotry—a home shattered by dynamite set off by hoodlums in the struggle to maintain strict residential segregation. It was the night of December 21, 1950, that the blast shattered the eighteen-thousand-dollar home of Mrs. Mary Leans Monk. The explosion, which came less than thirty-six hours after the United States Court of Appeals ruled unconstitutional the city's racial zoning law, injured a sleeping child who was hit by falling plaster.

The house had been unoccupied for several months while the issue was argued in court. When the verdict came, on December 20, Mrs. Monk, her son, William, and Mr. and Mrs. C. W. Askew and their two children moved in. Mrs. Monk was walking into her bedroom the night of the 21st when she heard a thud on the porch outside her bedroom. She ran out just in time to escape the blast, which tore half her bedroom wall away, wrecked the living-room, and damaged other rooms of the brick structure.

When detective G. L. Patty went out to investigate the bombing, he cracked: "The [court] decision must have been what she was waiting for, because she moved right in." Police found no witnesses. Nobody had seen "strangers" in the neighborhood, which is just outside the prescribed "Negro" section.

It was the fifth bombing of Negro homes in a short span of time. The city commission used this flareup of anti-Negro activity as an excuse for approving the segregation ordinance—an assumption that the solution was to keep Negroes out of "white" neighborhoods.

As I stood before the ripped building, an unoccupied, spoiled concession to intimidation and violence, I realized that it had been eight months since Dr. John Buchanan, a white Baptist pastor and head of a committee of five hundred Birmingham citizens, had demanded that "if the local police authorities are not able to find the violators, they should call upon the state forces, and if necessary the federal forces, to apprehend these law violators." A Birmingham paper joined the group in offering one thousand dollars for information leading to the arrest and conviction of the home-blasters. Apparently money must play second string to segregation in Birmingham: nobody knew a thing. Policemen, to whose diligence in enforcing segregation former Senator Glen Taylor can attest, were still following leads up blind alleys.

I went downtown and strolled past restaurants I would have been arrested for trying to enter. Yet the waiters, waitresses, cooks, and dishwashers—all the help except the person behind the cash register—were Negroes in practically every café. I found a cook plucking feathers off a chicken behind one place. I asked what he thought about his boss's racial-seclusion policy.

"Ain't it silly?" he ventured. "I make the biscuits with my black hands. Colored waitresses drag their sleeves in the gravy and stick their fingers in the coffee. That's just mellow fine. But any one of us is too dirty or too something to sit out front and eat."

. . . there are many streets in Birmingham on which a Negro dares not be seen on any side after sundown. Whites and blacks *may* be punished for riding together on the public street, even in a private vehicle, unless the relationship is obviously that of master and servant. Birmingham does restrict whites to one part of the courtroom and Negroes to the other. I found that in the courthouse, where the words "Justice to every man . . ." are inscribed above the elevators, a Negro can ride to his justice only in a Jim Crow elevator. Birmingham *does* prohibit the commingling of the two races, either in public or private hall, to discuss the political questions of the day.

Birmingham had doubly convinced me that segregation is not based on cleanliness, education, body odors, or economic status. It is the symbol of—it is synonymous with—white supremacy.

Montgomery, Ala. (1955)

12]   Bus Boycott

A court test of segregated transportation loomed today following the arrest of a Negro who refused to move to the colored section of a city bus.

While thousands of other Negroes boycotted Montgomery city lines in protest, Mrs. Rosa Parks was fined $14 in Police Court today for having disregarded last Thursday a driver's order to move to the rear of a bus. Negro passengers ride in the rear of buses here, white passengers in front under a municipal segregation ordinance.

An emotional crowd of Negroes, estimated by the police at 5,000, roared approval tonight at a meeting to continue the boycott.

SOURCE: *The New York Times*, December 6, 1955.

Spokesmen said the boycott would continue until people who rode buses were no longer "intimidated, embarrassed and coerced." They said a "delegation of citizens" was ready to help city and bus line officials develop a program that would be "satisfactory and equitable."

Mrs. Parks appealed her fine and was released under bond signed by an attorney, Fred Gray, and a former state president of the National Association for the Advancement of Colored People, E. D. Nixon. . . .

. . . . . .

Mrs. Parks was charged first with violating a city ordinance that gives bus drivers police powers to enforce racial segregation. But at the request of City Attorney Eugene Loe, the warrant was amended to a charge of violation of a similar state law. The state statute authorizes bus companies to provide and enforce separate facilities for whites and Negroes. Violation is punishable by a maximum fine of $500.

Other Negroes by the thousands, meanwhile, found other means of transportation or stayed home today in an organized boycott of City Lines Buses, operated by a subsidiary of National City Lines at Chicago.

The manager, J. H. Bagley, estimated that "80 or maybe 90 per cent" of the Negroes who normally used the buses had joined the boycott. He said "several thousand" Negroes rode the buses on a normal day.

Little Rock, Ark. (1957)

13] School Desegregation

It was Labor Day, September 2, 1957. The nine pupils who had been selected by the school authorities to enter Central High School—Carlotta Walls, Jefferson Thomas, Elizabeth Eckford, Thelma Mothershed, Melba Pattillo, Ernest Green, Terrance Roberts, Gloria Ray, and Minnijean Brown—were enjoying the last day of their summer vacation. Some of them were picnicking, others swimming, playing tennis, or just visiting with friends and relatives. About mid-afternoon young Jefferson Thomas was on his way home from the pool and stopped at my house for a brief visit. While Jeff was raiding the refrigerator, a news flash came over the radio that the Governor would address the citizens of Arkansas that night.

"I wonder what he's going to talk about," said Jeff. The youngster then turned to me and asked, "Is there anything they can do—now that they lost in court? Is there any way they can stop us from entering Central tomorrow morning?"

"I don't think so," I said.

About seven o'clock that night a local newspaper reporter rang my doorbell.

SOURCE: Daisy Bates, *The Long Shadow of Little Rock,* New York: David McKay, 1962, pp. 59–68. [Daisy Bates is a former newspaper editor and president of the Arkansas State NAACP.—Ed.]

"Mrs. Bates, do you know that national guardsmen are surrounding Central High?"

L. C. and I stared at him incredulously for a moment. A friend who was visiting us volunteered to guard the house while we drove out to Central. L. C. gave him the shotgun. We jumped into our car and drove to Central High. We parked a half block from the school. Under the street lights stretched a long line of brown Army trucks with canvas tops. Men in full battle dress—helmets, boots, and bayonets—were piling out of the trucks and lining up in front of the school.

As we watched, L. C. switched on the car radio. A newscaster was saying, "National guardsmen are surrounding Central High School. No one is certain what this means. Governor Faubus will speak later this evening."

Ahead of us we could see reporters rushing up trying to talk to the soldiers. However, it soon became clear that the guardsmen were under orders to say nothing. They remained silent.

The whole scene was incredible. "Let's go back home and hear Faubus!" I suggested.

The phone was ringing as we pulled into our driveway. An excited friend wanted to know what it all meant, what was going to happen. All I could offer was, "Listen to Faubus." As soon as I put down the receiver, the phone rang again. This time it was the father of one of the children. "What's going on, Daisy? What's going to happen?" All I could do was to give him the same answer.

On television, Governor Faubus creates almost the same impression he does in person. He customarily wears a dark suit, white shirt, and dark tie. He is a big man physically, and affects a big man's easy congeniality. He specializes in the folksy manner, fixing his unseen audience with an "I'm-right-here-with-you-good-folks" glance.

I don't recall all the details of what Governor Faubus said that night. But his words electrified Little Rock. By morning they shocked the United States. By noon the next day his message horrified the world.

Faubus' alleged reason for calling out the troops was that he had received information that caravans of automobiles filled with white supremacists were heading toward Little Rock from all over the state. He therefore declared Central High School off limits to Negroes. For some inexplicable reason he added that Horace Mann, a Negro high school, would be off limits to whites.

Then, from the chair of the highest office of the State of Arkansas, Governor Orval Eugene Faubus delivered the infamous words, "blood will run in the streets" if Negro pupils should attempt to enter Central High School.

In a half dozen ill-chosen words, Faubus made his contribution to the mass hysteria that was to grip the city of Little Rock for several months.

The citizens of Little Rock gathered on September 3 to gaze upon the incredible spectacle of an empty school building surrounded by 250 National Guard troops. At about eight fifteen in the morning, Central students started passing through the line of national guardsmen—all but the nine Negro students.

I had been in touch with their parents throughout the day. They were confused, and they were frightened. As parents voiced their fears, they kept re-peating Governor Faubus' words that "blood would run in the streets of Little Rock" should their teen-age children try to attend Central—the school to which they had been assigned by the school board.

Typical of the parents was Mrs. Birdie Eckford. "Mrs. Bates," she asked, "what do you think we should do? I am frightened. Not for myself but for the children. When I was a little girl, my mother and I saw a lynch mob dragging the body of a Negro man through the streets of Little Rock. We were told to get off the streets. We ran. And by cutting through side streets and alleys, we managed to make it to the home of a friend. But we were close enough to hear the screams of the mob, close enough to smell the sickening odor of burn-ing flesh. And, Mrs. Bates, they took the pews from Bethel Church to make the fire. They burned the body of this Negro man right at the edge of the Negro business section.

"Mrs. Bates, do you think this will happen again?"

I reminded Mrs. Eckford that Little Rock was a different city now. Different from 1927, when the lynching and the burning had taken place. True, Gover-nor Faubus spoke of blood. But in the next breath he had said that he called out the guardsmen to protect life and property against violence. Surely he meant the lives of the Negro students as well as white! No, it was inconceiva-ble that troops, and responsible citizens, would stand by and let a mob attack children.

The NAACP attorneys, Wiley Branton and Thurgood Marshall, appealed to Federal Judge Ronald N. Davies for instruction. Their question was, in effect: What do we do now? The judge stated that "he was accepting the Governor's statement at face value—that his purpose in calling out the Guard was to pro-tect 'life and property' against possible mob violence." Therefore, Judge Davies directed the school board again to put its plan for integration into operation immediately.

On the afternoon of the same day, September 3, when the school was sched-uled to open, Superintendent Blossom called a meeting of leading Negro Citi-zens and the parents of the nine children. I was not notified of the meeting, but the parents called me and asked me to be present. At the meeting Super-intendent Blossom instructed the parents *not* to accompany their children the next morning when they were scheduled to enter Central. "If violence breaks out," the Superintendent told them, "it will be easier to protect the children if the adults aren't there."

During the conference Superintendent Blossom had given us little assurance that the children would be adequately protected. As we left the building, I was aware of how deeply worried the parents were, although they did not voice their fears.

About ten o'clock that night I was alone in the downstairs recreation room, my mind still occupied by the problems raised during the conference. L. C. appeared in the doorway. With him was a local reporter whom I had known for some time.

Words began pouring from the young reporter. "Look, Daisy," he said anx-iously. "I know about the Superintendent's instructions. I know he said the children must go along to Central in the morning. But let me tell you, this is murder! I heard those people today. I've never seen anything like it. People I've known all my life—they've gone mad. They're totally without reason. You must know you can't expect much protection—if any—from the city police. Besides, the city police are barred from the school grounds!"

My friends voice took on a pleading quality, as if there were something I could do. "I swear there must have been about five hundred people at the school today," he continued. "And new recruits are pouring into the city from outlying areas. Even from other states. By morning there could be several thousand."

"What do you think we should do?" I asked him.

"I really don't know," he answered. "I really don't know."

The young reporter left. I sat huddled in my chair, dazed, trying to think, yet not knowing what to do. I don't recall how much time went by—a few minutes, an hour, or more—before some neighbors entered. One of them was the Reverend J. C. Crenchaw, President of the Little Rock branch of the NAACP.

His presence in my house immediately gave me an idea.

"Maybe," I said, "maybe we could round up a few ministers to go with the children tomorrow. Maybe then the mob wouldn't attack them. Maybe with the ministers by their side—"

Mr. Crenchaw caught on to the idea right away. "We can try, Daisy. At least we can try. Maybe this is the answer."

I called a white minister, Rev. Dunbar Ogden, Jr., President of the Interracial Ministerial Alliance. I did not know Mr. Ogden. I explained the situation, then asked if he thought he could get some ministers to go with the children to school the next morning.

"Well, Mrs. Bates, I don't know," he said. "I'll call some of the ministers and see what they think about it. You know, this is a new idea to me."

I said the idea was new to me, too; and that it had just occurred to me moments before. Tensely I waited for his return call. When it came, he sounded apologetic. The white ministers he had talked to had questioned whether it was the thing to do. Some of the Negro ministers had pointed out that the Superintendent of Schools had asked that no Negro adults go with the children, and that in view of this they felt they shouldn't go. Then he added gently, "I'll keep trying—and, God willing, I'll be there."

Next I called the city police. I explained to the officer in charge that we were concerned about the safety of the children and that we were trying to get ministers to accompany them to school the next morning. I said that the children would assemble at eight-thirty at Twelfth Street and Park Avenue. I asked whether a police car could be stationed there to protect the children until the ministers arrived.

The police officer promised to have a squad car there at eight o'clock. "But you realize," he warned, "that our men cannot go any closer than that to the school. The school is off limits to the city police while it's 'occupied' by the Arkansas National Guardsmen."

By now it was two thirty in the morning. Still, the parents had to be called about the change in plan. At three o'clock I completed my last call, explaining to the parents where the children were to assemble and the plan about the ministers. Suddenly I remembered Elizabeth Eckford. Her family had no telephone. Should I go to the Union Station and search for her father? Someone had once told me that he had a night job there. Tired in mind and body, I decided to handle the matter early in the morning. I stumbled into bed.

A few hours later, at about eight fifteen in the morning, L. C. and I started driving to Twelfth Street and Park Avenue. On the way I checked out in my mind the possibilities that awaited us. The ministers might be there—or again they might not. Mr. Ogden, failing to find anyone to accompany him, understandably might not arrive. Would the police be there? How many? And what if—

The bulletin over the car radio interrupted. The voice announced: "A Negro girl is being mobbed at Central High. . . ."

"Oh, my God!" I cried. "It must be Elizabeth! I forgot to notify her where to meet us!"

L. C. jumped out of the car and rushed to find her. I drove on to Twelfth Street. There were the ministers—two white—Mr. Ogden and Rev. Will Campbell, of the National Council of Churches, Nashville, Tennessee —and two colored—the Reverend Z. Z. Driver, of the African Methodist Episcopal Church, and the Reverend Harry Bass, of the Methodist Church. With them also was Mr. Ogden's twenty-one-year-old son, David. The children were already there. And, yes, the police had come as promised. All of the children were there—all except Elizabeth.

Soon L. C. rushed up with the news that Elizabeth finally was free of the mob. He had seen her on a bus as it pulled away.

The children set out, two ministers in front of them, two behind. They proceeded in that formation until they approached the beginning of the long line of guardsmen. At this point they had their first brush with the mob. They were jostled and shoved. As they made their way toward the school grounds, the ministers and their charges attempted to pass the guardsmen surrounding Central High. A National Guard captain stopped them. He told Mr. Ogden he could not allow them to pass through the guard line. When Mr. Ogden asked why, the captain said it was by order of Governor Faubus.

The ministers returned to the car with the students and Mr. Ogden reported what the captain of the guardsmen had said. I told him that in view of the school board's statement the previous evening that Central High School would be open to Negro students in the morning, it was my feeling that the students should go immediately to the office of the Superintendent for further instructions.

When we arrived at the office, the Superintendent was out. When he failed to return within an hour, I suggested that we appeal to the United States Attorney, Osro Cobb, since Federal Judge Davies had ordered the Federal Bureau of Investigation, under the direction of the United States Attorney, to conduct a thorough investigation into who was responsible for the interference with the Court's integration order.

Mr. Cobb looked surprised when we entered his office. I told him that we were there because the students had been denied admittance to Central High School by the national guardsmen and we wanted to know what action, if any, his office planned to take.

After questioning the pupils, he directed them to the office of the FBI, where they gave a detailed report of what had happened to them that morning.

I might add here that during the school year the FBI interviewed hundreds of persons. Many of those who had participated in the mob could easily have been identified from photographs taken in front of the school. Yet no action was taken against anyone by the office of the United States Attorney, Osro Cobb, or the Department of Justice.

Economic Aspects

The continuing CIO and AFL drives led to more southern blacks being unionized, as the case below of New Orleans shows. However, the black economic gains made during the war were not sustained afterward. This was certainly the case in Birmingham, where a comparison between the number of black industrial workers employed in 43 companies in 1939 and in 1951 showed that in all but three cases a significantly smaller proportion of blacks was used after the war than before it.

New Orleans, La. (1950)

14]   Blacks in Unions

Both American Federation of Labor and Congress of Industrial Organizations unions in New Orleans have Negro members in varying numbers. . . .

· · · · ·

New Orleans does not have a large number of major industrial plants. There are only five industries which may be considered in the category of large industries. These are:

Todd Johnson Shipbuilders and Dry Dock—now engaged primarily in ship repairs

Higgins Shipbuilding Company—since the war, engaged mostly in the building of pleasure crafts

Celotex

SOURCE: "A Review of the Economic Problems of New Orleans, La. Feb.–March 1950," Department of Research and Community Projects, National Urban League, pp. 44–58. (Unpublished manuscript.)

Blacks in Unions

Penick-Ford—engaged in molasses manufacturing
Lane Cotton Mills
All of these plants employ Negroes, but mostly as unskilled workers. Negroes
are members of labor unions in the above industries. Lane Cotton Mills has
the largest number of Negroes of any single employer, using approximately
300 in a total force of 1,600.

According to officials in both the AF of L and CIO unions, there are approximately 30,000 Negroes in labor unions in New Orleans, many of which
(unions) are interracial.

The General Longshore Workers Union, Local #1419, with a membership of
approximately 3,200 Negroes, is perhaps the largest Negro union in the nation.
Negro and white longshoremen are members of separate unions but work on
the same job and sign the same contracts. The union has five representatives in
the Central Trades Labor Council and is entitled to twelve delegates to the
State Federation of Labor. Members of both Negro and white longshoremen's
unions are members of the same Council. One meeting is held each quarter

Partial List of AF of L and CIO Union Members
New Orleans, Louisiana: 1950

UNION	TOTAL MEMBER- SHIP	WHITE	NEGRO
International Union of United Brewery Workers and Beer	141	141	0
International Brotherhood of Teamsters Local #965, AF of L	500	100	400
United Steel Workers of America Local #2369, CIO	280	274	6
Ship Carpenters, Caulkers and Joiners of America, #584, AF of L	325	300	25
Laundry Workers Joint Board Amalgamated International Workers of America	900	300	600
General Truck Drivers, Chauffeurs and Helpers, Local #270, AF of L	1,433	770	630
Distillery Workers, Local 168, CIO	120	80	40
United Steel Workers of America Local #2179, CIO	103	103	0
United Wholesale, Warehouse Workers, CIO	200	—	200
Textile Workers of America	2,500	1,997	503
Amalgamated Lithographers, Local #53 CIO	75	75	—
National Union of Marine Cooks and Stewards, CIO	6,000	3,500	2,500
Building and Common Laborers, AF of L	2,000	160	1,840
Longshoremen's, Locals #1418, #1419 AF of L	3,500	300	3,200
Transport Workers, Local #206, CIO	500	48	452

among the total Negro and white membership. At one meeting the Negro president presides and the white president serves as secretary. In the following meeting the order is reversed. Local #1419 has been one of the most politically active groups in the city. Recently a person was employed by the union on a full-time basis to teach union and non-union residents how to qualify to vote and how to use voting machinery.

The social service program of the union includes insurance and burial policies. The Monarch Life Insurance Company is owned and operated by Local #1419. The union and its enterprises provide employment for fifty-one persons (14 in unions, 6 in funeral homes, 31 in the insurance company).

. . . Both Negro and white union officials expressed the opinion that, on the whole, labor relations between Negroes and whites in New Orleans are exceptionally good. They agreed, however, that there have been evidences of discrimination toward Negroes which have impeded the building of a strong united front in labor.

The National Union of Marine Cooks and Stewards has done more to protect the interests of its Negro membership than any of the other local unions. . . . In the New Orleans local, Negroes hold positions as port agents, organizers, and patrolmen in the various ports.

In the International Brotherhood of Teamsters, Local #965, which is a mixed AF of L local, Negroes hold positions of president, vice-president, secretary-treasurer, and trustees.

Louis Stark, manager of the Laundry Workers of America, stated that the relationship between Negroes and whites in his local is good. The president of the union is colored. Negroes are also stewards and committeemen.

The president and general manager of the General Truck Drivers and Chauffeurs Union stated that there may be internal feelings between Negroes and whites toward each other, but these are not allowed to affect affairs in the union. The Negro elected officers, he stated, were chosen with good white support. The assistant business manager and organizer of the union are Negroes.

There are six Negro members in Local #2369 of the United Steel Workers of America, CIO, and all of these are good members according to Ralph J. Levison, president.

. . . . .

Negro plumbers are consistently denied membership in the local plumbers union. The local policy of the union states that a prospective member must have his application vouched for by a member of the organization. This rule is a disadvantage for Negroes because no white member has ever vouched for a Negro. Negroes in New Orleans who engage in plumbing work are under the supervision of white licensed plumbers. There are two certified Negro plumbers in the city; both are certified by the union and the city. Because of the union policy they have not been elected into membership in the union.

There is an almost unanimous acceptance in all AF of L and CIO unions of equal pay for equal work among Negro and white union members. The major problem among Negro union members is in the shipbuilding industry where they have difficulty in getting upgraded.

Blacks in Industries

It was the opinion of observers with whom the writer discussed the subject that there are employers who refuse to employ Negro union workers if their wages are to be the same as white workers. Several Negro craftsmen advised the writer that some contractors still just refuse to employ Negro union members. In the construction of the Le Garde Hospital in 1941, it is claimed that the white union painters refused to work on the job with Negro painters who were also union men in another local. The engineer in charge of the job designated a number of the buildings for Negroes to work on in order to provide them with employment. It should be pointed out that this type of discrimination no longer exists among white union painters.

Little is done in an organized way to foster workers' education by the AF of L or CIO.

The AF of L recently sponsored two workers' education meetings for business agents of their unions. These meetings, held at Dillard University, were attended by approximately 80 per cent of the business agents of all AF of L locals.

George Snowden is the leading Negro spokesman and a person of special influence in the AF of L union. He is a member of the Central Trades Council and head of the workers' education program which he initiated and had adopted by the Council. In 1948 he became a vice-president of the State Federation of Labor, the first Negro to be elected to that position in Louisiana. . . .

Birmingham, Ala. (1955)

15]   Blacks in Industries

The smallest proportion of Negro employment found is [in] the apparel industry where only 10 Negroes were employed out of over 400 workers in two apparel manufacturing firms. In sharp contrast, Negro workers make up 40 percent of the work force in the basic iron and steel industry and 50 percent in transportation equipment manufacture. [The] table [page 310] presents a summary of the percentage of Negro workers to total employment in the various industries represented by the firms included in the survey.

The figures upon which these percentages are calculated are in some cases the employer's best estimate and do not represent an actual pay roll count. This is particularly true of the figures for 1939. For this reason, a change from 1939 to 1951 of only a few percent is probably not significant. It should also be pointed out that the nature of the building construction business makes it difficult to give a precise proportion of Negro employment, which will vary considerably according to the character of the particular construction job. The

SOURCE: Langston T. Hawley, "Negro Employment in the Birmingham Area," Case Study No. 3 *Selected Studies of Negro Employment in the South*, Washington, D.C.: National Planning Association, 1955, pp. 232–43.

*Percentage of Negro Employment to Total
Employment in 43 Firms, By Industry Group.
1939 and 1951*

INDUSTRY GROUP	1951	1939
Manufacturing:		
Food	37	26
Textiles	11	9
Apparel	2	3
Lumber and wood products	34	° °
Paper and allied products	18	30
Furniture and fixtures	60	60
Stone, clay, and glass	48	45
Primary metals °	40	46
Fabricated metals	22	25
Machinery (except electrical)	19	20
Transportation equipment	50	50
Bituminous coal mining (commercial)	29	31
Building construction	40	40
Transportation	19	19
Public utilities: gas, electric and water	16	18

° Includes captive iron and coal mines.
° ° Data not available.

estimate shown here was concurred in by officials of all construction companies interviewed.

Since the figures presented in [this] table are averages, they tend to obscure important variations in the percentage of Negroes employed by the specific firms within the several industry groups. In the food industry, for example, the proportion of Negroes employed varies from 11 percent in a coffee plant to 63 percent in a grain and flour mill. Officials of these firms state there is nothing unusual about their proportions of Negro employment to total employment for their specific kinds of business in the Birmingham Area. In the case of two meat packing concerns, one has 20 percent Negro employment while the other has 40 percent. This came about during the war when the latter concern increased the employment of Negroes to alleviate a labor shortage and kept them on after the war in view of their satisfactory service. The firm with only 20 percent hired a somewhat larger percentage of White women during the war when pinched for labor.

Again, in the case of firms in the primary metals group there is wide variation. A small jobbing foundry has 90 percent Negroes comprising its work force, and the president of this company states that this is not at all uncommon for firms of his size (65 employees) in the foundry business in the Birmingham Area. Those firms in the primary metals group operating blast furnaces, rolling mills, and iron ore and coal mines have from one-third to one-half of their work forces made up of Negroes. Other firms making up an important part of the primary metals group manufacture cast-iron pipe, fittings, and industrial valves. These firms have from one-half to two-thirds of their total employment made up of Negro workers. The higher proportion of Negroes in this branch of the primary metals industry is due largely to the importance of foundry work in the manufacturing process.

In the fabricated metals group the proportion of Negro employment to total employment ranges from 6 percent to 31 percent for the individual firms surveyed. The firm having only 6 percent Negroes is a small (150 employees) manufacturer of metal lawn furniture, fire escapes, and stairways. Its work involves a fairly high degree of skill and it has relatively few common labor jobs; also, it has a long tradition of employing only White craftsmen and helpers. In general, each of the firms engaged in manufacturing light, structural steel shapes employs a smaller proportion of Negroes than is the case in the firms of the primary metals group.

As would be expected, wide variations in the number of Negroes employed relative to Whites were observed in the transportation and public utility firms in the area. The proportion of Negro employees ranges from 7 percent in an electric utility company to 44 percent in the maintenance shop of a common carrier bus company. One of the two major railroads included in the study has 20 percent Negro employment, and the other 14 percent. About one-third of the employees of the City of Birmingham's Water Works Board are Negro, while only 23 percent are employed in a large gas company where the work of the Negro—the installation and repair of pipe line systems—is very similar. The large proportion of Negroes in the maintenance shop of the bus company is due largely to the heavy use of Negro women in cleaning the interiors of the buses.

. . . . .

The higher proportion of Negroes employed in the food industry is accounted for largely by a meat packing firm of 250 employees which turned to Negroes during the war as a result of a tight labor market and retained the Negroes after the war's end. In 1939, this firm had 20 percent Negores in its work force. It is a unionized plant, paying the same wage rates to Negroes and Whites for the same work classifications. No other significant change in the use of Negro workers was found among the firms representing the food industry.

Two companies in the basic iron and steel industry reduced their proportions of Negro employment to total employment during the period 1939 to 1951. In the larger of these firms, the reduction was from 43 percent to 36 percent, while the smaller firm's proportion of Negro employment fell from 54 to 50 percent. A management official of one of these firms explained the decline in his company on the ground that improved technology, particularly in materials handling equipment, had displaced some Negro workers. No explanation was given by the other firm.

The slightly decreased proportion (from 25 percent in 1939 to 22 percent in 1951) of Negro employment in the fabricated metals industry is traceable to three fabricators of structural steel products. These three firms experienced considerable expansion in their total employment from 1939 to 1951. The character of their operations led to a larger expansion of relatively skilled jobs than of unskilled and semiskilled jobs. Since skilled jobs are traditionally filled by White workers, the employment expansion led to a relative decline in their use of Negro workers. This process of expansion was accompanied to some extent by the adoption of mechanical materials handling equipment which tended to hold down an increase in the employment of Negroes that probably would have occurred had such equipment not been available. The proportion of Negroes employed by fabricators of heavier iron and steel products—such as cast-iron pipe—which involve extensive foundry operations, remained remarkably stable during the period.

One large manufacturer of paper products (writing tablets, paper boxes, etc.) employed 30 percent Negroes in 1939 but only 19 percent in 1951. This decline in the proportion of Negroes occurred during a period when the company's total employment expanded 93 percent. The management of this company offered two principal reasons for this relative decline in the use of Negro workers: 1) the company shifted from hand trucking on its loading dock to gasoline and electric lift trucks, and 2) since the Fair Labor Standards Act requires the company to pay a minimum wage of 75 cents an hour, and there is an adequate supply of White labor willing to work for this rate, the company prefers White workers. The management official interviewed stated that this preference is based on the company's experience that White workers are better educated, understand instructions more readily, are more reliable, and, in general, are more productive than Negro workers.

Two cases of what may be termed "mass substitution" of White for Negro workers deserve special mention.

In one case a lumber manufacturer employing 235 people in 1951 was found to have had approximately three-quarters of his total employment comprised of Negroes in 1939 but none in 1951. This replacement of Negroes with all White workers was apparently the outgrowth of a labor dispute. An attempt was made to organize the company's workers, and a strike for recognition ensued. The company refused to recognize the union as bargaining agent and replaced the strikers with other workers. In the course of this replacement none of the Negro workers were taken back and an all-White work force resulted. The management official interviewed in this firm indicated that the reason Negroes were no longer employed is that they are "too susceptible to union organization."

The other case involved a coal mining company that employed 300 workers in 1951, about 4 percent of whom were Negroes. In 1939 this firm employed approximately 600 people of whom about 22 percent were Negroes. The company operates two mines in the Birmingham Area. The company president attributed the relative decrease in the use of Negro workers to what he believed to be a policy of the union (United Mine Workers of America) on upgrading. This policy as applied to Negroes would broaden the base of Negro job opportunities in and around the mines, and would require upgrading of the Negro to the more skilled jobs traditionally held by White workers.

The result of this union policy, stated the employer, is to create friction between White and Negro workers. He related that in one of the company's mines, as a direct result of the union policy, the White workers forced segregation upon the company. This segregation took various forms, both within and without the working environment. One occasion, a deputation of White miners who were members of the local union told the company "point blank" that the Whites would no longer work with Negroes. After this experience the company stopped hiring Negroes entirely at one mine, and apparently greatly reduced such hirings at the other mine. At present, the company's policy is not to hire Negroes in any circumstance which might lead to friction.

. . . . .

On the whole, ignoring relatively minor changes in the proportion of Negroes employed between 1939 and 1951, only three cases were found among the 43 companies surveyed where there was a significant increase in the relative importance of Negro workers in the total work force. On the other hand, eight firms (including the two cases of mass substitution) reported that they were using Negroes in significantly smaller proportions in 1951 than they had in 1939. From the standpoint of the absolute numbers of Negro workers involved, the decreases substantially overshadowed the increases.

In the firms surveyed, the overwhelming proportion of Negro workers was found among the unskilled and semiskilled occupations. With few exceptions these occupations break down into certain basic types of work: common, manual labor jobs, requiring only a few days training time and very little education; journeyman or craft-helper jobs, requiring very little skill and often calling for considerable physical exertion; and machine operations, both heavy and light, requiring at most a few weeks learning time and typically repetitive in nature. With respect to the unskilled jobs, it was found that while they are performed by both White and Negro workers, the latter do the dominant portion of this type of work. In the building construction industry, for example, it was estimated by the management officials interviewed that from 90 to 95 percent of all common labor is performed by Negroes. Much this same situation exists in the heavy industries which were investigated, particularly in the basic steel industry.

However, in the case of semiskilled jobs, such as machine operation, it was found that in most cases both White and Negro workers fill such jobs, and there was no discernible predominance of Negroes in them. This was not true, however, of the semiskilled jobs of packer, mortar mixer, chipper and grinder, garage helper and chauffeur, mule driver, air hammer operator, and tire changer. The Negro was definitely found to be predominant in these occupations.

Relatively few Negroes were found in the skilled and clerical occupations of the companies studied. Less than half—44 percent—of the companies interviewed had any Negro workers in skilled jobs, and only 9 of the 43 firms indicated that they had Negroes doing some degree of clerical work. No Negro workers were found in skilled occupations in the participating firms in the following industries: textiles; apparel; lumber; transportation equipment manufacture; gas, electric, and water utilities; paper and paper products; cement; and bed springs and mattress manufacture. Only one skilled Negro worker—an oven operator in a bread bakery—was found in the six firms interviewed in the food industry.

Negroes in skilled occupations were found most frequently in coal mining, train and engine service of railroads, foundries, and building construction. A

313

special word of comment is in order about skilled Negro workmen in railroads and building construction. In both of the major railroads included in the study, all of the skilled Negroes found were in train and engine service—that is, were firemen, brakemen, or switchmen. These Negroes were all long-service employees, and the officials contacted in both railroads stated that they had not hired Negroes in train and engine service for over twenty years. Thus, skilled Negroes on the railroads are apparently being gradually replaced with Whites through the attrition of turnover, principally by retirement.

Officials of the three building construction firms interviewed stated that they rarely employed Negro bricklayers or carpenters. It was their opinion that in the Birmingham Area, Negroes are employed in insignificant numbers—both absolutely and relatively—in these trades. This opinion was supported by an official of the Birmingham Chapter of the Associated General Contractors, and by trade union officials. In general, the investigation disclosed that the only important skilled trades in the building construction industry in which Negroes are employed in appreciable numbers are plastering, lathing, and cement finishing.

As already noted, few Negroes were performing clerical work in the companies surveyed. In all cases such work could be classified as clerical in only a limited sense. It involved, for the most part, such duties as filling out shipping notices, preparing shipping labels, assisting with inventory taking, and sorting mail. Interestingly enough, in all but a few cases, the management officials whose firms employed Negroes in these clerical capacities replied in the negative when asked whether Negroes were performing clerical work in their organizations. In seven of the nine firms employing Negroes in jobs which classify as clerical, only eight Negroes were so employed; the other two firms gave no information as to the number employed.

Negroes dominated the service occupations in the 43 firms studied. In fact, with the exception of the occupations of watchman and cook, no Whites were found to be performing the remaining service jobs. . . .

TWO ALL-BLACK
SOUTHERN TOWNS

Mound Bayou, Miss., and Grambling, La., are among the most famous all-black towns, of which there are more than five dozen in the United States. Grambling was made famous by Grambling College, an institution that has contributed a remarkably high number of black athletes to the nation. Mound Bayou was founded in 1887 by Isaiah T. Washington, a former slave of Joseph Davis, the brother of the Confederate president, Jefferson Davis, and himself a wealthy and politically influential man. Incorporated in 1898, it was still thriving in the 1940's, with a population of a little more than 1,000 under the mayoral management of Benjamin A. Green, a Harvard-trained lawyer. Significantly, Mound Bayou and Grambling were without police, jails, and other formal coercive agencies. The smallness of their size plus their origins in reaction to white discrimination produced well-knit communities whose social sanctions maintained a highly unusual degree of order and stability.

16]   *Mound Bayou, Miss. (1946)*

Peace abides in Mound Bayou where no white men dwell. The law is kept by the more than 1,000 Negroes who live here in a segregation of their own seeking, for Mound Bayou is an all-Negro town. For almost 60 years it has been that, with internal accord and freedom from external interference. Now a prosperous and prevailing community, it has the promise of a greater future.

The peace that abides in Mound Bayou is certified by the lack of law-enforcing machinery. For 15 years the town has had no jail. Even before that it could have been dispensed with, so seldom was it needed. In those 15 years there has been no major crime committed except one assassination that was really an outside affair connected with state politics. Misdemeanors have been few and far between, fights and the like of that. "You can't keep men from fighting," says Mayor Benjamin A. Green, "no matter how good Christians they are."

SOURCE: F. A. Behymer, "Mound Bayou, an All-Negro Town," *St. Louis Post-Dispatch*, April 8, 1946.

315

When something like that happens it is nothing to get excited about. Marshal Terrel, who runs a grocery and farms a little on the side, tells the misdemeanants to be at the mayor's office at 9 o'clock next morning to be dealt with at his discretion as ex officio justice of the peace. They show up ahead of time, in a broken and contrite spirit, and the mayor gives them a talking-to and lets them go or assesses a small fine.

"We all know each other here," the mayor says," and are interested in upholding the town's good name. If a man makes a little mistake, and is sorry, we forgive him. Citizens are taught to respect themselves and feel a personal responsibility. The eyes of the country are on us. We believe that the Negro, if given the opportunity, will do the right thing. He has the opportunity here and he does the right thing."

. . . . .

It is Mayor Ben Green,[1] with 27 years' service behind him, who now speaks of Mound Bayou and what it means and what of hope it holds for the solution of the race question that vexes the South. When he is asked if this sort of voluntary segregation is the answer to the South's perpetual problem, spreading more and more to the north, he considers before answering and at last says hesitantly, "I don't know. . . . But it's the best that we have found. It has worked out here. That is all we can say."

. . . . .

This thing of segregation, it is something that can't be created mechanically by compulsion. It has to grow, like it has grown in Mound Bayou. This is not like the segregation in the cities, imposed by white men, in which the Negroes get the worst of it. Negroes, the mayor says, don't object to grouping but to the Jim Crow accommodations, and discriminations that go with it. As a lawyer entitled to practice in the state and federal courts he sits with white lawyers around the counsel tables and the converse is easy and natural, with swapping of cigarettes, but when court recesses he can't go where the white lawyers go for lunch. He makes no comment. He merely mentions the fact.

Now take Mound Bayou. It shows what Negroes can do when they are on their own. Go look at our churches, says Mayor Green. As good as the white folks worship in. "Seems like we've got more churches than anything else. Let's see, there are two Methodist, M.E. and AME., two Baptist (the Baptists are always splitting up), the Church of Christ and, I almost forgot, the Episcopal. It's small but it's here. Then there are the folks who say millions now living will never die. We have some of them too."

. . . . .

And look at Mound Bayou's high school, as fine as can be seen in any white folk's town. And don't fail to look at the new Taborian Hospital. It's nearly new anyway, finished in 1942. Sponsored by the Knights and Daughters of Tabor. No finer hospital anywhere of its size. Headed by a civic-minded young surgeon, Dr. T. R. M. Howard, who also led the movement for the Good Will Park, opened last year. There's a Women's Civic Club working on beautification plans for the town.

[1] Harvard graduate of 1914 and World War I veteran.

Grambling, La.

Right now Mound Bayou is trying to have the proposed Federal hospital for Negro veterans located here. It's just the place for it, Mayor Green argues, for veterans would be among friends and they would be welcome. Any other place the white folks might object and that would make it unpleasant for the patients.

There's a new co-op gin opened three years ago to serve the 2,000 Negro farmers round about. That makes three gins for the town. They are part and parcel of the white men's ginning system of the state. It wasn't that way at first. The white gin owners ganged up on the first Mound Bayou gin, fixing prices without consulting the Negro owners here and putting them in a hot spot. The Mound Bayou gin boys turned the tables and fixed prices without consulting with the white brothers. That wasn't so good and the white ginners decided to play along.

Mayor Green, 57-year-old bachelor, five feet four, 125 pounds, looks upon the town that he has guided for 27 years and is properly proud of it. It's a good town, is Mound Bayou. To a stranger driving through on highway 61 it looks like any other Mississippi town, with all the improvements that a town that size should have. He reckons he will go on being mayor as long as the people want him. So far nobody has been able to take the job away from him, though there have been some hot elections. The town is solvent, even though it has to pay out the money about as fast as it comes in. There isn't much in it for him. As for pay, he gets a little something now and then, as he says. His reward is in the satisfaction of serving his neighbors in the little town of Mound Bayou where peace abides.

17]   *Grambling, La. (1948)*

Few Americans know that there are . . . all-Negro towns and settlements in America; not integral parts of some city or town, but separate, incorporated towns where the colored people operate their own post offices, stores, banks, schools and churches. . . . Take Grambling, Louisiana, for example.

Every evening at six, the weather permitting, the town of Grambling meets the train. An hour before train time, you can see the whole town, men, women, boys and girls, coming across the fields, from up and down the tracks, the sandy roads, the streams and swamps, and the pig trails, in all directions. All coming in quite a hurry. Ask anybody where he is going, and breathlessly he will answer, "T'meet the train."

From the excited crowd milling around the little weather-beaten station, capacity ten, you might imagine that some celebrity was coming to Grambling for a brief appearance. The train, a lumbering, five-coach, short-line affair of 1925 vintage, blows for Grambling a mile away. When it appears around the bend east of the town, the deep-voiced boys let go a whoop, a shout akin to that of the excited whalers in Moby Dick—"Yeee-hoo!" Late arrivals break into

Source: J. Andrew Gaulden, "DarkTown," *Tomorrow*, April 1948, pp. 53–55.

a run. And everyone clusters dangerously close about the tracks. Suddenly the train thunders through without stopping, picks up the mail from a contraption beside the track and bellows a goodby blow, as it disappears over the hill west of the village.

Just that quickly it's all over—the town has seen what it came to see. Within another hour a ghostly silence settles over the little village, until the next morning at five. Odd, this mass excitement over the arrival of a train which doesn't bother to stop, but that is Grambling, Louisiana.

An all-Negro town of 1,000, Grambling sprawls across the Illinois Central railroad in a clearing a few miles west of Ruston on the famous Dixie Overland highway, U.S. 80. It is two miles square, surrounded by corn and cotton fields, swamps, pastures, woods and rolling sand hills. Its Broadway, the one and only main street, is a mile-long stretch of road, half of it black-topped, the other half just plain dry-weather, red mud road. It reminds you of a frontier mining town after the frontier has moved on to another place. A slow-moving simple little village where life seldom goes beyond the bare essentials of uneventful existence.

A town is known by the way it amuses itself. In the all-Negro settlement, the people seem to be able to amuse themselves immensely. Grambling has its socials where to the music of an audiophone or piano and sometimes just a harmonica, you can see house-shaking jitterbugging comparable to that of the jumpingest "hepcats" anywhere in America, not excluding New York's Harlem. And box suppers where a man must buy his lady-love's shoe box consisting of a hunk of gingerbread, a half fried chicken, half a sweet potato pie, and now and then a big red apple. The box finished, you have a lot of fun sitting on the hard benches talking to your lady, exchanging rough-hewn jokes with the boys and marching around the kerosene lighted room to the rhythmic clap of hands and singing of folk songs.

The singing convention is the greatest "blow out" in the town's scheme of entertainment. Everybody goes—and everybody sings. From miles around they come, one big cluster of people without rank or regulation, sometimes inside, sometimes outside, to sing . . . nothing but sing, one song after the other, all day long . . . and sometimes two or three days. There are local conventions, county (Parish in Louisiana) conventions, district conventions and state conventions.

As in his singing, the Negro goes all out with his religion. Thus on Sunday in Grambling you inevitably go to church. All houses are empty, and once a month, the first Sunday, you carry a big basket of food along with you because church lasts all day. The minister, as one of them so well put it, "takes a text, then mystify, sprangles out, and then brings in 'rousements.'" You've got to bring in the arousements, for the people like to put some feeling into their worship. And you have to "see something" during your conversion if you want it to be accepted as sound. The outsider will perhaps consider it too highly emotional, but one thing he accepts—their unadulterated sincerity.

One of the pleasantest pastimes in Grambling is to sit around the foot of a great tree or on the edge of some rickety porch of a dusky evening and listen

Grambling, La.

to ghost stories. Any time you're in the mood, you can have your imagination pulled to the breaking point by skillful tellers of tall tales, surrounded by solemn grown-ups and wide-eyed, breathless youngsters. Dramatically, and with all the necessary sound effects, they tell you of the latest encounters with some grotesque inhabitant of the spirit world. These frightful sessions sometimes go on until past midnight; then everyone tries to convince everyone else that his is the shortest way home! Some, like the one about the "no-headed man in the long white robe" who walks every rainy night from Mr. Dyke's place to a fork in the road and back again with an inextinguishable blue light in his bony hand, have been told and retold with spine-chilling variations for generations.

In Grambling, the inhabitants have strange, and sometimes poetic names. You have an Oklahoma Red, Pudding Prescotte, Cottonhead Wilson, Nevada Johnson, Boss Head Brown, Memphis Tennessee Harris, Sunbeam Clark and Alligator Jones. And of course, there are several Huey Longs, Herbert Hoover Mounger, Joe Louis Smith, Kay Francis Turner, and an increasing and confusing assortment of FDR's.

In Grambling there is virtually no crime; only one murder in half a century (a triangle affair) and not a single other major crime in the last two decades! There are no police; not because of poor organization, but because the law there would be a useless and laughable monstrosity. When the county sheriff from near-by Ruston comes to Grambling, he is generally seeking steady, responsible and efficient workers.

The business section of Grambling would be a good place to film a movie of the Old West. The best view of it can be secured by standing at the south end of the one main street and looking north. To your left under a spreading bushy oak there stands, or rather leans, a shanty which calls to mind a little country store. But the boxed-in, one-by-six sign up over the door says U. S. Post Office. It is so small, as one patron put it, you have to come outside to turn around. You must "call for your mail" because there are only a few boxes.

When the mail comes in twice a day, you see Grambling, pure and undefiled—barefoot boys with their patched, cut-off-at-the-knee overalls and sling shots, scooting in and out among the elders and trying to edge in at the post office door; rheumatic, wrinkled old men and women, some practically sightless, some illiterate, so that when they get a card or a letter you see them halting some youngster or friend to have it read to them; students from the school, clean and mannerable, and their spry smiling teachers; and farmers who have left their mules at a row's end to come long-stepping across the fields to the post office for—well, what do they get?

Not a ton of mail as one might think. Actually when a dozen letters come in one day, it's a boom day! Getting a letter is an event, just like the arrival of the train each evening. Small crowds cluster around the lucky person, even if the letter is from the Speedo-Needo company telling how you can make fifteen dollars a day like Mr. Snickleworth did in Waycross, Georgia. If the letter happens to come from far enough away, say from a relative who has migrated to Michigan or California or from a soldier son or husband in North Africa or the South Pacific, it becomes a community topic of conversation for the next two

319

or three days. If you get a package, you will be followed home by a third of the kids and grown-ups, too, all of whom will stage a sit-down strike on your porch until you open up and show your $3.98 Sear-Roebuck shoes.

Across the street from the post office is Mike's barber shop and beauty parlor . . . but until Saturday, or special holidays when everyone wants to look his "Sunday-go-to-meeting-best," the shop is under lock and key. In Grambling, mama or sister gives daughter her hair-do and father and brothers cut each other's hair, generally with a pair of second-hand, screeching clippers or scissors. "Stump" hair-cuts, they call these, but you have a choice of several styles, namely, the "Sapsucker Ring," named for the resemblance to the appearance of the head of the green woodpecker; the "Syrup Bucket Special," so-called because it looks as if a syrup bucket was placed over the head and the hair cut up to it, and the "Jay Bird Tip Top," a clean cut except for the bangs at the front.

Across from Mike's barber shop is Bob's Café, which was once a shotgun shanty. (They call those long straight three-room shacks shotgun and shoot through to the back without hitting a thing.) It has the front porch knocked off and has been whitewashed and plastered up with soft drink signs. Inside, Bob—if he is not out in the back working his potato patch—"can serve you anything you want—so long as it's a hot dog and a big bottle of soda water." You can entertain yourself by dropping a nickel in the audiophone and listening to "G. I. Jive," "Boogie Woogie Bues," or some other hot jazz number.

Bob's Café is a novelty, but Reed's General Store is an institution. There you can get frankfurters, sardines, crackers, cookies and the inevitable bottle of soda water. Reed's is also the place to get your overalls, shoes, drugs, harness, medicine for man and beast, gasoline and kerosene, stationery, toys for the kids at Christmas—in fact, anything that it would take a whole town to supply you with elsewhere.

A few paces from Reed's are two other stores, Givens' and Williams', covered with a multitude of bright colored snuff, tobacco, food, patent medicine and soft drink signs, advertising what's inside. Except for a pressing shop there are no other businesses in Grambling.

Grambling is full of surprises. Right in the midst of people who have seldom seen the inside of a school, who know Joe Louis but who might miss naming the governor of their state by two administrations, and who carry rabbits' feet and black cat bones for luck and power, you can find college graduates, teachers with advanced degrees and singers who have won wide acclaim in surrounding areas. Here you will see many housewives cooking the noonday meal in heavy, soot-covered pots suspended from a tripod before a fireplace, and again some who cook in gleaming aluminum vessels on spotless white stoves, using modern butane gas for fuel. The majority of the farmers are poor, but some have spacious green acres well rotated, fertilized and terraced, with shelves and barns laden with good things to eat the year around. One old woman will take oak bark trimmings and place them under her bed each evening at sundown and take them out each morning at sunrise to cure her illness, while another knows about the sulfa drugs and how to administer them to the best advantage and safety—a strange mixture of the old and the new.

Grambling, La.

Concerning the new, there is one thing of which Grambling is particularly proud: "Louisiana Rural Normal"—a country college with country courses that trains country boys and girls to be practical country teachers in country areas. It is founded on the rock-bottom principle that the best education for the rural Negro of Louisiana's sand hills and soggy swamplands is the kind that's based on the lives they must live. Its program won the immediate favor and support of nationally known educators, state boards of education and philanthropic agencies.

Its faculty knows how to set a hen, prune a tree, can a pig, build steps or a sanitary toilet, decorate a room and lead a prayer meeting. Its president, Ralph Waldo Emerson Jones, M.A., Columbia University, is a shirt-sleeve administrator who knows how to grow a healthy flock of chickens as well as make a public speech. The curriculum is the life of the rural Negro—husbandry, homemaking, health and handicrafts, along with that fundamental information indispensable to everyone. The school keeps in contact with rural life through its unique Field Service Unit, a motorized teaching, surveying and planning group which goes to remote rural areas and for weeks on end actually lives and works with the people. And every prospective teacher does the same thing for twelve weeks. They all know what it's like, and they know it does little good to teach people Shakespeare and Spinoza when their pressing needs are a full stomach and a roof over their heads. Thus Louisiana Rural Normal and the idea it courageously advances are now permanent parts of progressive rural school practices in the South.

BORDER CITIES

Economic Aspects

During World War II, blacks made substantial economic gains, particularly after President Roosevelt's Executive Order of June 1941 banning "discrimination in the employment of workers in defense industries or Government," and his establishment of the federal Fair Employment Practices Committee with investigative powers. Between 1941 and 1945 urban blacks secured more jobs at better wages in a great range of occupations than ever before. In 1940 only 4.4% of black males held skilled jobs; by 1944 this figure had increased to 7.3%; and blacks in semiskilled jobs had increased from 12% to 22%.

Such gains were greatest in industrial cities, particularly those of the North. In the border cities the picture for blacks during the war was a mixed one. In St. Louis, which witnessed a phenomenal industrial expansion during the war, blacks were little represented in the building trades; more than 100 war plants refused to hire them, in violation of the spirit and letter of Executive Order 8802; and there was generally strong resistance to the use of women as industrial workers. Those St. Louis industries that employed black men and women in large numbers did so in segregated plants, but at least there blacks attained semiskilled, skilled, and supervisory positions. In Baltimore blacks were employed in a larger percentage of war industries and were integrated into the work force, though generally in a minimal way, and they were given few opportunities for technical training and upgrading.

St. Louis, Mo. (1944)

18]   Black Workers in War Plants

Early in 1940 when the National Defense program got under way, it was apparent that St. Louis, the queen city of the Mississippi, would become an im-

SOURCE: Richard R. Jefferson, "Negro Employment in St. Louis War Production," *Opportunity*, July–September 1944, pp. 116–19.

portant war production center. A city of varied industrial activities before the war, St. Louis had everything necessary for the speedy conversion of its peace-time industries to another arsenal of democracy. A network of railroad lines, long a definite advantage in its industrial and commercial development, plus a navigable stream, n..ade the city easily accessible for the steady flow of raw materials and finished products. A large local labor supply which could be supplemented by thousands of workers from neighboring towns gave it another decisive advantage. An alert city administration and energetic chamber of commerce lost no time in convincing gove: ment officials and leaders of big industry that St. Louis was the logical spot for war contracts to be filled by already existing industries as well as for the location of new industries.

It is not surprising then that the Federal Government had spent almost $1,700,000,000 in the St. Louis area by January, 1944. Several new plants were erected principally for the production of airplanes and ordnce, but the textile, iron, steel, clay, glass, and food industries soon felt the impact of war orders and business boomed throughout the area. The cost of new construction alone reached the staggering sum of $362,329,000 and approximately 20,000 construction workers were used during the first period of the war production program.

The total population of St. Louis in 1940 was 1,422,500 of which 109,000 were Negroes. By 1944 the estimated increase of 3.4 percent had raised the total to 1,471,300 in spite of selective service withdrawals. The total labor force grew from 628,100 in 1940 to 691,200 in 1944, an increase of approximately 10 percent. It is reliably reported that an even sharper increase in the total Negro labor force of 66,952 in 1940 had occurred during the same period due largely to the need for unskilled workers in the heavy industries and the absence of extensive war industries in the area immediately south of St. Louis.

Against this backdrop of expanding industrial production and an unprecedented demand for workers, an examination of the experiences of Negro workers reveals an amazing set of contradictions and discriminatory employment policies. Even during the period of large-scale construction it was clearly obvious that the traditional prejudices against Negro building mechanics would not yield to the pressure of stringent demands for skilled workers. Close to 3,000 Negroes were among the 20,000 workers used in the construction of the new plants, but with the exception of three Negro painters, they were confined to common labor and hod carrying. A combination of hostile union attitude and employer indifference was largely responsible for this situation and it persisted in spite of vigorous efforts of government agencies, the Urban League and other interested organizations.

Apparently there was little hope for extensive employment of Negroes in production jobs if their experiences in construction work were indicative of the attitudes of plant managers. Consequently few Negroes bothered to enroll in N.Y.A. and defense training courses. In this respect St. Louis differed little from scores of cities in which Negroes were discouraged in their attempts to train for semi-skilled and skilled work. But with the issuance of Executive Order 8802 a number of large industries, especially new plants, agreed to employ Negroes in substantial numbers. In July, 1942, the Curtiss-Wright Company and the U. S. Cartridge Company announced that they would accept Negro applicants for training for skilled and semi-skilled operators. By August the Curtiss-Wright Company had approximately 500 Negro workers in a segregated building on a variety of skilled jobs including welders, riveters, assemblers and inspectors.

Simultaneously, the U. S. Cartridge Company provided a segregated plant identical with other production units and employed a complete force of Negro production workers. The first shift went into production in October, 1942 and the second and third shifts started production in April and May, 1943. In June, 1943, thirty-three men were upgraded to jobs as foremen, thus completing the segregated production unit with the exception of several foremen, clerical workers, and administrative staff. At peak production the company employed a total of 4,500 Negroes, many of whom held jobs as machine operators, millwrights, inspectors, and adjusters.

If this form of segregation in industry can be looked upon with favor, it might be said that these firms made a reasonable effort to use the available Negro labor supply. However, other large industries attempted to restrict the number of Negroes to the population ratio of one to ten. Further, they made little or no effort to upgrade Negroes according to seniority or skills. Their flat refusal to comply with the spirit and letter of the Executive Order has precipitated a very unsatisfactory situation and has caused numerous strikes and work stoppages among dissatisfied Negro workers. The prejudice of white workers in the area is usually blamed for the failure to upgrade Negroes. In at least 100 important war production plants no Negro workers have been employed.

The employment of Negro women in St. Louis industries present a more discouraging picture as might be expected. Stronger resistance to their use except as maids and cleaners, or in segregated work-shops, has been encountered in almost every instance. With the exception of the Curtiss-Wright Company which employs about 200 women as riveters, assemblers, and inspectors, and the U.S. Cartridge Company which used almost 1,000 women as operators and inspectors, few plants in the area have attempted to use them. The lack of separate toilet facilities and the prejudices of white women workers are the main barriers to the wider use of Negro women, according to officials of many of 200 plants that refuse to employ them.

Perhaps the one bright spot in this picture is the development in the garment industry, although the policy of segregation has been followed even in this field despite our efforts to eliminate it. Since 1930 the Urban League of St. Louis has worked to secure employment opportunities for Negro women in some of the numerous textile plants. In the Spring of 1941 the Acme Manufacturing Company opened an all-Negro plant employing 28 operators, a packer and a foreman. With the assistance of the League's staff these workers were selected, trained, and subsequently accepted in the International Ladies' Garment Workers' Union.

Until March, 1943, no other manufacturer would consider the employment of Negro women. With depleted labor reserves and mounting war orders, several plants were forced to look elsewhere for workers and the Portnoy Garment Company was one of the first to consider the use of Negroes. While not willing

Black Workers in War Plants

to integrate Negroes in the plant, the Portnoy Company agreed to open an all-Negro plant if a suitable building could be obtained and qualified workers were available. Because of the exclusion of Negroes from the trade, there were few if any experienced operators except those employed by the Acme Co. However, the St. Louis and East St. Louis N.Y.A. projects had given training to approximaely 300 girls and a few had been trained at the Washington Technical School. From these groups, it was possible to recruit a sufficient number of operators to open the new plant on May 10, 1943. By the end of the year 60 women were employed and by May 1, 1944 the factory had 90 workers and was planning an expansion to accommodate an additional 40 operators.

As this new venture proved satisfactory other garment plants in the St. Louis area sought to employ Negro operators under similar conditions. The Industrial staff of the Urban League, after 13 years continued pressure, is now faced with the problem of recruiting trainees and providing training opportunities for Negro women who were not permitted to work in this industry before the war. At least 1,200 Negro operators are currently employed and another 200 could be used if they were available.

While officials in the plants now employing Negro operators have expressed satisfaction with their work, the problem of adjusting many workers to the rigid requirements of production line operations has frequently been disturbing. The first few months the turnover was extremely high and unexcused absenteeism often curtailed operations. To overcome these difficulties the Urban League initiated a workers' education program which included frequent plant visits, group and individual counseling, and community education. The results of this activity have already been reflected in the work records of the women and there is every reason to believe that Negro women will remain in this industry after the war. It should be noted that officials of the International Ladies' Garment Workers' Union have cooperated with the League in every phase of this project. With their continued assistance it is safe to predict that the policy of segregated workshops for Negro and white women will soon be discontinued. Three large plants have already begun a program of integration and League staff members are insisting that segregation of workers is not only undemocratic but entirely unnecessary.

Negro workers in the St. Louis area have not accepted the discrimination against them without protest. Through mass meetings and petitions they have expressed their disapproval of the situation even after they secured employment. No less than a half dozen all-Negro strikes have occurred in protest to discriminatory hiring or working policies. In June, 1943, Negroes employed in the segregated plan of the U. S. Cartridge Company struck because the company would not upgrade qualified Negroes to jobs as foremen. The company finally agreed to comply with their demands. A few weeks later the workers in the segregated Curtiss-Wright staged a sit-down strike protesting the lack of adequate cooling equipment. In August, 1943, 600 Negro workers in the General Steel Castings plant in Madison, Illinois, struck because of a number of grievances including differentials in pay rates and discrimination against Negro women workers. After several weeks of negotiations in which the Urban

League took an active part, 61 of the 62 grievance cases were satisfactorily adjusted.

In November, 1943 and March, 1944, 380 Negro employees of the Monsanto Chemical Company staged a series of work stoppages, one of which lasted 10 days. Long-standing grievances against both the company and the union were responsible for the difficulties, but the refusal to upgrade Negro workers was the major complaint. The League was instrumental in placing their grievances before the company and union officials and an acceptable settlement was finally negotiated. Minor incidents involving the introduction and integration of Negro workers in the industries in this area have been too frequent to enumerate, and they have served to further confuse a very tense and unsettled war production center.

. . . The stubborn resistance to the complete acceptance of Negro workers on the basis of their skills and capacities has prevented the full utilization of the available local labor supply. The steady influx of white workers from the cotton fields and worn-out farms in the surrounding states has increased already strong prejudices almost to the danger point. . . .

. . . Severe cutbacks have already been experienced in a number of plants forcing Negro workers to seek other jobs. Among those already laid off in war industries, the League has recently studied the problems of 34 residents of Carr Square Village (Low-cost Housing Project). These workers had been employed as skilled and semi-skilled operators in ten different war plants, but only 6 of the 34 were able to secure other jobs in war production and they were not employed in the jobs for which they were qualified. The remainder returned to unskilled work as janitors, maids, handymen, porters, and domestics. Earnings have been drastically cut in every case and the weekly average of slightly more than $40 per worker has been reduced to an average of less than $30 per week. This trend, if continued after the war, will return the majority of Negro workers in St. Louis to their pre-war status of marginal, low-paid jobs, and the consequent insecurity and social maladjustment which have long plagued Negro workers throughout the nation.

Baltimore, Md. (1944)

19]   Improved Status of Blacks

The break-through of more than twenty thousand Negro workers into Baltimore's 110 war industries since 1940 is a drama of epic proportions. It seems a far cry from Mr. Glenn L. Martin's testimony before the Congressional Committee on Inter-State Migration problems in 1941. He, at that time, insisted that he could not employ Negro workers in his plants because all of the white

SOURCE: Edward S. Lewis, "Profiles: Baltimore," *Journal of Educational Sociology,* Special Issue on "The Negro in the North During Wartime," January 1944, pp. 290–95. [Edward S. Lewis was executive secretary of the Baltimore Urban League from 1931 to 1942.—Ed.]

skilled workers would walk out. But in a recent radio broadcast he paid high tribute to the several thousand Negro workers now employed in this plant who are carrying on countless skilled operations involved in assemblying the famous Martin Bomber.

By the same token, the Bartlett Hayward Koppers Division, manufacturers of gun carriages, and the General Electric plant officials could tell how their plants emerged from the zero position, so far as Negro employment was concerned, to the point where they have a thousand or more Negro skilled workers in many departments.

Shipbuilding and steel industries also have their complement of Negro workers, and they are no longer confined entirely to hazardous unskilled jobs. In fact, it is an open secret that Baltimore's war employers have in recent months taken real pride in pointing out that the integration process has worked in their plants with a minimum of friction. Indeed, there has been evidence of rivalry between them to see who could claim first credit. This development can be put on the plus side of the ledger.

The negative factors in the equation cannot be overlooked and are everywhere apparent. Token employment in some Baltimore war plants is a stark fact. Training facilities for potential Negro war workers have been inferior from the start, and the educational authorities have only yielded inch by inch under relentless pressure of organizations like the Urban League and the National Association for the Advancement of Colored People to improve the facilities and quality of training offered. In-plant training facilities for Negroes have been almost nonexistent and upgrading of Negro workers has become the acid test for employers and some unions. A near riot broke out at the Fairfield Bethlehem Shipbuilding Plant because of the upgrading of Negro welders and both the company and the C.I.O. local were vulnerable on this issue.

Since the negative side of the union question has been mentioned, we might turn to a brief consideration of the positive side of the trade-union picture in Baltimore because there have been several significant developments that need appraisal.

When the Steel Workers Organizing Committee cracked the steel industry at Sparrow's Point and won the election, after many unsuccessful attempts, it opened the way to the organization of thousands of white and colored workers into the same locals. Colored organizers were used effectively in the campaign and these men had the support of the best civic and church leadership in Baltimore. Negro workers were elected to key posts and they have become a permanent factor in top leadership of C.I.O. steel unions. Negro workers are no longer shunted aside but are being taken in by newly formed C.I.O. locals in all major war industries.

The American Federation of Labor in Baltimore has become much more sensitive to discriminatory practices in its local unions. Genuine progress has been made in meeting this issue. Local 544 of Brotherhood of Carpenters was organized by the writer shortly before the Fort Meade construction job got under way. One hundred seventy-five Negro carpenters were employed on this job. This union, which started on a borrowed one hundred fifty dollars from an Urban League Board member, and from ten fellow workers, has jumped to a roster of over 500. The painters won a tough fight and were finally accepted in Local 101 of the Painters Union. Similarly the bricklayers, electricians, plasterers, and cement finishers have won recognition and the right to participate in these A.F. of L. craft unions.

Under the leadership of Harry Cohen, President of the Baltimore Federation of Labor, Negro members have been placed on all key committees of the Central Trade Union Council. There is not another Federation in the country that can show better Negro representation than Baltimore.

Another significant move involving not only A.F. of L. and C.I.O., but also the Brotherhood of Railway Trainmen, was the endorsement and support of a Negro member of the Motion Picture Operators Union for the position as delegate to Maryland's Assembly. This was the first time in the history of Maryland that organized labor had done such a thing. Although the nominee did not win, an important educational job was done on both sides of the fence.

One of the problems which the Negro community of Baltimore gets wrought up about is that of police brutality. A total of 14 Negroes have been killed by police officers since 1930 and nine of these killings occurred after the induction of Police Commissioner Stanton. Not a single policeman was brought to trial on these cases and the temper of Baltimore Negro citizens has steadily grown worse.

On February 1, 1942, Patrolman Edward R. Bender killed Private Thomas E. Broadus as the result of an argument about a taxi cab. Bender shot Broadus in the back and killed him while he was running from the scene of a brawl.

The news of a white cop killing a Negro soldier spread like the burning of dead grass in autumn. Soon the whole Negro community was aroused. Meanwhile the Grand Jury heard a few witnesses and found a presentment of lawful homicide, but a few days later the Grand Jury rescinded its action. It was this final action that capped the climax. A tremendous mass meeting was called by the newly organized Citizens Committee for Justice which included over 110 civic, labor, church, and welfare groups. The meeting was held prior to a March on Annapolis and was addressed by militant Adam Powell of New York City.

On April 24, 1942, more than 2,000 Negro citizens descended upon Annapolis and presented the following demands:

1. Investigation of the police administration in the Negro areas of Baltimore
2. Appointment of Negro police officers in uniform
3. Negro representation on all State institutions operated for Negroes
4. Official support for Executive Order 8802

Carl Murphy, President of the *Afro-American,* led this protest demonstration and there is no doubt but that the conduct of the hearing and the "dead-pan" seriousness of 2,000 Negroes in the State House made a tremendous impression on the Governor.

In May 1942, Governor O'Connor appointed a Commission on Problems Affecting the Negro Population to make an official investigation. The findings of this body confirmed the basis for the original demands and constructive recommendations were made in a report issued in March 1943.

Improved Status of Blacks

Since that time there has been some progress made on the police problems listed in the grievances of the Citizens Committee. Three Negro policemen have finally put on uniforms and it is reported that a fourth policeman will be added to the force—a good *beginning!*

No discussion of racial tensions in Baltimore would be complete without at least the bare mention of discriminatory practices in department stores. With one exception, all of the first-class department stores are Jewish-owned, and that fact arouses additional antagonisms in the Negro community. Some gentile groups with axes to grind connive to play both ends against the middle. The department-store muddle continues to stand out like a sore thumb.

Organizationally speaking, Baltimore's Negro community has been making real strides ahead. The Citizens Committee for Justice, Council of Negro Organizations, Urban League, the National Association for the Advancement of Colored People, and church groups are in every play when there are critical issues or knotty discrimination problems to be solved. There has been real unity of action present in the projects that have been cited, and there is a growing tendency to recognize the importance of "grand strategy" in planning pressure or educational campaigns. Had it not been for the work of this kind that is going on, Baltimore probably would already have had a race riot that would equal or surpass Detroit, New York, or Los Angeles.

Baltimore is singularly fortunate in having one of the best Negro weekly newspapers in the country—*The Afro-American.* This medium has close working relationships with all civic, welfare, and labor groups in the City. . . .

Baltimore's Negro community is in many respects an interesting study in contrasts. The patterns of segregation and Jim Crow that characterize southern cities are present, but do not dominate the scene. There are liberal and progressive forces at work here that have definitely challenged the status quo in industry, education, politics, and in housing. More than fifteen thousand Negro and white citizens recently assembled in Druid Hill Park to hear Paul Robeson sing and Lester Granger speak on the subject "Unity for Victory." Such a meeting in New York or Chicago is not news, but in Baltimore it portends a gleam of hope for better race relations if democracy is given a fighting chance to function.

Political and Social Aspects

More political action on the part of blacks and more communication between interracial groups led to somewhat improved race relations in the border cities. In one or more of the cities, as the selections below show, police brutality against blacks was moderated, discriminatory practices in white department stores were ended, teachers' pay was equalized, and hitherto white colleges and universities were opened to blacks. But as of 1950 there was still considerable segregation in public and private facilities; schools, hospitals, hotels, and, in St. Louis, major league baseball teams were still segregated.

During the 1950's the border cities, especially Baltimore, were to make rapid strides toward desegregation. A successful voter registration drive and effective participation in municipal politics gave Baltimore blacks representation and power in the city and state that was unparalleled in the South. The growth in black political power was accompanied by desegregation in education, employment, and housing.

Louisville, Ky. (1945)

20]   Improved Race Relations

Louisville, Kentucky, a city with many of the customs, manners, and prejudices of the Old South, is building a new fire station that will be completely staffed by Negro firemen. Additional municipal recreational facilities are being provided particularly for Negroes. These are only two examples of steps taken during the last three years to improve interracial relationships in a city where nearly 16 per cent of the population is Negro. Other steps include:

The number of Negro policemen was doubled in 1944 (increased from 15 to 30), two Negro officers were upgraded to the rank of sergeant, and two of the four women in the newly created crime prevention bureau are Negroes.

The salaries of all school teachers have been equalized at an additional cost of $65,000 a year. For years Louisville had two salary scales for school teachers. Negro teachers taught the same subjects as white teachers but the former received lower pay.

A 100-bed wing for Negroes has been added to the tuberculosis sanitorium where Negro patients are cared for by doctors, nurses, and housekeeping employees of their own race. In past years 45 per cent of Louisville's tuberculosis death rate was among its Negro citizens.

Louisville has six public housing projects, three of which are for Negroes.

Negroes now have representatives on several local boards and special committees and agencies. One-half of the members of the Louisville Interracial Committee appointed by the mayor are Negroes, and there is a Negro member on the library board and on the housing commission. Their race is also represented on various civic and war committees, such as the defense council, rationing boards, war fund board, and the mayor's legislative committee.

These steps were taken as rapidly as the community would accept them, and as a result there is little racial tension in Louisville today.

SOURCE: Wilson W. Wyatt, "City Takes Steps to Improve Interracial Relations," *Public Management*, April 1945, pp. 115–16. [Wilson W. Wyatt was mayor of Louisville when he wrote this.—Ed.]

Poor Health and Housing

Kansas City, Mo. (1946)

21]   Poor Health and Housing

In 1944, Negroes in Kansas City accounted for 10.9 per cent of the population and contributed 14.9 per cent to the total deaths. Adverse social and economic conditions are primary factors in the excessive rates of Negro morbidity and mortality. The principal causes of deaths among Negroes were diseases of the heart, nephritis, tuberculosis, pneumonia, cancer and syphilis. Influenza, tuberculosis, and syphilis, diseases which medical authorities agree are due largely to unfavorable sanitary conditions and low economic status, show greatest disparity between Negro and white death rates. Comparison between Negro and white infant deaths is interesting. The infant death rate among whites in 1944 was 31.80 per 100,000 population and among Negro infants it was 34.93 per 100,000 population.

Hospital needs among Negroes are served by General Hospital Number 2, a Negro institution administered by the Kansas City Health Department which has a capacity of 252 beds and 24 bassinets, and by Wheatley Provident Hospital, a private Negro-owned and operated institution which receives partial support from the Kansas City Community Fund. The total capacity of this institution is 67 beds and 5 bassinets. Negroes are not admitted to any other hospitals in the city except on rare occasions.

General Hospital Number 2 in 1946 had a staff of 14 white and 29 Negro physicians. In the nurse training school 98 student nurses were enrolled. The superintendent of the hospital is a Negro physician. Though the hospital renders extensive and valuable service to Negroes there are many inadequate provisions which seriously affect the services rendered. These include inadequate bedside equipment, improper ventilation in operating rooms and overcrowded conditions. One of the serious social and health lags in the city is the fact that no provisions are available for Negro convalescent patients. Wheatley Provident Hospital for a number of years has rendered a high type of medical service to Negroes. The hospital is old, new equipment is sorely needed, and the institution suffers because of inadequate funds.

. . . . .

. . . The Negro medical profession in Kansas City includes 52 physicians, 13 dentists, and approximately 125 nurses. Neither the Jackson County Medical Society nor the Kansas City Graduate Nurse Association will accept Negro members. . . .

Housing for the Negro population of Kansas City is considered by many the number one social problem and has been for many years. The problem is intensified because of the resistance of white property owners to the expansion of the Negro population outside of the few areas which were considered as the

SOURCE: National Urban League, Department of Research, Study of Kansas City, Mo., January–February, 1946, pp. 212–16.

"Negro districts." This attitude is formalized in the restrictive covenants among white property owners to prevent occupancy by Negroes, and in the difficulty experienced by Negroes in financing home purchases outside of the so-called Negro areas.

The bulk of the Negro population in Kansas City is concentrated in 13 wards. The largest concentration is found in Census Tract 12, where 9,638 units, or 48.1 per cent of the total occupied units, are occupied by Negroes. Census Tracts 26 and 32 have a Negro occupancy of 95.2 per cent and 97.6 per cent, respectively. Of 133,157 dwelling units in Kansas City, Negroes occupy 13,289, or 10.9 per cent. All recent housing studies in Kansas City indicate that Negroes are concentrated in the oldest sections of the city, and the homes they occupy are in dire need of repair. Many of the properties are incapable of physical rehabilitation. . . . In most of the sections where Negroes live, from 1 per cent to 19 per cent of the dwelling units have 1.51 or more persons per room. In some areas 6 to 10 persons are found occupying one room. The greatest crowding is indicated in the sections where rentals are lowest. Approximately 50 new private dwelling units for Negroes have been built in the city during the past 20 years. Out of the congested areas many serious social problems arise, which are reflected in the crime and health statistics.

On the west side of the city Negroes and Mexicans are living in contiguous areas, and on the north side Italians and Negroes live in the same neighborhood. In these areas the races live together with apparent amity.

In some areas occupied by Negroes, the homes are both modern and attractive. In many such areas formerly occupied by whites, the value of the houses has increased materially since Negroes took over because of the many physical improvements made by the new tenants. Nevertheless there have been varied devices used to restrict the movement of Negro home-owners. Among these are threats to discharge them from their jobs or refusals to hire colored residents in "white districts," and threats to plant termites in the Negro houses. During the past year injunctions have been filed against Negroes who have moved in [to] so-called white communities where it is alleged that the presence of Negro residents was in violation of restrictions prohibiting sales to Negroes. . . . The first tangible relief to the acute housing of Negroes since 1940 was the building of 100 units of demountable [sic] houses as a FPHA project. Approximately 100 houses have been built for Negro occupancy under FHA regulations.

St. Louis, Mo. (1950)

22] Discrimination Against Black Baseball Players

St. Louis, Mo., as a baseball town, has two major league teams, the St. Louis Cardinals and Browns, neither of which has a Negro player on its regular team.

Source: John H. Hicks, "St. Louis: Is It the Toughest Town for Negro Baseball Players?" *Crisis*, October 1950, pp. 573–76.

Discrimination Against Black Baseball Players

Yet for more than two years now, Negro players have crashed the field of major league baseball. With the Brooklyn Dodgers hiring Jackie Robinson as the first Negro player in the majors and the subsequent hiring of Negroes on teams in both the American and National Leagues, the trend pointed definitely toward another area of job and recreational opportunity for qualified Negroes.

With his sportsmanship and playing ability, Robinson scored a hit with baseball fans of the nation. He slugged his way into fame and threw the spotlight not only on himself but the race as a whole and caused other teams to turn in the direction of Negro baseball players.

It has generally been felt, largely through the success of Robinson, that the field of big league baseball is open to anyone, regardless of color, if that person can make the grade. However, doubt might arise as to whether St. Louis, the city with "the southern exposure," should be included.

. . . . .

Negroes in St. Louis comprise about 150,000 or one-sixth of the city's 900,000 population and in East St. Louis, Ill. (separated from St. Louis by the Mississippi River), they comprise about one-third of its 75,600 people.

People in the St. Louis area are baseball minded largely because of its major league teams—the Browns in the American League and the Cardinals in the National League. Among Negroes there has been a greater interest in baseball since Robinson donned the Dodger uniform. This is perhaps true of most cities in the country.

The over-all picture of Negroes in organized major league baseball might throw light on the question, "Is St. Louis the toughest town for Negro baseball players?"

There are nine Negroes on four teams. Luke Easter and Larry Doby with the Cleveland Indians in the American League and six others with three National League teams; four are with the Brooklyn Dodgers. The Brooklyn players are Robinson, Roy Campanella, Don Newcombe and Dan Bankhead. Hank Thompson and Monte Irvin play with the New York Giants and Sam Jethroe with the Boston Braves.

Other National League teams that do not employ Negro players, besides the Cardinals, are the Chicago Cubs, Pittsburgh Pirates, Philadelphia Phillies and Cincinnati Reds. There is none on the regular teams of the Detroit Tigers, Washington Senators, New York Yankees, Philadelphia Athletics, Boston Red Sox, Chicago White Sox and St. Louis Browns in the American League.

Is St. Louis the toughest town for Negro baseball players to crash? As far as being employed is concerned, the answer is no. In the competitive business of supplying entertainment in the field of baseball, the difficulty comes in finding good Negro players. . . .

The trend here, although progress seems slow, is a widening of economic opportunities and improved recreational, social, and educational facilities for Negroes.

Many changes for the better have taken place in St. Louis within the past ten years. . . .

The Catholic schools (elementary and high schools within the St. Louis area) and St. Louis University and its affiliated Catholic women's colleges have been opened to Negroes by Archbishop Joseph E. Ritter. Earlier during the year, the East St. Louis public school system, with 8,000 white students and 5,000 Negro pupils, abolished segregation.

Washington University, a privately endowed college in the city, has opened its graduate school, but not its undergraduate school. There are about 50 to 75 Negro graduate students enrolled.

Plans for modern housing for Negroes have been announced. There is no discrimination at the municipally owned Kiel Auditorium, where symphony concerts, circuses, and other types of entertainment are held. Negroes are not segregated at the Municipal Opera, an open air summer theater, a couple of the art theaters, Sportsman's Park; at one of the large downtown department store's lunch room and several eating establishments.

There are many organizations seeking to better race relations within the city. But St. Louis is far from being a Utopia. . . .

When Negro players come to St. Louis with their teams they are generally separated because of discriminatory practices by hotel owners and managers. A spokesman for the local NAACP pointed out that when Brooklyn comes to St. Louis its Negro players are not allowed to stay at the same hotel with the rest of the team. In other cities all members of the team live in the same hotel, he said.

The *St. Louis Argus*, a Negro weekly, revealed that Jackie Robinson, Roy Campanella, Brooklyn catcher, and Don Newcombe, pitcher, have taken rooms at an all-colored hotel. At times some of them have stayed in private homes, the newspaper disclosed.

. . . . . .

Besides the Brooklyn players the other major league players are also jim crowed by St. Louis hotels. The sickening part of the thing is that Sam Jethroe and Luke Easter, both from the St. Louis area, are treated like human beings in every city except their own, the NAACP spokesman declared.

Because of St. Louis' discriminatory practices, it perhaps may be one of the toughest towns for Negro players to crash from a psychological point of view.

However, if competent Negroes were hired by the teams in St. Louis they would be accepted or rejected according to their ability to produce. This has been demonstrated by the fans' acceptance of Newcombe, Doby, and the other Negro players. All that could be asked is that they be given a chance.

Baltimore, Md. (1959)

23] Black Political Spurt

Just five years ago, Baltimore was a Jim Crow seaport in a conservative state in a Dixie-minded section of the country. Today, Maryland's largest city, and the sixth biggest in the U.S., is a vibrant industrial center where use of the

SOURCE: Simeon Booker, "Baltimore: New Negro Vote Capital," *Ebony*, December 1959, pp. 131–38.

ballot has reaped more gains than a civil rights platform or a job promise, and produced a political yardstick for Negroes in every section of America.

In a city that was notorious for its treatment of Negroes (once barred from hotels and not allowed to try on clothes in downtown department stores), a sudden, spectacular spurt in vote registration has brought a desegregation pace in education, employment and housing equalled by only one other U.S. city, the nation's capital of Washington, D.C.

For the first time, Negroes in Baltimore are beginning to take their rightful place in municipal and state government. So tremendous is the achievement that Baltimore alone of the traditional southern cities can boast a race complement of a councilman and three state legislators besides many other Negroes on important commissions and boards. At the same time, no other area can boast a 40 per cent increase in Negro vote registration to an all-time high of 104,000 in a two-year period. Declared one Negro leader: "What other cities are trying now we did with fewer headlines."

The Baltimore vote story is an example of what determined registration drives can do as against the use of conferences, protests and mass meetings to achieve full civil rights. A year-round NAACP vote campaign functions on a block-to-block basis, touching every community. In some 50 churches and meeting places, an estimated 2,000 workers are regularly schooled in vote registration, then double back into their neighborhoods to keep the issue alive. Meanwhile, leaders of both parties, aware of the changing tide, consider the might of the Negro vote and have for the first time nominated qualified Negroes on tickets for major local and state offices.

Representative of the "new look" is the integrated legislative team from the heavily Negro Fourth District. The top machine candidate on the Democratic slate from the district is J. Alvin Jones, a University of Pennsylvania trained electrical engineer, and the only Negro in the Maryland Senate. Last year, fighting off threats of an all-Negro ticket headed by Sen. Harry Cole, first Negro elected to the state's highest body, Jones was named by the Democrats to lead an integrated ticket. When he defeated the racial thrust, he became spokesman for a new and powerful integration stand in politics throughout the state.

A veteran politician with a booming voice and an alert mind, Jones succeeded in getting a bill passed to ratify the 14th Amendment, a matter that had been before the legislature for 98 years. He has also pressed for more Negroes in important jobs, and is considered one of the Negroes closest to the present governor.

The first Negro women elected to the Maryland House of Delegates, Irma Dixon and Verda Welcome, form a conscientious, diligent team. Owner of a fashionable dress shop and wife of a businessman, Mrs. Dixon is a regular Democrat who refused to run on the all-Negro ticket, contending that "we cannot talk integration and practice discrimination ourselves."

A popular lawmaker among the whites because of her stand, she has served on a legislative committee investigating health plans and crime. Her first bill concerned equal pay for women and is slated for consideration at the next session.

Her colleague, Mrs. Welcome, is the wife of a wealthy surgeon and is regarded as the only independent candidate of the three Negro lawmakers, being the only candidate on the all-Negro coalition ticket to win after a bitter election. Told by Democratic bosses that she would be "knocked out" unless she withdrew, Mrs. Welcome accepted the challenge, financed her own campaign, and appealed to church and labor groups to give her support.

. . . The result is that Mrs. Welcome, to the delight of many Negroes, is very outspoken on issues, and even appears in picket lines protesting discrimination in public places.

On the local level, the city's first Negro councilman, 66-year-old Walter Dixon, dean of the Cortez Peters Business School in Baltimore, is serving his second term. His legislative battles include introducing a measure to outlaw discrimination in hotels and restaurants, which failed to pass but resulted in many places quietly eliminating the racial bars. . . .

Well trained as an educator, Mr. Dixon, a Howard University graduate, has taught at Howard University, Baltimore Junior College, North Carolina College, and served as teller at the District of Columbia Industrial Bank. His training and his experience make him an able discussant [sic] on fiscal affairs.

For the first time Negroes also serve in both state and municipal jobs as a result of their new political might. Possibly one of the few Negro traffic judges in the country is Judge Josiah Henry, who listens to 80-odd cases daily in the downtown police court. Twenty years ago, Judge Henry ran for the city council but was defeated because an insufficient number of Negroes were registered to vote. He continued his politicking and finally realized the dream. The first Negro assigned to Peoples Court, a small claims division, is Judge Everett Lane.

Meanwhile, Magistrate Calvin Douglass is assigned to the new $500,000 Western precinct station, described as one of the most modern buildings in the country. Two other Negroes, Bernard Morten and Nicholas Rice, serve as substitute magistrates. A veteran member of the Board of School Commissioners is Dr. Bernard Harris, Sr., while a new assistant City Solicitor is Atty. Jacques Leeds, whose wife is popular jazz singer Ethel Ennis.

On the staff of the city's legal department are Attys. James W. McAllister and Theodore Hayes. Ten years ago, it was considered unusual to have Negroes serving as messengers and clerks in downtown office buildings.

With appointment to key posts has come another breakthrough at a lower and more widespread level. Hundreds of Negroes work in state and municipal buildings as clerks, stenographers, receptionists, even building inspectors such as J. Gene Payne. During his single term as state senator, GOPer Harry Cole refused to use his vote to break a tie on an appropriations bill which Gov. Theodore McKeldin desired to pass. During the voting, Cole closeted himself in his office until the governor agreed to end employment discrimination. Then he voted McKeldin's bill.

Because of his fearlessness and courage despite the fact that he was a member of the minority six-man team in the Senate, Cole is regarded as the man who put Baltimore politics on a practical basis and showed Negroes what their participation could accomplish.

Black Political Spurt

With interest in politics at a high level, the NAACP now concentrates its campaign on a new goal of 150,000 voters sufficient to elect the state's first Negro congressman as well as officers at a county level. The program is directed by Rev. John L. Tilley, pastor of the New Metropolitan Baptist Church, and former executive director of the Dixie vote campaign.

The Baltimore project has been copied in seven cities, including Atlanta and Houston. It is considered the most unique in the country and is promoted by the Afro-American newspapers.

After forming a nucleus of workers from 50 churches, Rev. Tilley has made the entire Negro community vote conscious. Although forces are concentrated in the main Fourth District, workers are organized on a block-to-block basis in every neighborhood.

Typical of the helpers is Mrs. Margaret Dyer, mother of two grown children, who in two years has personally accounted for registering 2,500 new voters. She organized the women's groups at her Faith Baptist Church into squads of precinct workers, then extended the campaigning to neighboring areas. . . .

Still the dynamo of the herculean enterprise is soft-voiced, kindly Rev. Tilley, an inspired leader. A former Florida Normal and Industrial Memorial College dean, he accepted a pastorate in the city and immediately began neighborhood vote drives which caught the attention of NAACP officials. . . .

NORTHEASTERN CITIES

Political and Social Aspects

The Harlem riot of 1943 was essentially an explosive protest against second-class status and worsening ghetto conditions which were all the more intolerable in view of the major black contributions to the U.S. effort to defeat Nazi Germany. Harlemites found particularly galling the harassment, disrespect, and death that black soldiers met at the hands of white civilians. They also deeply resented the discrimination they faced in New York's war industries and the continued white economic control and exploitation of Harlem. A white policeman's harassment of a black woman, and the rumor of his killing a black soldier who came to her defense, triggered the expression of smoldering black anger against white property.

But wartime and postwar Harlem was to take some consolation in exercising greater political power than hitherto. In 1944 its first black congressman was elected: dashing, charismatic Adam Clayton Powell, Jr. In 1953 Harlem achieved another historic feat when its state assemblyman, Hulan Jack, was elected borough president of Manhattan, a position then regarded as the highest and most powerful ever held by a black man.

New York, N.Y. (1943)

24]   The Harlem Riot

. . . Last May 29 Judge William H. Hastie and Thurgood Marshall submitted a report on civilian violence against Negro soldiers to the National Lawyers' Guild, which in turn formally placed it before the War and Justice Departments. It was pointed out that recurrent violence in the civilian community directed against Negro members of the armed forces had increased in seriousness, in frequency and in the lack of any effective methods of control since a similar study had been made in November, 1942. . . .

Source: Walter White, "Behind the Harlem Riot," *New Republic,* August 16, 1943, pp. 220–22.

First Black Borough President

It is out of this sad record that the shooting . . . of Robert J. Bandy, a Negro MP, in a Harlem hotel by a white policeman on Sunday night, August 1, provided the spark which set off the explosion created by bitter, smoldering resentment against the mistreatment of Negro soldiers which was all the more dangerous because it had been pent up and frustrated. A five-minute shift in Private Bandy's movements that sultry Sunday night have averted one of the most destructive riots in American history, which took a toll of five lives, injured 307 and caused damage estimated to be in excess of $5,000,000. Bandy came to New York from a New Jersey camp to meet his mother, who had come down from Middletown, Connecticut, to spend Sunday with him and his fiancée. Bandy's mother checked out of the hotel around four o'clock in the afternoon and then set out with her son and his friend for dinner and a moving-picture show. It was an unfortunate, gratuitous circumstance that they returned to the hotel to pick up the mother's luggage just as an altercation developed when a policeman sought to eject an obstreperous Negro woman.

Bandy intervened, so the story goes, in an attempt to defend the woman. During the altercation he is alleged to have seized Policeman James Collins' night stick and to have struck the policeman across the cheekbone. He then turned away, refusing to obey the order to halt. The policeman drew his gun and fired, hitting Bandy in the left shoulder. Within a few minutes, the story had spread like wildfire throughout Harlem that a Negro soldier had been shot in the back and killed by a policeman in the presence of his mother. Blind, unreasoning fury swept the community with the speed of lightning. The available symbols of the oppressor, as was the case in Detroit's East Side, were the shining plate-glass windows of stores along One Hundred and Twenty-fifth Street. At the beginning, there was no looting. Nothing but blind fury was expressed. Later, from the more poverty-stricken areas of Harlem, poured those who entered the stores through the broken windows and began looting. . . . But let him who would criticize pause long enough to put himself in the place of the looters. Still barred from many defense industries in the area because of color, with dark memories of the depression years when 70 per cent of Harlem was on relief because Negroes are hired last and there were not enough jobs for white workers, hemmed in a ghetto where they are forced to pay disproportionately high rents for rat and vermin-infested apartments, the Bigger Thomases [1] of New York passed like a cloud of locusts over the stores of Harlem.

New York, N.Y. (1953)

25]   First Black Borough President

For the first time in the history of New York City a Negro [Hulan Jack] has been elected for Borough President of Manhattan. He was the choice of his

SOURCE: *New York Amsterdam News*, November 7, 1953.
[1] Bigger Thomas is the central character in Richard Wright's novel *Native Son* (1940).

party in the primary and the undisputed choice of the majority of the white and Negro voters who went to the polls on Tuesday.

The Borough President of Manhattan has a very important position. He has two votes on the Board of Estimate and this body actually governs New York City. He is also top man in his Borough and must supervise the work of the hundreds of people who are employed by his office and keep a watchful eye on the millions of dollars that are disbursed there.

NORTH CENTRAL CITIES

Social and Cultural Aspects

Between 1941 and 1945 the black population in Detroit jumped more than 50% and over the entire decade more than 100%. The black increase in Detroit during the war was matched by a corresponding white increase, most of which was from the middle South. Once again all the ingredients for a violent racial explosion were present: a deeply prejudiced white working class, an actively antiblack police force, high racial tension produced by competition for jobs, housing, and recreational facilities. These were ignited by rumor to set off the bloodiest racial confrontation thus far in the North.

At the same time black cultural interests were developing in a positive direction. Vibrant and aggressive black Chicago early and successfully insisted that black social studies be taught in the Chicago public schools. In Cleveland, Karamu House was established, soon becoming the single most influential center in the history of creative arts for blacks in the nation.

Cleveland, Ohio (1942)

26]   Karamu House of Black Arts

There is a street called Central Avenue which cuts through the dimly lit, squalid heart of the slums of Cleveland, Ohio. It is a Negro street. Its identification signs are beer joints and crumbling tenements, pawnshops, the home-relief station that is housed now in what used to be a branch office of the Cleveland Trust Company.

On hot summer nights the police cars cruise there watchfully, the thousand black kids turn to stick out their tongues at the cops, the men and women continue to walk and lounge, and the Negro laughter and curses rise rich and heavy toward the bits of sky between the close-packed roofs and chimneys.

SOURCE: Jo Sinclair, "I, Too, Sing America," *Common Ground*, Autumn 1942, pp. 99–106.

341

The doors of the small churches are open for the congregations to get some of whatever air has drifted into the Avenue between the ancient stone and steel. Once these were stores—a grocery, a confectionery, once in the "palmy" days of this neighborhood a dry-goods store; now they are the homes of the True Faith Baptist, the Jesus Only Church.

On these nights song flows out of them to mix with the laughter and curses, the shrill frail sound of children who cannot sleep in the furnace-like tenements: "Steal away, steal away! Steal away to Jesus!"

It is difficult to see the stars on Central. The ceiling is too low; the electric signs flash off and on, off and on, obscuring the view: *Bar B-Q, Drinks, Loans Made Here, Dine and Dance.* A hot wind drifts into the street and the young boys walk restlessly and sullenly; the girls break into sudden dance steps, in their hearts a tormented music.

This is the street where the battered, magical walls of Karamu House rise above the tenements—a fantastic, beautiful House within the core of industrial America.

Here Negro men and women and youths present Porgy and Emperor Jones. Here a group of Negro dancers rehearse for the recital they will give at the Institute of Music. They dance a poem by Archibald MacLeish, "The Western Sky." One of the stanzas says:

> Be proud to bear
> The endless labor of the free—
> To strike for freedom everywhere
> And everywhere bear liberty.

In the crafts studio boys and girls are working at lithographs and prints, or at metal trays, jewelry, bookends. And in still another room the Karamu Chorus is rehearsing for its monthly concert.

Karamu, which started in 1915, purely as a neighborhood house, has become famous as America's foremost Negro art center. The community soil has been turned with four singular spades—music, dance, pictorial and plastic arts, and theatre—and the upturned earth steams with richness and fertility. The Gilpin Players of Karamu Theatre, for example, are known as America's oldest and finest Negro theatre group. The Karamu Dancers at the New York World's Fair excited top newspaper and public comment and finally were photographed for *Life* Magazine as the exponents of a unique American art. The Karamu Artists have been shown at Cleveland's own art museum and in competitive exhibits throughout the country, achieving even the International Print Show and one-man shows at the Associated American Artists in New York and the Sullivan Memorial Library at Temple University in Philadelphia. As for the fourth shining spade, Karamu singing permeates the neighborhood. It rings through Porgy and is echoed in the twisted, crumbling houses up and down the street, where the women stand in their kitchens near stove or sink. It follows the men to factory or WPA job, the kids to school; it drifts for hours over the sidewalks, between pawnshop and home-relief office.

Karamu is a word taken from the Swahili, the most widely used African language. It means "places of feasting and enjoyment." It may also mean "center of the community."

. . . . .

Karamu is the story of how the Negro stepped . . . out of the dead-end streets onto the main highway, his hand outstretched not to ask for something, but to give—a gift so real, so challenging, it catapulted him into the thick of the crowd. Now he was walking in the center of the main road, as anonymous as they, yet as individualistic as they.

"This is mine," he was saying with dignity and joy, as he opened his hands to show his gift. "I bring this—it is my best."

Langston Hughes has cried out:

> I, too, sing America.
>
> I am the darker brother.
> They send me to eat in the kitchen,
> When company comes,
> But I laugh,
> And eat well,
> And grow strong.
>
> Tomorrow,
> I'll sit at the table
> When company comes.
> Nobody'll dare
> Say to me,
> "Eat in the kitchen,"
> Then.
>
> Besides,
> They'll see how beautiful I am.
> And be ashamed—
>
> I, too, am America.

Karamu House is now tied closely, in living affiliations, with all of the city. They are solid, working affiliations with such major institutions in Cleveland as the Museum of Art, the Institute of Music, the Museum of Natural History, Western Reserve University, and the Cleveland Play House. Exchange education and help: the lines reach out from Central Avenue into a thousand streets —bridges, over which walk people of all kinds and all colors.

At the twenty-fifth anniversary luncheon of Karamu House, more than 600 of Cleveland's civic and cultural leaders gathered to honor an ideal that had stepped from the slum darkness of their city into the light of nation-wide recognition.

Detroit, Mich. (1943)

27]   Antiblack Police Actions During Riot

Much of the blood spilled in the Detroit riot is on the hands of the Detroit police department. In the past the Detroit police have been guilty of both inefficiency and an attitude of prejudice against Negroes. Of course, there are
several individual exceptions.

In the June [20–23, 1943] riot . . . the police ran true to form. The trouble reached riot proportions because the police once again enforced the law
with an unequal hand. They used "persuasion" rather than firm action with
white rioters, while against Negroes they used the ultimate in force: night
sticks, revolvers, riot guns, sub-machine guns, and deer guns. As a result, 25 of
the 34 persons killed were Negroes. Of the latter, 17 were killed by police.

The excuse of the police department for the disproportionate number of Negroes killed is that the majority of them were shot while committing felonies:
namely, the looting of stores on Hastings street. On the other hand, the crimes
of arson and felonious assault are also felonies. It is true that some Negroes
were looting stores and were shot while committing these crimes. It is equally
true that white persons were turning over and burning automobiles on Woodward avenue. This is arson. Others were beating Negroes with iron pipes,
clubs, and rocks. This is felonious assault. Several Negroes were stabbed.

All these crimes are matters of record: Many were committed in the presence of police officers, several on the pavement around the City Hall. Yet the
record remains: Negroes killed by police—17; white persons killed by police—
none. The entire record, both of the riot killings and of previous disturbances,
reads like the story of the Nazi Gestapo.

Belle Isle is a municipal recreation park where thousands of white and
Negro war workers and their families go on Sundays for their outings. There
had been isolated instances of racial friction in the past. On Sunday night,
June 20, there was trouble between a group of white and Negro people. The
disturbance was under control by midnight. During the time of the disturbance and after it was under control, the police searched the automobiles of all
Negroes and searched the Negroes as well. They did not search the white people. One Negro who was to be inducted into the army the following week was
arrested because another person in the car had a small pen knife. This youth
was later sentenced to 90 days in jail before his family could locate him. Many
Negroes were arrested during this period and rushed to local police stations.
At the very beginning the police demonstrated that they would continue to
handle racial disorders by searching, beating and arresting Negroes while
using mere persuasion on white people.

A short time after midnight disorder broke out in a white neighborhood
near the Roxy theatre on Woodward avenue. The Roxy is an all night theatre

SOURCE: Thurgood Marshall, "The Gestapo in Detroit," Crisis, August 1943, pp.
232–33. [Thurgood Marshall, formerly chief counsel of the NAACP, is a Supreme
Court Justice.—Ed.]

attended by white and Negro patrons. Several Negroes were beaten and others were forced to remain in the theatre for lack of police protection. The rumor spread among the white people that a Negro had raped a white woman on Belle Island and that the Negroes were rioting.

At about the same time a rumor spread around Hastings and Adams streets in the Negro area that white sailors had thrown a Negro woman and her baby into the lake at Belle Isle and that the police were beating Negroes. This rumor was also repeated by an unidentified Negro at one of the night spots. Some Negroes began to attack white persons in the area. The police immediately began to use their sticks and revolvers against them. The Negroes began to break out the windows of stores of white merchants on Hastings street.

The interesting thing is that when the windows in the stores on Hastings street were first broken, there was no looting. An officer of the Merchants' Association walked the length of Hastings street, starting at 7 o'clock Monday morning and noticed that none of the stores with broken windows had been looted. It is thus clear that the original breaking of windows was not for the purpose of looting.

Throughout Monday the police, instead of placing men in front of the stores to protect them from looting, contented themselves with driving up and down Hastings street from time to time, stopping in front of the stores. The usual procedure was to jump out of the squad cars with drawn revolvers and riot guns to shoot whoever might be in the store. The policemen would then tell the Negro bystanders to "run and not look back." On several occasions, persons running were shot in the back. In other instances, bystanders were clubbed by police. To the police, all Negroes on Hastings street were "looters." This included war workers returning from work. . . .

Woodward avenue is one of the main thoroughfares of the city of Detroit. Small groups of white people began to rove up and down Woodward beating Negroes, stoning cars containing Negroes, stopping street cars and yanking Negroes from them, and stabbing, and shooting Negroes. In no case did the police do more than try to "reason" with these mobs, many of which were at this stage quite small. The police did not draw their revolvers or riot guns, and never used any force to disperse these mobs. As a result of this, the mobs got larger and bolder and even attacked Negroes on the pavement of the City Hall in demonstration not only of their contempt for law and order but of their contempt for law and order as represented by the municipal government.

Detroit, Mich. (1944)

28]   Influx of Migrants

. . . Since Pearl Harbor a half-million more people have come to Detroit and of these some 35,900 are Negroes and some 250,000 are whites from the hill country of the American South.

Source: Lewis E. Martin, "Profiles: Detroit," *Journal of Educational Sociology*, Special Issue on "The Negro in The North During Wartime," January 1944, pp.

At the beginning of the national defense program the so-called Negro problem in Detroit manifested itself sharply in the fields of employment, housing, and civil liberties. During peace times approximately 25,000 Negroes were employed in the auto industry and the majority of these were at the Ford Motor Company. They manned the foundries and in general were assigned the most arduous tasks with only a few skilled jobs open to them. A great many plants hired no Negroes at all and there were no Negro women workers in the entire industry.

After Pearl Harbor the manpower shortage and the pressures—governmental and civic—forced many of the industrialists to modify their employment policies and hire available Negro labor. The struggle of the Negro people for fair employment practices, however, was not won easily and as late as the spring of 1943 less than 100 of the 30,000 women recruited into the factories were Negroes. Today, however, there are 200,000 women in the Detroit war plants and 13,000 of them are colored.

The hiring of thousands of Negroes and the upgrading of those who were trained and qualified gave rise to "hate strikes" by white workers who, despite the threat of expulsion from the union, insisted on keeping certain jobs "white." A fortnight before the race riot of June 20–23, one of the largest hate strikes during this war period closed the Packard plant for a week and over 20,000 war workers took a vacation.

In the field of housing the story of the Detroit Negro does not vary greatly from that of other large northern urban centers. Through neighborhood agreements and covenants in property deeds the Negro has been pocketed into the slums and when these dykes failed to contain Negro expansion, white mobs have risen to the occasion. Two of the most notable instances of mob action involved the Sweet Case of 1925 and the Sojourner Truth riot of 1942. Dr. Sweet was threatened by a mob at his home in a so-called white neighborhood; he shot into the crowd, killing a man. He was successfully defended by Clarence Darrow. The 200-unit Sojourner Truth project was fought by whites who charged that the Government was moving Negroes into a white neighborhood.

While mob action in these cases made national and international headlines, countless incidents of near-riot proportions have accompanied almost every step of Negro expansion into new areas in Detroit. In the twenties Dr. Turner, a prominent Negro physician, was forced out of his home by whites and more recently Negro homes have been stoned and the lives of the occupants threatened. Several weeks following the riot of June of this year, one empty house which was for sale bore signs painted on the windows by hoodlums, "Niggers, Stay Out."

In the general field of civil liberties, the Detroit Negro a generation ago enjoyed considerable freedom and only a few public places would insult and refuse Negro patronage. With the coming of great numbers of Negroes, however, the liberal spirit of the town underwent a considerable change and the encroach-

280–83. [Lewis E. Martin, educated at Fisk and the Universities of Michigan and Havana, was formerly editor of the *Michigan Chronicle*, a black weekly.—Ed.]

346

ment of new forms of Jim-Crowism is increasingly apparent. Negro servicemen are not excepted from such treatment. Under the Michigan Civil Rights statute a mounting number of suits has been filed. The white juries, however, show a great reluctance to convict those guilty of violations. The law provides for a fine and punishments as a misdemeanor.

A contributing factor to the general unrest in Detroit among both groups is the inadequacy of recreational facilities. The tensions occasioned by this lack are greater today because of the pressure of the war and the pent-up feeling of the people. There are fewer recreational facilities in Detroit than in any city of comparable size in the country. The hasty construction of homes during the war period as in other boom times has proceeded without benefit of any thoughtful planning for social needs.

Chicago, Ill. (1943)

29]   Black Social Studies

Outstanding among steps in the direction of improved race relations is the fact behind the announcement made recently by Dr. William H. Johnson, Superintendent of Schools of the City of Chicago, of the inclusion of Negro achievement as a part of the regular city-wide program of social studies for the Chicago public schools. Not only is the announcement significant from a racial angle; but it is also of inestimable value from an educational point of view, since any measure which adds to the knowledge of historical facts is of benefit to all races of men.

For a long time, many agencies and organizations throughout the country have attempted to have Negro history included in school curricula in the belief that since the school is the chief agency of social improvement, it is the best place to improve inter-racial attitudes. It is believed that nowhere else in the United States, except in Chicago, has the Negro's contribution to America been authorized for city-wide study in the public schools.

Prominent among those responsible for this achievement is Mrs. Madeline R. Morgan, who through her principal, Miss Elinor C. McCollom, had the plan presented to Superintendent Johnson in March, 1941. Dr. Johnson immediately appointed Mrs. Morgan and Mrs. Bessie King, both elementary school teachers, to proceed with the gathering, assembling, and editing of the factual material about Negro achievement to be included in the Chicago public school curriculum. Both Mrs. Morgan and Mrs. King were relieved of all their teaching duties and devoted their entire time to this subject and work for eighteen months.

"For more than a year and a half," states Mrs. Morgan, "Mrs. King and I worked, blending the record of Negro achievements into the curriculum. After reading widely and consulting the courses of study in social science, we began

Source: "Chicago Schools Include Negro History," *Crisis*, February 1943, pp. 51–52.

to allocate the material to grades. Community life is studied in the primary grades (grades one to three). For these grades we chose to acquaint the children with Negroes in various occupations. We have stories for these grades that will show the Negro not only as private and public servants, but as educators, musicians and scientists. In grade three, we have presented a unit on Dahomey, Africa, which typifies a high degree of West African culture.

"For Grade four, Negro inventors in clothing and electricity are given. In Grade 5B, Chicago's first Negro pioneer settler, Jean Baptiste Point de Saible, is presented. Grade 5A, Virginia plantation life; Grade 6B, Negroes in discovery and exploration; Grade 6A, Africa; Grade 7B, Negroes during the Revolutionary period; Grade 7A, the Negro during the Civil War period; Grade 8B, Negroes in military life; Grade 8A, contemporary Negro leaders in Chicago. In each grade, Negroes in art, music and literature are included to fit as nearly as possible into the historical period in which they lived."

Chicago, Ill. (1945)

30]   Life in Bronzeville

Stand in the center of the Black Belt—at Chicago's 47th Street and South Parkway. Around you swirls a continuous eddy of faces—black, brown, olive, yellow, and white. Soon you will realize that this is not "just another neighborhood" of Midwest Metropolis.

Glance at the newsstand on the corner. You will see the Chicago dailies—the *Tribune*, the *Times*, the *Herald-American*, the *News*, the *Sun*. But you will also find a number of weeklies, headlining the activities of Negroes—*Chicago's Defender, Bee, News-Ledger,* and *Metropolitan News,* the *Pittsburgh Courier,* and a number of others.

In the nearby drugstore colored clerks are bustling about. (They are seldom seen in other neighborhoods.) In most of the other stores, too, there are colored sales people, although a white proprietor or manager usually looms in the offing.

In the offices around you, colored doctors, dentists and lawyers go about their duties. And a brown-skinned policeman saunters along swinging his club and glaring sternly at the urchins who dodge in and out among the shoppers.

Two large theaters will catch your eye with their billboards featuring Negro orchestras and vaudeville troupes, and the Negro great and near-great of Hollywood—Lena Horne, Rochester, Hattie McDaniels.

On a spring or summer day this spot, "47th and South Park," is the urban equivalent of a village square. In fact, Black Metropolis has a saying, "If you're

Source: St. Clair Drake and Horace Cayton, "Black Metropolis," *Negro Digest*, December 1945, pp. 74–82. [St. Clair Drake, Chicago-trained sociologist and coauthor of the classic *Black Metropolis,* is now professor of social anthropology at Stanford University.—Ed.]

trying to find a certain Negro in Chicago, stand on the corner of 47th and South Park long enough and you're bound to see him."

There is continuous and colorful movement here—shoppers streaming in and out of stores; insurance agents turning in their collections at a funeral parlor; club reporters rushing into a newspaper office with their social notes; irate tenants filing complaints with the Office of Price Administration; job-seekers moving in and out of the United States Employment Office. Today a picket line may be calling attention to the "unfair labor practices" of a merchant. Tomorrow a girl may be selling tags on the corner for a hospital or community house. The next day you will find a group of boys soliciting signatures to place a Negro on the All-Star football team.

And always a beggar or two will be in the background—a blind man, cup in hand, tapping his way along, or a legless veteran propped up against the side of a building.

This is Bronzeville's central shopping district, where rents are highest and Negro merchants compete fiercely with whites for the choicest commercial spots.

A few steps away from the intersection is the "largest Negro-owned department store in America," attempting to challenge the older and more experienced white retail establishments across the street.

At an exclusive "Eat Shoppe" just off the boulevard, you may find a Negro Congressman or ex-Congressman dining at your elbow, or former heavyweight champion Jack Johnson, beret pushed back on his head, chuckling at the next table; in the private dining-room there may be a party of civic leaders, black and white, planning reforms.

A few doors away, behind the Venetian blinds of a well-appointed tavern, the "big shots" of the sporting world crowd the bar on one side of the house, while the respectable "elite" takes its beers and "sizzling steaks" in the booths on the other side.

Within a half-mile radius of "47th and South Park" are clustered the major community institutions: the Negro-staffed Provident Hospital; the George Cleveland Hall Library (named for a colored physician); the YWCA; the "largest colored Catholic church in the country"; the "largest Protestant congregation in America"; the Black Belt's Hotel Grand; Parkway Community House; and the imposing Michigan Boulevard Garden Apartments for middle-income families.

As important as any of these is the large four-square-mile green, Washington Park—playground of the South Side. Here in the summer thousands of Negroes of all ages congregate to play softball and tennis, to swim, or just lounge around. Here during the Depression, stormy crowds met to listen to leaders of the unemployed.

Within Black Metropolis, there are neighborhood centers of activity having their own drugstores, grocery stores, theaters, poolrooms, taverns and churches, but "47th and South Park" overshadows all other business areas in size and importance.

If you wander about a bit in Black Metropolis you will note that one of the most striking features of the area is the prevalence of churches, numbering some 500. Many of these edifices still bear the marks of previous ownership—six-pointed Stars of David, Hebrew and Swedish inscriptions, or names chiseled on old corner-stones which do not tally with those on new bulletin boards.

On many of the business streets in the more run-down areas there are scores of "storefront" churches. To the uninitiated this plethora of churches is no less baffling than the bewildering variety and the colorful extravagance of the names. Nowhere else in Midwest Metropolis could one find, within a stone's throw of one another a Hebrew Baptist Church, a Baptized Believers' Holiness Church, a Universal Union Independent, a Church of Love and Faith, Spiritual, a Holy Mt. Zion Methodist Episcopal Independent, and a United Pentecostal Holiness Church. Or a cluster such as St. John's Christian Spiritual, Park Mission African Methodist Episcopal, Philadelphia Baptist, Little Rock Baptist, and the Aryan Full Gospel Mission, Spiritualist.

Churches are conspicuous, but to those who have eyes to see, they are rivaled in number by another community institution, the policy station, which is to the Negro community what the race-horse bookie is to white neighborhoods. In these mysterious little shops, tucked away in basements or behind stores, one may place a dime bet and hope to win $20 if the numbers "fall right." Definitely illegal, but tolerated by the law, the policy station is a ubiquitous institution, absent only from the more exclusive residential neighborhoods.

In addition to these more or less legitimate institutions, "tea pads" and "reefer dens," "buffet flats" and "call houses" also flourish, known only to the habitués of the underworld and to those respectable patrons, white and colored, without whose faithful support they could not exist. (Since 1912, when Chicago's red-light district was abolished, prostitution has become a clandestine affair, though open "street-walking" does occur in isolated areas.) An occasional feature story or news article in the daily press or in a Negro weekly throws a sudden light on one of these spots—a police raid or some unexpected tragedy; and then, as in all communities, it is forgotten.

WEST COAST CITIES

Economic and Social Aspects

As recently as the beginning of World War II, the black population on the West Coast remained relatively small. In 1940 the West accounted for 1% of the entire black population, compared with 22% for the North and 77% for the South. In that year Los Angeles was the only West Coast city with a black population of more than 50,000; as yet both San Francisco and Seattle had black populations of fewer than 5,000. Because it offered major job opportunities in the munitions industries, and a pleasant climate, the West experienced easily the greatest influx of blacks of any region during the war; over the decade 1940–50 its proportion of the national black population jumped from 1% to 4%. San Francisco, Seattle, and Los Angeles increased their black populations by 1,581.1%, 717% (from 3,789 to 27,167), and 231.8% respectively. This influx combined with the postwar recession, in which, typically, blacks were worst hit, to produce the predictable problems of housing shortages, unemployment, and racial antagonisms. However the migration to the West happened at a time when institutional American racism was being widely challenged, and, relatively speaking, blacks encountered more flexible and tolerant race relations there than elsewhere.

Los Angeles, Calif. (1945)

31]   Wartime and Postwar Racial Adjustment

Old-timers in the Sheriff's office will tell you that Los Angeles never had a Negro "problem" until the war. It is largely true—from the right side of the tracks. . . .

. . . . . .

SOURCE: Charles Bratt, "Profiles: Los Angeles," *Journal of Educational Sociology,* November 1945, pp. 179–86. [Charles Bratt, educated at Amherst College, has worked and traveled in many parts of the United States and China as a school teacher and labor relations and minority problems specialist.]

The strains created by the war derive chiefly from the fact that people have flocked into this area in the last five years by the tens of thousands. . . .

The strains increased throughout the entire war period in the form of an appalling housing shortage and fearful transportation overload. To the postwar heritage of these has now been added almost inevitable extensive unemployment. . . .

The gloomy over-all forecast is naturally of maximum importance to the Negro worker. While the special United States Census in April 1944 arrived at a figure of 134,000 for the number of Negroes in the county, estimates of their increased numbers have risen steadily until now responsible local officials "will settle for 200,000." War Manpower Commission employment figures, because of the nature of their coverage, never accounted for more than 27,000 "nonwhites" employed by "reporting" establishments—which was roughly 6 per cent of the covered payrolls. The extreme vulnerability of the Negro's wartime employment is indicated, however, as follows: In July of this year, shipbuilding was employing 40 per cent of the Negroes appearing on WMC reports (which was 11.2 per cent of total shipyard payrolls); aircraft was employing 22 per cent (3.0 per cent of aircraft payrolls); and rubber, iron and steel, and nonferrous metals together employed 18 per cent (an average of 11.8 per cent of these combined payrolls). There were, therefore, 80 per cent employed in those industries most severely affected by the ending of the war. Meanwhile, there are no known figures to show the distribution of the very large remainder of Negro workers in the labor force, but no possibility exists of their having become sufficiently integrated in stable civilian employment to prevent widespread Negro joblessness. . . .

Of considerable significance in analyzing job prospects is the fact that the vast majority of Negro men and women who found places in wartime industry acquired only partial skills because of the mass production methods used throughout. In so far as postwar job opportunities call for all-round knowledge of various crafts, the Negro worker shares the disadvantage of thousands of white workers who were wartime newcomers to the industrial field and were able to make a maximum contribution to production only because of the dilution of skills. Only supplemental training can remedy this situation but an apparent discriminatory trend in hiring practices will tend to discourage many Negro workers possessed of the diluted skills from embarking on extensive training unless they can be assured they are not already suffering two strikes against them in a highly competitive job market.

If the Negro's job future looks uncertain, then his housing future looks worse, based on his wartime experience. The county housing shortage is estimated at upwards of 100,000 family units. Five thousand validated applications are on file with the City Housing Authority alone (a significant number, considering the criteria for eligibility), 29 per cent of them from Negro families, 18 per cent from "other" racial groups, and the average waiting time before occupancy has been nine months. The end of the war has brought no relaxation in the demand for housing. On the contrary, all signs point to a continued in-migration, particularly of veterans and service-connected families —including additional minority veterans and families—which is not only canceling out the small outflow, but bids fair to worsen the already unbearable conditions.

Within this housing-shortage framework, Negro families have suffered more than any other group. Statistically, the estimates have it that there has been a 28.5 per cent overflow of Negro families above the number of dwellings available to them as against a 7.8 per cent overflow for families other than Negro. In absolute numbers this means that some 13,700 Negro families have gotten by somehow, through doubling up, tripling up, or by leading a miserable existence in abandoned store fronts or other places never meant for human habitation.

Attendant factors surrounding the basic problems of jobs and housing are the co-related problems of the large Mexican population (numbering 235,000), nearly as much victims of second-class citizenship as the Negro; the Japanese now being returned from the Relocation Centers; the Jim Crow prejudices of the newly arrived thousands of white southerners, often no more "assimilated" than their in-migrant colored brothers; the fostering of race hatreds by fascist leaders, and what might be described as the California pattern of tradition as regards minorities.

The so-called "zoot-suit" riots in 1943, on the one hand, involved only a small number of Negro youths as compared with Mexican youths and, on the other, was much more of a servicemen's fracas—chiefly sailors—than a civilian affair. It is the considered opinion of most thinking persons who made any attempt to penetrate the newspaper barrage that the outbreaks were not really symptomatic of seriously heightened racial tensions at that time but were the result of police and military laxness in permitting the prankishly lawless spirit of the American sailor to seize upon and make capital of minor barroom brawls.

The San Francisco "peace riots" in mid-August of this year which [was] generated out of hilarity and exuberance should give one pause at the possible results if hunger and hatred were the inciting forces. For several days in June of 1943 the newspapers had whipped up a factitious community hysteria and abetted a mob spirit, which could have had far more serious consequences had not a belated halt been called through a citizen's committee demanding that the Governor of the State take action.

Since 1943 there is reason to believe that far more serious antagonisms have been built up. There have been recently a number of "equal rights" incidents in restaurants "reserving" the right to refuse service. There are constant little incidents on city streetcars and buses and on the suburban lines growing out of who is going to sit beside whom or out of alleged jostling and petty irritations. The police and the leaders of Negro communities are mindful of such signs and are watching developments with some apprehension. These trivial incidents are regarded as nothing in themselves, except that they have been increasing even during the period when jobs have held up. Now the fear is beginning to be felt that with war-time morale and incentive slipping, with irritation inevitable from any contact with the hopelessly overloaded transportation system, with nerves on edge for many thousands of all races because of overcrowding in substandard living quarters, with many family incomes drastically

reduced or even wiped out—even a minor squabble might precipitate a basically serious clash.

The local Negro press reflects with some accuracy the disparate and contradictory tendencies within the prewar residential Negro community. On the
whole, however, it cannot be said that either the daily press or the weekly
Negro press has really grappled with the paramount problem of bringing about
the genuine assimilation and integration in the community of the thousands of
newcomers who now outnumber the prewar residents. Nor can it be said that
the churches, possibly the strongest single factor in shaping community
thought, have really embraced the problem either.

It can be justifiably charged that there is the same lack of a planned liaison
with the largest minority group, the Mexicans. There is a coming together of
leaders from both minority groups for specific campaigns like that for the State
FEPC but there is no co-educational effort directed at bringing together the
rank and file of both groups to fight their common battles. The nearest approach was the recent YMCA and Social Agencies-sponsored job get-together
for Mexicans and Negro adolescents in the Hollenbach District where gang
fights were breaking out among youth in the 12–15 year [old] age bracket.

On the positive side it should also have been said that the Housing Authority's occupancy-records show at the present time that approximately 25 per
cent of its units are occupied by Negro families and moreover that in a majority of the projects an excellent job has been done in establishing an interracial
pattern. There are any number of organizations working toward the establishment of interracial harmony. To mention only a few: there is an officially established County Committee for Interracial Progress, a Mayor's Committee for
Home Front Unity, and a re-vitalized Council for Civic Unity. In addition, an
ordinance that will set up a municipal Community Relations Committee is also
in the making.

There is hopefulness with youth. From among the generation which has
most recently moved out of the high schools and junior colleges, one could
find substantial numbers to attest to positive acceptance and popularity of
Negro, Mexican, and Japanese students in schools where attendance was predominantly white—the mark of esteem in many cases taking the form of election to top offices in student body organizations and the like.

There is no solution to minority problems in Los Angeles outside the solution of jobs and housing. And these are not minority problems; they are the
problems faced by the Nation, the State, and this community as a whole. It is
not a coincidence that maps showing the delinquency areas, the slum or
blighted areas, and the unrestricted areas, i.e., open to all races, can be super-
imposed one upon the other with almost no overlapping. In other words, the
problem of the well-being of the Negro and the Mexican is a straight-out economic and living-standards problem which can only be solved by wise planning of the community with the assistance of the Federal and State Governments. It is by such a solution that Los Angeles will stand or fall in its hope of
"becoming" a really great American city.

Seattle, Wash. (1958)

32]   Improvements in Race Relations

Seattle, the Queen City of the Pacific Northwest, has been described in many different ways. The dining car waiters and pullman porters who served the Pacific Northwest before World War II referred to Seattle as the city where a colored man could spend his money but could not earn a living, since he could not secure employment. Negro workers who came to Seattle during World War II called Seattle the New Promised Land. The trains they rode to Seattle were called freedom trains. In recent years, some race relations experts have called Seattle America's most democratic city.

What is the picture of race relations in Seattle today, approximately thirteen years after World War II? Has it been possible to maintain the policy of integration in America's last frontier? Are Negroes continuing to look to the Pacific Northwest for new opportunities and new freedoms?

Much progress has been made in public accommodations in Seattle. All of the outstanding hotels now serve guests regardless of race. This is a remarkable improvement since during World War II when prominent Negro guests were not always welcomed in the better hotels. It is now an accepted practice for Negro fraternities, sororities, and social clubs to utilize the facilities of all hotels for dances and public meetings. Restaurants encourage clientele from all segments of community life. However, there is occasional discrimination in taverns, cocktail lounges, and the cheaper hotels. A visitor to Seattle, if he is a member of a minority group, will experience discrimination in motels and trailer camps. All cemeteries either discriminate or segregate Negroes except those administered by the Catholic and Lutheran churches.

An excellent public education job and vigilance by many organizations is responsible for the favorable picture in public accommodations. Moreover, the State of Washington has a very strong civil rights law; the courts have been vigorous in assessing fines against public accommodation establishments that refuse service to minority groups. The largest amount of damages recorded in recent years in a civil rights case was granted a prominent Seattle citizen last year when she sued a reducing salon which denied her services. The salon has appealed to the State Supreme Court to reduce the damages awarded to the complainant.

The most serious problem in Seattle is housing. Although the Negro population has increased from less than 4,000 in 1940 to an estimated 25,000 in 1958, out of a total metropolitan population of 850,000, the area where the majority of Negroes live is approximately the same today as it was in 1940, since very few Negro families have succeeded in purchasing homes outside the central area. The reactions of white occupants to the free movement of Ne-

SOURCE: Lewis G. Watts, "Racial Trends in Seattle, Washington, 1958," *Crisis* June–July 1958, pp. 333–38.

groes in Seattle has been mixed. When a Negro family purchased a home in a white neighborhood, petitions were circulated to prevent the child from attending the local public school. Yet, in another neighborhood a Negro was given the leading role in an opera sponsored by a fashionable Episcopal church—he was a member of the only Negro family in a nearby housing development. The same factor produces the all-Negro neighborhoods in Seattle as in most American cities: the organized opposition of the real estate operators, neighborhood improvement associations, individual sellers, and the policy of the Federal Housing Administration and Veterans Administration. These groups have severely limited the housing opportunities in the open market for Negroes and other non-whites. Moreover, the apathy of many Negro home-seekers toward purchasing housing outside the central area, when there have been opportunities, has stimulated the development of neighborhoods which are predominantly Negro.

Most of the neighborhoods where Negroes and other non-whites predominate are blighted and are subject to urban renewal, rehabilitation, and conservation. The sections of Seattle where Negroes have been forced to live are the choice residential areas of the city. By "choice," I refer to scenic beauty. Many white families who previously sold property to Negroes in order to move to the suburbs are now moving back into the central districts, thereby competing with minority groups for property.

Tensions are developing. One cause is that white children form the minority in a number of Seattle's elementary schools. Many white families, fearing their children will be unable to cope with such situations, are sending them to private schools. Other white parents send their children to elementary schools located outside the district, where the majority of children are white. Real estate agents have capitalized on this factor and thus charge premium prices for houses located in some cases on the sides of streets where the children do not have to attend the public school in which the majority of the children are non-white. Last year, the Urban League joined with a citizens' group to petition the Seattle School Board to change the boundaries of two schools so that school populations would be more evenly balanced racially.

At the present time, there are seven elementary schools in Seattle which have more Negro and other non-white children than whites. The administrative staff of the Seattle public schools reports that the turnover of teachers in these schools is proportionately higher than in the rest of the city. In two schools, which, incidentally, have the largest number of non-white children, the turnover of teachers last year was over fifty percent. The administrative staff is attempting to correct this condition by instituting an in-service program in intergroup relations for teachers and principals who work in the elementary schools in areas where minority populations reside.

The School Board and the administrative staff of the Seattle public schools have done an exceedingly good job in race relations. The first Negro teacher was employed in Seattle in 1947, after most northern cities had already employed substantial numbers of Negro teachers. There are now over one hundred Negro and non-white teachers employed, which is excellent progress.

More Negro teachers would be employed if qualified ones could be found. Because of the recommendation of the Seattle Urban League, the first Negro teachers were assigned to schools located outside the predominantly Negro districts. The plan worked well. The Negro teachers are now assigned on the basis of need and qualification. As a result of careful screening, the quality of Negro teachers employed by the Seattle public schools has been so superior that the county schools have also employed Negro teachers, although very few Negro families resided in the school district. As further evidence of lack of prejudice and another testimony to the high quality of Negro teachers, one rather exclusive all-white neighborhood requested the superintendent of schools in Seattle to assign a Negro teacher to their school. In another case, a qualified Negro teacher was appointed principal of an elementary school in a neighborhood where not a single Negro family was residing.

Additional qualified Negroes would be employed in Seattle industries if they could be found. At the peak of its production in 1957, the Boeing Airplane Company of Seattle employed sixty thousand persons, of which an impressive number were Negroes. It is estimated that this company has employed only fifty Negro engineers since 1947, whereas many more would have been employed could they have been found. With few exceptions, all of the engineers were recruited outside of the State of Washington. Recently, several Negroes have been appointed to supervisory positions. There are many Negroes who have been employed ten or more years, but very few have applied for up-grading, and very few have participated in the in-service training programs offered by management. The majority of Seattle's Negro population is recently from the South, and most are still fearful of being aggressive on the job.

Other bright spots are found in the commercial establishments. All of the leading department stores employ Negro men and women in sales, clerical, and service departments. Up-grading to supervisory or prestige positions has not occurred, although some Negro sales persons have applied. The Pacific Telephone and Telegraph Company employs a large number of Negro women as telephone operators and clerical workers. One of the paradoxes in Seattle is that there is more acceptance of Negroes in professions, such as social work, medicine, law, engineering, nursing and teaching, than in the bread-and-butter jobs. Despite a fair employment practice law, Negroes are barred from such jobs as taxi drivers, bartenders, bellhops, waitresses (except at one department store), waiters, and service station attendants.

Only one department in the city government currently has a lily-white policy: this is the Seattle Fire Department. So far as is known, there has never been a Negro or any other non-white employed as a fireman in the city of Seattle, although a number have applied. Nertheless, the best opportunity for Negro employment has been in the federal and city civil service. Negroes are employed as policemen, transit operators, clerical workers, truck drivers, and laborers in all departments of the city. But up-grading is a problem in city civil service employment, even as in private industry.

With the closing of the Seattle Army Terminal and other defense installations, and the reductions of employment opportunities at Boeing, employment opportunities for Negroes in industry have declined. Very few Negroes have been employed in food processing, lumbering, fishery, metal fabricating, and the culinary trades.

. . . . .

Although in recent years the majority of Negroes who have migrated to the Pacific Northwest came from the farms and small towns of Mississippi, Arkansas, Louisiana, and Texas, the superior quality of the Negro population in Seattle has contributed enormously to racial progress and is the greatest hope for the future. Seattle has received its share of failures, but the overwhelming majority of Negroes who [have] migrated to Seattle since 1940 have made good. A reflection of this progress is shown by a survey of property valuation conducted by the Winston Realty Company, one of Seattle's outstanding realty firms. In 1940, the Negro citizens of Seattle owned dwelling units representing an investment of $800,000; but in 1957, the 25,000 Negroes owned an estimated 3,500 dwelling units, representing an investment of over $25,000,000.

A number of factors contributed to the "making good" of the Negro population in Seattle. Seattle is a young city, slightly over one hundred years old, and patterns of racial relations have not crystallized. The presence of a large Asian population and the fact that Seattle is a sea-coast city, the closest port to the Orient, has much to do with its good racial-relations climate. Moreover, many Seattle citizens have traveled in the Orient as seamen, business men, tourists or missionaries; and many Asians visit Seattle annually. Hence, a cosmopolitan atmosphere has been created which leads to less rigidity. In such an atmosphere the Negro has found acceptance in Seattle, and the tremendous industrial expansion of Seattle since World War II has created a need for additional manpower, thus making employment possible for Negroes.

A combination of factors has contributed to the employment of Negroes in Seattle industries. Until the recent closing of big defense installations and the reduction of employment at Boeing, Seattle experienced a tight labor market, which always enhances the employment opportunities of minority groups; this coupled with a strong FEPC law with effective enforcement powers created a receptive attitude toward the employment of Negroes in Seattle. The presence over the years of a carefully thought out Urban League program guided by an interested board has served as an energizer to all groups working in racial relations in Seattle.

Finally, the fusion of the immigrant Negro, who came principally from the South, with the small but stable Negro population that already resided in Seattle before 1940, has created a solid citizenry that is making an outstanding adjustment in a new community.

PART SIX

THE SIXTIES
AND AFTER

INTRODUCTION

The three general selections below discuss important aspects of black urban life. The first describes the new political opportunities for blacks in eight major American cities in which they form a significant proportion of the population. It also points out three factors that have tended to minimize black political effectiveness: relatively low registration, personal and ideological rivalry, and, for those who attain power, the weak tax base of the cities. The second document tells of the continuing serious underrepresentation of blacks in police forces, even in those cities where some genuine efforts have been made to attract them. The reasons for this condition include the persistence of the image of the policeman as the symbol of white oppression; and continuing discrimination against blacks in examinations, assignments, and promotions in the white-dominated police force. The third document chronicles aspects of the decay of the cities in the period following the urban riots. The federal and state governments have as yet devised no systematic rescue operation for the cities—a reflection of the fact that political and economic power resides more and more in the suburbs rather than the cities.

CITIES

General Aspects

1]   Black Political Power in Eight Cities (1970)

. . . Assuming the present urban patterns of black in-migration and white out-migration continue, black mayors in at least 19 large and medium-sized cities can be a reality before the end of the decade. These cities would include:

ATLANTA

Blacks who are 49 per cent of the city's population and almost 41 per cent of its registered voters have a better-than-even chance of capturing City Hall in 1973. The man most likely to spearhead that drive is husky Atty. Maynard Jackson Jr., who in last year's elections became Atlanta's first black vice-mayor when he defeated a veteran and respected white alderman by nearly 20,000 of the more than 85,000 votes cast. Although the only black in the mayor's race, Horace Tate, only placed third in a field of four, the elections produced some significant developments. According to the Voter Education Project, Inc. there was 1) a break-up of the traditional alliance between blacks and northside whites; 2) evidence that blacks along with a minority of whites determined the outcome of a number of elections, including those of mayor and vice-mayor; and 3) an increase in the number of blacks who were elected, they now occupy 30 per cent of Atlanta's elective offices.

BALTIMORE

"Whites are beginning to accept the fact that '71 is our year for a black mayor," reports State Sen. Clarence M. Mitchell III who himself plans a mayoral campaign. Other possible candidates include black City Solicitor George Russell and City Councilman Emerson Julian, brother of the distinguished chemist Dr. Percy Julian. . . .

Source: Alex Poinsett, "Black Take-Over of U.S. Cities?" *Ebony*, November 1970, pp. 77–78, 82, 84, 86.

Black Political Power in Eight Cities

CHICAGO

A local daily newspaper predicts this one-third black city will probably elect its first black mayor in 1979 or, at the latest, in 1983. . . .

[But] even when blacks achieve a population edge in Chicago or anywhere else, a simple majority will not be enough to overcome the obstacles of enormous white-controlled patronage, lack of black capital to finance mayoral campaigns and lack of black political sophistication as evidenced, for example, by the failure of many blacks to register to vote. . . .

DETROIT

Blacks, who are somewhat less than 40 per cent of the citizenry and registered voters, went to the mountaintop last November and saw that they could elect a black mayor. County Auditor Richard H. Austin, the first serious black candidate for mayor, lost to Sheriff Roman S. Gribbs but took better than 49 per cent of the vote total and nearly a fifth of the white vote. A switch in only 3,500 votes would have made him mayor. He is still considered a live prospect. . .

HOUSTON

Curtis M. Graves, first black man to run for mayor in this city, polled 32 per cent of the vote in the November election involving six candidates. A switch of 5,000 votes would have forced a runoff between him and the four-term incumbent, Louis Welch. The mayor received less than six per cent of the vote in black wards while Graves, a 31-year-old state legislator, got 10 to 11 per cent of the white vote. . . .

MEMPHIS

Rev. James M. Lawson Jr., a veteran of the freedom movement, predicts: "Within ten years we could have a black mayor and congressman." Already 30 per cent of the city's registered voters are black and three blacks sit on the 13-man city council. On the other hand, Atty. A. W. Willis ran a poor fourth in a field of seven in the 1967 mayoral election, receiving only 39 per cent of the black vote. . . .

PHILADELPHIA

Blacks are about 32 per cent of this city's population, but out of that percentage (some 700,000 people) "only about 50 per cent (350,000) are eligible to vote, according to Dr. Harry A. Bailey, black chairman of Temple University's political science department. "Of the 50 per cent eligible to vote, only about 60 per cent, or about 200,000 people, will bother to come out to vote." Black registration reached its peak in 1967 for the Johnson-Goldwater election in which 278,009 blacks registered, and has been going down since then. Most estimates indicate Philadelphia has some 200,000 unregistered blacks.

. . . . .

ST. LOUIS

Reapportionment of the city's 28 wards in 1971 should increase the number dominated by blacks from eight to 13, according to Teamsters Union official

363

Ernest Calloway, who is a close student of St. Louis voting patterns. He explains that the reason no black has made a serious attempt to run for mayor in the 44 per cent black city is that blacks think of themselves as a minority even while they are rapidly approaching a majority (estimated 50 per cent by 1975). Furthermore, black votes usually amount only to 25 to 30 per cent of the total cast in most city-wide elections, indicating many eligible blacks do not register and many of those registered do not vote.

Voter registration . . . is one of the keys to any serious effort at black political empowerment. [However,] some political observers fear the organizing of the black electorate to govern the cities may prove futile in the long run. On the one hand, they see a growing movement to subordinate city governments to the administration of regional metropolitan areas as a way of broadening the tax base. But they also see this trend as a way of thwarting black political empowerment. They suspect, in other words, that just as blacks are nibbling at the edges of political power, others are busily laying plans to snatch it away. Consolidations have already occurred in Nashville, Tenn., which is about 43 per cent black, [and] Miami, Fla. (28 per cent). After proponents of annexation in Richmond, Va., argued recently that it would prevent the city from becoming like predominantly black Washington, D.C., an annexation court awarded part of a suburban county to Richmond. And in 49 per cent black Atlanta, the Georgia House of Representatives narrowly defeated a bill in March 1969 to merge the city government with the governments of its surrounding Fulton County area.

2]   Failure of Black Police Recruitment (1971)

The cry of the nineteen-sixties for more black policemen has lowered to a whisper today, with only the District of Columbia among the nation's major cities able to lay claim to any real success in significantly increasing the number of blacks on its force.

From New York to New Orleans to Seattle, most departments have at best been able to add only a few blacks and to increase only barely the percentage of blacks among the total.

Responding to the racial crisis of the last decade, many cities announced at least a desire to have more black policemen, while some conducted recruitment drives. Black leaders and policemen do not believe many of the recruitment efforts were serious, and, at any rate, few of the efforts were successful.

Washington was the most successful, and Chicago and Atlanta got fairly good results.

Other cities employed gimmicks that failed or merely stepped up their tradi-

SOURCE: Paul Delaney, "Recruiting of Negro Police Is a Failure in Most Cities," *The New York Times*, January 25, 1971.

Failure of Black Police Recruitment

tional recruitment programs that had not worked in the past. Among those cities were Milwaukee, Charlotte, N.C., Seattle, New Orleans, Charleston, W. Va., Dallas, and Portland, Ore.

New York City's major recruitment project is the state-financed cadet training program, which tutors minority group members in an effort to help them pass police exams.

Sgt. William Perry, coordinator for this four-year-old program, said it had trained and placed on the force more than 400 members of minority groups. He termed the results "an upsurge," although the percentage of blacks on the force has risen only from 5 per cent to 7.5 per cent over the last decade.

A survey of recruitment efforts found the following:

Drives in most cities failed completely. The percentage of blacks on some forces is the same as it was a decade ago and in some cases has actually declined.

Police officials said they were desperately searching for Negroes for their departments, but in actuality little was being done in many places.

Discrimination on forces is still a problem that hurts recruitment. Many forces have token representation of blacks in the upper ranks, while some have none at all.

In the black community, the image of the police is still very negative. Black youngsters just do not want to be policemen. This attitude, combined with discrimination on the force, seems to be the major reason police recruiters meet with stiff resistance.

The need for black policemen became apparent during the sixties with the steady increase in crime in black communities and rioting in the cities. Along with more policemen, some blacks, mostly militants, were demanding community control of the police. The latter issue faded even before the efforts to recruit.

In Berkeley, Calif., however, a fight is under way over a plan to reorganize the police force into three community-ruled zones—one "black," one "white" and one "campus" for the University of California area.

The most aggressive campaign to recruit blacks was conducted in Washington. However, the situation here is not typical: It has the biggest percentage of black residents of any city, 75.

Four years ago, blacks made up only 17 per cent of the capital's force of 3,100 men. In September, 1968, the percentage was up to 24.4 per cent, or 786 blacks of 3,207 men. By last August, 1,000 more blacks had been added for a total of 1,797 of 4,994, or 35.9 per cent.

Washington did it by setting up recruit-mobiles in black sections, where written exams were given; recruiting on military bases; changing physical standards, such as lowering the height requirements and modifying the eye requirement, and changing the requirements on certain illnesses such as asthma and hay fever; conducting a "recruit-in-moviethon," where applicants and their dates attend free showing of Jim Brown and John Wayne movies, and a "radiothon" in which applicants were solicited over the radio and taxicabs were sent to pick them up and bring them to the station to take their tests.

Chicago has 2,100 black policemen on a force of 12,678, or 16.5 per cent.

The city is one-third black. There were 1,842 Negroes on the force in 1967 and 2,037 last spring.

Atlanta's force of 942 has 260 blacks, or 28 per cent. The percentage is up five points from the annual total during the last decade, according to Superintendent Robert Lane, who is in charge of training.

In New York, 2,400 of the 31,700 policemen are black, or 7.5 per cent. For years the percentage of blacks had remained at about 5 per cent, causing some blacks to charge the department with maintaining a quota system.

The Detroit force has 567 blacks out of nearly 5,100, about 12 per cent. Nearly 500 have been put on since 1966, with the bulk coming after the 1967 riots. The percentage of Negroes on the force in 1960 was 2.

Statistics in some other cities show Los Angeles with 350 blacks on a force of 6,705, or 5.2 per cent; Milwaukee, 50, of 2,098, or 2.3 per cent; Charleston, W. Va., 10 of 150, or 6.6 per cent; Charlotte, 22 of 459, or 4.5 per cent; San Francisco, 85 of 1,775, or 4.8 per cent; Dallas, 32 of 1,640, or 1.9 per cent; New Orleans, 83 of 1,359, or 6.1 per cent; Boston, 60 of 2,807, 2.1 per cent; Miami, 74 of 719, or 10 per cent; Hartford, 60 of 500, or 12 per cent, and Providence, R. I., 18 of 421, or 4.5 per cent.

In Philadelphia the number of blacks on the force has been declining the last few years. Philadelphia had 1,431 blacks on a force of 6,893, or 20.8 per cent, in 1967. This was down last year to 1,347 blacks out of 7,242, or 18.6 per cent.

"To get blacks, the only thing a police department has to do is to tell blacks they want black officers and mean it," commented Deputy Chief Tilman O'Bryant, one of the two top ranking blacks on the Washington force.

"You don't just go on the record in saying you want black officers," he said. "You've got to use just a little more effort to convince them you mean it. We've convinced the community here we mean it."

Many departments conduct recruitment drives by appointing a black to patrol the ghetto, sometimes with a small staff. Some use community organizations, such as the Urban League.

Other cities advertise in black papers and on radio stations aimed at the black community. Some departments have saturated the ghetto with posters, signs and billboards. The poster-billboard approach worked in Washington but apparently is failing in Philadelphia, where posters praise "the black in blue" and admonish residents to "cop in, don't cop out" and urge blacks to "join [Police Commissioner Frank] Rizzo's team." Philadelphia even hired a black advertising concern in an effort to stem the decline in blacks on the force.

Such efforts help most forces barely to maintain their current percentage of blacks.

A big problem is getting blacks who can pass the written tests. Larry Niles, recruitment officer with the Los Angeles police, said, "Negroes have more difficulty getting through the written tests. The tests give us people with over 100 I.Q. Whether it is a culturally fair test is another question." Detroit is attempting to eliminate the white middle-class "cultural bias" of its present tests.

Black policemen are convinced the tests are used to discriminate against them. White officials defend the exams as necessary to assure qualified officers.

A black policeman in Indianapolis said the test issue was a "sham," that "if an applicant is wanted on the force, the test wouldn't keep him off."

The testing problem has caused some cities to take steps, as New York has done, to help blacks to pass. Seattle has a training program to improve skills, while Boston intends to initiate one.

However, the major recruitment problem among blacks appears to be the negative image of the police in the black community, compounded by discrimination on the forces.

. . . . .

Many white officials are cognizant of the image problem. The Public Safety Director in Louisville, Ky., George C. Burton, commented, "It is a problem and we're working on it."

Mr. Burton's black assistant director, A. Wilson Edwards, said the department had created the image problem. He cited the fact that the city had only 42 blacks on its force of 624. He feels, though, the image is changing.

Discrimination in promotion is also a problem. Mr. Edwards said that many departments had at least one black in the upper ranks. But some, including Milwaukee, Charlotte and Dayton, Ohio, do not. In several cities, San Francisco and Portland included, the ranking blacks are sergeants.

Mr. Edwards, a veteran of 30 years on the force, retired as lieutenant in 1966 after helping set up police units in several African and Asian countries. He recalled years of bitter frustration in trying to get a promotion himself.

"Every time they gave the captain's exam and I finished first or second, they held the promotion list for a year," he said. "They gave the exams again and the same thing happened. I took the test five times. When I finally finished out of the top three, from which the appointment was made, the job was filled. I stopped taking it."

3]   Inner-City Deterioration (1971)

The weather-beaten plywood board is replacing the gleaming steel and glass skyscraper as a symbol of the American city.

Outside the central city, apartments and air-conditioned shopping plazas and theaters spring up. Miles apart but bound together by freeways making anything only a few minutes away from the auto-equipped resident of that outer city, suburbia.

But for those remaining in the central city cores—the black ghettos and the poor and even middle-class white areas around them—it is harder to buy food because the big supermarkets are going and the little stores are boarded up or torn down; it is harder to find a doctor or dentist; harder to fill a prescription or have a suit cleaned because the stores are gone; harder to buy a newspaper; call a taxi; find a pleasant park, a good restaurant or even a good corned beef sandwich.

SOURCE: Jerry M. Flint, "Inner-City Decay Causes Business Life to Wither," *The New York Times*, July 19, 1971.

The traditional commercial services are dying and the old urban cores have not yet been able to adapt to the new commercial pattern.

What is more, years after the racial riots along these same streets and after innumerable pledges to rebuild, the decay has intensified.

Four years ago this week, great riots occurred and today the streets, if anything, look emptier with large stretches of dusty cleared land and even larger stretches of shabby boarded-up storefronts. And reports from other cities—Pittsburgh, Chicago, Washington, for example—are much the same.

In a dozen cities examined as the summer began, the scene on these streets is similar: blocks abandoned, storefronts covered with plywood. Open stores are dingy, the fronts bricked up in the architectural style that dominates the ghetto of the nineteen seventies: "Riot Renaissance." If anything new is built on the old commercial arteries, it is probably another gas station or a gaudy drive-in.

There are exceptions. Here and there a bright shopping center exists. Not matching the glistening ones in the suburbs but reversing the general commercial decay. And some of the old shopping streets, such as 125th Street in Harlem, are still bustling and bright. But they are not typical.

Some blame a lack of federal money for the continued blight. Others blame the squabbling of citizens' groups, or high crime, or burdensome insurance, or freeze-outs by banks and private investors, or inability to gather large blocks of land needed for modern commercial services, or high costs for the obviously unwanted city blocks. Whatever the reason, the imagination and the will to rebuild the city cores seem lacking. . . . . .

Here are reports on the situation around the nation:

PITTSBURGH

The large core ghetto is called the Hill district. After the murder of Dr. Martin Luther King Jr. three years ago 100 stores were looted or burned. Most have not been rebuilt, and where the rubble was cleared away there's new debris: beer cans, whiskey bottles, trash.

"After the 1968 troubles we cut our hours. We close at 5:30 p.m., not open at night. Our black employees don't want to go out at night," said Leonard Edelson, a white co-owner of the bustling Hill Pharmacy. His store keeps its windows boarded up and is busy because "four major drugstores in the Hill were burned out" and because the welfare business has more than doubled in three years, he said.

He has to send a driver to pick up drugs each day because the suppliers pulled their men from the routes when they were attacked.

"There's nothing here to open up for," said Matthew Moore, a Pennsylvania state coordinator for the National Association for the Advancement of Colored People. "Drugs are flourishing so people are afraid to come out. The Hill is full of winos and junkies. People are afraid to carry money."

"Some services are available," he added wryly. "We control the bars, beauty shops, barbers and churches."

368

Inner-City Deterioration

BOSTON

The Boston ghetto stretches from the South End near downtown into Roxbury, its heart, and in it live four-fifths of the city's 105,000 Negroes. More than 50 stores along Blue Hill Avenue, a main thoroughfare, were damaged in the 1967 riot and most have not reopened. Some $56-million in pledges of aid for rebuilding never materialized, but some new black-owned or black-run businesses have opened, replacing white ones.

"So many Jewish shop owners got out of deep Roxbury that it amounted to a mass exodus" after the 1967 riot, said a spokesman for the Anti-Defamation League of B'nai B'rith. In one area 100 stores changed hands. Despite some new businesses and improvements the old core area is still "a business desert," said Robert M. Coard, executive director for the city's major anti-poverty agency.

BIRMINGHAM

Although the city says it tries to give the same treatment to the streets and sidewalks of Birmingham's ghetto as to other parts of the city one can see piles of trash lying about outside the biggest grocery store, boxes, paper, old produce and other refuse lie around for two or three days.

The only new restaurant in the area in five years, a quick-service hamburger franchise, changed management twice and has closed.

DETROIT

Twelfth Street, once a thriving Jewish commercial strip, then a busy honky-tonk black strip and the heart of the 1967 riot, is practically leveled, and residents must travel miles to find a large grocery or drug store. Even the pimps complain: "I used to make $100 a day on this street. Now I can't make a dime," one said.

On the east side of the city, on Mack Avenue, 127 vacant stores were counted in a two-mile stretch. A west side resident complained: "I called to have milk delivered and they said they don't have any trucks out here."

Detroit's car makers invested almost $10-million to set up black-owned automobile showrooms in inner city locations abandoned by whites, but now the companies have decided that even blacks can't do much business there.

CHICAGO

"In the past 10 years I would estimate that the attrition rate of ghetto business is 30 to 40 per cent, as high as 50 per cent in areas affected by the riots," said Pierre DeVise, a social scientist at DePaul University. "Madison Street [on the West Side of Chicago] looks like it was hit by a holocaust. Maybe only one-third of the stores operating there 10 years ago are still functioning. A three-block area lined by storefronts before 1968 lies completely vacant."

"See for yourself. Nothing has been replaced. The only new places are the gas stations moving onto some of this cleared land and one Midas muffler store," said Tommy Lee Durham, a black who owns a second-hand refrigerator store on Madison.

Cities: General Aspects

Construction of new stores has proved to be a failure in some cases.

Dr. Arthur Falls is a Negro and part of a 16-member syndicate that owns a shopping center in the South Side ghetto. He said $1-million was invested in the center four years ago. Now graffiti cover the walls of the stores, four of the seven are vacant, and chicken-wire, plywood or brickwork cover the windows.

There has been fire bombing and thievery and no profits, he said.

TRENTON

In the last five years two large department stores in Trenton have closed and some expect the remaining two to follow. Both downtown hotels are gone. Plans for a downtown shopping mall fell apart, and of the four movie theaters downtown all are expected to be closed by next month.

The seven black neighborhoods in Trenton are serviced by one small and one large supermarket. Bars and liquor stores abound, but a trip downtown is necessary for drugs or hardware, shoes or to see a doctor.

On the eight blocks of North Clinton Avenue there were 120 businesses in 1950; now there are 60. Every other store window is boarded up; alleys are filled with garbage and broken glass.

In most ghetto areas residents can't buy a newspaper because there are no stands and few stores, and carrier boys are scarce.

· · · · ·

LOS ANGELES

On Central Avenue in Watts nearly all the stores were destroyed in the 1965 riot and about one-third remain boarded up today. There are no major supermarkets in the business strips, Central and Compton Avenues and 103rd Street.

"If I get someone going to Watts in the daytime, and he looks O.K., I demand he pay in advance, and I take him. At night I won't go," said a white taxi driver. Services, which were scarce in the area before the riots, have not improved. And job transportation still seems the major concern.

WASHINGTON

Plywood is a big decorating item along Seventh and 14th Streets N.W. and H Street N.E., the old commercial corridors damaged in the 1968 riots. Black-owned stores are increasing but, said Cornelius Pitts, who owns the Pitts Motor Hotel just off 14th and has founded a black businessmen's alliance:

After the riots when whites were selling out to blacks, the new owners were paying substantially higher prices based on prior volume [rather] than volume justified afterwards. As a result, many have gone out of business, and a lot of the rest are just hanging on.

"I'm dying for lack of business," he admitted.

"I've been discouraged for the last year and half," said Rufus A. Isley, owner of two clothing stores and winner of a small Business Administration award a year ago. His side of the 3000 block of 14th Street looks as if the riots had occurred last month rather than three years ago.

Inner-City Deterioration

Harlem is exceptional, both within the nation and within New York City. The density of its mobile but constant population of about half a million people is part of a critical set of variables that set it apart even from Brooklyn's larger Bedford-Stuyvesant section.

"Harlem is different and the negatives are more aggravated than in other cities," said Hope Stevens, a prominent black Harlem lawyer who is also president of the predominantly white Uptown Chamber of Commerce.

It does not have to rebuild structures damaged in civil disturbances. Although there was an outbreak of violence following the death of Dr. King, property damage was not as extensive as in other cities.

But spiraling insurance costs, followed by a rise in prices for inferior goods, have been a source of aggravation. This has been accompanied by a high incidence of crime against property. One study by the Small Businessmen's Chamber of Commerce—a predominantly black group—estimated that crime last year cost the community "more than $2-billion."

"The cost of crime," said Mr. Stevens, "is passed back to the consumer. It doesn't drive the businesses out. They simply raise the prices."

Many of the larger white businesses are said to be "up for sale." But as one black businessman put it, "There are no banks or other agencies willing to give the black businessman a loan."

In all the cities studied, of course, many residents of the core areas, black and white, own automobiles and can drive to the suburban shopping centers. Any visitor to Northland, Detroit's major suburban center, can see that a large percentage of the buyers are blacks from the city.

"You don't know what a big thing it is for a black family to get in a car and go out to the suburbs to shop," said a black automobile dealer in Chicago. "That's where half my business goes."

And in some of the central cities, some of the shopping streets are succeeding.

In Philadelphia, not far from Columbia Avenue, a former riot area, there's a striking new shopping center, Progress Plaza, opened in 1968 with 17 stores and offices. One of its main backers was the Rev. Leon Sullivan, a leader in the black capitalism effort.

There's an A. & P. supermarket, two banks, shoe stores, a drugstore, appliance store, bookstore and others, all owned or managed by blacks. There have been no failures and the center's stores did $5-million in business their first year, Dr. Sullivan said.

In most places, however, the blight is widespread and deepening. For millions of people living becomes a little more inconvenient and a little uglier each year. . . .

SOUTHERN CITIES

Political and Social Aspects

In the early 1960's, like the late 1950's, southern cities were the main national venue of nonviolent, direct civil rights activities partly designed to end the kind of public segregation against blacks that had long been officially absent in the North. The student sit-in movement, which started on February 1, 1960 in Greensboro, N.C., spread in the next few months to the cities of the upper South, the Atlantic seaboard states, and Texas, and resulted in the desegregation of lunch counters in drug and variety stores. Out of these activities came the radical Student Non-Violent Co-ordinating Committee (SNCC). Other major civil rights organizations—NAACP, CORE, SCLC—were also active in southern cities, sometimes cooperatively. In the deep South the civil rights thrust was met with fierce resistance characterized by unrestrained police brutality, white mob violence, and murder of both black and white civil rights activists. But although the civil rights slogan, of the early 1960's—"Freedom Now"—was far from realized by 1970, there had been some noteworthy changes: the most obvious forms of jim crowism and segregation had been knocked down; political activities and representation had grown; interracial communication and business opportunities had improved. The documents that follow describe various aspects of this important period of transition in race relations in southern cities.

Greensboro, N.C. (1960)

4]   Lunch Counter Sit-in

A group of well-dressed Negro college students staged a sitdown strike in a downtown Woolworth store today and vowed to continue it in relays until Negroes were served at the lunch counter.

"We believe since we buy books and papers in the other part of the store we should get served in this part," said the spokesman for the group.

SOURCE: *The New York Times,* February 3, 1960.

372

The Politics of Desegregation

The store manager, C. L. Harris, commented: "They can just sit there. It's nothing to me."

He declined to say whether it was the policy of the store not to serve Negroes.

The Negroes, students at North Carolina Agricultural and Technical College here, arrived shortly after 10 A.M. and sat at two sections of the lunch counter.

At 12:30 P.M., the group filed out of the store and stood on the sidewalk in this city's busiest downtown street. They formed a tight circle, threw their hands into a pyramid in the center and recited the Lord's Prayer.

The spokesman said that "another shift" of students would carry forward the strike and it would continue "until we get served."

Richmond, Va. (1962)

5] The Politics of Desegregation

. . . Today, the progress that has been made in desegregation and non-discrimination in Richmond is one of the exciting racial stories in the South. Its pace astonishes many Richmonders, white and Negro.

The Negro vote, once the kiss of death, now is an asset; no candidate for City Council can afford to offend it and expect to win. The City has adopted a fair employment policy in municipal jobs, unique in the South, and Negro Richmonders have better job opportunities than ever before.

Negroes may stop at several formerly white-only hotels and dine at several formerly white-only restaurants. Some 130 Negro children, probably more, will be attending formerly white-only classes when the public schools reopen this fall.

Perhaps nowhere else in the country, certainly nowhere else in the South, do Negroes use their vote with more sophistication than in Richmond. It wasn't always so.

Not many years ago, the Negro vote in Richmond was a commodity to be purchased on the sly by white politicians from Negro salesmen who claimed they could deliver the goods. Public endorsement of a candidate by Negroes meant disaster, a fact used cleverly by more than one politician who would circulate a spurious Negro endorsement of his opponent.

During the days of massive resistance and accompanying racial rancor, Negroes tried "single-shot" voting for Negro candidates in City Council campaigns. But these candidates got only that vote and went down to defeat.

But things changed in 1960 with the emergence of the Crusade for Voters, headed by intellectual Negro leaders. Abandoned was the single-shot technique. Instead, the Crusade examined each candidate for City Council and en-

SOURCE: Robert E. Baker, "Richmond Quietly Leads Way in Race Relations," *The Washington Post*, July 29, 1962.

dorsed a full slate of nine candidates. The change was dramatic, as the case of Councilman Robert J. Heberle shows.

In 1957, Councilman Heberle urged Richmond to withdraw its financial aid to the Virginia National Guard in retaliation for the federalization of the Arkansas National Guard during the Little Rock crisis. In 1958, when President Eisenhower requested public officials to comply with the Supreme Court's school decision, Heberle, as Vice Mayor at that time, fired back a letter of refusal. In 1959, Councilman Heberle advocated that Richmond cut off local funds to any school that became desegregated.

By 1960, therefore, the Crusade for Voters viewed Heberle as an ardent segregationist and he was not among the slate of candidates it endorsed in the City Council elections that year. The 37 per cent of the vote that Heberle got wasn't enough for his re-election.

After two years out of office Heberle announced his candidacy for City Council in the June elections this year. He promised to serve and work for all the citizens. He gave his wholehearted support to the City Council's fair employment resolution, which had been approved unanimously shortly before the election.

With a touch of political genius, the Crusade for Voters endorsed Heberle and he led the field of 25 candidates with 51 per cent of the vote. The lesson was clear. The Negroes had bounced a segregationist from the Council, then returned him when he repented.

Lack of the Crusade's support in 1960 also knocked veteran Councilman Phil J. Bagley, Jr. from office. He was returned to the Council this June, however, without the Crusade's endorsement. Yet he still was to feel the influence of the Negro vote.

In Richmond, a new City Council elects the mayor from among its members, and the new Council in June was deadlocked: four votes for Bagley, four votes for Heberle and one vote for Eleanor P. Sheppard. The Crusade leadership said the Negroes would be displeased if Bagley were elected mayor.

On the 25th ballot, Mrs. Sheppard became the first woman mayor in the city's history. She had been endorsed by the Crusade.

Led and educated by the Crusade's leadership of Negro professional and businessmen and faculty members of Virginia Union College, about 8000 Negro voters went to the polls in June, two-thirds of the qualified Negro voters in the city. Some 14,000 white Richmonders voted, perhaps one-third of the qualified white voters.

The Crusade didn't announce its endorsements until just before election day, so the candidates worked to win the Negro vote right up to the deadline. The Crusade's selections included members of the two rival tickets, so one ticket wasn't tempted to use Negro support as an issue against the other.

Seven of the nine Council winners had received the Crusade's endorsement. The two losing endorsees came in 10th and 11th. No. 10 was a Negro. Another Negro candidate without the Crusade's endorsement came in 20th.

Negro Richmonders have matured as a political force. They also have matured in the use of their economic power.

The Politics of Desegregation

The Richmond Citizens Advisory Council was formed by representatives of 36 primarily Negro organizations 18 months ago to help Virginia Union students who had participated in sit-in demonstrations in Richmond department stores and restaurants. Even before the RCAC asked for funds, the Negro community raised $14,000 for that purpose.

The responsibility of the RCAC leadership was shown early when some Negro pickets at a department store carried signs offensive to Jews. RCAC leaders told the Negroes to remove such signs at once or the RCAC would withdraw its support of the picketing. Down came the signs.

Boycotting of the Miller & Rhoads and Thalhimer's department stores undoubtedly was effective. Shopping excursions to Washington stores were organized by the Negroes.

One of the RCAC leaders is J. Rupert Picott, executive secretary of the Virginia Teachers Association (Negro). He advised a Richmond hotel that teachers attending a VTA meeting would try to register at the hotel. The hotel management said it would prefer that the registrants be integrated rather than all-Negro—so some white teachers from northern Virginia came to Richmond and registered at the hotel, too.

Last year, the RCAC went into negotiations with the Virginia Transit Co., a private company with a municipal franchise that operates Richmond's buses, over the hiring of the first Negro bus drivers. Progress was slow. Finally, the Negroes indicated that a bus boycott might be called.

The transit firm then agreed to hire Negro drivers if the RCAC would postpone any action until after the company took up a new rate schedule with the City Council. The RCAC waited.

On March 5, four Negro applicants supplied by the Richmond Urban League began their training with the VTC. They began driving buses April 1.

Negotiations also have gained Negroes jobs as food checkers in chain supermarkets. The RCAC was surprised to learn that meat cutters in the back rooms, jobs sometimes available to Negroes, paid more than the food checkers, but they wanted Negroes as checkers because they are visible to the buying public, a symbol of progress that can be seen.

One of the remaining uncracked fields of segregation in Richmond is the motion picture theaters. Here the Negroes have no ready economic weapon because they haven't been admitted to the white-only theaters in the past and thus can't withhold their patronage now.

Negotiations are under way. It is felt that the theater owners are awaiting the outcome of a pending suit by Negroes against the Mosque and Parker Field.

The colorful Mosque is the city-owned auditorium which is leased to sponsoring organizations. The lease calls for adherence to the state law requiring segregated seating.

In fact, segregation at the Mosque is spottily enforced. Some "Twist Nights" in the Mosque ballroom have been integrated; operatic and symphonic presentations are generally segregated. In any event, Negroes are contesting the state segregated seating law.

Also segregated is Parker Field, the city-owned baseball park leased to the Richmond Virginians, the International League farm club of the New York Yankees. Negro baseball fans must sit in Section 16.

Negroes are testing the state law to force desegregation at Parker Field and it is likely that the baseball management hopes privately that they win. It would nourish the boxoffice if the fans now easily accommodated in Section 16 swelled to such numbers as to overflow several sections.

Negro leaders good-humoredly tell the story of an injured Negro player on the Virginians' team who didn't suit up for a recent game and sat in a white section to watch it. The player refused to move at the request of an attendant who then called a policeman. Recognizing the player, the policeman said he would have to move to the Negro section unless he put on his uniform.

The progress of the Negro in Richmond must be credited in part to the rise of firm, responsible and sophisticated Negro leadership which speaks softly and carries a big stick of political and economic power by commanding the support of the Negro community. But white Richmond and its leadership must also be credited for its good will and understanding.

The top academic senior this year at the Medical College of Virginia was Charles Fletcher Christian, 37, a Negro. But neither he nor the five other Negroes in the graduating class of 88 were sent invitations to the social functions of graduation week-end.

MCV President R. Blackwell Smith Jr. said the exclusion policy was designed "to conform to the social customs of the community." When MCV professors heard about it they voted 70 to 14 against such exclusion. The senior class petitioned the college administration to change the policy.

The Richmond Times-Dispatch said editorially that it was only right for the Negroes to be invited. It also asked understanding of the MCV officials involved. "Like most other Virginians, they have had to adjust their thinking to the changing times," it said.

The Richmond News Leader, while noting that it wasn't yielding in its opposition to school desegregation, said that the Negroes should be invited. "Any other policy is indefensible," it declared.

The MCV executive committee ruled that the Negroes wouldn't be denied admission if they appeared. The policy now is under study and it's unlikely that Negroes will be excluded in the future.

Comparison of the Negro Richmonder's lot today with that in the period of "massive resistance" causes astonishment in observers and participants alike. Yet the progress is not surprising in the light of Richmond's history of race relations before massive resistance.

The city led the South in bus desegregation and the employment of Negro policemen. A Negro won election to the City Council in 1948 with the help of white voters. City officials kept their offices open on Saturdays in 1947 to cooperate with a voter registration drive by the NAACP.

In 1951, the Virginia NAACP held an integrated convention at the Mosque and the city said, well, it's a private organization, and looked the other way. Back in 1925, the city suspended segregation ordinances and Jim Crow regulations when the Negro Elks held their national convention in Richmond.

Rising Expectations and Frustrations

Some observers see an end to the new political status of the Negro Richmonder if the city succeeds in annexing huge chunks of neighboring Henrico and Chesterfield Counties, reasoning that the white suburbanites would dilute the influence of the Negro vote. The annexation proceedings now are in court.

But others believe that the racial relations progress and the present era of increased racial understanding now have too solid a foundation to crumble. The 225-year-old city, a symbol of Virginia and the South, has turned a historic corner in race relations after a five-year detour.

It was in August, 1958, that the Richmond News Leader urged stubborn resistance to school desegregation as the zero hour neared in "massive resistance."

"Virginians," said the editorial, "are about to have an opportunity to demonstrate to the whole country—indeed, to the whole world—what it means to be a Virginian."

Today, Richmond is demonstrating what it means.

Atlanta, Ga. (1967)

6]   Rising Expectations and Frustrations

Rapid industrialization following World War II, coupled with annexations that quadrupled the area of the city, had made Atlanta a vigorous and booming community. Pragmatic business and political leaders worked to give it a reputation as the moderate stronghold of the Deep South.

Nevertheless, despite acceptance, in principle, of integration of schools and facilities, the fact that the city is headquarters both for civil rights organizations and segregationist elements created a strong and ever-present potential for conflict.

The rapidly growing Negro population, which by the summer of 1967 had reached an estimated 44 percent, and was scattered in several ghettos throughout the city, was maintaining constant pressure on surrounding white residential areas. Some real estate agents engaged in "blockbusting tactics" to stimulate panic sales by white homeowners. The city police were continually on the alert to keep marches and counter-marches of civil rights and white supremacist organizations from flaring into violence.

In September 1966, following a fatal shooting by a police officer of a Negro auto thief who was resisting arrest, only the dramatic ghetto appearance of Mayor Ivan Allen, Jr., averted a riot.

Boasting that Atlanta had the largest KKK membership in the country, the Klan, on June 4, 1967, marched through one of the poorer Negro sections. A massive police escort prevented a racial clash.

According to Mayor Allen, 55 percent of municipal employees hired in 1967

SOURCE: *Report of the National Advisory Commission on Civil Disorders,* New York: Bantam Books, 1968, pp. 52–54.

were Negroes, bringing their proportion of the city work force to 28 percent. Of 908 police department employees, 85 are Negro—a higher proportion of Negroes than in most major city police departments in the nation.

To the Negro community, however, it appeared that the progress made served only to reduce the level of inequality. Equal conditions for blacks and whites remained a hope for the future. Different pay scales for black and white municipal employees performing the same jobs had been only recently eliminated.

The economic and educational gap between the black and white populations may, in fact, have been increasing. The average white Atlantan was a high school graduate; the average Negro Atlantan had not completed the eighth grade.

In 1960 the median income of a Negro family was less than half of the white's $6,350 a year, and 48 percent of Negro families earned less than $3,-000 a year. Fifty percent of the men worked in unskilled jobs, and many more Negro women than men, 7.9 percent as against 4.9 percent of the respective work forces, held well-paying white collar jobs.

Living on marginal incomes in cramped and deteriorating quarters—one-third of the housing was overcrowded and more than half substandard—families were breaking up at an increasing rate. In approximately four out of every 10 Negro homes the father was missing. In the case of families living in public housing projects, more than 60 percent [were] headed by females.

Mayor Allen estimated there were 25,000 jobs in the city waiting to be filled because people lacked the education or skills to fill them. Yet overcrowding in many Negro schools forced the scheduling of extended and double sessions. Although Negroes comprised 60 percent of the school population, there were 14 "white" high schools compared to 9 Negro.

The city has integrated its schools, but "de facto" segregation as a result of housing patterns has had the effect of continuing separate schooling of nearly all white and Negro pupils. White high school students attended classes 6½ hours a day; Negroes in high schools with double sessions attended 4½.

One Atlanta newspaper continued to advertise jobs by race and in some industrial plants there were "Negro" jobs and "white" jobs, with little chance for advancement by Negroes.

. . . . . .

Since only one of the 16 aldermen was a Negro, and a number of black wards were represented by white aldermen, many Negroes felt they were not being properly represented on the city government. The small number of elected Negro officials appeared to be due to a system in which aldermen are elected at large, but represent specific wards, and must reside in the wards from which they are elected. Because of the quilted pattern of black-white housing, white candidates were able to meet the residency requirements for running from predominantly Negro wards. Since, however, candidates are dependent upon the city-wide vote for election, and the city has a white majority, few Negroes had been able to attain office.

Houston, Texas (1970)

7] Bleak Economic Picture

. . . In Houston, prosperity is labeled "white only" and in perhaps no other major urban center in the country is the exclusion of minorities—black and Mexican-American—so thorough and so exasperating. . . .

. . . Hiring practices, in fact, are so scandalous that the federal Equal Employment Opportunity Commission visited Houston for three days this past June to investigate.

Houston's population of 1.2 million is 25 per cent black and 7 per cent Mexican-American, but, the commission reported, the employment of minorities is woefully below that of whites. The National Aeronautics and Space Administration, for example, employs some 4,200 persons at the Manned Spacecraft Center, but only 3.4 per cent of its employes are black and only 2.4 per cent are Mexican-American.

Testifying at the hearings, the American Oil Company said that only 9.1 per cent of the employes at its Texas City refinery were from minority groups and admitted that of its 168 executives not one was black or Mexican-American. . . . As late as only two years ago American's black employes constituted only 5.9 per cent of the entire work force.

And at that, American turned out to be one of the more enlightened firms in Houston. Of the 37 firms invited to the hearings, only a dozen even bothered to send representatives to testify and even firms that have achieved good records of minority hiring elsewhere in the country have made a deplorable showing in Houston.

Among the discouraging statistics about the economic plight of black men and women in Houston that were disclosed at the hearings:

• One fifth of employment is concentrated in ten major companies, all of which increased their employment over the past few years. Still, in those ten companies only two per cent of all white collar jobs were held by blacks.

• The percentage of professional jobs held by black women actually dropped down from 11.4 per cent in 1966 to 6 per cent in 1969.

And, finally, the commission arrived at the staggering conclusion that despite its energetic economy, Houston ranked either 44th or 45th among the nation's 46 major urban centers in category after category measuring efforts at minority hiring. "For years, the Houston economy has been booming," the commission stated in a position paper. "Yet the industrial expansion and labor shortages that characterize its economic development have provided little opportunity for economic advancement for minorities. . . . Though most blacks are working, the jobs they find are in personal services, small businesses and declining industries."

SOURCE: "Houston," *Black Enterprise*, October 1970, pp. 42–44, 46.

Southern Cities: Political and Social Aspects

The commission's report seemed to be reinforced by a separate study of 225 of Houston's black college graduates conducted by a New York consulting firm, Recruiting Management Consultants Inc. Only 18 per cent of the graduates surveyed held jobs with business or industry that were suited to their training. A full one-third of the college graduates were placed in skilled production jobs where their white counterparts were high school dropouts.

And if things are difficult for a black man or woman seeking a career in Houston, in some respects life is even more difficult for the independent black businessman, who is confronted with a myriad of problems. Even the geography of Houston seems to work against the black businessman, for there is no single, large black community in Houston that might give a black business community some force and coherence, but rather a scattering of black enclaves in several parts of the sprawling city. The ten to fifteen thousand blacks living in the largest black area—Acre Homes—are, for example, thirty miles north of the second largest black community in Sunnyside.

A second problem is that unlike a more progressive city such as Atlanta, there is no long and solid tradition of black ownership in Houston. In fact, no one has an accurate count of how many black-owned businesses there are in Houston, although attempts are now being made to compile such a list. And, in the absence of a longstanding tradition of high quality and good service, even black consumers are reluctant to go to black-owned firms for more than barbeque, hair-straightening or gasoline. . . .

But certainly the biggest obstruction to black business in Houston is the inability to get loans and credit. Two years ago 23 banks pledged to lend $7.7 million to new businesses, but so far only $1.3 million has been disbursed. Out of 270 applicants 93 have been approved and 75 applicants have actually received money.

A few of Houston's black businessmen have been successful. Perhaps the most impressive success story is that of 32-year-old Johnny Burton, who borrowed $25 nine years ago to buy a sewing machine and started making shirts for his friends. Burton saved his money, opened his own tailor shop and in time has become tailor to some of the biggest names in show business, including James Brown, Smokey Robinson and the Temptations. When he opened his second store in the heart of downtown Houston last year the bank was only too happy to lend him $30,000, particularly since Burton put up $50,000 himself.

Much more typical, however, is the story of a 26-year-old economics graduate from Texas Southern University, Houston's largest black school, who decided to open a restaurant last year in Houston's black Third Ward. His troubles began with a delay in getting the loan from the SBA. "We were told the loan would take about two weeks," he recalls. "But it was four months before the loan was approved and we had the money." And then three days after he opened his restaurant, the Creole Hut, the Health Department closed it down because the businessman had not yet installed a sink in the sales area. When he reopened he was confronted with such problems as street repairs which made it difficult for people to get into his restaurant, the water and gas

380

being shut off without notice for long periods of time and three robberies. Defeated, he finally closed down the Creole Hut after several months.

Black contractors, including electricians, plumbers, bricklayers, painters and concrete finishers, confront a particularly maddening, although not uncommon, form of discrimination. These contractors have not been able to bid on city building contracts for jobs that amount to more than $2,000 because they cannot get bonding: . . . Black contractors, in fact, recently took their case to the Houston City Council. Qualifications for bonding are credit, capital and competence, observed Sawyer Bynam, a partner in a small construction firm. "But we have found out that there is another 'C'—color."

But as bleak as the situation is, there are at least some indications that black people are beginning to work together to become a forceful part of Houston's economy. Texas Southern, which is only a few blocks from the giant white University of Houston, enrolls some 5,000 students. Despite its shortcomings, including inadequate facilities and an underpaid staff, it still is an institution which has a potential for improving the life of Houston's blacks. TSU, for example, trains more pharmacists that any black school in the country.

One long-standing black organization, the Human Organizational Political Economic Development Inc. (HOPE), publishes a weekly newspaper, The Voice of HOPE, and is also trying to organize a housing project.

One of the most dynamic economic efforts has been mounted by Operation Breadbasket, the local chapter of the economic arm of the Southern Christian Leadership Conference. Under the leadership of Pluria Marshall, who ran a photographic studio for many years and consequently knows the black community's economics from the inside, Breadbasket has made some progress in bringing money into the community.

To get its story across Breadbasket has enlisted the support of local black celebrities, such as former AFL defensive lineman Ernie Ladd. And with such help Breadbasket has persuaded several local companies, including Mrs. Baird's Bread, the local Schlitz Beer distributor and the local Borden's milk distributor, to return a percentage of the money they make from the black community back to the black community in the form of higher salaries for black employes and contracts to black custodial firms and others who might do business with them.

Perhaps Breadbasket's most impressive accomplishment came last year when Marshall and twenty-five others picketed the local Burger King hamburger outlet because of the firm's failure to give the franchise to blacks. "We picketed for three or four weeks and there were three arrests," recalls Marshall. But in the end Marshall and his followers got their way and the franchise was given to a group of black businessmen, who formed a firm called RPM Development.

What kind of opportunity is there for black business in Houston in the future? One possible course is put forth by Bill Lawton, a 29-year-old law student and business advisor. Lawton believes that blacks should think not so much in terms of businesses owned by a single individual but rather in terms of larger, broader-based group efforts. He thinks, for example, that with the rising crime rate in the black community many Jewish and Italian grocery store owners are ready to get out. "A group of black grocers could set up their own grocer's supply and in that way cut their costs considerably," Lawton suggests.

. . . . .

Certainly the obstacles to black economic development in Houston are formidable: white racism, the geographic fragmentation of the black community and the absence of a long and sturdy tradition of black ownership. It would be illusory to pretend that problems such as these are going to disappear overnight. At the same time, Houston is an affluent city that has not yet been overwhelmed by its own deterioration. And Houston is a new city—or at least a new metropolis—and along with all the energy of its growth there is a new force of young black leaders looking for—and sometimes finding—new ways of meeting old problems.

Birmingham, Ala. (1971)

8] Interracial Communication

Birmingham, sometimes called "the Pittsburgh of the South," celebrates its 100th birthday this fall, still smarting from being labeled, a decade ago, as one of the most racist cities in the country.

Before the 1960's Birmingham was a typical slow-paced Southern city. A sprawling United States Steel works in the Fairfield section of town, to be sure, makes Birmingham of closer kin to Pittsburgh or Gary. But most residents of the city take greater pride in the neatness of the downtown area and their well-kept gardens than its steel industry. Indeed, before the racial disturbances of the sixties, the city rarely made headlines.

But in September, 1963, four little black girls died in a church bombing in Birmingham after there had been some ugly confrontations between Birmingham blacks demanding "freedom now," and city officials like Eugene "Bull" Connor and Jim Clark who vowed "never." The televised accounts of the city's raw racial strife brought Birmingham worldwide notoriety. To rights activists and newsmen the city became "Bombingham," a symbol of racial oppression.

Jarred by its newly acquired negative image, the city has now set out to change the view others have of this industrial hub. Gradually, progress in race relations has been made, such as in the desegregation of schools and places of public accommodation.

Chiefly because of local efforts to build a bridge between the black community and the white establishment, Birmingham this year boasts a new name: All-America City, an honor that was recently bestowed on it by a national magazine. There was one black Birmingham resident in the group that went to Portland, Oregon, to accept the All-America award from the magazine. He was

SOURCE: "Birmingham," *Black Enterprise*, September 1971, pp. 40–42.

Chris McNair, a professional photographer and the father of one of the four young victims of the bombing of the Sixteenth Street Baptist Church in 1963.

Bull Connor in his heyday once declared, "ain't no niggers and whites gonna integrate together around here as long as I'm police commissioner." Connor is no longer around and in most instances, racial harmony prevails. For instance, Connor would be amazed at what takes place every Monday morning in one of Birmingham's most posh hotels.

Over ham'n eggs and grits, a group of black and white community leaders, including law enforcement authorities and elected officials, have labored to remove the tarnish that still mars the city's image. The group, the Community Affairs Committee of Operation New Birmingham, was created in 1969 after black leaders called for a summit meeting with civic and business leaders to discuss racial matters. The meetings are closed, but some participants say they are remarkably candid.

For instance, as soon as the sessions began, reliable sources say, the blacks laid it on the line: they wanted better treatment by the police and a more equitable share of city services and jobs. Without such a commitment to equitable treatment, they warned, black leaders of the community couldn't be responsible for any additional racial explosions, which at the time appeared imminent.

.   .   .   .   .

According to the latest census tally, Birmingham's black population declined by some 9,000 persons. But because whites continue to move to the suburbs, the proportion of blacks in the city's total population of 301,000 actually increased, from about 39.6 per cent in 1960 to 42 per cent in 1970. Equally significant is the fact that the census clearly shows that blacks possess the numerical strength to gain more political power in Birmingham, a possibility that has not gone unnoticed by many observers in the city. Recently, an elaborate consolidation plan was devised to merge Birmingham with 26 surrounding municipalities which together have a total population of about 350,000. If the proposal is adopted it would produce one city of about 800,000 people. But the new city would be only about 30 per cent black.

The proposal nearly died in the state legislature after suburban residents let it be known they preferred "quality education," a not too subtle reference to the city's school problems, and "responsible government" to marriage with Birmingham. Naturally, many blacks also are hoping for the defeat of the merger. Black lawyer David Hood, who is chairman of the Jefferson County Democratic Progressive Council, said the plan would encourage suburban segregation while diluting black political power. . . .

Birmingham, of course, is not entirely without blacks in elective office. The city has one black councilman, out of a total of nine. Arthur Shores, a veteran lawyer, was first appointed to the city council to fill the seat of a white councilman who died in office. When Shores ran for reelection, he won easily. Many whites supported his bid for office because they considered him "responsible," as opposed to the "militant" candidacy of Tommy Wren, who was supported by the state's newly formed, predominantly black national Democratic Party of Alabama.

But more important, the specter of black political strength in the city has resulted in more liberal attitudes toward blacks from the white political establishment. Mayor George Seibels Jr. is a Republican who won election in the heavily Democratic city with the support of black voters. Seibels campaigned on a platform of better city services and more decent treatment of blacks by the police. Many of his aides insist that he intends to deliver on his promises. In terms of better services Seibels has generally high marks.

Statistics released last year by the federal government suggested dramatic changes in Birmingham schools, but although the city's formerly all white schools now have on their rolls about 20 per cent of the black student population, enrollment at black schools remains largely unchanged.

Slightly more than 30 per cent of the students in Birmingham and Jefferson County are black, and at that number, 80 per cent continue to attend totally black schools. . . .

The city is an economic paradox. Nature endowed the area with vast mineral resources, and as the iron and coal have been scooped out of nearby Red Mountain, other aspects of the local economy have also prospered.

Blacks, however, are only now beginning to share in the general prosperity. Birmingham's foundries and the industries that have spun off from the steel mills require many laborers and unskilled workers. For blacks especially, these were dead-end jobs before the Civil Rights Act of 1964 and a succession of Presidential executive orders. Today, although the picture has changed substantially . . . black lawyers have filed a succession of lawsuits attacking job discrimination because they believe that infinitely more progress is both possible and necessary. . . Not surprisingly, the construction industry is one of the chief offenders. Local NAACP officials put the proportion of blacks employed in the building trades at about one per cent. Grover Smith, the NAACP's Southern labor director, says this proportion holds true even in apprenticeship programs.

As far as black business is concerned, whether Birmingham offers adequate opportunities for entrepreneurship depends on whom you talk to. Like most Southern cities, Birmingham boasts a number of black businesses of the type that initially thrived in the sheltered market of segregation as well as some newer black-owned businesses in downtown Birmingham. One of the city's most successful businessmen, Arthur G. Gaston, is a reported millionaire who started in business in the life insurance field. The name of that venture is the Booker T. Washington Life Insurance Company. Gaston later built a string of funeral homes, a business school, a real estate company and a hotel-motel chain. Gaston's enterprises also include a savings and loan company and a restaurant-nightclub. Altogether, it is estimated that Gaston Businesses employ more than 500 people.

Some newer black businesses seem to be doing equally well. Laurie Forniss operates a women's clothing store. She says she met some hostility from white competitiors when she first opened the store, and as a result nationally known apparel makers would not sell to her. Now, she says, the business is flourishing, and although most of her customers are black, she gets "quite a bit" of white trade.

Other black business owners are less optimistic, particularly those who have recently opened shop in downtown Birmingham with the expectation of attracting customers regardless of race.

But whether they are businessmen, professionals or just plain ordinary citizens, black Birmingham residents are hopeful that their city will become an integral part of the "New South." They are convinced that the city has finally realized that racial harmony is prerequisite to continuing economic progress.

Memphis, Tenn. (1971)

9]   Improved Race Relations

It was only a little more than three years ago, that terror-filled April evening [April 4, 1968] in Memphis when Dr. Martin Luther King Jr. stepped out on the balcony of the Lorraine Hotel-Motel. With appalling determination, the assassin across the way steadied his rifle, took aim and fired. The world reeled back, struck numb with shock and grief and cities such as Philadelphia, Tallahassee, Baltimore and Washington convulsed with civil disorder.

And what about Memphis itself? After such an act, what hope could there possibly be for Memphis? Race relations in that mid-South river city were struggling under painful stress anyhow. Dr. King had come to Memphis, after all, to march with the city's sanitationmen, most of them black, in protest over their shamefully low wages. With the assassination forever imprinted on their memories, could any of Memphis's 250,000 black people and 375,000 white people ever look at one another again without fear and hatred?

The answer, surprisingly, is a hesitant and tentative "yes." The balance of the evidence of the past three years indicates that Memphis is making progress in its race relations. And in at least one critical area, black economic development, Memphis is making visible, and in some cases substantial, gains. Blacks and whites have joined together in building a new shopping center; the forward-looking chamber of commerce has led the way in securing a $1 million federal "special impact" program for the development of black business; belatedly, the city fathers have acknowledged Memphis's rich, black musical tradition as a municipal treasure and are starting to develop a tourist and convention center around Beale Street, the bustling thoroughfare immortalized in W. C. Handy's "Beale Street Blues." Even the sanitationmen are better off. Their current wage of about $4 an hour puts them at the same income level as secretaries downtown.

. . . . .

Certainly, a great deal remains to be done. Unemployment remains high in the black community. Some 85,000 Memphis residents, a large majority of them black, are on welfare, and, by one interpretation at least, fully one third of the black people in Memphis are firmly gripped by poverty. And any gains made by blacks seem dependent on the general prosperity of Memphis, which is

SOURCE: "Memphis," *Black Enterprise*, May 1971, pp. 26–29.

now going through a transition from an economy dependent on cotton and river trade to one very much dependent on industry.

. . . . .

. . . During the past 15 years the area within a 75-mile radius of Memphis has started to throb with new industry. Almost $2.5 billion has been invested in the Mississippi lowlands, more than 1,500 new plants and about 250,000 new jobs. (Like many other cities, industrial Memphis has had some setbacks and is feeling some of the contraction pains of the recession. In December, RCA phased out its Memphis plant production of color television sets, thus putting out of work some 1,600 people, half of them black.)

Who is responsible for this revival? An enterprising survey by the morning newspaper, the Commercial Appeal, last year revealed that these days, unlike the Crump era, Memphis is not run by a single man or even a single-minded oligarchy but rather by "a fluid, frequently competitive, almost structureless, combination of political, commercial and professional people."

The study identified 42 major decision-makers in the city, six black men among them:

Odell Horton, president of LeMoyne-Owen College and former Criminal Courts judge.

Ben. L. Hooks, president of Mahalia Jackson Food Products, co-owner of re-lated businesses and pastor of Greater Middle Baptist Church.

The Rev. James Lawson, pastor of Centenary Methodist Church.

Dr. Hollis Price, former president of LeMoyne-Owen College, special ad-viser to the Memphis Board of Education and news executive on the staff of WMC-TV.

Jesse H. Turner, executive vice president of Tri-state Bank of Memphis, member of the Shelby County Quarterly Court and former president of the Memphis branch of the NAACP.

Maceo Walker, head of the Universal Life Insurance Co.

Of the 42 leaders, 33 of them identified race, and primarily the poverty of the city's black community, as the number one problem confronting Memphis. Six months before Dr. King's assassination, black and white Memphis residents formed MACO—the Memphis Alliance of Community Organizations. "Essen-tially MACO is a kind of communications organization," explains Clifford Stockton, who has been running the chamber of commerce's human resources division for the past two years and is the first black man ever to hold an im-portant position at the chamber. "Whenever there is a real problem in the community, the same 33 organizational heads sit down and plan what can be done and then report back to their organizations for a followup."

Along with this new spirit of cooperation there is a sense—although not al-ways the substance—of dynamic activity in the black business community. Memphis has at its service one of the most informative black business directo-ries in the country and a list of businesses that range from soul food kitchens to the Main Stream Computer Service, a new and predominantly black-owned firm that is supplying computerized accounting to the community.

Three new projects are particularly interesting:

Improved Race Relations

Located on a nine-acre lot in a black neighborhood ten minutes from downtown Memphis, Metro is a shopping center with 18 separate businesses. Eleven of them are owned by blacks; four are jointly owned by blacks and whites and operated by blacks. "Blacks had no supermarket here and the idea was to create something economical to serve a social end," explains Lawrence Wade, who is president of Mutual Savings and Loan Association and is also a consultant to the group that operates Metro. "We want to train people to be upgraded in jobs and managerial classifications and the only way we could do that was to have a vehicle with which to work. . . ."
As a creation of the Memphis Business League's Project Outreach, Metro was started with loans from the Small Business Administration—$683,000 for construction of the plaza and $300,000 worth of capital for equipment and stock for individual black entrepreneurs. "Black businesses," says the 44-year-old Wade, "have a very good potential not only in Memphis but in certain other cities in the South and there is no question but that business in general is looking to the South for its growth."

SPECIAL IMPACT PROGRAM
A year ago the federal government made a $1 million grant for a special impact program to develop black business in Memphis. Under the direction of the Greater Memphis Urban Development Corporation (18 of the 24 board members are from the black community) the money is being put to work. An initial project is the Memphis Tubing Company, expected to start production of automobile tailpipes on July 1. The decision to make tailpipes was made in a sensible businesslike manner. "When they were doing the R&D for this," observes chamber of commerce executive Stockton, "they looked at the automobile business and looked for the part of the auto that sells even when new cars aren't selling. Old cars need new tailpipies."
Some of the other proposals that have been made for the special impact program are for the creation of a cable television company and for a "carcade" to teach automobile repair skills.

CONVENTION CENTER
Perhaps the most interesting, and certainly the most glamorous, aspect of business development in Memphis these days is the plan to turn the city into a tourist and convention attraction centered around Beale Street. Unlike New Orleans, which has long taken advantage of the allure of Basin Street and the Latin Quarter, Memphis has been slow to promote Beale Street's rich traditions.
Even so the "Memphis Sound" has been a factor in the city's economy, in particular such businesses as the largely black operated Stax Recording Company. "Because of all the shipping and promotion we do," notes Stax vice president Larry Shaw, "local trucking and paper industries appreciate our business."

387

Now Memphis has announced plans to develop a new "blue light" district, a colorful neighborhood of restaurants and nightclubs radiating out from W. C. Handy Park. As a first step, the city has passed an ordinance allowing the sale of liquor by the drink. Motel and hotel accommodations are expected to increase by some 5,000 over the next five years and there will be a new cluster of apartments at the end of Beale Street overlooking the Mississippi River.

Memphis is far from having solved all of its troubles, but after years of neglect black citizens and white citizens have at least started to cope with its problems. . . .

BORDER CITIES

Economic and Political Aspects

The following two documents together illustrate one of the present dilemmas of urban blacks: Though they have greater access to municipal political power (even when, as in the case of Baltimore, individual ambitions and ideological differences among blacks prevent its maximization), that access comes at a time when the economic base of the cities is weakened by the flight of the middle-class industries to the suburbs, as is strikingly the case in St. Louis.

St. Louis, Mo. (1968)

10]   Economic Troubles

The plight of the Negro poor is intertwined with a momentous change that has taken place in the economic functions of cities. Innovations in technology, transportation, and communication have undermined the traditional bases of urban economies. This undermining has weakened the cities' ability to provide industrial jobs, and to cope with the costs that the presence of the poor imposes. The nature of the change can be seen with special clarity in St. Louis.

For more than a century, St. Louis' North Side has been the locale of the poor. Generations of immigrants—Irish, Germans, Italians, Russians, Poles— have crowded its dingy streets, raised children in its bleak tenements and row-houses and ultimately, as their lot improved, moved out.

Today the North Side (or more precisely, the Near North Side) is inhabited overwhelmingly by Negroes, immigrants from the worn-out farms of the American South. Their conditions—poverty, crime, widespread illiteracy, disease, high infant mortality—are not much different from those of their predecessors, but their chances of following the old routes out of the North Side are

SOURCE: William S. Rukeyser, "The St. Louis Economic Blues," *The Negro and the City*, adapted from a special issue of *Fortune* on: "Business and the Urban Crisis," New York: Time-Life Books, Inc. 1968, pp. 96–103.

radically worse. Racial discrimination dims their prospects, of course; but perhaps even more significant is that the Negroes' predominance on the North Side has coincided with a far-reaching economic shuffle that has crippled St. Louis' ability to put them to work.

The situation is blurred by statistics that lump together growing and declining sections of the metropolitan area. For example, manufacturing employment in the St. Louis metropolitan area rose about 5 percent between 1959 and 1965. But this figure embraces two opposite trends. In St. Louis County over that span of years, manufacturing employment rose 42 percent; in the city, it *declined* 6 percent.

The contrast between core and hinterland is unusually pronounced in the St. Louis area because that city's boundaries were permanently fixed a long time ago. St. Louis has been fenced in, restricted to its current sixty-two square miles, ever since 1876, when the city shortsightedly cut itself free from the adjoining 497 square miles of St. Louis County. Back then, St. Louis had small reason to fear the consequences of going it alone. The city had been thriving since the days when its warehouses outfitted the pioneers, and its location on the Mississippi River seemed to guarantee its continued economic vitality. ("St. Louis," says a local real-estate developer, "was a well-developed commercial center when Chicago was a cow pastrue.")

Through most of its history, St. Louis County was quiet, thinly populated territory, economically dependent on the city. But in the years since World War II the county has outstripped the city in population, taken over the metropolitan area's fastest-growing industries, and built its busiest new shopping centers. The county seat, Clayton, has even become competitive with downtown St. Louis as a site for high-rise office buildings and apartments.

A quarter of a million people, virtually all of them whites, have moved out of St. Louis since 1950. Even with a large increase in the number of Negro residents over those seventeen years, the city's population has shrunk from 857,000 to under 700,000. By January, 1968, almost two out of five St. Louisans were Negroes, more than double the 1950 proportion. The whites who have moved out have included a large share of the city's better-educated and more prosperous people. The Negroes who have moved in have been generally ill-educated and poor.

Despite the population decline, a visitor to the central business district near the Mississippi River might conclude that St. Louis remains as economically vibrant as ever. The infusion of half a billion dollars of public and private money has transformed some of the more depressing downtown areas over the last decade. Along streets where grimy loft buildings and senile hotels once caused passing businessmen to yearn for suburbia, glassy office and apartment towers now cluster near Eero Saarinen's Gateway Arch and the new $29-million Busch Stadium. Recent additions to the skyline include a cylindrical riverfront hotel, a balconied office building, and the concrete shell of Pet Inc.'s new fifteen-story national headquarters.

Even away from the river, St. Louis still has the look and feel of a working town. Its factories churn out a myriad of goods ranging from potato chips to artillery shells. A two-story General Motors plant stretching for three blocks along Union Boulevard assembles more Chevrolets than any other facility in the world. On the South Side's Pestalozzi Street, the pungent odors of beer-making still waft from the massive red-brick headquarters plant of the nation's largest brewer, Anheuser-Busch.

But the office buildings provide few jobs for the unskilled, and the big factories are less numerous than they used to be. Since the early 1950's, manufacturing employment in the city has declined by about one-quarter. Many former manufacturing plants stand vacant, forlornly decaying.

The decline of industry in the city has been a bitter development for the North Side, where a survey found unemployment running above 12 percent late in 1966. Expanding employment in the county has provided relatively few jobs for city dwellers. At its huge plant seventeen miles from the North Side, McDonnell Douglas, by far the biggest employer in the metropolitan area, has actively recruited and trained St. Louis Negroes. But though McDonnell's work force has swelled from 22,000 to 42,000 since 1960, the company still employs fewer than 5,000 St. Louisans. The proportion of city residents on the payroll has actually slumped since 1960, from 17 to 12 percent.

One employment obstacle for North Side people is the lack of direct public transportation to where the suburban jobs are. It takes as much as two hours, and three buses, to get from the North Side to the McDonnell plant. With the help of a federal grant, the city planned to start a direct bus service in 1968, probably from the North Side to the McDonnell area. But the number of industrial jobs out there for unskilled and semiskilled city people is much smaller than the number of unemployed North Siders. Scattered around in the suburbs are quite a few service jobs that North Siders could fill, but the wages are generally not high enough to make up for the long trip.

For North Siders, the drop in city industrial jobs has not been offset by an expansion of other employment in the city. In the kinds of jobs accessible to them, the picture is grim. For example, some 7,600 positions in retail and wholesale trade evaporated between 1959 and 1966 as competition from the suburbs cut sales in St. Louis; retail sales declined by around 10 percent during those years.

The national trend toward white-collar employment and away from unskilled and semiskilled industrial jobs is even more evident in the older cities than in the rest of the country. Yet because low-income families can normally command only the most obsolete, undesirable housing, they must continue to live in cities. The incongruous result is that white-collar jobs for suburbanites become more plentiful in cities while jobs for unskilled and semiskilled city dwellers become scarcer. Unemployed St. Louis Negroes can mull the paradox as they watch the rush-hour commuter jams on the Mark Twain Expressway, which skirts the North Side slums on its way to St. Louis County.

St. Louis' leaders believe it is evident that their problems demand a reuniting of city and county, and they seem impatient with the coolness of voters, particularly those in the suburbs, toward the idea. "Before we can really go forward as we should," says Raymond R. Tucker, a former mayor of St. Louis, "we need metropolitan, regional government in the area. The interests of the county and the city are not basically opposed. They are identical."

391

Few suburbanites see it that way. Many enjoy boasting that they rarely have any call to go to the city any more. To them, the interests of the city and the county seem not identical but opposed. They want their borders carefully sealed against any importation of St. Louis' social and economic maladies. Samuel Bernstein, head of the city's business development commission, complains, "There seems to be a Mason-Dixon line—and at times a Maginot line—between the city and county."

On its own, St. Louis does not have the resources to cope with the problems of the North Side and other poor areas. Median family income in St. Louis County is about 40 percent higher than in St. Louis, but while the city government collected an average of $254 annually from its residents through taxes and other charges in fiscal 1966, the per capita tax bill in the county was only $153. Despite its smaller tax bite, the county had sufficient funds to outspend the city by a wide margin on schools—$117 per capita against the city's $86.

Skimping on education is a recipe for perpetuating poverty, but St. Louis has little choice. Its revenues, hard-won through tax rates that provide one more reason for businesses to leave town, are disproportionately committed to a whole range of public services linked to poverty, crime, and dilapidation. On health and hospitals, for example, the city spent $34 per capita in 1966, the county $8. For police protection the figures were $32 and $10; for fire protection, $13 and $6.

Far from using its powers to ease the city's financial squeeze, the Missouri state government worsens it. A recent study carried out for the city government indicated that Missouri gets almost a quarter of its revenues from St. Louis, but that only about one-eighth of state expenditures flow back to the city. So the city increasingly relies on the federal government for help. Federal outlays in St. Louis run in the vicinity of $575 million a year.

St. Louis is doing everything it can think of to reverse the decline of industry. To encourage companies considering a St. Louis location, the city government offers advice on sites and, often, generous tax abatements. In December, 1967, the Board of Aldermen established an industrial-expansion authority with power to issue tax-exempt bonds and condemn blighted property for industrial sites.

However, it is almost certainly futile for St. Louis, or any major city, to base its hopes for the future on attracting a lot of large factories. The city government, sensibly, is relying on its incentives chiefly to keep existing businesses from leaving. To many manufacturers, including some of the biggest employers, the benefits of being adjacent to a large pool of untrained labor are questionable, while the efficiency of operating spread-out one-story factories on suburban acreage is clear. Furthermore, the city's traditional assets of central location and access to rail and river transportation have been devalued by superhighways and electronic communications.

In the long run, St. Louis may come to view the retreat of noisy factories and fuming trailer-trucks as a disguised boon. The city already has strengths as a center of office employment and recreational and cultural activities. Building on these strengths might provide a more promising channel for municipal energies than competing with the suburbs for industrial plants. By working to make itself a more attractive environment for middle-class people, as well as for non-industrial enterprises, the city might begin to lure back some of the people whose move to the suburbs has been a reluctant reaction to urban blight. Their return would stimulate retail trade and service industries, and fortify the cultural life of the city too.

The North Side, however, does not fit into this vision of a possible future. A continuing substitution of white-collar for blue-collar jobs does not promise any great widening of employment opportunities for North Side people. And their poverty hobbles the city. Welfare and other services to the poor drain away resources that the city could otherwise invest in public facilities and services to make itself a more appealing place for suburban people to visit, shop in, and perhaps even move to. St. Louis needs a decongestion of economic liabilities as well as an expansion of assets.

Many people who have thought about the matter, in St. Louis and elsewhere, would agree in a general way with the view expressed by Father Lucius Cervantes, a Jesuit sociologist and brother of St. Louis' present mayor. "The answer," he says, "is to disperse the ghetto. Jobs are in a ring around the city. Allow the poor to follow the jobs." Father Cervantes has some ideas, possibly a bit quixotic, on how that might be accomplished: "Scatter the sites of public housing. With rent subsidies, move a Negro family into one house in each block in the suburbs."

If a cross-migration could come about, with some middle-class whites moving back to the cities they work in and some Negroes moving out to the suburbs to live and work, it would be possible to discern a less clouded future for St. Louis—as well as a less crowded future for the Mark Twain Expressway. Perhaps this is the direction of hope, for St. Louis and other cities too. But nothing like this can be expected, on a scale large enough to matter, without some new political arrangements. The power of the city stops at that 1876 boundary, and the county beyond wants nothing less than an inflow of Negroes from the city.

Some overarching authority would be required to open up the suburbs to large numbers of Negroes—perhaps some kind of metropolitan government imposed, or at least fostered, by state intervention. It is not a good bet that effective new arrangements will emerge any time soon. Yet unless things move in that direction, it is hard to see any future for St. Louis—and by inference many other U.S. cities—except deepening economic blues.

Baltimore, Md. (1971)

11]   Blacks in Politics

In the municipal elections of 1967 and the statewide elections of 1970 blacks in Baltimore successfully launched an unprecedented campaign to elect black

SOURCE: "Baltimore," *Black Enterprise*, November 1971, pp. 40–42.

officials to seats never before held by blacks. Joseph C. Howard became that city's first elected black Judge of the Supreme Bench; Milton B. Allen became the nations's only black States Attorney; Paul L. Chester was elected Clerk of the Court of Common Pleas, defeating a white opponent who had held the post for 25 years, and Parren J. Mitchell became Maryland's first black U.S. Representative by wresting the state's 7th Congressional District seat from Samuel N. Friedel, who had held it 18 years.

The victories came as a record number of blacks, more than at any time in the city's 242-year history, ran for public office. Representation on the state level increased as two more senators and five delegates were elected to both houses for a total of 17 blacks; four senators and 13 members of the House of Delegates and a majority in the Baltimore delegation. Black Baltimoreans were especially proud of this fact since blacks held no public office prior to 1955. Buoyed by these successful efforts other blacks were encouraged to seek the city's highest political offices: those of mayor, president of the city council and city comptroller, in the 1971 Fall primary. But in a larger sense it was demographic destiny that brought blacks into competition for the top municipal slots. Baltimore's black population increased over the past 10 years by just under 100,000, but this absolute growth coupled with the continuing exodus of white Baltimoreans to the surrounding suburbs resulted in a city population that was over 45 per cent black in 1970. In fact, long before the 1970 census was begun demographers and political experts alike predicted that 1972 would be the year that this immaculate city on the Chesapeake Bay would join Cleveland, Newark and Gary, Ind., as major American cities with black mayors.

However, cloakroom maneuvers and public denunciations failed to reduce the three-man field of black candidates to a possible shoo-in favorite son after everybody's choice, incumbent Mayor Thomas J. D'Alesandro, threw the race wide open by declaring he would not run for a second term in office. However, George L. Russell, the first candidate to declare himself, was thought to have had the best chance for victory.

A practiced politico who had served as a Supreme Bench judge, Russell had enough establishment contacts to gain appointment as City Solicitor in 1969. But while Russell had gained strong business and political ties as solicitor, it was felt that his basic weakness was a lack of rapport with grass roots people.

Another black hopeful was seasoned vote-getter State Senator Clarence M. Mitchell 3d, the 31-year-old minion of the city's powerful Mitchell family. The senator's father, Clarence Mitchell, Jr., is the Washington Bureau director for the NAACP, his mother Juanita is head of the Baltimore NAACP legal department and past president of the Maryland chapter. His grandmother, Lillie M. Jackson, is former president of the Baltimore NAACP chapter, and his uncle is Congressman Mitchell.

The third black candidate was William E. Roberts, an insurance broker who was relatively unknown until 1970 when he waged an admirable but unsuccessful campaign against Marvin Mandel in the race for governor. Roberts polled some 25,000 votes, a surprisingly good showing.

· · · · · ·

Blacks in Politics

All three men, each declaring himself to be the best choice, refused to withdraw and all three were defeated by City Council President William Donald Schaefer. And that was only part of the debacle.

Most of the blacks who sought lower offices in this primary also lost. Of the 21 blacks listed on the ballot only seven were nominated. Indeed, one of the blacks vying for seats on the City Council, Mary Adams, was nominated, and she defeated a black incumbent, Robert C. Marshall. All other incumbents were returned to office.

The surprising outcome has become the topic of speculation by armchair analysts and professionals alike. Why, they wondered, in this city of nearly one million people with its 474,000 registered voters evenly split racially, did blacks fail to capture a single city-wide post, even with a 41 per cent voter turnout (generally considered to be good)?

. . . . .

Perhaps the most acceptable theory behind the rout of the black office seekers is that no significant attack against Schaefer could be mounted. The odds-on favorite among the white aspirants had rarely antagonized blacks during his City Council tenure. In addition, he ran a rather mild primary campaign, leaving the mudslinging to others in the field. The strategy obviously paid off. When the votes were tabulated Schaefer had won with a plurality of 94,809 votes while Russell received 58,223, Mitchell 6,582 and Roberts 1,000. Nothing is so clear here than the fact that had Russell or Mitchell received all the votes for all the black candidates it would only come to 66,805, a figure 28,004 less than Schaefer's total. . . .

NORTHEASTERN CITIES

Political and Social Aspects

The documents below look on the brighter side of black urban life. The first rejects the commonly held thesis that the ghetto is pathological with "resentment, hostility, despair, apathy, self-depreciation . . ."; [1] it sees Harlemites as essentially cosmopolitan, stylish, and elegant. The second document describes the resourceful and rival political leadership of Harlem; while the third points to successful black economic initiatives in Philadelphia.

New York, N.Y. (1967)

12] Harlem's Positive Image

Mass media images of contemporary Harlem reveal only a part of the actual texture of the lives of the people who inhabit that vast, richly varied, infinitely complex, and endlessly fascinating area of uptown Manhattan. Those who create such images almost always restrict themselves to documenting the pathological. Thus not only do they almost always proceed in terms of the liabilities of Harlem but what they record more often than not also leaves the entirely incredible but somehow widely accepted impression that there are no negotiable assets of any immediate significance there at all.

But not only do the human resources of Harlem exceed the liabilities, even the existing material assets and possibilities do. There are thousands of run-down, poverty-ridden, vermin-infested tenements in Harlem which have long been unfit for human habitation and which are not only overpriced but also overcrowded. But even so, far from being one sprawling and teeming network of endless shambles, Harlem is an industry-free, ideally situated residential area with broad avenues and well-planned streets, and the convenience of its trans-

SOURCE: Albert H. Murray, "Image and Unlikeness in Harlem," *The Urban Review*, June 1967, pp. 12–17. [Albert H. Murray is a historian and urbanist.—Ed.]
[1] Kenneth Clark, *Dark Ghetto*, New York: Harper & Row, 1965, p. 11.

portation facilities is unexcelled by any other residential community in Manhattan. Nor do many other areas match the charm and elegance of its architecture. (Some of the least interesting buildings in Harlem, such as those in Delano Village near where the Savoy used to be, were constructed comparatively recently. They provide modest urgently needed comfort but little else.)

There may or may not be such a thing as a Moynihan Report image finder, a *Dark Ghetto* image finder, and so on, but there most certainly are focused viewpoints that exclude almost everything except that which substantiates Moynihan's Victorian notions about broken homes, Clark's (self-excepted) descriptions of black powerlessness and black self-hatred, and various pop art constructions of juvenile delinquency and uptown camp. But what is there to see if one lifts away these blinders?

Much has been made of the Harlem dweller's response to rats, discrimination, and poverty (but no more, incidentally, than Richard Wright made of Bigger Thomas' response to the same rats and the same discrimination and poverty in the Chicago of *Native Son*). What most observers almost always seem to be unaware of for some strange reason, however, is the incontestable fact that Negroes in Harlem, like those elsewhere, also respond to beauty, style, and elegance—even as their wonderful ancestors found delight in the magnolias and honeysuckles, the crepe myrtles and cape jasmines, the terrain, the fabulous thickets, woodland streams, and verdant hillsides, the gourd vines and trellis work near the cabins, the graceful lines of plantation mansions and even the deep richness of the soil they tilled during the darkest and most oppressive days of slavery.

It is true that most people in Harlem have little interest for articles in, say, *Vogue* or *House Beautiful* about the grillework on wrought iron gates, the ornamental griffins, period-piece bay windows, splendid archways, and charming courtyards to be found in the area. But after all, there are other and perhaps better ways of responding to such things. One can assimilate them, for instance, and simply live in terms of them, which is largely what they were made for in the first place. Obviously, there is much to be said for the conscious cultivation and extension of taste, but there is also something to be said for the functional reaction to artistic design (and honeysuckles) as normal elements of human existence. And there is, of course, also quite a bit to be said against fastidiousness and academic pretentiousness. (Not that Harlem can't use all the art history it can get.)

As James Weldon Johnson noted years ago, not very many New Yorkers in other parts of town seem to have as much involvement with their immediate neighborhoods as do the people of Harlem. Nor is the Harlemite's involvement a mark of oppression. It is a mark of openness. Most other New Yorkers seem to spend so much of their time hustling from one interior to another that they don't ever seem to see very much of their affluent and antiseptic neighborhoods except on the run, and they seem to see even less of the neighbors whose status locations they pay such high rents to share. On the other hand, weather permitting, the sidewalks and the brownstone doorways and steps of most of the streets of Harlem always hum and buzz with people in familiar contact with other people. The need for better housing and more adequate

397

community services in Harlem is a national scandal, but what many Harlemites do with what they have is often marvelous all the same.

The life style of Harlem Negroes of all levels, in fact, goes with the very best aesthetic features not only of Harlem but of New York at large. Harlem Negroes do not act like the culturally deprived people of the statistical surveys but like cosmopolites. Many may be indigent but few are square. They walk and even stand like people who are elegance-oriented. They talk like people who are eloquence-oriented. They dress like people who like high fashion and like to be surrounded by fine architecture. The average good barber shop and tailor shop in Harlem is geared to a level of sartorial sophistication that is required only from the best elsewhere. There is no telling what outside image makers think of the amount of formal wear sold and rented in Harlem, but one thing it suggests is that many of the social affairs sponsored by Harlemites scintillate. Not even the worst dressers in Harlem are indifferent to high fashion. They are overcommitted to it!

It is very curious indeed that at a time when Harlem Negroes encounter fewer restrictions, exercise more political power, earn more money, and have more involvements elsewhere than ever before, media reporters (following a writer like Clark) describe them as denizens of a ghetto, who are all but completely ostracized from the mainstream of American life—which media reporters refer to as the white world. The term ghetto does not apply to Harlem, if indeed it applies to any segregated housing area in the United States. Perhaps it applies to this or that Chinatown. It *does not* and *never has* applied to segregated areas where U.S. Negroes live. The overwhelming majority of the residents of Harlem, along with most other native-born U.S. Negroes, are part-white Anglo-Saxon Protestants, and Southern at that, with all the racial as well as cultural ramifications that this implies. Harlem contains a vast network of slum areas which are an ambitious social worker's absolute delight, but Harlem itself is no ghetto at all. No matter how rotten with racial bigotry the New York housing situation is, it is grossly misleading to imply in any way that the daily involvements, interests, and aspirations of Negroes are thereby restricted to the so-called black community.

Harlem Negroes are New Yorkers. (The mainstream is not white but mulatto.) Harlemites have their special cultural distinctions, as do New Yorkers who live in the Bronx, Queens, Greenwich Village and so on, but a Harlem Negro looking down Fifth Avenue from Mt. Morris Park is not nearly so cut off from the center of things as the word ghetto implies. He is looking toward midtown and downtown, where most people in Harlem work, and he feels as intimately involved with Macy's, Gimbels, Saks, and Bloomingdale's as his income and his credit card will allow. He, like most people in Harlem, is also aware that midtown is, among other things, Lena Horne at the Waldorf, Ella Fitzgerald at the Royal Box, Diahann Carroll at the Plaza, Jackie Wilson at the Copa, Count Basie at the Riverboat, and a wide choice of Negro prizefight champions and basketball players at Madison Square Garden. Nor is Leontyne [Price] without uptown followers—and competitors. The Harlem Negro knows very well that there are uptown lawyers and judges in the downtown courts, and that the Manhattan Borough President is almost always a Negro.

After all, he probably helped to put him (or her) there. Segregation in New York is bad enough, but it just isn't what it used to be. The national headquarters of the NAACP is at 57th street on Broadway, and the office of the NAACP Legal Defense Fund is at Columbus Circle.

But what useful purpose is really served by confusing segregated housing in the U.S. with the way Jewish life was separated from the gentile world in the days of the old ghettos? After all, in addition to physical segregation, the real ghettos also represented profound differences in religion, language, food customs, and were even geared to a different calendar. It is grossly misleading to suggest that segregated housing anywhere in the United States represents a cultural distance that is in any way at all comparable to the one that separated a Jewish ghetto from the life styles of various European countries.

Duke Ellington, whose music encompasses at least as much of the flesh and blood reality of life in the United States as do books like *An American Dilemma*, was well aware of the widespread hunger and filth and crime and political frustration in Harlem as long ago as when he wrote "Harlem Airshaft" (he had already written "The Mooch"), and so was William Strayhorn when he wrote "Take the A Train." But Ellington and Strayhorn and most of the other Harlem musicians, including the old rent party piano players, were—and still are—also aware of something else: that Harlem for all its liabilities generates an atmosphere that stimulates people-to-people good times which are second to none anywhere in the world. (Life in Paris is better celebrated in story but not in song and dance.)

The music of Harlem makes people all over the world want to dance. It makes the rich, the poor, the powerful and weak alike clap their hands and tap their foot in celebration of the sheerest joy of human existence itself. Not only that, but it disposes them toward affirmation and continuity even as, with the blues, it reminds them of their infernal complexity. (Incidentally, musicians and athletes are far more numerous, more symbolic, and more influential in Harlem than are the criminals and addicts.)

Images of Harlem that could have been derived only from the current fad in psychopolitical gossip about Negro self-hatred, only serve to charge an atmosphere already at the point of explosion. The system of racial exclusion in employment forces most people in Harlem to function far below their minimum potential even as it enables recently arrived white immigrants with no better qualifications than Harlemites to exceed their wildest dreams. Not even the most degenerate rituals of the South are more infuriating to multigeneration U.S. Negroes than the pompous impertinence of those European refugees who were admitted to the U.S. on preferential quotas, who benefit by preferential treatment because of the color system, and who then presume to make condescending insinuations about the lack of initiative, self-help, and self-pride among Negroes.

Meanwhile the least that is required of those who would help Harlem achieve its aspirations (some of which may very well be higher than many of those held in the most self-satisfied and self-restricted white communities and which are, if anything, even better for the nation at large than for Negroes) is that they disentangle themselves from the folklore of condescension and ap-

proach the people of Harlem with the attitude that good photographers seem
to take when they aim their cameras at the streets and the buildings.

New York, N.Y. (1970)

13]   Leadership in Harlem

"Who runs Harlem?" a question often asked during times of controversies
there, could better be asked, "Who runs 'what' in Harlem?"

For like all communities of its size, complexity, and history, Harlem is
moved by numerous interests and individuals with a variety of skills, styles,
commitment and effectiveness.

Congressman Adam Clayton Powell had been, until recently,[1] the all but in-
vincible political leader, and Manhattan Borough President Percy E. Sutton
appears to be the man who will replace him.

Mr. Sutton has patched up political differences with some other Harlem politicians and is generally seen as the leader of the best organized political force.

    .   .   .   .   .

Sidney von Luther, the 45-year-old State Senator-elect in Harlem, contends
that "the community is now in the midst of a political vacuum.

"The Powell machine is disintegrating, and the old-line politicians are not
able to pick up the pieces. Sutton is the only emerging political leader of significance here—the only man able to touch bases with all forces."

But leadership in Harlem stems not only from the organized political process
but also from religious, social and civic organizations and social activism.
Those most often identified as influencing the dynamics of Harlem include:

Jesse Gray, the leader of the rent strike, who has maintained considerable
influence over the years by articulating the needs and aspirations of the poor
and of the young in Harlem's Tenants Union and the Back Street Youth organizations.

A forceful speaker capable of swaying large crowds, Mr. Gray has proven an
imaginative activist. He has, however, lost every attempt to gain political office.

Livingston L. Wingate, the controversial head of the New York Urban
League and former director of Haryou-Act, who has most often taken the more
militant side of community issues and personally bridged wide philosophical
gaps between various Harlem schools of thought.

Mr. Wingate, an expert in labor law, was an aide to Mr. Powell for many
years.

Roy Innis, national director of the Congress of Racial Equality, which is

SOURCE: Thomas A. Johnson, "Power in Harlem Emanates from Many Bases," *The
New York Times*, December 6, 1970. [Thomas A. Johnson is a prominent black journalist now with *The New York Times.*—Ed.]
[1] Powell died April 4, 1972, at age 63.

400

headquartered in Harlem. He helped to develop the organization's black nationalist thrust. Mr. Innis was one of the first to advocate community control of schools and other public institutions. He was also a leader in the fight to open the Haryou-Act board of directors to larger numbers of Harlemites.

State Senator Basil A. Paterson, who ran unsuccessfully as the Democratic-Liberal candidate for Lieutenant Governor this year. An articulate, hard-working lawyer, and a thorough researcher, Mr. Paterson emerged as a leader of black state legislators, and gained a reputation of being well-informed on a large number of Harlem and statewide issues.

L. Joseph Overton, business agent for Local 338 of the Retail, Wholesale and Chain Store Food Employes Union, who has been involved in many civic organizations over many years. An extroverted, gregarious man, Mr. Overton is widely liked by many poor residents whom he has helped to find jobs and disliked by some young militants with whom he has clashed.

Mrs. Cora T. Walker, a lawyer who won a case against the New York City Department of Buildings four years ago, proving that the department had made her a target for official abuse. A former vice-president of the National Bar Association, she helped organize the Harlem River Consumers Cooperative, which, she charged in a successful court action, Mr. Overton was trying to put out of business.

In the area of Harlem politics, Congressman-elect Charles Rangel, one of Mr. Powell's most vocal supporters in the past, is scheduled to take his place in Congress in January. . . .

. . . . . .

With Mr. Rangel, Mr. Sutton has put together an aggressive political organization of mostly nonprofessional politicians in the "Martin Luther King Democratic Club," which was formerly the "John F. Kennedy Democratic Club."

While several organizations have produced public personalities who have made names outside the Harlem community, few, if any, could equal the history of the Harlem branch of the National Association for the Advancement of Colored People. Former branch chairmen include Mr. Sutton, Mr. Paterson and Mr. Overton. And visitors to state N.A.A.C.P. functions have noted that the affairs are heavily attended by Harlem-based activists.

Both the Christian churches and other religious organizations have provided leaders for Harlem over the years.

The late Malcolm X came out of Elijah Muhammad's Temple No. 7. And the temple's current spiritual leader, Minister Louis Farrakhan, currently exhibits an influence among those young activists connected with and those far beyond the confines of the mosque.

The Harlem Yorubas, who practice the Orisha Vodun religion of West Africa, have influenced many youths to adopt Yoruba names, study the Yoruba language and wear clothing common to West Africa.

The late Marcus Garvey attained his greatest success for the concept of African nationalism in Harlem, and his followers continue to influence the dynamics of Harlem. Many of the more traditional religious and political leaders will attest to the impact of Mr. Garvey.

Organizations like the African Nationalist Activist Movement and the African Jazz-Art Society and Studios are among the principal nationalist groups currently influencing the Harlem community.

Disputes like the fight for control of the Haryou-Act board of directors and the controversy over the new state office building have served to uncover and project Harlemites of significant influence. Participants in these running fights often look like a "Who's Who" of Harlem activism.

Philadelphia, Pa. (1971)

14]   Black Economic Initiatives

The most effective organization headed by a black Philadelphian is that of Rev. Leon Sullivan's Opportunities Industrialization Center which trains and reeducates thousands of previously unemployed youths. Since its inception OIC has grown to include more than 100 branch offices around the country and in Africa. It is a self-help program which Rev. Sullivan founded when he became fed up with the fact that for more than 100 years black Americans "have been outside the door of full opportunity of enterprise. We will move through that door," he declared, "by training, preparing, building and producing. We will prove to all Americans that all genius is color-blind."

The fiery pastor of Philadelphia's Mt. Zion Baptist Church predicts that during the decade of the '70s OIC will train one million Americans. These trainees, he said, "will earn $100 billion and will save governmental agencies about $24 million in relief revenues."

How close OIC will come to fulfilling that prediction is evidenced by the dozens of youthful inner-city workers trained as service station attendants, office machine operators and clerks by OIC.

Another Philadelphian who has made a mark on the black business community is Herman Wrice, President of the Young Great Society. A former gang leader, Wrice has probably done as much as any other individual at the local level toward helping young blacks to develop business interests and capabilities.

The Young Great Society has initiated several businesses which are profitable both in terms of dollars and sense. Wrice has convinced many gangfighters that they, too, have a stake in their community. So now, a number of past street warriors are working for YGS, operating moving companies, exterminating companies, and construction operations.

Minority businessmen are now operating businesses in a variety of fields in Philadelphia. Blacks in real estate are numerous. In addition, blacks operate funeral homes, cemeteries, gas stations, food chains, construction companies, insurance companies, and at least one data processing company, as well as other businesses.

SOURCE: "City in Profile: Philadelphia," *Black Enterprise,* July 1971, pp. 21–23.

Black Economic Initiatives

Some minority firms are also operating in the aerospace industry.

R. C. Robinson is the general manager of Progress Aero Space Enterprises, Inc. He came to Philadelphia a year ago from California where he was president of NARTRANS Corp., which is a subsidiary of North American Rockwell, Inc. Rev. Leon Sullivan chose Robinson, 39, for his background in aerospace. In the past few years Progress Aero Space Enterprises has grown steadily with the help of a large contract from General Electric Missile and Space Division. The expansion of the company has increased committed orders from $1.6 million in 1970 to $2.3 million in 1971. The number of employees—many of whom are trained by OIC—has increased from 98 to 130.

. . . . .

. . . Responding to pressure exerted by both local and national black groups, the Federal government established the Philadelphia Plan to break down the barriers against minority members in the building trades. This program, which has met with limited success, attempts to insure that representative numbers of blacks are hired to work on Federally-funded construction jobs that cost more than $500,000.

Another, more successful effort is the Apprentice Outreach Program, devised by the Negro Trade Union Leadership Council. This program is funded by the U.S. Labor Department and has trained and placed more than 200 young black men in high-paying apprenticeships. . . .

NORTH CENTRAL CITIES

Political and Economic Aspects

More than in any other region, black leaders in the cities of the Midwest have gained national attention by confronting the difficult problems of urban life. [Document 15]. In 1967, after skillful and determined struggles, Richard Hatcher and Carl Stokes became respectively mayors of Gary and Cleveland [Document 16]. Hatcher is still mayor of Gary; Stokes retired when his second term ended in 1971. Necessarily reform-minded, they both proved to be efficient administrators and were reasonably successful in stemming the tide of decay in their cities. Another city of the Midwest, Chicago, provides the best examples of recent black business successes: the Johnson Publishing Company and Johnson's Products, a cosmetic firm [Document 17].

Detroit, Mich. (1967)

15]   Background for Violence

. . . Between 1960 and 1967 the Negro population [of Detroit] rose from just under 30 percent to an estimated 40 percent of the total.

In a decade the school system had gained 50,000 to 60,000 children. Fifty-one percent of the elementary school classes were overcrowded. Simply to achieve the statewide average, the system needed 1,650 more teachers and 1,000 additional classrooms. The combined cost would be $63 million.

Of 300,000 school children, 171,000, or 57 percent, were Negro. According to the Detroit Superintendent of Schools, 25 different school districts surrounding the city spent up to $500 more per pupil per year than Detroit. In the inner city schools, more than half the pupils who entered high school became dropouts.

. . . . .

SOURCE: *Report of the National Advisory Commission on Civil Disorders,* New York: Bantam Books, 1968, pp. 89–91.

Some unions, traditionally closed to Negroes, zealously guarded training opportunities. In January of 1967 the school system notified six apprenticeship trades it would not open any new apprenticeship classes unless a large number of Negroes were included. By fall, some of the programs were still closed.

High school diplomas from inner city schools were regarded by personnel directors as less than valid. In July, unemployment was at a five-year peak. In the 12th Street area it was estimated to be between 12 and 15 percent for Negro men and 30 percent or higher for those under 25.

The more education a Negro had, the greater the disparity between his income and that of a white with the same level of education. The income of whites and Negroes with a seventh grade education was about equal. The median income of whites with a high school diploma was $1,600 more per year than that of Negroes. White college graduates made $2,600 more. In fact, so far as income was concerned, it made very little difference to a Negro man whether he had attended school for 8 years or for 12. In the fall of 1967, a study conducted at one inner city high school, Northwestern, showed that, although 50 percent of the dropouts had found work, 90 percent of the 1967 graduating class was unemployed.

Mayor [Jerome] Cavanagh had appointed many Negroes to key positions in his administration, but in elective offices the Negro population was still underrepresented. Of nine councilmen, one was a Negro. Of seven school board members, two were Negroes.

Although federal programs had brought nearly $360 million to the city between 1962 and 1967, the money appeared to have had little impact at the grassroots. Urban renewal, for which $38 million had been allocated, was opposed by many residents of the poverty area.

Because of its financial straits, the city was unable to produce on promises to correct such conditions as poor garbage collection and bad street lighting, which brought constant complaints from Negro residents.

Cleveland, Ohio, and Gary, Ind. (1968)

16]   Two Black Mayors

Throughout most of 1967, black power and Vietnam kept this nation in an almost continual state of crisis. The summer months were the longest and hottest in modern U.S. history—many political analysts even felt that the nation was entering its most serious domestic conflict since the Civil War. Over a hundred cities were rocked with violence.

As the summer gave way to autumn, the interest of the nation shifted a little from the summer's riots to the elections on the first Tuesday of November. An unprecedented number of Negroes were running for office, but public atten-

SOURCE: Jeffrey K. Hadden, Louis H. Masotti, and Victor Thiessen, "The Making of the Negro Mayors 1967," *Trans-Action*, January/February 1968, pp. 21–30.

tion focused on their elections. In Cleveland, Carl B. Stokes, a lawyer who in 1962 had become the first Democratic Negro legislator in Ohio, was now seeking to become the first Negro mayor of a large American city. In Gary, Ind., another young Negro lawyer, Richard D. Hatcher, was battling the Republican Party's candidate—as well as his own Democratic Party—to become the first Negro mayor of a "medium-sized" city. . . .

Normally, the nation couldn't care less about who would become the next mayors of Cleveland [and] Gary. . . . But the tenseness of the summer months gave these elections enormous significance. If Stokes and Hatcher lost . . . could Negroes be persuaded to use the power of the ballot box rather than the power of fire bombs?

Fortunately, November 7 proved to be a triumphant day for racial peace. Stokes and Hatcher won squeaker victories, both by margins of only about 1500 votes. . . .

．．．．．．

CLEVELAND

By early 1967, the city Cleveland had seemingly hit rock bottom. A long procession of reporters began arriving to write about its many problems. The racial unrest of the past several years had, during the summer of 1966, culminated in the worst rioting in Cleveland's history. This unrest was continuing to grow as several militant groups were organizing. Urban renewal was a dismal failure; in January, the Department of Housing and Urban Development even cut off the city's urban-renewal funds, the first such action by the Federal Government. The exodus of whites, along with business, shoved the city to the brink of financial disaster. In February, the Moody Bond Survey reduced the city's credit rating. In May, the Federal Government cut off several million dollars of construction funds—because the construction industry had failed to assure equal job opportunities for minority groups. In short, the city was . . . in deep trouble. And while most ethnic groups probably continued to believe that Cleveland was the "Best Location in the Nation," the Negro community —and a growing number of whites—were beginning to feel that Cleveland was the "Mistake on the Lake," and that it was time for a change.

Carl Stokes's campaign for mayor was his second try. In 1965, while serving in the state House of Representatives, he came within 2100 votes of defeating Mayor Ralph S. Locher. Stokes had taken advantage of a city-charter provision that let a candidate file as an independent and bypass the partisan primaries. Ralph McAllister had earned the enmity of the Negro community. The Republican candidate was Ralph Perk, the first Republican elected to a county-wide position (auditor) in many years. A second-generation Czech-Bohemian, Perk hoped to win by combining his ethnic appeals with his program for the city (Perk's Plan). He had no opposition for his party's nomination. The fourth candidate was Mayor Locher, who had defeated Mark McElroy, county recorder and perennial candidate for something, in the Democratic primary.

It was in the 1965 Democratic primary that the first signs of a "black bloc" vote emerged. The Negroes, who had previously supported incumbent Democratic mayoral candidates, if not enthusiastically at least consistently, made a concerted effort to dump Locher in favor of McElroy. There were two reasons.

Two Black Mayors

• Locher had supported his police chief after the latter had made some tactless remarks about Negroes. Incensed Negro leaders demanded an audience with the mayor, and when he refused, his office was the scene of demonstrations, sit-ins, and arrests. At that point, as one of the local reporters put it, "Ralph Locher became a dirty name in the ghetto."

• Stokes, as an independent, and his supporters hoped that the Democratic primary would eliminate the *stronger* candidate, Locher. For then a black bloc would have a good chance of deciding the general election because of an even split in the white vote.

Despite the Negro community's efforts, Locher won the primary and went on to narrowly defeat Stokes. Locher received 37 percent of the vote, Stokes 36 percent, Perk 17 percent, and McAllister 9 percent. Some observers reported that a last-minute whispering campaign in Republican precincts—to the effect that "A vote for Perk is a vote for Stokes"—may have given Locher enough Republican votes to win. The evidence: The popular Perk received only a 17 percent vote in a city where a Republican could be expected to receive something closer to 25 percent. Had Perk gotten anything close to 25 percent, Stokes would have probably been elected two years earlier.

Although he made a strong showing in defeat, Carl Stokes's political future looked bleak. No one expected the Democratic leaders to give Stokes another opportunity to win by means of a split vote. Nor were there other desirable elected offices Stokes could seek. Cleveland has no Negro Congressman [1] largely because the heavy Negro concentration in the city has been "conveniently" gerrymandered. The only district where Stokes might have had a chance has been represented by Charles Vanik, a popular and liberal white, and as long as Vanik remained in Congress Stokes was locked out. Stokes's state Senate district was predominantly white; and a county or state office seemed politically unrealistic because of his race. So, in 1966, Stokes sought re-election to the State House unopposed.

Between 1965 and 1967, Cleveland went from bad to worse, physically, socially, and financially. With no other immediate possibilities, Stokes began to think about running for mayor again. . . .

    . . . . .

The first part of his strategy was a massive voter-reigstration drive in the Negro wards—to reinstate the potential Stokes voters dropped from the rolls for failing to vote since the 1964 Presidential election. The Stokes organization —aided by Martin Luther King Jr. and the Southern Christian Leadership Conference, as well as by a grant (in part earmarked for voter registration) from the Ford Foundation to the Cleveland chapter of CORE—did succeed in registering many Negroes. But there was a similar drive mounted by the Democratic Party on behalf of Locher. (Registration figures are not available by race.)

The second part of the Stokes strategy took him across the polluted Cuyahoga River into the white wards that had given him a mere 3 percent of the vote in 1965. He spoke wherever he would be received—to small groups in

[1] In 1969 Louis Stokes, brother of Carl, was elected the first black Congressman from Ohio.

private homes, in churches, and in public and private halls. While he was not always received enthusiastically, he did not confront many hostile crowds. He faced the race issue squarely and encouraged his audience to judge him on his ability.

Stokes's campaign received a big boost when the *Plain Dealer*, the largest daily in Ohio, endorsed him. Next, the *Cleveland Press* called for a change in City Hall. . . .

More people voted in this primary than in any other in Cleveland's history. When the ballots were counted, Stokes had 52.5 percent of the votes—he had defeated Locher by a plurality of 18,000 votes. Celeste [2] was the man in the middle, getting only 4 percent of the votes, the lowest of any mayoral candidate in recent Cleveland history.

What produced Stokes's clear victory? . . . The decisive factor was the size of the Negro turnout. While Negroes constituted only about 40 percent of the voters, 73.4 percent of them turned out, compared with only 58.4 percent of the whites. . . .

. . . . .

Stokes emerged from the primary as the odds-on favorite to win—five weeks later—in the general election. And in the first few days of the campaign, it seemed that Stokes had everything going for him.

—Stokes was bright, handsome, and articulate. His opponent Seth Taft, while bright, had never won an election, and his family name, associated with the Taft-Hartley Act, could hardly be an advantage among union members. In addition, he was shy and seemingly uncomfortable in a crowd.

—Both the *Plain Dealer* and the *Cleveland Press* endorsed Stokes in the general election.

—The wounds of the primary were quickly (if perhaps superficially) healed, and the Democratic candidate was endorsed by both the Democratic Party and Mayor Locher.

—Labor—both the A.F.L.–C.I.O. and the Teamsters—also endorsed Stokes.

—He had a partisan advantage. Of the 326,003 registered voters, only 34,000 (10 percent) were Republican. . . .

—Stokes had 90,000 or more Negro votes virtually assured, with little possibility that Taft would make more than slight inroads.

THE GARY RACE

The race for mayor in Gary, Ind., was not overtly racist. Still, the racial issue was much less stable than it was in Cleveland. When Democratic chairman John G. Krupa refused to support Richard D. Hatcher, the Democratic candidate, it was clear that the reason was race. When the Gary newspaper failed to give similar coverage to both candidates and sometimes failed to print news releases from Hatcher headquarters (ostensibly because press deadlines had not been met), it was clear that race was a factor.

Even though race was rarely mentioned openly, the city polarized. While Stokes had the support of the white-owned newspapers and many white campaign workers, many of Hatcher's white supporters preferred to remain in the

[2] Frank P. Celeste, former mayor of Cleveland's east side suburb of Lakewood.

background—in part, at least, because they feared reprisals from white racists. Hatcher didn't use the black-power slogan, but to the community the election was a contest between black and white. And when the Justice Department supported Hatcher's claim that the election board had illegally removed some 5000 Negro voters from the registration lists and added nonexistent whites, the tension in the city became so great that the Governor, feeling that there was "imminent danger" of violence on election night, called up 4000 National Guardsmen.

Negroes constitute an estimated 55 percent of Gary's 180,000 residents, but white voter registration outnumbers Negroes by 2000 or 3000. Like Stokes, Hatcher—in order to win—had to pull some white votes, or have a significantly higher Negro turnout.

The voter turnout and voting patterns in Cleveland and Gary were very similar. In both cities, almost 80 percent of the registered voters turned out at the polls. In the Glen Park and Miller areas, predominantly white neighborhoods, Joseph B. Radigan—Hatcher's opponent—received more than 90 percent of the votes. In the predominantly Negro areas, Hatcher received an estimated 93 percent of the votes. In all, Hatcher received about 4000 white votes, while losing probably 1000 Negro votes, at most, to Radigan. This relatively small white vote was enough to give him victory. . . .

Chicago, Ill. (1970)

17]   Black Businesses

. . . There is no denying that Chicago is a segregated city. Most of its 1,300,000 black residents, more than one-third of the city's population, live along a strip on Chicago's South Side. And on the West Side, the scene of three days of racial violence following the death of Dr. Martin Luther King, close to 400,000 residents, many of them newly arrived from the South, are crammed into a 15-square-mile corridor of two- and three-story brick dwellings.

Ironically, Chicago's segregated housing pattern is seen as being largely responsible for the steady growth of black business in the city in recent years. Chicago's Black Book Directory, a directory of black-owned and operated businesses, contains a listing of approximately 4,000 businesses, 80 per cent of which are black-owned with the remainder operated or managed by blacks.

It is an impressive list which includes the Johnson Publishing Company headed by John Johnson, publisher of *Ebony*, the largest black magazine in the country, as well as three other magazines. Also listed is Johnson Products, a cosmetics manufacturing firm headed by George Johnson (no relation to the *Ebony* publisher) that recently went public and is enjoying surprising success despite a dip in the market.

Other top drawer firms listed are the black-owned and operated $34 million

SOURCE: "Chicago," *Black Enterprise*, September 1970, pp. 38–42.

Supreme Life Insurance Company and the Chicago Metropolitan Mutual Assurance Company. Black Chicago also supports four newspapers, the *Chicago Daily Defender*, owned by John Sengstacke, the *Chicago Courier*, the *Black Liberator*, and *Muhammad Speaks*, published by the Black Muslim followers of Elijah Muhammad, which, many insist, is the most widely circulated black newspaper in the country.

Of the 25 black-owned automobile dealerships in the country, no fewer than five' of them are located in Chicago. Black Chicago also has two banks, the same number as four decades ago, the largest of which is Seaway National Bank, and three Savings and Loan Associations.

Recently, Dempsey Travis, president of Sivart Mortgage Corporation, the oldest and largest of the country's black mortgage banking firms, announced the formation of the 52-member United Mortgage Bankers of America, a predominantly black group of mortgage bankers who hope to garner a larger share of the mortgage banking industry.

. . . . .

It is no accident that members of Chicago's black business community are aggressively seeking a larger share of the marketplace. They chafe at the knowledge that although blacks comprise more than one-third of the city's population, blacks own but five percent of the businesses there.

Chicago, Ill. (1971)

18] Operation Push

The Rev. Jesse L. Jackson, addressing some 4,000 cheering blacks, announced today (Dec. 18, 1971) the founding of a new organization for economic development and political action.

The announcement . . . followed Mr. Jackson's 60-day suspension by leaders of the Southern Christian Leadership Conference from his post as director of Operation Breadbasket and his subsequent resignation from both organizations last week.

The new organization will be known as Operation Push, which stands for People United to Save Humanity.

Wearing a blue vest and checkered shirt, Mr. Jackson conducted a spirited four-hour meeting at the crowded Metropolitan Theater on Dr. Martin Luther King Drive, near 47th Street. People sat in the aisles, lined the walls and made the sidewalk outside impassable.

The 30-year-old self-styled "country preacher" seemed to have drawn with him to this new location the audience that previously packed on Saturday mornings the Dr. Martin Luther King Workshop, another converted theater, on Halstead Street, that is owned by Operation Breadbasket.

SOURCE: Thomas A. Johnson, "Jesse Jackson Forms New Black Group for Economic and Political Action," *The New York Times*, December 19, 1971.

410

Operation Push

He said that Operation Push would follow whatever strategy was revealed to its members "and whatever is available at the time."

"We will be nonviolent as we can be, and violent if necessary," he said, adding that history had proved that black progress came in the United States only when black power existed.

The audience raised nearly $22,000 for the start of the organization.

Details of the new organization were not made public at the meeting or at a later news conference, although Mr. Jackson told his followers, "The problems of the seventies are economic, so the solution and the goal must be economic."

He said, "We must picket, boycott, march, vote and, when necessary, engage in civil disobedience." Then, almost shouting, he said: "We must express our power—the courts are too slow—the judges are too corrupt."

Political involvement was depicted as an important element of the new organization.

Mr. Jackson said that the organization would be "officially born" next Saturday, Christmas, "delivered by the soul saint."

"Santa Claus delivers gifts on Christmas and leaves you in debt for the rest of the year," he went on. "The soul saint's gift [Operation Push] will help us get out of debt."

Sources close to the organization Mr. Jackson will head said that there would be an attempt to organize young people and especially the newly enfranchised 18- to 21-year-old voters. A group of nationally known black leaders will also be formed as advisers. Last Sunday, some 25 black leaders expressed their moral, financial and physical support for Mr. Jackson, stating that he should not be lost to the movement.

WEST COAST CITIES

Economic and Social Aspects

In the 1960's the West Coast cities proved elusive as the promised land for blacks. The Watts riot of August 1965, with its heavy toll of life and property, was the worst in the United States since the Detroit riot of 1943. It was the harbinger of a series of major urban insurrections outside the South which extended over three summers. Since the riot, there have been in the south central Los Angeles ghettoes of Watts and Willowbrook some new job and business opportunities, and somewhat improved health and medical facilities. On the whole, though, for the masses conditions have either changed little or worsened. In 1970, 16.2% of blacks were unemployed—60% more than in 1963. But Los Angeles also has a relatively large middle-class black population —civil servants, teachers, workers in aerospace, construction, and auto industries—among whom there has been one of the highest rates of suburbanization in the country. In the San Francisco Bay Area, including San Francisco, Oakland, and Berkeley, there have been just enough political and economic gains to buoy up the optimism and hope of the black communities.

Los Angeles, Calif. (1965)

19]   The Watts Riot

. . . On the evening of August 11, as Los Angeles sweltered in a heat wave, a highway patrolman halted a young Negro driver for speeding. The young man appeared intoxicated, and the patrolman arrested him. As a crowd gathered, law enforcement officers were called to the scene. A highway patrolman mistakenly struck a bystander with his billy club. A young Negro woman, who

SOURCE: *Report of the National Advisory Commission on Civil Disorders,* New York: Bantam Books, 1968, pp. 37–38.

412

was accused of spitting on the police, was dragged into the middle of the street.

When the police departed, members of the crowd began hurling rocks at passing cars, beating white motorists, and overturning cars and setting them on fire. The police reacted hesitantly. Actions they did take further inflamed the people on the streets.

The following day the area was calm. Community leaders attempting to mediate between Negro residents and the police received little cooperation from municipal authorities. That evening the previous night's pattern of violence was repeated.

Not until almost 30 hours after the initial flareup did window smashing, looting, and arson begin. Yet the police utilized only a small part of their forces.

Few police were on hand the next morning when huge crowds gathered in the business district of Watts, two miles from the location of the original disturbance, and began looting. In the absence of police response, the looting became bolder and spread into other areas. Hundreds of women and children from five housing projects clustered in or near Watts took part. Around noon, extensive firebombing began. Few white persons were attacked; the principal intent of the rioters now seemed to be to destroy property owned by whites, in order to drive white "exploiters" out of the ghetto.

The chief of police asked for National Guard help, but the arrival of the military units was delayed for several hours. When the Guardsmen arrived, they, together with police, made heavy use of firearms. Reports of "sniper fire" increased. Several persons were killed by mistake. Many more were injured.

Thirty-six hours after the first Guard units arrived, the main force of the riot had been blunted. Almost 4,000 persons were arrested. Thirty-four were killed and hundreds injured. Approximately $35 million in damage had been inflicted.

The Los Angeles riot, the worst in the United States since the Detroit riot of 1943, shocked all who had been confident that race relations were improving in the North, and evoked a new mood in the Negro ghettos around the country.

Los Angeles, Calif. (1970)

20] Black Profile

. . . despite a flurry of black business activity in LA, the unemployment rate in the depressed south central black community continues to rise critically. At last report, the U.S. Labor Department said fully 16.2 per cent of the blacks there were unemployed. That's 60 per cent more than five years ago,

SOURCE: "The Elusive 'Promised Land,' Los Angeles," *Black Enterprise*, November 1970, pp. 45–48.

when the Watts revolt brought the attention of the entire nation to focus
on the deeply troubled community.

Los Angeles officialdom and its establishment have never been overly concerned about the welfare of their black brothers. Rather than seek to reverse the black unemployment trend, Mayor Sam Yorty blasted the labor
department for putting out such a report, claiming it did not reflect actual conditions.

Only recently has the city taken any interest in black economic development
—and that has been extremely limited. A program fashioned after the Philadelphia plan has been instituted to place more blacks in skilled trades and the
city has set up a small fund to provide bonding for black contractors bidding
on city projects. But blacks have little clout in places where it counts. The city
contract compliance department, which has been given responsibility for assur-
ing that blacks get a share of city business, has no ranking blacks in it. Neither
has the city administrator's office, which handles day-to-day operations. So
far, no black-owned firm has built a single city project in Los Angeles.

The city's lassitude about coping with the plight of blacks is not surprising.
LA's black community had been rather quiescent until the Watt's revolt. . . .

. . . . . .

Golden State Mutual Life Insurance Co. was the first major black business
in LA, built on the debit insurance policies so popular among black working
men. And today, it is looked upon as the most substantial and largest black
employer in the city, with assets of $33 million and a payroll of 300 people.

Today there are an estimated 12,000 black businesses in Los Angeles and
the city's black "gross product" is about $3 billion a year. Still, as is true across
the country, LA's black businesses employ only about two per cent of the
black work force. Civil Service jobs provide the greatest employment and the
aerospace industry is the second largest employer. Beyond that, it's thought
that more blacks are employed in the construction and auto industries than
any other.

Pitifully little is known about black economic development in Los Angeles.
No single agency has studied its development or even catalogued the businesses. Three years ago, however, four black businessmen sought to correct
that deficiency and set up the Black Business Directory to provide a sort of
Yellow Pages for black folk. It has been able to contact only about half the
businesses thus far.

Still, it is a beginning. And it has enabled Fletcher Brown, directory Executive Director, to pinpoint some growth dynamics. "We had 400 to 500 new
businesses formed last year, mainly service firms," he said. "But we detected
also an increasing emphasis on manufacturing. A lot of our aerospace engineers
are taking their specialties and turning them into businesses as aerospace suppliers." Los Angeles boasts more black technical people than any other city in
the country, primarily in aerospace. There are 3,000 to 5,000 people with academic degrees in the industry, Brown said.

As blacks have moved up the economic scale, they have broken out of the
prescribed south central ghetto, whose heart is Watts and Willowbrook. Blacks
have moved westward into such moderate- and high-income areas as Leimert

414

Park, Baldwin Hills and View Park. Conservative Pasadena (home of the "Little Old Lady in Tennis Sneakers") and adjacent Altadena have expanding black populations—and a resulting hotly contested school integration fight. Blacks also live in other widely scattered enclaves in the seashore community of Venice, the Long Beach port area, Pacoima in the San Fernando Valley, Duarte in the San Gabriel Valley and Pomona in the far eastern reaches of Los Angeles County. . . .

The size and vitality of the City of Angels' black community have produced more than a dozen black millionaires. Perhaps the best known and richest is Al Maddox, a low-key real estate entrepreneur. Maddox's wealth has been variously estimated at between $5 million and $30 million. Paul Williams, the country's best-known black architect, is headquartered in LA and is also reputed to be a millionaire. Another important member of the elite black establishment is H. Claude Hudson, president of Broadway Federal Savings and Laon Association, largest black-owned S&L in the country and one of LA's four black lending institutions.

Politically, blacks are beginning to exercise some muscle. Three blacks are now on the 14-man LA city council; four of the city's 14 state legislators are black and one of its seven congressmen is also black. Moreover, councilman Tom Bradley's breathtaking run for the Los Angeles mayor's office last year is looked upon as simply a prelude to the future. Even though he lost, by a narrow margin, to Yorty, Bradley is still "Mr. Mayor" to most blacks. And as one of his aides noted, 1973 is just around the corner. "We never stopped running after the last election," he said with determination.

It is only in the last few years that Los Angeles blacks have expanded their business horizons beyond the ghetto. As in other communities across the country, the riotous street revolt that wracked Watts caused a great deal of introspection and rededication to making life better in the ghetto. The resulting money flow and offers of help from white businessmen often were taken by blacks and transformed into businesses. . . .

San Francisco Bay Area, Calif. (1971)

21]   Black Mobility

There is a saying that everybody loves San Francisco. Make that blacks included. And not only are they visiting as tourists and settling permanently, but they have already achieved a political clout that is practically unmatched in the country. In addition blacks in the bay are also becoming a social and cultural force and now there is evidence that they are on the verge of a dramatic economic breakthrough.

Of course, this is not to hint that the bay area is mecca. It is not. In fact blacks in and around San Francisco face many of the same problems blacks

Source: Earl Caldwell, "San Francisco," *Black Enterprise*, June 1971, pp. 57–60.

do in other areas of the country. The difference is that there is now wide-spread belief in the bay that there is some light at the end of the tunnel.

For black folks, the bay area means San Francisco, Oakland, and Berkeley. They do not control those cities. Neither do they hold majorities in the population. Still it cannot be said though that they are not building strength in all three.

. . . . .

San Francisco is the city, the magic city. It is also the largest. The latest census count puts the population at 715,674. There are 96,078 blacks who comprise 13.4 per cent of the total population.

. . . . .

Oakland has the largest black population on the bay. Of its total population of 361,561 persons, 34.5 per cent or nearly 125,000 of its residents are black. Many of the blacks are poor and live in the ghettos of east and west Oakland.

Berkeley is the university town. The University of California is Berkeley. The city's population is 116,716. Surprisingly, there are 27,421 blacks in the city who comprise 23.5 per cent of the population.

In San Francisco, blacks are employed in good-sized numbers by the city. They drive the buses, work the cable cars and occupy a series of other jobs at various levels in government. They are also visible in various professional positions but the numbers are small. Unemployment among the blacks is high. Basically, they live in two areas of the city: the Fillmore district and Hunters Point. Fillmore is mixed, low- and middle-income people, low- and mid-income housing. Hunters Point is a poverty-ridden slum. It's hidden off on the east side of the city, back on a hill that is so isolated only the people who live there know for sure that it is in San Francisco.

A few weeks ago one of the major area papers conducted a poll among the people in the know in San Francisco to find what it called the ten most powerful men in the city. Joseph Alioto, the mayor, was selected most powerful. But it was a black man, assemblyman Willie Brown, who finished second. It was not a fix. Willie Brown is a damn powerful man. "He's got Ronald Reagan kissing his ——," those in the know say and add "if that ain't power, it's the next thing to it."

Willie is a hard-hitting, most righteously black legislator who is in his fourth term and whose power stems from the fact that he also happens to be the chairman of the state legislature's Ways and Means Committee. In other words, the big money that the state of California spends must go through him. Reagan can't do business with his budget until Willie Brown says it's okay. And all that from a 36-year-old who dresses mod, drives a Porsche, and holds the respect of even the most militant black students.

But what part of the tourist industry, San Francisco's major business, do blacks control? "You got to have a microscope to see it," a black business consultant said. Another black close to the industry complained that "we don't even get the fallout stuff."

On Fillmore Street, there is a small West Indian restaurant known as Connie's that is operated by Connie Williams, a black woman. It is a fine restau-

416

rant, one that has built something of a national reputation. And in a city that prides itself on the variety of food that it has to offer, Connie's is the only one with West Indian cuisine. But the fact is that there is not a single piece of literature put out by the convention and tourist bureaus that lists her restaurant. But what they do list is an exhibit on African and Afro-American history that is located just a few blocks down Fillmore from the restaurant.

There are other black-owned businesses that many tourists might find interesting but like Connie's none of those are promoted by the city. On Haight Street near Fillmore is the Black Man's Art Gallery, until recently the only black-owned gallery in the country. And there is no question that the art there is both unusual and unique. It is not protest art but black art, art based on a black African background.

There is an area of San Francisco on the fringe of what is generally considered the Fillmore district where there are a number of black clubs that offer both jazz and blues musicians. But tourists who watch the listings won't find them either. There is a single black-owned club downtown, the Celebrity Club of Geary Street, but it too is another of the places that tourists must find.

But the fact is, as Willie Brown points out, blacks don't really own the kinds of businesses in San Francisco that would enable them to collect any meaningful share of the tourist dollar. They own none of the clubs, hotels, motels, restaurants or any of the other services that tourists use. In fact, blacks own none of the significant tourist businesses in the bay area. The most significant role blacks play in the tourist industry in San Francisco is in entertainment. . . .

The question of course is why. Willie Brown says that black economic development has not matched that of politics simply because blacks have not had the resources to develop. "If the votes are there," he explained, "no amount of money can continue to prohibit you." In politics blacks have the votes. The black investment dollars have been lacking, but now money is arriving. According to Willie Brown the increase in investment power for blacks in the bay in the past five years has been "unbelievable" and he says that "in another five years" the black clout economically will rival that achieved in politics. If you accept that from his position that he is in a position to know, consider then the potential because Willie Brown adds that "this may very well be the most fertile ground in the country for black investment."

The largest black enterprise in the bay is the airport parking facility in San Francisco. It is operated by a five-man group (one is white) headed by Dr. Carlton Goodlet who also publishes a black newspaper, *The Sun Reporter*. Goodlet says that the airport parking facility is a $5 million business, thus making it the largest black-run public service in the country.

Berkeley, like San Francisco, offers an image that is often misleading but it too is chuck full of potential. In Berkeley, the new mayor, Warren Widener, is black. Two of the four councilmen elected in the recent municipal elections are black, and one of the holdover councilmen is black. And all that in a city where less than a fourth of the population is black. In Berkeley, the blacks live in the flatlands, down by the freeways and the railroad tracks and like their brothers who live in the Hunters Point section of San Francisco they are poor and often overlooked. Even some of the good liberals don't know that they are there. They work around the area where there are plants, at the university where there are jobs, and at the military bases around Oakland.

But there are a good many who don't work and the prime reason is that they cannot find jobs. With a black mayor, three councilmen and a congressman, Ronald V. Dellums, it would appear that the blacks do have something started though, and quite possibly they do. The blacks recently elected are protégés of Dellums'. They say that change is what they are all about. But the problem is whether they can transfer political power to economic power. And that is what must be done and that is the challenge. The problem is that the blacks who are elected in Berkeley were not elected by blacks alone and they have other obligations. They were elected by a coalition that includes other minorities but it also includes a good many students and as one observer remarked: "Okay, they—the students—are with the blacks today, but who knows where they will be tomorrow."

. . . . . .

In Oakland, the city just across the bay from San Francisco and next door to Berkeley, there is yet another story. It was the black majorities from Oakland that were crucial to the election of Dellums to Congress. But beyond that, Oakland has but one thing going as far as blacks are concerned and that is its potential. The white majority is dwindling. Visitors to the bay area, particularly those from the east, often take a quick look around and size up Oakland as being to San Francisco what Newark is to Manhattan. Forget it; there is no comparison.

Robert Allen, the black author of the book *Black Awakening in Capitalist America* who relocated in the bay area some 3 years ago, says that comparisons with his native Atlanta and Oakland are far more valid than those with Newark. As he points out, Newark is a used-up city. It is falling apart, has no tax base, whites are running off and even blacks are saying that maybe the city isn't worth the trouble. Nobody is running out of Oakland. It has a tax base and rather than falling apart it is a city where they are erecting tall, new buildings.

Dellums, who engineered his own election [and] helped build the successful coalition that has young blacks in power roles in Berkeley, has now led the way in putting together a coalition in Oakland. It tried for control of the city council a few weeks ago but failed. Still it showed promise. The coalition candidates drew record votes in losing.

But in Oakland, the value in winning would be in turning political power to economic power. The city has a major waterfront and significant industry. Power best used could give blacks a piece of that action and end their current plight. Just as they are in Berkeley, blacks in Oakland are confined to the flatlands, hidden under the freeways. Unemployment is near depression level in some neighborhoods. But the promise in Oakland is perhaps the greatest of all.

Once Oakland was known primarily among blacks as the city where the Black Panther party was founded. People now know, too, that Oakland blacks sent Ronald V. Dellums, the black man they call a radical, to Congress. Berkeley was just a college town. Now it's the place where they have that young black mayor and those young black lawyers whom they also call radical (both are in their twenties) sitting on the city council. Some people believe that Mayor Joseph Alioto may not run for mayor again in San Francisco. And it is a black man, the Rev. Cecil Williams, the minister of a big church (and as radical as a church can get) who is often mentioned as a prime candidate to succeed him. But even if San Francisco does not elect a black man mayor, there still is Willie Brown. Any way you look at it, San Francisco is not mecca and it is not likely to be either. But the black population on the bay is rising and the figures show that is not just because the people are making babies.

APPENDIX A

The Largest Cities in the United States, 1860–1970, in Terms of Black Population

The following statistics are derived from the decennial federal censuses. The numerical and percentage decennial change and, in some cases, the black and foreign-born white percentages of the entire population have been calculated by the editor himself. It is fair to say that there is a widespread feeling among scholars and the black community generally that for a long time there has been quite a serious undercount of blacks, particularly males, in the cities. For the decennials 1870–1960, by way of comparison, I have included the percentage of foreign-born whites.

The Largest Cities in the United States in 1860 in Terms of Black Population

CITIES	SLAVE	FREE	TOTAL BLACK	% OF TOTAL POPULATION
Baltimore, Md.	2,218	25,680	27,898	13.1
New Orleans, La.	13,385	10,689	24,074	14.3
Philadelphia, Pa.	—	22,185	22,185	3.9
Charleston, S.C.	13,909	3,237	17,146	42.3
Richmond, Va.	11,699	2,576	14,275	37.6
New York, N.Y.	—	12,472	12,472	1.5
Washington, D.C.	1,774	9,209	10,983	17.9
Petersburg, Va.	5,680	3,244	8,924	48.9
Savannah, Ga.	7,712	705	8,417	31.8
Mobile, Ala.	7,587	817	8,404	28.7
Louisville, Ky.	4,903	1,917	6,810	10.0
Montgomery, Ala.	—	—	4,502 °	50.9
Norfolk, Va.	3,284	1,046	4,330	29.7
Brooklyn, N.Y.	—	4,313	4,313	—
Memphis, Tenn.	3,882	198	4,080	21.7
Augusta, Ga.	—	—	4,049 °	48.0
Nashville, Tenn.	—	—	3,945 °	30.3
Cincinnati, Ohio	—	—	3,731	2.3
Columbia, S.C.	—	—	3,657 °	45.4
St. Louis, Mo.	1,542	1,755	3,297	2.0

° Breakdown into slave and free not available.

Appendix A

The Largest Cities in the United States in 1870 in Terms of Black Population

CITIES	BLACK POPU-LATION	CHANGE, 1860–70 NO.	CHANGE, 1860–70 %	% OF TOTAL POPU-LATION	% OF FOREIGN-BORN WHITES
New Orleans, La.	50,456	26,382	109.6	26.4	25.3
Baltimore, Md.	39,558	11,660	41.8	14.8	21.1
Washington, D.C.	35,455	24,472	222.8	32.5	12.6
Charleston, S.C.	26,173	9,027	52.6	53.5	10.0
Richmond, Va.	23,110	8,835	61.9	45.3	7.4
Philadelphia, Pa.	22,147	− 38	− 0.2	3.3	27.2
St. Louis, Mo.	22,088	18,791	569.9	7.1	36.1
Memphis, Tenn.	15,471	11,391	279.2	38.5	16.9
Louisville, Ky.	14,956	8,146	119.6	14.8	25.5
Mobile, Ala.	13,919	5,515	65.6	43.5	13.2
New York, N.Y.	13,072	600	4.8	1.4	44.5
Savannah, Ga.	13,068	4,651	55.3	46.3	13.0
Petersburg, Va.	10,185	1,261	14.1	53.7	2.3
Atlanta, Ga.	9,929	7,990	412.1	45.6	5.0
Nashville, Tenn.	9,709	5,764	146.1	37.5	10.9
Norfolk, Va.	8,760	4,430	102.3	45.6	3.8
Wilmington, N.C.	7,920	3,570	82.1	58.9	4.2
Vicksburg, Miss.	6,805	5,372	374.9	54.7	11.3
Augusta, Ga.	6,431	2,382	58.8	41.8	9.4
Cincinnati, Ohio	5,900	2,169	58.1	2.7	58.3
Natchez, Miss.	5,329	2,989	127.7	58.8	6.4
Columbia, S.C.	5,295	1,638	44.8	56.9	6.2
Little Rock, Ark.	5,274	4,421	518.3	42.6	9.2
Montgomery, Ala.	5,183	681	15.1	49.0	7.4
Brooklyn, N.Y.	4,944	631	14.6	1.2	36.5

Appendix A

The Largest Cities in the United States in 1880
in Terms of Black Population

CITIES	BLACK POPU- LATION	CHANGE, NO.	1870–80 %	% OF TOTAL POPU- LATION	% OF FOREIGN- BORN WHITES
New Orleans, La.	57,617	7,161	14.2	26.7	19.0
Baltimore, Md.	53,716	14,158	35.8	16.2	16.9
Washington, D.C.	48,377	12,922	36.4	32.8	9.7
Philadelphia, Pa.	31,699	9,552	43.1	3.7	24.1
Richmond, Va.	27,832	4,722	20.4	43.8	5.3
Charleston, S.C.	27,276	1,103	4.2	54.6	7.9
St. Louis, Mo.	22,256	168	0.8	6.3	30.0
Louisville, Ky.	20,905	5,949	39.8	16.9	18.7
New York, N.Y.	19,663	6,591	50.4	1.6	39.7
Nashville, Tenn.	16,337	6,628	68.3	37.7	7.0
Atlanta, Ga.	16,330	6,401	64.5	43.7	3.8
Savannah, Ga.	15,654	2,586	19.8	51.0	9.7
Memphis, Tenn.	14,896	−575	−3.7	44.3	11.8
Mobile, Ala.	12,240	−1,679	−12.1	42.0	10.1
Petersburg, Va.	11,701	1,516	14.9	54.0	1.6
Wilmington, N.C.	10,462	2,542	32.1	60.3	3.0
Augusta, Ga.	10,109	3,678	57.2	46.2	5.5
Norfolk, Va.	10,068	1,308	14.9	45.8	3.8
Montgomery, Ala.	9,931	4,748	91.6	59.4	3.9
Cincinnati, Ohio	8,179	2,279	38.6	3.2	28.1
Kansas City, Mo.	8,143	4,373	116.0	14.6	16.7
Brooklyn, N.Y.	8,095	3,151	63.7	1.4	31.4
Indianapolis, Ind.	6,504	3,573	121.9	8.7	16.8
Chicago, Ill.	6,480	2,789	75.6	1.3	40.7
Houston, Tex.	6,479	2,788	75.5	39.2	13.8
Boston, Mass.	5,873	2,377	68.0	1.6	31.6
Vicksburg, Miss.	5,836	−969	−14.2	49.4	7.9
Galveston, Tex.	5,348	2,341	77.9	24.0	22.7
Raleigh, N.C.	4,354	260	6.4	47.0	1.8
New Bern, N.C.	4,226	397	10.4	65.9	1.4

The Largest Cities in the United States in 1890 in Terms of Black Population

CITIES	BLACK POPU- LATION	CHANGE, 1880–90 NO.	%	% OF TOTAL POPU- LATION	% OF FOREIGN- BORN WHITES
Washington, D.C.	75,572	27,195	56.2	32.8	8.0
Baltimore, Md.	67,104	13,388	24.9	15.4	15.8
New Orleans, La.	64,691	7,074	12.3	26.7	14.0
Philadelphia, Pa.	39,371	7,672	24.2	3.8	25.6
New York (including Brooklyn), N.Y.	36,620	16,957	86.2	1.6	38.7
Richmond, Va.	32,330	4,498	16.2	39.7	4.2
Charleston, S.C.	30,970	3,694	13.5	56.4	5.6
Nashville, Tenn.	29,382	13,045	79.8	38.6	4.9
Memphis, Tenn.	28,706	13,810	92.7	44.5	8.3
Louisville, Ky.	28,651	7,746	37.1	1.8	14.6
Atlanta, Ga.	28,088	11,758	72.0	42.9	2.8
St. Louis, Mo.	26,865	4,609	20.7	5.9	25.4
Savannah, Ga.	22,963	7,309	46.7	53.2	7.7
Norfolk, Va.	16,244	6,176	61.3	46.6	3.2
Augusta, Ga.	15,875	5,766	67.0	47.7	2.2
Chicago, Ill.	14,271	7,791	120.2	1.3	40.9
Kansas City, Mo.	13,700	5,557	68.2	10.3	15.5
Mobile, Ala.	13,630	1,390	11.4	43.9	6.8
Montgomery, Ala.	12,987	3,056	30.8	59.3	2.9
Chattanooga, Tenn.	12,563	7,481	147.2	43.2	4.4
Petersburg, Va.	12,221	520	4.4	53.9	1.2
Cincinnati, Ohio	11,655	3,476	42.5	3.9	24.0
Wilmington, N.C.	11,324	862	8.2	18.4	2.5
Birmingham, Ala.	11,254	°	°	43.0	6.2
Macon, Ga.	11,203	4,619	70.2	49.3	2.6
Houston, Tex.	10,370	3,891	60.1	37.6	11.2
Jacksonville, Fla.	9,801	6,143	59.5	57.0	5.4
Little Rock, Ark.	9,739	5,232	116.1	37.6	4.3
Indianapolis, Ind.	9,133	2,629	40.4	8.7	13.7
Lexington, Ky.	8,554	971	12.8	39.7	5.0

° No information available

The Largest Cities in the United States in 1900
in Terms of Black Population

CITIES	BLACK POPU- LATION	CHANGE, 1890–1900 NO.	%	% OF TOTAL POPU- LATION	% OF FOREIGN- BORN WHITES
Washington, D.C.	86,702	11,130	14.7	31.1	7.0
Baltimore, Md.	79,258	12,154	18.1	15.6	13.3
New Orleans, La.	77,714	13,023	20.5	27.1	10.3
Philadelphia, Pa.	62,613	23,242	59.0	4.8	22.7
New York, N.Y.	60,666	24,046	65.7	1.8	36.7
Memphis, Tenn.	49,910	21,204	73.9	48.8	5.0
Louisville, Ky.	39,139	10,488	36.6	19.1	10.5
Atlanta, Ga.	35,912	7,824	29.3	39.8	2.7
St. Louis, Mo.	35,516	8,651	32.3	6.2	19.3
Richmond, Va.	32,230	− 100	− 0.3	37.9	3.3
Charleston, S.C.	31,522	522	1.8	56.5	4.5
Chicago, Ill.	30,150	16,879	111.0	1.8	34.5
Nashville, Tenn.	30,044	662	2.3	37.2	3.7
Savannah, Ga.	28,090	5,127	22.0	51.8	6.1
Pittsburgh, Pa.	20,355	9,190	117.1	4.5	25.4
Norfolk, Va.	20,230	3,986	24.5	43.4	3.4
Augusta, Ga.	18,487	2,612	16.5	46.9	2.4
Kansas City, Mo.	17,567	3,867	28.2	10.7	11.2
Montgomery, Ala.	17,229	4,282	33.0	56.8	2.1
Mobile, Ala.	17,045	3,415	25.1	44.3	5.3
Birmingham, Ala.	16,575	5,321	47.3	43.1	4.6
Jacksonville, Fla.	16,236	6,435	65.7	57.1	3.6
Indianapolis, Ind.	15,931	6,798	74.4	9.4	10.1
Little Rock, Ark.	14,694	4,955	50.9	38.4	5.4
Houston, Tex.	14,608	4,238	40.9	32.7	9.7
Cincinnati, Ohio	14,482	2,827	24.3	4.4	17.8
Chattanooga, Tenn.	13,122	596	4.7	43.5	3.3
Boston, Mass.	11,591	3,466	43.5	2.1	35.1
Macon, Ga.	11,550	347	3.1	49.6	2.0
Petersburg, Va.	10,751	470	3.8	49.3	1.2

*The Largest Cities in the United States in 1910
in Terms of Black Population*

CITIES	BLACK POPU- LATION	CHANGE, 1900–10 NO.	%	% OF TOTAL POPU- LATION	% OF FOREIGN- BORN WHITES
Washington, D.C.	94,446	7,744	8.9	28.5	7.4
New York, N.Y.	91,709	31,043	51.2	1.9	40.4
New Orleans, La.	89,262	11,548	14.9	26.3	8.2
Baltimore, Md.	84,749	5,491	6.9	15.2	13.8
Philadelphia, Pa.	84,459	21,846	34.9	5.5	24.7
Memphis, Tenn.	52,441	2,531	5.1	40.0	4.9
Birmingham, Ala.	52,305	35,730	215.6	39.4	4.3
Atlanta, Ga.	51,902	16,175	45.3	33.5	2.8
Richmond, Va.	46,733	14,503	45.0	36.6	3.2
Chicago, Ill.	44,103	13,953	46.3	2.0	35.7
St. Louis, Mo.	43,960	8,444	23.8	6.4	18.3
Louisville, Ky.	40,522	1,383	3.5	18.1	7.8
Nashville, Tenn.	36,523	6,479	21.6	33.1	2.7
Savannah, Ga.	33,246	5,156	18.4	51.1	5.1
Charleston, S.C.	31,056	− 466	− 1.5	52.8	4.1
Jacksonville, Fla.	29,293	13,057	80.4	50.8	4.3
Pittsburgh, Pa.	25,623	5,268	25.9	4.8	26.3
Norfolk, Va.	25,039	4,809	23.8	37.1	5.3
Houston, Tex.	23,929	9,321	63.8	30.4	8.0
Kansas City, Mo.	23,566	5,999	34.1	9.5	10.2
Mobile, Ala.	22,763	5,718	33.5	44.2	4.3
Indianapolis, Ind.	21,816	5,885	36.9	9.3	8.5
Cincinnati, Ohio	19,639	5,157	35.6	5.4	15.6
Montgomery, Ala.	19,322	2,093	12.1	50.7	1.8
Augusta, Ga.	18,344	− 143	− 0.8	44.7	2.2
Macon, Ga.	18,150	6,660	57.1	44.6	1.7
Dallas, Tex.	18,024	8,989	99.5	19.6	5.7
Chattanooga, Tenn.	17,942	4,820	36.7	40.2	3.0
Little Rock, Ark.	14,539	− 155	− 1.1	31.6	4.3
Shreveport, La.	13,896	5,354	62.7	49.6	4.8

*The Largest Cities in the United States in 1920
in Terms of Black Population*

CITIES	BLACK POPU-LATION	CHANGE, 1910–20 NO.	%	% OF TOTAL POPU-LATION	% OF FOREIGN-BORN WHITES
New York, N.Y.	152,467	60,758	66.3	2.7	36.1
Philadelphia, Pa.	134,229	49,770	58.9	7.4	22.0
Washington, D.C.	109,966	15,520	16.4	25.1	6.7
Chicago, Ill.	109,458	65,355	148.2	4.1	29.9
Baltimore, Md.	108,322	23,573	27.8	14.8	11.6
New Orleans, La.	100,930	11,668	13.1	26.1	7.1
Birmingham, Ala.	70,230	17,925	34.3	39.3	3.4
St. Louis, Mo	69,854	25,894	58.9	9.0	18.4
Atlanta, Ga.	62,796	10,894	21.0	31.3	2.4
Memphis, Tenn.	61,181	8,740	16.7	37.7	3.6
Richmond, Va.	54,041	7,308	15.6	31.5	2.7
Norfolk, Va.	43,392	18,353	73.3	37.4	6.0
Jacksonville, Fla.	41,520	12,227	41.7	45.3	4.5
Detroit, Mich.	40,838	35,097	611.3	4.1	29.3
Louisville, Ky.	40,087	− 435	− 1.1	17.1	5.0
Savannah, Ga.	39,179	5,933	17.8	47.1	3.9
Pittsburgh, Pa.	37,725	12,102	47.2	6.4	20.5
Nashville, Tenn.	35,633	− 890	− 2.4	30.1	2.0
Indianapolis, Ind.	34,678	12,862	59.0	11.0	5.4
Cleveland, Ohio	34,451	26,003	307.8	4.3	30.1
Houston, Tex.	33,960	10,031	41.9	24.6	8.7
Charleston, S.C.	32,326	1,271	4.1	47.6	3.2
Kansas City, Mo.	30,719	12,272	37.4	9.5	8.5
Cincinnati, Ohio	30,079	10,440	53.2	7.5	10.7
Dallas, Tex.	24,023	5,999	33.3	15.1	5.5
Mobile, Ala.	23,906	1,143	5.0	39.3	3.3
Portsmouth, Va.	23,245	11,628	100.1	42.7	2.8
Macon, Ga.	23,093	4,943	27.2	43.6	1.3
Augusta, Ga.	22,582	4,238	23.1	43.0	1.8
Columbus, Ohio	22,181	9,442	74.1	49.4	6.8

The Largest Cities in the United States in 1930
in Terms of Black Population

CITIES	BLACK POPU- LATION	CHANGE, 1920–30 NO.	%	% OF TOTAL POPU- LATION	% OF FOREIGN- BORN WHITES
New York, N.Y.	327,706	175,239	114.9	4.7	33.1
Chicago, Ill.	233,903	124,444	113.7	6.9	24.9
Philadelphia, Pa.	219,599	85,370	63.6	11.3	18.9
Baltimore, Md.	142,106	33,784	31.2	17.7	9.2
Washington, D.C.	132,068	22,102	20.0	27.1	6.1
New Orleans, La.	129,632	28,702	28.4	28.3	4.3
Detroit, Mich.	120,066	79,228	194.0	7.7	25.5
Birmingham, Ala.	99,077	28,847	41.1	38.2	2.3
Memphis, Tenn.	96,550	35,469	57.8	38.1	2.1
St. Louis, Mo.	93,580	23,726	34.0	11.4	9.8
Atlanta, Ga.	90,075	27,279	43.4	33.3	1.7
Cleveland, Ohio	71,899	37,448	108.7	8.0	25.5
Houston, Tex.	63,337	29,377	86.5	21.7	3.9
Pittsburgh, Pa.	54,983	17,258	45.7	8.2	16.3
Richmond, Va.	52,988	− 1,053	− 1.9	29.0	2.2
Jacksonville, Fla.	48,196	6,676	16.1	37.2	3.4
Cincinnati, Ohio	47,818	17,739	59.0	10.6	7.7
Louisville, Ky.	47,354	7,267	18.1	15.4	2.9
Indianapolis, Ind.	43,967	9,289	26.8	12.1	3.8
Norfolk, Va.	43,942	550	1.3	33.9	3.3
Nashville, Tenn.	42,836	7,103	20.2	27.8	1.2
Savannah, Ga.	38,896	− 383	− 0.7	45.7	2.9
Los Angeles, Calif.	38,894	23,315	149.7	3.1	14.7
Newark, N.J.	38,880	21,903	129.0	8.8	26.0
Dallas, Tex.	38,742	14,719	61.3	14.9	2.5
Kansas City, Mo.	38,574	7,855	25.6	9.6	6.1
Chattanooga, Tenn.	33,289	24,400	76.2	27.8	1.2
Columbus, Ohio	32,774	10,593	47.8	11.3	5.3
Winston-Salem, N.C.	32,566	11,831	57.1	43.3	1.0
Montgomery, Ala.	29,970	10,143	51.2	45.4	0.6

Appendix A

The Largest Cities in the United States in 1940
in Terms of Black Population

CITIES	BLACK POPU-LATION	CHANGE, 1930–40 NO.	CHANGE, 1930–40 %	% OF TOTAL POPU-LATION	% OF FOREIGN-BORN WHITES
New York, N.Y.	458,444	130,738	39.9	6.1	27.9
Chicago, Ill.	277,731	43,828	18.7	8.2	19.8
Philadelphia, Pa.	250,880	31,281	14.2	13.0	15.0
Washington, D.C.	187,266	55,198	41.8	28.2	5.1
Baltimore, Md.	165,843	23,737	16.7	19.3	7.1
Detroit, Mich.	149,119	29,053	24.2	9.2	19.8
New Orleans, La.	149,034	19,402	15.0	30.1	3.0
Memphis, Tenn.	121,498	24,948	25.8	41.5	1.5
Birmingham, Ala.	108,938	9,861	10.0	40.7	1.7
St. Louis, Mo.	108,765	15,185	16.2	13.3	7.3
Atlanta, Ga.	104,533	14,458	16.1	34.6	1.4
Houston, Tex.	86,302	22,965	36.3	22.4	4.0
Cleveland, Ohio	84,504	12,605	17.5	9.6	20.4
Los Angeles, Calif.	63,774	24,880	64.0	4.2	14.3
Pittsburgh, Pa.	62,216	7,233	13.2	9.3	12.6
Jacksonville, Fla.	61,782	13,586	28.2	35.7	2.3
Richmond, Va.	61,251	8,263	15.6	31.7	1.8
Cincinnati, Ohio	55,593	7,775	16.3	12.2	5.7
Indianapolis, Ind.	51,142	7,175	16.3	13.2	2.7
Dallas, Tex.	50,407	11,665	30.3	17.1	2.5
Nashville, Tenn.	47,318	4,482	10.5	28.3	0.9
Louisville, Ky.	47,158	− 196	− 0.4	14.8	1.9
Norfolk, Va.	45,893	1,951	4.4	31.8	2.5
Newark, N.J.	45,760	6,880	17.7	10.6	21.0
Savannah, Ga.	43,237	4,341	11.2	45.0	1.9
Kansas City, Mo.	41,574	3,000	7.7	10.4	4.8
Miami, Fla.	36,857	11,741	46.7	21.4	7.3
Chattanooga, Tenn.	36,404	2,115	6.4	28.4	0.9
Winston-Salem, N.C.	36,108	3,566	10.9	45.2	0.4
Shreveport, La.	35,975	8,756	32.2	36.6	1.5

The Largest Cities in the United States in 1950
in Terms of Black Population

CITIES	BLACK POPU- LATION	CHANGE, 1940–50 NO.	%	% OF TOTAL POPU- LATION	% OF FOREIGN- BORN WHITES
New York, N.Y.	775,516	319,072	69.6	9.8	22.6
Chicago, Ill.	509,437	231,706	83.4	14.1	14.5
Philadelphia, Pa.	378,968	128,088	51.1	18.3	11.2
Detroit, Mich.	303,721	154,602	103.7	16.4	14.9
Washington, D.C.	284,313	97,047	51.8	35.4	4.9
Baltimore, Md.	226,053	60,210	36.3	23.8	5.4
Los Angeles, Calif.	211,585	147,811	231.8	10.7	12.5
New Orleans, La.	182,631	33,597	22.5	32.0	2.5
St. Louis, Mo.	154,448	45,683	42.0	18.0	4.9
Cleveland, Ohio	149,544	65,040	77.0	15.6	14.5
Memphis, Tenn.	147,287	25,789	21.2	37.2	1.1
Birmingham, Ala.	130,115	21,197	19.5	39.9	1.2
Houston, Tex.	125,660	39,358	45.6	21.1	2.9
Atlanta, Ga.	121,416	16,883	16.2	36.6	1.3
Pittsburgh, Pa.	82,981	20,765	33.4	12.3	9.6
San Francisco, Calif.	81,469	76,623	1581.1	10.5	15.5
Cincinnati, Ohio	78,685	23,092	41.5	15.6	4.1
Newark, N.J.	75,627	29,867	65.3	17.2	16.1
Richmond, Va.	73,082	11,831	19.2	31.7	1.6
Jacksonville, Fla.	72,529	10,747	17.4	35.5	2.1
Indianapolis, Ind.	64,091	12,949	25.3	15.0	2.1
Norfolk, Va.	63,448	17,555	38.2	29.7	2.1
Louisville, Ky.	57,772	10,614	22.5	15.7	1.3
Dallas, Tex.	57,263	6,856	13.6	13.2	1.9
Kansas City, Mo.	56,023	4,448	10.7	12.3	3.5
Oakland, Calif.	55,778	47,316	559.2	14.5	9.9
Nashville, Tenn.	54,726	7,408	15.7	31.4	0.8
Savannah, Ga.	48,350	5,113	11.6	40.0	1.4
Columbus, Ohio	47,131	11,366	31.8	12.5	2.9
Mobile, Ala.	45,905	16,859	58.0	35.6	1.4

Cities in the United States in 1960 with a Black Population
of More Than 50,000 Arranged by Size

CITIES	BLACK POPU- LATION	CHANGE, 1950–60 NO.	%	% OF TOTAL POPU- LATION	% OF FOREIGN- BORN WHITES
New York, N.Y.	1,087,931	312,415	40.3	14.0	20.0
Chicago, Ill.	812,637	303,200	59.5	22.9	12.3
Philadelphia, Pa.	529,240	150,272	39.7	26.4	8.9
Detroit, Mich.	482,223	178,502	58.8	28.9	12.1
Washington, D.C.	411,737	127,424	44.8	53.9	5.1
Los Angeles, Calif.	334,916	123,331	58.3	13.5	12.6
Baltimore, Md.	326,589	100,536	44.5	34.8	4.2
Cleveland, Ohio	250,818	101,274	67.7	28.6	11.0
New Orleans, La.	233,514	50,883	27.9	37.2	2.3
Houston, Tex.	215,037	89,377	71.1	22.9	2.6
St. Louis, Mo.	214,377	59,929	38.8	28.6	3.5
Atlanta, Ga.	186,464	65,048	53.6	38.3	0.9
Memphis, Tenn.	184,320	37,033	25.1	37.0	0.9
Newark, N.J.	138,035	62,408	82.5	34.1	12.3
Birmingham, Ala.	135,113	4,998	3.8	39.6	2.5
Dallas, Tex.	129,242	71,979	125.7	19.0	1.9
Cincinnati, Ohio	108,754	30,069	38.2	22.9	8.7
Pittsburgh, Pa.	100,692	17,711	21.3	16.7	7.5
Indianapolis, Ind.	98,049	33,958	53.0	20.6	1.8
Richmond, Va.	91,972	8,890	12.2	41.8	1.4
Oakland, Calif.	83,618	27,840	49.9	22.7	9.6
Kansas City, Mo.	83,146	27,123	48.4	17.5	2.8
Jacksonville, Fla.	82,525	9,996	13.8	41.1	1.7
Norfolk, Va.	78,806	15,358	24.2	25.8	1.9
Columbus, Ohio	77,140	30,009	63.7	16.6	2.3
San Francisco, Calif.	74,383	− 7,086	− 8.7	10.1	19.3
Buffalo, N.Y.	70,904	33,204	88.1	13.3	10.3
Louisville, Ky.	70,075	12,303	21.3	17.9	1.0
Gary, Ind.	69,123	29,797	75.8	38.8	7.7
Mobile, Ala.	65,619	19,714	42.9	32.4	1.0
Miami, Fla.	65,213	24,637	60.7	22.4	16.9
Nashville, Tenn.	64,570	9,844	18.0	37.9	0.7
Boston, Mass.	63,165	20,421	47.8	9.1	12.4
Milwaukee, Wis.	62,458	39,716	174.6	8.4	7.7
Ft. Worth, Tex.	57,327	20,200	54.4	16.1	1.4
Dayton, Ohio	57,288	23,051	67.3	21.9	2.3
Shreveport, La.	56,607	14,365	34.0	34.4	0.9
Charlotte, N.C.	56,248	18,737	49.9	27.9	1.9
Savannah, Ga.	53,035	4,685	9.7	35.5	1.4
Jackson, Miss.	51,556	10,365	25.3	35.7	0.5

The Largest Cities in the United States in 1970 in Terms of Black Population

CITIES	BLACK POPULATION	CHANGE, 1960–70 NO.	%	% OF TOTAL POPULATION
New York, N.Y.	1,666,636	578,705	53.2	21.2
Chicago, Ill.	1,102,620	289,983	35.7	32.7
Detroit, Mich.	660,428	178,205	37.0	43.7
Philadelphia, Pa.	653,791	124,551	23.5	33.6
Washington, D.C.	537,712	125,975	30.6	71.1
Los Angeles, Calif.	503,606	168,690	50.4	17.9
Baltimore, Md.	420,210	93,621	28.7	46.4
Houston, Tex.	316,551	101,514	47.2	25.7
Cleveland, Ohio	287,841	37,023	14.8	38.3
New Orleans, La.	267,308	33,794	14.5	45.0
Atlanta, Ga.	255,051	68,587	36.8	51.3
St. Louis, Mo.	254,191	39,814	18.6	40.9
Memphis, Tenn.	242,513	58,193	31.6	38.9
Dallas, Tex.	210,238	80,996	62.7	24.9
Newark, N.J.	207,458	69,423	50.3	54.2
Indianapolis, Ind.	134,320	36,271	37.0	18.0
Birmingham, Ala.	126,388	− 8,725	− 6.5	42.0
Cincinnati, Ohio	125,000	16,246	14.9	27.6
Oakland, Calif.	124,710	41,092	49.1	34.5
Jacksonville, Fla.	118,158	35,633	43.2	22.3
Kansas City, Mo.	112,005	28,859	34.7	22.1
Milwaukee, Wis.	105,083	42,625	68.2	14.7
Pittsburgh, Pa.	104,904	4,212	4.1	20.2
Richmond, Va.	104,766	12,794	13.9	42.0
Boston, Mass.	104,707	41,542	65.7	16.3
Columbus, Ohio	99,627	22,487	29.2	18.5
San Francisco, Calif.	96,073	21,690	29.2	13.4
Buffalo, N.Y.	94,329	23,452	33.0	20.4
Gary, Ind.	92,695	23,572	34.0	52.8
Nashville-Davidson, Tenn.	87,851	15,396	21.2	19.6
Norfolk, Va.	87,261	8,455	10.7	28.3
Louisville, Ky.	86,040	15,965	22.8	32.8
Fort Worth, Tex.	78,324	20,997	36.6	19.9
Miami, Fla.	76,156	10,943	16.8	22.7
Dayton, Ohio	74,284	16,996	29.7	30.5
Charlotte, N.C.	72,972	16,724	29.7	30.3
Mobile, Ala.	67,356	1,737	2.6	35.4
Shreveport, La.	62,162	5,555	9.8	34.1
Jackson, Miss.	61,063	9,507	18.4	39.7
Compton, Calif.	55,781	27,516	97.4	71.0
Tampa, Fla.	54,720	15,876	40.9	19.7
Jersey City, N.J.	54,595	17,903	48.6	21.0
Flint, Mich.	54,237	18,212	50.6	28.1
Savannah, Ga.	53,111	76	0.1	44.9
San Diego, Calif.	52,961	18,951	55.7	7.6
Toledo, Ohio	52,915	12,900	32.2	13.8
Oklahoma City, Okla.	50,103	11,786	30.8	13.7
San Antonio, Tex.	50,041	8,436	20.3	7.6
Rochester, N.Y.	49,647	26,061	110.5	16.8
East St. Louis, Ill.	48,368	12,030	33.1	69.1

APPENDIX B

Comparison of the Percentage of Illiterates among Blacks and Foreign-born Whites of 10 Years Old and Over in 25 Major U.S. Cities [1] for 1930 and 1900

Percentage of Illiterates 10 Years Old and Over

CITY	1930		1900	
	BLACKS	FOREIGN-BORN WHITES	BLACKS	FOREIGN-BORN WHITES
New York, N.Y.	2.1	10.7	10.0	13.9
Chicago, Ill.	2.2	9.5	8.0	8.2
Philadelphia, Pa.	3.0	9.6	11.8	12.1
Baltimore, Md.	7.0	13.4	25.8	12.9
Washington, D.C.	4.1	4.8	24.2	7.0
New Orleans, La.	13.4	14.8	36.1	18.3
Detroit, Mich.	2.7	6.2	—	—
Birmingham, Ala.	14.7	12.0	40.3	13.9
Memphis, Tenn.	8.1	7.0	35.1	11.3
St. Louis, Mo.	5.2	8.0	21.3	9.8
Atlanta, Ga.	10.4	4.5	35.1	8.6
Cleveland, Ohio	4.4	12.1	—	—
Houston, Tex.	7.1	6.3	29.8	8.0
Pittsburgh, Pa.	3.5	10.8	14.6	15.1
Richmond, Va.	12.5	6.7	32.2	8.9
Jacksonville, Fla.	10.2	5.3	23.4	6.7
Cincinnati, Ohio	6.8	6.2	19.8	8.9
Louisville, Ky.	8.9	4.7	31.1	10.8
Indianapolis, Ind.	5.7	5.0	20.4	11.1
Norfolk, Va.	11.4	8.6	38.4	8.3
Nashville, Tenn.	9.9	3.1	32.4	9.9
Los Angeles, Calif.	2.3	3.0	—	—
Newark, N.J.	6.1	13.8	—	—
Dallas, Tex.	6.6	5.2	—	—
Kansas City, Mo.	4.9	10.3	19.4	8.8
Chattanooga, Tenn.	11.6	3.8	9.8	10.7
Columbus, Ohio	7.7	8.8	—	—

[1] The cities for which a % is not provided for 1900 had negligible black populations then.

433

APPENDIX C

Black Voting Age Population and Black
Municipal Representation in Cities
Over 50,000 With 20% or More
Black Population

SOURCES: 1970 Federal Census; the Joint Center for Political Studies, Washington, D.C.; and, in a few cases of municipal representation, the mayors' offices.

| | 1970 CENSUS | | | | AS OF APRIL 30, 1972 | | |
CITIES	TOTAL POPU-LATION	TOTAL BLACK POPULATION	BLACK % OF TOTAL POPULATION	BLACK % OF VOTING AGE POPULATION	TOTAL NO. OF COUNCIL OR COMMISSION SEATS	SEATS HELD BY BLACKS NUMBER	% OF TOTAL
Alabama							
Birmingham	300,910	126,388	42.0	38.4	9	2	22.0
Gadsden	53,928	11,088	20.6	18.3	3	0	0.0
Mobile	190,026	67,355	35.4	31.8	2	0	0.0
Montgomery	133,386	44,523	33.4	30.6	3	0	0.0
Tuscaloosa	65,773	17,345	26.4	28.9	3	0	0.0
Arkansas							
Little Rock	132,483	33,074	25.0	21.9	7	1	14.3
Pine Bluff	57,389	23,484	40.9	38.6	8	0	0.0
California							
Berkeley	116,716	27,421	23.5	20.2	8	3	37.5
Compton	78,611	55,781	71.0	66.0	4	3	75.0
Oakland	361,561	124,710	34.5	29.4	8	1	12.5
Richmond	79,043	28,633	36.2	31.5		1	
Connecticut							
Hartford	158,017	44,091	27.9	23.0	9	2	22.2
New Haven	137,707	36,158	26.3	18.2	30	5	16.7
Delaware							
Wilmington	80,386	35,072	43.6	36.7	12	5	41.7
Washington, D.C.	756,510	537,712	71.1	66.8	9	6	66.6
Florida							
Jacksonville	528,865	118,158	22.3	20.4	19	3	15.8
Miami	334,859	76,156	22.7	18.7	4	1	25.0
Orlando	99,006	29,177	29.5	24.2	5	0	0.0
Pensacola	59,507	19,709	33.1	16.9	10	1	10.0
Tallahassee	71,897	18,234	25.4	23.4	5	1	20.0
W. Palm Beach	57,375	14,020	24.4	20.8	5	0	0.0

435

| | 1970 CENSUS | | | | AS OF APRIL 30, 1970 | | |
| | TOTAL POPULATION | TOTAL BLACK POPULATION | BLACK % OF TOTAL POPULATION | BLACK % OF VOTING AGE POPULATION | TOTAL NO. OF COUNCIL OR COMMISSION SEATS | SEATS HELD BY BLACKS | |
CITIES						NUMBER	% OF TOTAL
Georgia							
Albany	72,623	27,517	37.9	35.9	6	6	31.5
Atlanta	496,973	255,051	51.3	47.3	19	3	18.8
Augusta	59,864	29,861	49.9	45.3	16	3	18.8
Columbus	154,168	40,422	26.2	24.5	16	0	0.0
Macon	122,423	45,715	37.3	34.0	15		
Savannah	118,349	53,111	44.9	40.6	6	1	16.7
Illinois							
Chicago	3,366,957	1,102,620	32.7	28.2	50	14	28.0
E. St. Louis	69,996	48,368	69.1	63.4	4	2	50.0
Indiana							
Gary	175,415	92,695	52.8	49.7	9	5	55.5
Kansas							
Kansas City	168,213	34,345	20.4	18.7	3	0	0.0
Kentucky							
Louisville	361,472	86,040	23.8	21.2	12	3	25.0
Louisiana							
Baton Rouge	165,963	46,198	27.8	25.0	10	1	10.0
Lafayette	68,908	17,167	24.9	21.9	5	0	0.0
Lake Charles	77,998	24,262	31.1	28.1	7	2	28.6
Monroe	56,374	21,540	38.2	33.6	2	0	9.0
New Orleans	593,471	267,308	45.0	39.7	7	0	0.0
Shreveport	182,064	62,152	34.1	31.0	5	0	0.0
Maryland							
Annapolis	25,592	20,676	41.7	26.7	8	2	25.0
Baltimore	905,759	420,210	46.4	43.7	19	5	26.3

Michigan							
Detroit	1,511,482	660,428	43.7	39.4	9	3	33.3
Flint	193,317	54,237	28.1	24.6	9	3	33.3
Pontiac	85,279	22,760	26.7	23.7	7	2	28.6
Saginaw	91,849	22,288	24.3	20.7	9	2	22.2
Mississippi							
Jackson	153,968	61,063	39.7	35.2	3	0	0.0
Missouri							
Kansas City	507,087	112,005	22.1	18.8	12	4	33.3
St. Louis	622,236	254,191	40.9	35.9	29	6	20.6
New Jersey							
Camden	102,551	40,134	39.1	34.0	7	2	28.6
East Orange	75,471	40,099	53.1	47.0	10	7	70.0
Jersey City	260,545	54,595	21.0	17.4	9	1	11.1
Newark	382,417	207,458	54.2	48.6	9	3	33.3
Paterson	144,824	38,919	26.9	21.4	11	2	18.2
Trenton	104,638	39,671	37.9	31.9	7	1	14.3
New York							
Buffalo	462,768	94,329	20.4	17.8	15	3	20.0
Mt. Vernon	72,778	25,883	35.6	19.3	5	1	20.0
New York	7,867,760	1,666,636	21.2	19.0	37	2	5.4
North Carolina							
Charlotte	2,411,178	72,972	30.3	27.3	7	1	14.3
Durham	95,438	37,018	38.8	35.8	12	2	16.7
Fayetteville	53,510	20,463	38.2	35.1			
Greensboro	144,076	40,633	28.2	26.6	7	2	28.6
High Point	63,204	13,690	21.7	18.7	8	1	12.5
Raleigh	121,577	27,594	23.0	21.3	7	1	14.3
Winston-Salem	132,913	45,533	34.3	31.6	8	4	50.0
Ohio							
Cincinnati	452,524	125,070	27.6	24.4	8	3	37.5
Cleveland	750,903	287,841	38.3	36.6	33	12	36.6
Dayton	243,601	74,284	30.5	27.1	5	1	20.0
Youngstown	139,788	35,285	25.2	22.5	7	1	14.3

| | 1970 CENSUS | | | | AS OF APRIL 30, 1970 | | |
| CITIES | TOTAL POPULATION | TOTAL BLACK POPULATION | BLACK % OF TOTAL POPULATION | BLACK % OF VOTING AGE POPULATION | TOTAL NO. OF COUNCIL OF COMMISSION SEATS | SEATS HELD BY BLACKS | |
						NUMBER	% OF TOTAL
Pennsylvania							
Chester	56,331	25,469	45.2	40.5	4	0	0.0
Harrisburg	68,061	20,911	30.7	25.4	7	1	14.3
Philadelphia	1,948,609	653,791	33.6	31.1	17	3	17.6
Pittsburgh	520,117	104,904	20.2	18.4	9	2	22.2
South Carolina							
Charleston	66,945	30,251	45.2	39.8	16	3	18.8
Columbia	113,542	33,998	29.9	26.1	4	0	0.0
Greenville	61,208	19,145	31.3	27.4	6	0	0.0
Tennessee							
Chattanooga	119,082	42,610	35.8	32.2	7	1	14.3
Memphis	6,235,320	242,513	38.9	36.2	13	3	23.0
Texas							
Beaumont	115,919	35,553	30.7	27.6	5	1	20.0
Dallas	844,401	210,238	24.9	22.3	11	1	9.1
Galveston	61,809	18,143	29.4	26.5	6	0	0.0
Houston	1,232,802	316,551	25.7	24.1	8	0	0.0
Port Arthur	57,371	22,994	40.1	35.1	6	1	16.7
Tyler	57,770	12,320	21.3	19.4	6	0	0.0
Virginia							
Chesapeake	89,580	20,669	23.1	21.6	9	2	22.2
Hampton	120,777	30,619	25.4	24.5	7	0	0.0
Lynchburg	54,083	12,583	23.3	21.0	7	1	14.3
Newport News	138,177	39,196	28.4	26.0	7	2	28.6
Norfolk	307,951	87,261	28.3	25.0	7	1	14.3
Portsmouth	110,963	44,320	39.9	36.0	7	2	28.6
Richmond	249,621	104,766	42.0	38.0	9	1	11.1

APPENDIX D

Shifting Racial Patterns in the Cities and
Suburbs of the 55 Largest Metropolitan
Areas Based on 1970 Census [1]

METROPOLITAN AREA	IN CENTRAL CITIES WHITE POPULATION [1]		IN SUBURBS WHITE POPULATION [1]		BLACK POPULATION [2]		% BLACKS IN SUBURBS
	1970	CHANGE SINCE 1960	1970	CHANGE SINCE 1960		CHANGE SINCE 1960	
New York	6,024	− 9%	3,425	+ 24%	217	+ 55%	5.9
Los Angeles– Long Beach	2,500	+ 5	3,504	+ 14	241	+106	6.3
Chicago	2,208	− 19	3,463	+ 34	126	+ 62	3.5
Philadelphia	1,279	− 13	2,664	+ 21	191	+ 34	6.6
Detroit	838	− 29	2,580	+ 28	97	+ 26	3.6
San Francisco– Oakland	725	− 17	1,856	+ 29	109	+ 61	5.4
Washington, D.C.	209	− 39	1,915	+ 58	166	+102	7.9
Boston	525	− 17	2,078	+ 11	22	+ 53	1.1
Pittsburgh	412	− 18	1,813	+ 4	65	+ 7	3.5
St. Louis	365	− 32	1,611	+ 27	125	+ 54	7.2
Baltimore	480	− 21	1,089	+ 36	70	+ 16	6.0
Cleveland	458	− 27	1,264	+ 23	45	+453	3.4
Houston	904	+ 26	680	+ 63	66	+ 7	8.8
Newark	168	− 37	1,325	+ 11	141	+ 64	9.6
Minneapolis– St. Paul	702	− 9	1,062	+ 55	2	+223	
Dallas	626	+ 14	669	+ 66	38	+ 5	5.4
Seattle–Everett	516	− 6	821	+ 63	3	+195	
Anaheim–Santa Ana– Garden Grove	430	+ 50	949	+132	3	+133	
Milwaukee	605	− 10	683	+ 27	1	+ 98	0.2
Atlanta	241	− 20	836	+ 73	56	+ 24	6.2
Cincinnati	325	− 17	903	+ 21	27	+ 26	2.9
Paterson–Clifton– Passaic	231	− 9	1,045	+ 18	26	+ 52	2.4

[1] SOURCE: U. S. News and World Report, March 1, 1971, p. 25.
[2] Figures given in thousands.

439

METROPOLITAN AREA	IN CENTRAL CITIES WHITE POPULATION [1] 1970	CHANGE SINCE 1960	IN SUBURBS WHITE POPULATION [1] 1970	CHANGE SINCE 1960	BLACK POPULATION [2]	CHANGE SINCE 1960	% BLACKS IN SUBURBS
San Diego	619	+ 17	632	+ 41	9	+ 83	
Buffalo	364	− 21	886	+ 14	14	+ 20	1.6
Miami	256	+ 14	815	+ 43	114	+ 58	12.2
Kansas City	391		704	+ 21	39	+ 15	5.2
Denver	458	− 1	702	+ 63	3	+143	
San Bernardino–Riverside–Ontario	279	+ 34	787	+ 40	27	+ 59	3.3
Indianapolis	608	+ 7	362	+ 31	3	+113	0.8
San Jose	417	+111	586	+ 38	7	+220	
New Orleans	323	− 18	394	+ 68	57	+ 27	12.5
Tampa–St. Petersburg	406	+ 5	494	+ 66	23	+ 25	4.4
Portland	353	+ 0.2	618	+ 39	2	+ 65	
Phoenix	543	+ 31	372	+ 74	5	+ 19	1.8
Columbus	437	+ 11	369	+ 32	7	+ 42	
Providence–Pawtucket–Warwick	320	− 7	564	+ 22	4	+ 73	
Rochester	244	− 17	576	+ 41	8	+ 82	1.4
San Antonio	598	+ 10	197	+ 63	10	+ 41	
Dayton	168	− 18	586	+ 30	19	+ 54	3.2
Louisville	275	− 14	449	+ 40	15	+ 16	3.3
Sacramento	207	+ 24	521	+ 25	11	+ 23	
Memphis	379	+ 21	99	− 6	46	− 35	31.7
Fort Worth	313	+ 4	362	+ 70	5	+ 17	1.3
Birmingham	174	− 15	346	+ 22	92	− 5	20.9
Albany–Schenectady–Troy	234	− 11	460	+ 22	3	+ 82	
Toledo	329	+ 19	302	− 2	4	− 19	1.4
Norfolk–Portsmouth	281	− 6	223	+ 78	36	+ 13	13.9
Akron	226	− 10	397	+ 29	6	+ 1	1.5
Hartford	112	− 18	498	+ 30	6	+ 62	1.3
Oklahoma City	308	+ 9	263	+ 45	4	+ 21	
Syracuse	174	− 15	434	+ 26	2	+ 87	
Gary–Hammond–East Chicago	219	− 16	300	+ 34	2	+ 4	0.6
Honolulu	110	+ 37	149	+ 52	5	+ 40	
Ft. Lauderdale–Hollywood	221	+128	320	+ 76	53	+ 60	14.2
Jersey City	203	+ 15	339	+ 3	7	+ 40	1.9

APPENDIX E

Black Police in American Cities

Nonwhite Personnel in Selected Police Departments, 1967

NAME OF DEPT.	NUMBER SWORN PERS.	NUMBER NON-WHITE SWORN PERS.	NUMBER SERGEANTS		NUMBER LIEUTS.		NUMBER CAPTS.		NUMBER ABOVE CAPTAIN	
			N.W.	W.	N.W.	W.	N.W.	W.	N.W.	W.
Atlanta	968	98	2	12	3	56	0	15	0	6
Baltimore	3,046	208	7	389	3	105	1	17	1	21
Boston	2,508	49	1	228	0	80	0	20	0	12
Buffalo	1,375	37	1	60	1	93	0	24	0	32
Chicago	11,091	1,842	87	1,067	2	266	1	73	6	66
Cincinnati	891	54	2	68	2	34	0	13	0	7
Cleveland	2,216	165	6	155	0	78	0	26	0	17
Dayton	417	16	1	58	0	13	0	6	0	4
Detroit	4,326	227	9	339	2	156	0	0	1	62
Hartford	342	38	0	32	1	16	0	9	0	2
Kansas City	927	51	7	158	0	36	0	11	1	14
Louisville	562	35	1	42	1	29	0	10	1	7
Memphis	869	46	0	0	4	192	0	45	0	44
Mich. St. Pol.	1,502	1	0	135	0	24	0	19	0	3
New Haven	446	31	0	20	0	16	0	12	0	6
New Orleans	1,308	54	7	107	1	51	0	27	0	10
New York	27,610	1,485	65	1,785	20	925	2	273	3	157
New Jersey S.P.	1,224	5	0	187	0	43	0	17	0	4
Newark	1,869	184	5	97	3	95	1	22	0	0
Oakland	658	27	1	95	0	25	1	10	0	3
Oklahoma City	438	16	0	32	1	19	0	11	0	6
Philadelphia	6,890	1,377	26	314	8	139	3	46	0	23
Phoenix	707	7	0	88	1	22	0	10	0	4
Pittsburgh	1,558	109	3	137	3	47	0	4	1	6
St. Louis	2,042	224	21	201	3	46	4	17	0	11
San Francisco	1,754	102	0	217	0	66	0	15	0	10
Tampa	511	17	0	50	0	12	0	13	0	8
Washington, D.C.	2,721	559	19	216	3	107	3	37	0	31
TOTALS	80,621	7,046	271	6,289	62	2,791	16	802	14	576

SOURCE: *Report of the National Advisory Commission on Civil Disorders* (New York: Bantam Books, 1968, p. 321).

Black Police in Key Cities, 1970

CITIES	% BLACK	TOTAL POLICE FORCE	TOTAL BLACK POLICE	% BLACK POLICE
Washington	71.1	4,994	1,797	35.9
Newark	54.2	1,500	225	15.0
Gary	52.8	415	130	31.0
Atlanta	51.3	942	260	28.0
Baltimore	46.4	3,300	420	13.0
New Orleans	45.0	1,359	83	6.1
Detroit	43.7	5,100	567	12.0
Wilmington, Del.	43.6	277	32	11.5
Birmingham, Ala.	42.0	660	13	1.9
St. Louis. Mo.	40.9	2,221	326	14.0
Portsmouth, Va.	39.9	195	14	7.5
Jackson, Miss.	39.3	270	17	6.2
Memphis	38.9	1,090	55	5.0
Cleveland	38.3	2,445	191	7.7
Mobile, Ala.	35.5	277	36	13.3
Oakland, Calif.	34.5	713	34	4.7
Winston-Salem, N.C.	34.3	300	20	6.6
Shreveport, La.	33.9	345	25	7.2
Philadelphia, Pa.	33.6	7,242	1,347	18.6
Chicago	32.6	12,678	2,100	16.5
Dayton, Ohio	30.5	422	22	4.1
Hartford, Conn.	27.9	500	60	12.0
Pittsburgh, Pa.	20.2	1,640	105	6.4
Dallas, Tex.	24.9	1,640	32	1.9
Miami, Fla.	22.7	719	74	10.0
New York	21.2	31,700	2,400	7.5
Los Angeles	17.9	6,705	350	5.2
Boston	16.3	2,807	60	2.1
Milwaukee	14.7	2,098	50	2.3
San Francisco	13.4	1,800	90	5.0

SOURCE: *Ebony*, May 1971, p. 124. Evidence above from selection 2, Part 6, "Recruiting of Negro Police Is a Failure in Most Cities," indicates that the figures represent the situation in the last months of 1970.

Black Police in the 50 Largest Cities in Terms of Black Population, April–September 1972.[1]

CITIES	% BLACK	TOTAL POLICE FORCE	TOTAL BLACK POLICE	% BLACK POLICE
New York, N.Y.	21.2	30,446	2,065	6.81
Chicago, Ill.	32.7	13,376°	2,129°	15.9
Detroit, Mich.	43.7	5,551	761	13.7
Philadelphia, Pa.	33.6	7,556	1,345	17.8
Washington, D.C.	71.1	5,063	1,805	35.7
Los Angeles, Calif.	17.9	c.7,000	c.360	5.0
Baltimore, Md.	46.4	3,441	446	13.0
Houston, Tex.	25.7	2,046	71	3.4
Cleveland, Ohio	38.3	2,281°	189°	8.3
New Orleans, La.	45.0	1,400	85	6.1
Atlanta, Ga.	51.3	1,206	272	22.6
St. Louis, Mo.	40.9	2,225	336	15.1
Memphis, Tenn.	38.9	1,038°	80°	7.7
Dallas, Texas	24.9	1,836	43	2.3
Newark, N.J.	54.2	1,460	211	14.5
Indianapolis, Ind.	18.0	1,091	108	9.9
Birmingham, Ala.	42.0	403	12	3.0
Cincinnati, Ohio	27.6	975	48	4.9
Oakland, Calif.	27.6	711°	50°	7.0
Jacksonville, Fla.	22.3	633	42	6.6
Kansas City, Mo.	22.1	1,296	97	7.5
Milwaukee, Wis.	14.7	c.2,300	48	2.0
Pittsburgh, Pa.	20.0	1,615	101	6.3
Richmond, Va.	42.0	549	75	13.7
Boston, Mass.	16.3	2,800	61	2.2
Columbus, Ohio	18.5	1,014°	39°	3.8
San Francisco, Calif.	13.4	1,927	77	4.0
Buffalo, N.Y.	20.4	1,380	27	2.0
Gary, Ind.	52.8	378	137	36.2
Nashville, Tenn.	19.6	534	56	10.5
Norfolk, Va.	28.3	523	31	5.9
Louisville, Ky.	32.8	674	43	6.4
Fort Worth, Tex.	19.9	655	19	2.9
Miami, Fla.	22.7	757°	85°	11.2
Dayton, Ohio	30.5	400°	22°	5.5
Charlotte, N.C.	30.3	497	26	5.2
Mobile, Ala.	35.4	299	37	12.4
Shreveport, La.	34.1	374	32	8.6
Jackson, Miss.	39.7	320°	20°	6.3
Compton, Calif.	71.0	141	59	41.8
Tampa, Fla.	19.7	565	15	2.7
Jersey City, N.J.	21.0	903	49	5.4
Flint, Mich.	28.1	367	9	2.5
Savannah, Ga.	44.9	207	42	20.3
San Diego, Calif.	7.6	1,065	26	2.4
Toledo, Ohio	13.8	686	41	6.0
Oklahoma City, Okla.	13.7	581	23	4.0
San Antonio, Calif.	7.6	950	29	3.1
Rochester, N.Y.	16.8	675	17	2.5
East St. Louis, Ill.	69.1	115°	65°	56.5

[1] Figures on police above were largely supplied by the offices of the chiefs of police but sometimes by the mayors' offices. Most of the statistics indicate the situation as of April 30, 1972; the others, which are asterisked, refer to the period between May and September 1972.

ADDITIONAL READING

This is a selective bibliography, listing only the main, available literature on blacks in cities not already referred to in the book. Useful as background to the period dealt with in this book are Leon Litwack, *North of Slavery: The Negro in the Free States, 1790–1860* (Chicago: University of Chicago Press, 1961); Robert S. Starobin, *Industrial Slavery in the Old South* (New York: Oxford University Press, 1970); and Richard C. Wade, *Slavery in the Cities: The South, 1820–1860* (New York: Oxford University Press, 1964).

There is as yet no comprehensive historical synthesis of blacks in cities, but the following literature does treat broad aspects of it: "Black Cities: Colonies or City-States?" *Black Scholar*, April 1970, entire issue; Arna Bontemps and Jack Conroy, *Any Place But Here* (New York: Hill and Wang, 1966); Joseph Boskin, *Urban Racial Violence in the Twentieth Century* (New York: Glencoe Press, 1969); Paul K. Edwards, *The Southern Urban Negro As a Consumer*, first published in 1932 and reprinted in 1969 by Negro Universities Press, New York; A. H. Fauset, *Black Gods of the Metropolis: Negro Religious Cults in the Urban North* (Philadelphia: University of Philadelphia Press, 1944); George W. Groh, *The Black Migration* (New York: Weybright and Talley, 1972); Ulf Hannerz, *Soulside: Inquiries into Ghetto Culture and Community* (New York: Columbia University Press, 1969). Charles Keil, *Urban Blues* (Chicago: University of Chicago Press, 1968); Thomas Kochman, ed., *Rappin' and Stylin' Out: Communication in Urban Black America* (Urbana: University of Illinois Press, 1972); William McCord et al., *Life Styles of the Black Ghetto* (New York: Norton, 1969); Emmett J. Scott, *Negro Migration during the War*, first published in 1920 and reprinted in 1969 by Arno Press, New York; Karl E. and Alma F. Taeuber, *Negroes in Cities* (Chicago: Aldine Publishing Company, 1965); Robert C. Weaver, *The Negro Ghetto*, first published in 1948, reprinted in 1967 by Russell and Russell, New York; T. F. Woofter, *Negro Problems in Cities*, first published in 1928, reprinted in 1969 by Harper & Row, New York; and James R. Wilson, *Negro Politics: The Search for Leadership* (New York: The Free Press, 1960).

Much of the literature deals with individual ghettoes, especially New York and Chicago. First New York: Howard M. Brotz, *The Black Jews of Harlem* (1964) New York: Schocken Books, 1970; Kenneth Clark, *Dark Ghetto* (New York: Harper & Row, 1965); John Henrik Clarke, *Harlem, A Community in Transition* (New York: Citadel Press Inc., 1969): Nathan I. Huggins, *Harlem Renaissance* (New York: Oxford University Press, 1971); Samuel M. Johnson, *Often Back: The Tales of Harlem* (New York: Vantage Press, 1971); Claude

McKay, *Harlem: Negro Metropolis* (New York: E. P. Dutton, 1940); Gilbert Osofsky, *Harlem: The Making of a Ghetto* (New York: Harper & Row, 1966); and Seth M. Scheiner, *Negro Mecca: A History of the Negro in New York City, 1865–1920* (New York: New York University Press, 1965); and for Chicago: Chicago Commission on Race Relations, *The Negro in Chicago:* A Study of Race Relations and a Race Riot (Chicago 1922); St. Clair Drake and Horace Cayton, *Black Metropolis:* first published in 1945, revised and enlarged Torchbook ed., 2 vols. (New York: Harper & Row, 1962); Harold Gosnell, *Negro Politicians: The Rise of Negro Politics in Chicago* (Chicago: University of Chicago Press, 1935); Allan H. Spear, *Black Chicago: The Making of a Negro Ghetto, 1890–1920* (Chicago: University of Chicago Press, 1967); and Arvarh E. Strickland, *History of the Chicago Urban League* (Urbana: University of Illinois Press, 1966). Other studies on individual ghettoes are W. E. B. DuBois's classic *Philadelphia Negro*, first published in 1899, now available in paperback (New York: Schocken Books); M. Elaine Burgess, *Negro Leadership in a Southern City* (Chapel Hill: University of North Carolina Press, 1962); John Daniels, *In Freedom's Birthplace: A Study of Boston Negroes*, first published in 1914, reprinted in 1969 by Arno Press, New York; Constance McLaughlin Green, *The Secret City: A History of Race Relations in the Nation's Capital* (Princeton: Princeton University Press, 1967); David M. Katzman, *Before the Ghetto: Black Detroit in the Nineteenth Century* (Urbana: University of Illinois Press, 1972); Elliot Liebow, *Talley's Corner* [Washington, D.C.] (Boston: Little Brown and Company, 1967); Geraldine Moore, *Behind the Ebony Mask* (Birmingham: Southern University Press, 1961); Elliot M. Rudwick, *Race Riot at East St. Louis* (Carbondale: Southern Illinois University Press, 1964); Daniel C. Thompson. *The Negro Leadership Class* [of New Orleans] (Englewood Cliffs, N.J.: Prentice-Hall, 1963); and Robert Austin Warner, *New Haven Negroes: A Social History*, first published in 1940, reprinted in 1967 by Arno Press, New York.

There is a book each on the first two black mayors of major American cities: Alex Poinsett, *Black Power, Gary Style: The Making of Mayor Richard Gordon Hatcher* (Chicago: Johnson Publishing Company, 1970); and Kenneth G. Weinberg, *Carl Stokes and the Winning of Cleveland* (Chicago: Quadrangle Books, 1968). And the black urban insurrections of the mid and late 1960's inspired its own literature: Paul Bullock, ed., *Watts: The Aftermath; An Inside View of the Ghetto by the People of Watts* (New York: Grove Press, 1969); Jerry Cohen and William S. Murphy, *Burn Baby Burn; The Los Angeles Race Riot*, August 1965 (New York: E. P. Dutton, 1966); Robert Conot, *Rivers of Blood, Years of Darkness* (Watts riot) (New York: Bantam Books, 1967); Robert Fogelson, ed., *The Los Angeles Riots* (New York: Arno Press, 1969); Ben W. Gilbert, *Ten Blocks from the White House; Anatomy of the Washington Riots of 1968* (New York: Frederick A. Praeger, 1968); Hubert G. Locke, *The Detroit Riot of 1967* (Detroit: Wayne State University Press, 1969); Van Gordon Sauter and Burleigh Hines, *Nightmare in Detroit; A Rebellion and Its Victims* (Chicago: Henry Regnery Company, 1968); and Tom Hayden, *Rebellion in Newark: Official Violence and Ghetto Response* (New York: Random House, 1967).

INDEX

Africa:
    cultural heritage of, 211-214, 348
    rituals of, in U.S. cities, 12-14, 139,
        144, 213-214
African nationalism, 209, 401-402
agriculture, 94, 155
    decline of, in South, 131
aircraft and aerospace industries, 352,
    357, 412, 414
Alexandria, La., 278-279
Alioto, Joseph, 416, 419
Allen, Ivan, Jr., 377-378
Allen, Robert, 418
American Baptist Home Mission So-
    ciety, 60-61
American Federation of Labor, 74,
    110, 159, 306-309, 327
    vs. CIO, 211, 214-220 *passim*, 236-
        241, 261, 262, 263
Anderson, Marian, 273, 280
Annapolis, Md., 279
anti-lynching legislation, 120, 280
architecture, urban:
    in Harlem, 112, 397
    in postbellum South, 21-22
    in "Riot Renaissance" style, 368
artisans, black (*see also* labor, black):
    in border cities, 33, 34-37, 39, 41,
        152-153, 158, 238, 327-328
    in North, 100, 104, 107-108, 196-
        197

artisans, black (*continued*)
    in South, 3, 8, 9, 22, 23, 66, 67-69,
        74-76, 81, 308-309, 381
artistic talent, black (*see also* cultural
    life, black), 170, 176-181, 342-
    343
artists, black, 180, 342, 417
athletic activities (*see also* baseball;
    sports), 163, 189-190, 349
Atlanta, Ga., 50, 60-63, 66, 78-79,
    151, 214, 216, 279, 284, 286,
    364, 366, 377
    racial conflict in, 53, 56-58, 140
    slums in, 63-65
    social and political gains of blacks
        in, 20-23, 137, 139-140, 288-290,
        362
Atlanta Baptist College, 60, 61-62, 63
Atlanta Inter-racial Committee, 139
Atlanta Negro Voters League, 286
Atlanta University, 60, 61, 63, 65, 179
Augusta, Ga., 6-7, 42, 50
Austin, Tex., 53
automobile industry, 134, 192, 195,
    275, 346, 412, 414

Baker, George (Father Divine), 242,
    243-248
Baker, Robert E., 373
Baldwin, Roger, 99
Baltimore, Md., 33, 34, 35-37, 39-42,

447

Index